Key Questions about
Biblical
Interpretation

Key Questions about
Biblical
Interpretation

OLD TESTAMENT ANSWERS

JOHN GOLDINGAY

Baker Academic
a division of Baker Publishing Group
Grand Rapids, Michigan

© 2011 by John Goldingay

Published by Baker Academic
a division of Baker Publishing Group
P.O. Box 6287, Grand Rapids, MI 49516-6287
www.bakeracademic.com

Printed in the United States of America

Library of Congress Cataloging-in-Publication Data

Goldingay, John.
    Key questions about Biblical interpretation : Old Testament answers / John Goldingay.
        p.   cm.
    Includes indexes.
    ISBN 978-0-8010-3959-1 (pbk.)
        1. Bible. O.T.—Hermeneutics—Miscellanea. I. Title.
    BS476.G649 2011
    221.601—dc22
                                                                    2011013277

Unless otherwise indicated, all Scripture quotations are the author's translation.

Scripture quotations labeled KJV are from the King James Version of the Bible.

Scripture quotations labeled NRSV are from the New Revised Standard Version of the Bible, copyright © 1989, by the Division of Christian Education of the National Council of the Churches of Christ in the United States of America. Used by permission. All rights reserved.

Scripture quotations labeled TNIV are from the Holy Bible, Today's New International Version®. TNIV®. Copyright © 2001, 2005 by Biblica, Inc.™ Used by permission of Zondervan. All rights reserved worldwide. www.zondervan.com

12   13   14   15   16   17   7   6   5   4   3   2

Contents

Part 3: Concerning the First Testament as a Whole

Part 4: Concerning the Torah, the Prophets, and the Writings

Acknowledgments

Chapter 1: "What Is Involved in Understanding a Passage from the Bible?" is taken from John Goldingay, "Interpreting Scripture," in *Anvil* 1 (1984): 153–62, 261–81. Used by permission.

Chapter 2: "What Difference Does It Make If You Are Premodern, Modern, or Postmodern?" is taken from John Goldingay, "Premodern, Modern, and Postmodern in Old Testament Study," in *Eerdmans Commentary on the Bible*, edited by J. W. Rogerson and J. D. G. Dunn, © 2003 Wm. B. Eerdmans Publishing Company, Grand Rapids, Michigan. Reprinted by permission of the publisher, all rights reserved.

Chapter 3: "Can We Learn from the Past? Luther and the Bible" is taken from John Goldingay, "A Case Study: Luther and the Bible," © 1982 *Scottish Journal of Theology*. Originally published in *Scottish Journal of Theology* 35, no. 1 (1982): 33–58. Reprinted with permission.

Chapter 4: "Can We Learn from the Hermeneutics of Liberation Theology?" is taken from John Goldingay, "The Hermeneutics of Liberation Theology," in *Horizons in Biblical Theology* 4 (1982–83): 133–61. Used with permission.

Chapter 5: "What Questions Does Evangelical Biblical Interpretation Need to Consider?" is taken from John Goldingay, "The Ongoing Story of Biblical Interpretation," *Churchman* 112 (1998): 6–16; "Going by the Book," *Third Way* 1, no. 12 (1988): 14–16; and "Current Issues in Evangelical Interpretation of Scripture," in *Anglican Evangelical Assembly Proceedings* 4 (ed. Colin N. Day; Church of England Evangelical Council, 1986), 19–29. Used with permission.

Chapter 6: "How Does Scripture Impact Our Life with God?" is taken from John Goldingay, *After Eating the Apricot*, © 1996, Paternoster. Used with permission.

Chapter 7: "How Should We Read Scripture in Church? Canon and Lection" is taken from John Goldingay, "Canon and Lection," in *To Glorify God: Essays on Modern Reformed Liturgy*, edited by Bryan D. Spinks and Iain R. Torrance, © 1999 Wm. B. Eerdmans Publishing Company, Grand Rapids, Michigan. Reprinted by permission of the publisher, all rights reserved.

Chapter 8: "How Might Preaching Be Scriptural?" is taken from John Goldingay, "In Preaching Be Scriptural: and Therefore Be Experiential, Be Oral, Be Interesting, and Be Imaginative," in *Anvil* 14 (1997): 87–94. Used with permission.

Chapter 9: "How Does the Bible Do Theological Reflection?' is taken from John Goldingay, "Modes of Theological Reflection in the Bible," in *Theology* 94 (1991): 181–88. Used with permission.

Chapter 10: "How Does Biblical Narrative Relate to Systematic Theology?" is taken from John Goldingay, "Biblical Narrative and Systematic Theology," in *Between Two Horizons: Spanning New Testament Studies and Systematic Theology*, edited by Joel B. Green and Max Turner, © 1999 Wm. B. Eerdmans Publishing Company, Grand Rapids, Michigan. Reprinted by permission of the publisher, all rights reserved.

Chapter 11: "How Does Biblical Story Shape Our Story?" is taken from John Goldingay, "Biblical Story and the Way It Shapes Our Story," in *Journal of the European Pentecostal Theological Association* 17 (1997): 5–15. Used with permission.

Chapter 12: "How Do We Preach on Narrative?" is taken from John Goldingay, "Preaching on the Stories in Scripture," in *Anvil* 7 (1990): 105–14. Used with permission.

Chapter 13: "Does Biblical Narrative Need to Be Historical?" is taken from John Goldingay, "'That You May Know That Yahweh Is God': A Study in the Relationship between Theology and Historical Truth in the Old Testament," in *Tyndale Bulletin* 23 (1972): 58–93. Used with permission.

Chapter 14: "How Does Christian Faith Relate to the First Testament?" is taken from John Goldingay, "The Old Testament and Christian Faith: Jesus and the Old Testament in Matthew 1–5, Parts 1–2," in *Themelios* 8, no. 1 (1982): 4–10; 8, no. 2 (1983): 5–12. Used with permission. http://thegospelcoalition.org/publications.

Chapter 15: "In What Sense Is It Appropriate to Read the First Testament Christologically?" is taken from John Goldingay, "The God of Grace and Truth," in the *Journal of Theological Interpretation* 2 (2008): 7–11. Used with permission.

Chapter 16: "What Defines Evangelical Study of the First Testament?" is taken from John Goldingay, "What Are the Characteristics of Evangelical Study of the Old Testament?" in *The Evangelical Quarterly* 73 (2001): 99–117. Used with permission.

Chapter 17: "In What Way Does Old Testament Theology Relate to the Canon?" is taken from John Goldingay, "Old Testament Theology and the Canon," in *Tyndale Bulletin* 59 (2008): 1–26. Used with permission.

Chapter 18: "How May We Interpret the Pentateuch?" is taken from John Goldingay, "Hermeneutics," in *Dictionary of the Old Testament: Pentateuch*, edited by T. D. Alexander and D. W. Baker, © 2003 InterVarsity Christian Fellowship/ USA. Used by permission of InterVarsity Press, P.O. Box 1400, Downers Grove, IL 60515. www.ivpress.com.

Chapter 19: "Can We Read Prophecy in Light of the Newspaper?" is taken from John Goldingay, "Palestine and the Prophets," *Third Way* 2, no. 7 (April 1978): 3–6; "Modern Israel and Biblical Prophecy," *Third Way* 6, no. 4 (April 1983): 6–8; and "The Jews, the Land, and the Kingdom," *Anvil* 4 (1987): 9–22. Used with permission.

Chapter 20: "Is There Prophecy Today?" is taken from John Goldingay, "Prophecy Today," in *The Spirit and Church* 3 (2001): 27–46. Used with permission.

Chapter 21: "How Does Poststructuralist Interpretation Work? Isaiah 40–55 as a Test Case" is taken from John Goldingay, "Isaiah 40–55 in the 1990s: Among Other Things, Deconstructing, Mystifying, Intertextual, Socio-Critical, and Hearer-Involving," in *Biblical Interpretation* 5 (1997): 225–46. Used with permission.

Chapter 22: "Is There Masculist Interpretation?" is taken from John Goldingay, "Hosea 1–3, Genesis 1–4, and Masculist Interpretation," in *Horizons in Biblical Theology* 17 (1995): 37–44. Used with permission. It appeared in revised form in *A Feminist Companion to the Latter Prophets*, edited by Athalya Brenner, © 1995 Sheffield Academic Press. Used by kind permission of Continuum International Publishing Group.

Chapter 23: "How May We Interpret Wisdom, Poetry, and Writings?" is taken from John Goldingay, "Hermeneutics," in *Dictionary of the Old Testament: Wisdom, Poetry, and Writings*, edited by Tremper Longman and Peter Enns, © 2008 InterVarsity Christian Fellowship/USA. Used by permission of InterVarsity Press, P.O. Box 1400, Downers Grove, IL 60515. www.ivpress.com.

Preface

Like the chapters in *Key Questions about Christian Faith: Old Testament Answers*, these papers sometimes arose from requests from other people, sometimes from my own wondering. All have been published elsewhere, but I have reworked them to different degrees, though I have not tried to bring the references up to date. Information concerning their original publication appears in the first footnote to each chapter. I am grateful to my successive faculty assistants Maria Doerfler, Michael Crosby, and Peter Alvarez for digitizing some of them, and to Tom Bennett for drawing up the indexes and helping with proofreading.

The reader will see even from the table of contents that I rather prefer the term "First Testament" to "Old Testament," but I am not worried about occasional inconsistency over this usage.

Abbreviations

BSac	*Bibliotheca sacra*
EvQ	*Evangelical Quarterly*
HBT	*Horizons in Biblical Theology*
IDBSup	K. Crim et al., eds. *Interpreter's Dictionary of the Bible: Supplementary Volume* (Nashville: Abingdon, 1976)
Int	*Interpretation*
JBL	*Journal of Biblical Literature*
JSOT	*Journal for the Study of the Old Testament*
JSOTSup	Journal for the Study of the Old Testament: Supplement Series
KJV	King James Version
LXX	Septuagint
MT	Masoretic Text
NJPS	New Jewish Publication Society Translation
NRSV	New Revised Standard Version
NT	New Testament
OT	Old Testament
RevistB	*Revista bíblica*
RSV	Revised Standard Version
SJT	*Scottish Journal of Theology*
Them	*Themelios*
TNIV	Today's New International Version
TynB	*Tyndale Bulletin*
VT	*Vetus Testamentum*
VTSup	Supplements to Vetus Testamentum

PART 1

Concerning Scripture as a Whole

1

What Is Involved in Understanding a Passage from the Bible?

In one sense, understanding is a quite straightforward task, one that we fulfill successfully all the time as we read newspapers or novels, watch plays or advertisements, and listen to confidences or weather forecasts or sermons or jokes. At the same time, it is a task that periodically catches us out. We can't see the point of the novel or the play, or we mishear the confidence and hurt the one who shared it. Further, beneath that recurrent experience of failure to understand lies something of a mystery: what is this thing called understanding, anyway? What makes it possible, what encourages it, what hinders it, what prevents it? How is it that communication takes place?[1]

Understanding Scripture is a particular instance of the general task of understanding. It, too, is in one sense a straightforward enterprise that quite ordinary people accomplish as effortlessly as they understand newspapers, television, or each other. It, too, however, catches them out periodically (partly because of the cultural differences that separate most modern readers from the Bible): they make little sense of ritual instructions in Leviticus or visionary material in Revelation, they are unsure (or are too sure) of what we are supposed to learn from stories in the Gospels or Acts, or they read Genesis 1–3 as more parabolic (or more historical) than it actually is. It, too, raises questions of baffling depth: what do we mean by understanding

---

1. First published in *Anvil* 1 (1984): 153–62, 261–81; it contains the seed thoughts for my *Models for the Interpretation of Scripture* (Grand Rapids: Eerdmans; Carlisle: Paternoster, 1995; Toronto: Clements, 2004).

Scripture, anyway? What makes it possible, what encourages it, what hinders it, what prevents it? How can I hear what these human authors were saying in God's name to their hearers? How can I hear what God wants to say to me through Scripture?

Another question arises out of the element of mystery about the task of interpretation, the mystery of which we are reminded when we have difficulty in understanding a text or when an interpretation that is compelling to us is unconvincing to someone else. Who knows whether we miss whole aspects of the meaning of particular texts, or fundamentally misconstrue them, even when we do not feel uncertain about their meaning or do not find our understanding contradicted by someone else? Texts, after all, cannot answer back ("No, I didn't mean that") as people can. If we feel we have grounds for being confident about the meaning of Scripture, we can obey and preach that meaning with confidence; but we cannot at the same time be open to being coaxed towards some other understanding of it. Openness to new understanding demands the willingness to yield old convictions.

The task of understanding can rightly be considered in the abstract, but discussion of it can then become rather rarified. Here I forego discussing the task in its "neat" or theoretical form and concentrate on particular instances of it, on what is involved in understanding specific types of material in Scripture. For understanding is a multiplex skill or art (understanding Hamlet, understanding the football results, understanding an atlas, understanding my wife . . .); ultimately a different approach is required for each form of the task. The varying objects of understanding with which Scripture presents us similarly require varying approaches. Further, as it happens, many of the different insights that have emerged from the study of interpretation at the rarified, abstract level over recent decades come into sharper focus and more direct relevance when applied to specific kinds of material.

To be comprehensive would involve examining one by one every scriptural genre, ultimately every scriptural text, but that would be to sacrifice ourselves to the concrete as fatally as we might otherwise do to the abstract. I propose instead to consider three broad scriptural genres—instruction texts, narrative texts, and prayer texts—which between them raise most of the issues we need to be concerned with. It may be no coincidence that they constitute examples of the three main ways of speaking that appear in Scripture: in instruction texts such as laws or prophetic oracles, God addresses people;[2] in narrative texts, people address each other; in prayer texts, people address God. They also constitute genres from the main divisions within the two Testaments (Torah, Prophets, and Writings, or historical books, poetic books, and prophetic books; Gospels and Epistles). They embody three forms of language, the discursive, the imaginative, and the existential.

With a little persuasion, they can also be harnessed to illustrate other diversities of approach to interpretation. For instance, texts may offer confrontation, reassurance, or response. Their meaning may be located within the text (in the inherent form and interrelationships of its various elements), beneath the text (in the common human

2. In chapter 6, I divide this second way of speaking into two.

experiences, feelings, and convictions that it concretely symbolizes and expresses), behind the text (in the aims and intentions of its author or the life setting of its tradition), or in front of the text (in the possible mode of being in the world that it sets before us). Interpreters may take one of several foci for their work: perhaps the world out there, the work's universe, the objective truth as the work conceives it; perhaps the needs of the audience it addressed and the effect it had on them; perhaps the personal feelings and experience of the author, to which the work gives expression; perhaps the inner dynamic of the work itself as a world of its own. They may regard texts as windows (onto another world), as mirrors (reflecting back insight on the interpreter's world), or as portraits (with a world of their own).[3]

Different genres cause different questions about interpretation to surface; I doubt whether any one philosophy of interpretation opens up all secrets. It is unwise to treat all texts as fundamentally expressive of an understanding of human existence (as Bultmann does), though some are. It is unwise to treat all texts as primarily didactic, concerned to teach something (an assumption for which Barr faults fundamentalists). It is unwise to treat all texts as "story and poem."[4] Like literary criticism, biblical interpretation needs to cultivate an eclectic, "open methodology."[5] Indeed, such a methodology will then recognize that the genres do overlap in their inner nature; the questions about interpretation consequently also overlap. A prayer text is also an instruction text; a narrative text reflects the experience of God and response to God that are more the overt concern of a prayer text. What a narrative tells a story about, an instruction text expresses as a theology or an ethic and a prayer text responds to in worship, commitment, and plea. So I make such distinctions in the sections that follow in order to let the issues emerge as sharply as possible; the distinctions themselves can then be allowed to become fuzzy in order for the insights to be applied across any artificial divides.

1. Instruction Texts

By instruction texts I mean material that overtly offers people direct teaching on belief and behavior; it is instanced by the laws, the prophets, Proverbs, the words

3. For analyses such as these, see M. H. Abrams, *The Mirror and the Lamp* (New York: Oxford University Press, 1953), 3–29; R. J. Karris, "Windows and Mirrors," in *Society of Biblical Literature 1979 Seminar Papers* (ed. P. J. Achtemeier; Missoula, Mont.: Scholars Press, 1979), 1:47–58, and his references; V. S. Poythress, "Analysing a Biblical Text," *SJT* 32 (1979): 113–38, 319–32; R. Lapointe, *Les trois dimensions de l'herméneutique* (Paris: Gabalda, 1967); Otto Weber, *Foundations of Dogmatics* (2 vols.; Grand Rapids: Eerdmans, 1981), 1:314–15; R. Jakobson, e.g., "Linguistics and Poetics," in *Style in Language* (ed. T. A. Sebeok; New York: Wiley, 1960), 353, 357; Luis Alonso Schökel, *The Inspired Word* (New York: Herder, 1965; London: Bums and Oates, 1967), 134–50, with his references to K. Buehler's *Sprachtheorie*; E. V. McKnight, *Meaning in Texts* (Philadelphia: Fortress, 1978), 152–53.

4. So David J. A. Clines, "Story and Poem," *Int* 34 (1980): 115–27.

5. So M. J. Valdés in *Interpretation of Narrative* (ed. M. J. Valdés and O. J. Miller; Toronto: University of Toronto Press, 1978), 10.

of Jesus, and the epistles. It is not with such material that either Testament actually begins; Genesis and Matthew are narrative texts. But it is convenient to consider instruction texts first.

The least controversial shibboleth of biblical interpretation for a century has been the conviction that any passage of Scripture should be understood against its historical background. Many instruction texts in Scripture offer some justification for that belief in that they themselves draw attention to their historical context. Most prophetic books begin by telling us something about the author's background and the period to which the message related, as if to say, "You need to see the oracles that follow as the work of this prophet in this context." The reasons for this are clear as we go on to read the prophets. One aspect of it is that their persons, lives, and personalities commonly enter into their message or embody it in some way; the way they express themselves and the kind of emphases they bring reflect their individuality. It is important to see Amos as a Judean prophesying in Ephraim, to see that Isaiah's name ("Yahweh is salvation") embodies a theme taken up by his message and that Hosea's marital experience shapes his interpretation of Yahweh's relationship with Israel. In a parallel way, an epistle characteristically begins by identifying its writer and its recipients; these introductions, too, often indicate key aspects to the epistle's significance. Paul's direct apostleship (Gal 1:1) is of key importance in Galatians, as is Paul himself in Philippians or 2 Corinthians; John's sharing on Patmos his brothers' and sisters' experience of tribulation is of key importance in Revelation.

The historical context often alluded to by the introductions to prophetic books or epistles can be illumined from sources inside and outside the canon. Inside the canon, Kings or Acts provides us with an account of the reigns referred to by the prophets or of Paul's visits to churches from where and to which he wrote his letters. Elsewhere, Middle Eastern sources offer us information on the international (and sometimes the national) context of the prophets, or sources from the Roman Empire illumine the background of the epistles. Nevertheless, neither of these sources is as helpful as one might expect. Kings and Acts have interests of their own that shape their presentation of Israelite and early Christian history. Often they do not give us the kind of background information that we might hope for. Extracanonical sources, for their part, rarely clarify the content of the biblical documents in any direct way, and often an interest in archaeology and Middle Eastern background constitutes a diversion from seeking to interpret texts themselves.[6]

In fact, the books themselves are our major resource for a knowledge of the situation that the prophets or the epistles address, of the question that they are concerned to answer. So one of the interpreter's first tasks in studying Amos or 1 Corinthians is to read through the book with this interest in mind: what were the various aspects of the needs, circumstances, beliefs, or lives of the readers that the writer needed to address? Even when you have understood clearly the words someone uses, you have

---

6. Cf. T. S. Eliot's analogous comments in *On Poetry and Poets* (London: Faber; New York: Farrar, Straus, 1957), 112.

not understood what this person meant until you know "what the question was (a question in his own mind, and presumed by him to be in yours) to which the thing he has said or written was meant as an answer."[7]

The fact that we learn most about an instruction text's historical context from the contents of the book itself perhaps explains the presence in Scripture of some exceptions to the generalization that most of the prophets and the epistles begin by telling us about their authors and background. A book such as Joel leaves us uninformed on its date; a document such as Hebrews tells us nothing of its authorship, but the contents of these works make clear what were the aims of their writers in relation to the needs they perceived. Biblical scholarship has been centrally concerned with establishing the nature of the actual historical process whereby Israelite and early Christian religion developed, and for this purpose to locate each of the biblical documents chronologically is of key importance. Whether we date Joel in the ninth, fifth, or third centuries (three favored possibilities) affects our understanding of this development. But it makes no difference to the meaning of the work itself. What matters is what kind of context the document was addressing, and the nature of that the document makes clear enough. It is this that decided what form of continuity and discontinuity the prophet had to manifest in relation to where the audience were, or that determined whether the prophet's ministry was fundamentally a reassuring one or a confrontational one.

The importance of appreciating the kind of circumstances a writer was addressing comes into especially clear focus when we contrast the contradictory emphases of different writers. Ezekiel 33:23–29 disallows appeal to the example of God's blessing of Abraham as a key to hope of return from exile; Isaiah 51:1–3 then offers that example as a key to hope of a return. Paul in Romans 4 declares, "People are justified by faith, not by works; you only have to look at the example of Abraham to see that"; James in James 2 declares, "People are justified by works, not by faith; you only have to look at the example of Abraham to see that." A large part of the reason for the differences between these two pairs of statements lies in the different contexts to which they were addressed. Only as we appreciate the circumstances of their audiences can we appreciate the significance of their statements.[8]

The fact that the prophets press us to understand their writings against their historical context exposes a fundamental weakness of the approach to predictive prophecy that appears in many Christian paperback bestsellers such as Hal Lindsey's *The Late Great Planet Earth*.[9] Here a prophet such as Ezekiel is read as if he were giving a coded preview of events in the twentieth-century Middle East. Reading Ezekiel that way ignores the hermeneutical hint with which his book begins and the pointers it gives to its audience as it goes along.

A historical approach to instruction texts, then, rules out one form of finding contemporary relevance in them. It does not rule out all concern with their contemporary

7. R. G. Collingwood, *An Autobiography* (London and New York: Oxford University Press, 1939), 31.

8. J. A. Sanders, "Hermeneutics," *IDBSup*, 404–5.

9. (Grand Rapids: Zondervan, 1970; London: Lakeland, 1971).

relevance. Indeed it makes a contribution to that, insofar as the distancing effect that a historical approach brings can help us grasp the text's real meaning.

An awareness of the historical nature of instruction texts emphasizes for us their human origin, even though it is among such texts that we also find the scriptural material that is overtly addressed from God to human beings. The laws are presented as dictated by God to Moses. The Gospels give us the teaching of the Son of God. In his letters Paul claims to write in words taught by the Spirit and, even when most tentative, associates the Spirit of God with his judgments (1 Cor 2:13; 7:40). Most strikingly, the prophetic books combine with their initial allusions to their human and historical origins the reminder that what you are to read is not merely human words but the vision or the word or the oracle that Yahweh revealed. The prophets also combine with their ongoing allusions to their historical context the repeated reminder that they function as God's direct messengers who declare "thus says Yahweh."

A first implication of this way of speaking is that the teaching in these books overtly makes special demands on its readers. Both the notion of inspiration and the notion of authority are especially at home with material of this kind. It speaks as the Word of God and expects to be treated as such. The interpreter is challenged to approach it with a special openness, and with a special expectancy. In his study of the phenomenon of translation, George Steiner includes an analysis of "the hermeneutic motion, the art of elicitation and appropriative transfer of meaning." Its starting point, he suggests, is an act of trust that "there is 'something there' to be understood." Without this, the effort to understand will soon collapse. "'This means nothing,' asserts the exasperated child in front of his Latin reader or the beginner at Berlitz" (the language school); but giving in to that tempting conclusion means never reaching understanding.[10] This is all the more true with the trusting conviction that I am reading words God spoke. For the task of interpretation, this conviction carries the significant implication that Scripture is neither unintelligible nor trivial, and it encourages me to persist in the effort to understand even where I am tempted to give up.

If the text I am reading is the Word of God, this will also mean that I relate to it as a person of prayer seeking to hear what God has been saying, as well as a person using my reason to decipher a human artifact. It makes interpretation a charism.[11] What by the exercise of the charism of interpretation I understand I can then go on to commit myself to; but it is also the case that what I commit myself to I can then go on to understand. My commitment to it can enable me to open myself to understanding. (It can also do the opposite; knowing I have to be committed to it may inhibit what I allow myself to perceive in it.) An academic or historical approach and a believing or theological approach are not in tension with each other. They can be partners. Either on its own is inadequate as a means to interpreting a text. To put it another way, I may think that in interpreting a text I am the subject in

10. *After Babel* (London and New York: Oxford University Press, 1975), 296–97.
11. So J. Macquarrie, *God-Talk* (London: SCM; New York: Harper, 1967), 152.

relation to it as object, the master in relation to it as servant. I am doing it the favor of letting it speak once more. But if this is the Word of God that we are reading, the interpretive movement is put in reverse. God is the subject and I am the object, God the master and I the servant. I am granted the favor of overhearing what God has said. At least, God may grant this; I cannot assume that or force God to speak. Hence "prayer must have the last word."[12]

A second implication of seeing instruction texts as the Word of God is that they can and should be brought into relationship with each other. A historical approach reflects and reveals the fact that these texts offer not a timeless theology or ethic but concrete, contextual insights and commands. This historicality of Scripture perhaps explains much of its ambiguity (as it seems to us) over topics such as what baptism means and who are its proper recipients. Even as merely human documents they might be taken to be the contextual embodiment of more far-reaching principles that we could seek to identify; as the words of God (who does not slip into irrational obiter dicta) they are certainly so. We are invited, then, to look behind them and relate them to each other. What Paul (and God) wanted to say to the Corinthians we discover from 1–2 Corinthians. What he might want to say to us we learn by considering that discovery in light of other Scriptures.

How Mark, Paul, and John conceive of the person of Christ is rather different, even when they use the same expressions (e.g., "Son of God"). If God spoke through them all, interpreting them as Scripture means considering them in light of each other after one has established what each writer meant individually. They will be capable of becoming part of a coherent whole, though at the level of thought and concepts, not necessarily of their own words. What Chronicles and Ecclesiastes imply about the attitudes and beliefs appropriate to the person of faith is very different, even though (indeed, especially because) the authors probably lived in approximately the same period. They need to be understood individually, often as in reaction to each other.[13] Interpreting them as Scripture also involves determining in what way and with what qualifications their messages will make a claim upon us when they are considered in light of each other.[14]

A third implication for interpretation is that, although their human and historical origin demands that we interpret them in accordance with their meaning as it would be understood by intellectually and spiritually competent contemporary readers such as God was originally addressing by means of human agents, their divine origin opens up the possibility that God might have meant by these words more than their human author or original reader would have understood. When New Testament authors tell us how First Testament prophecies have been fulfilled

---

12. Karl Barth, *Church Dogmatics*, I/2 (Edinburgh: T&T Clark, 1956), 531.

13. Cf. B. M. Ejxenbaum's comments on literary interpretation in *Readings in Russian Poetics* (ed. L. Matejka and K. Pomorska; Cambridge, Mass.: MIT, 1971), 17–18; also the discussion of intertextuality in, e.g., J. Culler, *The Pursuit of Signs* (London: Routledge, 1981), 100–118.

14. Cf. C. M. Wood, *The Formation of Christian Understanding: An Essay in Theological Hermeneutics* (Philadelphia: Westminster Press, 1981), 73–74.

(e.g., in Matt 1–2), they sometimes attribute to these prophecies meanings that were foreign to their human authors. In light of the Christ event and by the Spirit's guidance they are able to see significances in them that God could have known but that the prophet did not. The example of Hal Lindsey quoted above draws attention to the hazards of reading nonhistorical meanings into Scripture on the basis of extrascriptural information; but perceiving such meanings in light of other Scriptures is difficult to prohibit, though as difficult to test. It is also without so much point now that we have the New Testament to tell us directly about Christ; we can therefore allow the First Testament to press its own agenda upon us, not one determined by later considerations.

Yet even a historical approach to instruction texts may be able to justify finding more in them than their author knew; for prophecy, at least, is rather like poetry.[15] Like prophets, poets often feel that their message has been "given" them, and that they may not be able fully to express in words the vision they have seen, or that they cannot necessarily perceive all the implications of the words they have heard and expressed. The meaning of a poem may go beyond what the poet can indicate. Any further meaning an interpreter finds in the work is to be expected to be a deeper grasping of what the poet grasped. It will not be an allegorizing of it that reads into it a quite other meaning; it will be a fuller understanding, not an unrelated one.

Metaphor, in particular, invites the reader beyond the strictly circumscribable semantic significance of words; it expresses "what ideas feel like."[16] But it does more than that. While one needs to be wary of overextending a metaphor (Jesus is the true vine, but you can't ask what is the soil the vine grows in; God is our Father, but you can't ask who is our Mother), equally one needs to be wary of underinterpreting it. A metaphor points to a depth and breadth of meaning that may go beyond what the author had perceived. Its language is deliberately open and suggestive rather than totally defined and specific.

At the same time, metaphor trades on everyday earthly reality. To the urban Westerner, "vines" sound inherently spiritual; to the Palestinian, they were originally little more so than coffee or concrete are to us, and the metaphor worked because the writer was utilizing the everyday and down-to-earth to extend the boundary of the sayable. Interpreting biblical imagery, then, involves an attempt to hear everyday statements in their everyday significance and yet with their transcendent allusions.

In this respect, as in others, metaphor merges into symbol, whose central function is "to connect the clear and focused area of our experience with a dim but insistent kind of experience that is a constituent of consciousness but is, nevertheless, not clearly apprehended."[17] One way of distinguishing them is to see a symbol as a com-

---

15. Cf. D. N. Freedman, "Pottery, Poetry, and Prophecy," *JBL* 96 (1977): 21–26.

16. I believe this is Karl Shapiro's description of poetry in *The Bourgeois Poet* (New York: Random House, 1964).

17. William A. Beardslee, "Narrative Form in the New Testament and Process Theology," *Encounter* (Indianapolis) 36 (1975): 303, following Alfred North Whitehead.

munity metaphor, one widely accepted without (necessarily) being dead; one that "acquires a stable and repeatable meaning or association"[18] that enables it to be a means whereby a community evokes indirectly what cannot be articulated with the same power in a direct way.

Jesus is the real vine: a variety of significances and resonances from the First Testament belongs to the symbol, whether or not Jesus or John was immediately aware of all of them. God is our Father: a range of experiences of fatherhood and sonship (positive and negative) can help to unfold the meaning of the symbol. Of course symbols need to be understood historically; images of fatherhood vary in different cultures. At the same time, they are particular cultural embodiments of widely known archetypes. "There is one Father, from whom every family in heaven and on earth receives its name" (Eph 3:14).

So particular occurrences of the symbol need to be interpreted in relation to the archetype as well as in relation to its historical context. In using metaphor and symbol, writers are fitting their work into the larger whole comprised by reality as God constitutes it, creates it, sees it, and orders it. They are seeking to be open to God. Metaphor and symbol do trade on the familiarity of the down-to-earth, but they also trade on the fact that things like vines (or even coffee and concrete) have their own place in God's scheme of things. It is for this reason that they can bring to expression other realities of which we are only more vaguely aware, or only become aware through them.[19]

Metaphor and symbol with their openness and potential are not the only or sufficient ways of speaking of God, as (for instance) Sallie McFague sometimes implies in her suggestive book *Speaking in Parables*.[20] The creativeness of metaphor and symbol (intuitive, experiential, self-involving, allusive, plurivocal, holistic, open-ended, dynamic) needs to be complemented by the discipline of conceptual thinking (analytic, cerebral, distanced, defined, measured, nuanced) which tests it. Paul Ricoeur, with whose approach McFague identifies herself, recognizes this, noting that one can see taking place in Scripture itself a move from symbol to system and conceptualization (not, of course, to be understood as more advanced than symbol, as the two complement each other, and the latter is parasitic on the former).[21] Within Scripture, a special locus of this incipient theologizing is instruction material such as the wisdom teaching of Proverbs 1–9, the discourses in John, and the letters of Paul.

---

18. Norman Perrin, "Wisdom and Apocalyptic in the Message of Jesus," in *The Society of Biblical Literature One Hundred Eighth Annual Meeting Book of Seminar Papers* (ed. L. C. McGaughy; Missoula, Mont.: SBL, 1972), 2:553; cf. his *Jesus and the Language of the Kingdom* (Philadelphia: Fortress; London: SCM, 1976).

19. Cf. T. Hawkes's discussion in *Metaphor* (London: Methuen; New York: Harper, 1972).

20. (Philadelphia: Fortress; London: SCM, 1975); see, e.g., 29.

21. See, e.g., his "Biblical Hermeneutics," *Semeia* 4 (1975): 129–35; cf. G. Ebeling, *Word and Faith* (London: SCM; Philadelphia: Fortress, 1963), 93–94; also B. Wicker, *The Story-Shaped World* (Notre Dame, Ind.: University of Notre Dame; London: Athlone, 1975), 1–32, on the distinction between metaphor and analogy.

2. Narrative Texts

Discussion of poetry, metaphor, and symbol leads easily into consideration of narrative texts, for biblical narrative, like poetry, needs to be interpreted as literature if it is to be interpreted adequately. As Leland Ryken observes, the Bible "is in large part a work of literature," not a systematic theological treatise. Like McFague, he stresses that its theology and ethics are expressed in poems "about the weather, trees, crops, lions, hunters, rocks of refuge and human emotions such as love and terror and trust and joy"; the interpreter who does not seek to appreciate Isaiah or the Song of Songs as poetry, then, will not interpret them adequately. Even more clearly the Bible's stories are literary works, experiential and concrete theology, "full of the usual ingredients of literary narrative–adventure, mystery, brave and wise heroes, beautiful and courageous heroines, villains who get their comeuppance, rescues, guests, suspense, romantic love and pageantry." Thus "most parts of the Bible resemble the world of imaginative literature . . . more closely than they resemble the daily newspaper or an ordinary history book."[22]

Whether fundamentally factual or fundamentally fictional, a story creates a world before people's eyes or ears. In this respect, it is similar to a painting or a photograph (which again may be fundamentally fictional or fundamentally factual). It portrays the world that we live in, but "arranged into a meaningful pattern, in contrast to the fragmented pieces that make up our moment-by-moment living." It calls us back to the essential, the enduring, the fundamental, the truly real. It portrays for us "both a better and a worse world than the one we usually live with, and demands that we keep looking steadily at them both."[23] It may do that by conventions that are highly "unrealistic," such as those of C. S. Lewis's fantasy stories or Coleridge's *Ancient Mariner*, but this does not mean it is remote from reality. It may actually be closer to truth than documents that are completely factual but quite shallow or insignificant. Historical factuality is an important aspect of many biblical narratives, yet even narratives that are fundamentally historical are not mere archive or chronicle. Indeed, any writing of history involves making sense of data by bringing to them some vision of meaning capable of turning them into a story with a beginning, middle, and end. Facts do not speak for themselves; understanding them is always a hermeneutical enterprise. And the plots and configurations of history writing are the same as those of literature (or vice versa).[24]

Considering the features that make narratives more than collections of data is of great importance if we are to understand them. These features of their aim and method give works such as Kings or Ezra, Matthew or Acts, something in common

22. Leland Ryken, *Triumphs of the Imagination* (Downers Grove, Ill., and Leicester: InterVarsity, 1979), 22, 94.

23. Ibid., 85, referring to Northrop Frye's *The Educated Imagination* (Bloomington: Indiana University Press, 1964).

24. Cf. H. White, "Interpretation in History," *New Literary History* 4 (1972–73): 281–314; *Metahistory* (Baltimore and London: Johns Hopkins University Press, 1973).

with fictional narratives such as the parables or the largely fictional stories (as I take them to be) of Ruth and Job, Esther and Jonah.

All these biblical stories create a world before our eyes and ears. It is a world in which God promises blessing and shows a readiness to overcome all manner of obstruction, resistance, and delay in order to keep the promise. It is one in which God hears the cry of an oppressed and demoralized people, rescues them from their affliction, and draws them into a near relationship of worship and obedience. It is one in which a woman's life falls apart but is remade through the extraordinary loyalty of a foreign girl and the extraordinary love of a kinsman. It is one in which a prophet runs the other way when God calls him, has to be redirected by means of some foreign sailors and a bizarre monster, succeeds against his will in drawing his audience to repentance, but never comes to accept the nature of God even though he understands it quite well. It is one in which an extraordinary Galilean teacher and healer loses his life but regains it and promises to be with his followers always. It is one in which Palestinian artisans and Greek intellectuals begin to turn the world upside down by preaching about this man.

The world into which these stories invite us both attracts us and makes us hesitate to be drawn into it. It makes us draw near and draw back equally by its realism and by its vision. It is ruthlessly true to the suffering and sin that run through life and history: deprivation, animosity, fear, anxiety, hunger, guilt, injustice, immorality, loss, frustration, disappointment, grief, failure. This draws us because we want to be able to face these realities, to take account of them, to overcome them. It also makes us draw back lest these realities cannot be comprehended or overcome and lest to face them will thus bring a further pain that we can hardly bear or a cost that will be too high to pay. Stories can thus both reassure and challenge, support and confront, reinforce and unsettle; they may offer identity or disturb it. Different stories may "work" more one way or the other; some stories that are a comfort in one context would be false comfort in another (for instance, Chronicles if it were written in the time of Amos), some stories that are disturbing in one context would in another be a kick to a person already down (for instance, Kings in the time of the Chronicler).

Different types of story work in different ways. In the most intelligible introduction to structuralism in biblical studies that I know, J. D. Crossan remarks that "myth establishes world. Apologue defends world. Action investigates world. Parable subverts world."[25] Yet the best stories hold together comfort and confrontation, as they reflect life itself in holding together suffering and hope, cross and empty tomb, life in its gritty reality and death in which are the seeds of resurrection.

The Bible portrays a world in which the realities of sin and suffering can be faced, comprehended, and overcome, because active in it is also a God who blesses, who intervenes, whose providence works behind scenes, who refuses to give up when we insist on doing so, who in Christ walks earthly soil and in the Spirit walks in the

25. *The Dark Interval* (Miles, Ill.: Argus, 1975), 59.

midst of God's people. He finds his way to us in the midst of these very realities.[26] This portrait draws us, because we would like to live in such a world. It, too, makes us draw back, because we wonder whether that world actually exists. If we are to live in it, we have to be drawn into it the way a child is drawn into a story.

Indeed, we only really understand a story if we allow ourselves to be drawn into it. The parables, as the new hermeneutic has interpreted them, illustrate this point most clearly. Here Jesus begins by portraying the world that his hearers know well, the world of sowing and harvest, of shepherding and laboring, of weddings and funerals, of Pharisees, tax gatherers, priests, Levites, and Samaritans. He thus draws his hearers into his stories, because these stories manifestly relate to their world. They are at home in these stories, nodding in understanding as they unfold. But then Jesus' stories eject out of that world and somersault into a topsy-turvy one in which the tax gatherer finds God's favor, the Samaritan does the right thing, and people get a day's pay for an hour's work. The parables certainly create a new world, but the price is the destruction of an old one. They are understood only by those who are drawn into them and go through this world-destroying, world-creating process. Indeed, a good story has the power to draw you into it almost against your will. Story is characteristically open-ended, imaginative, experiential; it has the last word.[27] It is not only the parables that require a personal involvement if they are to be grasped. A narrative such as the story of Jesus, Simon the Pharisee, and the loose woman (Luke 7:36–50) requires an entering into the world of each participant as well as their common world if one is to hear it aright. The scientific ideal of objectivity in interpretation has its place, especially in interpreting instruction texts, but it is not up to interpreting story or prayer adequately.[28] The gospel story is designed to make something happen to people when they are drawn into its everyday but extraordinary world. It does not offer itself merely to the intellect. It addresses the whole being in the power of that reality that it portrays and that created it. It draws us into face-to-face involvement with the God of Israel and the Lord Jesus Christ active in our world, grasps us, and changes us as we come to link our story onto the one related in the biblical narrative. A "language-event" takes place.[29]

The Bible came into existence because people wanted others to share its world. The narrative texts of Scripture are as practical in purpose as the overt instruction texts. They are not just literature. To put this point another way, these texts that speak in the past tense, and refer to things that happened in the past, covertly relate to the future. By portraying a past or an imaginary or an other world they issue a promise, a challenge, or an invitation that opens up a future or a possible world. Even (especially) the Bible's stories about Beginning and End, while making a claim about

---

26. Cf. Amos N. Wilder, *The New Voice* (New York: Herder, 1966), 61–62.

27. So W. Brueggemann, *The Creative Word* (Philadelphia: Fortress, 1982), 61–62.

28. See further Hans-Georg Gadamer, *Truth and Method* (New York: Seabury; London: Sheed and Ward, 1975), e.g., 274–305.

29. Ernst Fuchs's term: see A. C. Thiselton, "The Parables as Language-Event," *SJT* 23 (1970): 437–68; R. W. Funk, *Language, Hermeneutic, and Word of God* (New York: Harper, 1966), 20–71.

linear history, also function like myths in that, because they portray a time when things are as they should be and are seen as they are, they "provide a paradigmatic or exemplary symbolic complex that is so raised above ordinary experience that it provides a norm and shape for it."[30]

Narrative texts thus seek the same commitment as instruction texts though they achieve this aim by more subversive means. They may be expected to imply the same beliefs and imperatives as instruction texts, but the story fleshes out the overt information and challenge of the didactic; perhaps the latter would be unintelligible without the former.[31] The story may sometimes express its didactic point quite overtly (cf. John 20:31); but this is rare, because if the story's didactics are too overt, the story itself becomes contrived and ceases to work as a story. It has to work indirectly, subliminally, if it is to work at all.

Characteristically, in instruction texts the form (the actual words the writer uses) is dispensable. The contents can be summarized, commented on, reexpressed, without necessarily losing anything. The ideas expressed in the words are what count. In contrast, a story cannot be paraphrased or summarized without losing something. The content comes via the story form and only via this form. The medium is the message. Admittedly, " 'narrative . . . is *translatable* without fundamental damage' in a way that a lyric poem or a philosophical discourse is not"; it is easier to understand another culture's stories than its thought patterns.[32] But narrative cannot be turned into straight didactic. The crucifixion story does things to the reader that a statement of the doctrine of the atonement does not. The latter will help me appreciate the story of the crucifixion more fully, and such a theology does need to be worked out, as happens in Scripture's own instruction texts; theology is not to be reduced to story.[33] Yet Christian theology is parasitic on the Christian story; the story gives it its raw material, and it is finally the story it serves, because it is the story (the gospel) that matters.

By describing narrative texts as a literature that opens up a world that we may enter, I have set an explicit or an implicit question mark alongside two common traditional ways of interpreting scriptural narratives, as designed to offer examples of the behavior that God does or does not approve, or as aiming to recount things that actually happened in history. Tradition does not in theory place exclusive emphasis on these two views of narrative; but homiletic practice has come close to an exclusive concern with the former, and exegetical practice has come close to an exclusive

---

30. Beardslee, "Narrative Form in the New Testament and Process Theology," 305; cf. his *Literary Criticism of the New Testament* (Philadelphia: Fortress, 1970), 21; James Barr, *Explorations in Theology* 7 (London: SCM, 1980) = *The Scope and Authority of the Bible* (Philadelphia: Westminster Press, 1980), 36, 126–27.

31. Cf. D. Tracy, "Metaphor and Religion," *Critical Inquiry* 5 (1978–79): 102; Gerhard Ebeling, *Theology and Proclamation* (London: Collins; Philadelphia: Fortress, 1966), 174.

32. H. White, "The Value of Narrativity in the Representation of Reality," *Critical Inquiry* 7 (1980–81): 5–6, quoting R. Barthes.

33. Cf. D. Ritschl and H. Jones, *"Story" als Rohmaterial der Theologie* (Munich: Kaiser, 1976).

preoccupation with the latter. Ever concerned to polarize from tradition when it perceives it, fashion is more recently inclined to be dismissive of both "moralizing" and historical positivism.[34] As usual, it is half right and needs to be considered with a cool head.

Three of the five New Testament narratives explicitly inform us of their purpose in writing: it is to tell us about Jesus in order to encourage in us a securely based faith in him (see Luke 1:1–4; John 20:31; Acts 1:1–5; we can here fudge the question of whether they refer to initial faith or ongoing faith). It is a fair inference that the aim of the major First Testament narratives, as well as that of Matthew and Mark, is comparable: it is to encourage faith and hope, repentance and commitment, in relation to Yahweh the God of Israel. Both Testaments relate God's story; God's person and activity are the narratives' supreme interest. They come into clearest focus.[35]

Human beings setting us examples are thus not a central feature of Scripture. One should not exaggerate the point: there are stories with a subordinate interest in pointing to a good example. There are also stories where human initiative, bravery, faith, or fortitude are central (e.g., Ruth, 1–2 Samuel, Ezra, Nehemiah, Esther). Yet even here it is doubtful whether they are exactly examples to be followed, partly because the characters are rather out of the ordinary for that (foreign heroines, Israelite kings, young princes, Persian officials, exiled queens), partly because it is as such that they, too, become part of God's story. Further, God's story advances despite as often as through human cooperation. Here, too, it is not a question of examples to be avoided; the story is too realistic to think that they will be. Rather, it portrays for us a world in which human sin and tragedy are real, but God's grace and providence are bigger, and it invites us to flee from moralizing to grace. The story of what God has done in Israel and what the God of Israel has done in Christ recounts the once-for-all events upon which the faith is based (its aetiology) and the characteristic pattern of events that it can look to see repeated (its paradigms). It offers mirrors for identity, not so much models for morality.[36] It portrays a world that should be, once was, and therefore can be again.

This takes us to the other traditional focus for the interpretation of scriptural narratives, the task of investigating how factual they are. This concern often assumes that the question Is the story true? can be reduced without remainder to the question Is the story historically factual? and further that understanding what the story means can be reduced without remainder to establishing what are the historical facts that underlie it. These two assumptions explain much of the past popularity of textbooks such as Bright's *A History of Israel*,[37] which has a reasonably conservative estimate of the First Testament's historical value and can be presumed, by recounting Israel's history, to be giving the reader an understanding of the meaning of the First

---

34. See, e.g., L. Keck, *The Bible in the Pulpit* (Nashville: Abingdon, 1978).

35. See Dale Patrick, *The Rendering of God in the Old Testament* (Philadelphia: Fortress, 1981), on this process.

36. So Sanders, "Hermeneutics," 406.

37. (First ed.; Philadelphia: Westminster Press; London: SCM, 1959).

Testament. These assumptions are mistaken. Some of the best stories in the Bible, the parables, are historically not true; they are fictions. Fiction's advantage is that it is not limited to representing what has happened; it can also represent what could happen.[38] Indeed, all biblical narrative is concerned with what could happen, not just with what has happened. We have noted that even narratives that are fundamentally historical are not mere archive or chronicle. The books of Kings offer the nearest thing to straight historiography in Scripture, but they, too, relate more than historical fact: they comprise a nightmare review of the history of Israel's relationship with God, an acknowledgment of the justice of the judgment of God, designed to draw Israel into an act of confession and thereby to open up the merest possibility of its having a future with God once again. The truth of the story involves much more than mere historical factuality, and the understanding of it is little furthered by books called *A History of Israel*.

This does not mean that the whole Bible could be fiction. Crossan asks, "is story telling us about a world out there objectively present before and apart from any story concerning it, or, does story create world so that we live as human beings in, and only in, layers upon layers of interwoven story?" and answers that the second is the case. God is unknowable, and "we can only live in story."[39] The creativity of the teller of Bible stories is well acknowledged. These stories do not claim to be directly God-given, as prophetic words do. They were works of the creative human imagination, as are stories outside the Bible. Acknowledging them as Scripture, however, implies that these particular stories indeed do reflect God's story. Their world may have been imagined, but we are not shut up to Crossan's gloomy view that it is merely imaginary. They are not stories that have sense, but lack reference.[40]

Part of the grounds for this conviction is the fact that the stories do commonly reflect factual history. They are more than history, not less than history. The belief that their vision of reality, their world, is true has part of its basis in the events they point to as evidence for that vision. Nevertheless, narrative exists in order to offer a patterned portrayal of events, to render a world, and this central aspect of its importance is ignored when interpreters are preoccupied with discovering what historical events are referred to by the various biblical narratives (the open, critical approach to the task) or with proving that historical events are referred to by the various biblical narratives (the apologetic, conservative approach to the task). These concerns equally distract the interpreter from the task of interpreting the narrative itself.

38. So R. Scholes and R. Kellogg, *The Nature of Narrative* (London and New York: Oxford University Press, 1966), 120–21, following Aristotle's *Poetics*; cf. Northrop Frye, *The Secular Scripture* (Cambridge, Mass., and London: Harvard University Press, 1976), 19; Tracy, "Metaphor and Religion," 100.

39. *The Dark Interval*, 9, 40–41; cf. Frank Kermode, *The Sense of an Ending* (London: Oxford University Press, 1966; New York: Oxford University Press, 1967), 36–40.

40. Cf. Paul Ricoeur, "Response" (to essays by Crossan and others), *Biblical Research* 24/25 (1979/80): 79; also D. Greenwood's discussion of "Poststructuralism and Biblical Studies" in *Gospel Perspectives* (ed. R. T. France and David Wenham; 6 vols.; Sheffield: JSOT, 1983), 3:263–88, and F. Lentricchia, *After the New Criticism* (Chicago: University of Chicago Press; London: Athlone, 1980).

Concern with the scientific factuality of Genesis 1 offers an instructive instance of the way a concern to investigate the historical events referred to by a narrative distracts attention from its actual meaning. Various aspects of the chapter's message (its world) become clear when one considers it in its contexts in the literary work to which it belongs (Genesis–Kings; Genesis–Exodus; Gen 1–11 and 12–50; Gen 1–2 and 3–11) and when one considers its own internal dynamic (e.g., its double climax in the creation of humanity and in God's rest; its structured form with its recurrent features such as God's speaking, God's seeing, and God's naming). Theologically, as the beginning of the Bible story, it is a most exciting chapter. Most of its excitement has been missed, however, when the focus has been placed on the relationship between its picture and the historical/scientific facts about world origins.

Similarly, such a focus is more of a hindrance than a help in interpreting the Gospels. Matthew and Luke offer markedly different accounts of Jesus' birth, the beginning of his ministry, and his resurrection appearances; but if the interpretive task concentrates on looking behind or harmonizing these differences, it ceases to follow the story Matthew or Luke told, the world they portrayed.

Investigating the history that lies behind a narrative can indeed fulfill two functions related to its interpretation. One, referred to above, is that if a narrative makes historical claims, the validity of these claims is a necessary though not a sufficient condition of the truth of the narrative. The other is that examining the differences between the events and the narrative's presentation of them (what they included, omitted, emphasized, reordered) will help us perceive aspects of the interpretation the narrative gives them. Comparing a new version of a story with an earlier one, too, can further the task of interpretation in this way.[41]

A concern with the historical events underlying a story or with the sources underlying its final form is still extrinsic to interpreting the story itself. Equally extrinsic to the story are the intentions of the author, except in the cases of Luke, John, and Acts, where (like Woody Allen and Hitchcock as directors, and some experimental novelists, I suspect) the authors insert themselves for a moment into their story. We often speak of interpreting a work in accordance with its author's intention, but that intention is elusive, in the case of the biblical books, except insofar as it is embodied or stated in the text itself.[42]

Knowing something of a narrative's historical background helps one to interpret it; Genesis 1 again offers an example, since various of its features gain their significance from its exilic context, and an awareness of that context enables us to spot those features. The significance of the parables can hardly be appreciated if one is unaware of the resonances of words such as "Pharisee" and "Samaritan" in the vocabulary of a first-century Jew. Without this we inevitably miss the scandal of Jesus' claim

41. See classically G. Bornkamm's study of Matt 8:23–27 in Günther Bornkamm, Gerhard Barth, and Heinz Joachim Held, *Tradition and Interpretation in Matthew* (London: SCM; Philadelphia: Westminster Press, 1963), 52–57.

42. See D. Newton-De Molina, ed., *On Literary Intention* (Edinburgh: Edinburgh University Press, 1976), for the debate on "intentionalism."

that God preferred the tax gatherer's prayer to the Pharisee's or of his impossible juxtaposition of the word "good" and the word "Samaritan."[43]

Often general features of Israelite or first-century life are an important part of the taken-for-granted background to biblical narratives. Nevertheless, the general value of efforts to establish the precise historical context of biblical narratives has been overrated. We can rarely (never?) place them geographically and historically with certainty and precision. Indeed, this may be inherent in their nature. Teaching texts work by revealing their background, intention, and message. Narrative texts work by being more reserved about these.

The key to the purpose and meaning of biblical narratives does not lie in data external to the text. It lies in the text itself. One perceives its meaning by means of an act of imagination, a guess, an intuition, more or less inspired, an act of divination.[44] Beginning from an insight—or rather a striking possibility—suggested by some aspect of the story, one jumps into the midst of the story and considers whole and part from this vantage point. Tentative purported insights thus have to be systematically explored and tested; interpretation requires a demanding combination of sensitivity, openness, enthusiasm, imagination, and the rigor and slog of hard work that develops ideas and tests them.[45] I do not wish to be reading an alien insight into the text, or more likely moving a marginal one into its center: this is an important insistence of E. D. Hirsch[46] against the more fashionable approach represented by Kermode, who inclines to the view that it is more important to be interesting than to worry about being right. I believe, for instance, that Genesis is the story of God's blessing—originally given, deservedly compromised, graciously promised, variously imperiled, partially experienced. That view is suggested by verbal clues in the text, but it must be tested by considering how the book's various episodes relate to this theme.[47]

Other biblical stories are more sparing in the clues they scatter, and leave us uncertain about their meaning. Is Jonah about how God deals with a reluctant prophet, or how God deals with a foreign nation, or even how God deals with a repentant Israel? What is the structure of Matthew, or Mark, or Luke? Responsible interpreters may formulate very different views on such questions. Others may not accept my understanding of Genesis, objectively clear and compelling though it seems to me.

Perhaps literary works have various meanings in different contexts or for different readers? This view offers openness and scope to the interpreter but threatens

---

43. Cf. A. C. Thiselton, "Understanding God's Word Today," in *Obeying Christ in a Changing World* (ed. J. Stott; 3 vols.; London: Collins, 1977), 1:107, quoting John Dominic Crossan, *In Parables* (New York: Harper, 1973), 64.

44. So F. Kermode, *The Genesis of Secrecy* (Cambridge, Mass., and London: Harvard University Press, 1979), 7, 16–17.

45. Cf. E. Haller, "On the Interpretative Task," *Int* 21 (1967): 161.

46. See his *Validity in Interpretation* (New Haven and London: Yale University Press, 1967); *The Aims of Interpretation* (Chicago and London: University of Chicago Press, 1976).

47. I have sought to do this in D. J. Wiseman and A. R. Millard, eds., *Essays on the Patriarchal Narratives* (Leicester: Inter-Varsity, 1980; Winona Lake, Ind.: Eisenbrauns, 1983), ch. 1.

arbitrariness. To insist (as Hirsch therefore does) that literary works have only one meaning (though they may have many applications or be capable of having fresh significance in different contexts) offers objectivity but threatens woodenness and makes much diversity of interpretation difficult to understand. We can appropriate some of the virtues of each of these views whilst sidestepping their drawbacks by affirming that part of the greatness of a good story may be a complexity that cannot be encapsulated in a single formula ("the story is about x"). Different readers will thus spot different facets of it. Interpreters may then be able to agree that there are several such facets: Ruth portrays how a Moabite comes into the center of the life and faith of Israel *and* how Yahweh takes an Israelite woman into terrible loss and grief but out the other side *and* what was the ancestry of King David.

Interpreters may also be able to agree on meanings that do not belong to the story, not so much because author or readers could or would not have envisaged them but because they are not natural to the story. Alongside looking for moral lessons, another preacher's instinct is to seek to reconstruct the psychology of biblical characters, because understanding our own and other people's feelings is so important in Western culture. A theologian's instinct, by contrast, is to seek to formulate the work's message in theological terms. But narratives rarely deal directly with either theology or the inner workings of the person (those concerns find nearer analogues in the material considered in sections 1 and 3 of this chapter), any more than with mere historical facts or moral examples. Interpreters need to be able to recognize when a text refuses to answer their questions, so that to press these will be to overinterpret them.[48]

To describe narratives as living portraits of an alternative world helps, finally, to align them with the future concern of books such as Daniel and Revelation and helps to interpret them. These books take the symbolism of didactic and the linear portrayal of narrative and project them onto the future. They arise out of contexts when the implicit promise of past narrative is insufficient, portraying a future that contrasts with the unhappy present, a world that should be, will be, and perhaps therefore can be.[49]

The existence of such forward projections of the line of biblical narrative draws attention to the further fact that each biblical story, while self-contained, also forms part of an overarching story extending from creation through the life of Israel and the Christ event to the new Jerusalem. This is of relevance to interpreting Scripture in that it means that no one biblical narrative can be finally understood out of the context of this overarching biblical story. Act 1 and Act 2 (First Testament events and New Testament events) can be understood only in light of each other.[50] The exodus cannot be understood out of the context of the exile or vice versa.[51]

48. Cf. Haller, "On the Interpretative Task," 160.

49. Cf. Beardslee, "Narrative Form in the New Testament and Process Theology," 305.

50. So John Bright, *The Authority of the Old Testament* (Nashville: Abingdon; London: SCM, 1967), 202–3.

51. Cf. John Goldingay, "The Man of War and the Suffering Servant," *TynB* 27 (1976): 79–113 (also at http://www.fuller.edu/sot/faculty/goldingay).

3. Prayer Texts

Biblical narrative grows as a new generation links its own story onto the story of God's dealings with his people in the past. The narrative from Genesis to Kings developed in this way. Chronicles-Ezra-Nehemiah adds the experience of the postexilic community to the story of Israel up to the exile. Luke adds part of the story of the early church to his Gospel; here in Acts the "implied author" explicitly introduces himself in the "we passages." In his letters, Paul links his story onto the story of Jesus (e.g., 1 Cor 15:1–11). How do we go about interpreting material in which people explicitly focus on relating their own experience?

One major tradition of studying interpretation over recent decades has treated written texts in general as the reflection of the particular historical (concrete, existential) experience of their authors, to which interpreters can gain access through their own analogous historical experience. This tradition's insights on interpretation provide us with a suggestive way in to interpreting prophetic or Pauline texts that directly reflect personal feelings, attitudes, and experience, such as Hosea, Jeremiah, Philippians 3, and Romans 7.[52] The material in the Bible that is most naturally susceptible to this approach is prayer texts such as the Psalms that, unlike most narrative or teaching texts, explicitly speak of the feelings, attitudes, and experiences of their authors.

The beginning of communication between people (parents and infants, foreigner and native, counselor and client) depends on two things they share. One is objects both can point to: mummy, daddy, teddy; tree, house, food; experiences of fear, loss, anger. The other is a mutual interest in these objects and a mutual involvement with them. If either party is not willing to look in the direction the other points, there can be no communication. In a parallel way, the beginning of our ability to hear what the Bible says is that we share things with it (we are also human beings relating in the one Spirit to the same God on the same basis) and that we want to grow in the understanding, relationship, and commitment to God expressed in these texts. Communication begins, then, on the basis of a shared interest in something people have in common. If a lion could talk, we could not understand it.[53]

Communication then develops by means of an ongoing conversation between such people. At first we only approximately grasp what the other person means; our categories of apprehension are rough and ready. A persistent, careful listening to the other person is needed if we are to come nearer to understanding what they are pointing to. We never totally grasp someone else's perspective, but that is the ultimate goal we nevertheless strive toward. Two friends or a married couple will recognize (perhaps ruefully) that they will never fully understand each other, yet they may also recognize that they understand each other a bit better each year. Their understanding develops as both are prepared to keep asking questions of each other and listening

52. Cf. Schökel, *The Inspired Word*.
53. Ludwig Wittgenstein, *Philosophical Investigations* (Oxford: Blackwell; New York: Macmillan, 1976), 223.

to each other's answers, to keep revealing themselves to each other and being open about how they see things. Asking the right questions is of key significance in a personal relationship, because they enable other people to express themselves to us.

Something similar is again true of the Bible. A strange conversation is involved because the outward form of the answers we shall receive from it is fixed. One aspect to the conversation, then, is that in seeking to discover the significance of these answers, I need to identify the question to which this text is a response. As I keep coming to it with the questions I can bring on the basis of what I have in common with it, it keeps responding. As particular aspects of its meaning grasp me, this enables me to formulate some further, fresh question that may free new facets of its meaning.

In an ordinary personal relationship, however, I am not merely concerned to understand another person. In learning to look at the world through their eyes I hope to understand not only them but also the world. I recognize that my own perspective on reality is limited by the fact that it is my perspective; it may be as good as anyone else's, but that does not mean I have nothing to learn. One of the devastating fruits of close friendship or marriage is the discovery that there are other perspectives on the world than my own. It is a positive fruit, however, because it can offer me the opportunity to broaden my horizon. So it is, again, with the Bible. I seek to empathize accurately with the psalmist's situation before God so that I can look at God and at life through the psalmist's eyes. Thus understanding involves learning to stand where someone else stands, seeking to look at the world through their eyes; and our shared involvement in the topic we are discussing is an indispensable aid towards a shared understanding. In parallel with this, our understanding of Scripture is facilitated by our sharing in a relationship with the God to whom the psalmist also speaks.

There is, however, a negative aspect to this feature of understanding; the involvement of which I have spoken is a potential liability as well as a potential asset. It may encourage us to identify our experience or our way of looking at things with the ones we are seeking to understand. We squeeze other people into our own mold and thus misunderstand them; we subsume what we think we hear within the categories of what we think we know already and thus miss distinctive features of what is said.

In a similar way, again, the experiences, needs, and desires we bring to the biblical text ("what rings a bell with me") are both an asset and a liability. They give us a starting point in asking questions of the text, but they may hinder us from hearing the things that the text was saying that do not correspond to what we have experienced or to what we are already interested in. We listen to the text's answers to our questions but ignore other aspects of the text that do not relate to these questions. As we may put it, only part of the text is "relevant." But if our questions, arising out of our experiences and interests, are to be our way in to understanding the text itself, then realizing that the text is actually the answer to a question rather different from the one we asked must lead not to our ignoring these other aspects of the text but to our seeking to formulate a new question that will open the way to hearing some of these other aspects. Generally, we hear "as though we know already, and can partly tell ourselves what we are to hear. Our supposed listening is in fact a strange mixture of hearing and our own speaking, and in accordance with the usual rule, it is most likely that our own speaking will be the really decisive event."[54] Thus a Latin American Roman Catholic perceives how prominent is the theme of political and national liberation in Scripture, which people in more privileged situations have often taken little note of, but misses the equal emphasis on spiritual liberation that also appears even in books such as Exodus. A North Atlantic evangelical notices the stress on personal salvation in the New Testament but misses the emphasis on the church. An Israeli Jew (or a Christian supporter of Israel) finds it easy to identify with the story of the conquest of Canaan in Joshua but may miss other features of the story such as God's concern to be fair to the existent inhabitants of Canaan. Our social context is thus particularly influential on what we are able to hear and what we miss. Some prayer texts (e.g., Ps 72) and some other parts of the Bible are difficult to hear in an industrial rather than an agricultural society. We may need to imagine ourselves in a developing country rather than a developed one in order to interpret them.[55]

The church's familiarity with and its commitment to Scripture is thus both a liability and an asset with regard to interpreting Scripture. Its familiarity gives us a way in to understanding it, but it may mean that the cutting edge of what it says is blunted; conversely, unfamiliarity with Scripture may enable us to hear it quite freshly or may make it difficult for us to hear it at all. Participation in the realities Scripture speaks of helps us to perceive them there and to respond to them; a purely clinical, analytical understanding misses the most vital dimensions of these texts. Yet this same assumed identification with Scripture unwittingly hinders our perceiving aspects of the text that do not already have equivalents in our faith. Those who are most committed to the biblical gospel may be hindered from understanding that gospel precisely by this loyalty.

In John, Jesus reminds us forcefully of this point. Those who are committed to doing God's will recognize teaching that comes from God (John 7:17). Yet those who were most familiar with the Scriptures and had committed themselves most unequivocally to following the Scriptures had the most difficulty in perceiving what they were pointing to. A further aspect to the charismatic nature of interpretation appears here. Interpretation involves the Holy Spirit not only because our imagination needs the shafts of intuition the Spirit has to give but also because our wills need the softening that the Spirit has to effect if we are to be open to costly new insights on the significance of Scripture for us. Interpretation is a moral issue. This relates to the fact that when we say "Jesus is Lord" or "Yahweh is a great God" we are not merely conveying information but declaring our commitment and our worship. The "deep structure" of these statements is similar to that of declarations such as

54. Barth, *Church Dogmatics,* I/2, 470; cf. W. W. Johnson, "The Ethics of Preaching," *Int* 20 (1966): 423.

55. On this problem, cf. R. L. Rohrbaugh, *The Biblical Interpreter* (Philadelphia: Fortress, 1978).

"We believe in Jesus Christ" or "We praise you, God." For such true statements to be truly interpreted, to be authentic on my lips, part of their significance must be to indicate my commitment—even if Bultmann went too far when he implied that "Jesus is Lord" indicates mainly or even exclusively that commitment ("for a certain performative utterance to be happy, certain statements have to be true").[56] We have to seek to understand texts in their historicity; but we have to do so out of our own historicity, the assumptions and horizons that affect how we see and what we see. Our personal situation and context shape the way we read, just as the authors' situations and contexts shaped the way they wrote, and we have to reflect as carefully about the former as we do about the latter. The image of the merging of horizons[57] has thus come to be used to describe the process of interpretation. I inevitably view the world from the vantage point where I stand, which fixes a horizon for me. If I can look at it from someone else's vantage point, my horizon is broadened. I can see reality more fully.

My historicity means I am not only in a different context from that of the text; I am in a later one, and all that has happened between the emergence of the text and my own life both links me positively to it and makes it difficult (impossible?) to hear it as I would have done when it was first uttered. Helen Gardner commented that *The Waste Land* in 1972 was a different poem from the one printed in October 1922 in *The Criterion*: familiar and famous, not new and exciting; fixed in a certain period of the past, not contemporary; located in the midst of the total T. S. Eliot corpus, not at the culmination of his then corpus.[58] Elvis Presley's records of the 1950s can be appreciated now in a way they could not then, even though (or rather because?) they cannot now strike us with the shock and offensiveness that they then had. The First Testament cannot be the same for the reader who comes to it as a Christian as it was for the believing Jew of pre-Christian (or post-Christian) times.

My historicity makes some texts more difficult for me to hear than others. In the 1920s, Romans suddenly became audible again in Germany, as had happened in the sixteenth century. During later decades of the twentieth century, 1 Corinthians 12–14 became audible again in many parts of the world. The Luther and the Barth for whom Romans came alive (let alone those who suddenly made sense of 1 Cor 12–14) themselves misheard their texts in marked ways, but at least some appropriation of them was now going on.

It is partly because different texts can be heard at different times that understanding a biblical text is not a once-for-all act. I can perceive aspects of it today, but miss others, which I may be able to see tomorrow. One generation becomes blind to insights that were once well appreciated (hence the value of using the commentaries of other centuries), but is in a position to perceive things long neglected. While

56. J. L. Austin, *How to Do Things with Words* (Oxford: Clarendon; Cambridge, Mass.: Harvard University Press, 1962), 45; cf. Anthony C. Thiselton, "The Use of Philosophical Categories in New Testament Hermeneutics," *Churchman* 87 (1973): 96.

57. See Gadamer, *Truth and Method*.

58. Helen Gardner, *"The Waste Land"* (Manchester: Manchester University Press, 1972), 1–2.

the story of biblical scholarship includes some ongoing development of insight and emancipation from error, like the one that characterizes the story of science, more fundamentally it is the story of each generation's attempt to appropriate the biblical message in its own context, and the story follows a zigzag line; insights are sometimes lost, sometimes regained.

A further aspect of our historicity is that the Bible as a whole is separated from us by the gulf that divides us from the biblical world (worlds, indeed), a gulf carved out by differences in people's beliefs and assumptions, in how they think, behave, react, feel, and experience life, which are unmentioned by the text itself because they do not separate author and original reader, though they do separate author and modern reader. Dennis Nineham often returns to this theme.[59] One may question his more extreme statements doubting whether any satisfactory understanding of the Bible is possible, with the theological inference he builds on these that contemporary Christian faith cannot base itself on the Bible. His work is valuable, however, because it presses on us the reality of the gulf referred to above. Understanding the Bible is a demanding exercise, like understanding Philo or Origen, Chaucer or Shakespeare. To appreciate these works in their original significance (like fully understanding any other human being) is an ultimately unattainable goal, yet it remains the interpreter's aim, even while recognizing that our having to view them in our different context is itself an aid to other aspects of their interpretation. The works themselves can transcend the gap that separates us from them, and in some ways the passage of time gives us a perspective that makes them easier to interpret.[60]

How, then, are we to perceive where lie the differences between our own experience and perspective and those witnessed to in the text? How may we safeguard against misreading our experiences and perspectives into a text that actually speaks of different ones? One of the chief significances of the methods of biblical criticism lies in the distancing from the text that they can give to the person who identifies with the text. Critical methods treat the text as an object independent of me; this may be a bad way to start reading the Bible, and it is certainly a bad way to end doing so, but on the way it may facilitate the move from a "first naivety" to a second, postcritical naivety, a move via a hermeneutic of suspicion to a hermeneutic of recovery.[61] The

59. See *The Use and Abuse of the Bible* (London: Macmillan; New York: Barnes, 1976); *Explorations in Theology* 1 (London: SCM, 1977); "The Strangeness of the New Testament World," *Theology* 85 (1982): 171–77, 247–55.

60. On this issue from a theological perspective see J. Barton, "Reflections on Cultural Relativism," *Theology* 82 (1979): 103–9, 191–99; Anthony C. Thiselton, *The Two Horizons* (Exeter: Paternoster; Grand Rapids: Eerdmans, 1980), 53–60; S. Coakley, "Theology and Cultural Relativism," *Neue Zeitschrift für Systematische Theologie und Religionsphilosophie* 21 (1979): 223–43; F. G. Downing, "Our Access to Other Cultures," *Modern Churchman* 21 (1977): 28–42; and from a literary perspective see Steiner, *After Babel*, 1–31; H. Gardner, *The Business of Criticism* (London and New York: Oxford University Press, 1959), 25–51; Lionel Trilling, "The Sense of the Past," in *The Liberal Imagination* (New York: Viking; London: Secker, 1951), esp. 187.

61. Paul Ricoeur's terms: see, e.g., *Freud and Philosophy* (New Haven: Yale University Press, 1970), 28–36, 496.

highly cerebral exercise of learning the biblical languages has its place here. The task of translation is, after all, the culmination of the act of interpretation, not a mere preliminary to it. It is an attempt to express the meaning of the words I have sought to understand. It parallels the counselor's attempt to reexpress in different words what the client said, to establish to both parties that the counselor has heard aright. While we can get an accurate enough understanding of a biblical text from a translation (better, by comparing translations), there are insights on the nuances of the text that seem to come only through close attention to its actual words, as counseling demands close attention to the very words of the client. Understanding something in a foreign language via an interpreter is quite possible, but unless the material is of a very down-to-earth kind, you are bound to miss something. Sharing someone's language is part of being willing and able to listen to him or her at all.

Another concern of criticism is to consider the Bible against its social context, seeking to identify the conventions of speech that lie behind its various texts. In any culture there is a range of attitudes, assumptions, ways of thinking, and ways of behaving that all who live in that culture accept without considering them. To such an extent are they taken for granted that we are not even aware of taking them for granted until we enter another culture that does not do so and has its own habits and assumptions. Now for us the Bible is such another culture, and one aspect of the complex task of understanding it is to discover its conventions of thinking and speaking. Form criticism deals with one aspect of this task by seeking to identify the basic genres or forms that appear in a literature and the social context (*Sitz im Leben*) to which they belong.

That such study is to be expected to illumine our understanding of a literature can readily be illustrated from our own culture. The various items that may come into our mailbox (a letter from a friend, an advertising circular, a bill, a wedding invitation, a greeting card) each have forms of their own. The kind of paper that is used, the format, the language, the opening and closing phrases, all constitute signals that take us a substantial way toward understanding the meaning of each item before we examine what the words actually say. One can imagine how difficult it would be for people in Africa in three thousand years' time to understand this material, given their unfamiliarity with the conventions that we take for granted.

This is our own position in relation to the Bible, a wide-ranging collection of works from a different age, a different culture, a different civilization. Form criticism seeks to recover the way things were said and written in that world and to devise the right kind of question-and-answer procedure that will open up the distinctive meanings (and expose the distinctive sets of possible misunderstandings) that belong to each genre.

As it happens, form-critical study of prayer texts has been a particularly fruitful exercise. The Psalms themselves were among the first subjects of the pioneer form-critic Hermann Gunkel, who analyzed basic ways of speaking to God represented in them. His work was taken further by Sigmund Mowinckel, who looked at the Psalms systematically as the vehicles of Israel's corporate worship, the expressions of its self-identity and the means of its mutual fellowship.[62] While such study takes us into the shared conventions of prayer texts, form is not all; a person uses form to express something unique. Comparing examples of various genres helps one to perceive the individuality of particular prayers and praises. Psalms 95 and 100, for instance, are psalms of praise with close parallels, except there is nothing in Psalm 100 that corresponds to the closing stanza of Psalm 95, where the movement of communication turns from congregation-God to God-congregation as God invites the enthusiastic worshipers to shut up for a minute and listen. (It is ironic that in the Church of England this last, distinctive section of Ps 95 came to be omitted from worship.) Sometimes the individuality of an author takes up a familiar form in order to make it do something quite different. My mail includes advertisements that are personalized in the hope that I may treat them as "proper" letters; newspapers include advertisement features designed to attract the credence given to editorial matter or satire that could be taken by the unimaginative (or the person from another culture) as a serious editorial. In the First Testament, Amos uses the form of an oracle of judgment on the nations to soften up Israel for an oracle of judgment against itself, the form of an invitation to worship to indict Israel about the true nature of its worship, and the form of a funeral dirge to picture Israel fallen by God's judgment (Amos 1:3–2:16; 4:4; 5:1–2). Such creative individual use of forms makes clear that texts such as the Psalms that reflect basic forms are not mere formal, institutional texts written to order for an institutionalized cult. They reflect the real experience of nation and individual. Claus Westermann has especially emphasized the point; it is significant that he came to his research on the Psalms from the background of the experience of the Confessing Church in the 1930s and from his personal experience of prison camp. Walter Brueggemann has taken this study further in light of Ricoeur's work on hermeneutics, seeing the Psalms as representing various stages of personal experience of orientation or equilibrium, disorientation, and reorientation in a new faith.[63]

In discussing how we interpret prayer texts, we have brought together two contrasting approaches to interpretation. One begins by assuming that our experience and the experience reflected in the text are parallel, so that the one can be understood in light of the other; it emphasizes the link between the two human experiences. The other approach seeks to distance the interpreter from the text and look at it "objectively" in light of its context rather than in light of the interpreter's experience. It is the differences between these two approaches that make them so important to each other. On its own, the objective, critical approach to Scripture falls short.

---

62. See, e.g., Hermann Gunkel, *The Psalms* (Philadelphia: Fortress, 1967); Sigmund Mowinckel, *The Psalms in Israel's Worship* (Oxford: Blackwell; Nashville: Abingdon, 1962).

63. See Claus Westermann, *Praise and Lament in the Psalms* (Atlanta: John Knox; Edinburgh: T&T Clark, 1981); Walter Brueggemann, "Psalms and the Life of Faith," *JSOT* 17 (1980): 3–32; Brueggemann alludes to Paul Ricoeur's *Interpretation Theory* (Fort Worth: Texas Christian University Press, 1976) and *Conflict of Interpretations* (Evanston, Ill.: Northwestern University Press, 1974), as well as works referred to above.

It falls short of the modern readers' hopes (they learn nothing from Scripture that can relate to their faith), and it falls short of the ancient text's hope (given that it was written and preserved in order to speak for and to people in their relationship to God). Karl Barth points out that it is precisely in following where the text in its humanity points, in treating it historically, that we have to grapple with the divine reality that is its concern.[64]

On its own, the approach that hastens to identify its concern with those of the text also easily falls short because it can encourage us to use the text merely to confirm us in the religious beliefs we had before we read it. We assume that the experience to which the text witnesses mirrors our own; we look down the well and see ourselves. So here objective, critical approaches can help us respond in trust and obedience to the scriptural texts themselves, because they help us actually to hear these texts aright. (Ricoeur remarks that Sigmund Freud in his *Moses and Monotheism* "thought he could economize on biblical exegesis" with the result that "he found, at the end of the analysis, only what he knew before undertaking it.")[65] "Whether in terms of the current 'contextual' emphasis in the World Council of Churches [WCC], or in terms of the charismatic movement, a polarization has emerged between the preoccupation with present experience and the study of the New Testament.... The hermeneutical task is to establish a relationship between two sets of horizons; those of the New Testament itself, and those of the interpreter's present experience and conceptual frame."[66]

That statement (which of course applies to First Testament study too) has a history going back long before the WCC and the charismatic movement. Indeed, the central tragedy of the history of biblical study over the past two centuries is that the objective, distancing, critical approach to Scripture and the obedient, trusting, experiential approach have proceeded in substantial independence of each other. The one is appropriate to the scholarly game and the exam treadmill, the other to believers on their knees praying or on their feet preaching. They are brought up on the second approach, struggle with the first approach to get a degree, and revert with relief to the first when they escape their professor's eye in the conviction that it is the application of the Bible in the contemporary world that counts; there is not enough time for the luxury of the distancing, critical approach. Our contemporary application of Scripture will be shallow and/or predetermined by the insights and experiences we bring to Scripture if we concentrate exclusively on contemporary application. Conversely, as we give ourselves seriously to understanding a passage for what it first meant to its writers and readers, the question of its application to us will often solve itself.

For an odd thing can happen when we do concentrate on that objective understanding. As we seek to enter the concrete fact of that past moment when some

---

64. *Church Dogmatics*, I/2, 463–70.
65. Paul Ricoeur, *Freud and Philosophy*, 349.
66. Thiselton, "The Use of Philosophical Categories in New Testament Hermeneutics," 98.

people very distant from us met with God, suddenly we find ourselves in that situation and see ourselves confronted by that God. We realize that it is in one sense a totally different situation from any we know, but it is our God meeting the same flesh and blood in Christ as we are. We can appreciate their testimony and make our response to that same God. We meet God precisely through entering into a particular situation whose distance from ourselves we emphasize—through, not despite, that distancing process.

It will be evident that the kind of historical study that can lead to this insight is not the mere analysis of sources and reconstruction of events on which biblical study has often concentrated. Such procedures can clarify what is unclear because of our historical distance from the text and thus remove some of the disadvantages of not being the writer's original audience, but they do not in themselves help us grasp the point the writer was making. The old Russian icon had to be "'discovered' not only physically—in that all the soot and more recent layers of paint have been removed—but also spiritually; we have learned how to look at it."[67] So it has to be with Scripture. Critical procedures open up the possibility of interpretation and help us to check purported interpretations, but they are not the task of interpretation itself. We understand Scripture only as we think ourselves into the text's perspective and let it interact with our own.

A reversal of movement in the process of interpretation thus takes place. As we have noted, I start as the subject, speaking, asking questions, being objective about the Bible, seeking to avoid reading into it the views I already hold or the experience I already have or the commitments I already accept. Then suddenly it becomes the subject, speaking, addressing, asking questions, challenging my views, my experiences, and my commitments; I am the object on the receiving end of its scrutiny. This exciting moment unveils whether I really regard the Bible as the word of God in human words, by acting on what I hear.

In the case of prayer texts and other works that directly reflect an author's own experience, that movement naturally has a different dynamic from ones we have considered in sections 1 and 2. There a word is spoken to me (or at least I put myself into the position of those to whom it was addressed). Here a word is spoken for me. The text is given to me to articulate on my behalf an experience, an attitude, a belief, a prayer. My response to it is to use it in this way, to allow it to call forth from me the praise, the prayer, the act of commitment, the protest, the declaration of trust that the text itself expresses. As well as having implied authors, texts have implied readers or ideal readers, and interpretation involves becoming such readers.[68]

Sometimes, admittedly, we find ourselves uncertain as to what kind of reader is anticipated by a text. Some texts are ambiguous. On occasion this is because we lack the right information that would enable us to see the text's meaning. At other times

---

67. N. S. Trubeckoj, in Matejka and Pomorska, eds., *Readings in Russian Poetics*, 119.
68. Cf. R. Cohen in Valdés and Miller, eds., *Interpretation of Narrative*, 5.

ambiguity is built into the text; it is there to put further questions to the reader, who learns precisely by having to decide how to read the text.[69]

Although this reader-response approach to interpretation is often appropriate to narrative, it comes into its own with prayer texts, which speak to me by asking me what, if anything, I would mean by taking this text on my lips. I as the subject questioning the text may be unable to discover whether a psalm that expresses a love for God's law arose out of a "legalistic" attitude (it can be read that way) or whether a psalm that praises or laments in stereotyped fashion arose out of genuine praise or prayer (it need not be read that way). But the text as the subject questioning me penetrates to my inner person (cf. Heb 4:12) to discover whether I have the prayer, praise, or commitment to express by means of this text; not just to discover whether I have them, but to evoke that response to God by offering itself as a vehicle for it.[70]

---

69. Cf. P. D. Miscall, *The Workings of Old Testament Narrative* (Philadelphia: Fortress, 1983), on this aspect of the Abraham and David stories; S. E. Fish, e.g., "Interpreting the Variorum," *Critical Inquiry* 2 (1975–76): 465–85.

70. Cf. Brueggemann, "Psalms and the Life of Faith," 17–19.

2

What Difference Does It Make If You Are Premodern, Modern, or Postmodern?

G. W. F. Hegel is credited with a three-stage model for understanding the history of thought.[1] First, some theory or thesis is accepted. Subsequently, a counterthesis or antithesis gains acceptance. Then a synthesis combines the truths in the first two.[2] Current conventional wisdom implies a Hegelian understanding of the history of biblical interpretation. In the first millennium there was premodern interpretation, the second millennium saw the development of modern interpretation, and in the third there is postmodern interpretation. Calling this the conventional wisdom implies a recognition that it may look silly in a few years' time. Associating it with Hegelianism implies a recognition that it imposes categories on the history; for instance, some features of Jewish practice in the first millennium had features in common with the modern as well as the premodern. In addition, it reflects our

---

1. An expanded version of material first published in John W. Rogerson and James D. G. Dunn, eds., *Eerdmans Commentary on the Bible* (Grand Rapids: Eerdmans, 2003), 13–20. I adapt the opening paragraph, and some subsequent paragraphs, from *An Ignatian Approach to Reading the Old Testament* (Cambridge: Grove, 2002), 3–7, and some other paragraphs from volume 1 of *Old Testament Theology* (3 vols.; Downers Grove, Ill.: InterVarsity, 2003; Carlisle: Paternoster, 2006).

2. Admittedly the Hegelian scheme seems not to derive directly from Hegel, as Calvinism does not derive directly from Calvin: see, e.g., Gustav E. Mueller, "The Hegel Legend of 'Thesis-Antithesis-Synthesis,'" in *The Hegel Myths and Legends* (ed. Jon Stewart; Evanston, Ill.: Northwestern University Press, 1996), 301–18.

need to understand matters in a way that provides them with structure and provides history with closure. It is still a helpful framework. It may help us consider aspects of the way these three ages approach the nature of the biblical text, its origin, its historical reference, and its exegesis, and suggest ways our postmodern context opens up possibilities for the aims and practice of biblical study and enables us to appropriate the strengths of premodern and modern while sidestepping their respective weaknesses.

1. Premodern

a. Text. The New Testament illustrates the nature of premodern attitudes to the text of the First Testament. While assuming that these Scriptures are the inspired words of God, it quotes them in ways that show it did not infer a need to be inflexible over the details of the text.

The New Testament's first quotation comes from Isaiah 7:14, which says, "There, the maiden is pregnant and is going to give birth to a son. You[3] will call him 'God-is-with-us.'" The text in Matthew 1:23 corresponds to the fairly literal LXX version except that the LXX reads, "they will call." Matthew 2:6 goes on to introduce a quotation from Micah, "You, Bethlehem in the land of Judah, are by no mean least among the rulers of Judah, for from you will come out a ruler who will shepherd my people Israel." Micah 5:2 [MT 1] itself says, "You, Bethlehem in Ephrath, small to be in the clans of Judah, from you will come out for me one to be ruler in Israel." Here Matthew does not follow the fairly literal LXX version. While the change from "clans" to "rulers" could indicate free translation or a different reading of an ambiguous text, this is not true of the replacement of Ephrath by Judah or of the addition of "my people." Further, Matthew reverses Micah's point about Bethlehem's insignificance and adds the "for" that reworks the link between Micah's clauses.

These not-untypical opening quotations illustrate how the New Testament can quote the scriptural text with relative exactness, or with small changes, or with far-reaching adaptations. It can translate it from the original or quote it from an existent Greek translation. It shows no concern to quote Scripture with precision.

The textual data presented by the New Testament compare with those presented by the Qumran scrolls. One Isaiah scroll (1QIs[b]), for instance, presents a text very close to the MT, but another (1QIs[a]) presents a text with many more detailed differences. None of these differences changes the nature of the scriptural message. In substance the texts are the same, but they differ in many details. The Qumran community, like the early Christian community, did not sense that their commitment to the Scriptures entailed a concern for a single text form.

b. Origin. Premodern works may be explicit about their authorship, or may be anonymous, or may be pseudonymous. Paul includes his name in letters, and John

---

3. The verb is second person singular feminine (i.e., the prophet is now addressing the woman).

includes his name in Revelation. Genesis–Kings and at least two of the Gospels are anonymous, though the communities that treasured these works were inclined to link them with famous names: the Pentateuch became the five books of Moses, and two anonymous Gospels came to be associated with Matthew and Mark, while Hebrews came to be Paul's. There are thus a number of pseudonymous works and no anonymous works in the KJV of the New Testament.

What was going on here? Why should the authorship of a work be of interest? First, it may buttress the work's authority; for Paul, the authority of his writings derives in part from his being an apostle and from his specific relationship with churches he founded. Second, it can put flesh on the bones of a document. We can imagine Solomon contemplating his achievements and possessions in the testimony in Ecclesiastes, and Paul interacting with the churches he visited.

The instincts that made people provide anonymous works with a link to known persons will have had similar backgrounds. It can again put flesh on a document's bones. The association of David with psalms where he is not mentioned either in the body of the psalm or in its heading makes it possible to imagine them on the lips of a concrete person known from the First Testament story. It can also undergird a work's authority. It will have been because of its contents that Hebrews became an authoritative document; attributing it to Paul then buttressed or symbolized its authority. Moses, Joshua, and Matthew were in a position to tell the story of the exodus, the conquest of Canaan, and the story of Jesus, so they were appropriate people to link with accounts of these events that had gained acceptance in Israel or in the church. Papias's story about Mark writing down Jesus' story in accordance with the way Peter told it[4] undergirds that Gospel's authority while also providing readers with a vivid and attractive picture of the Gospel's origin. One attributes a document to someone whose name will enhance it; choosing an unknown person would defeat the object of the exercise. Readers can feel that the Bible came from important people who had lived lives close to God and could speak reliably about God's ways. Thus Jeremiah becomes the pseudonymous author of the anonymous poems in Lamentations. Books first gain the community's assent and recognition as given by God, and are subsequently linked with an appropriate human author.

These are examples of anonymous writings becoming pseudonymous within Jewish and Christian tradition. I imagine the same instincts had earlier led to anonymous material becoming pseudonymous in the form in which it appears within Scripture itself. The Book of the Covenant, the Priestly Code, and the Deuteronomic Code did not come from Moses, but their anonymous creators saw their work as expounding the significance of Mosaic faith for their various times. When the Qumran community attributed a document to Moses, it was declaring the conviction that it had Mosaic authority; while its authors might have been making a cynical claim, more likely they,

4. See *Ante-Nicene Christian Library* (repr., Edinburgh: T&T Clark; Grand Rapids: Eerdmans, 1989), 1:154–55.

too, believed their work expressed Mosaic faith.[5] It is difficult to be sure of the original significance of the expression *ledawid* in the headings to many psalms, but it came to be understood as an indication of authorship, and this made it possible to imagine David writing these individual psalms in concrete situations in which he needed to reach out to God, and eventually to see David as the writer of the other psalms in which he is not mentioned. Convictions about authorship thus become hermeneutical keys to understanding books. The book of Daniel points to another conviction. Why did second-century visionaries ascribe their visions to Daniel, a figure from previous centuries? The link of content suggests Daniel's visions had inspired theirs. The Holy Spirit brought into being the visions in Daniel 7–12 by inspiring people's reflection on Daniel's own vision in Daniel 2 and on other Scriptures (rather as the Holy Spirit subsequently brought into being the visions in Revelation by inspiring John's reflection on material in the First Testament Scriptures). Something similar is true about the inclusion in the book called Isaiah of much material that did not issue from Isaiah ben Amoz. There, too, the Holy Spirit inspired much of that material by encouraging people to reflect on the oracles of Isaiah to see what God had to say to later centuries in light of what Isaiah himself had said.

   c. Reference. Until the eighteenth century, readers understood First Testament narratives in a "realistic" way, treating them as factual accounts of God's involvement in Israel's life over the centuries, though doing this unreflectively without asking questions concerning whether the biblical story corresponds to what actually happened. They also took for granted that the narrative corresponded to the story of their own lives in the sense that they interpreted and judged the story of their lives by the Bible story. In the eighteenth century, both these assumptions came apart.[6] People came to interpret and evaluate the Bible story by their own story, as people still do, asking whether it is relevant, not whether we are. In addition, they became preoccupied by the difference between the history of Israel and the story the First Testament tells and the difference between the Jesus of history and the Jesus of the Gospels. It requires some effort of the imagination to put ourselves back into a context where this was not so. Today when someone says, "Jonah was three days and nights in the sea monster's belly," he or she will have a view on whether the statement refers to something that happened historically or that happened in a story. When Jesus said those words, neither he nor his hearers need have worked with that antithesis.

   The etymology of the words "history" and "story" tells an instructive tale in this connection. Both derive from a Greek root that provides parts of the defective verb *oida*, "to know" (e.g., *iste*, "you know"). A *histōr* is a person who knows, a wise person; *historein* refers to learning by investigating something and then to narrating what one has learned, and *historia* is an inquiry or its results, specifically a narrative. The biblical narratives are thus instances of *historia*. They offer insight in narrative form

---

5. On the range of reasons for pseudonymity, see Bruce M. Metzger, "Literary Forgeries and Canonical Pseudepigrapha," *JBL* 91 (1972): 3–25.
   6. I here follow Hans Frei, *The Eclipse of Biblical Narrative* (New Haven and London: Yale University Press, 1974). See further chapter 5 (section 3) below.

that results from inquiry. That itself might suggest that the material their authors have investigated includes factual material but need not be confined to that. This corresponds to the nature of history writing in the ancient world.

The point may be made in another way by considering the nature of much of the scriptural story as midrash, Chronicles being in part a midrash on Kings, and Matthew on Mark and Chronicles. As midrash it retells a story to show what it now signifies for people, in light of other Scriptures and other convictions regarding God's word to the people now. When this retelling involved changing words attributed to Solomon or Jesus, the authors presumably realized that what they were writing was not straight history. They and their readers could apparently live happily with that, perhaps rather like Shakespeare and the people who watch his plays, or the scriptwriter and viewers of movies such as *Erin Brockovich* or *A Beautiful Mind.*

Jesus and the New Testament writers can refer to Exodus as "the book of Moses," to material from different parts of Isaiah as "Isaiah," and to the Psalms in general as "David's." Whereas they might seem to be implying a conviction about the actual authorship of the different books, their words more parallel statements such as that the sun rises (e.g., Matt 5:45; 13:6), which hardly indicate a position on the question whether the earth revolves round the sun as opposed to the sun revolving round the earth. In such texts, Jesus speaks conventionally and phenomenologically. He is not making pronouncements about questions of authorship or cosmology. The same argument does not apply to his treating the Scriptures as having incontrovertible theological and ethical authority. This is also a premodern attitude, but one with more far-reaching implications. Working with conventional ways of speaking about cosmology or about the human authorship of books is one thing; working with conventional views regarding the authority of the books is another. If Jesus is sharing the mistaken views of his day on this question, or making a concession to conventional views, this affects the substance of his teaching in a significant way.

d. Exegesis. Actual interpretation, interaction with the text's meaning, in the premodern period is again conveniently illustrated for us by the New Testament's interpretation of the First Testament. The First Testament Scriptures decisively shaped and resourced Jesus' self-understanding and the early Christians' understanding of Jesus and of the church. They did so in an imaginative and intuitive rather than an analytic and systematic fashion. Matthew wants to understand the surprising story of Jesus' birth and early life, and does so by putting a verse of the Scriptures alongside an incident within it that gives him and his community some insight regarding what on earth that was about and what it meant (see Matt 1:18–2:23). Paul wants to provide a rationale for the material support of apostles or to shake a congregation into living more uprightly or to underline how Jesus must reign over everything, and one of the ways he does so is by incorporating passages from the Scriptures into his argument (see 1 Cor 9:9; 10:1–13; 15:27). Premodern interpretation can thus generate powerful application of Scripture directly addressing new contexts and the questions arising there. The understanding of Jesus and of the church that we derive from the New Testament could not have existed without this use of the Scriptures. God used it to mediate key insights for Jesus himself as his Father addressed him in words from Psalm 2, Genesis 22, and Isaiah 42, "You are my son, my beloved, with whom I am well-pleased" (Mark 1:11) to set before him crucial insights on his identity and vocation.

Such use of Scripture utilized exegetical principles recognized in its context and also suggests some theological principles: the Scriptures are the Spirit-inspired words of God to Israel, Jesus is the climax of Israel's story, and a Christian congregation is a local embodiment of what Israel was called to be. But this use of Scripture did not emerge from such a conscious hermeneutical/theological framework. Premodern interpretation was intuitive. It started from present context and from faith convictions and moved back to the Scriptures. The serendipitous way New Testament writers quote from the text is one symbol of that. Their angle of vision did not predetermine what they saw there, though it did determine the *kind* of thing they saw. It also meant that their interpretation would hardly convince someone who did not accept their starting point, their faith in Jesus; it was not designed to do so. However, the argument of Acts suggests it might be expected to convince people when it formed part of a larger picture: namely, when there were extraordinary events that needed explaining and such interpretation opened the way to a plausible explanation. One might describe it as "charismatic interpretation." It involves the Holy Spirit inspiring people to find God saying things to them through a text that ignores the meaning the text had when the Holy Spirit inspired it as an exercise in communication between God and people in its original context.

New Testament interpretation of Genesis 1–3 provides many examples of the interpretation of Scripture in light of current issues and convictions, and it sometimes troubles Christians, particularly those of a feminist persuasion. Most notoriously, 1 Timothy 2 supports the requirement that women keep silent in church with a reference to Adam's being formed before Eve and Eve's being the one who was deceived and became the transgressor, not Adam. The passage "uses data from Genesis 2–3 selectively to suit the needs of the argument at hand."[7] It does not work within a modern framework.

Jesus, too, uses Scripture in a way that ignores the meaning it had for its original writers and readers. In Luke's version of his story, the first incident in his ministry provides an instance (see Luke 4:16–21). Jesus takes up a first-person testimony from centuries before (I understand it as that of a prophet in the sixth century). It is not a prophecy in the sense of a statement about the future, and there is no basis in the text for taking it as anything other than a statement about the prophet's own vocation. But Jesus says it is "filled" or "fulfilled" or "filled out" in his ministry (Luke uses the ordinary verb *plēroō*, which means "fill").

---

7. David M. Scholer, "1 Timothy 2:9–15 and the Place of Women in the Church's Ministry," in *Women, Authority, and the Bible* (ed. Alvera Mickelsen; Downers Grove, Ill.: InterVarsity, 1986), 193–219 (see 211).

His riposte to the Sadducees about resurrection is another noteworthy example of his premodern interpretation. The Sadducees provide a *reductio ad absurdum* of the brother-in-law rule from Deuteronomy 25:5. Because they accept only the Torah, not the Prophets or the Writings, he needs to respond to them from there, and does so by referring to God's being "the God of Abraham, the God of Isaac, and the God of Jacob" (Exod 3:6), then adds, "He is not God of the dead, but of the living." When God makes a commitment to someone, he implies, this commitment can hardly die when they die. This profound piece of theological interpretation emerges through working backwards from a current question. It does not belong to what Exodus was in itself communicating.

2. Modern

Modern interpretation came into existence in the West through the collocation of the Renaissance, the Reformation, and the Enlightenment. The Renaissance gave birth to an interest in the human side to texts from the past and to a desire to understand them in their own right. The Reformation took up this emphasis and declined to let the interpretation of Scripture be determined from outside itself, and specifically by the authority of the church. The Enlightenment urged that nothing be accepted on the basis of tradition; everything should be tested and can be questioned.

a. Text. Whereas the Qumran community happily treasured manuscripts that differed from each other (such as 1QIs[a] and 1QIs[b]), during the first millennium the Masoretes made it their business to establish *the* one true text of the Scriptures. The premodern context of this work was reflected in their assumption that the true text was the one that truly represented the tradition; the Masoretes *were* the "tradition-ers." With the Renaissance, this concern for the true text took a new form when scholars came to assume that the *true* text was the *original* text. Seeking to establish the original text became the first stage of critical study of either Testament.

This concern gained an extra level of theological importance in the context of reflection on the doctrine of Scripture in the context of the growth of critical study of Scripture. Charles Hodge, A. A. Hodge, and especially B. B. Warfield encouraged a novel development of the doctrine of Scripture by formulating their doctrine of Scripture's infallibility or inerrancy (they used the word "infallibility," but "inerrancy" is the more recent equivalent).[8] One of their strategies for coping with apparent mistakes in Scripture that seemed in tension with this doctrine was to attribute infallibility to Scripture "as originally given," to the original text that textual criticism sought to establish. In this connection, conservative study thus accepted the same aim as liberal study, and added another level of theological importance to it.

b. Origin. With the development of modernity biblical critics asked what was the evidence for (for instance) the tradition that Moses wrote the Pentateuch, and

8. See, e.g., B. B. Warfield, *The Inspiration and Authority of the Bible* (Philadelphia: Presbyterian and Reformed, 1948; London: Marshall, 1951), 420.

concluded it was poor. The books make no statement about authorship, and it is almost a thousand years after Moses' day that he comes to be connected with them. They refer to circumstances from centuries after Moses' day and manifest repetitions and changes in handling questions that suggest they bring together several versions of stories and teachings rather than being written by one person over a short period. So scholarship looked for alternative understandings of the books' origin and eventually settled into a consensus that the books issued from the interweaving of several versions of the story of Israel's origins that dated from the early monarchy, the seventh century, and the exile or later. This provided a more coherent account of the data, one that corresponds to the way we know books such as the early Christian "Harmony of the Gospels" (traditionally attributed to Tatian) came into being. It sometimes enables us to link the Torah with specific historical contexts, and it provides grounds for dating the material that do not depend on faith.

Study of the prophetic books went through a parallel process, operating on the assumption that their authority stemmed from links with great figures such as Isaiah and Jeremiah. Study therefore focused on getting behind the books to the words of the prophets themselves, where authority lay (as an undergraduate I remember being puzzled by the random-looking choice of chapters in Isaiah for exegetical study, eventually realizing they were chapters that some professor had thought really came from Isaiah ben Amoz; it was the link with the prophet himself that made them of paramount importance). Modern conservative study believed with liberalism that the books' authority was tied up with their being written by the people tradition said, and it therefore tried to find evidence that one could still reasonably believe that all Isaiah was written by Isaiah and all Jeremiah by Jeremiah. It thus again added another level of theological importance to critical research, in connection with authorship, and sought to use modern methods to support premodern convictions.

c. Reference. Perceiving the difference between the history the Scriptures tell and the actual history of Israel and of Jesus presented scholarship with a fateful choice. In which history would it now interest itself? In the context of modernity there was no contest. "History is God nowadays."[9] Scholarship abandoned the history the Scriptures tell in order to investigate the history behind it. In some sense the theology of the scriptural story depends on its historical factuality, and this study opened up the possibility of establishing historical factuality without presupposing faith, though in practice the results of the venture were discouraging. Modern conservative study agreed with modern liberal study that the historical nature of the Scriptures was vital to their authority, and tried to present evidence that one could still reasonably believe that the narratives themselves are thoroughly historical.

d. Exegesis. Modern interpretation further assumed that the key to understanding the meaning of Scripture was to project oneself back into the time of its authors. The meaning of Scripture lay in what the authors intended to say. Biblical criticism

---

9. J. Reumann, "*Oikonomia*-Terms in Paul in Comparison with Lucan *Heilsgeschichte*," *New Testament Studies* 13 (1966–67): 147–67 (see 147).

declined to be bound by the church's tradition regarding Scripture's meaning, whether this was more catholic tradition or more protestant/evangelical tradition. It also took further a Reformation principle, for the Reformation was, among other things, an argument about the interpretation of Scripture. It had not been the case that the pre-Reformation church ignored Scripture. Rather, the Reformers thought the church misinterpreted it. They affirmed that it must be read in accordance with its intrinsic meaning. They saw other people as treating it as if it was a wax nose that could be twisted to any shape you want, though they were themselves subject to the same critique.[10] The Reformation thus brought into focus the problem of conflicts of interpretation: what happens when people disagree on the meaning of texts, as Catholics, Protestants, and Anabaptists did?

The strengths and weaknesses of modern interpretation formed a mirror image of those of premodern. In theory, it opened up new possibilities of entering into what was going on between (for instance) Jeremiah and God and of escaping from the interpretations of the Christian tradition that had overlaid the Scriptures. In practice, it led interpreters into a marsh of critical study in which they wandered round in circles unable to find any firm footing and forgetting why they had ventured there, and from which they never returned.

Modernity made a different assumption from that of premodernity about the way a text comes to speak to people. It was not quite that one was intuitive, the other rational; both involved the intuitive and the rational. Premodernity assumed that the royal road to good interpretation was the assumption that the text spoke to our current concerns. It then found that it did so, though it might be limited to seeing what spoke to its existent concerns and its nature did not allow for these to be broadened out so that they matched the text's concerns. Modernity assumed that the royal road to good interpretation was the setting aside of our concerns in order to focus on the text's, but there were problems with its practice. To begin with, it did not work, as countless dull biblical commentaries by both liberal and evangelical writers testify. One reason was that modernity did not live by its own principles. The text was concerned to feed a community's self-understanding by reminding it of God's involvement with it, but modernity was preoccupied with questions about history that it naively treated as if they were also the text's preoccupation. It never reached the text's agenda. A historical approach to interpretation produced thin interpretation. An ironic but sad aspect of this is the way the marsh consumed evangelicals as well as liberals. Evangelical commentaries were also dull and predictable, but in different ways from liberal commentaries, largely confining themselves to paraphrasing the text and reassuring their readers that the events were historical, really. They were a world away from the dynamic of Calvin, who had the good sense to live after the Renaissance but before the Enlightenment.

Another ironic aspect to the story is the way modern conservative/evangelical scholars tried to come to terms with the nature of premodern interpretation,

10. On this image, see chapter 3 below (section 1).

especially as represented by the New Testament. I am aware of having used a number of strategies in this connection. One is denial, and the attempt to show that at each point the meaning the New Testament attributes to the text is the same as the meaning it would have had for its writers and first readers. In some examples this is a plausible claim; that is broadly so with the passage from Micah 5 quoted in Matthew 2, noted above. But other examples in Matthew 2 make this an unrealistic general claim, and examples could easily be multiplied. It is unlikely that Deuteronomy 25:4 actually did mean to authorize the payment of ministers, so that 1 Corinthians 9:9 then offers an exegetically sound understanding of it.

Another strategy is to seek to understand the rationale for the New Testament's method of interpretation but to fence off the modern reader from using it. As Richard Longenecker neatly put it, we can follow the New Testament's exegetical method in the sense of understanding it, but not in the sense of using it ourselves.[11]

A third strategy is theological damage limitation. This involves seeking to show that there is a theological rationale for the interpretation in question. One can argue that there is a typological correspondence between a scriptural text such as Hosea 11:1 and its use in Matthew 2:15. This might be true, but there is no hint of it in the text, and we are imposing an alien rationale on the process that suits our modern thinking.

A fourth is hermeneutical damage limitation. We can argue that the New Testament generated its exegesis by first-century methods, but produce the same results by means of modern exegesis. The text's point can be made using hermeneutical principles acceptable to us. The phrase I have just used gives the game away. The basis for our interpretation lies in modern ways of thinking. To put it more sharply in theological terms, modernity is our authority for understanding the nature of interpretation. Scripture is not our authority for understanding the nature of interpretation.

A fifth strategy is to argue that the New Testament's exegesis is acceptable for its own day as God's condescension to the methods of exegesis of its day, but that it is unacceptable for our day because we now see that historical exegesis fits the nature of the gospel. The New Testament's acceptance of nonhistorical exegesis then parallels its acceptance of slavery: it was a necessary condescension to its age, but the historical nature of the gospel means that historical exegesis is a fruit of the gospel, like emancipation. This makes it puzzling that God still uses nonhistorical exegesis, which suggests God likes it and that we need to formulate a positive theological account of it.

When I myself expounded theories like these, I was sidestepping an uneasy conscience. Evangelical understanding of Jesus' approach to interpretation has treated it as more like his comments on scriptural authority than his comments on cosmology. I became no longer satisfied that this will do. I could no longer accept what the evangelical understanding implies about the common experience of Christians over

---

11. See Richard N. Longenecker, "Can We Reproduce the Exegesis of the New Testament?" *TynB* 21 (1970): 3–38; cf. *Biblical Exegesis in the Apostolic Period* (Grand Rapids: Eerdmans, 1975).

the centuries that God has spoken to them through charismatic interpretation of Scripture. I knew that premodern exegesis was alive and well in my own experience from time to time. God sometimes spoke to me by making Scripture signify something different from what it "really" meant. God had no need to do that: it would have been quite possible to direct my mind to some passage of Scripture that actually said what God wanted me to hear or to give someone else a message from God for me. Instead, God chose to use Scripture in a premodern way. Perhaps for God and for us, by becoming Scripture these texts have gained an importance that makes God inclined to use their words in ways that need not correspond to their original meaning. Perhaps there is a depth and richness about Scripture that derives from the depth, richness, and mystery of the reality to which it points. At its best, allegorical interpretation is then a way of relating the whole of Scripture to that mystery.[12]

Both premodern and modern interpretation were powerful in what they affirmed but weak in what they (implicitly or explicitly) denied. We could consider them in deconstructionist fashion, noting the points at which each was implicitly granting what it explicitly denied. Premodern scriptural interpretation often did not concern itself with the historical sense of Scripture even though it was committed to the historicality of God's speaking and acting. Modern interpretation aimed at objectivity in interpretation and wanted to discover what the text referred to historically, but its priorities and methods were actually different from those of the scriptural text. In absolutizing the importance of history, it brought its subjective priorities and aims to the text and ignored other aspects of the text that it claimed to be seeking to interpret. The text was concerned with questions about God, truth, and life, but modern study systematically bracketed these questions that are at the center of the text's own agenda. The nearest it would get to these was to consider matters such as faith, ethics, and spirituality, questions about what human beings believed or did rather than what was true or right. Modern study would rarely even reach these matters. It thus failed to live up to its own professed concern to do justice to the texts' own agenda.[13]

This is not to imply that we should revert to premodern interpretation. The problems that modern interpretation sought to handle were not imaginary. I find it to be more the case in the United States than in Britain that students come to study Scripture with a framework of beliefs that derive more from evangelical tradition than from Scripture, concerning matters such as creation, the fall and sin, divine omniscience and omnipotence, the impossibility of God's having a change of mind, the significance of prayer and the nature of worship, the nature of the atonement, and the necessity of scriptural historicity and inerrancy. Studying Scripture in a modern way thus continues to be important in order for us to distance ourselves from Scripture as we are familiar with it, to let it say what it has to say in its own terms. Our present understanding is probably wrong at some points, and we need

12. Cf. Andrew Louth, *Discerning the Mystery* (Oxford and New York: Oxford University Press, 1983), 110, 121.

13. Cf. Brevard S. Childs's comments in *Isaiah* (Louisville: Westminster John Knox; London: SCM, 2001), e.g., 307.

delivering from our framework of interpretation. We need to understand Scripture historically.

We also need to recapture the power of premodern interpretation, which focuses more on the question "What does this signify for me?"—or rather, for *us*, because the premodern assumption is that Scripture belongs to the Christian community and that the natural place to study it is in the company of other people. So we ask, how does Scripture address questions that are important for us? How does it bring to the surface issues that we are not quite facing? How does it bring good news regarding the anxieties we do not face because we dare not do so in case there is no good news? How does studying it in the company of other people enable me to see things that I would otherwise miss or rescue me from misperceptions that issue from my personal agenda?

Modern interpretation assumed that in principle texts were always of univocal meaning. If we had enough information, we could discover what they meant. That assumption proves fruitful, but it is not always so. Sometimes the information available to us seems unlikely ever to generate an agreed interpretation. Whether this is because we lack the necessary information or because the text has more than one meaning, premodern interpretation is happy with not being sure which meaning of the text is correct, because it can work profitably with the process of looking at texts with several possible meanings, asking what happens when I look at this text in light of its different possible meanings.

Modern interpretation assumed that textual work is an affair of the mind, and it can give only a formal place to the Holy Spirit's activity in the interpretation of Scripture. Like Calvin, Ignatius of Loyola had the good sense to live after the Renaissance but before the Enlightenment, and his approach to interpretation assumes there are mysteries about our understanding of ourselves and our understanding of God that take more than intellectual resolving. The Holy Spirit uses Scripture to penetrate through our blindness to enable us to see ourselves before God. We can think in linear fashion about such shafts of insight; indeed, we are wise to do so, as part of the process of discerning whether they are indeed shafts of insight. But the insight comes more intuitively and imaginatively than linearly. Ignatian interpretation thus complements more rational, linear, objective, distancing forms of biblical study. Modern interpretation assumed that biblical narrative was history, with the high boredom potential of that designation. Ignatian interpretation assumes that biblical narrative is story—not that this implies the story did not happen, but that we need to enter into it as story, into the lives of the characters and the unfolding of the scene, and find our own place there. Modern interpretation replaced the authority of the church and its tradition by the authority of scholars. For personal Bible study, people then needed commentaries or Bible study notes written by experts, which mediated between Scripture and people. Ignatian interpretation assumes that God speaks to people directly through the words of Scripture. A wise pastor or a group of Christians provide the safeguards and the stimulus that other written material might provide.

Discovering the significance of Scripture for us is more like watching the spark that comes when a shovel strikes rock than excavating precious metal from inside the rock.[14] In what sense does Paul uphold Moses' Teaching rather than overturning it? His argument in Romans 3–4 is that his gospel (the shovel) reaffirms and works with an essential but neglected aspect of Moses' Teaching. It fits with the specific narrative shape of that Teaching in the way the latter deals with election, promise, and divine demand as it expounds the rightness of God.[15] Whereas modern interpreters attempt to keep their interpretation on the rails by using the right method of exegesis, Paul does that by working within the right theology.[16] At the same time, his argument in Romans recognizes that he needs to be able to demonstrate that he has the right theology by showing that it matches the actual inherent meaning of the Scriptures.

Historical interpretation can stimulate analogical imagination.[17] It may test the interpretation of a specific text, but it may also test the validity of our large-scale construals of the text. For instance, *does* Moses' Teaching revolve around the story of God doing the right thing? *Is* Christian faith about our individual lives and our individual relationship with God (in light of which we then interpret the First Testament)?

3. Postmodern

"Postmodern" is of course a notoriously polyvalent term. I am not here concerned with the broader postmodernity of which "deconstruction" is a "virtual synonym"[18] but with postmodern attitudes to the areas already outlined. Postmodern attitudes are formulated in reaction to modern ones. They start from the difficulties of modern attitudes even as modern attitudes had started from the difficulties of premodern ones. They remain aware of the difficulties of premodern views, so they do not imply a reversion to premodern ones as if those were right all along and what we need to do is forget the aberration that comprises modernity. Postmodern study starts from the fact that liberal modern study cannot find any alternative answers to the questions that emerge from premodernity, only more and more questions, and that evangelical modern study cannot find any more evidence for its convictions but can only reassure you that traditional views are as good as any other. Postmodern study seeks to combine premodernity and modernity in a new way. It recognizes that one of the traditions of which we now need to be critical is the tradition of the academy, which is part of modernity. My seminary has long been committed to "believing criticism." One can now see this as involving the attempt to be premodern

---

14. I adapt a metaphor from Richard B. Hays, *Echoes of Scripture in the Letters of Paul* (New Haven and London: Yale University Press, 1989), 155.

15. Ibid., 157.

16. Ibid., 161.

17. Ibid., 190.

18. Mark Brummitt and Yvonne Sherwood, "The Tenacity of the Word," in *Sense and Sensitivity* (Robert Carroll Memorial Volume; ed. Alastair G. Hunter and Philip R. Davies; London and New York: Sheffield Academic Press, 2002), 3–29 (see 5).

and modern at the same time, which is easier now that postmodernity has dawned. The "believing" part implies the premodern conviction that the whole of the Bible is true, the whole of it is given by God, and the whole of it makes demands on us. The "criticism" part implies recognition that the church's interpretation of Scripture and the academy's interpretation of Scripture are fallible and that we should never assume that what we have been told about the Bible by the church or by scholars is right. We are critical about what anyone says the Bible says.

a. *Text.* In the third millennium, the aim of textual criticism neither need nor can be the establishing of the original text of the Scriptures.

The discovery of the Qumran scrolls had paradoxically conflicting implications for textual criticism. It reinforced the conviction that nothing too disastrous had happened to the text of the Masoretic tradition in the thousand years between the copying of the scrolls and the production of the great Masoretic codices around AD 1000. In 1945, our oldest complete Hebrew texts were only a thousand years old and were thus nearer to us in age than to anyone who lived in First Testament times. In 1950, we had substantial texts of Isaiah and other books that were two thousand years old and were thus nearer to their authors' age than to us, and these texts are substantially the same as the Masoretic texts. But the many small differences between (for instance) 1QIs^a and 1QIs^b also reinforced the suspicion that since pre-Christian times there have been several textual traditions. We have no basis for guessing whether any of them is closer to the original text.

Indeed, it has become unclear what we mean by the original text of a First Testament book. Textual history collapses into redactional history. What do we mean by the original text of Isaiah? More pressingly, what do we mean by the original text of Jeremiah, given the possibility that the shorter LXX text is older than the longer Masoretic text? Should we see the authoritative form of the text as the canonical one (virtually a tautology, that)?[19] If Roger Beckwith is right and we define the canonical Scriptures as the works deposited in the temple,[20] is this the text that textual criticism seeks to establish? But how would we know what this text was? It would be nice if the temple scrolls were the ones taken up in the Masoretic tradition, but is there any evidence that this was so? And in trying to identify such a single tradition, are we imposing categories on the process? Further, we are ignoring that implication in the New Testament that there is no need to reckon that the First Testament's authority requires there to be only one text form.

A postmodern attitude to textual criticism will be quite at home with pluralism, as we are at home with a plurality of translations. The implication of the New Testament's attitude is that the Holy Spirit could be involved in the process whereby different

19. Cf. Brevard S. Childs's discussion of "Text and Canon" in *Introduction to the Old Testament as Scripture* (London: SCM; Philadelphia: Fortress, 1979), 84–106, and of "The Hermeneutical Problem of New Testament Criticism" in *The New Testament as Canon* (London: SCM, 1984; Philadelphia: Fortress, 1985), 518–30.

20. See *The Old Testament Canon of the New Testament Church and Its Background in Early Judaism* (London: SPCK, 1985; Grand Rapids: Eerdmans, 1986).

texts of the Scriptures developed, as the Holy Spirit was involved in generating the first versions of stories, psalms, sayings, and oracles, and then in the redactional process whereby they were collected, supplemented, and updated. We have no basis for determining what is the one text of the First Testament, nor any need to do so. We can treat both MT Jeremiah and LXX Jeremiah as inspired and look for edification in each. Instead of being either-or people, we can be both-and people.

The argument does not point toward recognizing the LXX canon, though the Anglican Church's openness to being edified by the books in the longer canon fits my general argument. While some New Testament writers have read and been influenced by books in the longer canon, they never refer to them as Scripture or quote them. Nor does it imply accepting all textual variants as equally valid, as we do not accept all prophecy as equally valid. The question is, Where may we see the Holy Spirit's work in the development of the text? That may lie in deliberate reworking or in misunderstandings and mistakes that generate edifying readings. Alongside a premodern openness to seeing divine involvement in textual development we can maintain a modern spirit that asks questions about the nature of this development. Textual criticism thus remains a critical task, one that involves spiritual discernment. Its critical principles include (for instance) what is oldest and what makes sense to the modern critical scholar, but also (for instance) Augustine's interpretive criterion, what encourages love?

Here are examples. In Psalm 1:5, the MT declares that the faithless will not stand in the judgment when the "company of the true" assembles. It apparently refers to an event in the present life of the community. But in the LXX, people will not rise *again* at the judgment, so that the LXX refers the psalm to the final judgment. Psalm 5:8 MT prays, "Direct your way before me," meaning be purposeful and focused in your action, while in some LXX mss it prays, "direct *my* way before *you*." Psalm 7:11 MT declares that God is always expressing indignation, which is good news because it means God consistently acts against oppressors, while the LXX declares that God is *not* always expressing anger, which is good news because it means God is merciful to us. In each case the LXX says something edifying and encouraging or appropriately challenging within the readers' framework. One can see the Holy Spirit's work in that. However, precisely in doing this, in each case it conforms the text to its readers' expectations. It makes it say something they would be less likely to find surprising. This does not sound like the work of the Holy Spirit, because being surprising is one of the Spirit's characteristics. We do not need the Holy Spirit to say things we would have thought of anyway. Postmodern textual criticism is simultaneously affirming and questioning.

b. Origin. Modern study was predicated on the assumption that we could discover when books were written. We now have to face the fact that there are virtually no assured results of modern criticism. We know very little about the dating of most First Testament books. Opinions differ, and presuppositions and fashion are influential on what scholars think. Scholarly writing makes much use of statements such as "it seems likely," implying "there is no hard evidence for this," and statements such as "most scholars think," implying "this is a view that will soon be outdated." Current interest in interpreting the First Testament against its sociological background only relocates the problem, because we have no more basis for knowledge about the sociological than about the historical. And it is almost laughable that scholarship should be currently so keen on interpreting the First Testament against the historical and social background of the Persian period, when we know very little of either and there is no more evidence for dating the books against this background than there was against the alleged "Solomonic enlightenment."

I say "virtually no assured results" because I must not exaggerate the point. In particular, there is a difference between the Prophets and the other books. It is an assured result of modern criticism that Isaiah 40–55 needs interpreting against the background of the late sixth century as well as that Daniel's visions need interpreting against the background of the second century, and I still enjoy inviting students to read Genesis 1 against the background of the exile. But we do not know when most of the First Testament was written, *and we never will know.* Another recurrent word in scholarly writing is "yet," as in "we are not yet clear," "scholars are not yet sure." This gives the impression that First Testament research is like medical research and that one day we will know the answers to questions that currently puzzle us. There are grounds for this confidence in medical research; this process has happened in the past. There are virtually no such grounds in First Testament research. None of the major questions that scholars discussed in the nineteenth century has been solved.

This does not mean readers can revert to premodern views, because the data that led to the modern theories are still there. We can know that Moses did not write the Torah and that there are several collections of teaching and compilations of stories brought together there that represent ways God guided the people over the centuries. But we can have no theory about the nature of this process to replace the premodern one that Moses wrote it, or the modern Wellhausenian consensus. Therefore we cannot build First Testament interpretation on convictions about date and authorship. We do not get anywhere by trying to understand Job, Jonah, or Ruth against their historical context or in light of their author's intentions, except insofar as talk of the author's intentions is another way of talking about the actual content of the books (what the author intended was to say what the book says). Apparently the same is true about (for instance) the Pentateuch. The communities that generated and preserved the Scriptures declined to incorporate the kind of data that would help us fix them historically. Modernity thought we needed this, but God does not seem to have agreed.

So postmodern study implies that the question about authorship and dating is the wrong question. In the postmodern era, we simply (?) read the books without knowing who wrote them or when. We thus focus on what can be known from the text rather than on questions that run into the sand.

But with modernity, we do not take for granted that we know what the text says and that it says what we have been told it says. In this sense we approach it critically. We seek to read it with open eyes; we do not revert to what tradition says it says.

This aspect of criticism is at least as important as it ever was. We use whatever keys seem to unlock aspects of the text, trying different ones until one opens the lock without forcing it.

c. Reference. In the aftermath of the Enlightenment, "history" and "story" with their common etymology came apart. "History" came to refer to the facts, the events that (might) lie behind a narrative. "Story" came to refer to the narrative, with the implication that it had little value except insofar as it spoke of events that did happen. It was history that now came to count, so that Thucydides and Exodus were valued only for the factual material they contained. Liberals and evangelicals agreed that if Exodus is not factual, its authenticity or value disappears.

Modern historical study has presupposed that we are in a better position to determine where the facts lie than the authors of the narratives were, as well as having the motivation to do that, but this other aspect of a historical approach to Scripture also produces disappointing results. It would be nice to think that current skepticism about Israelite history issued from end-of-millennium malaise and/or postmodern convictions[21] and that in a decade or two things will have settled down. But more likely First Testament study went through a loss of (false) innocence at the end of the second millennium. In seeking to discover the events that lie behind the story, we are again asking questions the text will not answer. If end-of-millennium malaise allowed this fact to emerge, now that it has emerged, it cannot be evaded. The problem is not just a temporary one. The twentieth-century consensus was always just a consensus. Once the boy has commented that the emperor has no clothes, the clothes can never be restored. We cannot abandon the idea that the First Testament story needs to be basically historical. But we have to trust God that it has the historical value it needs to have, on the basis (for instance) that Jesus would hardly have relied on this book as he did if it did not have the historical value it needed to have, and would hardly have therefore encouraged us to base our thinking and lives on it. But we cannot prove that this is so by using critical methods.

Ziony Zevit defines history as "a true story about the past" of the kind that a law court seeks to establish, concerned with facts.[22] The definition fits the history Zevit seeks to write. But for the First Testament "histories," Jan Huizinga's definition is more illuminating: "History is the intellectual form in which a civilization renders account to itself of its past."[23] Such an account of the past needs to have some relationship with historical events, but a civilization's "past" includes more than the

---

21. So Ziony Zevit, *The Religions of Ancient Israel* (London and New York: Continuum, 2001), 1–80; William G. Dever, *What Did the Biblical Writers Know and When Did They Know It?* (Grand Rapids and Cambridge: Eerdmans, 2001), 245–62. But even Dever is skeptical about Israel's ancestors and the exodus; his confidence starts only with David.

22. *The Religions of Ancient Israel*, 27.

23. "A Definition of the Concept of History," in *Philosophy and History: Essays Presented to Ernst Cassirer* (ed. R. Klibansky and H. J. Paton; Oxford: Clarendon, 1936), 1–10 (see 9), as quoted by W. W. Hallo, "Biblical History in its Near Eastern Setting," in *Israel's Past in Present Research* (ed. V. Philips Long; Winona Lake, Ind.: Eisenbrauns, 1999), 77–97 (see 83). I do not think it matters if the way people use Huizinga's definition does not exactly correspond to its meaning in the

events in which it has been involved, and "giving account of the past" has naturally included—indeed focused on—the passing on of its traditions in general, which have varied relationships to actual events. Like Western dramatists and scriptwriters, even when telling the story of a historical person ancient "historians" were at home including material of a "fictional" kind—both traditional material ("legends") and material newly created by the author. Genesis 1 is not the last piece of true imaginative fiction in the Bible. The inclusion of such imaginative fictions fits with the nature of history writing in the ancient world. God's inspiring the biblical historians did not make them write as if they were modern historians but as really good ancient historians.

There is then a paradox here. Moderns and postmoderns are quite happy with the interweaving of fact and fiction in Shakespeare and in movies, and as theatergoers we are not so different from premodern readers. Conversely, perhaps premodern reading of Scripture was not so different from our own. Some readers would assume that narratives indeed related what actually happened, like viewers assuming that soap opera characters are real people. Other readers would know that there was probably some difference between the narrative and the actual events and might sometimes be able to guess where it lay, but would mostly focus on the narrative, like a theatergoer watching a Shakespeare play or a film based on facts. It was the context of modernity that made Gerhard von Rad describe the substantial divergence between the First Testament narrative and the actual course of Israel's history as a grievous burden.[24] In a postmodern context, that seems an understandable but extreme view. The considerations about the nature of history writing I have just noted do not eliminate the burden, but they do reduce it so that it becomes bearable.

There are disadvantages to our uncertainty about the precise historical value of the First Testament, but it also brings such significant advantages that I might be prepared to see it as a result of divine providence rather than divine oversight. If we cannot establish what events lie behind the First Testament, that pushes us to focus more on the text. Adopting modernity's understanding of history as the privileged lens through which to view the First Testament has skewed the perceptions of both liberal and evangelical study. Even if we could establish exactly what actually happened in these events, and even if these were identical with the text itself, the proper subject of First Testament study would still be the First Testament, not the history. It would still be the text with its selectivity and arrangement. The narrative gives us the truth and not merely the facts.

In the premodern era, the church believed it lived its life in the context of God's story with Israel, and in the modern era, scholarship invited readers to be critical of the tradition of interpretation that they had received. Evangelical tradition says it is really important that the events of First Testament history happened but that they

---

context of his work, as K. Lawson Younger implies (*Ancient Conquest Accounts* [Sheffield: Sheffield Academic Press, 1990], 26–27).

24. *Old Testament Theology* (2 vols.; Edinburgh: Oliver and Boyd; New York: Harper, 1962), 1:108.

are then of no further relevance to our thinking or life today. What matters is that God is involved in my personal life. Modern interpretation supported this view by seeing biblical narrative as history, with the high boredom potential of that designation. Postmodern interpretation assumes that biblical narrative is story and that we need to enter into it as story, into the lives of the characters and the unfolding of the scene, and find our own place there. It invites the church to be self-critical about its assumption that we evaluate the relevance of the First Testament story by our story and to start living by the First Testament story.

d. Exegesis. Partly as a consequence of the thin nature of modern interpretation, premodern interpretation persists and is still the dominant form of interpretation in the church, which is virtually unscathed by critical interpretation. This appears in the use of Scripture in lectionaries and in the prooftext approach to Scripture in ecumenical documents. It appears in the use of the Bible in preaching and in people's spiritual reading.

Worse, as I have noted, God uses Scripture that way. I offer three personal examples. As an ordinand I went through a period of spiritual uncertainty—not over whether the Christian faith was true but over whether it applied to me. I was no longer sure whether I belonged to God. What brought me reassurance was the impact of Deuteronomy 17 when it was read in seminary chapel one day, in particular the phrase relating to the Israelites' having come out of Egypt: "You shall not return that way again." That came to me as a promise that God had taken hold of me and would not let me go. The irony is that in context it is a challenge, not a promise. God used the text unhistorically, atomistically, and directly. God had no need to do that and could have given me this reassurance via the intrinsic meaning of some other passage of Scripture. God's using Scripture that way implies that when texts become part of Scripture as a whole they become semi-independent of the historical and literary specificity of their origin. They are open to being read as part of this larger whole and to having a significance deriving from that larger whole. Indeed, one might say that in a sense they have a new level of literal meaning. And they speak to people without going via an analytic process.

Then, as a seminary professor I was once in a service where our bishop was preaching. As he climbed the pulpit steps I knew that afterwards I had to offer him the words that come from Psalm 45, "the LORD has anointed you." The next day, his wife called to say how important that had been to him because he was feeling exhausted and discouraged. In context, however, these are words addressed to a king of Israel on the occasion of his marriage. In Hebrews 1 they are applied to Christ.

Third, when I was contemplating accepting a post in the United States, a student had God say to her, "Tell John 'Judges 18:6.'" This verse includes the words "Go in peace. Your journey is before the LORD." This played a part in helping me to make the decision to make the move, or to do so with confidence. In context the words are addressed by a priest to a group of Danite spies who are on a journey to reconnoiter in the north and to prepare the way for their clan to kill all the people of Laish (kidnapping the priest on the way). It is not clear whether we are to take the words of the priest (who was rather unorthodox by the standards of the Torah) as actually the words of Yahweh.

I add one other instance, not from my own experience. The KJV version of Proverbs 29:18 offers the suggestive and edifying maxim, "Where there is no vision, the people perish." But the verb is *pāraʿ*, which means "to let go" or "let loose." Thus the NRSV has "where there is no prophecy, the people cast off restraint," and the TNIV "where there is no revelation, people cast off restraint." This is also a suggestive and edifying maxim, but a different one.

Modernity's understandable mistake was to attempt to sideline this form of interpretation in order to promote its own. But sidelining simply drove it underground (and not very far underground). Paradoxically, if we want the positive aspects of modern interpretation to have an impact on regular Christian interpretation, we need to work with premodern interpretation, not against it. The prospect and the challenge of postmodern interpretation are to bring together the strengths of premodern and modern in such a way as to sidestep the limitations of each. We are the victims of a split between academic study and person-involving study. Our postmodern context gives us the opportunity to put these two back together. The nature of postmodern interpretation is to try to move beyond the antitheses of premodern and modern.

Postmodern interpretation will enthuse over the way the Holy Spirit inspires imaginative leaps in the use of Scripture that give the words a significance that may have little to do with their meaning in their grammatical and historical context. But it will not make that a default assumption about the nature of interpretation, for reasons that emerged in the context of the Reformation and the Enlightenment. Such use of Scripture can be a means of making affirmations that are actually unscriptural, and we need means of being able to argue about whether what someone says is indeed a word from the Lord. If it does not correspond to the text's original meaning, we need to treat it as we would a purported prophecy, being open to the possibility that it came from the Spirit, but not assuming that. We also need to keep in mind that most prophecy is either false or trivial. A similar problem with "free" interpretation (bigger than the problem of whether it is false) is that it often simply confirms us in what we already believe rather than allowing God to break through. Studying Scripture in a modern way is important because we need to distance ourselves from Scripture as we are familiar with it in order to let it say what it has to say in its own terms. Our present understanding is probably wrong at some points, and we need delivering from our framework of interpretation. We need to understand Scripture historically, and the Holy Spirit is involved in the process whereby we seek to do so. But we also need to be open to leaps of inspired imagination.

I have used various approaches to Bible study over my life. I have used the method that involves reading through a book over a period of days or weeks, reading study notes to help me understand it and to see how it applies to me (and I have written such notes). I have used the old IVP "Search the Scriptures" system, working systematically through the whole Bible over three years. As a lecturer in an Anglican theological college, I was in chapel every day listening to the Scriptures read systematically, and I would then go home and reflect on what they had to say to me. And for much of our married life my first wife and I read the mélange of Scripture verses in "Daily Light" each evening.

Looking back over that, and talking with other people about their experience of reading Scripture, I see that each of these methods has its strengths and snags. Bible study notes are fine, but it's easy for them to come between the Bible and us. We learn from the notes rather than from the Bible. I know people who used a set of notes called "Everyday with Jesus," but they used to joke that people treated them as "Everyday with Selwyn Hughes," the notes' author. Our need for the notes suggests we don't find the Bible itself can speak to us.

With an approach such as "Search the Scriptures," reading Scripture easily becomes a mainly academic exercise, an affair of the head. "What does the passage teach us about God, about Jesus, about the Holy Spirit?" We don't have to get stuck there, but it's easy to do so.

I found that reading several passages of Scripture in chapel in the company of other people and then reflecting on them on my own was almost guaranteed to generate helpful insights and words of encouragement for the situations I had to face. But I am aware now that it was my needs that set the agenda for this selective attention to the readings for the day. In turn, "Daily Light" has already predigested the Bible before I read it.

I have mentioned Ignatius of Loyola, who was born in 1491 and was thus a contemporary of Luther and Calvin. He was a Spanish soldier of aristocratic background, a Christian with the usual enthusiasm of a young man for life and love. Recuperating at home after being wounded in battle at thirty, through reading the life of Christ and reflecting on his own life he came to a dramatic realization of its pointlessness. It led him to reshape his life and dedicate it to God as a monk. He then found himself involved in encouraging spiritual growth among both lay people and monks. The "Exercises" on the life of Christ that he thus developed were designed to encourage people to reflect on what their lives were about and where God might be directing them.

Over against the methods described above, this approach first puts you in the company of the Bible and nothing else. I exaggerate slightly; Ignatius did after all devise a scheme, and the scheme may provide significant guidelines for a week's reading. But you spend each day with a few verses of the Bible and nothing else. The theological conviction underlying the approach is that the Holy Spirit who inspired Scripture really does get involved with people when they do that.

Second, it encourages the whole person, not just the head, to engage with God and with Scripture. In a rather contemporary touchy-feely way, it keeps asking what feelings the Scriptures arouse in us. It does that in the conviction that the feelings will be a clue to what is happening in our inner being and to what God wants to deal with. It emphasizes the engagement of the imagination, perhaps the most famous feature Ignatian meditation is known for. Reading the Gospels, in particular, is especially a matter of reading stories, and it invites you to enter into stories, to take part in them, to identify with characters, to discover what you say to Jesus and what Jesus says to you. The imagination also comes out in other ways. For the whole of my time one morning I "camped in" (to use an expression one Ignatian group used) the phrase "O Lord, you are my God," reflecting on what that implied for me.

Third, it gives you shorter rather than longer amounts of Scripture to deal with, sometimes just a verse or two for several days. That can be hard work, and one of the important questions becomes Why is this hard work? It is when we don't feel we are getting much out of it that something really important may be going on. The text is raising questions we want to avoid. If we are committed not to jump from this passage to another, then we may be driven into finding what those questions are.

Paul's interpretation of Deuteronomy 25:4 derived from his conviction that Scripture speaks. It is a living word that addresses *us*, and it was designed to do so (see, e.g., Rom 15:4; 1 Cor 10:11). He is following the precedent of Deuteronomy itself (e.g., Deut 5:2–3).[25] The reason it addresses us is not merely that it is the Word of God or that we belong to the same people as it originally addressed. It addresses us because we live at the climax of the ages and thus at the point toward which the Scriptures were themselves working. There is no theological gap between us and the text, as is presupposed when we reckon that God acted and spoke in different ways in biblical times. There is hermeneutical continuity and no hermeneutical gap between text and interpreter. The Spirit, given in connection with this being the age of consummation, ensures that this is so.[26]

---

25. Hays, *Echoes of Scripture*, 167.
26. Cf. ibid., 185–92.

3

Can We Learn from the Past?

Luther and the Bible

It is my impression that in Britain there is more awareness of the importance of John Calvin as a biblical expositor and theorist on the doctrine of Scripture than there is of the parallel significance of Martin Luther; but perhaps I am generalizing from my own experience of realizing the creativeness of Luther's work much later than I did that of Calvin, or perhaps it reflects Britain's not being a very Lutheran context. While Calvin's doctrine of Scripture is more clearly formulated and his exegesis is tighter, often the issues that are raised and not entirely solved in Luther are the ones that continue to trouble and fascinate biblical scholars and theologians. His new hermeneutic foreshadows many aspects of the problem of the status and interpretation of the Bible as this has since unfolded; indeed, he was a decisive stimulus to this development.[1]

---

1. First published in *SJT* 35 (1982): 33–58. An extensive selection of Luther's writings in English translation appears in *Luther's Works* (henceforth referred to as *LW*, followed by a volume and page number), volumes 5–30 comprising biblical commentaries (ed. Jaroslav Pelikan; St. Louis: Concordia, 1955–86) and volumes 31–55 other works (ed. H. T. Lehmann; Philadelphia: Fortress/ Muhlenberg, 1955–86). Valuable secondary works in English include P. Althaus, *The Theology of Martin Luther* (Philadelphia: Fortress, 1966); H. Bornkamm, *Luther and the Old Testament* (Philadelphia: Fortress, 1969); Jaroslav Pelikan, *Luther the Expositor* (*LW* Companion Volume; St. Louis: Concordia, 1959); J. S. Preus, *From Shadow to Promise: Old Testament Interpretation from Augustine to the Young Luther* (Cambridge, Mass.: Harvard University Press; London: Oxford University Press, 1969); Gerhard Ebeling, *Luther: An Introduction to His Thought* (Philadelphia: Fortress; London: Collins, 1970), also "The New Hermeneutics and the Early Luther," *Theology Today* 21 (1964–65):

The Reformation constituted a moment when the Bible came alive in an unparalleled way, particularly in the life of Luther. In 1512, he became a lecturer in biblical studies at the new University of Wittenberg. He gave his first lecture course between 1513 and 1515 on the Psalms, and even these early lectures (see *LW* 10–11) mark him as a Christ-centered exegete and theologian with a profound commitment to treating the Scriptures as his resource for a knowledge of God, of God's purpose, of Christ, and of the nature of Christian living.

Luther wrestled with Scripture not merely with the anxiety of a new lecturer or the ambition of a scholar but with the personal concern of someone unsure of his position before God. It was eventually through his study of Scripture that the light dawned and he came to see himself as accepted by God despite his unworthiness, on the basis of his faith in Christ. In the preface to one of the collected editions of his writings (*LW* 34:337), he recalls: "at last, by the mercy of God, meditating day and night, I gave heed to the context of the words [of Rom 1:17], namely, 'In it the righteousness of God is revealed, as it is written, "He who through faith is righteous shall live."' . . . This is the meaning: the righteousness of God is revealed by the gospel, namely, the passive righteousness with which merciful God justifies us by faith. . . . Here I felt that I was altogether born again and had entered paradise itself through open gates. There a totally other face of the entire Scripture showed itself to me." Luther relates how he checked his insight by other parts of Scripture, found it confirmed by Augustine, and set anew to his task of lecturing on the Psalms. His work was already Christ-centered; it was now to be more grace-centered and gospel-centered.

While the passage of a quarter of a century may have sharpened the picture,[2] there is no doubt that Luther's spiritual pilgrimage at its beginning and subsequently was directed by the Bible. Further, while political, social, ecclesiastical, intellectual, and other factors provided the background and stimulus for the subsequent reformation of the church, Luther's biblical study and his grasp of (or his being grasped by) the teaching on justification by faith that he found in Romans is at the heart of the reason why reform took the form it did. While he was a voluminous writer, he claims to wish really to direct attention only to Scripture. Thus he prefaces another edition of his works (*LW* 34:284) by observing that "all other writing is to lead the way into and point toward the Scriptures, as John the Baptist did toward Christ, saying, 'He must increase, but I must decrease' [John 3:30], in order that each person may drink of the fresh spring himself. . . . Neither councils, fathers, nor we, in spite of the greatest and best success possible, will do as well as the Holy Scriptures, that is, as well as God himself has done. . . . Therefore it behoves us to let the prophets

---

34–46; see also S. L. Greenslade, ed., *The West from the Reformation to the Present Day* (vol. 3 of *The Cambridge History of the Bible*; Cambridge and New York: Cambridge University Press, 1963).

2. The chronology of Luther's spiritual experience is notoriously controversial. He may have come to this moment of realization earlier (e.g., while or before lecturing on the Psalms); it may even be misleading to look for one such "moment." See G. Rupp, *Luther's Progress to the Diet of Worms* (London: SCM, 1951; New York: Harper Torchbooks, 1964), 3–6, 26–35.

and apostles stand at the professor's lectern, while we, down below at their feet, listen to what they say." For Luther, then, doing theology consists in discussing the meaning and implications of passages of the Bible. "His theology is nothing more than an attempt to interpret the Scripture. Its form is basically exegesis. . . . There is no precedent for the way Luther, as an exegete and as a preacher, thinks in constant conversation with Scripture."[3]

1. Taking Scripture in the Straightforward, Natural Sense

Church leaders and theologians were quite prepared to debate with Luther on his grounds, on the teaching of Scripture. But Luther found this debate frustrating, because at the crucial points his opponents seemed to refuse to interpret Scripture in what he saw as the straightforward way. They silenced the text itself. The dispute with Latomus (e.g., *LW* 32:217) and *The Bondage of the Will* (e.g., *LW* 33:24, 90, 161–63) offer many examples. The pope silences the text by declaring that he alone has the authority to say what Scripture meant. Theologians do this by assuming that its meaning is fixed by the interpretation of the Fathers.[4] The "enthusiasts" do it by claiming that the Holy Spirit communicates directly to them what Scripture means. Erasmus does it by maintaining that Scripture is often unclear and ambiguous, so that it cannot be used to establish theological points in the manner Luther sought to adopt. Latomus, Zwingli, and Erasmus again, do it by interpreting it "figuratively" ("God hardened Pharaoh's heart" means only that God gave Pharaoh occasion to harden his own heart). In a letter to Spalatin (*LW* 48:59) Luther laments that even his teacher Jodokus Trutvetter does it by reading Scripture within the framework of Aristotelian philosophy.

Luther insisted that interpretations should arise from the text of Scripture itself, not be brought to it from outside. The goal of interpretation is to understand what the author meant to say, and authors should be understood in the straightforward, natural sense unless this produces manifest nonsense. It is a recurrent conceit in writings of the period that Scripture must not be treated as if it had a "wax nose," capable of being turned in any direction you fancy, and Luther agrees.[5]

Luther's more literal and historical approach to Scripture was an important feature of the Reformation. It was through wrestling for such an understanding of Romans that he found his peace with God, and it was this same approach that underlay his theological critique of the church. Yet there is no one-to-one relationship between

3. Althaus, *The Theology of Martin Luther*, 3–4.
4. Pelikan (*Luther the Expositor*, 113) comments that "in Luther and Eck we see opposed to each other a fundamentally inductive and a fundamentally deductive method of Biblical exegesis."
5. But the phrase is not distinctive or characteristic of Luther; Basil Hall (*The Cambridge History of the Bible*, 3:48) credits its origin to Geiler of Kaisersberg, a pre-Reformation preacher. Luther notes that he was accused of treating Scripture as if it were wax that could be shaped in any way one wished, when he finds the Trinity in Gen 18 (*LW* 3:191).

historical exegesis and the Protestant Reformation. Before Luther, literal, historical interpretation was being urged from the Renaissance, and it is accepted by Erasmus (though not with sufficient consistency in practice, in Luther's view).[6] Luther often expresses his approval of the earlier literal exegesis of Genesis by Nicholas of Lyra (c. 1270–1340) (e.g., *LW* 1:93), though even he could be led astray by allegory (e.g., *LW* 1:184). And after the reform movement was begun, in the treatise on the words "This is my Body" (*LW* 37) Luther chastises Zwingli for abandoning literal interpretation, while subsequently allegory and unhistorical approaches generally have been popular in pietism.

The insistence on interpreting Scripture in the natural, straightforward way depends upon the prior claim that the Scriptures are, in fact, fundamentally of clear and unambiguous meaning. In *The Bondage of the Will* (*LW* 33:24–28, 91–100), Luther acknowledges that there is a mystery about many truths of Scripture, but it is the mystery of *how* they can be true (for instance, how Christ can be both human and divine), not of *whether* they are true or what they mean. He acknowledges that Scripture often seems a mystery to people, but this is because of the veil over their own minds, not because of the veiledness of Scripture. He acknowledges that many individual passages remain a mystery to us, as he laments in his commentaries, because of our incomplete knowledge of the original languages. But he asserts that nevertheless the subject matter of Scripture, its fundamental teaching, is quite clear. The claims it makes for itself to reveal the truth (e.g., Ps 119), and the character of the God who stands behind it, presuppose that it should be clearly intelligible. "Holy Scripture must necessarily be clearer, simpler, and more reliable than any other writings" (*LW* 32:11). Thus it will not do simply to point out that Scripture has produced heresy as well as orthodoxy, as Luther's opponents did at Worms (*LW* 32:119, 128–29). It does not do so when understood in the natural way (*LW* 33:163).

Believing this to be the case, Luther goes about the task of interpretation as if it is the case. His early dispute with Latomus (*LW* 32:133–260) over the interpretation of passages concerning human sin, such as "All our righteousnesses are as filthy rags" (Isa 64:6) and "There is not a righteous man on earth who does good and never sins" (Eccles 7:20), illustrates this well. He strives for a historical meaning (discussing whether Isa 64:6 refers to the Assyrian, Babylonian, or Roman period), a contextual meaning (the verse is considered in connection with vv. 5–11 as a whole), a literal meaning ("all" is not to be reduced to "much of," as if it were hyperbole), a grammatical meaning (arguing on the basis of the tenses in Eccles 7:20), a single meaning (Rom 7 cannot be referred both to humanity under the law and to humanity under grace), and a natural meaning (whereas his opponents apparently have to twist passages to make them fit their preconceptions).

Unfortunately, though we can applaud Luther's aims, we cannot necessarily applaud his results. Key exegetical discussions such as the ones just referred to do not satisfy us, even though we can accept his theory of exegesis. In his debate with

---

6. See Hall's comments, *The Cambridge History of the Bible*, 3:85.

Zwingli, Luther's interpretation may seem literalist rather than literal. His understanding of the Song of Songs as Solomon's song about the kingdom God has given him, an "encomium of peace and of the present state of the realm" (*LW* 15:195), does not carry conviction, even though we agree with Luther in seeking a literal rather than an allegorical interpretation of the Song. Although Luther is committed to the straightforward, natural meaning, he cannot be sure of finding it.

The nature, aims, and methods of literal interpretation have been much discussed since Luther's day.[7] Is the goal of such interpretation to establish the meaning the author intended? Or is a statement to be read in its own right without being circumscribed by what its author had in mind, which is itself elusive? In the act of interpretation, are we trying to gain an objective understanding of some words, or to get into the mind of an author, or to relive the author's experience, or to grasp what the author grasped, or what? How do we go about this task, when we have defined it, and how do we test our efforts? These theoretical questions continue to demand discussion; yet, although they remain unresolved, the task of biblical interpretation necessarily goes on. And although the conclusions we reach on the interpretation of particular texts may have changed, our methods are still for the most part similar to Luther's.

Luther used the straightforward, natural sense of Scripture to vindicate and refine the insights of the Reformation, but the sword he wielded was two-edged. It would work against Protestantism's beliefs as well as for them. In Geneva, the now widely accepted view that the Song of Songs was written as a secular love poem was propounded by an ordinand named Sebastian Castellio. Calvin did not dispute this interpretation, but the young man's insistence on it, and his consequent rejection of the book's inspiration, led to his being refused ordination.[8] Similar disruptive consequences followed from attempts merely to establish the actual text that the human authors of the Bible wrote. The Huguenot scholar Louis Cappel discovered that the standard edition of the Hebrew Scriptures, the MT, does not represent exactly what the various authors wrote and sometimes needs correcting in light of its own marginal variants and the distinctive renderings of old translations such as the Septuagint. Such insights promised advances in ascertaining what the biblical authors wrote, but they seemed to threaten belief that the Bible was God's Word, and in 1675 the Swiss Reformed Church made it an article of faith that the traditional text, vowels and all, represents the oracles of God passed on to Christianity by the "Jewish church." The traditional text was not to be emended; those who did so would "bring the foundation of our faith and its inviolable authority into perilous hazard."[9] The fear expressed here is

7. And before: see B. S. Childs, "The Sensus Literalis of Scripture," in *Beiträge zur alttestamentliche Theologie* (Walther Zimmerli Festschrift; ed. H. Donner et al.; Göttingen: Vandenhoeck, 1977), 80–93.

8. The account is included by R. H. Bainton in *The Cambridge History of the Bible*, 3:8–9.

9. Quoted from J. H. Leith, *Creeds of the Churches* (New York: Doubleday, 1963; rev. ed., Richmond: John Knox, 1973), 309–11. For background, see Philip Schaff, *The Creeds of Christendom* I (New York: Harper, 1884), § 61. It is nice to be able to note that this "Helvetic Consensus Formula"

similar to the one voiced today by those concerned at any apparent compromise over commitment to a particular understanding of Scripture's inerrancy.[10]

Luther's stress on a historical approach to the biblical text could also lead to troublesome results. One fruit of the centuries of biblical study since Luther has been a clearer awareness of the variety manifested by the lives, attitudes, assumptions, and worldviews of people in different cultures. Many modern readers are separated from the biblical culture (better, cultures) not only by two to three thousand years but also by the difference between west and east, North Atlantic and Middle Eastern, urban and agricultural/pastoral, democratic and monarchic/imperial, post-Christian and unquestioningly religious, and so on. Scholars therefore wonder whether it is possible for us to hear the various biblical writers in any complete sense, given the huge differences between us and them in all those things that are unstated because they could then be taken for granted. Can we understand the Bible at all?[11] One may note first that Luther assumed that human beings were always the same (see his comment on Ps 1, *LW* 14:290), so that there is little problem in principle in understanding people of different ages. In *Against Latomus* he notes the further principle that the same Spirit indwells believers under both covenants (*LW* 32:176). And the fact is that by listening to these writings Luther was able to hear things he had not heard before; it is impossible to prove that those things came from the insights of these writers, but this seems the commonsense inference, and it suggests that a reader in a different situation from that of a document can hear something if not everything. Of course Luther was not separated from his sources by as great a gulf as we may be. He belongs to pretechnological society. Yet in other respects he is a modern person. He constitutes one of the links between us and the biblical text, part of that tradition that bridges an old world and a new world which, as such, can help the latter understand the former.

Again, Luther asserted that faith must be based on history, and he began to work out the implications of the historical nature of revelation. His fundamental case against allegory rests here, as his discussion of Isaiah 13 reveals. "For playing games with the Sacred Scriptures has the most injurious consequences if the text and its grammar are neglected. From history we must learn well and much, but little from allegory. . . . Let history remain honest. It teaches, which allegory does not do. . . . In history you have the fulfillment of either promises or threats. . . . Console yourself with this in every trouble. Do not lose hope, consider that God is truthful and that He can accomplish what He has promised, even though there were a hundred Babylons to be destroyed" (*LW* 16:136–37). Faith and hope are based on what has actually happened.

---

was drawn up by a man named Heidegger, a name that recurs in connection with a very different approach to interpretation later. The formula had a much wider range of concerns than the doctrine of Scripture.

10. See further the discussion in chapter 2 above.

11. See D. E. Nineham, *The Use and Abuse of the Bible* (London and New York: Macmillan, 1976), chs. 1 and 4; and see chapter 1 (section 3) above.

Luther assumed that the biblical narrative related actual history, whereas much subsequent historical research has seen a gap between the story the Bible tells and the events it refers to.[12] Indeed, the Bible itself makes clear that there is such a gap, by the differing portrayals that it offers of events in First Testament history (in Kings, Chronicles, and the Prophets) and in the life of Christ (in the Gospels). We have no direct access to historical events themselves. Can the story be valid if it does not actually represent the history?

It is easy to imagine what might be Luther's attitude to the minutiae of modern scholarship's endeavor to recover the actual history behind the text, though the task in principle is one in keeping with his recognition of history's importance. It is also easy to envisage Luther's impatience with a historical-critical method that, though tracing its ancestry to Luther, rules out a priori an event such as the resurrection and, indeed, methodologically excludes God from history. However, the man who can recognize that the book of Judith (or that of Tobit) is unhistorical yet can comment that "the words spoken by the persons in it should be understood as though they were uttered in the Holy Spirit by a spiritual, holy poet or prophet who, in presenting such persons in his play, preaches to us through them" (*LW* 35:337, 339, 345) might have found it easier to cope with the view that the Gospels are portrait rather than photograph than some other moderns who share his commitment to Christ and to Scripture.

Although the Bible is so important to Luther, he is not narrowly biblical in his theology. He will listen not only to the Scriptures but also to the Fathers, to the subsequent teaching of the church, to reason, and to human experience. The aim of his polemic is to put an end to what are relatively novel practices and to call the church back to more ancient ways. He opposes the overthrowing of tradition when it is not inconsistent with Scripture. Though concerned for the priority of text over tradition, he also asserts the priority of tradition over rationalism and over enthusiasm.[13]

After many years of negative attitude to tradition, in some quarters Protestantism is coming to a new realization of its positive value. After all, if we believe that the Holy Spirit has been present and active in the church, it is odd to assume that we can simply ignore the ways the church has felt led to formulate doctrine and to interpret Scripture over the centuries. Of course tradition can be misleading: it can have been wrong for its day or irrelevant for ours. But it can also offer an illuminating way in to perceiving aspects of the meaning and implications of Scripture that we might otherwise miss or be unclear on.[14]

---

12. On this development, see Hans Frei, *The Eclipse of Biblical Narrative* (New Haven and London: Yale University Press, 1974); again see the discussion in chapter 2 above and in chapter 5 (section 3) below.

13. On Luther and tradition, see Pelikan, *Luther the Expositor*, ch. 4.

14. From different perspectives, see B. S. Childs, *Biblical Theology in Crisis* (Philadelphia: Westminster Press, 1970), 139–47; P. Stuhlmacher, *Historical Criticism and Theological Interpretation of Scripture* (Philadelphia: Fortress, 1977; London: SPCK, 1979), 31–35, 79–80; Richard Bauckham, reviewing Hans Küng's *On Being a Christian* in *Them* 4 (1979): 73.

However, taking up an image he attributes to Bernard of Clairvaux (though apparently it cannot be located in Bernard's writings), Luther emphasizes that the Fathers and the church's tradition are the stream that issues from a spring that is Scripture itself; and a spring always tends to be purer than the brook that flows from it (e.g., *LW* 41:20, 26–27). Thus the written Scriptures are the fount from which the church's proclamation is to flow. They are also a check on whether that proclamation is in accordance with truth. The apostles' attitude to the First Testament illustrates this double principle (see Luther's comment on 1 Pet 1:11, *LW* 30:22–23). Thus, where necessary, even the Fathers are to be subordinated to the Scriptures. Only Scripture "has never erred." The apostles alone are "infallible teachers" (cf. *LW* 1:121; *LW* 32:11; *LW* 34:113). "For St. Augustine writes that he had learned that only those books that are called canonical should be given the honor of belief in their absolute truth, and that he believed the rest of the learned fathers, no matter how holy and sanctified, only if they wrote the truth" (*Luther at the Diet of Worms*; *LW* 32:118).

What exactly are "those books which are called canonical"? One aspect of this question is, "Which pre-Christian Jewish books belong in the Bible?" Protestants, and to some extent Roman Catholics, are now used to there being a clear distinction between the First Testament (works in the Hebrew canon accepted by Jews) and the Apocrypha or deuterocanonical writings. The Latin Bible Luther inherited, however, did not make this division. Generally he makes no distinction in authority between the First Testament and deuterocanonical works, and he introduces quotations from the latter with phrases such as "it is written," "the Bible says" (e.g., *LW* 31:47).

On some occasions, however, he does declare his view that quotations from the deuterocanonical books are not legitimate evidence in a debate. Only the books written in Hebrew really belong in the canon. Even then, he is wary of giving this argument too much force, so he adds the further point that an important doctrine ought not to be based on one passage in an out-of-the-way book, or that the passage is obscure and ambiguous and therefore again cannot have a doctrine based on it (e.g., *LW* 32:96–97; *LW* 33:110–11).

Luther's ambivalence over the longer canon reappears in his prefaces to the deuterocanonical books. The complete Luther Bible of 1534 gives them the general title "Apocrypha: these books are not held equal to the Scriptures but are useful and good to read." We have noted his view of Judith and Tobit. First Maccabees "would not have been unworthy of a place among the Scriptures." Second Maccabees, however, is of composite authorship, and is unedifying and unhistorical in parts. "Just as it is proper for the first book to be included among the sacred Scriptures, so it is proper that this second book should be thrown out, even though it contains some good things. However, the whole thing is left and referred to the pious reader to judge and to decide" (*LW* 35:350, 352–53).

An earlier remark to Erasmus (who had appealed to Ben Sira to establish a point) opens up another aspect to the question of which books belong in the canon. "You compare Proverbs and The Song of Solomon (which with a sneering innuendo you call the 'Love Song') with the two books of Esdras, Judith, the story of Susanna and the Dragon, and Esther (which despite their inclusion of it in the canon deserves more than all the rest in my judgment to be regarded as noncanonical)" (*LW* 33:110). In other words, not only are books outside the Hebrew canon treated as Scripture; books inside that canon are not beyond questioning. Yet phrases such as "in my opinion" and "referred to the pious reader to judge and to decide" are to be noted. Perhaps Luther recognizes that his own difficulty in appreciating certain books may be (to use a modern term) culture relative.

Luther discriminated similarly between New Testament books, giving Hebrews, James, Jude, and Revelation a subordinate position primarily because they seemed to proclaim the central gospel message less clearly (*LW* 35:394–99). Despite this verdict, he does use the books. Even Esther is quoted more than once (*LW* 34:130; *LW* 35:61) and his second preface to Revelation (*LW* 35:399–411) introduces the book's teaching much more positively than the first. According to Pelikan, "from his own experience he could testify that often a Christian found one or another book of the canon difficult or useless to him at a particular time, only to discover later on that it was just what he needed in a time of trouble or temptation. Had such a person been permitted to re-edit the canon on the basis of his passing mood, he would have been deprived of the patience and comfort of the Scriptures when he needed them most."[15] Thus Luther does not seek formally to reopen the question of the canon. Perhaps his expressions of opinion on what it ought to include are no more attempts at change than were the parallel remarks of the rabbis reported in the Talmud. His antipathy to James is partly explicable as a reaction to the awareness that its teaching was too congenial to Catholicism, and his antipathy to Esther reflected the popularity of that book with the Jews (though it has troubled many other Christians since). What this suggests is that we have to take a historical approach to the activity of the interpreter himself. Even exegetes who make objectivity their supreme goal have to recognize that all their judgments are historically conditioned.

On what basis can Luther ascribe a unique status to the Scriptures of the two Testaments as the church's normative, indeed "infallible," theological resource? The question of why Scripture should be given supreme status is not prominent in Luther or in the Lutheran tradition.[16] Luther argued for the acceptance of the (First Testament) Scriptures on the basis of the apostles' example. He argued for the acceptance of the apostles' testimony (the New Testament, as he saw this to be) on the basis of their connection with Christ but also on the basis of the Fathers' example. This last argument suggests that the acceptance of the Scriptures is based on the church's tradition and thus plays into the hands of the Catholic Church. It was the church that prescribed what was in the Bible (and thus that decides what the Bible means).

15. *Luther the Expositor*, 87.

16. See John Bowden's remarks on Bultmann's conservatism at this point, in his "Translator's Preface" to W. Schmithals, *An Introduction to the Theology of Rudolf Bultmann* (London: SCM; Minneapolis: Augsburg, 1968), xiv; and Ellen Flesseman-van Leer's "letter," "Dear Christopher, . . ." in *What about the New Testament? Essays in Honour of Christopher Evans* (ed. Morna D. Hooker and C. Hickling; London: SCM, 1975), 234–42.

In response to this argument, the Reformed churches declared that the church accepts Scripture not on human testimony but on that of the Holy Spirit, who spoke to the prophets and apostles, who now testifies to Scripture's truth in the heart of believers, and who also enables them to grasp its meaning.[17] This position is self-consistent and reflects how many Christians come to their acceptance of Scripture, but it offers no way of arguing for or against the position it safeguards. Either you see the light, or you do not.

Luther's position depended on the New Testament's connection with the apostles. He recognized and utilized the fact that this argument was two-edged. If given writings were not apostolic, what then? Luther queried whether Hebrews, James, Jude, and Revelation were apostolic (*LW* 35:394–99), either in the sense that they were written by apostles, or in the sense that they preached apostolic doctrine, as Luther understood it. Although Luther does not seek formally to reopen the canon, his approach raises the question whether the canon's bounds are finally settled.

The basis on which Luther considers which books belong in the canon is also reminiscent of rabbinic discussion. The rabbis, too, discussed questions of authorship (whether books came from the period of inspiration, from Moses to Ezra) and of content (books such as Ezekiel that seemed to conflict with the Torah were the subject of dispute). Within Protestantism a systematic investigation of the origin of the biblical books was undertaken in the centuries after Luther, partly following his example. The implication is that questions of authorship carry implications for questions of authority; but though questions of authorship come to have a prominent place in discussions of the canon in the patristic period, it is doubtful whether such considerations lay at the heart of the process whereby documents such as the Gospels originally commended themselves to churches.

Luther believed that the First Testament comprised those books that were written in Hebrew. But we now have the Hebrew original of Ben Sira (Ecclesiasticus), and other apocryphal books were probably also written in Hebrew. So language is not the key to canonicity. Further, some apocryphal books belong to the same period as some canonical books. Do these belong in the canon? Or do some canonical books not really belong? What is the difference between canonical and extracanonical writings? Both came into existence by a historical process, and they are not formally distinguishable from each other. The formation of the canon was itself a historical process; the Bible did not drop from heaven in its complete form.

The other aspect of Luther's critique raised questions about the content of certain writings. Esther, 2 Maccabees, and James seemed to conflict with other books, which Luther regarded as more central. Althaus infers that in his critique of the canon

---

17. See J. Calvin, *Institutes of the Christian Religion* (1559), I.vii. There are hints of this understanding in Luther: it is "by the testimony of the Holy Spirit in his own person" that someone recognizes the gospel message as God's Word, and since Scripture itself can be identified as God's word (see Althaus, *The Theology of Martin Luther*, 38, 50–53), presumably this conviction comes by the same means. For this argument in the modern period, see G. C. Berkouwer, *Studies in Dogmatics: Holy Scripture* (Grand Rapids: Eerdmans, 1975), 30–66.

Luther "in principle abandoned every formal approach to the authority of the Bible."[18] Whether or not this is true of Luther, it has become true of most biblical study since.

Luther's willingness to be critical of canonical books has to have put alongside it his description of the Scriptures as infallible. He was willing to give blank check assent to whatever Scripture said, even if it seemed to make no sense to him.[19] This can be interpreted as a relic of medievalism that cannot be held onto without falling into legalism, but an alternative view is that it cannot be abandoned without falling into subjectivism. If biblical criticism can find itself in Luther's freedom in discussing Scripture, Protestant confessionalism and fundamentalism find themselves in his talk of infallibility.

Another key topic of modern canonical discussion is the question of a "canon within the canon." The phrase has several meanings. It can signify a recognition that we inevitably tend to pay serious heed only to that part of Scripture that seems relevant to us, or it can denote an identification of part of Scripture as its center or as the real word of God within it. In the latter senses, recognition of a canon within the canon stems from an awareness of diversity within Scripture. If the Scriptures are inspired by God, they may be expected to speak with consistency, and it will be possible to interpret them in accordance with each other. This principle, however, can lead to reading them in the flat and taking exegetical and theological shortcuts instead of listening to the various writings in their distinctiveness as they are read in their historical contexts. Luther recognized that there was diversity in Scripture, and he proposed to use the gospel as he understood it (primarily from Romans) as the basis for passing judgment on other parts of Scripture (*LW* 35:365–80). In fact, the principle of *sola scriptura* (by Scripture alone) is subordinate to the more fundamental proposition *solus Christus* (Christ alone). With regard to the canon, Luther's central principle is, Does it point to Christ? Does it express the gospel? If writers speak of Christ but they are outside the canon (whether they are apocryphal or patristic), then let them be heard. If they do not speak of Christ, then they may be ignored even if they have canonical status. The point is explicit in the *Theses Concerning Faith and Law*: "41. The Scriptures must be understood in favor of Christ, not against him. For that reason they must either refer to him or must not be held to be true Scripture." For instance, the commandments are to be kept "in Christ," apart from whom we can do nothing. "49. Therefore, if the adversaries press the Scriptures against Christ, we urge Christ against the Scriptures" (*LW* 34:112).

Luther here opens the door in Protestantism to the belief that the Word of God is not more than the canon of Scripture (as Catholicism taught) but less than it. His criticism is not "in the name of reason or in the name of a scientific world-view or the modern understanding of existence," but in the name of the gospel itself: "Sacred Scripture is its own critic."[20] But is it possible to produce a nicely self-coherent

---

18. *The Theology of Martin Luther*, 85.
19. Ibid., 51–52.
20. Ibid., 86, 81.

Bible by relegating certain books to an appendix? Is an alleged understanding of the Bible not called in question by an inability to deal positively with some parts of the biblical material?

2. The First Testament as a Christian Book

Luther's Christ-centeredness is reflected in the way he interprets the First Testament, which is very prominent in his theological discussions as well as his lectures. It is radically clear in his first lectures on the Psalms. He begins the printed preface to the edition prepared for his students (*LW* 10:6–7) with a series of passages of Scripture ending with 1 Corinthians 2:2, "I decided to know nothing among you except Jesus Christ and Him crucified." From these passages he infers that "every prophecy and every prophet [David and his psalms would be included] must be understood as referring to Christ the Lord, except where it is clear from plain words that someone else is spoken of." Thus, for instance, Psalm 1 "literally" describes Jesus' way of life, Psalm 2 his rule despite opposition, Psalm 3 his complaint at his enemies. The Psalms can be applied allegorically or tropologically to the church and the individual believer, because they share his blessings. They can even be applied to David, as a First Testament believer, and may have been applied by David to himself (*LW* 10:52, on Ps 4:1). They can be applied to "the faithful and seeking synagog" and to people in general "seeking and hoping to be saved by Christ" (*LW* 10:196, on Ps 42:7). But the literal reference is to Christ himself. They are his veiled testimony, revealed as such by his coming and by the New Testament's approach to them.

Luther's approach to interpretation in these first lectures is thus radically Christ-centered. But it is also radically unhistorical, like that of most of his predecessors. The Psalms have no (literal) meaning for those who first wrote and sang them. In them Christ speaks his own prayer and testimony; the psalmist is merely his mouthpiece. Surprisingly, Luther needed in a sense to become less Christ-centered, a development we can perceive as we look at his later treatments of some of these same psalms (in *LW* 14). The subject is no longer necessarily Christ himself (and other believers only by extension). It is any believer, in affliction (Ps 6), longing for the vindication of the righteous (Ps 37), rejoicing in God's law (Ps 1). Particularly striking, Psalm 94 no longer reflects the conflict between Christ and the Jews of his day, with people of First Testament times appearing only in "a mystical sense" (vv. 5–6; so *LW* 11:242–51). It is "clearly a prayer that is common to all the pious children of God and members of His spiritual people . . . be they Jews, Christians, or patriarchs." In First Testament times "the pious and faithful Jews prayed it against . . . the Gentiles, who raged about them and continually persecuted them; and the false prophets, who arose in their midst and misled the people" (*LW* 14:243).

Luther's developed position on the Psalms, then, includes the idea that many of them are the prayers and praises of the Israelite congregation seeking God's face and looking for the fulfillment of God's promise in the coming of the Messiah. They are thus natural models for the prayer and praise of the church that is the spiritual successor to the "faithful synagogue" and looks for the coming of Christ in its own life and at his final coming.[21]

The assumption that the believers in both Testaments had the same relationship to God in Christ through the Word also underlies the way Luther read the narratives, the prophets, and the worship regulations of the First Testament. Theologically, Israel and the church are one people of God, and Israel's story is the story of the church. Patterns in the experience and life of (faithful) Israel correspond to patterns in the experience and life of the (true) church. Thus Genesis, "an exceedingly evangelical book" (*LW* 35:237), offers "beautiful examples of faith, of love, and of the cross, and warning examples for the godless" (*LW* 35:173). Luther's *Lectures on Genesis*[22] illustrate at length what he means. He is only taking further a tradition that goes back to the New Testament.

While an important step toward a historical understanding of the First Testament is taken in Luther's treatment of the Psalms as Israel's praise and prayer, another possible step remains untaken in that the psalms that explicitly refer to the king are still assumed to be literal prophecies of Christ. The prophetic books proper, of course, are also frequently seen as consciously promising the coming of Christ, as is Moses himself on occasion (e.g., Deut 18:15–16). In this approach, Luther is content to follow the New Testament, though here, too, there is development. Earlier, Luther apparently saw the messianic psalms as spoken by Christ, unbeknown to the psalmist (who is ignored). Now he envisages the psalmist consciously declaring God's promise of the Messiah to come. Their literal, historical meaning is what they meant to the psalmist.[23]

This understanding of the First Testament as literally prophesying Christ remains central in Luther's approach to the First Testament, particularly when he offers a theoretical formulation of the First Testament's significance. In *A Brief Instruction on What to Look for and Expect in the Gospels* (*LW* 35:113–24), he declares that "the apostles . . . want themselves to be our guides, to direct us to the writings of the prophets and of Moses in the Old Testament so that we might there read and see for ourselves how Christ is wrapped in swaddling cloths and laid in the manger [Luke 2:7], that is, how he is comprehended [*Vorfassett*] in the writings of the prophets," and he laments people's unwillingness to read the First Testament to learn of Christ. Luther believes, indeed, that the First Testament explicitly speaks of the two natures of Christ, divine as well as human, in passages such as in Genesis 4:1 and 1 Chronicles 17:17; he argues forcefully that this is the natural way to understand

---

21. For this threefold coming of Christ in fulfillment of God's promise, see the treatment of Ps 115:1 (*LW* 11:396–97) with Preus's comments (*From Shadow to Promise*, 192–95); and more generally Luther's *Preface to the Psalter* (*LW* 35:253–57).

22. *LW* 1–8; on these, see Pelikan, *Luther the Expositor*, ch. 5.

23. On this development, see Preus, *From Shadow to Promise*, ch. 12. In general, however, I think Preus may draw a little too sharply the distinction between Luther's hermeneutic at the beginning of his first Psalms course and the one he reached by the end of it.

the Hebrew, though he acknowledges that it is only in light of the coming of Christ that this becomes the natural reading. It remains veiled to the Jews. Similarly he finds a trinitarian understanding of God sometimes expressed (e.g., in Gen 1:26; 2 Sam 23:1–3; Ps 2).[24] Thus, while Luther sees progress in the outworking of salvation history in the biblical period (there is a before Christ and an after Christ), he does not see a development in revelation. The same Holy Spirit speaks throughout, and the teaching of Scripture as a whole (and especially the more thoroughly worked out teaching of the New Testament) provides the framework for understanding the literal meaning of its different parts.

We may doubt whether this principle actually makes it appropriate to understand biblical texts in a way that contrasts with the meaning attaching to them in the historical context in which the Holy Spirit inspired them, but the positive truth Luther here reminds us of is that God has always been three Persons and that Father, Son, and Holy Spirit were involved in creation and in the history of First Testament times. Even if a trinitarian or christological exegesis of the passages referred to above is inappropriate, a trinitarian or christological understanding of First Testament times is not only appropriate but necessary.

In the description of the life and hopes of the people of God, and in the strictly messianic prophecies, Luther finds a strong thread of continuity between the Testaments. The First Testament is directly applicable to the life and thought of the Christian. His third category for understanding the First Testament emphasizes the element of discontinuity. "The Old Testament is a book of laws, which teaches what men are to do and not to do . . . just as the New Testament is gospel or book of grace, and teaches where one is to get the power to fulfill the law. Now in the New Testament there are also given, along with the teaching about grace, many other teachings that are laws and commandments for the control of the flesh. . . . Similarly in the Old Testament too there are, beside the laws, certain promises and words of grace, by which the holy fathers and prophets under the law were kept, like us, in the faith of Christ. Nevertheless, just as the chief teaching of the New Testament is really the proclamation of grace and peace through the forgiveness of sins in Christ, so the chief teaching of the Old Testament is really the teaching of laws, the showing up of sin, and the demanding of good" (LW 35:236–37); compare the sermon on How Christians Should Regard Moses (LW 35:155–74). The First Testament, that is, fulfills a negative function of revealing the divine standards that humanity cannot keep. The fact that Moses himself looks forward to Christ indicates that he did not even see his own law as the last word. Moses' best pupils are those who see his demands clearly and are driven to Christ by the impossibility of fulfilling them (LW 35:245–46).

But once they come to Christ, as far as they are concerned "Moses is dead" (LW 35:165). Do the First Testament laws, then, have no function in the Christian era

24. See the treatise On the Last Words of David (2 Sam 23:1–7) (LW 15:265–352) for these christological and trinitarian discussions; also (on the Trinity in Gen 1:26) LW 1:57–59. Bornkamm (Luther and the Old Testament, 114–15) notes Luther's relative restraint over this point, however: for instance, he does not find the Trinity in Gen 18.

except that of driving people to Christ? Luther allows only slight qualification of this negative. First, modern rulers can learn from them as they seek to fulfill their calling. They were given simply to be the national law code of the Jews, and as laws they are binding on no other state, but they are instructive for people of other races in that they comprise one particular (indeed, a notable) embodiment of the natural law written in the hearts of all humanity (*LW* 35:164–68; *LW* 40:96–99). Luther is far short, however, of envisaging the First Testament as functioning as the framework for a Christian state, as the Reformed tradition came to do.

A second qualification is that the law can fulfill certain functions in the Christian life. Luther is concerned to leave no loophole for the reemergence of justification by works, and his emphasis is therefore placed on the conviction that Christ is the end of the law. In principle Christians need the law neither as a guide to the mind of God (the Spirit indwelling them can guide them into writing new law codes, in fact: *LW* 34:112–13), nor to convict them of sin (because they have already been drawn to Christ and made righteous in him). But Luther is aware, and emphasizes, that no Christians realize this ideal short of heaven. They are righteous, but at the same time still sinners. In this world they therefore still need the law to clarify for them what are the expectations that by the grace of Christ and the activity of the Spirit they are to fulfill, and thus, by reminding them of their sin, to keep drawing them to Christ for forgiveness (cf. the comments on Gal 2:18, *LW* 27:232). Thus the Decalogue has an important place in Luther's teaching and in his own spirituality (*LW* 47:109–13), though he does not formulate the notion of the law as "training the Christian in good works"[25] as explicitly as Melanchthon did. Here, once again, Luther's emphasis is the one he learned from Paul.

3. Appropriation

Luther prides logic and argument in his biblical study. He is concerned to get the text and the translation from Hebrew and Greek right and to take due account of the biblical books' historical background. In his Prefaces (*LW* 35:225–411) he discusses the books' origins and speculates as to how far they were actually written by those whose names appear at their head. The "letter" must be studied. But one also has to listen to the Spirit who speaks through the letter.[26] Mere historical study is lifeless and

25. The phrase comes from Althaus, *The Theology of Martin Luther*, 273. I think Althaus underestimates Luther's persistent distinctiveness on this point; see Gerhard Ebeling's discussion of the threefold use of the law in *Word and Faith* (Philadelphia: Fortress; London: SCM, 1963), 62–78. But the law-gospel antithesis is a complex one: see Althaus, *The Theology of Martin Luther*, ch. 19; Ebeling, *Luther*, chs. 7–8.

26. On this antithesis, see Ebeling, *Luther*, ch. 6. Luther's praise of Nicholas of Lyra is tempered further by his finding failure here: the Jewish exegetes from whom Lyra learned so much nevertheless also tended to mislead him when they inevitably (from a Christian perspective) missed dimensions of meaning beyond the merely historical (see Luther's *Treatise on the Last Words of David*, *LW* 15:269).

pointless. Luther is thus not coldly objective and uninvolved. His exegetical method involves him in projecting himself into the situation and feelings of the characters he seeks to understand, as his commentaries on Genesis and Psalms illustrate.

From a study of Psalm 119, he offers three principles for biblical study: *oratio, meditatio, tentatio* (LW 34:279–88). First, prayer: for we must not suppose that Scripture becomes clear to mere human reason. Second, reflection: Luther urges outward reading and rereading of a book as part of giving serious and continuing attention to it. The emphasis on outward reading corresponds with that on oral proclamation: the gospel began as a preached message that demands a response, and it "should really not be something written."[27] Third, and most strikingly, conflict (*Anfechtung*: a key term in Luther): Luther found in his own inner and outward experience what he read of also in the psalmists and prophets, that somehow the word of the Lord became most clear in his affliction. "Theological thinking and speaking does not occur apart from doubt and temptation, and faith's overcoming of temptation; rather it is and remains a thinking within this process, that is, thinking within the framework of *Anfechtung*."[28]

Elsewhere, in a lecture on the same psalm he notes that the psalmist prays for understanding (Ps 119:125), as if having none, but aware of the need to keep increasing in insight. Indeed, what was "Spirit" yesterday is "letter" today. We never finally grasp any passage or any doctrine. It has to be reappropriated afresh each time we approach it (*LW* 11:497).[29] Luther's own exegetical attitude illustrates his point: twenty years after his first Psalms course he begins an eleven-lecture treatment of Psalm 51 by acknowledging how little he understands and how he still stands under the Scriptures in the same way as his students do. "I cannot promise that I shall lecture satisfactorily, for I admit that I have not fully grasped the Spirit who speaks there. Still it gives us an opportunity and a basis for thought and study, so that I can become a student with you and await the Spirit" (*LW* 12:303).

Luther assumes that our involvement with the text helps us as exegetes to understand its meaning. Our understanding of its meaning would then be expected to have implications for our life and for the contemporary church. As it does not occur to Luther to seek to speak to his own day without a fresh listening to Scripture, so it does not occur to him to teach the Bible "academically" without in the same breath noting how it applies to the contemporary situation. His assumption of a basic oneness between people of all periods undergirds his attempt to apply Scripture as well as his endeavor to understand Scripture. As we have seen, his theological-historical understanding of the relationship between Israel and the church as both enjoying salvation in Christ enables him to relate much of Genesis, Psalms, and the Prophets to the church of his day as directly as he does the New Testament, and without their being substantially hindered from speaking their own message by being treated as only the New Testament in disguise.[30]

---

27. So *A Brief Instruction on What to Look for and Expect in the Gospels* (LW 35:117–24 [123]); cf. Pelikan, *Luther the Expositor*, 63–65 and ch. 3 as a whole.
28. Althaus, *The Theology of Martin Luther*, 34.
29. Cf. Ebeling, *Luther*, 99–100.
30. Cf. Preus, *From Shadow to Promise*.

Nevertheless, Luther recognizes that not all biblical acts are recorded for us to imitate and not all commands are given for us to obey. They are situational and culture relative. Whether or not we are entitled to follow Jacob's example of deceitfulness (Gen 30:31–43) depends on whether we are in a precisely similar situation to Jacob (*LW* 5:386).[31] The command to Israel to slaughter the Amalekites (Exod 17:8–16) cannot be assumed to justify a peasants' revolt, as contemporary liberation theologians claimed; this command was not addressed to the German peasants. The laws of Moses in general were not directed to Christian believers.

If the Bible does not apply to believers in this direct way, how does it speak to them? In Luther's day, allegorical interpretation provided the standard approach to this question.[32] In the medieval period, the literal, historical sense of Scripture, while theoretically the sole norm for doctrine, in practice yielded prominence to the figurative, allegorical sense, which could find meaning in writings that otherwise seemed irrelevant and unhelpful. It could generate applications of Scripture with reference to Christian doctrine (the allegorical sense proper), or to the life of the believer (the tropological sense), or to the life of heaven (the anagogical sense). Thus—to give a standard example—a reference to the city of Jerusalem as the city of God could be applied allegorically to the church, tropologically to the individual believer, or anagogically to heaven. More specifically, the law concerning marriage to a woman captured in war (Deut 21:10–14) refers to the acquisition of eloquence or the conversion of the Jewish people to Christ. The method was kept on the rails theologically by the requirement that its lessons had to be consistent with the faith itself, as established by the literal, historical sense of Scripture.

Luther knew that the allegorical method had the authority of Paul's example (Gal 4:22–31) (*LW* 16:327), and he was willing to use it as a method of drawing out applications from the text. But his use of it is very different from what he finds in his predecessors. First, he disagreed with the theology that underlay the allegories of writers such as Jerome and Origen: "they direct everything to manners and works, whereas everything should rather be applied to the Word and to faith" (*LW* 9:7). Allegory need not presuppose this framework (as Luther's own allegories are in part designed to show), but it is always in danger of being a means of missing the thrust of Scripture's message, the gospel of grace. Luther's own conversion had come about through his wrestling with the literal, historical meaning of Scripture.

Even when used in accordance with a sound theology, allegory is an approach to be used with restraint, because of the importance of the principle nominally accepted by all that the literal, historical sense has to be the foundation of all else. We have noted his positive emphasis on historical interpretation in his discussion of Isaiah 13. Negatively, in the same discussion he comments: "Let us forewarn here

---

31. Bainton, *The Cambridge History of the Bible*, 3:15, offers further examples.

32. Luther often refers to this as "figurative interpretation," a term which also covers exegetical approaches that avoid the natural sense of statements such as "God hardened Pharaoh's heart" or "This is my body." Probably Luther liked to associate these two together, but it may help clarity to keep the distinction, especially as allegory itself has several meanings.

concerning allegory that it may be handled wisely in the Spirit. . . . You use allegory as an embellishment by which the discourse is illustrated but not established. . . . Allegory does not pertain to doctrine, but to doctrine already established it can be added as color. The painter's color does not build the house. . . . Even so faith is not established by means of allegories" (*LW* 16:136–37; cf. *LW* 1:231–34, on Gen 1–3 as a whole). The basis of faith is the fact that God has spoken and then acted in fulfillment of this word. Allegorical application must build on that, not replace it.

Luther's *Lectures on Deuteronomy* include, exceptionally, a systematic allegorical application. Commenting on Deuteronomy 21:10–14, referred to above, for instance, Luther first discusses the original social and ethical significance of the law, then rejects a first allegory (Jerome's) but approves a second (his own) (*LW* 9:213–14). In the other commentaries, allegorical application is more occasional. Thus, although Luther sees the problem about applying legal, and some narrative, material to his own day, he cannot solve it, particularly so long as he resists the development of a notion of the use of the law for the guidance of the Christian and of the state, because of his fear of a reintroduction of legal righteousness.

4. An Integrated Approach?

We began by noting that Luther was a decisive stimulus to the development of biblical interpretation over the next four centuries. Many of the issues that came to be raised during this period were variants on one theme: what is the relationship between historical and theological study of Scripture, between the study of the lecture room and that of the pulpit, between prayer and thinking, between (as Luther would put it) the letter and the Spirit?

The goal of biblical interpretation is to treat Scripture at once theologically and historically, at once in a literal and an applied way. Its aim is to listen to it as the Word of God and as the word of human beings, to seek its own particular meaning and its relevance to us. It is difficult to hold these two complementarities together. This is, of course, the case with several other elements in Christian belief. One example is belief in both the humanness and the deity of Christ. Another is allowance for both a sovereign choosing on God's part and a free responding on the part of human beings as aspects of what is involved in coming to faith in Christ. It is easy to place excessive, perhaps exclusive, emphasis on one or the other of the twin aspects of these beliefs, perhaps on the grounds that the one prima facie excludes the other. Christian faith characteristically accepts such polarities, however, and we have to strive at each point for a "both-and" rather than an "either-or."

It would be an exaggeration to claim that Luther had a perfectly balanced, integrated approach that realized the ideal just described. Nevertheless, he, and Calvin even more markedly, maintain an extraordinary balance in their commitment to a theological (yet also with a desire for a historical) approach and in their striving for literal (and yet also applied) interpretation. The balance of their attitudes is the more remarkable when one considers how difficult subsequent centuries have found the maintaining (still less the developing) of it. In practice, one side of Luther develops in biblical criticism and in the Enlightenment, the other side in pietism.[33]

A concern for literal, historical interpretation has its background not merely in the Reformation but also in the Renaissance, and it was pursued not merely in church circles but in those of the Enlightenment. The development of scholarly biblical study was, indeed, centrally a quest for a historical approach to Scripture. The theological value of Scripture was not outside the concerns of this study, but it was subordinated to the historical question. Furthermore, many scholars who sought to approach the Bible "without dogmatic or creedal bias"[34] were deeply affected by all sorts of other biases: rationalism, romanticism, evolutionism, and so on. This drew most scholarly work even further away from the study of Scripture as God's Word. Still less in this scholarly tradition was Scripture read with the personal involvement and urgency characteristic of Luther, or with the energy of Calvin, who, "having first established what stands in the text, sets himself to re-think the whole material and to wrestle with it, till the walls that separate the sixteenth century from the first become transparent."[35]

This aspect of the way biblical criticism was developing alienated those who were concerned to treat the Bible as the Word of God and to listen to its message for their day. Criticism seemed to make no contribution to those ends. It could be left to people such as Hobbes and Spinoza, Hegel and Wellhausen, as at best irrelevant, at worst dangerous. What was needed for the understanding of Scripture was the illumination of the Spirit, not the work of human reason.

Controversy with Catholicism also pushed Protestant pietism toward a biblicism that ignored the human and historical origin of Scripture. Catholicism made the Bible dependent on the church for its authority and its interpretation. Thus Protestantism placed all its emphasis on the fact that the Bible was God's Word, vouchsafed for and interpreted by the Holy Spirit and not by mere human beings.

So for three centuries theological, applied study and literal, historical study proceeded in growing independence of each other. The loss to those who were concerned for the Bible as God's Word was considerable, as may be seen from works such as those of the great Baptist preacher Charles Spurgeon. Spurgeon described Calvin's commentaries, for instance, as "of priceless value," not least because of Calvin's fairness to the text, never extracting teaching out of it that the text itself could not be fairly reckoned to contain (Spurgeon instances Calvin's treatment of Gen 1:26, where he does not find the doctrine of the Trinity—though he does find plurality

---

33. Cf. the remarks of B. Hagglund, "Renaissance and Reformation," in *Luther and the Dawn of the Modern Era* (ed. H. A. Oberman; Leiden: Brill, 1974), 156–57. See also Ebeling's essay on "Luther and the Beginning of the Modern Age" in that volume, and ch. 6 of his *Luther*.

34. W. G. Kümmel, *The New Testament: The History of the Investigation of its Problems* (Nashville: Abingdon, 1973; London: SCM, 1973), 13.

35. Karl Barth, *The Epistle to the Romans* (London and New York: Oxford University Press, 1933), 7.

within the Godhead).[36] But Spurgeon himself is much less historical in his approach, as may be seen by comparing his work on the Psalms[37] with Calvin's commentary. Spurgeon's is devotionally helpful, but it often has little to do with the literal, historical meaning of the Psalms.

The loss that the divorce of these two approaches brought to historical study was much greater. Its achievements were huge. We do understand far more about the historical origins of the various books of the Bible than previous Christian centuries have. We can listen to Jeremiah or Isaiah as they could not. But historical study fell fatally short of an adequate listening to the Bible. It was not listening to what God had to say through these human writers; and its historical approach was vitiated by the influence that the philosophies of the time exercised on its theories. Historical criticism, which hoped to let the Bible speak afresh, ended up leaving the Bible with apparently nothing to say.[38] This was part of the background to twentieth-century interest in hermeneutics. We still have to seek an approach that listens for God's Word to us today but accepts (indeed rejoices in) the historicality of the texts in which we hope to hear it, a literal and historical understanding of Scripture that is at the same time open to hearing "thus says the Lord."[39] Historically, the impasse that resulted when people followed up Luther's lead was perhaps inevitable. But this only emphasizes the challenge that remains, to be rational without being rationalist, devotional without being pietist, biblical without being biblicist. Both pietists or fundamentalists and practitioners of the historical-critical method can claim Luther's support for what they affirm,[40] but he confronts each of them over what they deny. It is doubtful if he would acknowledge any of these grown-up children as his sons; at best he might want to bang their heads together, concerned himself to hold together what each stood for. Where Luther is unclear, more recent study has rarely progressed much beyond him; while where more recent study has moved beyond him, it has usually done so at the cost of resolving tensions Luther was wiser to accept.

36. *Commenting and Commentaries* (London: Passmore and Alabaster, 1876; repr., London: Banner of Truth, 1969), 36; see also 4–5; and John Calvin, *Commentaries on the Book of Genesis* (repr., Grand Rapids: Eerdmans, n.d.), 1:92–93. Calvin is here, as quite often, more literal and historical in his approach than Luther is.

37. *The Treasury of David* (London: Passmore and Alabaster, 1884).

38. For recognition of this, see J. D. Smart, *The Strange Silence of the Bible in the Church* (Philadelphia: Westminster Press; London: SCM, 1970); W. Wink, *The Bible in Human Transformation* (Philadelphia: Fortress, 1975), ch. 1; also various articles in *Theology Today* 33 (1976–77): 66–73; 219–23; 354–67.

39. Cf. Kümmel's "Conclusion," *The New Testament*, 405–6; J. M. Robinson, "The Future of New Testament Theology," *Religious Studies Review* 2, no. 1 (1976): 17.

40. See on one hand H. Lindsell, *The Battle for the Bible* (Grand Rapids: Zondervan, 1976), 56–59; J. W. Montgomery, "Lessons from Luther on the Inerrancy of Holy Writ," in *God's Inerrant Word* (ed. J. W. Montgomery; Minneapolis: Bethany, 1974), 63–94; on the other, James Barr, *Fundamentalism* (London: SCM; Philadelphia: Westminster Press, 1977), 172–86; Kümmel, *The New Testament*, 20–26.

4

Can We Learn from the Hermeneutics of Liberation Theology?

While it may be tempting to dismiss Latin American liberation theology as a fad of the 1970s or a dead end that was succeeded by postcolonial interpretation, its broader influence on interpretation in the context of feminism, African American interpretation, and other forms of liberation theology means it continues to raise questions about theology and about hermeneutics that appropriately concern biblical scholars as well as other theologians and ethicists. In the work of many liberation theologians, indeed, the Bible had a more important place than it often has in contemporary theology, but their methods of interpretation and their results were very different from those of what is customarily called biblical theology.[1]

In the first part of this chapter I note some characteristic features of liberation theology's approach to biblical interpretation, which constitute the challenge it issues to conventional approaches. I then discuss aspects of this approach that have been matters of debate within liberation theology: what is the relationship between theology and praxis, how negotiable is the belief that liberation is the Bible's central theme, how are particular Bible passages to influence us today, and how far our understanding of the truth has to go via the Bible.

1. The Challenge of Liberation Theology's Approach to Interpretation

Liberation theologians believe that understanding the Bible is not the objective, scientific affair that biblical scholarship traditionally assumed it to be. What we see in the Bible is substantially influenced by what we are prepared to see there.

1. First published in *HBT* 4 (1982–83): 133–61.

In part, liberation theology is here only applying to biblical interpretation an insight that is true of all forms of study. The scientific ideal pictures a person standing receptively before the data of nature or of history or of some text and seeking to understand these data on their own terms, according to their categories, in keeping with their emphases. But in fact understanding always depends on bringing to the data some hypothesis that makes sense of them. One then seeks to perceive whether the data fit the hypothesis or whether some different hypothesis is needed.

Rudolf Bultmann long ago emphasized that tentative preliminary understandings of this kind are thus the way one opens oneself to the biblical text.[2] Liberation theology adds to this the further insight that one's opening of oneself to the text involves not merely the mind but also the will and deed. It is not merely possible, preferable, or dangerous for the way we live to influence the way we read the Bible. It is inevitable; this is a feature of human understanding in any sphere. Any reading of Scripture takes place against the background of some commitment, "reactionary, reformist, or revolutionary"; so what is important is to be self-conscious about one's bias, rather than pretending to speak from "some sort of ideologically aseptic environment," and to be self-critical about it.[3]

The Bible itself makes clear that understanding is helped forward, not held back, by a commitment to the ways of the Bible's God and thus hints that the attempt to understand it objectively and scientifically may not be fruitful because the knowledge and truth that the Bible are concerned with are not mere academic attainments. Knowledge (da'at) implies recognition and acknowledgment; truth ('emunah) involves constancy and faithfulness. To be willing to live by the truth is a precondition of seeing the truth (cf. John 7:17). The Bible is not merely a document of history that can be treated as a means to an end such as tracing the development of Israelite religion or investigating the events of Israelite history. It expresses, invites, and demands commitment to the one of whom it speaks and to those for whom this God is concerned. To study it "objectively" is to adopt an approach inappropriate to its nature. Liberation theology thus doubts whether the academic theology of study and university is theology at all, and questions whether the kind of understanding of Scripture that lacks the context of a desire to do what it says is true understanding at all.

What is the nature of the commitment that opens one to the message of Scripture? In a context of oppression, at least, the obvious answer is commitment to liberation, to the releasing of the bonds of all forms of exploitation and oppression. The belief that such a commitment is the means to understanding Scripture finds its vindication in the way it opens the interpreter's eyes to the prominence of the theme of liberation in Scripture. Further, behind the theme of liberation is another assumption much

---

2. See R. Bultmann, *Essays Theological and Philosophical* (London: SCM; New York: Macmillan, 1955), 234–61; *Existence and Faith: Shorter Writings of Rudolf Bultmann* (New York: Meridian, 1960; London: Hodder, 1961), 289–96, 314–15.

3. J. Míguez Bonino, *Revolutionary Theology Comes of Age* (London: SPCK, 1975) = *Doing Theology in a Revolutionary Situation* (Philadelphia: Fortress, 1975), 99; cf. J. L. Segundo, *Liberation of Theology* (Maryknoll, N.Y.: Orbis, 1976; Dublin: Gill and Macmillan, 1977), 7–8.

more prominent in Scripture than it has often been in biblical interpretation, the assumption that the God of the Bible is the God of the whole person, and that creation, redemption, covenant, and kingdom are matters of body as much as of soul. Yahweh is the warrior God, a God involved in history. The latter is a cliché of twentieth-century theology if there is one, but it is a principle liberation theology took seriously by taking it politically.[4] God is the one who does what is right, as J. P. Miranda has emphasized in studies of the Pentateuch and the prophets, of John and of Romans.[5]

Although some of Miranda's more original work relates to the New Testament, the biblical themes just noted are more obviously First Testament ones, and liberation theology consistently makes creative theological use of that opening three-quarters of the Bible that usually has little influence on theology. In particular, liberation theology perceives that the pattern whereby God does right by Israel is one that applies to all nations, because Yahweh *is* the God who does what is right.[6] Liberation theology's affirmation that there is only one history, so that sacred and profane are not to be separated, undergirds this point, as does the further emphasis in the work of Gustavo Gutiérrez on the link between creation and salvation history.[7]

Traditional academic study of Scripture thus finds itself under fire for its objectivizing, uncommitted approach to Scripture. Traditional confessional study of Scripture, although not guilty of that error, finds itself in the same firing line for a different reason. It allows its doctrinal formulations and its piety to determine what it notices in Scripture. The exodus story, for instance, is not ignored in such biblical study, but by being treated typologically it is depoliticized. The prophets are read, but more for their possible references to the first coming of Christ and to circumstances leading to his second coming than for their message to their own hearers. The New Testament is read out of an interest that is "religious" in the narrow sense (a concern focusing on people's personal relationship with God), and so the New Testament's revolutionary political implications are missed. Such biblical study is committed, but it is a commitment to a theology and a piety that does not open up Scripture broadly enough.

If the theme of liberation is so prominent in Scripture, how was it that theology and piety missed it for so long? The answer is that various forms of ideological prejudice blinded both scholarship and church to this theme. Unbeknown to us, our theology and interpretation are shaped by social mechanisms as well as by the sources to which we ascribe formal authority. It would be nice to think that data produce theories and that a collection of theories forms a view of reality as a whole. But in practice our total way of looking at reality normally determines what kind of theories we think up and thus how we interpret data.[8] The work of Miranda, Míguez

4. So A. Kee, ed., *The Scope of Political Theology* (London: SCM, 1978), 16–17, quoting Hugo Assmann, *Practical Theology of Liberation* (London: Search Press, 1975), 76; cf. I. Ellacuría, *Freedom Made Flesh: The Mission of Christ and His Church* (Maryknoll, N.Y.: Orbis, 1976), 131–41.

5. See, e.g., J. P. Miranda, *Marx and the Bible* (Maryknoll, N.Y.: Orbis, 1974; London: SCM, 1977).

6. Cf. ibid., 88–106.

7. G. Gutiérrez, *A Theology of Liberation* (Maryknoll, N.Y.: Orbis, 1973; London: SCM, 1974), 49–60.

8. Cf. James H. Cone, *God of the Oppressed* (New York: Seabury, 1975; London: SPCK, 1977), 39–61 and elsewhere. Segundo offers some nice examples of what he calls "the ideological infiltration

Bonino, and others shows how a study of Marxism opened liberation theologians to aspects of the biblical message that we might otherwise miss or make too little of: for instance, the Bible's concern with justice, its approach to capitalism, its understanding of human beings as workers, its belief that this world is not finished, and its stress on praxis and on the recognition of truth through involvement.

The awareness that interpretation is so influenced by considerations we bring to the material does not imply a hopeless relativism over whether we can reach anything that really deserves to be called knowledge. People can transcend their cultural history.[9] It does imply that biblical interpretation needs to be as incisive, critical, and systematically suspicious in its understanding of itself and its own present as it is in its approach to the ancient documents of the faith, if it is to grow in its perception of Scripture's significance.[10] Herod, the Pharisees, and Satan demonstrate clearly enough that the people who know the Bible are not necessarily those who can see and respond to what God is doing in their day. Indeed, biblical learning can be not only useless but also destructive of the very foundations of the faith.[11]

So texts "have to be 'made to speak,' even as texts, through the secular sciences," which also enable us to "relate the 'word' to the facts of present-day human experience."[12] Both exegetical understanding of the text in its own terms and contemporary application of the text are facilitated not only by present commitment to liberation but also by this interaction with the secular sciences.

These assumptions are fundamentally positive insights that constitute a challenge to the biblical interpretation of university and church. But each conceals ambiguities, many of which are matters of debate within liberation theology itself.

2. What Is the Relationship between Theology and Praxis?

Commitment to God's ways makes it possible to understand God's words. But on what basis do we commit ourselves to some action as in accordance with God's ways? Assmann[13] speaks as if an act of commitment contains its own justification, given the impossibility of establishing truth independent of the sphere of historical reality and given the "inescapable importance of the ethical leap, the political choice." But the agonizing of Mathieu, the philosopher "hero" of Sartre's trilogy *The Roads to Freedom*, hovering between inability to commit himself and commitment without reason, illustrates more realistically the dilemma of finding a basis for commitment. Some ideology or faith must lie behind an act of commitment.[14]

---

of dogma (*Liberation of Theology*, 40–47); cf. also Miranda's comments on the manipulative presupposition underlying preoccupation with being "in itself'" (*Marx and the Bible*, vii–ix, xviii–xx).

9. Cf. Cone, *God of the Oppressed*, 49.

10. Cf. Segundo, *Liberation of Theology*, 9; he goes on to illustrate a four-stage hermeneutical circle in process.

11. Cf. ibid., 81–82; H. Bojorge, "Para una interpretación liberadora," *RevistB* 33 (1971): 67–71 (67).

12. Assmann, *Practical Theology of Liberation*, 64.

13. Ibid., 105.

14. So Segundo, *Liberation of Theology*, 101.

Many acts appear so clearly right that they may seem to carry an intrinsically self-evident justification. Yet this is because we do not actually come to them with an empty head and heart but with a set of assumptions about God and the world, about truth and life, about love, mercy, and justice, and so on, whose guiding lines embrace these acts unambiguously. Although commitment leads to new insight and to the refining of previous assumptions, commitment itself operates on the basis of a framework of insights already assimilated, as the hypotheses scientists or historians bring to their evidence presuppose the framework of a view of reality overall. Thus Marx's famous eleventh thesis on Feuerbach turns out to risk oversimplification: in order to change the world, one needs to understand it.[15] It ought to be the case that Christians, having a clearer understanding of the world, are in a position to create a more adequate concrete praxis than that of Marxism.[16]

It is right to suspect and question the assumption that the right way to do theology is to infer contemporary application from objective exegesis or systematic theology. But practical theology or critical reflection on praxis in the light of the word[17] can and must be complemented by applied theology or critical reflection on theology in the light of praxis. The two function in a necessary and natural dialectic. Further, while a historical-critical approach to interpretation is limited in what it can achieve, and while it can subvert interpretive insight if it becomes an end in itself, it can nevertheless serve practical obedience to Scripture.[18] First, it can be a means toward appropriating Scripture and being appropriated by Scripture. It does not have to stop short of responding with the whole person to the reality that one perceives the text is pointing to, even though in practice it very often does so stop short. Second, the distancing effect of objectivizing interpretation can help me distinguish my faith and commitment from the one embodied in the text, so that I can make a response to what the text actually says and not merely to what I have always assumed it said. Third, when my current commitment leads me into some new interpretation of a text, historical-critical interpretation can facilitate my checking this interpretation. Systematic theology can fulfill similar positive functions as long as it is firmly linked with applied theology and interacting with practical theology.

3. How Negotiable Is the Belief That Liberation Is the Bible's Central Theme?

Commitment to liberation opens up central and neglected aspects of Scripture. Is liberation *the* key to understanding Scripture?

15. Cf. J. P. Miranda, *Being and the Messiah* (Maryknoll, N.Y.: Orbis, 1977), 5–6.
16. J. A. Kirk, *Liberation Theology: An Evangelical View from the Third World* (London: Marshall; Atlanta: John Knox, 1979), 200–201.
17. Cf. Gutiérrez, *Theology of Liberation*, 3–19.
18. Cf. Míguez Bonino, *Revolutionary Theology Comes of Age*, 101–2; Miranda, *Being and the Messiah*, 73. Miranda's two books show him putting this conviction into practice.

James Cone notes that black theology is accused of a bias for the Mosaic tradition rather than the David-Zion tradition, the First Testament rather than the New Testament, Israel's prophets rather than its sages. Is this bias arbitrary? His reply is that the hermeneutical principle for understanding Scripture is the revelation of Christ as liberator.[19] This response seems only to restate the problem. On what basis is this biblical theme given an absolute status that enables us to ignore other biblical themes? As Cone recognizes, the Bible does have other themes. Some are as central to it as liberation and cannot be subsumed under it: themes such as peace or God's rule or worship or commitment to Christ (compare Luther's *was Christum treibet*). None of these opens up the whole of Scripture, not even the last, as Luther unwittingly demonstrated in his treatment of James. Liberation does not constitute a grand master hermeneutical key to biblical interpretation. Scripture is not a house on a uniform lock system. It is more like a landscape that may with profit be viewed from many vantage points. Some offer fuller perspectives overall than others, but none reveals everything.

Tradition and its doctrinal formulations can suggest other vantage points for surveying the landscape, which will enable us to check whether we are seeing certain features out of perspective. They are not absolutes (only the text itself is that), but they are no more relative than my own present perspective is, and they thus deserve critical attention as sources of possible insight. For the same reason, liberation theology would be unwise to refuse to talk theology with other Christians, on the grounds that only the oppressed can evaluate the actions of the oppressed.[20] Liberation theologians are in as much danger as anyone else of seeing their own face at the bottom of the hermeneutical well, and thus in as much need as anyone else of working in hermeneutical fellowship with believers in other contexts both past and present to widen their perspective and test their visions. Even criticism from one-sided perspectives should surely be welcomed as offering reminders of what we may have forgotten or taken too much for granted or failed to integrate with our new emphases. When Christians committed to political theology react with hysteria or rhetoric to such critique, it neither commends their case nor bodes well for their chances of refining their vision.

While a commitment to liberation can open one's eyes to aspects of the biblical text that had long been missed, it can also make one read this interest into them when it is not there, or miss some other theme of importance to praxis, or misconceive the actual nature of the Bible's own understanding of liberation, which may differ from the one we bring to the Bible.[21] Exodus, for instance, pictures Yahweh bringing about an act of political liberation for an oppressed people, but its account of this act emphasizes the personal supernatural activity of God, the goal of the service

19. Cone, *God of the Oppressed*, 81–82.
20. So C. Banana, "The Biblical Basis for Liberation Struggles," *International Review of Mission* 68 (1979): 417–23 (422); cf. Cone, *God of the Oppressed*, 206.
21. Cf. the analysis by J. Mejía in "La liberación: aspectos bíblicos: evaluación crítica," *Liberación: dialogos en el CELAM* (Bogota: CELAM, 1974), 271–307.

of God, and the aim of the acknowledgment of God by oppressed and oppressor. We would be wise to be open to hearing these features of its account that may not immediately correspond to what modern readers' situation predisposes us to hear.[22] Indeed, here may be the vital and distinctive aspects to the biblical testimony. In ancient Israel, and in modern Latin America, to speak of God as warrior and of the theological significance of human violence may be inevitable if we are to offer any theological interpretation of life as it actually is. To be God at all, Yahweh must be God the warrior (it is part of being God in a warring cosmos), so that the Bible's telling affirmations regarding God in this connection lie not in its assertion that God is a warrior (which is common to many religions) but in the way it portrays God making war.

Commitment to liberation functions as a preliminary understanding of a central aspect of Scripture, but this preliminary understanding must not be allowed to freeze as a final understanding of liberation or of Scripture as a whole. Otherwise liberation theology is the hopeless prisoner of a hermeneutical vicious circle. Even liberation theology needs liberating from its own questions so that it can allow itself to be questioned by Scripture.[23] If it refuses this, it may in the end even do praxis itself a disservice, for if liberation is the gospel message, "what will theology say when there are no people to liberate?"[24]

4. How Are Particular Biblical Passages to Influence Us Today?

The preceding paragraphs have begun to imply the question how much of the Bible we are to seek to apply to our own situations and how we go about that task. The Bible manifests a rich diversity in the contexts it reflects and the attitudes it takes up. The theologizing of the First Testament substantially revolves around two very different experiences, the triumph of deliverance from Egypt and the humiliation of exile in Babylon, while the theologizing of the New Testament has to hold together the shame of crucifixion and the victory of resurrection. The ethical insight of the Bible embraces the ideals embodied in creation and in the rule of God proclaimed by Christ and also the condescensions to Israel's hardness of heart whereby God adapts the ideal standards to the reality of the people they are designed to shape. The world is seen both as the sphere of God, in which we are to be involved, and as the sphere of evil powers, from which we are to distance ourselves. There are times when God commands violent action and times when Jesus commands turning the

22. See further J. Goldingay, "The Man of War and the Suffering Servant: The Old Testament and the Theology of Liberation," *TynB* 27 (1976): 79–113 (89–93); also at http://www.fuller.edu /sot/faculty/goldingay.

23. Cf. Míguez Bonino, *Doing Theology in a Revolutionary Situation*, 87; Bojorge, "Para una interpretación liberadora," 68–70.

24. A. Fierro, *The Militant Gospel: An Analysis of Contemporary Political Theologies* (London: SCM; Maryknoll, N.Y.: Orbis, 1977), 211.

other cheek, times for emphasizing people's physical and political needs and times for emphasizing their need of forgiveness and inner renewal, times for looking to the past and times for looking to the future, times for a stress on order and times for a stress on conflict. This diversity in Scripture reflects the complexity of reality itself, the variety of the situations Scripture addresses, and the differences between what is absolutely true or right and what people can cope with at a particular moment.

Cone's approach to the diversity of Scripture's testimonies is to regard these as a resource within which we can identify ones that seem appropriate to our circumstances and ignore others. For instance, he appeals to texts that refer to breaking the chains of oppression but does not view texts about turning the other cheek or going the second mile or about slaves obeying their masters as binding the contemporary black community.[25] Segundo takes the broadly situational approach further in asking whether it is realistic to look for any passages in the Bible that directly relate to our situation. In any period, God relates to the circumstances people experience and to questions as they see them; so no biblical response is directly applicable today. From the biblical writers' responses to their situations we learn not the content of our response to ours but the way we should respond, making our own decisions in light of an analysis of our situation (to which the use of secular resources will be of key importance) and of the guidance of the Spirit. We enter upon this task in faith knowing that there is no final verifying of our interpretive intuitions this side of heaven, yet also knowing that these are both received and tested within the context of the people of God corporately indwelt by the Spirit.[26]

Liberation theology only half-recognizes, however, that whether or not we believe that some scriptural passages directly address situations like ours, any form of commitment to Scripture implies opening ourselves to all the dimensions of its testimony. For if, on one hand, scriptural narratives and laws do function more as paradigms in whose light we formulate our response to our own situation than as direct warrant or precedent,[27] then we need to expose ourselves to the full range of biblical paradigms if we are to have our thinking led into biblical ways in a thoroughgoing fashion. If, on the other hand, we do find passages more directly addressing our kind of context, we still need to check this discovery by the rest of Scripture. Because of Scripture's diversity, almost anything can be given a veneer of justification from it. Both right and left can use it ideologically. Thus André Dumas, while recognizing that our application of specific scriptural insights will depend on circumstances, nevertheless urges that we pay attention to the various biblical political models and points out that political and liberation theology's own change of emphasis during the 1970s from the exodus and the hope of the resurrection to the exile and the cross only partially indicated a difference in situation: "theology has reflected moods, rather

25. See, e.g., *God of the Oppressed*, 62–81; *A Black Theology of Liberation* (Philadelphia: Lippincott, 1970), 68, 108–9; *Black Theology and Black Power* (New York: Seabury, 1969), 139–40.

26. See Segundo, *Liberation of Theology*, 33–34, 110–22; cf. Cone, *God of the Oppressed*, 197–200; Míguez Bonino, *Doing Theology in a Revolutionary Situation*, 103.

27. So Míguez Bonino, *Doing Theology in a Revolutionary Situation*, 103.

than presenting proclamation and doctrine."[28] The swing of mood might have been unnecessary if exodus had been seen in light of exile, and hope in light of the cross. The theology of the right may only notice the side to the Bible that is less overtly political, while the theology of the left may see liberation behind every text; each ends up with too narrow a perspective.[29]

The diversity within Scripture as a whole can be markedly reduced if the specific emphases of the First Testament can be eliminated. The overall picture of biblical attitudes is then significantly modified: hence Segundo's observation that the whole of theology has been conditioned by the attitude it takes (or rather, by its failure to formulate an attitude) to the question of the relationship of the two Testaments.[30]

In practice, the First Testament has commonly been silenced in the Christian church, being unconsciously ignored and unread, or consciously regarded as superseded by the New, or assimilated to the New by interpretive devices such as typology and allegory. Gutiérrez protests against such "spiritualizing" exegesis, and one may grant that the New Testament is itself more this-worldly than it has often been taken.[31] But it is easy to exaggerate this point, and in reasserting the importance of many fundamentally First Testament themes, liberation theology may seem to have reverted from New Testament perspectives to First Testament ones without noticing, still less reasoning this out.[32]

So how do the various parts of the Bible relate to each other? Liberation theology has emphasized the intrinsic importance of the exodus to both Testaments; the exodus narrative is its "privileged text."[33] The exodus from Egypt indeed dominates Israel's faith as it looks to the past, shapes its hopes as it looks to future release from the bondage of exile, and supplies one interpretive key to understanding the achievement of Christ. But the hermeneutical significance of setting exodus and exile or exodus and Christ event alongside each other can be understood in two ways. Traditional theology reads the exodus in light of subsequent events and is inclined to spiritualize it. Liberation theology stresses the opposite implication, that the nature of the Israelites' liberation should continue to form the focus of a biblical understanding of liberation.

In fact, the interpretive process should surely be seen as a dialectical one. When different events are juxtaposed for interpretive purposes, they throw light on each other. Because the New Testament regards the First Testament as God's word, its appeal to the exodus from Egypt and to the hope of a new exodus invites us to take

28. A. Dumas, *Political Theology and the Life of the Church* (London: SCM; Philadelphia: Westminster Press, 1978), 46, 99.

29. Cf. J. Smolik, "The Theology of Revolution," *Concilium* 7/5 (1969): 73–78, on the variety of patterns of social existence in the NT.

30. Segundo, *Liberation of Theology*, 113; cf. my *Approaches to Old Testament Interpretation* (rev. ed.; Leicester and Downers Grove, Ill.: InterVarsity, 1990; Toronto: Clements, 2002), 11.

31. Cf. Gutiérrez, *Theology of Liberation*, 166–67; P. Bigo, *The Church and Third World Revolutions* (Maryknoll, N.Y.: Orbis, 1977), 81.

32. So Fierro, *The Militant Gospel*, 325.

33. Kirk, *Liberation Theology*, 95; Assmann, *Practical Theology of Liberation*, 35; J. S. Croatto, *Liberación y libertad* (Buenos Aires: Mundo Nuevo, 1973), 21–61; Gutiérrez, *Theology of Liberation*, 153–60.

seriously what God was actually doing and promising then, with both its political and its spiritual aspects. But because the story of the exodus belongs to a collection of Scriptures that includes the exilic and early Christian writings that refer to it, the significance of the exodus has to be seen in their context. The later First Testament writings (especially Isa 40–55) continue to emphasize political bondage but also place more stress on bondage to rebellion against God on the part of oppressed and oppressor alike.[34] Then the New Testament, arising out of a context when the Jews are once again unjustly oppressed, nevertheless makes little reaffirmation of God's commitment to political liberation and uses the exodus story as a means of picturing liberation from sin, not in its original political significance.[35]

Yet it would be a mistake to see the New Testament as having a depoliticizing effect on biblical perspectives. Christ brings a new fullness, confirmation, and fulfillment to First Testament promises, but he does not spiritualize them.[36] How can he? He can do more than they envisaged, but if they were God's words he cannot do less. He brings a radicalizing of the First Testament: the inner problem of Israel's spiritual bondage, which prevents its creative enjoyment of political freedom, manifests itself clearly enough in Exodus but comes to the forefront of consideration in the New Testament, yet without any denial of the importance of what Exodus majored on. The exodus both explains later events and is illuminated by them.[37] It is not God's only act, but it is God's act. We cannot use the First Testament as if we did not have the new horizon provided by the New, but neither is our use of the First Testament limited to the way the New uses it. The insights of each Testament are set in the context of Scripture as a whole, and a fully biblical perspective involves living with the various tensions between these insights.[38] The danger that theology and biblical interpretation always risk is a simplifying of the complexity of reality and of the Bible itself.

In light of such considerations, Cone's choice of texts is particularly open to the suspicion of being ideological. First, it involves setting aside a moral position that Christ the liberator took up. Now this might be justifiable; on the question of slavery, at least, most Christians do not assume he spoke a timeless word regarding Christian praxis. The problem is that Cone asserts rather than argues the point; and we have noted that it is not the case that disciples in New Testament times were in a markedly different situation vis-à-vis their oppressors than modern disciples. Then Cone's choice of texts ignores the hermeneutical clue Christ himself suggested for viewing First Testament texts that sat in tension with the view Christ wished to commend, in seeing them as not simply reflections of different situations but of human hard-heartedness (Mark 10:5). Indeed, it might be possible to defend an ethic of liberation along these lines; the oppressed can cope only with exodus, they are not

34. See further Goldingay, "The Man of War and the Suffering Servant," 93–104.
35. Cf. J. M. Breneman, *El éxodo como tema de interpretación teológica* (San José: privately published, 1973), 28.
36. Cf. Gutiérrez, *Theology of Liberation*, 166–68.
37. Cf. Breneman, *El éxodo como tema de interpretación teológica*, 27.
38. Cf. Dumas, *Political Theology and the Life of the Church*, 24–46.

up to the Sermon on the Mount. Scripture does not always expect people to live by God's ultimate word. But again, Cone asserts rather than argues. Further, he ignores rather than responds to possible understandings of the development of thinking on liberation and politics within the Bible, despite his commitment to "speaking across cultural lines" on the basis of the Bible and "looking at the message of Scripture exegetically" to see whether it does "center upon the proclamation of the liberation of the oppressed" in the way he believes.[39]

A parallel question mark sits alongside Segundo's ignoring of the development he acknowledges in Scripture that leads to a greater concentration on issues that are less overtly political.[40] Might not the educative process he identifies in Scripture be a cumulative one that takes the people of God to a stance that has a more developed understanding of bondage and liberation? Segundo asks rhetorically whether Israel should be expected to act differently if it finds itself in the same situation now as at the beginning of its story.[41] Is this impossible? Can people hear the message of the exile and of the cross only when they have experienced the disappointment of exodus/resurrection hope? Is it not possible to learn from history instead of having to repeat it?

A traditional approach to finding the unity in the diversity of the theological statements in the Bible is to look for themes, motifs, truths, or emphases that underlie the external differences. Míguez Bonino takes up this possibility, suggesting "the reading of the direction of the biblical text," especially the witness of the faith's paradigmatic events, which point "to certain directions which such concepts as liberation, righteousness, shalom, the poor, love help us to define."[42] In the variety of responses to situations that are collected in Scripture certain patterns may emerge.

One aspect of this study is an examination of how Scripture itself goes about expressing itself in the world's terms. Abraham and David take up Canaanite concepts and language and Paul takes up Greek ones, and thus theology follows biblical precedent in doing something similar today. What one has to be wary of is taking over the world's concepts and language without transforming them, and one of the aspects of the Bible's exercises in theologizing that we need to examine is the direction in which it modifies nonbiblical concepts and language when it takes them over.

As there are directions that underlie the diversity of the biblical texts, so there will be directions that underlie the situations in response to which the faith has to find its embodiment. If this is so, then it again qualifies any emphasis on the uniqueness of the situations we face and the difficulty of applying Scripture directly to them. Dumas, for instance, examines the paradigms of resistance and submission in Scripture, then comments that neither must be absolutized but both practiced, "depending on the circumstances, what they require and what they make possible."[43] He does not as-

39. Cone, God of the Oppressed, 37–38.
40. Segundo, Liberation of Theology, 111.
41. Ibid., 115.
42. Míguez Bonino, Doing Theology in a Revolutionary Situation, 42.
43. Dumas, Political Theology and the Life of the Church, 46.

sume that the infinite variety of situations we experience makes them impossible to compare with each other, but rather that certain directions underlie them.

One pattern running through Scripture is a combining of two purposes. One is legitimation: it reassures the hearers of God's involvement with them in their particular situation and provides them with a context of meaning for their experience. Exodus assures the oppressed Israelites that God will liberate them and assures later generations of God's involvement in bringing them to Canaan. Isaiah 40–55, the Gospels, Acts, and Revelation give parallel assurances in later contexts. But Scripture also fulfills a second, more confrontational purpose: as well as encouraging them, God challenges people in some way. In Exodus, this challenge concerns their acknowledgment of God and their service of God. In Isaiah 40–55, these themes reappear in a radicalized form (to use Dumas's word), though the sinfulness of the people also finds emphasis, especially in Isaiah 48. In Jesus' teaching, challenge and gospel are interwoven from the first in his exhortation to repentance in view of the coming of the rule of God. In Revelation the challenges to the churches in chapters 2–3 precede the promise of deliverance and judgment on oppression.

God's Word consistently confronts as well as reassures the oppressed. It does not function ideologically in offering only legitimation. One would expect that this would continue to be the case today. The passages we have just noted illustrate ways the biblical text confronts both Western theology and liberation theology. For each (but in opposite aspects of the text) there is both legitimation or reassurance and confrontation or challenge. Each theology is open to the temptation to find only the legitimation, and each may need to listen to the other theology in order to hear the challenge. When one compares the stance of each, it is striking that neither can actually find itself in any of the overall stances of either Testament.

Our interest in the Bible will be to allow ourselves to be both reassured and confronted by the total message of passages to which we feel drawn because they speak to our circumstances and our questions, and also by other passages that bring totally different challenges and encouragements. Passages that seem to undermine the commitment we have already made will be ones to which we pay particular attention if we want to open ourselves to constructive criticism. They will not be ones we quickly seek to subvert by declaring them historically conditioned or situational and irrelevant. Thus any liberation theology needs to be as concerned to ponder the fact that political liberation was not central to Jesus' overt teaching and activity, in a context when this would have been quite possible and natural,[44] and that the rest of the New Testament concentrates more on how Christians are to hold on under pressure than on how they are to make a revolution, as it is to work out the real political implications of the New Testament message. The study of "the political Christ" illustrates more clearly than any the interwovenness of prior commitment and exegetical study.[45] Once again, we risk seeing our own face at the bottom of the hermeneutical well. Theology has a habit of careering from overemphasis on one

---

44. Segundo, *Liberation of Theology*, 110–12; Dumas, *Political Theology and the Life of the Church*, 42.
45. Cf. Fierro, *The Militant Gospel*, 165–67.

insight, treating one half-truth as the whole truth, to some opposite overemphasis or half-truth. It swings from other-worldliness to politicization, from passivity to revolution, from rejection of the world to assimilation. Attentiveness to the diversity of scriptural paradigms may aid us in holding the tension between these various poles.[46]

5. Who Is Interpreting What?

Hermeneutics is concerned with understanding. In the narrow sense, it refers to the way people go about understanding something written (or some artifact). It studies the way we grasp the meaning of a document and work out its implications for ourselves. But the documents we seek to understand are themselves exercises in understanding. Their authors had seen or heard something that they then expressed in writing. Their writings are thus expressions of understanding by someone else before they are the object of my understanding. They are exercises in hermeneutics before they are the object of my exercise in hermeneutics. In general, then, when I seek to enter into their way of looking at reality, I do so on equal terms with them. I feel free to evaluate them on the basis of my own understanding of reality; they may confirm it, complement it, modify it, or be judged by it.

The Bible, too, is an exercise in hermeneutics before it is an object of hermeneutics; it is the interpretation of God's mind by figures such as prophets and apostles. When I seek to understand the Bible and the truth to which it witnesses, am I therefore also ultimately on equal terms with it? Or does the notion of its being Scripture involve my being committed to the assumption that its exercises in hermeneutics were successful and can be the judge of mine? Looked at this way, the question of biblical hermeneutics collapses into the question of biblical authority and inspiration (as in other contexts the reverse happens).

In the context of liberation theology, this question takes the following form. If theology involves "critical reflection on praxis in the light of the Word," it involves an openness to Scripture modifying one's commitment, modifying one's initial understanding of Scripture in relation to liberation, and modifying the Marxian perspective that facilitates one's understanding of Scripture. On the other hand, liberation theology emphasizes God's current involvement in human history, and if our history reflects this involvement, we will naturally expect to gain insight on God's purpose from a consideration of and a sharing in that involvement. Both Scripture and history, then, reflect God's activity, and each throws light on the other. But what is their relative revelatory status?

Liberation theology is often equivocal on this question. Raúl Vidales, for instance, speaks of a "dialectical activity" that "obliges the theologian to re-read the Bible from the context of the other 'Bible' known as human history" in the conviction that "human history is the manifestation of the Christ-fact"; "God's activity is manifested in effective human efforts to create a more just and fraternal society in line

46. Cf. Dumas, *Political Theology and the Life of the Church*, 13.

with his promise." Here contemporary event and biblical word seem to have parallel significance; hence the possibility of a dialectical relationship between them. Yet later Vidales speaks of theology's need to maintain its critical function over against both church and society by means of its constant reference to "its vital underlying source and principle: the word of God."[47] So what is the relationship between the two "Bibles"? Again, Cone says that "the dialectic relationship of the black experience and Scripture is the point of departure of Black Theology's Christology"; "the black Christian ethic must start with Scripture and the black experience. We must read each in light of the other, and then ask, 'What am I to do?' "[48] But how do you deal with priorities and tensions between these theological resources? Gutiérrez manifests parallel ambivalences over the relationship between current experience and the overt statements of the biblical text.[49] In the end, is praxis to be subjected to critical evaluation and reinterpretation in light of the Word, or is the Word to be subjected to critical evaluation and reinterpretation in light of praxis?

Some Latin American theologians have noticed the fence on which liberation theology seeks to sit and have sought to climb off it, though not without leaving a hand on the palings to keep themselves steady. On the basis of the assumption that seeking to understand the will of God today is parallel to that attempt to understand the will of God embodied in Scripture, rather than subordinate to it, Assmann infers that we cannot check our Christian commitment by setting it in light of the faith revealed in the Bible, because the faith appears there, too, only in historical embodiments. The Bible is "the history of successive interpretations" of Christianity. And anyway, "How can we talk candidly of the 'gospel' when there is so much truth in what one committed Christian once said to me: 'The Bible? It doesn't exist. The only Bible is the sociological bible of what I see happening here and now as a Christian'?" For the theology of liberation, "its 'text' is our situation, and our situation is our primary and basic reference point," not any other resource such as Scripture.[50]

Segundo, too, sees the various biblical messages as essentially human crystallizations of the faith in particular contexts.[51] In a telling footnote on the "gratuitousness" of the love demanded by the New Testament, he remarks that such love "redounds to the advantage and maintenance of the status quo" and infers that "the suspicion of ideological interpretation, which seems quite logical when applied to historical theology, penetrates as far as the sacred writings themselves. Since the latter are already an interpretation, why should they be free of 'ideology'?"[52] Similarly political

47. See R. Vidales, "Methodological Issues in Liberation Theology," in *Frontiers of Theology in Latin America* (ed. R. Gibellini; Maryknoll, N.Y.: Orbis, 1979), 34–57 (40, 47).

48. Cone, *God of the Oppressed*, 113, 205.

49. So Kirk, *Liberation Theology*, 61–65; Fierro, *The Militant Gospel*, 326–27.

50. So Assmann, *Practical Theology of Liberation*, 60–61, 104.

51. Segundo, *Liberation of Theology*, 116–17.

52. J. L. Segundo, *A Theology for Artisans of a New Humanity 5: Evolution and Guilt* (Maryknoll, N.Y.: Orbis, 1974), 125.

theology explains the gap between the Christ of faith and the Jesus of history by seeing the former as a dehistoricized, depoliticized version of the latter.[53]

If our attempts at understanding relate as directly to reality itself as Scripture's do, then our attempt to understand the acts of God described in Scripture is also parallel to Scripture's own attempt to understand those acts, rather than subordinate to it. Indeed, we may in some respects be in a better position to understand an event such as the exodus if we have our experiences of exodus (or at least of bondage) to facilitate this. For events in Latin America are also God's acts, and because they are events of a similar kind, acts of liberation on behalf of the oppressed, they provide a means of understanding the original event independent of the scriptural interpretation of it, and thus a means of apprehending something of the event's "reserve of meaning."[54] Here we are following Scripture's own example, for within Scripture earlier understandings of the significance of the exodus are transformed in light of the subsequent events of exile and the coming of Christ. Latin American experience, as a further context of God's revelatory activity, can bring out yet more aspects of the meaning of that event.

In interpreting the historical event of the exodus in light of current events, Croatto seeks to remove from the scriptural narrative of the exodus two "mythic" features. One is its mythic function: it may encourage us to believe that the act of God that is constitutive of the present and that brings us salvation is one that belongs to the past, whereas in reality biblical revelation breaks with myth and establishes a constant tension between primordial event and present history.[55]

The other feature is its mythic language. The historical reality in the exodus story is the event itself, experienced as of special and promissory significance, which reveals that God is at work and engenders a conscientization of humanity (Exod 14:31), an end to the hopeless acceptance of oppression and an insight into God's purpose to deliver. The event comes first and the new awareness follows subsequently, but this awareness is then back-projected and mythologized as Yahweh appearing to Moses at the beginning of the story. Historically, Moses was not a leader because he was called in this way: he is "called" (that is, a call narrative becomes attached to him) because he was a leader. Symbolic and mythic images such as the plagues, the miraculous sea crossing, and the pillar of cloud give further metaphorical expression to the conviction that God was active in the event.[56]

So the picture of the event as issuing from God's call and God's promise is painted in light of the actual event.[57] It is Latin American experience of how liberation

53. So Kee, *Scope of Political Theology*, 18–20; cf. Fierro, *The Militant Gospel*, 215–16 with his quotation from Pannenberg.

54. Croatto, *Liberación y libertad*, 27–29; "Dios en el acontecimiento," *RevistB* 35 (1973): 52–60 (52–57); cf. S. Ruiz, "Teología biblica de la liberación," in *La liberación: dialogos en el CELAM*, 337–70 (347–48); also Goldingay, "The Man of War and the Suffering Servant," 106–13, for a discussion of Croatto's views.

55. Croatto, "Dios en el acontecimiento," 53.

56. Cf. *Liberación y libertad*, 52–54.

57. Ibid., 32–34.

comes about that reveals that this must have been the case. Again, the current event in which God's revelatory activity is perceived is a human activity, and thus the exodus is understood in these terms. Similarly Fierro describes grace as "the transcendent side of the believer's freedom," "the idea with which theology represents authentic human freedom."[58] He perhaps goes further than Croatto; his critique of the unreflective or uncritical or rhetorical use of language in political and liberation theology may suggest that he would see Croatto as preserving only the language of Christian orthodoxy.[59]

The understanding of Yahweh's action and of ours that Croatto expresses is not alien to Scripture. Scripture is capable of seeing Yahweh's activity as an immanent providence giving transcendent meaning to events that can be described in human terms. This perspective appears in the opening chapters of the exodus story (Exod 1:1–2:10). Scripture is capable of describing human battles as ones in which Yahweh is involved; Exodus 17 provides a notable example, so that Patrick Miller can describe "holy war" as a "synergism," "a fusion of divine and human activity."[60] Precisely in this light it is striking that Exodus attributes the constitutive, paradigmatic act of deliverance solely to Yahweh. Human activity could hardly be further minimized. It is implausible to reckon that Croatto's understanding of the exodus is one shared by Exodus itself when rightly interpreted. The interpretation in light of the contemporary event rules out that offered in Exodus.

Miranda's position on the question of the relative importance of biblical text and modern situation differs from those of Assmann, Segundo, and Croatto. He questions the validity of "empirical theology." While agreeing that God is active in present history, he points out that "opposing and irreconcilable ideologies" claim to recognize where that purposeful activity can be seen. The only way to judge whether any of these claims is Christian is to return to the Bible and its portrait of Jesus and his significance, understood by "verifiable, scientific exegesis."[61]

As Cone also recognizes, Scripture has an objective givenness that means it can stand over against me and my "story."[62] It is partly on this basis that Dumas advocates "meta-textual" existence, a life lived in dialogue with the biblical texts, rather than a metaphysical one such as dogmatic theology tends to encourage, or a meta-historical one such as Marxism's. Meta-textual existence involves "trying to listen to a God who is other than our aspirations or our energies," and it avoids the risk of putting one's fancies in place of what one might hear.[63]

Further, Marxism is itself a historical phenomenon, a reaction to particular circumstances. It too is "dependent upon a social a priori" and is "open to error."[64] So,

58. Fierro, *The Militant Gospel*, 293.
59. Ibid., 318–29, 339–47.
60. P. D. Miller, *The Divine Warrior* (Cambridge, Mass.: Harvard University Press, 1973), 156.
61. Miranda, *Being and the Messiah*, 80–81.
62. Cone, *God of the Oppressed*, 103–4.
63. Dumas, *Political Theology and the Life of the Church*, 47–51, 54–55.
64. Cone, *God of the Oppressed*, 44.

while Marxian insight can enable the suspicious interpreter to expose hidden biases in theology and interpretation, Marxism itself should not be absolutized. Its effectiveness in subverting certain ideologies in certain circumstances does not mean it could not itself function ideologically in other circumstances or that it is not so functioning at other points.[65]

Meta-textual existence introduces more, not less, realism into one's politics than an absolutizing of Marxism, because at key points the Bible's insights are more profound than Marxism's.[66] We have noted already that history as we experience and make it is an inherently ambiguous affair. The revelation that history offers will become truly clear only when the last piece is added to its jigsaw. So can we perceive the meaning of history before then? Pannenberg sees the anticipatory revelation in Christ himself as the key to understanding history.[67] The Bible offers the further insight that the purpose of the interpretive word of prophet and apostle was to explain the meaning of events. Word and event belong together in the biblical understanding of revelation, but the former explains and the latter confirms.[68] Liberation theology is right that current history reveals the activity of God, but what it reveals we do not know until someone interprets it for us.

The Bible offers to be the means of our interpreting history. It does that in two main ways. First, it forms our overall thinking as we seek to immerse ourselves in it and let our attitudes and lives be shaped by it. It thus forms the "ideology" in light of which we interpret our experience and make our decisions. Then it is also the norm to which we refer as we seek to reflect critically on our praxis.

"Ideology" (that is, theology) and praxis are both ways into seeing the meaning and implications of Scripture or ways of avoiding Scripture. Both may be embodiments of what Scripture says, or ways of concealing the meaning of Scripture. Theology and praxis interact critically with each other. But at least until God's revelation in the whole of history is complete, we need Scripture to inform and to judge both theology and praxis. That, at least, is what Scripture offers to be for us. To accept this offer is the alternative and preferable way off the fence referred to above. "The one and only thing that can maintain the liberative character of any theology is not its content but its methodology."[69] This will involve Christian believers in fellowship and in the Spirit searching the Scriptures from the context of commitment to the Christ of the cross and the empty tomb, and allowing the Scriptures' own meaning to challenge both church and world.[70]

65. So Kirk, *Liberation Theology*, 191–92.

66. Dumas, *Political Theology and the Life of the Church*, 130; cf. the critiques of Marxism in the works of Kirk and Míguez Bonino.

67. Wolfhart Pannenberg, *Basic Questions in Theology* (2 vols.; London: SCM; Philadelphia: Fortress, 1971), 2:21–27.

68. Cf. my discussion in "The Man of War and the Suffering Servant," 58–81.

69. Segundo, *Liberation of Theology*, 39–40.

70. Cf. J. A. Kirk, *Theology Encounters Revolution* (Leicester and Downers Grove, Ill.: Inter-Varsity, 1980), 183.

5

What Questions
Does Evangelical Biblical Interpretation
Need to Consider?

T he year I moved to the United States, 1997, saw a double twenty-year anniver-
sary in Britain.[1] In 1977, the second National Evangelical Anglican Congress
had taken place, and the same year saw the publication of the symposium *New Testament Interpretation* by members of the Tyndale Fellowship, edited by I. Howard
Marshall.[2] The former event was significant for introducing the evangelical constitu-
ency to the word "hermeneutics"; the second was significant as an indication that
evangelical scholarship was in a position to join in debate on a more equal footing
with the rest of the scholarly world. At the same time, these events raised the questions What distinguishes evangelicalism's involvement with Scripture from that of
the rest of the church? and What distinguishes evangelical scholarship from the rest
of scholarship? James Barr in *Fundamentalism*, also published in 1977,[3] could only
see an unprincipled inclination to "maximal conservatism"; that was hardly enough.
Over succeeding years, the answers to those questions have hardly become clearer.

1. This chapter combines material from "Current Issues in Evangelical Interpretation of
Scripture," in *Anglican Evangelical Assembly Proceedings* 4 (ed. Colin N. Day; Church of England
Evangelical Council, 1986), 19–29; "Going by the Book," *Third Way* 1, no. 12 (1988): 14–16; and
"The Ongoing Story of Biblical Interpretation," *Churchman* 112 (1998): 6–16.
2. (Exeter: Paternoster; Grand Rapids: Eerdmans, 1977).
3. (London: SCM; Philadelphia: Westminster Press, 1977); see, e.g., 85–89.

1. Is There a Hermeneutical Gap?

Talk of "hermeneutics" easily frightens people, and it does so with reason. Ironically, people who talk about the interpretation of Scripture are often difficult to understand. This is partly because hermeneutics, as the word is used in academic circles, is an intrinsically complex and subtle aspect of philosophy. Philosophy is entitled to be difficult to follow, involving as it does the attempt to handle in as careful a way as possible some questions that are both very simple and very deep, questions such as What do we mean by the word "God"? or How can we talk in human language about God? Hermeneutics is concerned with a question of that kind, namely, What do we mean by "understanding," and how does it come about?

Anthony Thiselton's work on "Understanding God's Word Today" in the preparatory papers for that 1977 congress accepted that there is indeed a significant "hermeneutical gap" between ourselves and the biblical text. It referred with sympathy to the emphasis in a report of the Church of England's Doctrine Commission, *Christian Believing*, on "the pastness of the past" with its questioning whether we can enter into the experiences of first-century Jews who expected an imminent end of the present world order. "The whole difficulty of standing alongside the men and women of the past," he notes that report urging, is "far more fundamental even than questions about the truth of the biblical writings."[4] That is a worrying thought for people who presuppose that this standing alongside is possible as we read Scripture in the context of and as foundational for our day-by-day relationship with God. I recall a senior evangelical scholar gently asking for "not too much of this 'gap' talk." Yet Mr. Thiselton, as he then was (by 1997, of course, many of the authors of those 1977 volumes were doctors, deans, and university professors, and even an archbishop), in effect pointed out that if we deny the issue the Doctrine Commission was raising, we are hiding our heads in the sand, whereas if we acknowledge it, we are in a position to do something about it. We belong to the same humanity as the Bible writers, we are members of the same people of God, we are put right with God on the same basis as they were, and we are indwelt by the same Holy Spirit as the one who inspired them. We have quite enough in common with them for understanding to be possible. If we do not take understanding for granted, it can become actual.

When I was preparing to move from Britain to the United States, from time to time people would say to me, "Oh, you must be feeling this or that" (disoriented, in-between, excited, sad, apprehensive about moving after twenty-seven years in Nottingham . . .). Actually my predominant feeling was none of those; because of my personal circumstances, anxiety about how the move would work out for my disabled wife, Ann, overrode all those other feelings. If people had not assumed that they knew how someone in my position would feel, they could have discovered how I felt. If they had recognized that there might be a gap, they and I could bridge it.

4. Anthony C. Thiselton, "Understanding God's Word Today," in *Obeying Christ in a Changing World* (ed. John Stott; 3 vols.; London: Collins, 1977), 1:94.

If we will recognize that there is a gap between us and first-century Jews (and First Testament Israelites), then the Holy Spirit, the human authors, and we can bridge it.

2. Scripture's Historicity and Ours

Related to this point is the fact that the single most important insight of the study of hermeneutics over the past century is that both the Bible and we ourselves belong in history. A better way to put it is to say that we belong in separate histories. It has long been a familiar idea that the Scriptures themselves belong in history and have to be understood in light of the historical contexts in which they came into being. A crucial insistence of contemporary study of hermeneutics is that we as interpreters also belong in history and have to go about understanding in light of the historical contexts in which we live. We "have to" do so in the sense that we cannot avoid it. The particular experiences as human beings and as believers that we bring to the text, our perceptions and our questions regarding life and regarding God, shape what we see in the text.

This fact about understanding (which is not peculiar to Scripture) is both an asset and a drawback. It is an asset, insofar as it is our having some questions and some experiences in common with the text that makes it possible for us to understand it at all. If we did not have these, we would not be able to begin to understand. It is a drawback insofar as we can become satisfied with understanding those aspects of the text that correspond to the questions and experiences we brought to it, instead of using these as our point of entry to understanding wider aspects of the text that do not have close points of contact with our previous experience and questions but may nevertheless be very important (or rather, may consequently be very important). Your questions decide what sort of answers you are going to find; your lenses determine what you see. I read Scripture as a twentieth-century, Western, male, middle-class, heterosexual, middle-aged, comfortable, intellectual clergyman; as a person with his own joys, pains, loves, and temptations. All that makes it possible for me to see certain things in Scripture; it also limits my horizon, at least when I fail to keep in mind the fact that it is likely to do this. We all come from experience to Scripture, and we had better be aware of this if we are not to be trapped by it.

Our coming to Scripture out of our experiences and questions affects the way preachers handle texts. We may be drawn to a particular passage because of its relevance to a certain theme. There is a place, no doubt, for the sermon that simply takes up those aspects of the text that relate to the theme we want to preach on. But staying with the text beyond those to other themes with which it associates our theme may well adjust our agenda to God's and enable us to see our theme in better perspective. We cease to be limited to the questions we brought to the text and begin to have our horizon broadened. The same is true with our devotional use of Scripture. If the passage I read in my devotions does not seem relevant to my life with

God at present, this may be because my agenda needs adjusting to God's. Often it is a matter of moving from our predominant individualism to the Bible's characteristic concern with the people of God corporately. As preachers and as congregations, we will be wise to refuse to be satisfied with a use of Scripture that is concerned for what seems immediately relevant and stops short of what God thought was relevant when inspiring the text.

The principle applies to our interpretation of Scripture on a broader front. Christians commonly find themselves most at home in particular parts of Scripture or with particular scriptural themes. These speak to them especially directly; they correspond to the questions, needs, and experiences they bring to the text. For traditional evangelicalism, it has commonly been Romans 3–8 and the theme of justification that have fulfilled this function (followed, perhaps, by aspects of John's Gospel and the theme of new birth). For charismatics, it may be the accounts of Jesus' ministry of healing and signs in the Synoptic Gospels, or parts of Acts or 1 Corinthians or Ephesians. For evangelicals who stress social involvement, it may be Jesus' proclamation of God's rule or the Sermon on the Mount.

Now it is possible to argue that Jesus' work of atonement, or his signs and wonders, or his teaching, or his proclamation of God's rule, or the Sermon on the Mount does constitute the heart of the gospel, or at least the aspect of the gospel that speaks most powerfully in certain contexts. If we want to live by Scripture, however, we will not be satisfied with affirming those aspects of Scripture that speak to questions and needs we are aware of and thus provide us with our way in to grasping Scripture and being grasped by it. We will want them to be only a way in, a point of entry that sets us on the road of understanding and appropriating other aspects of Scripture. What can happen in practice is that we get stuck in the part of Scripture from which we start. When we read other parts of Scripture, we reinterpret these in light of our starting point. One can perceive this in liberation theology's reading of Romans and in evangelicalism's typologizing of Exodus and its pietistic or purely predictive reading of the prophets. One perceives it also in the difficulty that each group has in recognizing other groups' use of Scripture, so that traditional evangelicalism is puzzled by the way some other evangelicals talk about the reign of God, while the latter sometimes speak as if God has good things to say only to the poor (if that were true, God would never have appeared to Paul and never have inspired Romans). One can perceive it also in the way the groups read their favorite texts. Evangelicalism reads Romans as if it were concerned to minister to "the introspective conscience of the West"[5] and ignores the key significance for Paul of chapters 9–11 on the destiny of Israel; while social-activist evangelicalism ignores the fact that Jesus' central concern is also the destiny of Israel, even when he is talking about the poor, and liberation theology reads Exodus as if it were describing only a humanly inspired

5. See Krister Stendahl, "The Apostle Paul and the Introspective Conscience of the West," *Harvard Theological Review* 56 (1963): 199–215 = Stendahl, *Paul among Jews and Gentiles* (Philadelphia: Fortress, 1976), 78–96.

act of political liberation and not a God-given experience of release from political service to the service of God.[6]

None of us can interpret Scripture on our own. It is an inherently corporate enterprise. In group Bible study, one is commonly amazed at what other people perceive in Scripture, insights that are really there but that they can see as others could not because they started from where they were. I have sometimes had a group of people helping me prepare a sermon, and that can issue in greater riches from Scripture for those who will hear it than would issue from my reading of Scripture alone. The point also applies on a broader front. The whole church needs the ways into Scripture that its different parts can offer us: the Fathers, the Puritans, liberation theology, academic theology, the suburban as well as the urban church. Reading Scripture through the eyes of others is one safeguard against getting stuck with those aspects of the richness of Scripture that correspond to our immediate needs.

We will be able to find a starting point within Scripture for a message that speaks to the experiences, needs, and context in which we live; the question is whether we are moving from grasping those insights to seeing them in the context of Scripture as a whole. That is involved in interpreting Scripture, in interpreting Scripture by Scripture, and in accepting the authority of Scripture and the inspiration of Scripture. There are new things to be learned from Scripture every day and every decade, as we become aware of new questions to bring to it. It is a wondrous treasury that the church is never going to exhaust. There is no reason for the opening of Scripture in the church ever to be a boring event. I remember a sermon that suggested that if the Scripture Union, the British society formed to encourage Bible reading, should ever redesign its badge, it should be changed into a pair of raised eyebrows (at first I typed that as "a prayer of raised eyebrows," which is also worth thinking about). God invites us to come to Scripture expectant of our eyebrows being raised.

3. The Form of Scripture

The human authors of Scripture play a part in the overcoming of the hermeneutical gap. It was also in about 1977 that Brevard Childs spent a sabbatical year in Cambridge working at his canonical approach to Scripture, study that would issue in his *Introduction to the Old Testament as Scripture*, to be followed by *The New Testament as Canon*.[7] During that year, he took part in an informal seminar at Tyndale House. He was not actually so impressed by the evidence that British evangelical scholars were flocking to show themselves experts at the historical-critical enterprise, because he was moving in an almost opposite direction. He resolutely pursued his project of studying Scripture as canon and wrote a series of huge books in this connection, though somehow he did not set the world of scholarship alight with them. He has

---

6. See further chapter 4 above.
7. (London: SCM; Philadelphia: Fortress, 1979); and (London: SCM; Philadelphia: Fortress, 1984), respectively.

observed that the effect of his work on biblical theology "has been minimal on the field of biblical exegesis."[8] His work is more respected than seen as the way forward. In his two big books of 1979 and 1984 Childs put forward the thesis that the human authors of the individual books of the Bible as we have them have "shaped" these books to give them a form that will enable them to "function as canon." The opening and closing paragraphs of Hosea and of Ecclesiastes, for instance, provide guidelines for the reading of these books. One characteristic of this canonical shaping was sometimes to remove historical particularities that could obscure the fact that these writings were designed to speak well beyond their original context. Thus Childs points out how few concrete references to exile in Babylon appear in Isaiah 40–55 despite the critical consensus that this setting is the chapters' origin.[9] The historical focus of critical study misses the canonical focus of the books themselves.

Childs's point is not that critical readers must personally accept the books' shaping to function as canon but that they ought at least to recognize it. A parallel point was made by Rolf Knierim in relation to the implication that there is something unprofessional or undisciplined about the theological exegesis of biblical texts, as if interpreters who discuss theological issues were imposing on the text agenda of their own that is alien to it. "Since the substantive statements of the biblical texts are basically theological, the theology of a text belongs to its exegesis from the outset. . . . Theological exegesis is not a separate method in addition to the other methods, or an appendix to them. It is not rooted in the theological interest of the exegete, but in the nature of the text."[10] In the same way, Childs notes a canonical concern as an interest of the text, not merely an interest of the Jewish or Christian interpreter. If one does personally allow one's reading of Scripture to be conformed to the shaping that Childs identified (as evangelicals are presumably committed to doing), this contributes to the bridging of the alleged gap noted above. The books themselves are shaped to reach beyond that gap.

Childs's canonical approach has some similarities with two other significant approaches to interpretation that have aroused much interest over the same period, though their own background lacks the religious dimension of Childs's canonical criticism.

One is more general interest in the final form of the biblical text of a work such as Isaiah. In an extraordinary development, the unity of Isaiah has become a focus of study. This is not to imply that scholars who have followed up this interest go back for a moment on the conviction that the book called Isaiah contains material from several authors who lived in several centuries. One basis for this that is not shared by evangelical scholars will be the assumption that it is simply impossible to refer

---

8. *Isaiah* (Louisville: Westminster John Knox; London: SCM, 2001), xii.

9. Current interest in locating Second Isaiah in Palestine does something different with the data Childs notes. See, e.g., P. R. Davies, "God of Cyrus, God of Israel," in *Words Remembered, Texts Renewed* (J. F. A. Sawyer Festschrift; ed. J. Davies et al.; JSOTSup 195; Sheffield: Sheffield Academic Press, 1995), 207–25; cf. P. R. Davies, *In Search of Ancient Israel* (Sheffield: JSOT, 1992), 40–42. I myself see a rhetorical significance in the data (see *The Message of Isaiah 40–55* [London and New York: Clark, 2005]).

10. *The Task of Old Testament Theology* (Grand Rapids and Cambridge: Eerdmans, 1995), 60–61.

to the events of the sixth century when you live in the eighth. It needs to be noted that the general trend of First Testament study is now if anything more agnostic or atheistic or secular than it was in 1977. (I am perpetually struck by the fact that a number of prominent First Testament and New Testament scholars are people who once believed and now do not. If I stopped believing, I cannot imagine wanting to continue to invest time and interest in these texts once I had decided that they are not the Word of God after all. These scholars pursue the study of the Bible as others do the study of Latin or French literature, or study it as an important cultural artifact that cannot be ignored even if—perhaps especially if—its influence on our culture has been a bane as much as a blessing.)

The other approach looks at the biblical narratives as narratives, using the techniques that one might apply to fiction and considering how a narrative uses plot, character, and point of view. Much of this study deliberately ignores questions of historicity, and conservative evangelical scholars have thus been able to work on the same basis as liberal or secular scholars and publish books with similar-sounding titles on "literary approaches to the Bible."

A significant stimulus to this movement was Hans Frei's *The Eclipse of Biblical Narrative*,[11] a historical study of the way approaches to biblical narrative have fallen apart since the Reformation. Calvin, for instance, Frei points out, assumed a unity between the biblical narrative and the events that actually happened in the Middle East in scriptural times. He also assumed a unity between that story and the story being played out in his own day, or assumed that there should be such a unity. The normative status of Scripture means we tell our story in light of that story, we fit our story into that story, we evaluate our story in light of that story.

Since Calvin's day, both unities have collapsed. Perceiving a gap between the biblical events and the biblical story, mainstream (liberal) theology originally chose to attribute authority to actual history rather than to biblical story, though the more recent interest in narrative interpretation jumps in the other direction. It also reversed the authority between biblical history/story and ours. Instead of interpreting and evaluating our thinking and experience by Scripture, it evaluated Scripture by ours. Instead of fitting us into Scripture, it fitted Scripture into us.

These moves require more than mere disavowal by evangelicals. With regard to the first fractured unity, we should recognize that one motivation for the critical study that gave priority to history rather than text was a desire to escape the authority of ecclesiastical dogma. The text was in bondage to the church and its tradition; historical-critical work sought to study Scripture free of that bondage. On the other hand, the general dominance of history in secular thinking meant that history became the locus of revelation for theologians; and evangelicals joined others in working within this framework. William Foxwell Albright, who became a hero for many evangelicals, was overtly pursuing a project that actually has the appearance of being

---

11. (New Haven and London: Yale University Press, 1974). See further chapter 2 (section 1c) and chapter 3 (section 1) on Luther.

in tension with evangelicals' own gospel. B. O. Long describes him as "transposing traditional theological claims for the uniqueness and truth of biblical revelation into the idiom of objectivist historical narrative."[12]

In Britain, Bishop David Jenkins affirmed a belief in the incarnation and the resurrection, but by the way he interpreted scriptural narrative raised questions about his orthodoxy. Incarnation, he affirmed, was not a hyperbole imposed on Jesus; resurrection is not a metaphor for a change that took place within the disciples. In Jesus, God truly became a human being, and after his death Jesus actually came back to life. But incarnation did not involve virgin birth, and resurrection did not involve the revival of the same body that Jesus had had before his death.

I do not believe that Jenkins is right, nor (as far as the resurrection is concerned) that his view is really coherent. My concern at present, however, is with a question about biblical interpretation that his views raise. He doubts the factuality of the virgin birth and the empty tomb not merely on philosophical or theological grounds (perhaps not at all on these grounds, at least overtly) but on critical or exegetical grounds. He does not view the Gospel accounts of these events as historical material. They are midrash, fictions that give imaginative concrete expression to the truth about the incarnation and the resurrection. They are not factual narrative.

Here, too, I disagree with him, but I acknowledge that there is an issue of interpretation that requires careful handling. I do not see why God should not have inspired some fiction within Scripture. It would not do if the whole Bible were fiction, because it could not then be a message, a gospel, about something God has done for us. But some of the Bible could give imaginative expression to the way God deals with people—not to the way people merely imagine God deals with people, but to the way God really deals with people. Indeed, I believe this is the case: I take it that the book of Job, for instance, is largely fictional. In form it is close to being a play, it is nearly all in verse, and it parallels other ancient works that seem to be fictional. It is an inspired fictional portrayal of a man's life that brings out many issues concerning God and God's ways with us. Its being fiction in no way lessens its capacity to speak the truth about God and humankind. It may even do so more effectively by not being limited to the precise facts of one person's experience.

Grounds similar to the ones that lead me to conclude that Job is fictional lead many scholars to take the Gospel accounts of Jesus' birth and resurrection as partly fictional. If I believe they are wrong, this is because I see the critical situation differently, not because I think the question they ask is an inherently illegitimate one.

It is inevitable that people will come to different conclusions on these questions, because determining what is fact and what is fiction is one of the most difficult of critical enterprises. I do not mean it is difficult to tell when an author is trying to be factual but makes a historical mistake (though that is also the case). I mean it is

---

12. *Planting and Reaping Albright* (University Park: Pennsylvania State University Press, 1997), 134. See William Foxwell Albright's *From the Stone Age to Christianity* (Baltimore: Johns Hopkins University Press, 1940; 2nd ed., 1946; repr., Garden City, N.Y.: Doubleday, 1957); *History, Archaeology and Christian Humanism* (London: Black, 1965).

difficult to tell whether an author is trying to be factual or not. Indeed, Frank Kermode in a study of Mark's Gospel asks whether it is ever possible to be sure whether an author is writing fact or fiction.[13] Fiction authors are quite likely to try to make their fiction as like fact as possible (not so as to deceive, but so as to make it a lifelike story), so that by definition we may not be able to tell the difference between the two.

Scripture contains both fact and fiction. This is not the same as to say that it contains fact and error. I have noted that regarding Scripture as inspired may logically require regarding it as without error. Yet faith in Scripture's inspiration does not require that Scripture be without fiction. Indeed, the awareness that Scripture contains not both fact and error but both fact and fiction is a liberating one. It invites us into the imaginative approaches to interacting with Scripture that we might use with other literature of the imagination, and to the possibility of avoiding getting bogged down in a study of scriptural narrative that makes it as boring as school history.

4. The Importance of Historical Interpretation

If taking history too seriously is Scylla, coming to despise history is Charybdis. At present a vocal movement of First Testament scholars urges that the whole First Testament was written in the postexilic or Second Temple period. All the so-called histories of the preexilic, First Temple period are actually fictions. There is no clear historical knowledge to be had not only of Abraham or Moses but even of David or Hezekiah, whose supposed building of a famous tunnel to safeguard Jerusalem's water supply might be redated to the Hellenistic period.[14] This development can make common cause with the emphasis on reading Scripture as narrative, which can represent an antihistorical strand within biblical study in two senses. First, in reading a work such as a Gospel as a narrative, with techniques developed in the interpretation of fiction, it prefers to ignore the question of any reference to realities outside the story, such as the figure of Jesus. From an orthodox Christian angle that is inadequate; it is incompatible with the nature of the gospel, which refers to such an objective person. Indeed, its inadequacy may be argued on broader grounds. To judge from passages such as Luke's opening (Luke 1:1–4) and John's conclusions (John 20:30–31; 21:24–25), the Gospels present themselves not as fictions but as narrative works whose point depends on their historicity. If interpreters choose to interpret them as fictions, they must at least acknowledge that they are reading them against the grain, reading them allegorically.

13. See Frank Kermode, *The Genesis of Secrecy: On the Interpretation of Narrative* (Cambridge, Mass., and London: Harvard University Press, 1979), 116.

14. See P. R. Davies, *In Search of "Ancient Israel"* (Sheffield: JSOT, 1992); John Rogerson and P. R. Davies, "Was the Siloam Tunnel Built by Hezekiah?" *Biblical Archaeologist* 59 (1996); and broader discussion of the question *Can a "History of Israel" Be Written?* in the volume of that name edited by L. L. Grabbe (Sheffield: Sheffield Academic Press, 1997). For critical (i.e., more conservative) discussion of the theses, see, e.g., the discussion in the *Biblical Archaeology Review* 23, no. 2 (March 1997); 23, no. 4 (July 1997); A. Hurvitz, "The Historical Quest for 'Ancient Israel' and the Linguistic Evidence of the Hebrew Bible," *VT* 47 (1997): 301–15.

That first antihistorical strand links with the other. I have just presupposed that our interpretation of a text should correspond to its author's intention. Is this so? Reading in light of an author's intention raises theoretical and practical difficulties. We have no access to an author's intention except the text itself, and authors such as Luke and John who explicitly state their intention are the exception rather than the rule (and anyway, suppose such statements as those in Luke and John, just noted, do not represent the actual author's view or are part of the fact-like presentation of a fiction?). Further, guesswork regarding intention may subvert interpretation. It has been a common view that the intention of the authors of Ruth and Jonah was to oppose the nationalism of the Second Temple period. While openness to other peoples is indeed one theme in these two books, they contain other prominent themes that are obscured when the urging of that openness is privileged by its being identified univocally as the author's intention. To judge from the evidence of the books, their authors had several intentions, expressed in several themes.

Nevertheless the importance of the traditional emphasis on the author's intention is to affirm that the text does have a meaning of its own. It is not the case that texts are meaningless until someone reads them and responds to them. E. V. McKnight emphasizes the tag that it is readers who "make sense" of texts,[15] but in the process he changes the meaning of the tag. I hope that readers make sense of this book. By that I mean I hope they make *my* sense, that they understand what I intended to say. If they gain other insights that I did not intend, that is fine, but it does not count as "making sense." If the book is nonsense but they are nevertheless able to articulate something for themselves as a result of reading it, that is at least something, but it does not count as "making sense."

As with the historical reference of narratives, one might defend the conviction that texts have meanings of their own on at least two grounds. The specifically Christian ground is the knowledge that the Scriptures are a body of writings that issued from God's speaking objectively, historically, and intentionally. The more general ground is the fact that they issued from human authors doing the same, as some make explicit. To interpret them in a way that ignores the meaning their writers gave these writings and ignores what they were intending to do in writing is again to offer an allegorical interpretation. Interpreters cannot be forbidden this right, but the nature of the act should be acknowledged. Indeed, it might seem that some ethical obligation attaches to seeking to understand something in light of what its author meant rather than simply using it as a canvas onto which to project insights of our own.

5. An Openness to the Whole of Scripture

Brevard Childs's first volume on interpretation, *Biblical Theology in Crisis*,[16] had given the phrase "canonical interpretation" a different significance from ones he emphasizes

15. See, e.g., *The Bible and the Reader* (Philadelphia: Fortress, 1985), 12.
16. (Philadelphia: Westminster Press, 1970).

later. There he noted among other things the way different parts of Scripture treat individual themes in different ways. Recognizing Scripture as canon implies taking all Scripture seriously and suggests the need to move from diversity to synthesis in the study of biblical themes. This is a move that still needs implementing in the study of biblical theology. Since the 1960s the stress has been on diversity in Scripture as different parts of Scripture bring a different message to different contexts. Postmodernism encourages that affirmation and is disinclined to ask about how individual emphases might fit into a more comprehensive picture. I would expect one feature of evangelical study to be a concern to make that move.

It is not surprising if Scripture has many complementary ways of understanding the nature of sin (for instance, as failure, as transgression, as rebellion, and as unfaithfulness) or salvation (for instance, as justification, as healing, as regeneration, and as pardon), and indeed of understanding the nature of God (for instance, as father, creator, and redeemer). God, sin, and salvation are deep and mysterious realities that are illumined by a number of understandings. All the images Scripture uses will elucidate some aspect of them. It is easy for these understandings to become dead metaphors, mere theological concepts, and one task of interpretation and preaching is to let them again be the living realities that they are within Scripture itself. That is facilitated by disentangling them and seeking to appreciate one metaphor at a time. We then have a collection of insights comparable to a collection of portraits, all different but not incompatible, like a collection of portraits of some often-painted person.

Such a collection of paintings might contain irreconcilable interpretations. Our knowledge that Scripture is God's inspired Word means we can be sure that its portraits belong together (at another level, all reflect the work of one artist) and that all illumine their subject. They are not a collection from which we pick and choose according to our preferences. They are normative as a collection. None may be ignored; none that are peripheral may be made central; none from outside may be admitted to the collection itself (even if portraits outside the collection may indeed express true insights).

In practice, evangelical study of Scripture can easily impose unconscious constraints on itself that make us less biblical in substance than in name. An example is the study of a book such as Leviticus and its treatment of sacrifice. A number of New Testament writings, particularly Hebrews, take up this aspect of Leviticus as a key to understanding the significance of the death of Christ, and do so fruitfully. It is difficult to see how the doctrine of the substitutionary atonement of Christ would ever have been formulated without the aid of that strand of the First Testament Scriptures. Hebrews thus illustrates for us the way those God-breathed First Testament Scriptures are able to instruct us concerning salvation and faith *in Christ Jesus* (2 Tim 3:15–16).

But paradoxically, the success of Hebrews in its interpretive work narrowed down the focus within which the church has subsequently read Leviticus. There is much more to the significance of Leviticus for our understanding of Christian worship than we have noticed, because we have allowed the prism provided by Hebrews to restrict us to one aspect of Leviticus's significance. In Romans 15:16, Paul himself points to another aspect for an understanding of evangelism.

The New Testament provides the explicit witness to Christ that enables us to see the First Testament in focus, as the First Testament provides us with the "many and various" ways of God's speaking without which we could not understand Christ. Without the New Testament, the First Testament might be an unfocused enigma, but it is possible for us to turn the New Testament into something that narrows our vision. Its witness gives us our normative focus on Jesus as the center of the Christian message and gives us one normative way of reading individual First Testament passages, but not the only way of working out the implications of that focus for individual passages or books. Our belief in the God-breathed nature of Leviticus invites us into a commitment to the book itself in its historical and contextual meaning, including those aspects of it that are not taken up in Hebrews or in other parts of the New Testament. As it happens, the study of this book has been remarkably fruitful over recent decades, on the part of Jewish, secular, and Christian writers.

The involvement of conservative scholars in this study of Leviticus[17] illustrates how it is possible to be a "conservative" evangelical and not be confined to past insights and ways of thinking. The implications of that word "conservative" deserve consideration. In Britain, the phrase "conservative evangelical" came into use in the 1950s to distinguish people who wanted to be seen as neither "fundamentalist" nor "liberal evangelical" and believed that there was a space in between. In the United States, the word "neo-evangelical" was used in a comparable way (though the word "evangelical" is used more broadly and more pejoratively than in Britain). Fundamentalists seemed to have closed minds, but liberals seemed to have given too much away. Over subsequent years, many of the conservative evangelicals of the 1960s came to designate themselves "open evangelicals" without facing the question of what distinguishes them from the liberal evangelicals of an earlier decade. While many of the specific issues have changed, I doubt whether there is any difference in the nature of the stances implied by the terms. The open evangelicals of the 1990s were the liberal evangelicals of the 1950s.

To be conservative implies a commitment to conserving truths and positions rather than surrendering them in light of alleged new insights. To be liberal implies a freedom over against long-accepted positions. In principle these do not seem incompatible positions. I am not unhappy when I am reviewed simultaneously by liberals as too inclined to see Scripture as God's revelation and by conservatives as making too many concessions to scholarly theories.

Both positions have downsides. To be liberal often seems to imply an unprincipled willingness to follow the spirit of the age. To be conservative often seems to imply that one can only come to conclusions that have been reached before. Anything new must be wrong, and the purpose of scholarship is to vindicate and support what

---

17. E.g., Gordon Wenham, *The Book of Leviticus* (London: Hodder; Grand Rapids: Eerdmans, 1979).

we know already; there is no new insight to be gained. Paradoxically, conservative evangelicals can be the group most bound to the church's tradition of interpretation of Scripture rather than to Scripture itself.

That classic passage in 2 Timothy on the nature and significance of the First Testament Scriptures (which we may presumably also apply to the New Testament) emphasizes their role in connection with teaching, rebuking, correcting, and training. In *Obeying Christ in a Changing World*, Anthony Thiselton implicitly questioned evangelical preoccupation with what Scripture "teaches," and in his *Fundamentalism*,[18] James Barr directly attacked this preoccupation.

The clash with 2 Timothy 3:16 may be more apparent than real. There is more to "teaching" than "teaching"; that is, there is a narrow and a broad application of the word. In the narrow sense, "teaching" suggests the explicitly didactic, the kind of plain setting forth of the truth to which Paul refers in 2 Corinthians 4:2. There is much of that in Scripture, and it is the characteristic stuff of systematic theology or of statements of faith. Yet when Jesus tells a parable, he is concerned to teach and thus to fulfill the role described in 2 Timothy 3:16, but he does so by avoiding setting forth the truth plainly. Elsewhere Scripture "teaches" by asking questions or offering worship or writing poems or relating dreams. There is nothing wrong with concern for Scripture's "teaching" if we use the word in a way that can embrace the many approaches to teaching that Scripture embraces. Long before the reminting of that word "hermeneutics," when our forebears discussed hermeneutics they emphasized that poetry had to be understood as poetry, vision as vision, symbol as symbol.

An openness to the whole of Scripture implies a stance toward the question of how we handle diversity in its teaching. There has always been disagreement over the biblical teaching on topics such as baptism, or the return of Christ, or divorce and remarriage, or the role of women in church life. I do not think that all these disagreements reflect our sinfulness in not being willing to face the unequivocal teaching of Scripture. Sometimes they reflect the fact that Scripture speaks with more than one voice, and our problem lies in doing justice to its variety of voices.

The issue is handled most explicitly when Jesus considers divorce and remarriage (Mark 10:2–12). Here Jesus points to the tension between the view of marriage and divorce implicit in the creation story and the instructions regarding divorce in Deuteronomy. The former, he says, expresses God's original intention; the latter makes allowance for Israel's stubbornness. Marriages break down, even within God's people, so there is teaching to cover what to do in this situation.

Jesus is not replacing the teaching of the First Testament with a higher standard of his own. Indeed, it is quite difficult to find topics on which the New Testament's teaching is consistently "higher" than that of the First Testament (the New Testament can be pretty nasty about sinners and can pray for their punishment as fervently as the First Testament, for instance), and quite possible to point to topics where the First Testament seems more illuminating than the New Testament (as is the

---

18. See 76.

case regarding God's concern with society). Within both Testaments we find more and less absolute views of marriage, divorce, and remarriage, as on other topics. Interpreting Scripture's view on such matters involves doing justice to all strands of its teaching. It testifies both to an ideal of lifelong monogamous marriage and to the need for a realistic approach to the fact of marriage breakdown. Historically, churches have been better at the first than at the second, though they now need to avoid abandoning their testimony to lifelong monogamous marriage by too easy an appeal to individual "pastoral considerations."

The question of the place of women in family, society, and church involves a similar attempt to do justice to a variety of scriptural material. It is quite possible to make an apparently biblical case for women forgoing leadership roles in each of the three contexts, family, society, and church; it is also possible to make an apparently biblical case for women exercising these roles. The situation parallels that with slavery. Scripture provides abundant material both to support and to subvert this institution, too, and it was used both by abolitionists and by their opponents during nineteenth-century debates in ways that closely parallel our discussion of the place of women.[19] People who believe that women should be subordinate at home and in church need to be able to show how the arguments used to support this view would not lead us to accept the institution of slavery; people who incline to the Christian feminist view need to be able to show what authority texts such as 1 Timothy 2:8–15 have for us. (My own view is that Gen 1–2 again portrays God's ideal for humanity, which does not involve any hierarchy in the relationship between the sexes or any division of areas of responsibility; passages such as 1 Tim 2 model a way of handling the situation when matters get out of hand in a certain direction, but do not ask to be applied to situations that do not require them.) Both sides in debates on women's ministry are inclined to selectivity in the proof texts they quote to support their case.

Might it be God's will that Christians hold different views on topics such as divorce and feminism? I have suspected that this might be the case with baptism, since some important aspects of its significance find clear expression in the baptism of babies born within church families while other aspects of baptism find clear expression when baptism is the moment of someone's personal profession of faith. In church life, as well as in theory, we need to be able to offer an interpretation of Scripture that does justice to its diversity, a diversity that reflects the complexity of the matters it handles and reflects the tension between ideal and reality that it faces.

6. How We Handle the First Testament

There is an amusing contrast between the attitude to the First Testament taken by traditional evangelicalism and that taken by the Church of England report on

19. See the illuminating discussion by W. M. Swartley in *Slavery, Sabbath, War, and Women* (Scottdale, Pa.: Herald, 1983).

Urban Priority Areas, *Faith in the City*.[20] For *Faith in the City* the place where real authority lies in Christianity is in the teaching of Jesus, then in other aspects of the New Testament. It finds, though, as people interested in the social implications of the faith often do, that it is not the New Testament but the First Testament that has most to say on that subject.[21] Now it is quite possible to argue that the New Testament is concerned for the poor as well as for the poor in spirit, but is a bit pathetic to feel obliged (as I perceive some social-activist evangelicals also to be doing) to base your theology of the poor on a minority concern of the New Testament, when the Bible that Jesus himself gave us overtly and indisputably majors on that topic, in a book such as Deuteronomy (as the report notes). It is also amusing (though sad, too) to find the report totally ignoring Scripture when it discusses the gospel and other faiths,[22] if this is because the conclusion it wants to come to finds little support from the New Testament. It can, however, be supported from the First Testament. *Faith in the City* finds (or rather is apparently unaware of) a tension between its formal attitude to the First Testament and its attitude in practice: the First Testament is found to speak with authority, though it lacks the form of authority.

Evangelicalism has traditionally had the opposite difficulty. It is formally committed to accepting the authority of the First Testament, but in practice does not do so. Its understanding of the church and of Israel is not significantly influenced by the First Testament's understanding of Israel as the people of God; its praise and prayer are not significantly influenced by the Bible's own manual of praise and prayer, the Psalms (for that matter, evangelicalism's approach to Israel, to worship, and to the ministry has not been much influenced by the New Testament); its understanding of redemption is not significantly influenced by that of a book such as Exodus (which invented the idea). It avoids the thrust of these by hermeneutical devices such as typology, which makes the First Testament mean something different from what its authors thought it meant, or by the theory of progressive revelation, which makes it possible for the New Testament to be treated as effectively superseding the First Testament, which has the form of authority but not the reality.

James Barr's *Fundamentalism* contains its misapprehensions about evangelicalism but also its penetrating insights, and one of the latter is this criticism, that for evangelicalism the Bible often has the form of authority but not the reality.[23] Doctrinally we are committed to a theology of the Word, but precisely that commitment can hinder us from actually being a people of the Word, because the fact that we accept that theoretical commitment provides us with a false sense of security, as if it guaranteed a real commitment to Scripture. The result is that it does the opposite. We love to tag texts onto things, as if that made them biblical. One ironic example is our talk of Scripture as "the Word of God"; in Scripture, phrases such as "the word

20. *Faith in the City: A Call for Action by Church and Nation. The Report of the Archbishop of Canterbury's Commission on Urban Priority Areas* (London: Church House, 1985).

21. See §3.11–13.

22. See §3.26–28.

23. See 36–38.

of God" or "the word of truth" are not used to refer to Scripture. The scriptural word for Scripture is Scripture.

An evangelical commitment to Scripture involves believing that God spoke and speaks through the whole Bible, and an evangelical hermeneutic involves listening to the whole and seeking to take account of the whole. It looks at the First Testament in light of the New Testament and vice versa, and it allows the intrinsic meaning of each part of the First Testament to stand and to contribute to that biblical perspective on the whole of life to which we aspire. It is easy for evangelicalism not to accept the authority of Scripture. People who affirm that authority most strongly as part of their formulary can be among those who sidestep much of Scripture in practice.

7. Scripture in Culture and Us in Culture

Consideration of subordinationist and feminist hermeneutics leads to a further question. How far are the Scriptures tied to and limited by the particular cultures in which they emerged? Feminist hermeneutics and gay hermeneutics sometimes sidestep texts that might challenge their position by declaring that Paul (somehow it is usually Paul) was "a man of his day," limited by the state of knowledge and assumptions of his day, and therefore cannot be held to views that he would hardly have maintained when increased knowledge shows those assumptions to be mistaken.

It was the glory of Paul to be a person of his day. When he invited people to envisage what Christ had done for them as an act of redemption or reconciliation or propitiation or justification or healing, these were not so much the technical terms of a theologian's world of discourse as shorthand expressions for the experiences of everyday life. Whether you were a slave, or a slave owner, or an ordinary free person, slavery, slave purchase, and manumission were familiar realities of your day. To use these and other such familiar realities to communicate the gospel and its implications to believers and to unbelievers was to speak as a man or woman of your day to other men and women of your day. They were not mere sermon illustrations but powerful life metaphors and symbols that carried the dynamic reality of what they referred to. In this sense, the prophets and Jesus before Paul indeed spoke as people of their day. They too had taken everyday life experiences and turned them into metaphors and symbols. These were means of preaching from inside people's worlds, inside the worlds of family life and farming, of birth and marriage and death, of business and politics and religion.[24] Prophets such as Amos and Isaiah had developed the nastier technique of entering these worlds and then turning them upside down with their punch line that revealed that mysteriously God's world, while one with his people's, differed radically from it. Jesus had perfected this technique in parables that portrayed a familiar world (Pharisees, priests, Samaritans, employers and employees, brides and grooms) yet one that turned surrealist during the course of the

24. See further chapter 1 (section 2) above.

story, so that God ignores the delegates at a prayer breakfast and goes to talk to the members of the Iranian parliament. Amos, Jesus, and Paul are indeed men of their day, as well as being men of God; they could therefore bring God's world and our world together in their preaching. Our preaching sometimes indicates that we are not very familiar with either world.

Is the price of being people of your day that you are limited by the perspectives of your day? There is one sense in which this is true. In our world (at least in Britain) the release of slaves and the offering of animal sacrifices are not part of everyday life. The temptation to boil a kid in its mother's milk is not the most serious one we have to contend with (as might have been the case in First Testament times, to judge from its threefold mention in the Pentateuch). We want to know what to do about the bomb and abortion, about experiments on embryos, and whether to let Muslims take over redundant church buildings. It is a consequence of Scripture's speaking directly to the concerns of its day that it often does not do so to ours. God paid this price in speaking specifically to people who lived in concrete situations; what God said directly to them may not be immediately intelligible or applicable to people in other contexts. We have to look behind the metaphors for the transcultural experience captured by them, and to give new life to that in our day. We have to look behind the warnings and commands for the transcultural perspectives on life and death that they embody, and look for equivalent concrete commitments (not merely for the principles on which they are based, for these in themselves will be too abstract) that will embody God's way of seeing and behaving for our day.

There are some pointers to how we may do that in *Faith in the City*. The Commission refuses to attempt a "deductive" theology of the city,[25] and there is little theology in the report, even in the chapter dealing with theological perspectives and priorities. The report insists that theology has to emerge from facing actual questions, and it indicates how such a theology might be expected to emerge. It does this not so much by the way it actually goes about doing theology, but by the way of studying Scripture it commends, an imaginative reflecting on Scripture in the very context of issues and questions that people have to face.[26] This can be not just a way into perceiving how Scripture applies today, but a way into an understanding of the historical meaning of Scripture, a way into exegesis, a way of seeing more of what is actually there. It is not something that our objectivist and deductive approach to education in general teaches us, but if we gain a vision for it, we can regain the facility to read Scripture this way. It requires an empathy.

That word is sometimes used of approaches to hermeneutics that fail to take seriously that Scripture is objectively God's Word. The Bible offers instruction on who God is and how God relates to us, but it does that partly through its affirming the nature of some people's religious experience, their experience of God. The Psalms, Jeremiah, and Paul are often testimonies to religious experience, so approaches to interpretation

25. See §3.43.
26. See §3.35–36, with note 2 on page 80.

that see the task as involving the attempt to enter empathetically into an account of someone's experience seem quite appropriate. We also need that empathy in entering into the experience of the people in whose company we interpret Scripture, so that we can bring Scripture's world and their world together. Scripture has the capacity to speak across cultural gaps to the world in which we live. I have found Charles Elliott's *Praying the Kingdom* very suggestive as it models a reading of Scripture out of the urgent world contexts in which we have to live.[27] (It also models ways whereby we may avoid falling from escapist pietism into an activism that behaves as if we have the task of seeing that the kingdom comes, an issue very important in the context of an evangelicalism that has paid lip service to grace more often than it has lived by grace.)

Scripture is thoroughly time-bound, but books such as Elliott's, or Jacques Ellul's *The Meaning of the City*, or Dale Aukerman's *Darkening Valley* (on the nuclear threat),[28] show how it also transcends its time. Perhaps this is because our culture is not, after all, so utterly different from the cultures of the Bible. Poverty, class, race, other faiths, work, and politics are the Bible's concerns. The world of television soap operas is the world of the Bible. It has a wondrous capacity to keep speaking in cultures quite different from the ones in which it arose. This reflects the fact that it is not merely the result of impressive human insight (though it is that) but also the result of God's enabling people to reach insights that they would not have achieved without God's enabling.

It is this that Israel and the church were responding to when they saw to the preserving of some of their writings and when, by a cumbrous process, some of these writings came to have a special status as Scripture. We cannot prove that the church made the right decision in recognizing the books that it did; we are left in the end with the invitation to trust the providence of God over the matter. It is equally impossible to prove that the writings that were chosen were ones free of any error or shortcoming due to the limitations of their writers. Yet if these writings have a depth about them that transcends mere human capacity, so that they are rightly regarded as "inspired," God-breathed, it would seem more logical to assume that this inspiration protected them from being spoiled by the time-bounded position of their human authors than to assume that if the latter had only lived in a more enlightened age they would have avoided some of their errors. I cannot prove that this is so; it is a logical statement of faith, but it is a statement of faith. So in the presence of a genuine tension between what Scripture says and what modern insight says, I would rather take the risk of trusting the former.

8. A Practical Commitment to Scripture

With regard to the second aspect of Frei's "eclipse," as evangelicals we need to be aware that our dogmatic commitment to Scripture does not in itself guarantee a substantial

27. Charles Elliott, *Praying the Kingdom* (London: DLT, 1985).
28. Jacques Ellul, *The Meaning of the City* (Grand Rapids: Eerdmans, 1970); Dale Aukerman, *Darkening Valley: A Biblical Perspective on Nuclear War* (New York: Seabury, 1981).

commitment. I continue to be frightened by James Barr's critique in *Fundamentalism* that our commitment to Scripture is merely a badge that we wear; the Bible is our supreme religious symbol.[29] That may actually make it more difficult for us to read Scripture accurately, because we know we are committed to agreeing with what we find in it. We are therefore in ongoing danger of having to make it mean what we can accept, because we do not share the luxury enjoyed by people of more "liberal" conviction of being able simply to disagree with it. This is one reason why we will value the study of Scripture by people we know we disagree with, whether liberal or secular or Jewish, because they may be free to see in Scripture things from which we have to hide. To put it another way, we should be worried if there are no aspects of Scripture's teaching that we wish were not there and/or that we believe simply because they are there rather than because we like them and can make sense of them.

I am not fond of giving orders, of telling people what to do; it suits me better to help people think through in light of Scripture what they should do, help them come to a decision rather than tell them what to do. That no doubt reflects the influence of personality and of the spirit of the age, though neither of those in itself makes it wrong. I am therefore puzzled or sad to find that Scripture portrays God as so fond of telling us what to do. It is not how I would go about being God if I were God, and I could wish it were otherwise. But that is how it is, and I am not God, and my submission to Scripture involves me in accepting that this is how God is, and in seeking to come to terms with it.

I am also attracted to process theology's way of understanding God's sovereignty, as guaranteeing to bring about the fulfillment of God's purpose but as not deter-mining ahead of time how to do so. It emphasizes the interrelation between human acts and divine acts, and it is inclined to see God as responding to human acts and making them part of a pattern, more than to see God forming detailed plans and then sovereignly implementing them. Again, personality factors and aspects of the spirit of the age incline me to this understanding, and again that does not in itself make this understanding wrong. Indeed, it is present in Scripture, and these influ-ences thus enable me to do justice to an aspect of Scripture's understanding of how God's sovereignty is at work in the world. But if I want to let Scripture shape and not merely confirm my thinking, I also have to own Scripture's emphasis on the way God decides beforehand that certain things should happen (e.g., Acts 4:28).

Anyone who thinks that he or she is happy to affirm all of Scripture needs a dose of self-suspicion and needs to find where he or she is avoiding its thrust. As human beings who fall short of God's glory, all of us are reluctant conformers to Scripture to one degree or another. What distinguishes evangelical involvement with Scrip-ture from that of the rest of the church at this point is that we commit ourselves to conform anyway.

This leads me finally to an attempt to portray two broad approaches to inter-pretation. They are ideal types in the sense that no one operates by either of them

29. E.g., 11.

all the time, and features of one may become combined with features of the other. That I take to be a good thing, because both models are valuable, and they need each other. The first is more at home with didactic material in Scripture such as the epistles, with which evangelical interpretation has usually been happier; the second is more at home with the narrative and poetic material in Scripture. The first is more traditional, the second is more trendy.

The two approaches can be characterized by means of a series of further comparisons. One is analytic: it discovers things by taking texts apart, by analyzing them into parts. The other is holistic: it responds to texts as wholes. One is deductive: it disciplines itself to starting from texts and moving from there to life. The other is experimental: it moves from life to texts. One is concerned with what Scripture says to us individually, the other with what Scripture says to us communally. One views the studying of Scripture as naturally something people do on their own. The other views it as something people naturally do together. One is highly cerebral, an exercise that majors on hard and careful thinking. The other is more impressionist. One tends to focus on otherworldly concerns, the other tends to be more interested in this world. One concentrates more on getting our thinking right, the other more on getting our actions right. One is objective in its approach, the other more participatory. One tends to look for timeless truths; the other tends to be highly situational. One is inclined to be abstract, the other concrete. One in its preaching tends to be unapplied, the other to be involved in the application of Scripture to people's lives. One tends to be confident about ascertaining Scripture's meaning; the other may be fearful of missing it because of our capacity to avoid the truth.

We need to exercise both these approaches to interpretation, so that we may get a bit nearer to that eschatological goal of a complete grasp of Scripture and by Scripture, when we will have no more questions and see face to face.

6

How Does Scripture
Impact Our Life with God?

How does Scripture relate to our individual lives with God? There seem to me to be two complementary aspects to the answer: there are times when Scripture determines the agenda and we respond, and other times when we set the agenda and Scripture responds. In considering these, I want to come at them obliquely, starting from an issue and a story.[1]

1. Scripture and Our Worldly Drivenness

First the issue. With my disabled wife Ann, I once spent a weekend at the L'Arche community north of Paris. L'Arche is a fellowship of mentally handicapped people and their companions, living together. After we came back I read Henri Nouwen's journal of a year he spent at L'Arche.[2] One interesting aspect was Nouwen's account of the contrast and tension between the life he had spent as a theologian and lecturer on life in the Spirit in a divinity school in the United States, the life he then lived at L'Arche, and what he subsequently found when he returned to the United States. It rang bells with my experience in the church in Britain, not least in the theological college where I worked. Nouwen talks about the competitiveness of the life of his divinity school and of his sense of being forever busy but never sure whether he

---

1. First published in John Goldingay, *After Eating the Apricot* (Carlisle: Paternoster, 1996), 1–15; also at http://www.fuller.edu/sot/faculty/goldingay.
2. *The Road to Daybreak* (New York: Doubleday, 1990).

was really on the right path. He found that the mere move from divinity school to community for the handicapped made no difference in itself, because the competitiveness and compulsive busyness were internalized. They were parts of our culture that Nouwen knew were part of him.

People sometimes suggest that a theological college or divinity school is too cut off from the real world. The truth may be the opposite. It is a microcosm of the world, very like the world, haunted as the world is. Not surprisingly, this can also be true of people in ministry. A colleague once told me about research suggesting that one major reason why people were not offering themselves for the ministry was that they were not attracted by the frantic, harassed, under the cat-o'-nine-tails nature of the way ministers live. Ordinands come out of a world—that is, a church—that is compulsively busy and harassed, are on their way back into such a world, and while they are at theological college behave the same way; and the world looks the other way for inspiration because all it sees in us is the mirror image of itself.

When Nouwen went back to North America and found himself talking with people from the Senate and from business, he discovered two things. One was the importance of taking Jesus into this world of busyness so that one was not sucked into its way of being. The other was that what people wanted to talk about was Jesus, partly because they themselves did not like their way of being.

How might we separate ourselves from that drivenness that characterizes the world and the church? This question raises managerial issues, but also personal ones. Because the world and the church are likely to stay haunted, we need to develop the ability for ourselves to stay separate from it. God is likely not to be calling us into the desert as a witness against the world and the church in its drivenness. God is likely to be calling us to the tougher task of staying in the city, in the church, in the world, but dwelling in our own place of stillness there. To put it another way, the world, the church, the theological college have all the temptations of the desert. They make us face the demons inside ourselves, and we had better learn to live with these temptations, with our own demons, precisely because what we find outside ourselves in the world and the church is what we also find inside ourselves.

Living with Scripture is a potential key to being able to do so. Anthony Bloom tells a story about a woman who after breakfast each morning would go to her room and put her armchair in a position that would enable her to ignore all the other things that might worry her, so that she could sit in quiet, peacefulness, and stillness. There she would knit before the face of God for fifteen minutes, until the room was suffused with God's presence. There she would experience how, "at the heart of the silence," there was the One "who is all stillness, all peace, all poise."[3] In the evangelical tradition the place of knitting is played by the Bible. You go into your little room as that woman did, you light your candle if you find that helpful, and you open the Bible and submerge yourself in it. You know it is the story or script of an alternative world, a world different from the world's world and the world's church, a

3. *School for Prayer* (London: DLT, 1970), 61.

world (for instance) not characterized by compulsive busyness and competitiveness designed to reassure you that you actually do exist. You want not to be conformed to this world but to be conformed to the image of Jesus, to be transformed by the renewing of your mind, and you know that the Bible is of key importance to that end.

If you are a theological student, you know that studying the Bible in the lecture room and for the writing of papers can play a significant part in this, but you know that this study is also part of a system that easily gets allied with competitiveness and busyness, and you know that you need to be distanced from that. It is also important to sit on your own in the quiet with the Bible and your candle and/or your knitting and/or your cup of coffee. Thus you sit not on your own but with God and with the book God gave us to be the means of conforming our mind to that alternative world, so that we can live in the everyday world in light of the nature of this real alternative world of God's.

Being transformed by the renewing of your mind involves recognizing that your whole framework of thinking and attitude tends to be adrift. It involves being given a whole new framework. It is for this reason that reading the Bible systematically is so important. It is for this reason that a system for reading the entire Bible is important, because it refuses to let us off with reading only favorite parts of Scripture or reading Scripture to find the answers to questions we already have. It is for this reason that the weekday lectionary used by some denominations is so valuable, because it is less affected by the selectivity that inevitably characterizes the Sunday lectionary.

2. Scripture: Story, Way of Life, Vision, Testimony

What is it about Scripture that enables it to rework our frame of thinking? Its most prominent characteristic is that it is distinctively a story in which we locate our own story.

Nowadays we are a very existential people. Only the present counts, only what I have experienced counts. The really important thing is telling my story. Yet in reality we are what we are because of the story in the midst of which we live. We are who we are because we belong to our particular century, because we live in our particular decade, because we live where we live. When people studying church history in two hundred years' time write papers on the church in the twentieth and twenty-first centuries they will think we were very odd. Living where and when we do has many advantages, but it also involves limitations, ways our perspective is skewed. Scripture sets us in the context of a different story, a story that extends from a Beginning to an End, a story that has Jesus at its crucial point. It sets us in the context of a story in which things happen that we have not experienced (yet). It does not thereby take away from our importance; it enables us to see our story more clearly by seeing it in context. Reading part of Scripture's story can therefore do amazing things to us.

Such reading needs to take us right inside the story, so that we relive it. We need to allow ourselves to be sucked into it. When my mother-in-law watched soap operas on television, she did not merely watch them. She took part. Marshall McLuhan once taught us that television was cool communication; it does not involve us and our imagination, as radio does. Ann's mother had not read McLuhan. When someone was about to do something unwise, she would urge them not to (unfortunately they took no notice, rather like us reading the Bible). I once went with some colleagues to see *The Taming of the Shrew*. The performance was in the round, to encourage the audience to feel part of it, and when there was a rhetorical question addressed to the audience, one of my colleagues (who was not a Westerner and did not feel as bound by the rules as the rest of the audience) answered the question out loud; the cast never relaxed again. That is the way to read the Bible, taking its stories as told for us, its questions as addressed to us.

There are other ways in which Scripture shapes us. It is, second, a set of commands, values, and principles to live by; sometimes its stories illustrate and inculcate these (or their opposites). Someone in my family who does not go to church once commented on the difference between Christians and Jewish people. For Jewish people their faith is something that shapes their everyday lives; for Christians it is more a matter of what they do on Sundays. That is the impression the outsider gets. If you ask Asians about the nature of their religion, they will tell you about what they do; if you ask Westerners about their religion, they will tell you about what they believe. See what we have done to our Asian religion!

Parts of the First Testament lay great emphasis on observances governing cleanness and taboo; these observances that distinguished the people of God from other people were later terminated within New Testament faith. Christians have often wanted to reestablish such observances, to make themselves look and behave differently so as to provide protective boundaries around their community. My own generation was thus brought up with an alternative subculture: Christians did not go to the pub or the cinema and did not shop on Sunday. The contemporary younger generation tends to have an opposite attitude. Christians are now entirely at home in the pub. We have moved from having a silly kind of distinctive Christian lifestyle to not having one at all. Scripture's nature is, among other things, to give us a set of priorities different from the world's, at points where it needs to be. For instance, in the world the family is often idolized; Jesus says turn your back on your family. Scripture is a set of commands and values and principles to live by, so we look to it to transform our priorities in life.

Third, Scripture is a nightmare and a dream of the future. The calling of the prophets is to share God's nightmares and dream God's dreams, and then to pass them on to the people of God. These nightmares and visions are not bound inevitably to take place. They are disasters that hang over the people or blessings that God wants to give them, but whether they come true depends on the response people give to God. Scripture thus holds before us possible scenarios and invites our response.

Fourth, Scripture is people's testimony to how experience with God has worked for them, testimony to shape our experience. It is often assumed that the way we experience things comes from inside us: it is part of us, a given, expressing who we really are. That is a fallacy. We experience things the way we do because of the way we have been shaped, the way we have been taught. The process thus involves a mixing of what is inside us and what has come to us. Liturgy, for instance, is designed to shape us, or rather it does inevitably shape us, whatever its own nature. It is for that reason important that the liturgy is of the kind that we would want to shape people. That is why it is important that liturgy is commonly stiff with Scripture; it is in this way that Scripture trains us in the way we experience life. If Scripture reflects the truth about God, it appropriately shapes us so that we truly experience God. In the same way Scripture is designed to be a key shaping factor with regard to the way we pray. The Psalms offer us a clear model of how life with God is, of what praise and prayer are like and how they work. The Epistles add to that. As far as I can see, how we actually praise and pray reflects very little of the way Scripture does so. We praise and pray in the way of our tradition.

We belong, then, to a driven society, a driven church, a driven ministry, and Scripture is a resource into which we escape to give it opportunity to conform our story to God's, our way of life to God's, our visions and nightmares to God's, our experience to the one God offers. Scripture sets the agenda.

3. Scripture in Response to Our Agenda

It is also possible and important to come at the question of Scripture and our lives with God from the other end, from when we set the agenda.

A few years ago, I went through an experience of particular personal loss. The ultimate in loss is literal bereavement, but we go through other sorts of losses in life, losses that are little bereavements. Changing jobs can be like that, especially if it involves moving house and changing churches; it can take quite a while to get used to life after those little deaths. We experience losses like these when our children leave home, or when a key relationship in our life comes to an end, or when our church gets amalgamated with another one, or when we are made redundant. I went through something a little like one of those, something that indeed felt a fearsome bereavement. For months on end I lived much of the time with a deep hole inside me, a pain that really seemed physical, a heart that ached inconsolably. I would get up in the early hours and cry out to God from my armchair, sitting in the early morning sun that shone through our patio windows in the winter and during that particular lovely sunny winter belied the way I felt. I would cry out "Will it be all right?" I knew God always said yes, and I knew that it would be all right in due course. I had read books on real bereavement and watched people go through it, which did help me believe that the tunnel would come to an end, but you also have to live with the darkness in the meantime.

There were one or two things that helped sustain me. One was students and colleagues who I knew I could ask to pray with me and whose prayers were always a blessing. But another, and the most astonishing, was the Bible. It was the most astonishing, not because of the mere fact that it proved capable of being an encouragement, a resource, a well, a rock, through that experience of hopelessness, emptiness, desert, and drowning. I would have taken for granted that the Bible could be a help from time to time. What was astonishing was the consistency with which it did so.

One of the keys was this. If you are an ordinand and are finding it impossible to cope with life, one of the natural things to do is to give up coming to chapel. If you are the principal of the theological college, however, as I was, and if you have a reasonably average superego telling you what to do, you cannot do that. You have to go to chapel anyway. So each morning I would join with other people there, join them aware of that deep gaping hole inside, the hurt in my heart that I knew would heal one day but was not healed then. I would join them, with that pain inside me, and listen to the Scriptures being read and join in the reading of the Psalms, and *every single day* there was something in those Scriptures that directly addressed me, consoled me, challenged me, or made a promise to me.

I wonder now whether I am exaggerating, painting an experience of Scripture other than it was, but that is how I remember it. Perhaps it was not really every day and I have misremembered it in that way. Perhaps it was only four days out of five—though as Meatloaf once said, even two out of three ain't bad. What I do know is that if the cloud outside was overwhelming me and the hole inside was consuming me at 7:55 a.m., one way or another through the Scriptures and/or someone's ministry and/or just sitting with God, by 8:55 a.m. the hurt had not been healed, because it had to take its time, but balm had been applied to it, and I could face another day. And in that process in which God did not fail me, the Scriptures played a key role. They were the indispensable and the most consistently soothing anointing.

Fortunately I can demonstrate to myself that I am not making it all up because I kept a kind of journal in an old school notebook. I cannot remember why I started doing so, though I do know that it became important because when I was being overwhelmed by the gaping hole at 4:00 a.m. and I was hesitant to wake some hapless student or colleague to ask them to pray with me (though I know they would not have minded) it became my resource book. Indeed, it became my comfort blanket. I carried it round with me in case I needed a fix from time to time. I would be fearful of being separated from it, because it was the evidence that God still existed and cared about me, in that God was speaking to me through the Scriptures. When at those moments I could not remember anything about what I believed and what might be the grounds for hope, it contained all these golden pages with things that God had said to me, that the Scriptures had said to me.

Recently I again wondered what sort of things these were, and I worked through my red notebook to see if I could categorize them. Now the schema I have just used for articulating the kind of thing Scripture is (story, imperative, vision, testimony) has become deeply engrained in me, and it is probably inevitable that it partly also shapes the way I categorize my experience of Scripture. But it does not entirely do so, which may suggest I am not fudging the evidence too much. Further, I found that I could trace an interesting order in the prominence of the different functions of Scripture as I went through that healing process. Early on, not surprisingly the most common thing I found Scripture did for me was provide me with means of articulating my feelings to God. Yet what I found as I read back in my book was that it hardly ever just did that. What it did was set a conversation going, something like the conversation in Psalm 42, where the psalmist asks, "Why are you so downcast, trust in God!" The psalm makes clear that talking to yourself in prayer is important.

One day, for instance, we apparently read Psalm 107 in chapel. I noticed and noted that this psalm is all about people being in distress, darkness, and affliction, but that it keeps moving on to "But God took them out of their trouble." The next day we read Psalm 108, which starts "My heart is fixed, O God, my heart is fixed," and I noted "It didn't feel very fixed last night" when I had felt depressed and oppressed, but then that "It's God's mercy and God's glory that are decisive—I mustn't think it depends on me" and on my capacity to stay fixed. The next week we had reached Psalm 119 and I noted verse 57: "Yahweh, you are my portion." "My portion": my means of support and life, something and someone especially for me. The same day, I am amused and embarrassed to report, I received a special blessing from a lesson from the book of Baruch in the Apocrypha, a lesson that acknowledged to God that "it is the living who mourn their fall from greatness, who walk the earth bent and enfeebled, with eyes dimmed and with failing appetite—it is they, Lord, who will sing your praise and applaud your justice." There was a promise there to lay hold of. The next week it was 2 Timothy, where Paul is made to say that his life is already being poured out on the altar, that he has run the great race and finished the course, that there now awaits him the garland of righteousness; and I wrote, "I do not want a garland of righteousness. I want to be loved, to be talked to, to be appreciated, to be understood. But I am willing to be poured out. I will run. I will finish the course."

As I hinted, what strikes me now as I read the way people's testimony to their experience in Scripture was interacting with my experience is that Scripture was indeed giving me means of articulating my experience, but all the time it did not confine itself to doing that. It was moving me on, not just mirroring where I stood. Here were people who had been where I was and therefore had authority to say things to draw me on, which (on reflection) is what one might expect.

When I did this analysis of my notebook, I expected the way Scripture gives its testimony and shares its prayers to be prominent. I was surprised at the second function I found running through what I'd written, which was Scripture directly being confrontational, demanding.

"The person who wants to come after me must deny self and take up their cross and follow me," we read one day early on. My loss was not my cross in the strict sense, but there is something a little like taking up the cross in what you do with painful experiences rather than giving in to self-pity. "Reckon others better than yourselves; look to each other's interests," we read in Philippians 2. There are times when you have to give way to someone else. I have rights, but I do not have the right to claim them, we read in 1 Corinthians. My rights lie in the gospel, not in anything else I am entitled to claim. While there was an element of confrontation in the way scriptural testimony sought to draw me on, there is a more explicit element of confrontation in passages such as these. In our situations of need God does not simply say, "There, there," does not merely exercise accurate empathy. God challenges us about moral issues, about the stance we take to these situations. In a strange way that is part of the good news. "God's judgments are in all the earth; he confirmed it to Jacob as a statute," I noted in Psalm 105. In relation to our destiny, what we call God's law is good news, it is promise. Israel never saw the law as a burden. It was a delight; it was a wonderful gift of God.

Less surprising was the third role: I found Scripture fulfilling. It was telling me stories with an implicit promise. That was not surprising; I have already noted that the most prominent feature in Scripture is story. Much of the material in my journal comes from October and November, the weeks leading up to Advent and Christmas. At the beginning of the church year, we read the Abraham and Sarah narrative, and that is the kind of story that is in Scripture to offer implicit promise to us. Genesis 15 is where God affirms the promise that there will be a future, and I wrote: "There will be unpredictable grace for me in fulfillment of God's promise, and I have to trust. If it was predictable [if I could see how it could work out], it wouldn't be unpredictable [it wouldn't have the characteristic nature of promise, of being something that surprises you when it comes true]. I can't see how the future can work out happily—[but] that's why there has to be trust [the kind of trust Abraham had to show, which led God to approve of him]." I still find this paradox difficult but important. I cannot see how the future can work out in a way that honors what had come before, but if I could, it would cease to have to be a matter of trust.

Two weeks later we reached Genesis 22, Abraham's offering of Isaac, and I wrote about "holding the most precious thing[s] on an open hand before God. God doesn't take them away without restoring them in some way." But I still do not know what that means. Later those stories became linked in my mind with Jesus' silly remark about the girl who was not dead, just asleep. What looks like the end may not be the end.

Of course there is an ambiguity about our relationship to stories about the past. When we got into Advent, the lectionary moved on to Isaiah 40–66, and I noted the verse that Gerhard von Rad puts at the front of the second volume of his *Old Testament Theology*: "Stop brooding over days gone by: I am going to do something new."[4] In the new year when we read John 2 one Sunday after Epiphany, I noticed the marvelous comment about Jesus keeping the best wine till the end. Scriptural stories contain implicit promises for the future.

There were two other ways in which I found Scripture ministered to me. Scripture was a way of looking at what goes on, something that gave me new perspectives. At the end of the old church year we read Ecclesiastes, and I made a note of the passage about there being a time for this and a time for that, about accepting changes of the time, about accepting what is possible. Alongside Ecclesiastes the same morning we read Paul declaring that as far as he was concerned life was Christ, and that if he

4. (Edinburgh: Oliver and Boyd; New York: Harper, 1965), 1.

was to go on living in the body there was fruitful work for him to do. So, I noted, there was no reason to balk at actual loss or the prospect of loss, because there would still be fruitful work to do. Passages like that were another way of God's being confrontational, but they were doing so by inviting me to look at the whole situation in different ways, giving me new perspectives.

In addition, Scripture often reminded me of facts about God. I wrote out much of Psalm 46 one morning, about God being a refuge and strength, and accessible help, and about there being a river whose streams make glad. I also wrote down Matthew 10:29, I suspect when Professor David Ford memorably preached on it after his wife had had a stillborn child. It tells how no sparrow falls to the ground "without your Father": not so much that your Father wills it, causes it, or plans it, but that your Father knows it and determines to get a grip on it, to do something creative with it and with its consequences, and somehow to bring new life out of death.

In due course I stopped writing verses down in my notebook. The process of inner healing that God built into our minds and bodies was taking place, and the pain of loss came to be mostly memory. Indeed, I have heard that when a fracture heals, the join is actually stronger than the bone around it, so that if you break that limb again it will be at a different place. I know that in several senses the place of that healing is one that is less vulnerable than it was before, when I did not even know it was vulnerable. I would still say that the pain of loss is "*mostly* memory," because when you touch a scar you commonly still feel something there. Jacob always limped, after someone insisted on wrestling with him. Indeed, one would not want the loss to have gone completely from memory, because that would be to forget the thing one lost and to stop valuing it. But the pain is nearly all gone. The irony then is that the pain therefore no longer drives me to God. It stopped driving me to Scripture, desperate to hear God speak to me through it. The stimulus that drove me in my helplessness to Scripture was no longer there.

Having realized all that in connection with doing this analysis of my little red book, however, once or twice I have again come to Scripture with expectancy and openness, despite the fact that I am not feeling especially bereaved, and I have found it has the same power to speak. So it still invites me into two forms of openness to Scripture. On a regular basis it sets the agenda as I listen to its story, its priorities, its nightmare and vision, and its testimony; it wants to shape me. And it invites me, as I need, to come to it as who I am, with my agenda, and to let it respond to me with its testimony, its confrontation, its stories with implicit promises, its new perspectives on my agenda items, its reminders of the facts about God.

7

How Should We
Read Scripture in Church?

Canon and Lection

The Episcopal or Anglican Church, the Roman Catholic Church, the Lutheran churches, and many Reformed churches govern the reading of Scripture on Sundays and on weekdays by a lectionary, a list of passages that all churches will be reading.[1] Traditionally, each denomination had its own lectionary, but in the late twentieth century "common lectionaries" became, well, common. So did revising them. Revising the lectionary could seem an esoteric and marginal enterprise until one takes account of the fact that to many ordinary church members, lectionaries "are 'the Bible.' "[2] Choosing material for reading means omitting other material, and that "makes a lectionary no less than a new canon."[3] If that is so, lectionaries really matter. Theologically, then, what should we expect of a lectionary? Behind that question stands another. What is the place of Scripture in worship? In considering that question, I comment on two lectionaries produced in the 1970s to 1990s. One was devised by the Joint Liturgical Group (representing British and Irish Protestant denominations) and appears in the Church of Scotland's *Book of Common Order* (1979) and the Church of England's *Alternative Service Book* (1980). The other is the

---

1. First published in *To Glorify God: Essays on Modern Reformed Liturgy* (ed. Bryan D. Spinks and Iain R. Torrance; Edinburgh: T&T Clark; Grand Rapids: Eerdmans, 1999), 85–97.
2. J. Reumann, "A History of Lectionaries," *Int* 31 (1977): 116–30 (see 116).
3. G. S. Sloyan, "The Lectionary as a Context for Interpretation," *Int* 31 (1977): 131–38 (see 131).

Revised Common Lectionary[4] included in the *Book of Common Worship* (1993) of the Presbyterian Church (USA) and in the Church of Scotland's *Common Order* (1994).

1. Scripture and Lectionary

Scripture and lectionary form overlapping, though not concentric, circles. On one hand, use in worship will have been one cause and one result of material becoming Scripture, though we cannot say that worship was the invariable matrix of the canon or that everything that came to be Scripture was used in worship. On the other, Scripture has had a prominent place in much Christian worship, but never an exclusive one.

The early history of the lectionary is controverted.[5] For all the abundance of imaginative and attractive theories, we are not sure how Scripture was read in pre-Christian Judaism or in the Judaism of Jesus' day, or whether the church took on a Jewish lectionary system, or whether there was a link between the production of some early Christian documents and Jewish lectionaries or their being read in worship. The very nature of Christian faith would make it unsurprising if the development of lectionaries, like that of canons and creeds, belonged to a second rather than an initial stage in its story. At the beginning, "biblical faith . . . was not in its own nature a scriptural religion."[6] The first Christians were close to the gospel events and their witnesses, and they neither needed nor possessed Gospels. Yet the very character of that faith made it natural that Christian faith became a biblical faith, precisely to keep in touch with those gospel events and the people who first witnessed to them. It was also natural that Christian worship became lectionary-based. Underlying the development of the Bible's place in Christian worship there were thus theological factors concerning matters such as the nature of that faith and its intrinsic relationship to events of the first century, and arguments about the propriety of different lectionaries have to be conducted on theological rather than historical grounds. It was been said that "a new lectionary will inevitably be shaped by the two factors of tradition and contemporary need."[7] It will inevitably also be shaped by politics. It needs to be shaped by theological principle, too.

The Christian Scriptures are a fuzzy-edged double collection of writings that emerged from the history of Israel, the early history of Judaism, the opening decades of the Christian movement, and the early centuries of catholic Christianity, a collection that by and large subsequent Christian churches have felt committed

4. Consultation on Common Texts, *The Revised Common Lectionary* (Nashville: Abingdon, 1992).

5. See, e.g., J. A. Lamb, "The Place of the Bible in the Liturgy," in *From the Beginnings to Jerome* (ed. P. R. Ackroyd and C. F. Evans; vol. 1 of *The Cambridge History of the Bible*; Cambridge and New York: Cambridge University Press, 1970), 563–86.

6. James Barr, *Holy Scripture: Canon, Authority, Criticism* (Oxford: Oxford University Press; Philadelphia: Westminster Press, 1983), 1.

7. Martin Dudley, "The Lectionary," in *Towards Liturgy 2000* (ed. M. Perham; London: SPCK, 1989), 35–42 (41).

to. These Scriptures are those churches' resource and norm for their understanding of the gospel and of the life that expresses the gospel. Their use in worship is one reflection of that commitment. Thus use in worship extends beyond their place in lectionaries; it appears, for instance, in their influence on the content of set and extempore prayers. But their place in lectionaries represents the churches' systematic formal acceptance of that commitment. The reading of the Scriptures in worship, and the manner and extent of that reading, fulfills a role in the realm of symbol as well as in terms of specific content. It indicates a recognition that Christian faith is determined not by what we think today but by what happened back then.

What might therefore be expected to characterize the Bible's place in lectionaries? Characteristically, a lectionary covers the Scriptures systematically if selectively, and it does so by providing two, three, or four readings for each service. One feature of the Scriptures of which this is a sign is that these Scriptures are characterized by various forms of diversity, of which the plural "Scriptures" is also a sign. A multiplicity of readings has more prospect of doing justice to that diversity. A lectionary might thus be expected to aim to make the most of its potential to harness and do justice to the Scriptures' diversities.

First, there is the twofold nature of the Testaments that comprise them. The Christian faith is a gospel centering on the Christ event; the Scriptures come from before Christ and after Christ. If Justin's depiction of the church reading from the apostles and prophets[8] refers to reading from Christian writings and from the Jewish Scriptures, this will evidence that the twofoldness of the Scriptures has been reflected in the church's liturgy from an early period.

Second, there is their manifold form. They constitute (for instance) history or story, moral instruction, reflection on human problems and experience, resources for praise and prayer, and declarations regarding the promised or threatened future. These communicate in different ways and communicate different content.

Third, there are differing balances and emphases within these genres. The history and story are concerned with what God has done and with what human beings have done. The instruction concerns the obligations of nation, church, family, and individual. The reflection balances conviction and doubt. The praise and prayer balance confidence and protest. The prophecy balances nightmares and visions.

Fourth, there is the combination of more than one form of witness to events and reflection on them. There are two accounts of the story of Israel during the monarchy in Samuel-Kings and Chronicles, and more than one account of many of the stories concerning Israel's origins incorporated into the preceding books beginning with Genesis. There is the synoptic presentation of the story of Jesus in Matthew, Mark, and Luke and the distinctive presentation of John. There is the earlier witness of Mark and Paul and the later reflection of Matthew, Luke, John, and other Epistles.

8. *First Apology* 67.

How are things with lectionaries? I was brought up as a Christian with split ecclesial loyalties. First thing on Sunday mornings I attended a Prayer Book Communion at my parish church, where the two readings came from the New Testament Epistles and Gospels. The centrality of the Gospel reading was signaled by the fact that we stood for it. I guess there would have been a brief homily, probably on the Gospel, though I confess I do not remember. Later on Sunday morning and in the early afternoon I sang in an Anglican cathedral choir during Morning and Evening Prayer. There a prominent place was given to the systematic singing of the Psalms and to the reading of set passages from both Testaments. The sermon would likely allude to these readings, though I think the preachers would in general grant that the greater prominence of the reading of the Scriptures in the service was paradoxically matched by a greater independence over against the specific content of the Scriptures in the preaching. On Sunday evenings I attended an independent church where each service gave a prominent place to one reading from the Scriptures, often working sequentially through a book chosen by the minister. This reading then provided the raw material for the sermon. There was no doubt that the Scriptures mattered in this liturgy, though I realize with hindsight that the reading of them was subject to ministerial whim and the whim of ecclesial tradition.

I write, then, as someone especially aware of the positive potential of the lectionary principle because of my background in a church that did not use a lectionary (and with that awareness reinforced by my periodic contemporary experiences of churches that do not use a lectionary, including the many flourishing Church of England parishes that ignore the lectionary). I also write as an Anglican who lived through much of the revision of the Church of England's calendar and lectionary in the context of the broader revision of its forms of worship and the more far-reaching revolution represented by the triumph of the parish communion movement, the abandonment of twice-a-Sunday worship for once-a-Sunday worship, and the burgeoning growth of all-age/family worship that avoids being liturgical in the traditional sense. In addition, I write as someone whose parish church in inner-city Nottingham in England happened to be one that was asked to road-test the Revised Common Lectionary (RCL) as part of the Church of England's asking itself whether it wished to adopt it.

2. The Two-Year Lectionary

The Church of Scotland's *Book of Common Order* (1979) included the two-year lectionary developed in the 1960s by the Joint Liturgical Group (henceforth I refer to both the group and its lectionary as JLG). With its revision of the calendar it was accepted by a number of other British denominations as well as appearing in the Church of England's *Alternative Service Book 1980*. In the way just noted, in the Church of England Holy Communion had become the main service and most people go to church only once. Whatever is read at Holy Communion therefore constitutes the church's Scriptures for them. The creative developments of the JLG lectionary were therefore of great importance.

The finest of these was associated with a revision of the liturgical calendar whereby the church's year effectively began five weeks before Advent with a season recalling creation and the story of Israel, leading neatly into the Advent season itself. The church thus lived, read, and thought through the story of creation and salvation over the nine Sundays before Christmas, beginning with Genesis and working through the outline of the story up to Christ. This draws our attention to that meta-narrative as a whole and also gives us a "creation Sunday" counterbalancing the focus on salvation history that otherwise dominates the calendar. Jürgen Moltmann called for the introduction of such a feature into the liturgical year in the context of his call for an "ecological theology." He issued this call at the end of a century that had brought about and was beginning to witness a monumental act of de-creation, the catastrophic destruction of nature itself, of our and God's home in the world.[9] JLG had already generated that creation Sunday at the beginning of the church's year, with the First Testament providing the "control" lection in the period that follows.

Given that the Church of Scotland was subsequently the first British church formally to abandon JLG in *Common Order*, it is an irony that this creation season was a gift of the Church of Scotland to the broader church.[10] From 1948, A. A. McArthur experimented with this modification of the church's year so that it celebrated more of the Christian faith and qualified the extent to which the church's year is primarily a christological cycle. In the 1960s, the Anglican Bishop of Knaresborough, Henry de Candole, developed the proposal into the pre-Advent structure taken up into JLG and adopted by the 1979 Scottish book and the 1980 English book.[11]

JLG had its problems; its treatment of the First Testament has been faulted, its treatment of the long Pentecost season leaves it disjointed, and its thematic approach is half-hearted. Nevertheless it is regrettable that JLG's strong features came to be compromised by the results of liturgical revision in Britain in resources such as *Promise of His Glory*[12] (which ignored JLG's principles) and then to be formally abandoned.

Liturgists had found JLG untraditional, unkerygmatic, unchristological, and unecumenical. To the first objection one might suggest that innovation should not in itself be seen as a fault. In any case, the history of the church reveals great variation in the calendar and lectionary. They neither emerged laid down from the beginning, nor developed consistently and coherently over the centuries.[13] Nine Sundays before Christmas was a British innovation, but historically a defensible one given the absence of a universal tradition regarding the length and nature of the Advent season.[14]

9. "The Destruction and Liberation of Nature: Towards an Ecological Theology" (lecture at St. John's Theological College, Nottingham, October 1995).

10. For what follows, see, e.g., T. J. Talley, "The Year of Grace," in *The Identity of Anglican Worship* (ed. Kenneth Stevenson and Bryan D. Spinks; London: Mowbray, 1991), 27–35.

11. "Can We Rationalize the Christian Year?" *Theology* 63 (1960): 486–90 (see 488).

12. (London: Church House Publishing/Mowbray, 1991).

13. As Dudley notes, "The Lectionary," 35–42 (see 39); cf. G. S. Sloyan, "Some Suggestions for a Biblical Three-Year Lectionary," *Worship* 63 (1989): 521–35 (see 523–27).

14. See Bryan D. Spinks, "Revising the Advent-Christmas-Epiphany Cycle in the Church of England," *Studia Liturgica* 17 (1987): 166–75 (see 171–73). But Spinks does not enthuse over "Nine Sundays before Christmas."

To the second one might first respond that the story from creation to the coming of Christ might surely be seen as kerygmatic. One might also respond by asking what is so wrong with being didactic as well as kerygmatic. Indeed, there is a fundamental point of substance here.

The Reformation led to the development of different attitudes to the reading of Scripture. In the radical reformation and the free churches, lectionaries were abandoned. Within the Church of England, the *Book of Common Prayer* provided a scheme of Sunday worship involving Holy Communion, Morning Prayer, and Evening Prayer. It thus contains three lectionaries. The first follows a millennium's Western practice in providing simply Epistles and Gospels. The second and third provide First Testament and New Testament lessons working through each part of the Scriptures.[15] The Psalter was also to be said or sung systematically. Cranmer's vision was of people going to all three services on Sunday as well as attending Morning and Evening Prayer during the week. In the event, the chief Sunday services became Morning and Evening Prayer. Thus whereas the normal Scripture diet in the Roman Catholic Church continued to be the epistle and gospel, in the Anglican church it was lections from each Testament that people heard read. This happened to implement even better the Cranmerian doctrine of the place of the First Testament and New Testament Scriptures and the Cranmerian vision of a teaching church.

The fact that Cranmer's plan was unrealistic, or at least unrealized, should not be allowed to obscure the force of its theology and its vision. The flourishing of the Parish Communion movement and the move to once-a-Sunday worship have meant the revolutionary move that the reading (and preaching) of the Scriptures at the Eucharist are the only reading now shared by the congregation as a whole. The Eucharist has to bear a heavier burden than it once might have done. It cannot continue to be christomonist rather than trinitarian or kerygmatic to the exclusion of teaching.

Underlying the third objection is the conviction expressed in the Episcopal Church in the USA when it decided to follow the three-year lectionary rather than JLG that "the Church Year is a Christian Year, an epitome of the Christian era, the 'time of Christ' between his two advents." It is not a "chronological review of the whole of salvation-history."[16] To put the response to objection two in another way, what distinguishes JLG at this point is not that it is inherently unkerygmatic but that it has a broader understanding of the kerygma, an understanding that is more trinitarian and less christomonist. It is theocentric rather than christocentric.

The fundamental underlying point of substance here again relates to the fact that the three-year lectionary is in its origin and nature explicitly a eucharistic one. J. Reumann observes that there is a vital difference between a lectionary created for

15. Strictly, the *Book of Common Prayer* provides a daily lectionary that does that; a "table of proper lessons" provides alternative First Testament provision for Sundays and holy days, working more selectively through the First Testament as a whole.

16. See the quotation from *The Church Year* (New York: The Church Hymnal Corporation, 1970), 10, in Talley, "The Year of Grace," 31.

a service of the word and a Eucharist.[17] The three-year lectionary is by its nature a eucharistic lectionary.

Its basic nature goes back to its origins. The eucharistic lectionary has naturally focused on the gospel events and thus on the Gospels and the Epistles. If the First Testament features, it does so in such a way as to lead into the Gospel in some sense, in keeping with the service's agenda. It might do so by relating the prophecy of which the Gospel relates the fulfillment, or the old standard that is replaced by the revolutionary new standard of the gospel, or the type of which the gospel brings the antitype, or the partial revelation of which the gospel brings a fuller revelation, or some piece of background or context, or a metaphoric parallel.[18] Whichever it is, the agenda is set by the issues the Gospel raises, and the First Testament reading adds nothing; perhaps it was precisely this prophetic/typological hermeneutic that led to the dropping of First Testament lections from the Western lectionary.[19] It was a strength of JLG that it reversed this momentum.

A fourth objection to JLG, that it was unecumenical, may seem a strange one, because its production was arguably more inherently ecumenical than the one that produced RCL; perhaps "unecumenical" is code for "not involving the Roman Catholic Church." But ecumenicity is a desideratum that would have to be weighed against other desiderata. It is a commonplace that we do not want ecumenism to mean the acceptance of a gray lowest common denominator; I am not clear that British ecumenically-minded liturgists faced the cost of replacing JLG with its assets by RCL with its snags. No doubt one would pay the price if the other gains were significant; but I am in any case unclear why a common lectionary is reckoned to be a good idea. There must be more to it than the facilitating of attempts by local clergy in the United States to meet together for sermon planning.[20] And in any case, the amount of permitted variation in RCL surely means that the notion of a common lectionary with its advantages has died the death of a thousand qualifications.

3. The Three-Year Lectionary

JLG represents one of the two streams of lectionary revision that developed in the 1960s. A nourishing fruit of Vatican II was a desire to rework the use of Scripture in the Eucharist; it was this that led to the three-year lectionary family to which RCL belongs, on which most recent work has been done in North America (twelve of the

17. Reumann, "A History of Lectionaries," 117.

18. See G. Ramshaw, "The First Testament in Christian Lectionaries," *Worship* 64 (1990): 494–510 (see 503–10), and the comments of L. H. Stookey with particular reference to forms of typology, "Marcion, Typology, and Lectionary Preaching," *Worship* 66 (1992): 251–62.

19. See R. Boon, "Bringing the Old Testament to Its Legitimate Place and Function in the Church's Liturgical Reading of the Scriptures," *Studia Liturgica* 17 (1987): 19–25 (see 20, 25). But Sloyan wonders if the influx of pagans into the church was rather the key factor in the dropping of First Testament lections: see "Some Suggestions for a Biblical Three-Year Lectionary," 527.

20. RCL, 75; cf. 10.

fourteen members of the task force that produced RCL are from the United States and Canada). In the process of its revision, the task force was especially concerned to be sensitive about questions of racism and anti-Semitism and to respond to criticism from liberation and feminist perspectives (though in connection with the material on women it is still possible to point to a number of coins that remain lost; one is surprised to find John 8:1–11 and 16:16–33 missing).[21]

RCL's great strength and great weakness is that it "accepts the cornerstone of the Roman lectionary," the semi-continuous reading of the three Synoptic Gospels over a three-year period.[22] The term "semi-continuous" denotes a lectionary that prescribes readings coming sequentially from Scripture but that is selective in that it omits some or many sections; it thus contrasts with continuous reading such as the synagogue's reading right through the Torah and with the eclectic prescription that characterizes JLG. As I write, the past year has been "the year of Luke" and the coming year will be "the year of Matthew." I asked some people at church whether they had noticed that the Gospel readings for the past year had worked through one Gospel, and they had not, but I am still prepared to believe that in principle such reading is A Good Thing.

Our congregation's reaction may illustrate further how contextual features affect one's reaction to lectionary reform, because we had been reading Luke over the summer holiday period. I recall a conversation with an Australian Anglican priest. For her, the continuity through the Sundays after Pentecost was a great asset because in the southern hemisphere that is ordinary time, whereas for me the discontinuity of JLG was no great disadvantage because that is holiday time and many people go away for some time during the period.

Nevertheless RCL's cornerstone raises a number of questions. For instance, why should the three Synoptic Gospels become the canon within the canon? They have a history of being so within the Roman Catholic Church, as is illustrated by the rich development of Ignatian meditation that has paralleled the process of lectionary revision. They have traditionally had this position in the Church of England's eucharistic lectionary. But the Church of England also has a Morning and Evening Prayer lectionary with a different dynamic, and it has arguably been more important historically because these were the services to which most people went. While JLG was ecumenical from the beginning, RCL is thus a scheme that bears the marks of its Roman Catholic origin. Why should other churches take over its principle? Within the evangelical tradition, John has been the favorite Gospel (as it is for JLG), though Romans has been the key New Testament book. Why should the Synoptics have priority over these? The assumption that might have been made in the 1960s was that the Synoptics were more or less the historical Jesus while John was pure theology, but both aspects of that antithesis are false. The Synoptics have their theology; John

---

21. See C. J. Schlueter, "The Gender Balance of Texts from the Gospels in the Revised Common Lectionary and the *Lutheran Book of Worship*," *Currents in Theology and Mission* 20 (1993): 177–86.
22. RCL, 13.

has its history. The fact that the first three Gospels are "synoptic," broadly looking at Jesus from a similar angle, surely suggests that if we are to have a three-year lectionary, John should feature through one of the three years.

The more radical question is Why should a Gospel always control the lectionary? Why could (say) Romans not do so? In many nonliturgical/nonlectionary Protestant churches, Romans has probably had a more prominent place in reading and preaching than any Gospel. Why not? Once again, one recalls that it is not the case that the Gospels are straight history rather than later theological reflection. They are themselves narrative theological reflection, and they come from a significantly later period than a number of the Epistles.

The difficulty with RCL's use of the Synoptic Gospels is not merely that they feature so prominently in the lectionary. It is that they largely control what other parts of Scripture are read and how they are read. This is especially so with the First Testament. Its typological approach to the First Testament has been a standard critique of the three-year lectionary. RCL is pleased with what it has achieved in the process of developing the earlier versions of the three-year lectionary. It questions the typological or prophetic approach and the practice of simply omitting the First Testament, as many Western eucharistic lectionaries did, and does not want the First Testament lection to be apparently unlinked to Christian belief and prayer. (There may be a fallacy here, and if so it is a telling one. If we start from the assumption that First Testament is part of Christian belief and prayer, why is there a problem?) It allows for some optional semi-continuous reading of the First Testament broadly related to the Gospel, during the weeks after Pentecost, but it does not discuss the possibility of making the First Testament the controlling lesson for part of the year. RCL worked hard to meet criticisms of the Roman lectionary's handling of the First Testament, but it did not go nearly far enough. There is still "a kind of nervousness throughout the Lectionary that not every problem raised by the Hebrew Scriptures may be seen as solved by the incarnation, death and resurrection of Jesus Christ."[23] Not only does RCL generally use the First Testament as illustration for the Gospel. From Easter to Pentecost even the first reading comes from the New Testament, and we have three New Testament lessons, Acts becoming the control reading (which in itself is reasonable enough). There is no season when the First Testament provides the control reading.

One factor that caused our congregation to be bemused by RCL was the length of its readings, or more often their shortness. Among liturgists, one of the critiques of the JLG readings is that they are too long. I presume the critique refers to their total length, since I have the impression that they average only nine or ten verses and rarely go below six or above thirteen. In RCL, the readings are often either shorter or longer. Two Sundays away from when I write, the First Testament lection is Malachi 4:1–2a; blink and you have missed it. Conversely, our congregation was restive about the length of some Gospel readings.

---

23. Sloyan, "The Lectionary as a Context for Interpretation," 137.

RCL's own positive principles prevent its dealing with the place of the First Testament in an ultimately satisfactory way. The principle that underlies the prioritizing of the Gospels is that "it is the paschal mystery of the saving death and resurrection of the Lord Jesus that is proclaimed through the lectionary readings and the preaching of the Church."[24] The theological framework I outlined in the opening part of this chapter indicates the weakness of that statement from a Reformed or Anglican perspective. It is the lectionary's task to reflect the nature of Scripture, and Scripture has more than the paschal mystery of the saving death and resurrection of the Lord Jesus, even though that lies at its heart. A fundamental underlying point of substance here again relates to the fact that the three-year lectionary is, in its origin and nature, explicitly a eucharistic one. RCL has adapted it partly in order to make it more suitable for a service of the Word, not least by the provision of the optional semi-continuous First Testament readings.[25] But it has not changed its basic nature. One could imagine a scenario in which RCL provided the readings for eucharistic celebration but in which it was accompanied by other more broadly-based provision for other services. But we hit against that fact that nowadays for most people the "principal" service is the only service.

Making the Gospels the canon within the canon serves to make it impossible to hear anything that does not come in the Gospels. RCL's use of the Psalms provides a spectacular example. It describes the set psalm as "a congregational response and meditation on the first reading" that as such is not intended as another reading.[26] The first reading (usually but not universally from the First Testament) is itself of course usually chosen to link with the Gospel. So the Psalms can never bring their own agenda. It is surprising that RCL says that the lectionary seeks to "respect the breadth and diversity of the psalter" while acknowledging that "the more familiar psalms are repeated occasionally."[27] On its own principles it could not be seeking to respect the Psalter's breadth and diversity if it is at the same time letting the choice of psalms be determined by the first and thus generally by the Gospel reading.

What happens in practice is this. In RCL about 105 psalms appear in whole or in part spread over about 352 occasions. Thus on average each psalm that does appear does so more than three times. Of the forty or so psalms that never appear, at least thirty-two are lament or protest psalms. Now these are a form of prayer that occupies about half the Psalter, so nearly half of them never appear. In other words, the Psalter as a whole puts onto the lips of the people of God three chief ways of speaking to God (praise or worship, confession or thanksgiving, and lament or protest) and implies by its proportioning that the last of these is particularly important. RCL ignores this datum and follows the church's customary focus (shared by JLG, indeed) on the kind of psalm with which the church has been more comfortable, ignoring the awareness that has grown over a number of years that the Psalter knew what it was

24. RCL, 12.
25. Ibid., 15.
26. Ibid., 11.
27. Ibid., 77.

doing when it invited the people of God to spend much time expressing to God their grief, hurt, anger, pain, and loneliness, so that it can be ministered to and responded to.[28] In a parallel way, passages from Job appear six times in the Sunday lectionary. Only two come from the protests of Job that dominate the book, and of these one is Job 19:23–27a, the famous "I know that my redeemer lives" passage, chosen to parallel the Gospel for the day with its hopefulness (Luke 20:27–38) and carefully demarcated down to the half-verse in such a way as to exclude the expressions of pain and uncertainty that are integral to it in its context.

Using RCL has made me more aware that as a preacher I had become a bit bored with the JLG lectionary; or at least, I was delighted to have some new passages surfacing. In addition, while I personally have always felt free to ignore the alleged theme that the *Alternative Service Book* told me ran through the lections (I understand it was quite intentional that finding the page where the themes were listed was somewhat difficult, because the idea was that neither preachers nor the Scriptures themselves should be constrained by these), I understand that many preachers who were used to this thematic principle were put into a state of panic about a set of lections that lacks a theme. In itself this seems a good reason to abandon themes. On the other hand, in our urban congregation another cause of bemusedness about RCL was its abjuring of themes (most of our congregation has come into the church since 1980, when themes became normal in the Church of England's lectionary).

A subsequent Anglican liturgical volume, *Patterns for Worship*,[29] included some discussion of "the Bible-reading part of our worship" that, as well as noting that many churches do not use the official lectionary provision, comments on "a reluctance to use the Old Testament, even in the Advent to Christmas period when it is the controlling reading." It suggested that "the importance of 'story' should be allowed to have an effect on the way the lectionary is constructed" but then observes "glaring omissions" in the JLG Sunday lectionary of stories, such as Lot, Hagar, Ishmael, Isaac, Joseph, Moses in the bulrushes, the spies in Canaan, the fall of Jericho, Achan, Deborah, Barak, and Samson, as well as Gospel stories such as Mary and Martha, the man born blind, Jesus calming the storm, Legion, the pool of Bethesda, and the story of the rich fool. In general, JLG has been characterized as insufficiently attentive to narrative and therefore less concrete and less accessible than it might have been.[30]

A three-year lectionary obviously has the capacity to do justice to a wider range of Scriptures than a two-year one. It is then a surprise to find that, granted its famous scope to read sequentially through three Gospels, the use of the Psalms is not the only instance of ways in which we are actually deprived. In keeping with Christian tradition, Genesis does better than other narrative books, but we never read God's words of judgment on Adam and Eve in Genesis 3:16–24 or the story of Cain and Abel or most of those First Testament stories that *Patterns for Worship*

28. See G. Ramshaw, "The Place of Lament within Praise," *Worship* 61 (1987): 317–22.
29. (London: Church House Publishing, 1995), 6–10.
30. Dudley, "The Lectionary," 39–40.

misses from JLG. We read Genesis 1 on a Sunday only once every three years (on Trinity Sunday). Genesis thought that a patriarch's passing of his wife as his sister was so important that it tells such a story three times, and a feminist psychoanalytic interpretation offers an intriguing suggestion as to the reasons;[31] RCL includes none of them. It includes not one passage from Chronicles and no stories about Daniel. "The Lectionary is all but silent on the marvel of creation and the paradox of the grandeur and wretchedness of human life" (e.g., Psalms, Job, and Gen 1).[32] JLG also fails at a number of such points, but it could be reworked so as to meet the points within the terms of its own principles; RCL could not.

Bryan Spinks faulted JLG for focusing on God's goodness and avoiding God's severity in its readings from a book such as Isaiah.[33] Among passages Spinks points to, Isaiah 1:12–17 and 5:1–7 appear in RCL; Isaiah 1:2–9; 2:12–22; 3:16–26 do not (the last might now draw the ire of those who found sexism in the predecessors of RCL). Five passages from Amos 6–8 broaden out the one passage from Amos in the JLG lectionary. So RCL may be less inclined to offer false comfort and reassurance to modern society. But the prophets were concerned about the affairs of the nations and gave much space to declaring God's will regarding the peoples and international events of their day (e.g., Isa 13–23; Jer 46–51; Ezek 25–32). Not one of these passages appears. The encouraging side to the prophets still dominates, and specifically the passages that could be reckoned most explicitly to "point to" the New Testament. Isaiah is said to be read "intensively" in Advent in such a way as to allow it to "contextualize" itself.[34] What this means is that we read Isaiah 2:1–5; 11:1–10; 35:1–10; 7:10–16 (Year A); 64:1–9; 40:1–11; 61:1–4, 8–11 (Year B). These are not a cross section of readings from Isaiah that can "contextualize themselves." They could not be, because the choice of them is subordinated to themes from the Gospel reading. (Elsewhere, Isa 6:1–8 still appears cut off from that of which it is the introduction.) G. S. Sloyan observed with regard to the various forms of the three-year lectionary as they existed in the 1970s, "If we assume that one of their major intents is to give Christian hearers a feel for the whole Bible, we must declare their plan a failure."[35] The supporters of RCL would hardly agree that this was or should be one of their major intents. Whereas the lectionary for the principal service each Sunday should seek to reflect Scripture as a whole, RCL does not attempt to do so. We need a lectionary that does this by combining some of its strengths with some of those of JLG.

31. See J. Cheryl Exum, "Who's Afraid of 'The Endangered Ancestress,'" in *Fragmented Women* (Sheffield: Sheffield Academic Press, 1993), 148–69.

32. Sloyan, "The Lectionary as a Context for Interpretation," 137.

33. "Christian Worship or Cultural Incantations?" *Studia Liturgica* 12 (1977): 1–19 (see 6–7).

34. RCL, 15.

35. "The Lectionary as a Context for Interpretation," 138.

8

How Might Preaching Be Scriptural?

In his 1877 *Lectures on Preaching*, which remains one of the best books on the subject, Phillips Brooks remarked that "preaching in every age follows, to a certain extent, the changes which come to all literature and life."[1] I can see this as I reflect on changes that have come about (and need to come about) in my own preaching over the years, in subconscious conformity to Brooks's dictum.

1. Experiential

Our methods of communication might be expected to profit from reflecting Scripture's own methods.[2] While it is particularly obvious and significant that Scripture communicates by means of story and specifically of parable as well as by direct address, this is not the end of the insight to be gained from a consideration of the methods God has used in communicating with us. The great block of Scripture that differs from either of these is the Psalms. In the address of Torah, prophecy, or epistle, God or God's agents speak to us directly, and they have provided the dominant mode for preaching over the centuries. In contrast, in the story in Scripture human beings speak to each other, tell each other the gospel story, God's story, and we listen in on their storytelling and story-hearing; this suggests a model for preaching.[3] In

---

1. Phillips Brooks, *Lectures on Preaching* (repr.; New York: Dutton, 1902), 20. This chapter was first published in *Anvil* 14 (1997): 87–94.
2. I sought to work out the implications of this conviction in *Models for Interpretation of Scripture* (Grand Rapids: Eerdmans; Carlisle: Paternoster, 1995; Toronto: Clements, 2004).
3. So Fred B. Craddock, *Overhearing the Gospel* (Nashville: Abingdon, 1978).

psalmody, human beings speak to God, and with characteristic paradox and self-effacement God lets their speech about themselves, their experience, their needs, their awarenesses, and their blessings do as a guide to God's nature and God's ways of dealing with us. This feature of Scripture is not quite confined to the Psalms; it appears in prophets such as Hosea and Jeremiah and also in Paul's reflection on his own experience. But the Psalms are the great repository of God's communicating with us by means of having people talk about their experience of the activity of God and the absence of God. Their implication for the nature of preaching is that it can appropriately take the form of address to God that the congregation again "overhears." Having realized this, I have once or twice preached on a psalm by meditating on it Godward out loud, offering God the actual prayers and praises, the questions and the confessions, that emerge for me from this psalm, and inviting the congregation to join me in these prayers or to substitute the ones they need to utter on the basis of this text. I was preaching, but praying, on the basis of the fact that having people do that within Scripture was a way of communicating with us that God had reckoned appropriate.

It is not only in expounding the Psalms that I find myself talking on the basis of experience in the pulpit (the metaphorical pulpit: the liturgical architecture of St. John's Theological College, Nottingham, of All Souls, Radford, Nottingham, and of St. Barnabas, Pasadena, the places I have preached most often over the past thirty years, means that I do not very often enter literal ones). We live in an experience-obsessed age, and this is naturally as much a characteristic of the church as it is of the world. The downside is that experience can be the criterion for judging everything, but the fact that experience has a prominent place in Scripture suggests that we should therefore not merely dismiss stress on experience as of the devil. In Scripture, God gives it a place alongside God's address of us and our overhearing the gospel story.

Thomas Troeger suggests that there is good precedent in the history of preaching for an emphasis on the importance of the preacher's experience, for homiletics since Augustine has stressed the preacher's personal qualities. Traditionally this has been expressed as a requirement for holiness. In the late twentieth or twenty-first century it is personal authenticity that is the measure of homiletical credibility.[4] Of course person and preaching have always interacted. Troeger quotes a poem by C. H. Sisson expressing appreciation to the preacher John Donne for his human extravagance and passions, and asking him to come and speak to the men whom Sisson imagines waiting for their train to London for their important jobs in the city, and tell them God is interested in the vain and the ambitious and the highly sexed. As Brooks again famously put it more than a century ago, preaching is truth through personality.[5] Troeger notes, "A disembodied preacher cannot credibly proclaim the incarnate Christ. . . . No preacher can grab us by the entrails who is not in touch

---

4. "Emerging New Standards in the Evaluation of Effective Preaching," *Worship* 64 (1990): 290–307 (299).

5. *Lectures on Preaching*, 8.

with his or her own fundamental humanity. That is why Sisson says earlier in his poem: 'Bring out your genitals and your theology.'" He adds, "'I will awaken deep experiences in others to the extent that I am able to reach myself.'"[6] "An authentic contemporary homiletics . . . begins at the level of human suffering and the trust and empathy awakened when our pain is recognized by another," and this capacity to own one's own suffering and recognize someone else's is often what communicates the gospel of "Emmanuel, God with us, the identification with human suffering, a willingness to lay aside the prerogatives of transcendence to be fully present with a world in pain."[7]

Troeger suggests that in North America a "homiletic of personal authenticity for the pulpit" is emerging through the impact of women clergy.[8] My limited experience suggests that in Britain women are as inhibited as are men in being themselves in preaching, as in other contexts they seem as reserved as men in owning their feelings, perhaps because we have required them to behave like honorary men. But perhaps the ordination of women to the priesthood might give new impetus both to women and to men toward such authenticity in life, ministry, and preaching.

Obviously my bringing my experience into the pulpit could be for me and my congregation merely an indulgence in self-display or an ecclesial equivalent to the Oprah Winfrey show. Perhaps a criterion for whether it avoids being this is whether it actually facilitates communication between human beings and God via Scripture. The Psalms, the prophets, and Paul are not talking about their experience for its own sake but for the sake of the development of this relationship. And that is presumably in principle what the pulpit is about ("presumably," though a lot of student sermons I have heard seem preoccupied with telling people that they ought to do this or that—a lot more than is proportionate to God's concern with telling people to do this or that, to judge from the Bible).

"One of the reasons people show up on Sunday morning is [an] inarticulate yearning and wishfulness for a lost communion. . . . The task of the preacher is to bring to speech that deep yearning. In that speech the preacher also dares to respond from the other side; to speak for the God who has authorized and evoked the yearning, who yearns as we do for another beginning."[9] In other words, the preacher does what the Psalms do: give voice to the longing plea of people and also to the loving response of God. For "speech is the central act of communion. . . . We may be tempted to distorted, safe speech. Or we may settle for silence, because faithful speech is too risky and requires too much." But if we are reduced to chatter, silence, or platitude in our supposed meeting with God and say less than we know, hurt, or long for, then (as with human relationships) there is no actual meeting.[10]

6. Troeger, "Emerging New Standards," 299–300; the second quotation is from the research on homiletics of H. van der Geest.
7. Troeger, "Emerging New Standards," 305–6.
8. Ibid., 302.
9. Walter Brueggemann, *Finally Comes the Poet* (Minneapolis: Fortress, 1989), 43.
10. Ibid., 44.

"It is speech and only speech that bonds God and human creatures" (you may think that a hyperbole, but it bears thinking about). "The preaching task is to guide people out of [their] alienated silence . . . into a serious, dangerous, subversive, covenantal conversation" such as makes communion possible.[11] In correspondence to the nature of the Psalms, the preacher begins "from below" by voicing the worshipers' hurt, rage, hopelessness, guilt, and need, goes on to mediate that powerful, intervening response of God that the plea urges (but whose actual nature remains free and unpredictable and not necessarily comforting in the way we might have hoped), and then brings this conversation to its consummation in doxology, in responsive praise and celebration.[12]

2. Oral, Interesting, Imaginative

The apparent safeness of platitude is the preacher's common alternative to personal authenticity (did Kierkegaard really say, "God did not become a man in order to make trivial remarks. He had plenty of followers who would do that"?). Rhetoric, furthermore, is the preacher's alternative to conversation. The impossibility of rhetoric is another feature of our day. There are no doubt a number of reasons why rhetoric has become impossible. One has been that it is guilty by association, for until recently it was possible to claim that the only context outside the pulpit in which people came across the preacher's rhetoric was the political speech, and we all know how much notice we take of that. But nowadays even politicians have often abandoned rhetoric. For some years party-political broadcasts have illustrated the point; more recently, speeches at party conferences are even being affected. One of Ronald Reagan's speechwriters explains how he was enabled on television to abandon the elevated station of traditional public speech to become "more personal, narrative and graphic."[13] We might be tempted to despise the development as a piece of manipulation, and rejection of authority is a fundamental feature of postmodernity, but for the preacher at least the development may nevertheless restore to communication something of the nature of the gospel rather than taking away from it, for the gospel itself, after all, is personal, narrative, and graphic.

The story-shapedness of Scripture and of preaching is a familiar theme; the personalness of Scripture and of preaching has been our theme in section 1 above. What of the graphicness of Scripture and of preaching? Reagan's speechwriter ghosted for him as what he was; she thought cinematically. Of course as a mass medium the cinema gave way to television, and the preacher had to think televisually. Now television has given way to You Tube, which extends the challenge.

The written word has also given way to the visual. Traditional Western preaching belonged intrinsically to the Gutenberg era. Sermons worked with the strict linear

11. Ibid., 49.
12. Ibid., 51–77.
13. Troeger, "Emerging New Standards," 290.

rhetoric of the printed word and presupposed people's ability to follow a developing sequential logical argument from introduction through points to conclusion. "The different sections of a discourse are presented as links in a chain, leading the listener irresistibly to an appreciation of the speaker's main ideas. . . . These different sections are not repetitive and they are not interchangeable. Their logical sequence, like the words and sentences that comprise them, rely on the reader's capacity to retain the author's argument without oratorical assistance, and to reflect on his ideas as one might re-read certain passages in books or articles that require further study and thought."[14] The rhetoric of the printed page belongs to the era of Gutenberg that has yielded to the era of James Logie Baird that is itself now passing. Yet in one respect that is a return to something more like the oral culture of biblical times, so that it might facilitate rather than hinder the preaching of Scripture. Oral rhetoric is circular or repetitive or spiral rather than linear.[15]

That is actually the nature of the argument of Romans. While Romans was a written text from the beginning, it was received aurally and was evidently generated by someone who thought orally. Its argument forms a spiral rather than following a neat line. Commentators provide the student with neat accounts of its structure, but they oversimplify the nature of the text. In Romans 3–8, for instance, Paul does not deal with a sequence of different topics but several times discusses the nature of the gospel and of Christian experience from a sequence of perspectives. Oral rhetoric involves constant flashbacks and devices to make it easier for the audience to remember where it has been, and these are characteristic of the epistle. The death of the written word encourages the preacher to recover the obvious but neglected oral nature of preaching that corresponds to the oral nature of Scripture.

The nature of televisual communication makes more radical demands on us. The communication of the Baird and post-Baird era will assume that people are used to pictures, images, and sound effects. They respond to a gestalt, a total experience, an overall ambience of the kind that is created by an audio-visual montage. They expect communication to come at them in sound bites (sometimes now I make one point after the First Testament lection, one after the Epistle, and one after the Gospel). They are accustomed to zapping from one channel to another rather than concentrating devotedly on one channel, and they will be doing so as we preach, switching to programs within their own imagination even though we cannot see them reaching for the remote or checking their emails like students in a class. They no longer follow the preacher like sheep following a shepherd. They are used to magazine programs of the kind that comprise sequences of flashes of news, entertainment, and advertisement rather than exploring a theme. Such programs could seem to be a completely heterogeneous montage linked only by empty spiel, though they do have an underlying agenda, which is to keep people watching. The programmers

14. Bernard Reymond, "Preaching and the New Media," *Modern Churchman* 34, no. 5 (1993): 19–29 (21).
15. Reymond diagrams the rhetoric of orality in "Preaching and the New Media," 20.

know they will not have people's total or sustained or unwavering attention; they will be satisfied to keep them switched to this channel.

An implication of the nature of such televisual communication is that the graphicness of our communication needs to take account of the instinct to zap, so that our preaching will include devices to win people's attention back.[16] We need to ask what is the underlying aim of our communication, the equivalent to getting people to keep watching so that the advertisers or the government will continue to support us. There is no reason why our underlying concern should not be fulfilled in the Baird or internet age; we do need to see the criteria that must be met if we are to achieve this.

The instinct to zap brings out a paradoxical side to televisual communication. Marshall McLuhan described television as a medium of cool communication; it does not involve its audience, in the manner of radio or the theater. Preaching is performance in the manner of the theater rather than that of television. Traditionally it has not much involved the audience, but it has the capacity to do so. When I moved from a suburban church with an elevated pulpit to an urban church with no pulpit, one of the changes it brought to my preaching was to involve the congregation. I asked them nonrhetorical questions and got interesting answers. They contributed to the sermon. They were more like the studio audience than the people at home who are only half-watching. In that context and in the televisual age, communication need not be confined to words or even to words and pictures (I would not now preach on "You are the salt of the earth" without passing round a bag of chips). Preaching has the capacity to be more than graphic.

Television is better at raising questions than closing off answers. It suggests more than it can establish, it stimulates more than reinforces existent convictions, it illustrates more than establishes dogma; it of course engages sense and feeling and not merely logic.[17] This contrasts with the traditional nature of doctrine and preaching but perhaps not with the nature of Scripture itself.

A preacher in the United States has to deal with the gospel's being old hat there. In Britain at least, one might reckon that outside the church this is no longer so; we have the possibility of bringing the gospel to the world as something with the charm of novelty. But within the church, where preaching is actually done and where the gospel first needs to be heard if it is to be taken elsewhere, it is old hat. So "the task and the possibility of preaching is to open out the good news of the gospel with alternative modes of speech," dramatic, artistic, concrete speech that "when heard in freedom, assaults imagination and pushes out the presumed world in which most of us are trapped," living reduced lives on the basis of reduced speech. Preachers are "poets that speak against a prose world," people who propose "that the real world in which God invites us to live is not the one made available by the rulers of this age," who offer "an evangelical world: an existence shaped by the news of the gospel." They mediate the Bible with its "generative power to summon and

16. See further Reymond, "Preaching and the New Media."
17. See ibid., 28.

evoke new life," its guarantee that "prophetic construals of another world are still possible, still worth doing, still longingly received by those who live at the edge of despair, resignation, and conformity."[18] The gospel is graphic, and Scripture is graphic. Our living in the age of Baird rather than Gutenberg is not a reason for being depressed.

18. Brueggemann, *Finally Comes the Poet*, 3–4.

9

How Does the Bible
Do Theological Reflection?

According to Gustavo Gutiérrez's definition, theology involves "critical reflection on Christian praxis in the light of the Word."[1] There is more to be
said about the nature of theology; theology is proactive as well as reactive, and its
resources extend beyond Scripture even if Scripture plays a key role in it. But in so
far as there is some truth in the formulation, how does such reflection on praxis or
on events or on experience proceed?

In their book on supervision and pastoral care, *Helping the Helpers,*[2] J. Foskett and
D. Lyall note that reflection on experience has characteristically taken discursive,
analytic form and suggest a move to a more narrative mode in which this reflection
takes the form of storytelling. Their suggestion followed the contemporary emphasis
on storytelling in a number of disciplines. In the Bible, itself a manual of theological
reflection, both the discursive and the narrative are prominent; nor are they the only
modes in which the Bible formulates its theological thinking.

For some time, attempts to express a doctrinal understanding of Scripture have
been in disarray. One reason is the nature of the models that have long governed
theological thinking concerning Scripture but that for the most part do not come from
Scripture itself. Models such as inspiration, authority, and revelation may illumine
some parts of Scripture (prophecy, law, apocalypse), but they are less enlightening

1. G. Gutiérrez, *A Theology of Liberation* (Maryknoll, N.Y.: Orbis 1983; London: SCM, 1984), 13.
See further chapter 4 above. The current chapter was first published in *Theology* 94 (1991): 181–88.
2. J. Foskett and D. Lyall, *Helping the Helpers* (London: SPCK, 1988); see esp. 48–49.

when applied to the whole, and none matches the nature of the most prominent and arguably most significant genre in Scripture, narrative. Our theological thinking about the nature of Scripture needs to begin from the distinctive nature of narrative, law, prophecy, apocalypse.[3]

I want here to make a parallel point about the nature of theological reflection insofar as it is attempted in light of Scripture. The varied forms taken by theological reflection within the Bible itself, in epistle, wisdom, narrative, prophecy, law, and psalmody, suggest a variety of complementary approaches to contemporary theological reflection, whether in relation to commitments we have (Gutiérrez's concern), to pastoral experiences (Foskett and Lyall's starting point), or to questions raised by church life (as in my examples below).

1. Discursive and Narrative

We may begin with the discursive, analytic form, which appears most systematically in Paul. Paul, indeed, is *the* great discursive theologian in Scripture, but his systematic, analytic thinking characteristically takes the form of contextual theological reflection. This is especially apparent in 1 Corinthians, which takes up a series of issues in church life in Corinth such as divisions within the congregation, aspects of their sexual practice and their worship, and their eating of meat dedicated to idols. What it does is declare the fruit of reflection on these in light of a Christian understanding of creation, the story of Israel, the incarnation, the cross, the resurrection, and the future appearing of Jesus.

Contextual theological reflection is also prominent in Romans, superficially the least situational of Paul's letters and the one that seeks to expound the eternal gospel. At the heart of the exposition and of the letter is Paul's discussion of the place of Israel in God's purpose: Israel's failure on the whole to recognize Jesus as its Messiah is an inescapably urgent contextual problem for Paul. If he cannot give a satisfactory theological account of it, this event fatally undermines his gospel with its stress on the promises of God and the lasting faithfulness of God. It is for this reason that Romans 9–11 has such a central place in the letter. Paul has reflected on the question theologically, and he has done so in light of Scripture in a more formal sense than is his way in 1 Corinthians. The pocket edition of the *New Jerusalem Bible* normally lists in the margin scriptural references and allusions within passages, but in Romans

---

3. See now my *Models for Scripture* (Grand Rapids: Eerdmans; Carlisle: Paternoster, 1994; Toronto: Clements, 2004). This fact underlies the periodically lamented oddness of saying "This is the word of the Lord" after any and every lesson (e.g., T. G. A. Baker in *Theology* 93 [1990]: 268). One might, however, note that conservative enthusiasm for this phrase and liberal unease about it may share a common false premise, that its significance is to make a statement about the mere authorship of the passage in question. That is not so. When a prophet said, "This is the word of the Lord," the implication was, "so it will do its work, it will be effective": a useful reminder with regard to (say) some expression of doubt from Ecclesiastes or some story about the incompetence of the disciples, as well as to a passage from the prophets.

9–11 it gives up the attempt and offers only a note that these are too numerous to list. That fact reveals the prominence of Scripture in this piece of theological reflection; it was as Paul pored over the Scriptures or worked through them mentally that illumination came regarding the mysterious purpose God was implementing, the offering of the gospel to the nations as a result of the temporary defection of those to whom it originally belonged. In 1 Corinthians and in Romans Paul thus models a process of theological reflection that looks at contextual issues in light of the gospel and/or in light of Scripture, and does so in analytic, discursive form.

When I joined the church to which I belonged for my last decade in England, my eyebrows rose at two regular events. One took place each Sunday. As we came to the end of our worship, the members of a black-led church began to arrive for their service, which started as we talked together over refreshments in the community center downstairs. The gathering of these two separate congregations for worship and fellowship seemed a contradiction of the gospel with its talk of all ethnic groups being one in Christ.[4] The other event took place each Ramadan, when the local Muslim community was allowed to use the community center for their prayers. That, too, seemed a contradiction of the gospel in the sense of a denial of New Testament declarations about people coming to the Father only via Jesus and about there being salvation through no one else. Analytic, discursive theological reflection in light of the gospel and of direct statements in Scripture seemed to put a question mark by the church's policy. Admittedly there is more to be said, as I shall note below.

Foskett and Lyall's suggestion regarding theological reflection was that we need to move from a discursive mode of this kind to a narrative mode. Scripture models the latter as well as the former. Genesis to Kings is an epic narrative leading in due course to the exile, and it constitutes, among other things, a *tour de force* of narrative theological reflection on the experience of exile. It suggests answers to urgent questions regarding why Israel came to be in exile, what hope it may be able to entertain for the future, and what response is called for to its present experience. The books of Chronicles retell the same story as that in Genesis to Kings on a smaller scale and along different lines, because the context on which they need to reflect is different; they offer an interpretation of the situation of the postexilic community, in narrative form.

The Gospels and Acts are also works of contextual theological reflection, though we are less certain of the circumstances in which they were written. That perhaps reflects their predominant concern with the facts about Jesus and the beginnings of the church. But they are also concerned to use these to illumine the situation of the churches to which they are written, offering theological reflection on issues such as

4. An equivalent in the United States is the existence of separate black and white churches in the Episcopal Church. There are three churches in the Diocese of Los Angeles that were founded in the same areas as existing white churches, specifically to provide places of worship for African American Episcopalians. In 2009, the Diocese of Los Angeles held a service of apology and repentance for the way it had treated African American Christians, part of a broader movement along these lines within the Episcopal Church.

the relationship between Jews and Christians and between the life of the synagogue and the life of the church.

The nature of biblical narrative points to a form of theological reflection that involves telling a modern story and showing how it relates to the gospel story and the scriptural story. Part of the background to the relatively recent development of black-led churches separate from white-led churches in Britain is the story of the white-led churches' failure to welcome their brothers and sisters in Christ when they began to come to Britain in the 1950s. In her contribution to a symposium called "You Have Created Me Black," Eve Pitts gives one humiliating account of this experience (humiliating for a white Christian, that is, particularly one who actually lived at the time in the part of Birmingham, England, where the events took place, as I did).[5] It was this kind of experience that led to the formation of black-led churches in Britain. But the scriptural story includes the account of the conflict and split between Paul and Barnabas that led to the development of two separate Christian mission ventures in the Mediterranean world. The first story (that of the conflict and split) makes it morally impossible for white Christians to criticize black Christians for forming separate churches. The second story (the twin missions) gives grounds for hope that even developments that reflect the sin of the people of God can be harnessed to the purpose of God.

The Muslims who said Ramadan prayers in our community center were also people who came to Britain with grounds for expecting a different reception from the one they experienced. But the growing strength of Islam in Britain needs to be seen against a broader background that coheres with this, the scandalous fact that Islam is a consciously post-Christian religion. Its building of the Dome of the Rock on the Temple Mount in Jerusalem expressed (among other things) an understandable distaste for the Christian religion as people in the Middle East experienced it. Are the existence and the flourishing of Islam a judgment of God upon the state of Christianity? To allow Muslims to say their prayers in a community center attached to a Christian church could be a way of accepting that judgment. It might also be a step on the road of commending Christ to Muslims. Theological reflection in light of the scriptural story might also recall the mixed attitude to other religions expressed by the story told in the First Testament, which includes Abram's openness to Melchizedek and Elisha's indulgent stance toward Naaman (Gen 14:18–24; 2 Kgs 5:18–19) as well as the strictness of Joshua or Ezra.

The contexts in which we do our theological reflection also offer us ways into perceiving aspects of the biblical story that we have not perceived before. I had always seen Ruth as an essentially pastoral idyll until I read it from the context of an urban priority area and realized how it mirrored life there. It is, after all, the story of a man who loses his livelihood, his home, and in due course his life, before he is even middle-aged. It is the story of a woman who also loses her livelihood, her home, and in due course her husband, so that she is the archetypal inner-city figure, the single parent, until she also loses her sons, and all that by the time she is in her

---

5. See *Spirituality and Social Issues,* The Way Supplement 63 (1988): 4–5.

forties (hence her understandable evaluation of the way God has treated her). It is the story of a younger woman who is the equivalent to the Sikh or Muslim girl next door, marrying cross-culturally and cross-religion, drawn to Naomi's God through Naomi despite what Naomi has to say about her God, and thus reflecting how unpredictable are God's ways of reaching into the world. It is the story of an older man who apparently has everything except a wife and family and who unexpectedly gains both. And it is the story of a baby through whom God gives a lasting significance to four people who look totally insignificant.

2. Prophecy, Policy Making, Worship

Their editors draw attention to the fact that the Hebrew prophets were contextual theologians by placing at the beginning of most of their books a note indicating in one form or another both the awareness that their work is of divine origin (e.g., "the vision of Isaiah ben Amoz") and the awareness that it came into being in particular contexts ("which he saw concerning Judah and Jerusalem in the days of Uzziah, Jotham, Ahaz, and Hezekiah"). The prophets' work is thus designated as theological and contextual. Their oracles presuppose both these features, on one hand affirming that "this is the word of Yahweh" and on the other commonly drawing attention to the nature of the concrete situations to which they speak.

Their theological reflection took the form of an attempt to drive Israel to face nightmares and to dream dreams. The facing of nightmares is more prominent before the exile, when the prophets are those who see that calamity is coming upon Israel and Judah, offer a theological interpretation of that calamity in terms of a divine judgment that responds to people's failure of love for Yahweh and love for each other, and strive to persuade them to return to Yahweh before it is too late. The prophets are people who can bring together what they can read in the newspapers, what they can see in worship and in society, and what they know from Israel's gospel story.[6] When a bishop of Liverpool warned a British prime minister that calamity was imminent in his city because of the way local government was being exercised, he acted like a prophet insisting that nightmares be faced, without necessarily prescribing the detailed nature of the political action that needed to be taken.

With the exile came a transition from the facing of nightmares to the dreaming of dreams, the offering of avenues of hope for a demoralized people. Once again the prophets are confronting their people, but now with unbelievable good news. "Yahweh has anointed me to proclaim good news to the poor, he has sent me to bind up the brokenhearted," says the Isaiah who preaches in Palestine after the exile (Isa 61:1). He sees people who are afflicted, broken in spirit, captive, imprisoned, cut off from God. His response is not to do anything or to urge anyone else to do anything, but to preach, to talk to people about freedom, grace, joy, rebuilding, and

---

6. This paragraph depends partly on remarks by John Barton, "History and Rhetoric in the Prophets," in *The Bible as Rhetoric* (ed. M. Warner; London: Routledge, 1990), 51–64.

pride. All he does is make promises to people, because what they need is hope. He brings good news, but news about the future, about something God is going to do. He is aware that human agencies cannot bring about freedom or grace; these are God's gifts, and therefore there has to be preaching about them as well as action. Pending God's action, the invitation to the people is to dream God-given dreams (though in some contexts these may then inspire human action).

In the contexts in which we minister, hope is commonly people's most pressing need, not least where there may seem to be no room for action. Physical and human desolation is often an obvious reality in urban areas, but the suburbs know as profound a misery issuing from people's oppression by their wealth and their jobs, and as profound a heartbreak issuing from their experiences with their children and their marriages. Theological reflection here, too, means discerning God's dreams.

These certainly include dreams for the church such as are expressed in the vision of a numberless worshiping multitude in Revelation 7. These come from all ethnic, political, and linguistic groups, and they offer the dream to set against the present reality of Afro-Caribbean or African American Christian worship largely separated from Caucasian Christian worship, and of Muslims turning their backs on the worship of the Lamb. They also help us to see where there is some hint of fulfillment of this dream. There are occasions in urban areas when black, brown, and white, young, middle-aged, and old, women and men, middle class, artisan, and underclass all meet for worship, and such occasions constitute anticipations of the worship of heaven and encourage the dreaming of dreams.[7]

The prophets invite us to discern what nightmares and dreams Scripture encourages. The prophets are not particularly practical people; they are not social reformers, but the Bible does also model the translation of story and vision into policy, in the Torah. It pictures the Torah as all given by God through Moses, at Mount Sinai (in the case of Exodus and Leviticus) and in the Plains of Moab (in the case of Deuteronomy). It thus declares it to be of heavenly origin and significance. The various bodies of Torah differ from each other, however, and do so because they speak to the needs of different contexts. It is particularly clear how Deuteronomy constitutes a restatement of Yahweh's expectations of Israel as these are expressed in Exodus 19–24. The Pentateuch locates this restatement in the Plains of Moab on the eve of the people's actually taking up life in the promised land; historically it reflects the actual experience of life in the land and its pressures. Seen either way, Deuteronomy is a piece of contextual theology that systematically develops the old theological idea of the covenant so that it becomes a framework for understanding the faith and life of Israel as a whole. It turns theological concepts, stories, and dreams into practical policies and models the way we may do so.

Scriptural systematics makes me insist that black and white worship together, the dreams of Scripture's visionaries promise that they will, the stories of how things

---

7. For this point (and one in the next paragraph), see John Goldingay, "The Bible in the City," *Theology* 92 (1989): 5–15 (reprinted as "Is God in the City?" in *Key Questions about Christian Faith: Old Testament Answers* [Grand Rapids: Baker Academic, 2010], 272–81); on which, indeed, the present chapter is in part a subconscious methodological reflection.

were in scriptural times cause me to make allowances for the fact that they do not yet do so and that God can cope with that fact. Yet this must not allow me to sit back content with a situation that falls short of God's dream. Torah impels me to venture this fourth form of theological reflection that turns dreams into policies. The drastic policy would be for the white churches to repent, close down the white-led churches, and ask to be admitted to the black-led churches. The less drastic one would be to seek in concrete ways to develop means of worshiping and working together and to give people from ethnic minorities visible leadership roles in white-led churches, such as may take us nearer the realization of the dream.

Scripture's fifth mode of theological reflection takes the form of worship. The Eastern tradition, affirmed at this point by Karl Barth, reminds us that theology and doxology are one. Theology is worshipers thinking about their worship, as they must; worship is theologians turning their thought into worship, as they must. Arguably the densest theology in Scripture takes the form of worship, in the Psalms.

The Psalms, too, are a contextual theology. Their prayer issues from urgent situations of need on the part of individuals or groups and it wrestles before God with the theological questions raised by God's acts and by God's failure to act. Their praise issues from concrete experiences of God's acting in response to such prayer, or of God's speaking some word that throws new light on a situation, or of the suppliant's seeing afresh some theological truth that enables a situation to be coped with. Their whole spirituality takes people through a cycle, or spiral, of theological orientation (when they know who God is, who they are, and how life works), followed by disorientation (when some contextual experience shatters those convictions), followed by reorientation (the attaining of some new perspective that does justice to both these earlier sets of experiences and truths).[8] They are a manual of contextual theology formulated in praise and prayer. They invite us to make our worship part of our theological reflection, and our theological reflection part of our actual life with God. In light of their pattern, we rejoice before God in the fact that the gospel makes one new person out of people of all races, lament before God about that not being true in experience and urge God to make it so, and glory before God in hints of its fulfillment such as are provided by the occasions described above.

People who are interested in theological reflection are commonly people committed to active work in the church and the community. They especially need to perceive how incomplete is their theological reflection issuing from activity and in activity unless it is complemented by theological reflection in the form of worship. The converse is also true. The fourth and fifth modes of theological reflection in Scripture belong together. There are congregations and ministers who are instinctively more involved in community development and ones who are instinctively more involved in worship. Each needs to see that both aspects of Christian discipleship are present in their own lives, and each needs to affirm the other emphasis as part of what the body of Christ requires.

8. See W. Brueggemann, *The Message of the Psalms* (Minneapolis: Augsburg, 1984).

PART 2

Concerning Narrative

10

How Does Biblical Narrative
Relate to Systematic Theology?

1. Narrative and Theology

When I watch a film or listen to music or read a novel, as a narrow-minded in-tellectual I cannot help thinking about it: about its significance, about its insight on life and God. Indeed, I am such an ivory-towered academic that I cannot stop myself reflecting on what my wife used to call "waste-of-time" films or music, by which she means popular art designed simply to entertain or make money or make someone famous.[1]

I indulge in this weakness during the film or song or novel, grinning to myself or uttering some exclamation under my breath. I did so during the film *The Truman Show*. Tru(e)man has just discovered that his whole life has been lived on a soap opera set; all the people he thought loved him have been playing parts. The God/Devil/Director figure, Christoph (at least one syllable short of being a Christ-bearer), then tells him, "It's all deception out here in the real world, too, you know" (I reproduce the quotation from memory and may have sharpened its import to match my agenda, rather in the manner of the New Testament's use of the First Testament).

---

1. First published in *Between Two Horizons* (ed. J. B. Green and M. Turner; Grand Rapids: Eerdmans, 1999), 123–42.

Then, after listening to the song a few times, or completing the novel, or leaving the cinema, I will probably be compelled to think back over the lyric or novel or film as a whole. I do it every time I play to a class Leonard Cohen's song about God and David, "Hallelujah." I do it every time I watch *When Harry Met Sally*, still wondering whether it is true that men and women can never be friends because sex will always get in the way (and still not sure what is the film's own implicit take on that). I did it after I first saw *Leaving Las Vegas* in Britain, as I spent three hours (with a break for pizza) attempting to explain to a seminarian why her seminary principal should want to see such an unchristian film; and I did it again after watching the video with a small group of seminarians down the freeway from Las Vegas (the answer being that it expresses such gloomy realism yet also such hope as it portrays the difference loving and being loved can make to a man who has sentenced himself to death and to a woman whom life has sentenced to a living death). I did it on leaving the cinema open-mouthed at *The Truman Show*'s breathtaking discussion of whether it is best to live in a clean, unquestioning, problem-free hermetically sealed world such as a film set or a Garden of Eden, or whether it is best to live a "real" life outside, with all its ambiguity.

In films the plot also counts, though as I come to think about it, the plots tend to be simple (man goes to Las Vegas to drink himself to death, and does so). We know that George Clooney will in some sense get the woman, in *One Fine Day* or *Out of Sight*; the question is how, and how far, and for how long. We suspect that Tom Hanks will succeed in *Saving Private Ryan*, despite the false clue when we see a Ryan dead on the Normandy seashore; the only question is how.

Further, films depend on believable characters (well, some films do), though film is a tough medium for the conveying of character, and character comes out more in novels. Perhaps this is partly because characterization in films comes via the character of the actor, and most actors are playing themselves. I reflected on this recently when rewatching *Sophie's Choice* on television and seeing Kevin Kline behave the same way as he would a decade later in *A Fish Called Wanda*; and I reflected on how much more the novel *Sophie's Choice* conveyed than the film did.

Doing theology on the basis of biblical narrative parallels one's reflection on a film, a novel, or a song. One may do it in the same four ways.

First, individual moments in a narrative convey insights. A famous reflection by Günther Bornkamm on the story of Jesus' stilling of the storm, in its two forms in Mark and Matthew, brings out this event's message in the different versions of these two evangelists.[2] In Genesis, three stories about one of Israel's father figures passing off his wife as his sister comprise attempts to come to terms with male ambivalence at female sexuality.[3] Exodus 19–40 includes a long series of attempts to find ways of speaking about God's presence as real while also recognizing the fact of God's

---

2. See Günther Bornkamm, Gerhard Barth, and Heinz Joachim Held, *Tradition and Interpretation in Matthew* (Philadelphia: Westminster Press; London: SCM, 1963), 52–57.

3. See J. Cheryl Exum, "Who's Afraid of 'The Endangered Ancestress'?" in *The New Literary Criticism and the Hebrew Bible* (ed. J. Cheryl Exum and David J. A. Clines; JSOTSup 143; Sheffield:

transcendence; John Durham has suggested that God's presence is the theme of Exodus 19–40, as God's activity is the theme of Exodus 1–18.[4] Exodus 19–40 is thus an exercise in narrative theology.

Second, biblical narratives have plots, and a key aspect of their theological significance will be conveyed by their plot.

On the large scale, the plots of the four or five New Testament narratives (is Luke-Acts one or two?) are at one level simple, like those of many films. There are two of these plots, the story of the beginnings, ministry, killing, and renewed life of Jesus of Nazareth, and the story of the spreading of his story from Jerusalem to Rome. The plots are simple but theologically crucial. The New Testament theological message is contained in the plot about Jesus, because that message is a gospel, and the New Testament ecclesiology is contained in the plot about the spread of the gospel.

Yet there being several versions of the first plot draws attention to the fact that there are many ways of bringing out its theological significance. To put it another way, it has many subplots. It is also the story of how Jesus starts as a wonder-worker and ends up a martyr. It thus raises the question of the relationship between these two. Is the former the real aim and the latter a deviation and a way of ultimately achieving the former? Or is the former a dead end succeeded by the latter? Or do the two stand in dialectic tension? Again, the Gospel story portrays Jesus choosing twelve men as members of his inner circle, which might confirm men's special status in the leadership of the people of God. It then portrays him watching them misunderstand, betray, and abandon him, so that the people who accompany his martyrdom and first learn of his transformation are women—which might subvert men's special status in the leadership of the people of God.

Third, biblical narratives portray characters. From a theological angle, they concern themselves with two correlative pairs of characters: God and Israel, Jesus and the church. They "render" these characters[5] sometimes by offering titles for them (El Shaddai, Yahweh; holy nation, royal priesthood; Son of God, Son of Man; body of Christ, flock of God). They render them by describing them with adjectives or nouns (gracious, long-tempered; family, servant; good shepherd, true vine; household, temple: the examples show that the boundary between "title" and "description" is fuzzy). They render them most by describing them in action, because that is the way character emerges. It has become customary to distinguish between showing and telling. The Gospels rarely "tell" us things about Jesus (e.g., "Jesus was a compassionate person"). Instead they "show" us things. They portray Jesus in action (and in speech) and leave us to infer what kind of person Jesus therefore was. In this respect they are much more like films than novels; in general films have to show rather than tell.

Sheffield Academic Press, 1993), 91–113; also in Exum, *Fragmented Women* (Sheffield: Sheffield Academic Press, 1993), 148–69.

4. See his *Exodus* (Waco: Word, 1985).

5. On the notion of rendering, see Dale Patrick, *The Rendering of God in the Old Testament* (Philadelphia: Fortress, 1981).

Fourth, biblical narratives discuss themes. I have suggested two examples from the Gospels: Mark discusses the relative position of women and men in leadership among Jesus' followers and the relationship between what Jesus achieves by works of power and what he achieves by letting people kill him. In the First Testament, Esther is directly a discussion of how Yahweh's commitment to the Jewish people works itself out; it also implicitly makes theological statements or raises theological questions about the nature of God's involvement in the world and the significance of human acts in accepting responsibility for history, about the nature of manhood and womanhood, about human weakness and sin (pride, greed, sexism, cruelty), about the potentials and the temptations of power, about civil authority, civil obedience, and civil disobedience, and about the significance of humor. Jonah is about the disobedience of prophets and Yahweh's relationship with the nations and the possible fruitfulness of turning to God. The stories in Daniel are a narrative politics discussing the interrelationship of the sovereignty of Yahweh, the sovereignty of human kings, and the significance of the political involvement of members of God's people.

The task of exegeting biblical narratives includes the teasing out of the theological issues in such works.

It has not commonly been assumed to be so. A school friend of mine is now a professor of Latin; in comparing his textual work and that of biblical exegetes some years ago, I was depressingly struck by the similarity in the apparent aims and procedures. One might never have guessed that biblical narratives had a different set of concerns from those of Ovid.

Biblical narratives came into being to address theological questions, or at least religious questions. The teasing out of their religious and theological implications is inherent in their exegesis. It is not an optional additional task that the exegete may responsibly ignore if so inclined. Greek or Roman, English or American literature, and Russian or French films will always have an implicit theology, but teasing this out may not always be an essential aspect of their study. With biblical narrative, theological issues are the texts' major concern, and the exegete who fails to pay attention to them and focuses on (for instance) merely historical questions has not left the starting line as an exegete.[6]

The exegete may undertake the task by the four means suggested above. First, it involves teasing out the theological implications of individual stories within the larger narrative. The agenda here cannot be predicted: discerning it depends on the exegete's sensitivity to recognizing a theological issue. Second, it involves standing back and giving an account of the distinctive plot of the story (for instance, that of Chronicles as opposed to Kings or that of Matthew as opposed to Mark) so as to show what is the gospel according to this Gospel. Third, it involves realizing a portrayal of the two or four characters in the story. According to this narrative as a whole, Who is God and Who is Israel? In the case of a New Testament narrative,

---

6. Cf. chapter 5 (section 3) above.

in addition, Who is Jesus and Who is the church? Fourth, it is a matter of analyzing the narrative's various insights on its own specific theme(s).

There is no method for doing this, any more than there is for interpreting a film or for any other aspect of the interpretive task (I have suggested that it is no more or no less than an aspect of that). It requires a more or less inspired guess as to what the theological freight of this narrative might be, and then discussion with other people (perhaps via their writings) to discover whether my guess says less or more than the narrative: whether they can help me notice things I have missed or eliminate things I am reading into the text. This guess comes from me as a person living in the culture in which I live, and it needs to recognize the specificity of that, so that my reading fellowship needs to embrace people from other ages and other cultures, and people of other beliefs and of the opposite sex. But it can also benefit from the possibility that this enables me to see something of how this narrative speaks to people like me in my culture in the context of its debates.

2. The Difference between Systematic Theology and Biblical Narrative

The theological work I have just described will stand somewhat short of interaction with systematic theology.

Systematic theology means different things to different people.[7] Traditionally, it has denoted the discipline that gives a coherent account of Christian theology as a whole, showing how the parts comprise a whole. Consciously or unconsciously, it undertakes this task in light of the culture, language, thought forms, and questions of its time; it is not written once for all.[8]

Such descriptions of systematic theology's task suggest several observations from the perspective of biblical studies.

First, it is a telling fact that "systematic" and "theology" are both Greek-based words. The discipline emerged from the attempt to think through the gospel's significance in the framework of Greek thinking. Thus the key issues in the theological thinking of the patristic period concerned God's nature and Christ's person, and these were framed in terms of concepts such as "person" and "nature" as these were understood against the background of Greek thinking. Subsequent theological explication of the atonement and the doctrine of Scripture similarly took place in terms of concepts and categories of the medieval period and the Enlightenment. Their being able to use scriptural terms may obscure the fact that their framework of thinking is that of another culture.

---

7. See Colin E. Gunton, "Historical and Systematic Theology," in *The Cambridge Companion to Christian Doctrine* (ed. Colin E. Gunton; Cambridge and New York: Cambridge University Press, 1996), 3–20.

8. See, e.g., the definitions in Sinclair B. Ferguson and David F. Wright, eds., *New Dictionary of Theology* (Leicester and Downers Grove, Ill.: InterVarsity, 1988), 671–72; Donald W. Musser and Joseph L. Price, eds., *The New Handbook of Theology* (Nashville: Abingdon, 1992), 469.

This points us toward the awareness that not only are individual ventures in systematic theology contextual. The enterprise is inherently so, dependent as it is on that collocation of Jewish gospel and Greek forms of thinking. Thus Alister McGrath has noted that ancient Greece and traditional African cultures resemble the scriptural writers in tending to use stories as a way of making sense of the world. Just before the time of Plato a decisive shift occurred; "ideas took the place of stories," and a conceptual way of thinking gained the upper hand and came to dominate Western culture.[9]

The arrival of postmodernity has then brought implications for systematic theology. While one great contemporary German theologian, Wolfhart Pannenberg, has written a three-volume systematic theology on something like the traditional model,[10] another great contemporary German theologian, Jürgen Moltmann, has written a series of "systematic contributions to theology" on a similar scale but declines to call these "systematic theology."[11] Admirers may nevertheless see them as suggesting the way forward in systematic theology, insisting as they do on creativity, coherence, rigor, critical thinking, and the conversation between the modern world and the Christian tradition, but being suspicious of grand schemes. If systematic theology seems a misguided enterprise, one response is thus to replace it by a wiser enterprise. But another is to assume that this will simply leave the term "systematic theology" with its value status to unwise exponents of it, and therefore rather to set about the different task that one does approve of and to appropriate the term "systematic theology" for that.

Perhaps it is indeed the case that humanity's rationality necessitates analytic reflection on the nature of the faith; at least, the importance of rationality to intellectuals necessitates our analytic reflection on the nature of the faith, as one of the less important aspects of the life of Christ's body. Yet such rational and disciplined reflection need not take the form of systematic theology, of the old variety or the new. For long it did not do so in Judaism, where the two key forms of reflection were haggadah and halakah. This reflection took the form of the retelling of biblical narrative in such a way as to clarify its difficulties and answer contemporary questions, and the working out of what behavioral practice was required by life with God. We need to distinguish between the possible necessity that the church reflects deeply, sharply, coherently, and critically on its faith and the culture-relative fact that this has generally been done in a world of thought decisively influenced by Greek thinking in general as well as in particular (e.g., Platonic or Aristotelian).

The nature of reflection in Judaism draws attention to the need for systematic theology to do justice to the essentially narrative character of the gospel in both Testaments if it is to do justice to the nature of biblical faith. First Testament faith centrally concerns the way God related to Israel over time. It relates the story of

9. *Understanding Doctrine* (London: Hodder, 1990; Grand Rapids: Zondervan, 1992), 34.
10. *Systematic Theology* (Grand Rapids: Eerdmans, 1991, 1994, 1998).
11. See, e.g., *God in Creation* (London: SCM; Philadelphia: Fortress, 1985), xv.

how Yahweh did certain things, such as create the world, make promises to Israel's ancestors, deliver their descendants from Egypt, bring them into a sealed relationship at Sinai, persevere with them in chastisement and mercy in the wilderness, bring them into their own land, persevere with them in chastisement and mercy through another period of unfaithfulness in the land itself, agree to their having human kings and make a commitment to a line of kings, interact with them over centuries of inclination to rebellion until they were reduced to a shadow of their former self, cleanse their land, and begin a process of renewal there.

New Testament faith sees itself as the continuing of that story. Like the First Testament, the New Testament takes predominantly narrative form, and the form corresponds to the nature of the faith. Its gospel is not essentially or distinctively a statement that takes the form "God is love" but one that takes the form "God so loved that he gave."

Second-century Christians found the need of a "rule for the faith," an outline summary of Christian truth that could (among other things) guide their reading of Scripture. The two great creeds that issued from the fulfilling of that need, the Apostles' Creed and the Nicene Creed, do not actually summarize the fundamentals of biblical faith (neither mentions Israel),[12] but at least they take a broadly narrative form. In this respect they are a far cry from the Westminster Confession or the Thirty-Nine Articles of Religion. Similarly, systematic theology has commonly been shaped by the doctrine of the Trinity, and recent years have seen an increased emphasis on the importance and fruitfulness of thinking trinitarianly.

The focus on the Trinity rather than on narrative highlights the problem of seeking to work at the relationship of systematic theology to Scripture in general, and to biblical narrative in particular. Let us grant that the doctrine of the Trinity is a (even the) logical outworking within a Greek framework of the implications of statements of the more Greek-thinking writers within the New Testament. It is then two stages removed from most of the New Testament narratives (because they are narrative, and because they are less inclined to think in Greek forms). Further, it is three stages removed from most biblical narrative (which was written before Bethlehem and Pentecost made trinitarian thinking possible, let alone necessary). If one starts from biblical narratives and asks after their theological freight, the vast bulk of their theological implications does not emerge within a trinitarian framework.

That is even true (perhaps especially true) if we are interested in theological implications in the narrowest sense, in what biblical narrative tells us about God. For all its truth and fruitfulness, the doctrine of the Trinity seriously skews our theological reading of Scripture. It excludes most of the insight expressed in the biblical narrative's portrayal of the person and its working out of the plot. There is a paradox here. Some of the key figures in the development of the doctrine of the Trinity emphasized

---

12. It is noteworthy that "the Jewish people and Christian theology" has become one of the topics which needs to be considered in *The Cambridge Companion to Christian Doctrine* referred to above (see 81–100, by Bruce D. Marshall).

how little we may directly say about God, particularly God's inner nature. Theology nevertheless involves the venture to think the unthinkable and say the unsayable, but in doing so it ignores the theological potential of the things that Scripture does say.

There is a further sense in which scriptural reflection on God's nature is inextricably tied to narrative, expressed in Jack Miles's *God: A Biography*.[13] To use systematic theology's own terms, revelation as well as redemption is tied to narrative. God's person emerges in a series of contexts. God is a creator, then a destroyer. God relates to a family in the concerns of its ongoing family life such as the finding of a home, the birth of children, and the arranging of marriages; God then relates to a nation in the different demands of its life, which includes God's becoming a warmaker. Entering into a formal relationship with this people takes God into becoming a lawmaker and a deity identified by a sanctuary (albeit a movable one) and not merely by a relationship with a people. The revelation of God's person is inextricably tied to the events in which God becomes different things, in a way that any person does; it is thus inextricably tied to narrative.

Systematic theology's theological and philosophical framework imposes on it a broader difficulty in doing justice to much of the biblical material. By its nature traditional systematic theology, in particular, is concerned with the unequivocal; it presupposes a quest for unity. Biblical faith indeed emphasizes that Yahweh is one, but then relaxes in implying paradox within that oneness. For instance, it emphasizes God's power but generally portrays events in the world as working themselves out not by God's will but in ways that reflect human and other this-worldly considerations; indeed, the emphasis in biblical narrative in particular is very predominantly on the latter. It emphasizes God's wisdom and knowledge but also portrays God asking questions and experiencing surprise and regret. Starting from its Greek framework, traditional systematic theology affirms God's power and knowledge ("omnipotence" and "omniscience") and then has to subordinate any theological account of the reality of human decision making except insofar as it emphasizes the "necessity" for God to give human beings "free will" (further alien ideas imported into Scripture) and/ or has to offer an allegorical interpretation of statements in scriptural narrative that indicate God's ignorance or God's having a change of mind.

Narrative is by nature open-ended, allusive, and capable of embracing questions and ambiguity. I have noted two features of Mark's Gospel that illustrate this fact. It is a feature of Genesis 1–4, where the three stories (1:1–2:3; 2:4–3:24; 4:1–26) keep offering different perspectives on what God is like and what human beings are like and on the goodness or otherwise of life in the world. These keep the reader ricocheting between them in a way that is simultaneously bewildering and enriching—or at least they would do that, if we were able to escape the lenses that the categories of systematic theology impose on the chapters.

While concerned to work out the implications of biblical narrative, by its nature systematic theology (traditional or postmodern) does not take narrative form. It

13. (New York and London: Simon & Schuster, 1995).

thereby has difficulty in maintaining touch with the narrative nature of the faith upon which it seeks to reflect, and therefore with the object of its concern, and it has difficulty in maintaining touch with the narrative contexts out of which aspects of God's character emerge and thereby in understanding the significance of these aspects of this character.

From the side of biblical studies, over the past two decades there have been two powerful attempts to relate the Bible to the concerns of systematic theology, on the part of Brevard Childs and Francis Watson. There is something wrong with me, because I find Childs's work in particular disappointing. The opening chapter headings for his *Old Testament Theology in a Canonical Context*[14] expose one major problem here, for they indicate that the chapters concern "The Old Testament as Revelation," "How God Is Known," and "God's Purpose in Revelation." The entire framework of thinking is introduced into biblical study from elsewhere, in this case not from the Greek thinking of the patristic period but from the agenda of the Enlightenment age. In turn, Watson opens his *Text, Church, and World* with his concern for "an exegesis oriented primarily towards theological issues" but goes on that "at least in my usage, the terms 'theology' and 'theological' relate to a distinct discipline—that of 'systematic theology' or 'Christian doctrine.'"[15] He restates the point at the opening of his *Text and Truth*.[16] The exegete who expounds the theological significance of the text expects to do so in the terms of the existent Christian doctrinal tradition. Jon D. Levenson has tartly commented on Gerhard von Rad's famous study "Faith Reckoned as Righteousness" (Gen 15:6), "Within the limited context of theological interpretation informed by historical criticism—the context von Rad intended—his essay must be judged unsuccessful. Within another limited context, however—the confessional elucidation of Scripture for purposes of Lutheran reaffirmation—it is an impressive success." It is for this reason that Jews have not been interested in biblical theology.[17]

In other words, Christian theological interpretation of Scripture is always inclined to come down to the elucidation of our already-determined Christian doctrines (and lifestyles) by Scripture, either accidentally (von Rad) or deliberately (Childs, Watson).

3. From Narrative to Theology

Scripture's focus on narrative might seem to imply that the whole enterprise of thinking critically and analytically about biblical faith is doomed to failure. Pointers within Scripture suggest that this is an unnecessary fear.

14. (London: SCM, 1985; Philadelphia: Fortress, 1986).
15. (Edinburgh: T&T Clark; Grand Rapids: Eerdmans, 1994); see 1.
16. (Edinburgh: T&T Clark; Grand Rapids: Eerdmans, 1997); see 2–4.
17. *The Hebrew Bible, the Old Testament, and Historical Criticism* (Louisville: Westminster John Knox, 1993), 61. Von Rad's essay appears in *The Problem of the Hexateuch and Other Essays* (Edinburgh: Oliver and Boyd; New York: McGraw-Hill, 1966), 125–30. R. W. L. Moberly also makes the point in "Abraham's Righteousness" in *Studies in the Pentateuch* (ed. J. A. Emerton; VTSup 41; Leiden and New York: Brill, 1990), 103–30 (111).

First, non-narrative books such as the Psalms, the Prophets, and the Epistles abound in material that has taken the first step from narrative to discursive statement, while keeping its implicit and explicit links with the gospel, the story running through the two Testaments. The statement "God is love" is grounded in a narrative statement about the way "God showed his love among us" (1 John 4:8–9). The statement "Yahweh our God Yahweh one" (Deut 6:4) is implicitly grounded in narrative statements such as "I am Yahweh your God who brought you out of Egypt" (Deut 5:6).

This example illustrates how the point about the possibility of moving from narrative to theology can be made in terms of Hebrew syntax. While biblical narrative is conveniently able to express itself by means of the finite verbs characteristic of Hebrew and Greek, the First Testament also makes use of Hebrew's "noun clauses" (such as "Yahweh our God Yahweh one") whose name indicates that they lack verbs. I do not imply the fallacy that the language's syntax reflects distinctive ways of thinking, only that the use of this particular syntax in theological statements shows that biblical theological thinking is not confined to narrative statements.

Second, narratives themselves incorporate discursive statements. Exodus tells of moments when God offers some self-description in response to questions from Moses. Before the exodus, God declares, "I am who I am" and speaks as "Yahweh, the God of your ancestors, the God of Abraham, the God of Isaac, and the God of Jacob." After the exodus and the people's faithlessness, God offers an extensive adjectival self-identification as compassionate and gracious, long-tempered, big in commitment and faithfulness, keeping commitment for 25,000 years, and forgiving, not ignoring wrongdoing (presumably that of people who do not seek forgiveness) but punishing it for 75 or 100 years. In both cases the statements are inextricably linked to narrative and gain their meaning from the narrative contexts in which they are set, but they are open to our reflecting on them as statements offering insights on God's nature that hold beyond their narrative context.

In between these two ways of linking narrative and discursive statement is a narrative such as John's Gospel. A film may sometimes seek to escape its form by having a narrator tell us things or by putting instructive speeches on its characters' lips. The *Pasadena Weekly* commented on how *You've Got Mail* incorporates Nora Ephron's "digressions into social commentary about the computer age, commercialism and blah, blah, blah." The Deuteronomists work in this way, but John does it most systematically. He and Paul are the two biblical thinkers who have most in common with systematic theology's way of thinking, but this technique enables John to do his theology in the writing of narrative as Paul does in writing discursively.

Scripture includes fundamentally factual narratives such as Kings and Mark and fundamentally fictional narratives such as Ruth and Jesus' parables. By "fundamentally" factual or fictional, I indicate a recognition that factual narratives in Scripture (like factual narratives elsewhere) include fictional elements, while fictional narratives incorporate factual elements (and are arguably always based on factual human experience). My working assumption is that most biblical narratives, like most other narratives, stand on the spectrum between bare fact and pure fiction. The latter two are ideal or notional types, extremes that are useful to define but of which there are no instances. Outside Scripture, both fact and fiction can be the means of conveying truth and depth, untruth and triviality. Every night it is possible to watch television news that is breathtaking in its combination of factuality and triviality.

Most weeks I watch one or two films that may be breathtaking in their combination of fiction and deep truth. Within Scripture, both fact and fiction are entirely true narratives and deeply significant ones. The truth in the factual is that which can be conveyed through facts, while the truth in the fictional is that which can be conveyed through fiction.

The two then have differing relationships with systematic theology. On one hand, a factual narrative seeks to keep systematic theology on the narrative straight and narrow, to drive it to keep thinking narratively, on the basis of the nature of the gospel that systematic theology is seeking to explicate. On the other, fictional narrative is more inclined to be the discussion of a theme or the interweaving of several themes, and it seeks to keep systematic theology from its traditional besetting temptation to be too straight and narrow, to be rationalist. I have noted that part of narrative's genius is its capacity to embrace ambiguity, discuss complexity, and embrace mystery.

Traditional systematic theology's strength is its analytic rigor and its emphasis on the law of noncontradiction, but that is also its limitation. Taking biblical narrative seriously has the capacity to release it from this limitation. Systematic theology could construct a discursive equivalent to the narrative discussion of the notion of God's presence and of God's transcendence and immanence such as appears in Exodus 19–40, but it would need to be one that preserved the richness and paradoxical nature of what a narrative presentation makes possible.

(By this example I have subverted my distinction between factual and fictional narrative and demonstrated the point that this distinction is a notional one; observations I have made about Mark also establish the point. I assume that Exodus is telling us about historical facts in a sense that Jonah or the parable about the good Samaritan is not, but the nature of its narrative shows that it has fiction's strengths and not merely the narrowness of factual narrative.)

If the Prophets and the Epistles show Scripture taking a step toward the way of thinking more characteristic of systematic theology, their nature also lays down another marker for the enterprise. They are also parts of Scripture especially concerned with the commitment of God's people to the gospel's behavioral implications. They thus suggest the need for systematic theology to be kept in relationship with commitment.[18] The collocation of haggadah and halakah as Judaism's two traditional ways of undertaking sustained reflection on Scripture coheres with this observation.

Biblical narrative itself has practical concerns. The Torah and the Gospels incorporate much material that explicitly delineates the way of life expected of Israel

18. See, e.g., Stanley Hauerwas, "On Doctrine and Ethics," in *The Cambridge Companion to Christian Doctrine* (ed. Colin E. Gunton; Cambridge and New York: Cambridge University Press, 1996), 21–40.

and of disciples. Further, the narrative itself is designed to shape a world view, but a world view within which people then live. The point can be illustrated from its handling of the theme of God's creation of the world. Scripture frequently takes up the theme of creation, but never for its own sake. In retelling the creation story, it always has some world-shaping to do. A work such as Moltmann's *God in Creation* is thus likewise concerned to work out the significance of creation in our own context.

There is a point to be safeguarded here. I have noted that biblical narrative talks more about human acts than about God's acts. Nevertheless its understanding of the significance of these human acts is generally rather gloomy. It is like that of film noir such as *LA Confidential*. In the end, film noir declares, everyone has their weaknesses; there are no unmitigated heroes. Biblical narrative agrees, but adds that God is also decisively involved in its story. In this sense Scripture puts its emphasis on God's acts rather than on human acts. We leave church less sombered than we leave the cinema.

Perhaps narrative can decisively shape human character. Certainly people who want to shape character often try to do so by telling stories, and people who want to have their characters shaped often seek this by reading them, though they commonly then find that biblical narrative is different from what they expected (but what would be the point of the Bible if it were what we expected?). Even the biblical narrative that is nearest to film noir, 1–2 Samuel, shapes character by portraying for us people with weaknesses and strengths like ours (Hannah, Peninnah, Eli, Samuel, Saul, Michal, Jonathan, David, Abigail) handling pressures and crises that are usually greater than ours, and by inviting us to set their stories alongside ours. Yet the shaping of character is rarely the direct aim of biblical narrative; we are not told stories about Abraham, Moses, Jesus, or Paul chiefly in order that we may let our characters be shaped by theirs. The primary concern of biblical narrative is to expound the gospel, to talk about God and what God has done, rather than to talk about the human characters who appear in God's story. The commonsense view that biblical narrative is concerned to shape character is surely right, but the narrative assumes that expounding the gospel is the way to do so.

The narrative also interweaves imperatives, in a variety of ways. Yahweh's promises to Israel's ancestors give them a responsibility to exercise for other peoples (Gen 18:17–33). Or, Yahweh's acts on Israel's behalf are sovereign deeds that establish Yahweh's lordship over Israel and look for a submissive response that takes certain forms ("I am Yahweh your God who brought you out of the land of Egypt: you are to have no other gods"). Or, Yahweh's acts embody priorities Israel is expected to share ("I delivered you from serfdom; you are not to treat people the way you were treated there"). Or, Yahweh's acts establish a distinctiveness about Israel that mirrors Yahweh's distinctiveness and requires to be embodied in its life ("You are to be holy as I am holy").

Biblical narrative thus suggests for systematic theology a context in concern about a relationship with God and a life lived for God. It is not merely an exercise in describing abstract truth. Nor is this merely a matter of acknowledging that systematic truths need to be applied. As happens in human relationships, the apprehension of truths about the person and the expression of these in relationship is dialogical.

Apprehending truths about the person feeds the relationship, but living in the relationship unveils truths about the person. As liberation theology has shown, a commitment to right living generates insight on the theological interpretation of Scripture as well as the other way round. Biblical narrative suggests that insight on theology and on lifestyle cannot be pursued separately. This awareness of the context of relationship leads to a further observation, that the Psalms (arguably the densest theology in Scripture, at least in the First Testament) hint that an appropriate form for systematic theology is that of adoration, thanksgiving, and lament, or at least that a context in the life of adoration, thanksgiving, and lament should be a fruitful one for theological reflection on biblical narrative.[19]

At least that is so in theory. In practice it is not evident that piety produces profound theology or serious interaction with biblical narrative. I am not yet ready to give up the hope that Christian doctrine and lifestyles might be shaped by Scripture, though I do not have great expectation that this will ever happen. If it is to do so, of key importance will be not the reading of scriptural narrative in light of what we know already and how we live already, but the reading of scriptural narrative through the eyes of people such as Jack Miles and Jon Levenson, who do not believe what we believe or practice what we practice.

4. Reflecting on Theology in Light of Narrative

If systematic theology did not exist, it might seem unwise to invent it, or at least unwise to begin the devising of grand schemes that are bound to skew our reading of Scripture and from which postmodernity delivers us. But systematic theology does exist, and it fundamentally shapes the church's thinking. In the context of considering the relationship between scriptural narrative and systematic theology, this suggests three functions for it.

First, systematic theology has the task of critical reflection on the theological tradition in such a way as to tweak the latter so that it does better justice to the prominence of narrative in Scripture.

The doctrine of Scripture itself suggests an example. Tradition has bequeathed to us a series of concepts that have shaped its formulation of Scripture's theological status and significance, concepts such as authority, canon, inspiration, inerrancy, infallibility, and revelation. Like the concept of Trinity, none of these appear in so many words in Scripture (except for one possible reference to inspiration in 2 Tim 3:16), and their significance in theology derives from questions that have arisen over the centuries such as the problem of authority, the question about reason and revelation, and the development of historical criticism.

---

19. Geoffrey Wainwright's *Doxology* (London: Epworth; New York: Oxford University Press, 1980) is "a systematic theology written from a liturgical perspective" (ix).

This need not make the use of these concepts unjustifiable; concepts from outside Scripture might enable us to articulate Scripture's own thinking. In practice, these concepts obscure Scripture's own implications regarding its nature, and they do this in particular with regard to the prominence of narrative in Scripture. Authority, revelation, and inspiration are not concepts well-fitted to bring out the theological status of a body of Scriptures that is dominated by narrative (they suit the Qur'an and the Book of Mormon rather better). The concepts of "witness" and "tradition" have more capacity to do this.[20] The nature of scriptural narrative makes it necessary for systematic theology to reflect on matters such as the nature of narrative itself and the nature of history, on narrative interpretation and on historical criticism, and these have more capacity to help theology do that.

Second, systematic theology has the capacity to encourage reflection in light of scriptural narrative on the church's more everyday assumptions regarding a topic such as the nature of God's involvement in the world and the implications of this for the practice of prayer.

Christians commonly emphasize the omniscience, omnipotence, omnipresence, and timelessness of God, assume that God has a detailed plan for the world and for their lives, and reckon that God works out in history a sovereign will framed before all eternity. That is part of their implicit systematic theology. Thus prayer never really involves informing God of something that God did not know (even of our own feelings), nor does it involve overcoming God or causing God to do something different from what God intended (such as show mercy when God did not intend to do so).[21]

The understanding of God implicit in such convictions derives from the same meeting of the Christian faith with Greek thought that we considered in section 2. Such Greek thinking emphasizes that God is the great absolute, independent of the world and unaffected by constraints. Such an understanding of God could perhaps not have come to shape Christian thinking unless there had been overlapping statements in scriptural material such as the Psalms and the Epistles. However, quite different assumptions about God feature prominently in biblical narrative. Here God is committed to the achievement of certain long-term aims, and sometimes acts in history, but does not decide how most events work out in history. If sovereignty means that what happens is what God wants to happen, God is not sovereign. As we have noted, specifically God is capable of being surprised, frustrated, grieved, and angered by events, and of becoming aware of failure to realize some intent. God thus has changes of mind and tries one plan after another. In responding to events and making new plans, God consults with human beings and as a result does

---

20. See my *Models for Scripture* (Grand Rapids: Eerdmans; Carlisle: Paternoster, 1994; Toronto: Clements, 2004).

21. See, e.g., Jonathan Edwards, "The Most High a Prayer Hearing God," Sermon xxxv in *The Works of President Edwards* (New York: Leavitt, 1854), 4:561–72. I am told that this is the text which most shapes thinking about prayer and practice of prayer by Christian students throughout the Greater Los Angeles universities and colleges.

things that would otherwise not have happened or refrains from doing things that otherwise would have happened.

In Christian thinking, the first kind of statement about God (as omniscient and outside time) is allowed to determine an allegorical interpretation of the perspective of biblical narrative, which is not allowed to mean what it says. Like the rule for the faith, "doctrine provides the conceptual framework by which the scriptural narrative is interpreted." In theory "it is not an arbitrary framework, however, but one that is suggested by that narrative. . . . It is to be discerned within, rather than imposed upon, that narrative."[22] In practice, in this instance, this process is short-circuited; the relationship between scriptural narrative and Christian doctrine becomes a vicious circle in which the narrative's significance is narrowed down to what doctrine allows it to say.

One result is that prayer that involves asking for things becomes much less significant than prayer as portrayed in biblical narrative. Indeed, the relationship between God and humanity becomes much less than is portrayed in biblical narrative. We never say anything that God does not know already or anything that makes a difference to God; the relationship becomes one-sided, and in this sense it is not really a relationship at all. Biblical narrative has a dynamic understanding of humanity's relationship with God and of humanity's involvement in God's purpose in the world. God acts in interaction with human activity and speech. In reflection on biblical narrative, systematic theology has the opportunity to encourage Christian thinking toward a more whole understanding of our relationship with God and of prayer's possibilities.[23]

Third, systematic theology has the capacity to facilitate reflection in light of scriptural narrative on current issues.

Recent decades have seen urgent questioning about what it means to be human in light of differences between the sexes, between races, and more recently between able-bodied people and handicapped people.[24] In reflecting on what it means to be human, traditional systematic theology has commonly emphasized the notion that we are made in God's image. The difficulty with this procedure is that "in God's image" is an extremely opaque expression, open to our reading into it whatever we wanted to emphasize about humanity's nature. Thus traditional systematic theology assumed that the divine image lay in human reason or morality or human capacity to have

22. Alister E. McGrath, *The Genesis of Doctrine* (Oxford and Cambridge, Mass.: Blackwell, 1990), 58–59.

23. See further John Goldingay, "The Logic of Intercession," *Theology* 99 (1998): 262–70, reprinted as "How Does Prayer Work?" in *Key Questions about Christian Faith: Old Testament Answers* (Grand Rapids: Baker Academic, 2010), 182–89.

24. I have discussed the last in "Being Human," in *Encounter with Mystery: Reflections on l'Arche and Living with Disability* (ed. F. M. Young; London: DLT, 1997), 133–51, 183–84, reprinted as "What Does It Mean to Be Human?" in Goldingay, *Key Questions about Christian Faith*, 42–55. Alistair McFadyen's systematic reflections on what it means to be a human person begin with his experience as a psychiatric nurse: see *The Call to Personhood* (Cambridge and New York: Cambridge University Press, 1990), 1–2.

a spiritual relationship with God. One place where the image certainly did not lie was in the body, despite the fact that images are usually physical. More recently the divine image has been seen in the capacity for relationship, which suits our concern about relationship. The disadvantage of Genesis's description of humanity as made in the divine image is that this phrase is not further explained in the context (or only allusively so). It is open to being understood in whatever way suits us.

A more positive way to put it is to see God's image, like God's reign, as a symbol rather than a concept. It is thus open-ended and dynamic, a stimulus to thought as much as a constraint on thought. If the description of humanity as made in God's image had appeared in a discursive work such as Deuteronomy or Romans, it might have been explained discursively (as happens in connection with talk of images in Deut 4). In contrast, we have noted that the nature of narrative is to show rather than tell. Placed at the beginning of the biblical narrative, the declaration that human beings are made in God's image is not to be understood as an isolated comment but neither is it simply a blank screen on which we are invited to project whatever suits us. It is to be understood in light of the narrative of whose introduction it forms part. As is the case with the word "God" itself, it is the narrative as a whole (for instance, from Genesis to Kings) that tells us what is "the image of God" and thus what it is to be human. Systematic reflection on the nature of humanity as made in God's image needs to be reflection on this narrative, not merely reflection on this opaque but stimulating phrase. Systematic reflection on what it means to be human will involve reflection on the succeeding biblical narrative of the lives of people such as Cain and Abel, Abraham, Sarah, and Hagar, Jacob and Esau, Ruth and Naomi, Saul, David, and Jonathan. All these lives raise issues about what it means to be human that can contribute to a systematic understanding of what it means to be human. Indeed, I assume that this is partly why they are there.

11

How Does Biblical Story Shape Our Story?

Christian spirituality has often emphasized the power that resides in our telling our story and hearing other people tell theirs.[1] This telling plays a powerful role in connection with our growth as Christians and our contributing to our brothers' and sisters' growth in Christ. Christian tradition has also assumed that the story the Bible tells is designed to make us grow, to shape the identity of the church and the individual. Pentecostals have emphasized the importance of sharing testimony as an approach to sharing in Bible study.[2] They believe in a "hermeneutics of testimony."[3] In considering the power of telling our own story, not least in connection with the interpretation of Scripture, it is illuminating to reflect on the power of Scripture's story.

Narrative, story, history dominate Scripture. Sometimes we set "story" and "history" over against each other, as if a narrative is either factual history or "only a story," but when we put it that way, we imply that factual history is what really counts. Story is mere entertainment. I do not want to imply an antithesis of that kind between story and history. With biblical narrative in general, it is important both that it relates to events that actually happened and that it is not a mere chronicle of happenings, but more than that; it is a narrative that brings out a message in the story and shows

---

1. First published in *The Journal of the European Pentecostal Theological Association* 17 (1997): 5–15.
2. See Jackie David Johns and Cheryl Bridges Johns, "Yielding to the Spirit," *Journal of Pentecostal Theology* 1 (1992): 109–34 (esp. 124–27).
3. See Paul Ricoeur, "The Hermeneutics of Testimony," *Anglican Theological Review* 61 (1979): 435–61 = Ricoeur, *Essays on Biblical Interpretation* (Philadelphia: Fortress, 1980), 35–61; though I am using the phrase in a different connection.

how it relates to its hearers. To say "story" is to say that this is not mere dry-as-dust history but a narrative with something to say to us.

The dominance of narrative, story, in Scripture is indicated by the way more than half the First Testament and more than half the New Testament is story. Although at one level Christian tradition has always recognized the importance of story, you would not guess this from the nature of Christian theology or from the nature of much writing on Christian spirituality.[4] Until story became a fashionable subject in the late twentieth century, the discursive form of theology that characterizes great works such as Thomas Aquinas's *Summa Theologica*, Calvin's *Institutes*, or Barth's *Church Dogmatics* seemed the natural way to do proper theology. It is indeed *a* natural and biblical way to do theology; it takes up the discursive method of Paul. But narrative is Scripture's more dominant way of doing theology, and it is therefore odd that subsequent Christian theology has not tended to take narrative form. It is especially odd given the fact that the reason for narrative's dominating Scripture is itself theological. It corresponds to a fact about the content of Scripture, to a central aspect of the Christian faith. The Christian faith is not a set of timeless truths, assertions that are always true about God and us. Christian faith is a gospel, a piece of news about something God once did. Its characteristic expression takes the form not of statements such as "God is love" or "God is three and God is one" but of statements such as "God so loved the world that he gave. . . ." The Christian faith is a narrative statement. One would therefore reckon that story would be a natural way to do theology or to do spirituality.

My starting point suggested another, related reason why story is a natural way to do theology. Alongside the way the gospel is story-shaped is the fact that human experience itself is story-shaped. This fact underlies the significance of story to spirituality. If I want to tell you who I am, I am likely to do so by telling you something of my story. The story-shapedness of Scripture corresponds to the story-shapedness of human experience as well as the story-shapedness of the gospel. I imagine that all these links are more than coincidence. Scripture is story-shaped because the gospel is story-shaped; the gospel is story-shaped because human experience is story-shaped. Very likely the logic also works the other way round. If it is important to human experience that it is story-shaped, and if human beings are made in God's image, then this points to the idea that God's experience is story-shaped, that God lives in narrative sequence. That is how Scripture describes God. God moves from not being incarnate, to being incarnate, to knowing from the inside what it is like to be a human being. As with human beings, God has a consistent nature and in this sense an unchanging nature, but Scripture also portrays God as living in narrative sequence, as human beings do. Human experience is story-shaped because the gospel is story-shaped because in some sense God lives in narrative sequence.[5]

4. See chapter 10 (section 2) above.

5. Jack Miles, *God: A Biography* (New York and London: Simon & Schuster, 1995) works out the implications of this notion.

Scripture is dominated by story and this story is designed to shape us, especially as we set our story alongside its story. How does that work?

1. Stories Told More Than Once

First, the scriptural story is a story told more than once, told in more than one way. A full two-fifths of the First Testament, from Genesis to Kings, comprises a mammoth single narrative running from creation via the story of Israel's origins and triumphs to its decline and fall and its return to the Babylon whence it came. The books we may think of as separate works (Genesis, Exodus, Leviticus, and so on) are not finally separate and self-contained works. They are more like long chapters in a very long work, or like the seasons of a long-running television series. None is fully complete on its own. None but Genesis has a clean start, and none but 2 Kings has a clean end. We know that 2 Kings has brought the long narrative as a whole to a real end only because turning over the page at the end of 2 Kings in the English Bible, we find ourselves back at the beginning, back with Adam, in 1 Chronicles 1:1. The English Bible follows the order in the Greek Bible. In the Hebrew Bible, the order is different; over the page from 2 Kings comes Isaiah, which makes at least as clearly the point that the Bible's great opening narrative has come to an end. Either way, Chronicles (which comes at the end of the Hebrew Bible) goes on to retell the entire story of Genesis to Kings in a new version. Following the Greek and English order, Ezra-Nehemiah (and in a sense Esther) continues that new version of the story. In the New Testament, one telling of the gospel story is succeeded by another, and another, and another, and then by a book that advertises itself as the continuation of the third of these; Acts continues Luke as Ezra-Nehemiah continues Chronicles.

What is going on here? Why is there more than one version of the stories in both Testaments?

The two great First Testament narratives were written for the Judean community in two different contexts. In its final form, at least, the first was written for a people under God's judgment by means of Babylon. The second was written for their descendants, when God had to some extent restored them by means of Persia. The community was in a different position in those different centuries. God needs to say different things to us according to where we are with God, and these narratives reflect this fact. The two narratives bring out different lessons from Israel's story. They emphasize different aspects of God's concerns and of God's ways of relating to the people. Whereas we can thus infer who were the audiences of those two great histories, the four Gospels do not tell us who were their equivalent targets, and the matter is a subject of scholarly speculation that will never come to final conclusions. But it is clear enough that these four retellings of the gospel story were devised to drive home its significance to people in different contexts.

The implication is that we need to understand the conversation between story and context in Scripture and see how story is being related to context and how context has the capacity to bring out the significance of story. Our uncertainty about the specific context of the Gospels does not significantly hinder us in this task, because we can securely enough infer from the narratives the *kind* of context to which they were written, especially by comparing them with each other. Matthew tells the story for Jewish Christian readers, for instance; Matthew and Luke are both more overt than Mark in telling their story for people living after the resurrection, telling it for the church itself. The differences between the Gospels are not reason for alarm but reason for encouragement as we see God inspiring the telling of the story in different ways for different people. Their example invites us to go on to retell the First Testament and the New Testament story in such a way as to bring home the gospel to people in their own context. The church in Britain, for instance, may seem a people of God that has gone through decline and disaster like that which came on the Judean community in the sixth century. The books of Kings model for us the telling of such a story in a way that owns such decline and disaster rather than hiding from it. It will own failure where there has been failure. It will recall reasons for hope that may lie not in human potential but in divine promise, in the fact that God has not finished with us. We need to tell our story not as mere history or as mere sociology but as a narrative portraying what God has been doing along the way and where God will want to take this story.

(It is a common scholarly theory, especially in the United States, that there had been a first edition of this narrative going back to the time of Jeremiah and Josiah, at the end of the sixth century. If this is so, it is a nice coincidence that the U.S. church has not reached the exile that the church in Europe has reached but is rushing toward it, like Judah in Jeremiah's day, so that it needs to tell its first edition of such a story and invite itself to halt the rush.)

2. Stories of Individual and Community

As a whole, the two great First Testament narratives are the stories of the people of God, with the stories of individuals told in the setting of that community story.

In general, the biblical story is designed to enable us to discover who we are. This involves our telling our own story, but doing so in the context of the Bible story. We find ourselves by setting ourselves in that other story. It shows us who we are and what our story means. For the early Pentecostals, "by interpreting their daily life and worship in terms of the significant events of biblical history, their own lives and actions were given significance."[6] "As they name reality, testimonies speak of tragedies, of failures, of fears, of oppression and of violence. However, they offer alternative realities when placed in dialogue with the Christian story."[7] We are not limited to our own interpretation of our experiences or left without the means of finding the meaning of our griefs. We find their meaning by setting our story alongside the scriptural story.

6. Steven Land, *Pentecostal Spirituality* (Sheffield: Sheffield Academic Press, 1993), 73.
7. Cheryl Bridges Johns, *Pentecostal Formation* (Sheffield: Sheffield Academic Press, 1993), 126.

The way telling our story is fashionable in Western culture means it can seem implicit that our story is self-interpreting and self-validating. The fact that things have happened to me in this way may seem to prove that my experience, self-understanding, and way of seeing things must be authentic. In reality, we tell our individual stories in light of a worldview, a "grand narrative." A culture has an implicit understanding of what it means to be human. The Christian conviction is that the biblical story is the real "grand narrative" in whose context the short stories of our communities and our individual lives have to be set if we are to understand them aright. This does not mean simply paying attention to the sections of the biblical story that seem of evident relevance to us. That makes us the point of reference. Rather, we let the biblical story as a whole set the framework for the way we look at our story.

Our identity is both a matter of who we are individually and of who we are in the context of a community. In the two great First Testament narratives, many ordinary individuals appear. Some, such as David, become much more than ordinary individuals. Others, such as Hannah, remain ordinary individuals but turn out to have a special significance for the story of the people as a whole. Hannah, that is, suffers, prays, and receives an answer to her prayer, like many individuals, but her answer turns out to affect the whole community. It involves the gift of a son who is the prophet who anoints Israel's first king and later de-anoints him and designates his successor.

British prime minister Margaret Thatcher once declared that "there is no such thing as society."[8] More recently, social trends have suggested that soon the majority of British people will be living on their own. As happens in many areas, the United States is far ahead of Britain in this development. We think and live primarily as individuals, and we experience the sadness of that, because God designed us also to live with the fulfillment as well as the challenge and frustration of being in relationship as part of communities. The relationship into which God draws us is not merely a one-on-one relationship with a single other person but a relationship in community that means we discover how much we gain when we give up part of our individual freedom. The two great First Testament narratives portray that double reality before us. They invite us to read Scripture for its capacity to rescue us from individualism so that we see and live our individuality in the context of communities. They point us to the discovery that our formation as people takes place in relationship with other people, not in isolation from them. The narratives are there to enable us to discover who we are, individually and corporately.

The stories of Abraham, Sarah, and Hagar, of Jacob and Esau, and of Joseph and his brothers are examples of stories that may help us discover ourselves. Genesis presents Abraham, for instance, as a man who believed Yahweh's word (Gen 15:6). It also presents him as a man who was capable of behaving in ways that look very questionable (for instance, in the story of Hagar that follows that act of faith). On other occasions, it offers no clue to whether he acts in faith or simply does what

8. *Woman's Own*, October 31, 1987; see http://www.margaretthatcher.org/document/106689.

Yahweh says because it is Yahweh who says so. Both Testaments invite believers to take Abraham as a clue to understanding how life works between Yahweh and Israel and between Yahweh and the individual believer. All three features of Abraham's story relate to that. As communities and individuals, we live in the context of God's promise, invited to trust it. At the same time, we are reassured that it is not surprising when a church or an individual fails in relationships with other people or with God; that is how things have been since Abraham. Nor is it surprising when things are ambiguous. Church and individual are urged to consider the path of their own following to see whether it is indeed a life of faith, even when we do externally walk in the way to which God points.[9]

3. Stories with a Plot

Both those great First Testament narratives are stories of promise, expectation, achievement, failure, and hope. You could say the same about the Gospels. They are stories with a plot.

Admittedly the balance of these plot elements in the two narratives varies, and that again reflects their context. Genesis–Kings emphasizes hope in its earlier stages, in the promises to Israel's ancestors. Promises are then fulfilled, and subsequently extended in God's commitment to David and to Zion, but they are apparently undone as Israel lapses back into subordination to foreign powers, reduction in numbers, loss of territory, destruction of its sanctuary, and the deposing of its kings. Yet the story keeps reminding us of the promises, as if to say "Perhaps there could yet be life in them. . . ."

Chronicles has a different dynamic, in some ways a more modern one. It covers the first three-quarters of the older story at breakneck speed in 1 Chronicles 1–9, like a video on fast-forward or the resumptive summaries at the beginning of an episode in a series. It does this just by means of a simple sequence of names; but the sequence goes beyond the point at which the main story will then start, the time of Saul, to close with the names of people who returned from Babylon on the other side of the community's acts of sacrilege. It thus ends up giving readers a preview of where the story will go as well as a reminder of where it has been. Sacrilege, invasion, destruction, and deportation are not to be the end. Ezra-Nehemiah continues the story, as its overlap with Chronicles makes explicit. Quite likely, to be even more modern, Chronicles is the prequel to Ezra-Nehemiah, the latter being written first. Chronicles thus invites the Second Temple community to see itself as the beneficiary of the generous mercy and faithfulness of Yahweh, though also (it must be said) of Yahweh's continuing toughness, or at least the faithfulness (and toughness) of aides such as Zerubbabel, Ezra, and Nehemiah themselves.

The two narratives point to our telling the story of the people of God in a way that reveals its plot, reflects grace, and owns failure.

9. See further my treatment of such stories in John Goldingay, *After Eating the Apricot* (Carlisle: Paternoster, 1996); www.documents.fuller.edu/sot/faculty.goldingay.

The difference between annals and stories is that stories have plots. They have a beginning, a middle, and an end; they are going somewhere. Plots are not intrinsic to history as we experience it. Like life, history "is a tale told by an idiot, full of sound and fury, signifying nothing."[10] It is storytellers who give plots to their tales, plots that need facts but might not emerge from facts until all the facts of history are known. Their plots bet on the reality of God and the truth of God's promise and God's grace, and rely on such known facts to make their bet plausible enough to base life on. They make it possible to own sacrilege, failure, and calamity because they set these in the context of a plot that refuses them the status of having the last word. Scripture enables us to tell our story in such a way as to face the facts about our hurt and pain, and the facts about the way we thus are or feel distanced from God.

Within postmodernity there are no grand narratives. There is no universally accepted overarching story. The biblical narratives imply an overarching story, but their actual stories are told on a smaller scale. They invite us to bet our lives on the truth of their sweeping but slightly-less-than-grand-narratives, to live our lives by them and prove their truth by proving that they can be lived in. They invite us to invite other people to take the plot of promise and achievement, sacrilege and failure, mercy and grace as the plot that will one day be proved to be the grand narrative, as the plot that provides the grid for understanding the shape of their own lives, as individuals and as communities, at moments of need, achievement, guilt, and calamity. They are lives given by God's generosity in grace and sustained by God's promise.

4. Stories Facing Sex and Violence

Israel's first opening great narrative incorporates a "chapter" comprising a self-contained story of sex and violence in the book of Judges. Judges illustrates how the heart of a story may sometimes be the many-faceted treatment of a particular theme. While Judges has a plot, its theme is at least as significant to its meaning. It thus parallels Genesis, which is arguably a story about God's promise, and Exodus, which is arguably a story about God's presence.[11] Such themes may run through a narrative. The theme may follow a trajectory, a sort of plot, so that we could not put the individual episodes in the story into a different order and leave the book unchanged in meaning. In Genesis, the promise moves from bare word to certain degrees of fulfillment, though also to its imperiling as the descendants of Abraham leave the land of promise. In Exodus, Yahweh is first God present acting, then God present speaking, then God present being. In Judges, the stories of sex and violence work toward a horrific ending in its closing chapters that more than vindicates its concluding comment on everyone's doing what was right in their own eyes in the absence of a state structure to constrain them in any more orderly direction.

10. William Shakespeare, *Macbeth*, 5.5.16.
11. See respectively David J. A. Clines, *The Theme of the Pentateuch* (Sheffield: JSOT, 1978); J. I. Durham, *Exodus* (Waco: Word, 1987).

From the beginning in this great narrative as a whole, sex and violence have been loci and expressions of human sin (Gen 4; 6), but in its account of their interweaving Judges brings the exposition of this motif to horrific highpoint. There are at least three books with the phrase "money, sex, and power" in the title or subtitle.[12] They point to three aspects of life that make big promises, offer big temptations, and open up huge pits beneath human beings. They raise three sets of questions that need facing in human life and relationships, and thus in the shaping of people as disciples. They are the three often-unacknowledged key issues in ministerial formation and ministerial failure. Hearing and telling the story of Judges has the potential to help us come to terms with our instinct for sex and violence. Men in particular need to put this book alongside our own instincts and the facts of our own stories, and/or to let it enable us to own these, though women may also find encouragement here, not least as the nature of their own experience is so clearly recognized.

5. Stories That Show and Tell Character

With some irony, after Judges this great narrative soon becomes the story of a man who could manage the state but not his own life, the story of David, a man for whom sex and violence were indeed realms of his failure. Yet a distinguishing feature of his story is its ambiguity and complexity. Like many a biblical story, much of it is told without offering any judgment on the tale. Interpreters sometimes distinguish between stories where we are shown things and stories where we are told them. A storyteller can tell the audience that a person is brave or honorable or can show them as honorable by describing things they do and leaving the audience to work out that this is true of them. The nature of film is to work by showing rather than telling; a story with a narrator can use the narrator to tell the audience what to think. In general, biblical stories show rather than tell. They then show a character such as David with all the complexity that attaches to human beings in real life, with the strengths and weaknesses and inconsistencies that are characteristic of real human beings. There is edification lying in the stories of saints as people who live with consistent integrity and faith. These inspire and edify. Stories of believers with the inconsistency and complexity of other human beings inspire and edify in another way. They can enable us to look into ourselves for the equivalent inconsistency and complexity, to face the oversimplifications of ourselves in which other people may indulge (and which may suit us ourselves, too), to see how far we are involved in the issues that David (for instance) was.

When Samuel-Kings does offer judgments on David, when it tells as well as shows, the problem is that there are too many of these judgments, or rather that they are too varied. David is the man after God's own heart, who followed Yahweh with all his heart, and whose heart was wholly true to Yahweh (1 Sam 13:14; 1 Kgs 14:8; 15:3). He is also the man who acted in a way that displeased Yahweh, who despised Yahweh's word, and

12. E.g., Richard J. Foster, *Money, Sex, and Power* (San Francisco: Harper, 1985).

who utterly scorned Yahweh (2 Sam 11:27; 12:9, 14). We are confronted by ambiguity as well as by complexity, by its being unclear which of two ways to read David; and this too may help us reflect on ourselves, or encourage other people to reflect on themselves.

One way to fit together the two sets of judgments on David is to see them as one expression of an inconsistency built into his life, a tension between David as a public figure and David as a private figure. In matters of state (as general or king or patron of the temple) David was characteristically incisive, faithful, and successful. In matters of private life (as friend, husband, father) he was characteristically weak, inconsistent, and unprincipled. The trouble is that leadership and private life cannot be kept separate; they inevitably contaminate each other. David's weakness as private human being produces weaknesses in his exercise of leadership. His story can thus encourage us to reflect on our exercise of our leadership and on the nature of our private lives, and on the interrelation of these, and to provide us with raw material for encouraging other people in that reflection.

6. A Story Facing Up to the Day of Small Things

We have noted that Genesis–Kings and Chronicles-Ezra-Nehemiah come from different contexts. The former especially speaks to people who know their own failure and need to be helped to own it to themselves and before God. The latter speaks to people who have known God's chastisement and restoration, yet not seen a fulfillment of God's promises that is as splendid as they might feel they had been led to expect. They remain a small group of survivors from the days of national glory, people with a small stake in the holy place and a little sustenance there, but still subject to the authority of an alien empire. Chronicles-Ezra-Nehemiah is thus a story with an aim, that of encouraging people to perceive the grace and commitment of Yahweh in their being in a position to resume life in Jerusalem and renew the temple there (Ezra 9:8–9).

The nature of narrative is to conceal its author, who disappears behind the story in a way that prophets may not disappear behind their prophecy. We do not know who was the author of Chronicles, and in this sense we cannot know the intention of the author in telling this story. Yet the nature of this narrative is not to conceal its intention or aim. It is designed to encourage the people of God, and it models the way our telling of the biblical story can be an encouragement to the people of God. It invites them to see God's involvement with them in the "day of small things" (Zech 4:10) and not to miss that God's involvement because it is not as impressive as the involvement we read of in other stories.

7. Short Stories about God's Involvement with Individuals

The First Testament includes a number of short stories about God's involvement in the lives of individuals. Although I deal with these last, in seeking to develop an understanding of stories there would be something to be said for starting with these short stories so that we can then move on to longer ones. Given their smaller scale, it may be easier to see in them how a story moves from problem to resolution or how plot and character interweave. They give us practice in gaining the understanding of a story as a whole that is then able to see how individual episodes fit into this whole.

One of these short stories relates how God works behind the scenes via a woman's acts of commitment. In the book of Esther, Queen Vashti is a woman who cannot be pushed around at the whim of a husband, even if he is a king and even if it costs her, and Esther is a woman who will use her position as Vashti's successor to bring deliverance from a royal official who wanted to use his position to eliminate her people even if it involves her in risk. We do not exactly get inside the characters in this story, discovering what makes them work, because they function more as embodiments of types (Ahasuerus the pompous king, Vashti the feisty queen, Mordecai the successful Jew, Esther the shrewd woman, Haman the stupid man). The story invites us to tell it so that people in positions that combine potential and vulnerability can look for God doing that in ways that correspond more directly with our own general experience of God's activity via human initiatives and apparent happy coincidences.

Another is a story about human friendship. Ruth is a tale with three characters, and it illustrates how sometimes the way to hear and to tell a story is to focus on the characters and to look for any indications of the way their character develops through the story. This happens to Naomi as she moves through loss and bitterness to hope and blessing. Different hearers may be able to identify more with thirty-something Ruth, or middle-aged Naomi, or lonely Boaz and be able to look for God at work in their ordinary lives as God was in theirs. Here as in Hannah's story, God gives their ordinary insignificant lives a place in God's great purpose, because the child they share turns out to be King David's grandfather. We tell the story so that people may look for God working through their relationships and through them, working out a purpose.

The First Testament's other great short story is a tale about how not to be a prophet. There is more to the book of Jonah than this, and that reflects the way a story may have more than one theme running through it. But if we are asking how Bible stories shape our story, especially how it shapes the story of people involved in God's service, then the natural angle from which to consider Jonah is its being a story about a prophet who gets everything wrong: his vocation, his prayer life, and his theology. God tells him where to go, and he runs in the opposite direction. When there is a crisis and other people are praying, he is asleep. When he realizes that God is gracious and compassionate, he objects. His story has the capacity to stop us taking ourselves too seriously or taking ourselves at our face value. Like Esther, it is full of irony, a powerful and a risky feature of a story, risky because irony is easily missed as parables are easily misunderstood; but then straight statement can also easily enough be ignored.

One way Jonah seeks to break through to its hearers is by ending with a theological question. It is the most intriguing, surprising end to a book in the First Testament, equaled in Scripture for its power in this respect only by the original ending of Mark's Gospel (Mark 16:8). For someone concerned for the shaping of people, importance attaches to raising questions as well as to answering them, and leaving them unanswered is sometimes important if people are to own their answers. It has been said that the place for the text in a sermon is the end, so that Scripture is the last thing people hear.[13] I offer the alternative observation that a biblical way to close a sermon is to ask a question and leave people to work out the answer for themselves.

13. So David J. A. Clines, "Note for an Old Testament Hermeneutic," *Theology News and Notes* 21 (1975): 8–10.

12

How Do We Preach on Narrative?

We noted in chapter 11 that more than half of each Testament comprises a series of narratives. The First Testament is dominated by two versions of an epic that begins with creation and takes us through the story of Israel (Genesis to Kings and Chronicles to Nehemiah). It also includes a number of shorter stories focusing on individual men and women such as Ruth, Jonah, and Esther; Daniel and Job, too, partly fit this category. The New Testament, in turn, is dominated by four versions of a new kind of story, an account of a Messiah who is unsuccessfully crucified; one of these continues with a report of aspects of the early years of the church, persecuted equally unsuccessfully.[1]

Stories in general, and biblical stories in particular, create a world before people's eyes and ears and invite people to live in that world as the real world, even if it contrasts with the world of their current experience. In issuing that invitation, a story communicates in a different way from direct statements of what people are encouraged to believe and do. It leaves the hearers to do more of the work if they are to learn from it. Perhaps precisely because of that, it may communicate more powerfully than a direct statement does. Everybody responds to stories: hence television is dominated by them, and advertising and documentaries characteristically focus their attention on what the product does for a specific family or on the way government policies affect people on a particular street. Stories are a key resource

1. First published in *Anvil* 7 (1990): 105–14 and incorporated in revised form in John Goldingay, *Models for the Interpretation of Scripture* (Grand Rapids: Eerdmans; Carlisle: Paternoster, 1995; Toronto: Clements, 2004).

by which Scripture communicates, and therefore a key challenge to the preacher. How do they themselves suggest we go about preaching on them?

I was brought up on that classical form of expository preaching that works by seeking to explain systematically and explicitly the central message of a text and the way its various parts contribute to this message, addressing people's minds as clearly and directly as possible. When I learned to preach, that was the form of preaching I sought to adopt. It remains a powerful and effective means of opening up the significance of Scripture, vastly preferable to the three-point "thoughts that have occurred to me that I am prepared to attribute to the Spirit and inflict on you" that are often the fare of pulpits. But it is mainly appropriate for Bible texts that are themselves directly expository, such as the Prophets, the Sermon on the Mount, and the Epistles. It is less appropriate to the history/story material in Scripture. A common homiletic approach to the latter is to summarize the story at the beginning of the sermon and then ask, "Well, what do we learn from this?" At this point the sermon falls flat on its face as we abandon the text's story form and turn it back into the kind of direct teaching that those other parts of Scripture offer.

I was just beginning to realize this and wondering how to develop an approach to preaching that would deal better with story texts when I came across a book called *Communicating the Word of God* by John Wijngaards.[2] It looks at appropriate ways of preaching on many different kinds of scriptural material, but it was the chapter on history/story that especially interested me. I was due to preach on Abraham at about the time I read it, and I decided to try a method Wijngaards suggests, retelling part of the story fairly straight, then reflecting on that part (perhaps talking about a modern experience that might be equivalent), then telling more of the story, then reflecting again, then relating yet a further episode of the story . . .

As I preached the sermon, I quaked at the knees, feeling I was taking people back to an old-fashioned Sunday school. Yet I do not remember ever receiving more appreciative comeback from a sermon. I proved to myself that there is a power about stories that reaches adults as profoundly as it reaches children. Like children, they will collude with you if you tell the story in a way that invites them to forget that they know it (avoiding the use of phrases such as "As we know . . ."), so as to enable themselves to be drawn into its wonder once again.

1. What Stories Aim At

"As the Father sent me, so I am sending you" (John 20:21). Jesus' commissioning of his disciples suggests one motive that will have underlain the telling of stories about him. He is the model for people who come to share his calling; as he lived and worked, so should they. Similarly, stories about Abraham or Sarah, Joshua or Ruth, Daniel or Esther, Stephen or Paul were preserved partly to offer examples for other

2. (Great Wakering: Mayhew-McCrimmon, 1978).

believers called to live by faith, exercise leadership, withstand the pressures of life in a foreign land, or witness boldly before Jews and Gentiles. It is this function of stories that is taken up by a passage such as Hebrews 11. Stories illustrate the commitments that the faith entails.

Using biblical stories to provide examples of how believers should or should not behave is thus a quite biblical procedure. Yet books on preaching often protest at such a moralizing approach, and the protest is eighty percent justified. While this way of using stories is common (especially with children and in family services), in Scripture it is much less so. There are theological and spiritual reasons for this. It focuses on God's word to people as a challenge to them to perform certain acts or to manifest certain characteristics, and this is its fundamental limitation. In contrast to it, the focus of the biblical story lies on what God has done for us. Taking stories as examples of what we should do or be risks turning the faith into something we do, rather than something God has done. It also causes problems when we read about things that God did or told people to do (such as slaughtering the Canaanites) that we rightly sense are not for us to imitate.

Perhaps the reason preachers are tempted to use stories in this way to a greater extent than Scripture itself does is that as preachers we may be inclined to feel that we only fulfill an aim and actually achieve something if we tell our congregations what to do; they can then go and do it. Perhaps Scripture gives this concern less prominence because it recognizes that when as believers we do not act or live as we should, it is commonly not because of ignorance, so that being given the right example will show us something we do not know. We need to be affected at a different level in order for our attitudes and behavior to change. Merely being given the correct positive or negative example may not help a great deal.[3]

At least as commonly as Scripture uses stories to illustrate the commitments the faith entails, it utilizes them to illustrate the experiences the faith may involve. The stories concern God and God's ways with God's people; they show us how God characteristically relates to people like us. They encourage and challenge us not by giving us a clearer picture of what we should or should not do or be, but by giving us a clearer picture of who God is. The stories in Genesis, for instance, focus more on the way God deals with Abraham and Sarah than on the way Abraham and Sarah relate to God. Their emphasis is on God's purpose, God's promise, God's initiative, God's blessing, God's covenant undertaking.

Occasionally Genesis does express implicit or explicit approval of human attitudes and actions (e.g., Gen 15:6; 22:16), but this is relatively rare. More commonly it is difficult to tell whether people are doing the right or the wrong thing or acting from right or wrong motives, as is reflected in the long-standing difference of interpretation of passages such as the Hagar story in Genesis 16. If Genesis saw Abraham and

---

3. The objections to this approach to preaching on narrative texts are discussed by Sidney Greidanus in *Sola Scriptura: Problems and Principles in Preaching Historical Texts* (Toronto: Wedge, 1970); see also his *The Modern Preacher and the Ancient Text* (Grand Rapids: Eerdmans; Leicester: InterVarsity, 1988).

Sarah primarily as examples to us, rights and wrongs would surely have to be made clear. If the stories mainly function to show how *God* fulfills a purpose for the world, despite as much as through human actions and circumstances, clarity about human motivation is less important. It is thus natural that when Isaiah 51 comes to appeal to the story of Abraham and Sarah, it is to the story as an example of what God can do that it appeals, not to the story as an example of what human faith can achieve.

Similar considerations probably lay behind the telling and preserving of stories about Jesus. The burden of these is not centrally to set Jesus forward as an example of what we are called to go out and do. More fundamentally they show us what Jesus can be and do for us. In appropriating these stories, we do not see ourselves as taking Jesus' position but as taking that of disciples (or opponents) for whom or despite whom Jesus can achieve his purpose.

To take stories as illustrations of the experiences that the faith regularly involves comes closer to their intrinsic nature, but it leaves certain problems unresolved. Not all stories embody characteristic experiences of faith. In particular, what is the purpose of the stories of great miracles? If God marvelously delivered Israel at the Red Sea, rescued Daniel from the lions, brought back to life the widow's son at Nain, and resurrected Jesus from death, we cannot infer that God with any frequency acts in that way for later believers. Martyrdom is an infrequent occurrence, but it is more common than miraculous rescue. So what is the point of such miracle stories in the Bible? What message is the preacher to draw from them? They bring out particularly clearly a question that arises with many stories, in that they do not indicate what God may do with us, any more than what God expects of us.

Such stories manifest a characteristic they share with the biblical story as a whole: they bring to life the events on which the faith is based. This faith is itself a gospel, a piece of good news about something that has happened. It is good news with implications for the present and for the future, but it is news about events that are essentially past. Thus John tells us that he wrote his story of Jesus so that people might come to believe (or might carry on believing) that Jesus is the Messiah and might thus find life in him (John 20:30–31). Luke's explanation of the purpose of his Gospel (Luke 1:1–4) is similar. In 1 Corinthians 15, Paul assumes that the story of Jesus' resurrection is important, not because it models the kind of experience of new life Christians may have in this life (though this point is made elsewhere), but because Jesus' resurrection was the once-for-all event in the past that makes inevitable our own rising from the dead at the End.

First Testament stories, too, were written to bring to life the once-for-all past events on which faith for the present and for the future has to be based. The Abraham story reminded Israel that they possessed their land only as God's gift, in fulfillment of God's promise. The exodus story reminded them that they had been only a herd of demoralized serfs in a foreign country, and would still be that but for the exercise of Yahweh's power on their behalf. The books of Kings showed how Israel ignored Yahweh's expectations over centuries and thus explained why they had ended up in exile. The fundamental function of stories in both Testaments is to bring to life the events on which the faith is based. They are events that may not be repeated in our experience, yet ones that remain of crucial importance for us.

Biblical stories are not limited to fulfilling one of the three aims just described; their depth may derive partly from their fulfilling several functions at once. Yet one function will usually be more important in any one story than others. Ruth relates how God's providence takes two women through bereavement and exile and into new life ("the experiences that the faith may involve"), but it also makes these events part of the introduction to the story of David ("the events on which the faith is based") and implies that Ruth and Boaz are models of caring for a widow in need and for a girl in need (and of how to get yourself a husband?!). Disagreements about the present relevance of some stories (for instance, the use of Exodus in liberation theology or the use in renewal circles of stories in the Gospels and Acts about healing or raising the dead) are sometimes disagreements about whether these stories relate solely "the events on which the faith is based" or also offer paradigms of how God may act now or how we should act now.

The answer may not be the obvious one. To return to Joshua: readers are often repelled by its stories of extermination in the past, as they are by the visions of extermination in the future in Revelation, taking these as accounts of what happened or what will happen. But they may not be that. The opening of Judges makes clear that Israel did not actually slaughter the Canaanites as one might have inferred from Joshua, and critical and archeological study points away from Joshua's being a straightforwardly historical work. Such narratives and visions have been called "sanguinary fictions" that "reflect in the contemporary modes of the imagination men's acute sense of the struggle against the encroachments of the primeval chaos and for the viability of the human."[4] They are not merely accounts of events on which the faith is based (past or future) but also expressions of or invitations to present faith, hope, and commitment in the context of threatening chaos.

2. How Stories Preach

The Gospels suggest four ways of going about telling a story so as to enable it to be effective. One is by simply telling it. Interpretive comments by the narrator are rare; events speak for themselves. While many First Testament narratives work on this basis, Mark's Gospel is the most powerful driving straight narrative in Scripture. This breathless accumulating chain of stories manifests a "lack of relaxation or indulgence"; "every incident is a summons to recognize the mystery of Jesus and to follow him."[5] In this sense, the story is quite straightforward in its message and way of working. At the same time, readers who begin trying to give themselves to individual stories in Mark find that in their straightforwardness they are puzzlingly

4. Amos N. Wilder, *The New Voice* (New York: Herder, 1969), 59.
5. John Drury, *Tradition and Design in Luke's Gospel* (London: DLT, 1976; Atlanta: John Knox, 1977), 32.

opaque. They rarely tell us what to learn from them beyond what they contribute to the thrust of the Gospel as a whole. This work in which Mark first "took the momentous step of presenting the (Pauline) gospel of the cross entirely as history" has the "primeval power" of something done "powerfully and roughly for the first time," compared with the "more elegant and digestible" work of subsequent masters such as Matthew and Luke,[6] which do much more of the work for their readers. There is a theology implicit in Mark's story of Jesus, but it is less overt than those of the other Gospels.

The reminder this issues to the preacher is the power of the bare story. The philosophy of story presupposes that stories can communicate and convey a world without the storytellers necessarily making explicit what principles or lessons they want people to draw from them. Mark's Gospel points us toward a style of preaching that is simple, the mere retelling of a story, but may be extremely powerful. The preacher finds it difficult to believe that the congregation will get the point and feels a responsibility to make explicit and to underline what that point is, but by doing so we may destroy the dynamic of the story itself, which gets home in power precisely by working more subliminally.

Matthew's Gospel illustrates a second way of telling stories, by building an application of the story into the way one tells it. Matthew contemporizes Mark in order to draw his readers into his story. This is the way he makes his story work as "preaching," as the bringing home of a message from God intended to change the faith and life of the hearers. Mark had told a story about the disciples in a storm on the lake, for instance, a story firmly located in the historical ministry of Jesus (Mark 4:35–41). Where Mark tells about the disciples taking Jesus into the boat, however, Matthew says they "followed" him into it (Matt 8:23). It might have been a coincidence that Matthew uses the technical term of Christian discipleship; but he has already added to Mark's story the account of how Jesus warned one would-be disciple about the cost of following him, and has urged another to follow him rather than putting it off (Matt 8:19–22). So the recurrence of the term is less likely to be accidental. Getting into the boat is an act of following Jesus. The storm is then the kind of experience that sometimes comes to Christian disciples, "Save, Lord" is the way the church prays in crises (contrast Mark's "Teacher, do you not care . . ."), "of little faith" is its Lord's assessment of his followers (Mark's "have you no faith?" is less appropriate to people who have made their initial commitment in faith) (Matt 8:23–26).[7]

In subtle ways, Matthew brings home the story's application to the church's life by the way he retells the story. Similarly the preacher's occasional sentences expressing what Jesus "said" in the sense of "would have said" to people like us make it possible to keep the story form, with its potential for reaching mind, heart, and will, yet also

---

6. Ibid., 6.

7. See further Günther Bornkamm in Günther Bornkamm, Gerhard Barth, and Heinz Joachim Held, *Tradition and Interpretation in Matthew* (London: SCM; Philadelphia: Westminster Press, 1963), 52–57.

make it possible to indicate how the story applies to us without appending another sermonette on the end that risks destroying its impact.

There is another implication of the difference between the approaches of Matthew and Mark. Mark is mainly concerned with "the events on which the faith is based," with the Jesus of Galilee and Jerusalem to whom its readers have committed or should commit themselves. Matthew is more concerned with "the experiences that the faith may involve" and "the commitments that the faith entails," with the Christ event's continuing concrete implications for discipleship. In the First Testament, Kings is more like Mark: it is an account of how the exile came about, an "act of praise at the justice of the judgment of God,"[8] not an attempt to draw detailed lessons from the distant past for ongoing life in the present. Genesis and Chronicles may be more like Matthew, retelling the story not only out of a concern that people may come to the right act of faith in regard to the events of the past, but also wanting them to see the story's implications for ongoing life (for instance, the significance for people in Babylonian exile of Sabbath, abstaining from blood, and circumcision, and the significance for people after the exile of David's arrangements for the temple and of the defeats and triumphs of preexilic history).

John's method of contemporizing the story of Jesus is less subtle than Matthew's. He offers examples of something like the procedure that subsequent preachers have often used (the one that is otherwise rarer in Scripture itself), whereby the point of the story is driven home by direct teaching material attached to the story to bring out its theological and ethical implications. Even here, however, the teaching can be presented as the words of Jesus rather than as the words of the evangelist (one might compare First Testament sermons such as that in Josh 1), so that the framework of the story form is kept.

A fourth form of biblical storytelling is instanced by Luke, which continues the gospel story into the life of the church. Our story is thus linked onto the biblical story. This process had a long history in First Testament Israel, most clearly in the way Ezra and Nehemiah continue the story told in Kings and Chronicles. It also probably underlies the accumulation of the history in Genesis to Kings as a whole, which was repeatedly brought up to date by having new episodes linked onto it, as well as by being itself retold in updated ways. The eventual result of this process that contributed to the development of the Scriptures as a whole is the macro-story that stretches from Beginning to End with Christ at its center. Because it looks forward to the End as well as back to the Beginning, it embraces our story.

It is possible to present a sermon by setting a biblical story and a modern story side by side, but whether or not we do precisely that in the pulpit, Luke's work offers a suggestive clue to a way we may go about preparing the sermon (or studying Scripture for ourselves). We are seeking to set an appropriate aspect of our story alongside the biblical story, linking our story onto God's story.

8. Gerhard von Rad, e.g., *Old Testament Theology* (2 vols.; Edinburgh: Oliver and Boyd; New York: Harper, 1962), 1:343.

3. How Stories Engage Their Readers

Stories engage their readers. How do they do this, and how do we enable them to do this in the retelling? The following observations are not universals, but they may be useful generalizations.

First, stories have a beginning, a middle, and an end; they are structured. They have a plot of some kind. We are presented with a problem that is to be solved; quite likely there are difficulties to be overcome on the way or consequences when the main events are over. In Gospel stories an aspect of them may lead to a significant remark by Jesus, and it is for the sake of this remark as much as for any other reason that the story is told. Interpreting a story involves discovering how its plot works; it may then be natural for the sermon's structure to follow that of the biblical story. The sermon may not have a structure in the sense of four points beginning with the letter r, but it will still (for the congregation's sake) be a structured entity rather than a ramble, in the more subtle way that a story is.

Second, stories offer a concrete portrayal of a series of events against a particular historical, geographical, social, and cultural background. There is movement from one area to another, political and religious heroes and villains pass before the audience's eyes, pressure points of economic or family or social life are alluded to or emphasized. For the story to grasp its modern hearers, the significance of these allusions has to come home. It is possible to convey this information in a ham-fisted way; there is no need to incorporate all the learning that may be gleaned from valuable works such as de Vaux's *Ancient Israel* or Jeremias's *Jerusalem in the Time of Jesus*,[9] and one should spare the congregation the phrase "When I was in Israel" as rigorously as the phrase "The Greek word means," invaluable though a visit to the scene itself and a knowledge of the biblical languages are to understanding and preaching on biblical stories. The skilled storyteller brings to life the concreteness and thus the reality of a story by more subtle, low-key explanations of the meaning of this detail or that, in the course of the imaginative reconstruction of a significant scene.

A third feature of biblical stories is that they invite their hearers to identify their life and circumstances with those presupposed by the story. In this way the story makes clear in the telling that it is about the hearer as well as about the subject. Features that mark biblical stories as unhistorical often originate with this characteristic. We have noted it in a Gospel story such as the stilling of the storm, which makes Jesus and his disciples use the language of the life of the church. In the First Testament, Chronicles pictures priest and people of previous centuries behaving the way they would in the Chronicler's day. The preacher, in retelling the story, similarly encourages the congregation to see the story as about people like them in situations like theirs, not by telling them that it is so but by using the kind of language that makes it so.

To this end, as well as portraying the scene, the setting, and the action, the preacher may look at the events through the eyes of each of the characters in the story. One

---

9. Roland de Vaux, *Ancient Israel* (London: DLT; New York: McGraw-Hill, 1961); Joachim Jeremias, *Jerusalem in the Time of Jesus* (Philadelphia: Fortress; London: SCM, 1969).

needs to be wary of psychologizing characters, imposing on the story modern interest in and modern forms of expression of the inner workings of people's minds, and also of biographizing them, since biblical stories also lack our interest in the way characters develop over time. Yet we can ask what an event would mean for the kind of person involved, and how these characters would relate to each other, noting especially what we can learn from the words, feelings, and actions that are attributed to them. For a fourth feature of many stories is their focusing on individual people with whom the hearers are invited to identify. Luke 7, for instance, offers its hearers a series of brief sketches involving a galaxy of players: Jesus, centurion, slave, elders, friends, crowd (vv. 1–10); Jesus, disciples, crowd, widow, mourners, youth (vv. 11–17); John, his disciples, Jesus, crowd, recipients of Jesus' ministry, Pharisees, lawyers (vv. 18–35); Pharisee, sinful woman, Jesus, guests (vv. 36–50). The stories engage their hearers by offering them various characters with whom to identify. Different hearers then grasp different facets of the stories' significance, so that group meditation on a story naturally leads different people to focus on and identify with different characters in a way that can then be illuminating for the whole group. Different facets also come home to particular hearers at different times in their lives; there is no once-for-all hearing of a story. Our task as preachers is to open up as much as possible of the resources that lie in these various character portrayals, all of which can disclose for people aspects of the gospel. It is to help people to get into the story, identifying with characters and situations as if hearing it for the first time, so that in doing so they can respond to the gospel in the way they must.

13

Does Biblical Narrative Need to Be Historical?

The Christian church received the First Testament from Christ and recognized in it the voice of God speaking "in many and various ways" (Heb 1:1).[1] This divine-human communication came down to us expressed predominantly in narrative forms, which dominate in the Torah and Prophets and are prominent in the Writings. Given that narrative forms may be used for many purposes (historiography, the novel, the fairy tale, and so on), why does the First Testament use narrative? How far is its narrative intended to be historical? How far does its message depend on history? Further, how far must our acceptance of the truthfulness of its message depend on being sure of the historicity of the events it narrates? If we could prove by historical method that some of the Israelites' forebears escaped from slavery in Egypt in the thirteenth century, and even if we were prepared to see a supernatural agency at work in this, such a measure of verification of the narrative in Exodus would not necessarily bring with it the validation of the First Testament's theological interpretation of this event.[2] Such historical verification does not ensure theological validation. Is historical veracity nevertheless a sine qua non of theological validity, a necessary though not a sufficient feature if we are to accept it as theologically true? Does the First Testament's revelation-value hang on its history-value? To approach

1. Originally published as " 'That You May Know That Yahweh Is God': A Study in the Relationship between Theology and History in the Old Testament," *TynB* 23 (1972): 58–93.
2. R. Tomes is indeed prepared to grant in part the Exodus account of the Israelites' deliverance from Egypt, but not its mainstream interpretation of the event ("Exodus 14," *SJT* 22 [1969]: 455–78).

the question from the other direction, "Why is an understanding of the Bible as fictive considered to undermine its truth and integrity?"[3]

1. Revelation and History in Theological Debate

The heyday of a stress on a link between revelation and history was the 1950s and 1960s. In the United States, it was one of the emphases of the biblical theology movement; thus G. E. Wright asserted that "the primary and irreducible assumption of Biblical theology is that history is the revelation of God."[4] In Germany in a different context, it was a central theme in the work of Wolfhart Pannenberg, the key figure in generating a symposium called *Revelation as History*.[5] Yet during the 1960s it also came to be regarded as questionable whether revelation in history was after all an idea peculiar to Israel in the Middle East,[6] whether it is an adequate formulation of the First Testament's attitude to revelation,[7] and even whether the idea of revelation is appropriate to Christianity at all.[8] I therefore begin with some reconsideration of the appropriateness of these terms.

The prima facie impression that the First Testament gives, of a close interest in certain events that happened on the historical plane, is surely neither misleading nor surprising. The books of Kings, at least (which admittedly offer the clearest example), seek to give precisely this impression by devices such as providing relative dating and references to other sources. This interest is only to be expected in light of the widespread assumption that the events of history have meaning.[9] Nevertheless, if it were possible to proscribe theological terms, then "history" might make a good candidate for such treatment. It was long a word with value status in theology,[10] so that any theological position had to claim to be "historical" if it hoped to be taken seriously. Someone who believed that the First Testament literature, the tradition, had a revelatory value independent of whether the events it speaks of happened, or that truth is known through personal human experience in the now, ipso facto does not believe in a revelation through history. Yet because of the value status attached to history, the tradition came to be described as "historical tradition" and

---

3. Thomas L. Thompson, *The Mythic Past* (New York: Basic, 1999), 5. The present chapter is the oldest in this collection and the one whose references are most systematically dated, but Thompson's question shows how the subject does not go away.

4. *God Who Acts* (London: SCM; Chicago: Regnery, 1952), 50.

5. (New York: Macmillan, 1968; London: Collier-Macmillan, 1969); cf. Pannenberg's own essays on this theme in *Basic Questions in Theology* (2 vols.; London: SCM; Philadelphia: Westminster Press, 1970), e.g., 1:15.

6. B. Albrektson, *History and the Gods* (Lund: Gleerup, 1967).

7. J. Barr, *Old and New in Interpretation* (London: SCM; New York: Harper, 1966), 65–102.

8. F. G. Downing, *Has Christianity a Revelation?* (London: SCM; Philadelphia: Westminster Press, 1964).

9. Albrektson, *History and the Gods*, passim.

10. Barr, *Old and New in Interpretation*, 65.

experience as "historical experience," when the rationale for a theology of tradition or a theology of experience should lie elsewhere.[11]

The ambiguity of the word "history" has facilitated its wide use in theology.[12] The remark usually attributed to Oscar Wilde, "Any fool can make history, it takes a genius to write it," capitalized on two fundamentally different areas that the word covers, "things that have happened" and "our account of things that have happened," but it has had many theological successors. Without intending to trade on them, Gerhard von Rad uses "history" and "historical" in half a dozen senses in his discussion of the proper subject matter of First Testament theology.[13] The adjective "historical" applied to the tradition or to experience seems to mean no more than that they came into existence on the plane of human history, as part of the historical process; but then how else could they?

As well as being both loaded and ambiguous, "history" is in another connection too narrow a word. Its use in First Testament study relates primarily to the great events of Israel's national experience, as opposed to the events of ordinary life that the wisdom literature is more concerned with. This distinction, and the value status attached to "history," combine to divorce the historical and prophetic works from the wisdom books and to make the former seem more important than the latter, when in reality historian and prophet on the one hand, and sage on the other, agree in picturing God acting and God being revealed in events on the historical plane, but the former concentrate on those of national history, the latter on those of everyday life. Even this distinction should not be sharply drawn. Kings, for instance, is also concerned with God's activity in everyday affairs and in the world of nature, which is also often distinguished too sharply from that of history. Conversely, the wisdom books are concerned with national and political affairs.

The word "events" is more useful for correlating with "revelation" in connection with the First Testament. It is a less loaded and less ambiguous word than "history," and also a word better suited to the breadth of what the First Testament has to say about God's activity.[14] I shall try to use the word "history" only in a neutral way as a still convenient way of speaking of things that happen (primarily to the nation) as part of the historical process.

Is it appropriate to speak of "revelation" in connection with events, whether of history, of personal experience, or of nature? Perhaps the word "revelation" should

11. Thus M. J. Buss defends the nonhistorical nature of the First Testament on the grounds that categories of time and space do not apply in the subatomic world; he infers that ultimate reality is Being rather than History (in J. M. Robinson and J. B. Cobb, eds., *Theology as History* [New York: Harper, 1967], 137–38). Philosophy of language could provide a comparable basis for a belief in the revelatory value of tradition apart from a historical reference.

12. Barr, *Old and New in Interpretation*, 66–70.

13. *Old Testament Theology* (2 vols.; Edinburgh: Oliver and Boyd; New York: Harper, 1962), 1:105–15; further, Albrektson, *History and the Gods*, 87.

14. Barr, *Old and New in Interpretation*, 26–27, suggests the word "situations" to indicate the setting of God's revelatory action; "events" denotes where the activity is seen and the revelation thus verified. A. Richardson, *History Sacred and Profane* (London: SCM; Philadelphia: Westminster Press, 1964), 223–27, speaks of "disclosure situations."

be allowed to go the same way as "history," for the First Testament does not speak of "God revealing himself" anywhere near as often as theologians came to, and it uses such language rather rarely in connection with events of history.[15] This reflects the fact that the problem of revelation or epistemology is a modern concern. The Bible is more concerned about religion without morals than about morals without religion, and normally speaks "from faith to faith." It sees the essential human predicament not as ignorance but as sin, and therefore it sees humanity's essential need not as revelation but as redemption or reconciliation.[16]

Nevertheless, the First Testament does speak of "Yahweh revealing himself" or "making himself known." The niphal of *galah*, *ra'ah*, and *yada'* first occurs in connection with Yahweh's encounter with human beings in human-like form, and its use in the Psalms (e.g., Pss 9:16 [17]; 48:3 [4]; 102:16 [17]) probably has such overtones. Some verses in the prophets come nearest to speaking of a divine self-revelation in events of history (Isa 40:5; Ezek 20:5, 9; 35:11; 38:23). A stress on God "acting to reveal himself" invites the comment that when God (or anyone else) acts, this is primarily in order to effect something, not just "for show." Yet precisely because it was assumed that acting is the means of God's will being put into effect, throughout the Middle East "it is thought to be possible for men to know how the gods are disposed by observing what happens. . . . Defeats and disasters are interpreted as evidence of the anger or displeasure of the gods, and similarly success and prosperity are held to reveal their favor and mercy."[17]

This does not mean there is a revelatory character inherent in history as such.[18] Historical events are not self-interpreting; they can be given an interpretation only within an already existing framework of beliefs, that the gods may be assumed to be active, powerful, purposeful, consistent, moral, merciful, and so on. An event can be understood as an act of God only by being associated with the accepted truths about God.

Even within such a tradition, interpretation cannot be assumed to be unnecessary, as the differences of opinion between Jeremiah and his prophetic contemporaries show,[19] and when God's *sod* is revealed to the prophets (Amos 3:7), this does not seem always to be a concession to unbelief.[20] Exodus and conquest show God's benevolence and faithfulness to Israel but not their grounds: is it Israel's faithfulness or Yahweh's love? "The difference between these two alternatives is immense: it is the difference between law and gospel, between man's merits and undeserved divine

---

15. Downing, *Has Christianity a Revelation?* 20–47.

16. C. Braaten, *History and Hermeneutics* (Philadelphia: Westminster Press; London: Lutterworth Press, 1968), 14; cf. Downing, *Has Christianity a Revelation?* 123–25, 274–83.

17. Albrektson, *History and the Gods*, 100. Pannenberg, *Basic Questions in Theology*, 1:16–22, seeks to elucidate wherein the uniqueness of Israel's historical consciousness lay.

18. As Richardson (e.g., *History Sacred and Profane*, 225–26) and Pannenberg (e.g., *Basic Questions in Theology*, 1:61, 66) sometimes seem to imply.

19. E.g., Jer 23:9–40. Cf. R. Davidson on Jeremiah and the tradition, "Orthodoxy and the Prophetic Word," *VT* 14 (1964): 407–16.

20. As Rolf Rendtorff (in Robinson and Cobb, eds., *Theology as History*, 129) seems to suggest.

grace. But no naked events will decide which alternative is right; they are mute—or rather, they are ambiguous. Something must be given in addition to the events: the word of revelation."[21]

If this is true of the great moments in Israel's history such as the exodus, it is even more true outside these, especially insofar as the events of Israel's history are in large part the working out of the frustration of God's will rather than the fulfillment of it. The regular process of history is anti-revelatory;[22] any fool can make history, it takes God to right it. This negative view of history as the tale of human opposition to God comes to the fore in many apocalypses. God's revelation comes in connection with acting to end history and bring in the new age, and it comes not as "the last candle at the end of a history-long candlelighting service" but as light bursting in on darkness.[23]

The very nature of history, then, seems to demand that in order to communicate by means of history, God will need to speak. The very natures of humanity and God make the same demand. The faculty of verbal communication is a basic constituent of personality.[24] As Martin Heidegger put it, language constitutes our humanity; it is what distinguishes humanity from the rest of the animate and inanimate world. It is, furthermore, a basic means of personality making itself known: "through speech the essence of a personality receives expression more fully than through any other means of self-expression."[25] It is presumably (though this is indeed only a matter of inference) for reasons such as these that the God of the First Testament not only acts but also speaks.

What then is the relationship between the speaking and the acting? As far as the effecting of God's will is concerned, it is no doubt mistaken to try to distinguish too closely between speaking and acting (and indeed willing). Decision, word, action are all one. In the area of epistemology, however, it is important to distinguish word and deed, for they function in different ways. It is God's words that reveal God's nature and purpose, but precisely because words that really come from God find fulfillment in events, the events, God's actions, also fulfill an epistemological function, not so much as revelation but as confirmation of purported revelation. "Yahweh's history with Israel is the place where the truth of his revelatory word is knowable in that it is carried out."[26] Thus word and deed are both important to God's self-revelation. The First Testament writers "kept real historical facts indissolubly together with the accompanying words of interpretation. Facts without words are blind; and words without facts are empty, to paraphrase one of Kant's famous utterances."[27]

21. Albrektson, *History and the Gods*, 118.

22. Buss, in Robinson and Cobb, eds., *Theology as History*, 145–47. Rudolf Bultmann expounds the thesis that First Testament history is a history of failure in his essay on "Promise and Fulfillment," in *Essays on Old Testament Interpretation* (ed. Claus Westermann; London: SCM, 1963) = *Essays on Old Testament Hermeneutics* (Richmond: John Knox, 1963), especially 72–75.

23. W. R. Murdock, "History and Revelation in Jewish Apocalypticism," *Int* 21 (1967): 167–87 (187).

24. Barr, *Old and New in Interpretation*, 77–78.

25. J. Lindblom, as quoted in Albrektson, *History and the Gods*, 119.

26. Walther Zimmerli, in Robinson and Cobb, eds., *Theology as History*, 45.

27. Braaten's description of some nineteenth-century theologians, *History and Hermeneutics*, 23.

The implication of this debate in the 1960s is thus that "revelation as history," far from being the central concept in the First Testament, is not really a biblical notion when put simply thus. But it is true that events on the historical plane, both those of national and those of everyday personal experience, fulfill an essential function ancillary to the words by which God's will and ways are known, in that these events provide an external check for, a vindication of, the purported divine words. Theological assertions appeal to events for their validation, the assertions depend on the historical veracity of the events, and thus the historical verification of the events opens up the possibility of accepting the theological assertions. They will not guarantee it or force it; although the fall of Jerusalem fulfilled and proved Jeremiah's words, the devotees of the Queen of Heaven read the event in a very different way from him (Jer 44:15–23), and people without ears to hear will continue to fail to understand (cf. Isa 6:9). But for people with a gleam of insight, the Ebed-melechs and the Baruchs (Jer 39:15–18; 45:1–5), the event that confirms the word also enlarges the vision.

On the other hand, if the words of prophets remain unfulfilled, this at least casts doubts on their theology; and if historians, through the inadequacy of their sources or because of the construction they place upon them, make assertions about events that the events do not justify, then these historians' theology, too, has doubts cast upon it. This is so not because historicity has a mystical significance but because this is the ground upon which historians or prophets have chosen to base themselves; by historical verification they have committed themselves to stand or fall.

In connection with this debate, I now consider what happens when we ask what implications regarding revelation and verification emerge from the books of Kings and of Job, which exemplify something of the diversity of the books in the First Testament.

2. Revelation and Verification in the Books of Kings

Both in Kings and in Job, God is known or speaks by many different means; others might be added from elsewhere in the First Testament, notably revelation through personal encounter (human relationships). Indeed, "there is no reality, thing, or event which cannot become a bearer of the mystery of being and enter into a revelatory correlation";[28] nor is any one of these media normative and the rest secondary. In connection with Kings, however, they may be divided for convenience into three main categories.

1. The personal presence of Yahweh, manifested to people, is experienced in various ways. Twice a self-revelation of God to Solomon is described (*nir'ah*, 1 Kgs 3:5–15; 9:1–9), in terms reminiscent of appearances of God in preceding books. Here, and in the account of Micaiah's vision (1 Kgs 22:19–22) as in other accounts of God's self-manifestation and of being taken into Yahweh's council, the climax and

---

28. Paul Tillich, *Systematic Theology* (3 vols.; Chicago: University of Chicago, 1951; London: Nisbet, 1953), 1:131.

purpose of the experience is not the experience itself but the verbal exchange, and especially the divine word, to which it leads.[29] The writer's real interest lies here, and the word's coming in the context of such an experience of God guarantees with regard to Solomon or Micaiah the authority and fulfillment of the word that they are given or that they give. When Yahweh appears to Elijah, this similarly leads into a verbal exchange and divine word (1 Kgs 19:13–18), whatever the significance of the *qol demamah daqah*, the "low murmuring sound" (v. 12).

There is also in Kings another kind of appearing of God, in the context of worship, which is not of secondary importance to an accompanying word. A major theme of Kings is Yahweh's name coming to dwell in Jerusalem (e.g., 1 Kgs 11:36; 14:21), Solomon's building a house for the name (e.g., 1 Kgs 5:3, 5). Solomon's dedication prayer makes it clear that the name (1 Kgs 8:16–20) is Kings' favorite surrogate for God in person (8:12–13, a quatrain older than the body of the prayer),[30] a "spiritualization of the theophany" insofar as "the name is regarded as to such an extent an expression of the individual character of its owner that it can in fact stand for him, become a concept interchangeable with him."[31] Yahweh's dwelling in the temple is also spoken of in terms of Yahweh's glory in the cloud (1 Kgs 8:10–11) and of the presence of Yahweh's eyes and heart (9:3). Even though the temple appearance may have often led into the utterance of a word from God, as the Psalms may suggest, the stress in Kings reminds us that "revelation" in the First Testament does not mean so much the revealing of a God (or of theological truths) previously unknown but the coming of the presence of the already known God.

2. Nevertheless, the theme of God speaking is prominent in Kings. Theophany does often lead to theology; indeed the expression "the word of Yahweh came to . . ." (e.g., 1 Kgs 6:11; 17:2, 8; 19:9) points to something as real as a personal appearing, in verbal form. Yahweh is present speaking.[32]

The forms of the divine utterances are very varied. Many are words of promise, of Yahweh's presence and blessing to king and people (e.g., 1 Kgs 6:11–13; 11:37–38) or of Yahweh's action to deal with some particular situation (e.g., 1 Kgs 20:13–14; 2 Kgs 7:1; 19:7). They may also be words of warning, especially of the disastrous consequences of disobedience, upon which Yahweh's judgment is declared (e.g.,

29. Cf. J. K. Kuntz, *The Self-Revelation of God* (Philadelphia: Westminster Press, 1967), 68–69.

30. See J. Gray, *I and II Kings* (2nd ed.; London: SCM; Philadelphia: Westminster Press, 1970), on the passage.

31. Walther Eichrodt, *Theology of the Old Testament* (2 vols.; London: SCM; Philadelphia: Westminster Press, 1967), 2:40.

32. This is even clearer in 1 Sam 3, especially v. 7, "the word of Yahweh had not yet revealed itself [*yiggaleh*] to him," and v. 21, "Yahweh again appeared (*hera'oh*) at Shiloh, for Yahweh revealed himself (*niglah*) to Samuel at Shiloh by (*b*) the word of Yahweh," but also passim in the description of this audiovisual experience. Cf. also Isa 22:14. Note also Zimmerli's description (in Robinson and Cobb, eds., *Theology as History*, 43–44) of the phrase "I am Yahweh" as a self-presentation formula that expresses Yahweh's making himself present in his word, though this interpretation has been the subject of debate (J. Moltmann, *Theology of Hope* [London: SCM; New York: Harper, 1967], 112–16).

1 Kgs 13:1–5; 14:7–16; 2 Kgs 17:13; 20:16–18). They may be words of command and commission (especially in the Elijah stories), of information and guidance (again in connection with Elijah; also, e.g., 1 Kgs 14:5; 22:5–28; 2 Kgs 3:11–19; compare Elisha's surprise that Yahweh has not told him something, 4:27). Most striking is the attribution to Yahweh of false promises, misleading guidance, untrue information (1 Kgs 22:19–23; 2 Kgs 8:10).

Kings does not picture Yahweh's speaking thus as a novel phenomenon. The prophets' words have to be seen against the background of the body of Yahweh's words that have been handed down from the past but have maintained their relevance to each new generation. This tradition included words of promise, especially the divine commitment to David's house made through Nathan that legitimated the succeeding line (e.g., 1 Kgs 2:4; 8:15–26; 2 Kgs 21:7–8). It included a whole range of words of command, "the commands that Yahweh commanded Moses" (2 Kgs 18:6, cf. 14:6; 17:12–16, and the description of and reaction to Josiah's Torah scroll, which he is pictured as regarding as part of the tradition albeit new to him). It included warnings of judgment that were bound eventually to come about (1 Kgs 2:27; 16:34), and in at least one area, the exodus, theological interpretation of earlier activity of God (8:53).

3. As well as by appearing and speaking Yahweh is known through acts in the world. The range of this activity is as wide as life itself, covering the affairs of nations, the phenomena of nature, life and death, health and prosperity, whole peoples, kings, prophets, priests, and ordinary individuals. Most of this diversity can be seen just in Solomon's prayer (1 Kgs 8:12–61), which also makes clear that it is a mistake to try to categorize this activity into areas such as "nature" and "history" distinguished from one another in a modern way, still less to speak of Yahweh as, for instance, God of history rather than God of nature.[33] Yahweh is the God of all the earth and all the events that occur on the earth may be viewed as Yahweh's work.

Hence the wisdom and prosperity of Solomon (1 Kgs 5:7; 10:9), the flourishing of Israel (8:59–60), the answering of prayer, or the meeting of challenge (8:43; 18:24, 36–39; 2 Kgs 5:15) may lead to the acknowledgement that "Yahweh, he is God." Yahweh's uniqueness, reality, power, favor, and wrath (though that is all)[34] are made known to people through events interpreted as Yahweh's actions.[35] This does not mean that the will of Yahweh is read off from events through their inherent revelatory character (though this may be the assumption of Adonijah, 1 Kgs 2:15, and it may be the attitude lying behind the enigmatic "there came great wrath upon Israel" in 2 Kgs 3:27).[36] Events may lead only to people asking the right questions (1 Kgs 9:8; 2 Kgs 3:9–12), they will often be susceptible of more than one interpretation (Isaiah and the Rabshakeh looked at the Assyrian invasion rather differently, 2 Kgs 19:22–26; 18:25), and prima facie they may suggest implications that would be difficult to accept; the violent deaths of Joash and Josiah, two faithful kings, are not interpreted

---

33. Cf. Albrektson, *History and the Gods*, 11–12, 19, 22–23.
34. Cf. Albrektson, *History and the Gods*, 113–14, following Köhler.
35. Cf. "natural revelation" according to Paul (Rom 1:19–20), which is similarly limited.
36. Cf. Gray, *I and II Kings*, on both these verses.

by Kings, though Chronicles later seeks to fill the gap. Even when regarded as the works of God, events are mute or ambiguous. If lessons are to be learned from them, they must be explained. Thus Kings matches its picture of events as the outworking of Yahweh's will with a picture of Yahweh linking word with event, the two bound together for the purpose of revelation.

The precise relationship between word and event varies. Sometimes the word provides a retrospective interpretation of the event (1 Kgs 12:24: Yahweh explains that the revolt of the ten clans was the divine will). More characteristic of Kings is the pattern of word preceding event, so that they provide each other with interpretation and confirmation. Before they occur, major events, especially the rise and fall of kings, are announced and interpreted. Kings' impressive exposition of the breaking up of the Solomonic state provides the best example. Yahweh declares the rejection and coming punishment of Solomon for his failure to abide by the received words of Yahweh (1 Kgs 11:11–13). A note of the adversaries Yahweh raised up against Solomon follows (11:14–26), and leads into Yahweh's word through Ahijah to Jeroboam, declaring that he is to receive the ten tribes (11:27–39), which was "the reason why he lifted up his hand against the king" (v. 27a). Once given, this word cannot be frustrated, whether by Solomon (v. 40; cf. Ahab's futile efforts to avoid the fulfillment of Yahweh's word, 22:29–38), or by the wise counsel of the old men (12:1–15: "it was a turn of affairs that came from Yahweh so that he might fulfill his word"), or by Rehoboam (12:16–24: "you shall not go up . . . for this thing is from me"). The miserable cycle of word–resistance–inevitable fulfillment is hardly complete before it begins again (13:1–34).

Without the tradition, which is the background of the whole, and the prophetic words given by Yahweh to the particular situation, which reveal the particular meaning of the sequence of events, these events would say nothing, or would invite the inference that history has no meaning. Why should the achievement of the Solomonic age come to nothing? Why should bad counsel triumph over good? Why should an undistinguished but good man lose out to a flamboyant but wicked one? If this is the working out of a divine purpose, what is that purpose? The event needs the word, of tradition and of prophet, if there is to be an answer. On the other hand, without the events that "establish" (*yaqim*, e.g., 1 Kgs 2:4) or "fulfill" (*lemalleʾ*, e.g., 2:27) or "confirm" (*yeʾamen*, e.g., 8:26) the words of warning or promise, if the words "fall" (*napal*, e.g., 8:56), they are worthless. If the prophet's word is not fulfilled, then Yahweh has not spoken by him (22:28). Yahweh, who answers the prophet by fire, is God; Baal, who fails to do so, is not (18:24, 36–40; the area of God's activity here is, in our terms, not history but nature and worship). When Yahweh's word is fulfilled, then people will be forced to acknowledge that Yahweh is God (e.g., 20:13, 28). The word needs the event, if it is to be validated.

How the mechanics of the relationship between word and event, of the functioning of Yahweh's word in history, are to be conceived is a complex question. The conviction expressed by David's concern about Shimei's curse that hangs over his house (1 Kgs 2:8–9) implies that power can reside in the words of someone of personal strength, especially words of blessing and cursing.[37] To put this in modern terms, words have creative possibilities, a self-fulfilling potency; they can "do things," create new historical situations.[38] They do not return void. They have a power that is not limited to (though no doubt it includes) the effect they have on the psyche, the morale, of the person to whom they are addressed. But this conception of the power of the prophetic word as word differs from the conception of God speaking and thereby effecting the divine will independently of whether the word is announced through a prophet; that is, the word is addressed to the situation it is meant to affect, for instance to some part of the natural world (e.g., Ps 33:6–9).[39] The model here is not the power of word as word but the authority of a king's command, which inevitably finds fulfillment (cf. 33:10–11).

A more subtle feature of the relationship between word and event also needs to be taken into account. "As a rule the promises do not enter so literally into a fulfillment as one would assume that they would if they were the word of God effecting history";[40] the same is true of the warnings. This reflects the fact that the object of declaring promises and warnings is as much to win faith and repentance as to set Yahweh's power at work, and it is in this moral way, too, that God's word affects history, by affecting people. God's words are both conditional and situational. They are not cold announcements of what is inevitably predestined to occur; how they are fulfilled depends on what reaction they meet with, and on how the total situation has changed when the time for fulfillment comes.

The viewpoint of Kings may include all these three angles on the relationship between word and event at one time or another.

We might systematize as follows the way Kings pictures the means by which Yahweh and Yahweh's truth are known. First, at any moment nation and individual stand within or under a received body of divine teaching that should form their self-understanding, their hopes, and the aims and principles according to which their lives are lived. The tradition derives its authority from the fact that it is the tradition and that it does illumine people's situation. This does not mean that hope for the future is based on "the tradition of Yahweh's saving acts" and not on any acts themselves;[41] if anything, the opposite is the case. Solomon appeals (1 Kgs 8:51) to what Yahweh did at the exodus, not just to the tradition about it. But this is a false antithesis, because it is on the basis of verification in events that new material is continually being added to the tradition, so that although people would hardly ask each time they sought the tradition's insights whether its teaching had been verified in events, in principle it could be assumed to be so verified. Then, second, at any

37. So J. Pedersen, *Israel I-II* (London: Oxford University Press, 1954), 169.

38. Cf. A. Richardson, following Martin Heidegger, *Religion in Contemporary Debate* (London: SCM; Philadelphia: Westminster Press; 1966), 97–99.

39. Albrektson, *History and the Gods*, 53–67, quotes this passage and others from the First Testament and other documents, though without drawing this distinction.

40. Pannenberg, in Robinson and Cobb, eds., *Theology as History*, 259.

41. So Rendtorff, in Robinson and Cobb, eds., *Theology as History*, 47–48.

moment nation and individual may know God's presence in self-manifestation in the temple.

At particular moments, against this double background, Yahweh may appear to king or prophet (either in response to a situation that has arisen or spontaneously, sometimes to the eyes but perhaps more often just to the ears) and declare the divine will by way of promise, warning, or command. This experience of Yahweh's real presence is self-authenticating and provides authentication for the word to which it leads. Indeed, it makes it possible to hold onto a belief in what has been declared even when events for a time seem to belie it[42] and when it would indeed be much easier to forget it (compare Jeremiah's "confessions"). But the word receives verification that no one ought to doubt when events, if only in the long term, bear it out; and as they verify the word they provide evidence that Yahweh is God.[43]

3. Revelation and Verification in Job

The book of Job raises urgently the question, How may God be known?—indeed, May God be known? Job sees his life fall apart without apparent reason and finds himself alienated from the God he thought he knew well, the God of grace and faithfulness and love. He seeks to reach this God again, to gain an explanation of his suffering, but as in a nightmare finds that when he does so it is a different God, a confrontational adversary. From the supernatural side, too, the possibility of a genuine relationship between God and humanity is questioned, for the Adversary "maintains that there is a terrible unreality in the relations between God and man . . . honour and integrity are not basic in them" in that "man, even in his relations with God, is inescapably and incurably selfish."[44] How then may God and truth be known?

1. Through the tradition. "Do ask of a generation, and consider what their ancestors discovered. . . . Will they not teach you, and tell you, and utter words out of their understanding?" (Job 8:8–10). Bildad voices a fundamental assumption of wisdom thinking, that beliefs that have proved themselves over the generations deserve respect. But Job's friends represent a tendency to treat the tradition as the last word. They forget that its formulations have the drawbacks as well as the virtues of generalization and, like scientific theories, are always open to refinement. They treat them as absolute, in a scholastic way, and deny the reality of experience that conflicts with them. "Rather than revise their theology, they are prepared to rewrite Job's life."[45] If Job questions the tradition, they soon put him in his place (15:1–35).

---

42. Cf. David Noel Freedman, "The Biblical Idea of History," *Int* 21 (1967): 32–49, with regard to the conviction that Yahweh is Lord of history (32–34).

43. Cf. Zimmerli's debate with Rendtorff in Robinson and Cobb, eds., *Theology as History*, 45–47, on the phrase "You/they will know that I am Yahweh."

44. J. Wood, *Job and the Human Situation* (London: Bles, 1966), 33.

45. R. Davidson, *The Old Testament* (London: Hodder; Philadelphia: Lippincott, 1964), 173.

Job desperately wants to hold on to the received picture of God, but the inflexible exposition of it by his friends has robbed it of any strength (Job 13:12), made it windy words that only comfort the speaker (16:1–5). Fancy the tradition marveling at the attention God pays to human beings: indeed, God gives them attention, but only to give them trouble (7:17–18; contrast Pss 8:4; 144:3). Thus while Job reaches out toward new possibilities (e.g., Job 16:18–21; 19:23–27: perhaps the difficulty of interpreting these passages is an allegory of this factor of "reaching out"), his friends, as even Elihu sees, can do no more than reiterate old irrelevances (32:6–15). Instead of going back to the tradition to see if there might be yet new truth to find there, they have ossified it.

2. *Through experience.* The wisdom tradition is "the accumulated folk wisdom of a coherent traditional culture, based on the observation and evaluation of human experiences."[46] This openness to what the events of everyday life have to contribute toward an understanding of life is one of the distinguishing marks of wisdom throughout. It is the grounds of Ecclesiastes' pessimism (1:12–2:26) and of the paternal instruction in Proverbs (e.g., 7:6–26). There is furthermore a tendency for wisdom teaching to become linked with the life of a wisdom teacher, which provides part of the authentication of what the teacher goes on to say.[47] The wisdom literature promises that its teaching will be validated by the listeners' own experience (e.g., Ps 34:4, 6, 8); its teaching works (Prov 3:1–10), even though sometimes it may be tempting to doubt this (e.g., Ps 73). As the prophet's word is validated by events of history, then, the teaching of the wise is verified by the events of their own life and the consequent experience of their pupils. But as the concrete events of human living were the rock from which the tradition was hewn, so that it reflects their complexity and the capricious element in human life (compare the paradoxes in Proverbs, notably 26:4–5), so its link with human experience remains its lifeline. As the tradition ossifies, it cuts the lifeline and sacrifices its capacity to speak in relation to future experience.

Wisdom's purported, but insincere, appeal to experience recurs in Job (e.g., 4:7–8; 5:2–7, 19–26). Job himself accepts that the truth about life can be known from experience. That is the trouble, insofar as his gross suffering cannot be said to be the result of gross sin (see the protests of Job 6 and Job 21, especially in relation to the confident assertions that precede them). Job and his friends seem to be describing different worlds. Indeed, Job himself errs in the opposite direction from them; he too generalizes too whole-heartedly from his limited experience, and in his agony sees things bleaker than they really are (Job 24). But neither he nor his friends have recourse to the leap of faith solutions to the problem of human suffering accepted by other nations, such as belief in an afterlife, in magic, in reincarnation, or in demons. All agree that truth must be verifiable, and vindication after death is very much second-best.[48]

46. R. B. Y. Scott, "The Study of the Wisdom Literature," *Int* 24 (1970): 20–45 (29).

47. So H. H. Guthrie, *Wisdom and Canon* (Evanston, Ill.: Seabury-Western Theological Seminary, 1966).

48. Belief in an afterlife is more justifiably taken into account after Christ, when his resurrection has rescued such belief from being mere speculation.

Job will not belie his experience, avoid the facts of human life, or abandon his claim to (relative) innocence (Job 29–31); neither will he abandon his belief in a fundamental order in the universe deriving from the just God who is behind it. He is left with the tension between "the protecting God of the tradition and the destructive God of Job's experience" who "both exist together,"[49] until after God appears and points to an area of the tradition where a way of coping with the tension may be found. Then Job is approved, precisely because he has faced up to the facts (42:7–8);[50] he is restored and given even greater blessings than before, with the implication that ultimately the tradition must be right and experience will reflect the love and faithfulness of God to those who are themselves faithful. Job's restoration cannot be taken to imply that everyone in such a predicament will be similarly restored (the book's aim is precisely to refute such thinking), any more than the escapes of Daniel and his friends guarantee those of other people in such situations; but these "special cases" do assert the faithfulness and power of God, even though ultimately they do not solve the problem of how that faithfulness and power are proved in our experience. They only encourage a conviction that somehow they will be.[51]

3. *Through human reason.* It is Elihu who expresses wisdom's confidence in and commitment to the use of reason in attaining understanding. He is confident of the perceptiveness of his God-given mind (Job 32:8, 18; 33:4) and encourages the friends to use theirs (34:1–4). Job, who is also open to intellectual adventure (e.g., 16:18–21), has long ago concluded that their minds are closed, and that of Yahweh's doing (17:4). They resist any challenge to accepted patterns of thought (20:1–29 may indicate explicitly that Zophar is tempted to follow Job in his speculation but manages to control himself).

Reason has its limitations (Job 11:7–8; 28:12–13). Its rigorous exercise in Job provides no solution for the book's problem, but it does demonstrate that it is not impossible to envisage solutions (the cosmic significance given to this particular man's sufferings by the prologue). Its whole approach is to see the problem as one to be thought and argued through to the limits to which our God-given reason can take us. Thus it is dealt with not by theological assertion but by posing the question and discussing it from various angles in order to grasp the whole, portraying it in the round.[52] The book provides a series of snapshots and leaves the resultant whole to speak for itself: Job attacks divine justice, the friends human justice, but both are wrong in what they attack, right in what they affirm, for even when it is

---

49. Von Rad, *Old Testament Theology*, 1:413.

50. Cf. N. H. Snaith, *The Book of Job* (London: SCM; Naperville, Ill.: Allenson, 1968), 5.

51. First Maccabees, with its account of the martyrs dying cheerfully in their confidence of resurrection, expresses the same conviction. Again we see how the First Testament needs the resurrection faith, though it cannot yet have it.

52. P. Humbert, "Le modernisme de Job," in *Wisdom in Israel and in the Ancient Near East* (ed. Martin Noth and D. W. Thomas; Leiden: Brill, 1955), 150–61 (155), notes how this gives Job an almost Hegelian flavor, though L. Köhler, *Hebrew Man* (London: SCM; Nashville: Abingdon, 1956), 158–60, connects it rather with the courtroom.

near impossible to do so, "man must not relinquish his own righteousness, nor must he relinquish God's. . . . Even if the righteous fails, he must still believe in righteousness as the supreme law, firmly resting in God."[53] In that they make this point, the dialogues must not be misunderstood, under the influence of the story framework, as the story of Job the faultless hero of faith versus the friends who are totally misguided. In the dialogues Job does everything but curse God while the friends do their best to interpret the situation with the limited resources available to them. Understanding the teaching of the book as a whole involves taking account of the contributions of the friends as well as that of Job, both being subject to the judgment of the book as a whole.

Job has a distinctive place in the First Testament as the consciously creative product of the human mind, the nearest thing in the First Testament to a drama or a philosophical discourse, the testament of the author's own trust in the spirit that God breathes into us.[54]

4. *Through religious experience*.[55] In his opening exposition Eliphaz claims that his teaching has the backing of visionary experience as well as of the tradition (4:12–21). He has listened in at God's council (15:8), seen (*hazah*) the fate of the wicked (15:17). Elihu, too, speaks of God communicating with people through dreams (33:14–18) and angels (33:23–30).

At the book's climax no angel but Yahweh in person answers Job out of the whirlwind. Job is granted the confrontation with God that he has sought all along, but it turns out to be not his grilling of God but God's of him, reducing him to silence (40:1–5; 42:1–6). He is granted a place in God's council so that he can look at the universe from God's angle. Once again God's self-manifestation does not mean making known some new truths; rather, God points Job to the created world, which was important in the tradition of wisdom thinking, was part of the wise person's (indeed of everyone's) experience, and gave human beings scope for the exercise of their reason.

Though refusing to answer the question, Why am I suffering thus? God implies that there is an answer, but does not tell Job what the reader knows about the background to his affliction in the scene in the heavenly court. Job has come near aspiring to the total knowledge that is only God's,[56] whereas God insists on Job's accepting limits, on being God and keeping some secrets. Indeed, God lifts the veil a little so that Job can see how many more riddles and marvels there are that Job has not yet thought of.[57]

---

53. Pedersen, *Israel I-II*, 373.

54. Humbert sees this as the chief mark of Job's "modernity" ("Le modernisme de Job," esp. 153).

55. While one must not set up an antithesis between sacred and secular, Job does imply a distinction between the wisdom gained from everyday experience of ordinary life and the special supernatural revelations that come through visionary and theophanic experiences. It is interesting that such revelatory experiences, which are so important in Job, are among the non-wisdom features listed by J. L. Crenshaw ("Method in Determining Wisdom Influence upon 'Historical' Literature," *JBL* 88 [1969]: 129–42 [129–31]) as indications that the Joseph narrative ought not to be described as a wisdom narrative.

56. Cf. E. Jones, *The Triumph of Job* (London: SCM, 1966), 105.

57. Cf. von Rad, *Old Testament Theology,* 1:416.

Thus God leads Job to "the point where he can continue to suffer, trusting God without understanding."[58]

5. *Through the created world.* While Job comes to a climax with God appearing, the medium is the vehicle for a message. Job is reduced to silence not merely by a new vision of God but by a new vision of God's world.

The wisdom tradition "thinks resolutely within the framework of a theology of creation,"[59] providing an extended exposition of insights also expressed in Genesis 1–3. Creation's theological importance is much more immediate than it is in the history works; here "creation" suggests not just a long ago first event but the present status of the world and humanity in relation to God. By looking at creation thus, wisdom is able to learn from nature without being bewitched by it. It can assert both that serious attention to wisdom's creation theology helps one to have right religious attitudes (see especially Job 38–42) and that "true religion is the first principle of wisdom" (to paraphrase Prov 1:7), virtually its converse.

Eliphaz, whose first speech anticipates so much of what follows, urges on Job something very like the solution he eventually accepts from God, to commit himself to the God of creation (5:8–10). But at this stage the creation speaks to Job more of God's awesomeness than of God's grace (Job 9; also 26:5–14, though many critics transfer this section to Bildad). And "these are but the edges of his ways, and what a whisper of a word do we hear of him! But the thunder of his mighty acts who can understand?" (26:14). Like Eliphaz, Elihu believes in a "faithful creator" (34:12–15), but like Job and in substantial anticipation of God's address, he is even more over-awed at the majesty of the creator (35:1–8; 36:24–37:24).

God's appearing provides the definitive statement of this theme. God scans the created world and points to how it embodies the divine wisdom, authority, and power (Job 38–39). But it does more than that, for this much Job has been prepared to grant already, though without making the response now dragged from him (40:1–5). It also embodies the way God's power is exercised for good ends, which is what Job doubts (40:6–41:34). Job can do nothing about unjust power in the world, but Yahweh has put the chaos-powers in their place, reducing Leviathan to a plaything (41:5). God's wisdom and power are thus shown to be constructive, purposeful, and gracious. God is the basis of order and stability in human life. Job comes to acknowledge God's power and purpose as he sees God not in the temple or in mighty acts but in the created world (42:1–6).

4. A Comparison

A comparison of the epistemologies of Kings and Job reveals closer parallels than one might have expected.

58. Jones, *The Triumph of Job*, 110.
59. Walther Zimmerli, "The Place and Limit of the Wisdom in the Framework of the Old Testament Theology," *SJT* 17 (1964): 146–58 (148).

1. Both stand within a tradition of accepted belief from within which they interpret the situations they face. For Kings these include the special relationship between Yahweh and Israel in which the Davidic king plays a key role, Yahweh's undertaking to look after king and people in the future as in the past, and the moral demands God makes upon them that are a condition of all this being realized. For Job they include that if someone is blameless and upright, reveres God and turns away from evil, God will grant protection, blessing, and increase.

2. Both expect this teaching to be actualized and thus validated in experience. Job, however, is concerned with the events of personal experience and everyday life (though God's activity in history is mentioned: see 12:23 and the rest of this paragraph). God is expected to be active here, honoring those who honor God. Kings is more interested in the events of national experience, incidents that have dates (though again the contrast should not be too sharply drawn, for Elijah and Elisha have dealings with ordinary individuals).

3. Both accept that the tradition keeps being supplemented, applied, or refined through God's speaking, either in person or through intermediaries such as angels or through dream experiences (more in Job) or through prophets (Kings). Commonly in Kings and sometimes in Job (the experiences of Eliphaz and Elihu), these revelations are intimately linked with events of national or personal experience, in that they interpret past events or predict future ones, as the tradition in the form that it has at the moment consists of interpretations of earlier events and warnings and promises about the future. New such prophetic and other words continued to find inclusion in the tradition until this process ceased and writings were no longer added to the canon;[60] henceforth the tradition as a whole functions as the sole "word."

4. Neither Job nor Kings knows all the answers; there are points at which the tradition's teaching seems not to be proved by experience. It is in what they do with this problem that the distinctiveness of the two approaches emerges.

While Kings offers no explanation of the violent deaths of two good kings, Joash and Josiah, this "problem" does not seem to bother it. Perhaps it presupposes a trust that the positive teaching that it puts forward and can verify through most of the history it relates would also be applicable to these problem areas if all the facts were available, or at least that there are explanations of these apparent exceptions that prevent their invalidating its general thesis. Even though functioning as a creative historian implies the exercise of the mind and human discernment,[61] the author does not seem to have exercised these very hard in seeking out such explanations, unlike the Chronicler (see 2 Chr 35:20–22).

Job is more concerned with the exceptions than with the general truth that faithfulness and unfaithfulness ultimately get their reward. Kings might be so concerned if it were not convinced that Israel's experience in the exile was a good illustration of

60. It is customary to speak of the canon being "closed," but we have no evidence of any decision to close it, and it seems unwise simply to assume that there was one. Maybe the community stopped finding itself adding writings to its canon (we do not know what was the process whereby this happened).

61. Cf. Luke's description of his historical method (Luke 1:1–4).

the general truth. In seeking to ease the problem, Job emphasizes the part that can be played by human reason, even more perhaps by human imagination, in its own approach and by the words it puts into the mouths of its protagonists. It suggests that the thesis that God is faithful and good is overwhelmingly verified by God's activity seen in the created order. It is here that it locates its grounds for trust that the apparent exceptions to the thesis do not invalidate it.

The contrast between these two approaches to revelation and verification might be summarized as follows. Kings asserts: "The exile is to be understood as the judgment of the holy God on a disobedient people, in fulfillment of the warnings and chastisements given it over the years. To see that this is true, you only have to look at the history of God's dealings with this people to see that Yahweh is such a God and it is such a people." Job asserts: "No matter how strong may be appearances to the contrary, it is always true that God is faithful. If you doubt this, look at the created world and see how it manifests the power and goodness of that God." The books thus suggest two falsification principles: Kings, "If the history did not happen like this, then my thesis about our situation and about God is unproven"; Job, "If creation is not orderly and reliable, if the cosmos is not after all a friendly place, then, Job, you still have your problem."

5. Historiography Ancient and Modern

Verification in history is thus crucial for Kings as it is not for Job; by it Kings commits itself to stand or fall. It claims to explain why the exile came about, and in doing so to explain God's ways, and the two explanations depend on each other. Its use of a narrative form, its relating of things that are supposed to have been said and to have happened, is seriously meant. The theology is dependent on the events; their veracity is a sine qua non of the validity of the theology.

The narrative form in Job fulfills a different function. While modern theologians have usually discussed theodicy or suffering in an abstract, theoretical way, a biblical writer (like a dramatist or novelist) is usually concrete in thinking and communicating, choosing a narrative form for theological or philosophical reflection. With Aeschylus or Camus it is inappropriate to ask, "Did this happen?" So it is with Job. If we ask the book, "How do you know that what you say about God and about suffering is true and is relevant to me?" the affirmation "It happened" would be insufficient. Job is a very special case; Job's seeing God is no guarantee that I will. The answer to the question is rather, "Look in the direction that the book points, at the created world, and see that it is like that." It is by this, not by its historicity, that Job stands or falls; here (and as these lines were first written in the week of an earthquake in Peru it is a serious matter) lies its falsification principle.

Concluding that there is little historical truth behind Job would not have serious consequences for our estimate of its theological validity.[62] With Kings and the

---

62. The same applies to Jonah, which may be regarded similarly as the dramatization of a theological point in concrete form; it also appeals to creation (Jon. 4:6–11).

other First Testament history works, the converse will be the case. They do appeal for validation to history, to events that they base their argument on. They thus need to be historically trustworthy.

They are widely regarded as being far from this. "Two pictures of Israel's history lie before us, that of modern critical scholarship and that which the faith of Israel constructed, and for the present we must reconcile ourselves to both of them. . . . The fact that these two views . . . are so divergent is one of the most serious burdens imposed today upon biblical scholarship,"[63] precisely because the biblical historians elect to stand or fall by their interpretation of history. What are we to do about the divergence between these two pictures?

Part of the problem is that we are not reconciled to the way Israelite historians, like their ancient colleagues elsewhere, practice their art in a way so different from that of modernity. While the nature of the difference is well understood, we have been so wedded to the modern way of writing history that the ancient way cannot appear to us as an alternative way and not just a primitive and inferior one. The difference between history and non-history and the real importance of the former is very real to us, and we assume that the historian's first duty is to relate only what he or she knows actually happened, as it actually happened.

In the realm of the stage and film this is not so. The play and film *Oh What a Lovely War*[64] illustrate the relevance of this to an appreciation of the way ancient history works. It is drama and propaganda and history, looking back to what happened in the First World War and letting the facts it relates more or less speak for themselves. Speeches from the war years are repeated verbatim, news headlines are read and statistics quoted, mock-ups presented of life in the trenches and in battle. Yet the whole is cast in a surrealistic framework, a pierrot show, which contrasts starkly with the reality and horror of battle. This is a history work, concerned with events that happened and with their interpretation and relevance, and its point depends on the accuracy of its history, but it makes its point by utilizing diverse material with a diverse relationship to what actually happened. Authentic speeches are delivered in a make-believe context; officers turn into merry-go-round figures; scenes in the trenches or on the field come from the imagination of the author, although they are meant to exemplify the kind of thing that went on or to express the kind of attitudes that people took. There is little attempt to recreate the actual event, as happens in other war films, yet this might be judged a more serious historical presentation than them. It is a propaganda piece, but one whose very propaganda validity depends on its being a veracious interpretation of what actually happened.

The biblical history works are closer to this than to most modern history works. Kings is certainly interested in what actually happened from Solomon to the exile, and its theological points concern these events, but within its historical and theological

---

63. Von Rad, *Old Testament Theology,* 1:107–8.
64. Theatre Workshop, Charles Chilton and others (London: Methuen, 1965).

framework it includes material diverse in form and in relationship to events as they happened.[65]

1. The succession narrative, which comes to an end with 1 Kings 1–2, concerns itself with actual people and events, but the recounting of the protagonists' conversations stems from the author's imagination. In these Kings seeks to represent the attitudes and relationships of the period. Probably historical method is unable to tell us whether it does so fairly, but its thus working more like a modern historical novel than a modem history work does not mean it cannot have done so.[66]

2. The Rabshakeh's speeches in 2 Kings 18 are written up so as to bring out their theological significance, for they signify a contempt of Yahweh and thus a challenge to trust Yahweh nevertheless and not to trust in human beings or resources. All this is regarded as implicit in the Rabshakeh's words; it is therefore given expression as from his lips.[67] Such an attempt to bring out the implication of events needs to be assessed in its own right, and not according to exclusively positivist assumptions; it is something to be grateful for, as more meaningful than bare chronicle.[68] Admittedly, interpretation can easily become the imposition upon a story of preconceived ideas that ill fit it; it has been said of Spengler and Toynbee that "they have written some good poetry but a lot of bad history,"[69] and if this is true of the biblical historians, then they have failed in the task they set themselves.

3. A similar kind of interpretation and theological judgment can be seen in Kings' practice of arranging narratives in an order that is not chronological but theological. The skillful arrangement of the account of the dissolution of the Solomonic empire begins with an account of Solomon's sins, particularly in the matter of foreign marriages, which has been kept back so that it can be associated with the troubles of his old age (1 Kgs 11). In the case of Josiah, to underline the importance of the reforms that followed the discovery of the Torah scroll, Kings holds back its account of miscellaneous reforms that probably date from before the discovery so that it can be given prominence (2 Kgs 22:1–23:3; 23:4–20).

4. The main Josiah narrative and the earlier description of Hezekiah's conduct during the Assyrian crisis (especially 2 Kgs 19:14–19)[70] exhibit a different kind of writing up that seems to be intended to glorify the heroes and set them forth as examples; Hezekiah is "the type of the faithful king."[71] In such a "tale . . . told in order to edify" in which "the contrast between good and bad is brought out sharply,"[72]

---

65. Cf. Barr, *Old and New in Interpretation*, 81.

66. As R. N. Whybray, *The Succession Narrative* (London: SCM; Naperville, Ill.: Allenson, 1968), seems to assume.

67. Cf. B. S. Childs, *Isaiah and the Assyrian Crisis* (London: SCM; Naperville, Ill.: Allenson, 1967), 84–90.

68. Cf. Richardson, *History Sacred and Profane*, 234–40; D. E. Nineham, "Eye-Witness Testimony and the Gospel Tradition," *Journal of Theological Studies*, new series, 11 (1960): 253–64 (262–64).

69. D. Thomson, *The Aim of History* (London: Thames and Hudson, 1969), 24.

70. Childs, *Isaiah and the Assyrian Crisis*, 99–100.

71. Ibid., 103.

72. K. Koch, *The Growth of the Biblical Tradition* (London: Black; New York: Scribner, 1969), 198.

and more so later in the stories in Daniel and in Ben Sira, the hero figures not so much as an actor in the divine-human drama as an embodiment of divine-human wisdom and righteousness.[73]

5. Some stories already referred to might also be considered in light of the distinction between *Historie* and *Geschichte*. On at least one definition this is similar to the distinction between history and story, which "has a different effectiveness from that of historical writing, bridging the gap between the present and the past, and showing that what appears as past events contains a hidden relevance to the present. The narrator and his hearers identify themselves with the deeds and sufferings of their forebears. . . . The later narrators' experiences of God and the world affect the stories of earlier periods."[74] Yet showing the relevance of the past to the present is a common aim for history itself. Furthermore, although God can speak through fictional stories (as Jesus' parables show), one would have to ask how the historical interest of books such as Kings affects the question of the purported inclusion there of stories that are substantially unhistorical. In terms of the distinction between *Historie* and *Geschichte*, "can anything become *geschichtlich* which was not first *historisch*? Can anything become historically significant, if it did not first actually happen?"[75]

6. The Importance of Historical Veracity

Kings worked with a different ideal of history writing from a modern one, but this need not make it less responsible or less valuable. Nor does this difference conflict with a concern for what actually happened, in that it seeks to trace the working out of the will and word of God precisely in what happened in Israel's history. This commitment to matching word and event, interpretation and historical actuality, means that even when we have made due allowance for a different attitude to historiography, we must still grapple with the questions raised by the two pictures of Israel's history.

The exile means that Judeans are forced to ask fundamental questions about their relationship with God, as they strive to find meaning in their situation. Kings suggests to them the "perspectival image" that the tradition puts forward for looking at their situation, the "memory impression" that can be left by an event or series of events and that people can then use to interpret their own experience.[76] It has the nature of an aetiology, explaining the present situation in terms of the tradition's account of God's dealings with Israel in the centuries leading up to the fall of Jerusalem. Is

73. Cf. Guthrie, *Wisdom and Canon*.

74. Koch, *The Growth of the Biblical Tradition*, 154–57. The English translation renders the German word *Sage* by "saga," but this is misleading; *Sage* is nearer "story."

75. S. Neill, *The Interpretation of the New Testament* (London and New York: Oxford University Press, 1964), 234; cf. von Rad, *Old Testament Theology*, 1:125.

76. V. A. Harvey, *The Historian and the Believer* (New York: Macmillan, 1966; London: SCM, 1967), 266–89.

the validity of such an image independent of a correlation between the tradition's account of the events it relates and the events themselves?

· According to Van A. Harvey, "If one thinks of revelation as a paradigmatic event that casts up images that alter our interpretation of all events, this requires that we distinguish between two kinds of belief, and accordingly between two kinds of certitude: the belief that the actual Jesus [or Israel] was as the perspectival image pictures him, and the belief that the perspectival image does illumine our experience and our relationship to that upon which we are absolutely dependent. . . . Faith finds its certitude, its confirmation, in the viability of the image for relating one to present reality."[77] Can this approach be applied to the First Testament, so that what matters is not whether Jerusalem was delivered from Sennacherib, but "the perspectival image" this story suggests, its understanding of humanity before God?[78]

Our consideration of revelation and verification implies that this is not the case. Theological (or anthropological) validity is tied up with historical veracity. Further, the very perspectival image we are considering is of a God who has been active in guiding and protecting the people and whose graciousness and power have been demonstrated by these actions. If this picture does not correspond to historical reality, then its illumining our experience and our relationship to that upon which we are absolutely dependent is neither here nor there except as a psychological prop. If Yahweh did not speak and then fulfill this word, or not punish waywardness, or not rescue Jerusalem, then promise and fulfillment, divine justice working itself out among human beings, and Zion theology are but nice ideas. Israel developed these historical narratives so profusely because "the faith needed them."[79] Because Israel's faith, the perspectival images it offers, is so bound up with history, this feature of the First Testament viewpoint cannot be treated as a husk that can be discarded without affecting the kernel. Indeed, even if it were legitimate to seek to separate kernel from husk in this way,[80] the possibility of doing so is questionable; "it hangs the passion of faith on the slenderest of threads."[81]

Rolf Rendtorff attempted to outflank the problem of the apparently unhistorical nature of First Testament historiography by pointing out that really it is historical in the sense that, just as much as the events it describes, it is the result of the activity of God in history. "The working out of the 'interpretation' is itself an historical event. . . . In speaking of God's activity in the history of Israel we cannot be satisfied with the alternative between the two versions of history, the one produced by historical-critical research and the other portrayed by the Old Testament. For Israel's history occurred both in the outer events which are customarily the object of the critical study of history, and in the various stratified inner events which we bring together in

---

77. Ibid., 281–83.
78. Ibid., 289.
79. Von Rad, *Old Testament Theology*, 1:109.
80. As Buss seeks to do (in Robinson and Cobb, eds., *Theology as History*, 144–45).
81. Harvey, *The Historian and the Believer*, 193–94; cf. the whole section, 187–94.

the concept of tradition."[82] Thus Kings, whatever its value as a source for the history of the monarchy, is of first importance for an understanding of the exile.

Seeing the formation of the tradition as reflecting God's activity in Israel's history and thus as a factor in her history is important in understanding both the tradition and the history. Nevertheless the words "historical tradition" seem here to have been retained while their meaning has been transformed. We have been cheated. The tradition can be described as historical after all, it is implied, so all is well; but the assurance is given only by trading on the ambiguity of the word "history" and on the value status attaching to it, and at the price of implying a wrong kind of theological priority of history over the tradition.

More seriously, this approach suffers from the same drawbacks as the "perspectival image" solution, and indeed sharpens the problem. It suggests that, whereas the tradition makes no claims to being produced by God's activity, but many assertions that God's activity may be seen in the events it records, the opposite is the case: a divinely produced tradition, but little by way of divinely produced acts. And precisely this tradition which is said to be divinely produced gives a profoundly misleading picture of the area of the activity of the one whose activity produced it. If God was really active in the production of this tradition, then surely the events it describes must have happened. This objection still seems to hold if it is maintained that there are historical events to which the tradition corresponds but that these are later events which the tradition has back-projected—for instance, if later military exploits "impressed on the historical memory the picture of a conquest and drove from the consciousness the much less dramatic and, in parts, the less glorious events of the period of peaceful settlement."[83]

If the events were largely otherwise, then surely the tradition that bases itself on them must be abandoned. This is an alternative reaction to von Rad's dilemma. The events as they actually happened, as we now know them through historical research are the real *Heilsgeschichte*, and we must seek to interpret the meaning of these.[84] The string between the kite of interpretation and the ground of events is cut, not so that the kite can fly free, but so that it can get lost.

In regard to this position, the assumption that some history can be known at all is worth noting. It is easy to swing from the false thesis of positivism to the false antithesis of historical relativism, "nothing can be known."[85] "Neither the fact that much historical knowledge is missing nor the fact that much historical knowledge wavers in the twilight zone of conjecture and minimal probability means that all

---

82. Rolf Rendtorff, in Braaten, *History and Hermeneutics*, 113. Cf. Pannenberg in his appreciation of von Rad's *Old Testament Theology*, especially *Basic Questions in Theology*, 1:90–93.

83. M. Weippert, *The Settlement of the Israelite Tribes in Palestine* (London: SCM; Naperville, Ill.: Allenson, 1971), 141.

84. See J. M. Robinson's discussion of Franz Hesse's position in "The Historicality of Biblical Language," in *The Old Testament and Christian Faith* (ed. B. W. Anderson; London: SCM; Philadelphia: Westminster Press, 1964), 124–58.

85. Harvey can come close to this position: see (e.g.) *The Historian and the Believer*, 282.

historical knowledge is problematical and must be less certain than knowledge gained by immediate sense-perception."[86]

Furthermore, it seems mistaken to exclude a priori the possibility of historical certainty even about extraordinary events, of which Christ's resurrection is the paradigm case. If it is unscientific to be gullible about what purports to be miracle, it is also unscientific arbitrarily to rule out the possibility that an event may be unique, miraculous. Historical sources must be treated on their merits as sources, rather than prejudged by means of presuppositions.[87] Indeed, a religious understanding of events such as the exodus can be relevant to determining that they are historical events; religious insights may not only help to interpret events known otherwise but "may also help to find solutions to historical problems as such."[88] Not that "intuitions" operate independently of evidence,[89] but they may lead to a different interpretation of evidence.

Nevertheless with regard to the First Testament events, it would still have to be granted that the nature of the sources precludes a confident historical judgment with regard to much of the history. For some of it—notably the end of the preexilic kingdom—a measure of certainty is possible; but for the details of the monarchy that is the concern of Kings, or the key First Testament complex of events from exodus to conquest on which such varied views are held, certainty on historical grounds is impossible. How, then, are we to relate the negative results reached by the application of historical method to these events, to our recognition of the authority and value of the First Testament tradition that makes it impossible to write off this tradition?

7. The First Testament and the Historical Method

Long ago Ernst Troeltsch raised the question of how the church would deal with the revolution that the historical method must bring to theology. "Once the historical method is applied to biblical science and church history," he wrote, "it is a leaven that alters everything and finally bursts apart the entire structure of theological methods employed until the present."[90] Three reasons are advanced why it must be so applied. First, "Christianity must build its religious thought upon it or else be consigned to the limbo of those countless other antiquated forms of religious belief that were unable to make their own accommodation to the Zeitgeist."[91] Again, "for men who live in the sphere in which the Enlightenment has become effective, authoritarian

---

86. D. P. Fuller, *Easter Faith and History* (Grand Rapids: Eerdmans, 1965; London: Tyndale, 1968), 258; cf. Pannenberg, *Basic Questions in Theology*, 1:54–56.

87. Cf. Pannenberg's discussion of historical method, *Basic Questions in Theology*, 1:38–80; also Braaten, *History and Hermeneutics*, 98–101.

88. Cf. H. D. Lewis, *Our Experience of God* (London: Allen and Unwin; New York: Macmillan, 1959), 150.

89. Cf. Pannenberg, *Basic Questions in Theology*, 1:50–51.

90. Harvey, *The Historian and the Believer*, 5.

91. Ibid., 5–6.

claims are no longer acceptable" and we must look for "a manifestation of divine reality which meets the test of man's matured understanding as such."[92]

It is not just by concession to the modern non-Christian world that Christians reason thus; they, too, are post-Enlightenment people. "Actually, Troeltsch believed the church had no real option, because it is impossible even to think without the new assumptions. They have already penetrated to the deepest levels of Western man's consciousness. They are a part of the furniture of his mind."[93]

But then, third, the post-Enlightenment "morality of knowledge" is itself to be regarded not as an unchristian expression of unbelief but as a form, albeit a secularized one, of faith. Faith is not to be identified with assent, even to the Bible as the Word of God; it is, in Tillich's words, "the courage to be," to accept the total ambiguity of the human situation, to trust in being itself, "the accepting of the acceptance without somebody or something that accepts."[94] The integrity and autonomy of the historian are aspects of this "faith," and the historian is "justified by faith" in facing up to data with the radical honesty of the historical method. Conversely, "the really destructive atheism is fear of facts. . . . It is the existential denial that the world is God's."[95]

The rigorous exercise of the historical method, however, need not lead to agnosticism about biblical history, unless presuppositions about what may and may not be allowed to have happened are permitted to prejudice the way it is exercised. Such presuppositions set aside, the historical Jesus is not quite so elusive. The fact that we received the First Testament from this Jesus, so that it has his authority, complicates our position as we seek to look at it through the eyes of the historical method. Indeed, faith is not to be equated with assent, even to the Bible as the Word of God; but neither is it to be identified with a brave and autonomous stand before impersonal Being. It is rather a bowing before the personal God and Father of our Lord Jesus Christ, whom Christ implies to be the author of the biblical tradition and of the events the tradition relates. Our act of faith is not in Being and in the historical method but in God and in the tradition. As a result of this act of faith that is a reaction to historical knowledge of Jesus Christ we gain a conviction about the validity of the First Testament tradition that can survive without the support of the historical method. It is in this sense, in regard to the First Testament, that one can agree that "the real call of today . . . is to make a turn of 180 degrees and bring historical science, especially in so far as it has gained a dominant position within theology itself, under the judgement of revelation."[96] The pressure to attribute ultimate authority in First Testament studies to the historical method is to be resisted; like the scientific method, it stands under the revelation of God in the tradition, not over it. This being the case, the pressure to yield to the consensus viewpoint on

92. Pannenberg in Robinson and Cobb, eds., *Theology as History*, 226, 229.
93. Harvey, *The Historian and the Believer*, 6.
94. Ibid., 147.
95. Alexander Miller, as quoted in ibid., 137.
96. Erwin Reisner, as quoted in Harvey, *The Historian and the Believer*, 128.

the ultimate importance of the historical method is simply one that will have to be resisted, like other epistemological and moral pressures.

The historical method does have a subordinate function in our study of the First Testament, as an aid to investigating and establishing the events that the tradition tells us of. But when it leads to negative results—for instance, when we find that historical science cannot substantiate the deliverance of Jerusalem from Sennacherib[97]—we need not feel obliged to be skeptical or agnostic about the incident, because of our trust in and commitment to God and the tradition. We are like someone who "can be confident that a jury will find his friend innocent of a crime—since he 'knows' independently that this friend is innocent, although he must wait for the judgement of the jury."[98] We know that Israel's account of the events of its history will not be discredited.

Commitment to God and to the tradition carries with it conviction that the tradition and the events do in fact correspond, even where we cannot demonstrate how. Where they seem to conflict, we must be misinterpreting the tradition or mis- interpreting the data available to us as historians. We recognize that we are far short of the total amount of information we need on the one hand as exegetes of ancient documents from an alien culture and on the other as historians of remote events. The verification that the First Testament regards as indispensable to the validation of its theology may not be one attainable by the application of the historical method, unless the data available to us increase dramatically. When Kings was written, the situation was different. You could go and look the matter up in the archives, at least in theory. For us, certainty about the historical trustworthiness of the First Testament historical narratives has to be grounded on the validation they receive from Christ.

We have to continue to live with the "two histories," abandoning neither the events as they actually happened nor the First Testament's picture of them. But we do so believing that there is in reality but one history, experienced by Israel and described and interpreted in its tradition, both of them under the hand of God who is thus the guarantee of their unity and the grounds of our confidence that the credibility gap between them will be closed in the fullness of time. In the meantime, we whose concern is that theology should be seen to be validated by history, that the world may know that Yahweh is God, may work at the points of tension (to change the metaphor) in the expectation that they may be resolved.

---

97. So Childs, *Isaiah and the Assyrian Crisis*, 118–19.

98. Harvey, *The Historian and the Believer*, 196; though (as Harvey avers) the analogy cannot be applied to that historical-critical investigation that may precede faith in Jesus.

PART 3

Concerning the First Testament as a Whole

14

How Does Christian Faith
Relate to the First Testament?

C hristian faith focuses on Jesus Christ, and we learn of him from the New Testament. So what significance attaches to the First Testament, the Hebrew-Aramaic Bible, the Torah, the Prophets, and the Writings, the Scriptures accepted by the Jewish religious community to which Jesus belonged? Within the New Testament there is variation in the extent to which different books refer to these Scriptures and some variety in the way they use them. As it happens, however, the opening pages of the New Testament offer a particularly instructive set of concrete illustrations of what the First Testament means in the context of the gospel of Christ.[1]

1. The First Testament Tells the Story
of Which Christ Is the Climax (Matthew 1:1-17)

To the eyes of most modern readers, the opening verses of the New Testament form an unpromising beginning, with their unexciting list of bare names. Our attention soon moves on to the inviting stories in Matthew 1:18–2:23. But the Jewish reader who came to faith in Christ through reading these verses responded to them in a way Matthew would have appreciated. This reader had seen that the genealogy embodies a particular assertion about Jesus. It establishes that he was a Jew. Indeed, it is a genealogy of a particular kind: his ancestry not only goes back via the exile to

---

1. First published in *Them* 8, no. 1 (1982): 4–10; 8, no. 2 (1983): 5–12.

Abraham but also marks him as a member of the clan of Judah and of the family of David, and thus gives him a formal claim to David's throne. It is a genealogy that (unusually) includes the names of several women, names that draw attention to the contribution made by some rather questionable unions to this genealogy even before and during David's own time, so that the apparently questionable circumstances of Jesus' birth (Matt 1:19) can hardly be deemed unworthy of someone who was reckoned to be David's successor. It is a genealogy arranged into three sequences of fourteen names, a patterning that expresses the conviction that the Christ event comes about by a providence of God that has been at work throughout the history of the Jewish people but now comes to its climax

The genealogy appeals to the historical past, to real history. Matthew assumes that a person has to be a descendant of David to have a claim to David's throne, and a descendant of Abraham to have a "natural" share in Abraham's promise, still more if he is to be recognized as *the* seed of Abraham. Matthew has in mind legal descent; someone can be adopted into a family and then come to share that family's genealogy as fully as if they had been born into it. Thus Jesus has a claim to David's throne via his adoptive, legal father Joseph. In this sense, Matthew is talking about the real ancestry of Jesus, the real historical antecedents to the Christ event. At the same time, he schematizes the past when he appeals to it. There were not factually fourteen generations from Abraham to David, from David to the exile, and from the exile to the Christ (Matt 1:17). By shaping the genealogy as if there were, Matthew creates something more artistic and easier to remember than it might otherwise be, and something giving explicit expression to the way a providence of God had been at work in the ordering of Israelite history up to Jesus' time, as it was in his birth, life, death, and resurrection.

These two aspects of Matthew's appeal to the historical past are consistent features of the Gospels and of First Testament narratives. The evangelists are concerned with the real historical Jesus, but they tell his story in a schematized way, selecting and ordering material in order to make the points of central significance clear. Matthew 4 tells us of three temptations Jesus experienced; Luke 4 includes the same temptations but orders them differently. Matthew tells us of the beginning of Jesus' ministry in Capernaum; Luke precedes this by the account of his rejection at Nazareth, which comes later in Matthew. It is not that either Matthew or Luke has made mistakes in his presentation, but that sometimes a reordering or rewriting makes a story's significance clearer than a merely chronological account does.

The First Testament narratives that were among the evangelists' models, such as Genesis and Exodus, Kings and Chronicles, were likewise concerned with real historical events, but they, too, select, order, and rewrite their material so as to make the message of history clear for their contemporaries. Much of the material in the opening part of Matthew's genealogy comes from Chronicles, which well illustrates this combination of a concern for real people and events with a presentation making explicit their significance for the writer's day. It is the latter interest that explains the substantial difference between Samuel-Kings' and Chronicles' presentation of the same story.

Matthew's example, then, directs us toward a twofold interest in the First Testament story. We are interested in the real events of First Testament times that led up to Christ. It is this instinct, in part, that made generations of students feel that their library was incomplete without a volume on the history of Israel on their shelves. If this history is the background to the Christ event, we had better understand the actual history of Israel. We are also interested in the way this history has been shaped as narrative by the writers of both Testaments. We are not reading mere chronicle or annal but a story whose message is expressed in the way it is told. So as well as books retelling the history of Israel, we need books on the interpretation of biblical narratives to help us interpret the story of Israel as the First Testament itself tells it.

In practice, it is easy to let one interest exclude the other. Either readers assume that we are concerned only with the events, and ignore the literary creativity in biblical narrative, or they become so aware of this creativity that they cease to recognize the fact and/or the importance of the fundamental historicity of Israelite history. Like the First Testament narratives themselves, Matthew implies that both matter.

Matthew assumes, then, that readers need to know something of the history behind Jesus if they are to understand Jesus himself aright. This assumption applies to every historical person or event. We understand other people aright only if we know something of their history, experiences, and background: it is these that have made them what they are. We understand complex political problems such as those of the Middle East only if we understand their history. We understand the Christ event aright only if we see it as the climax to a story reaching centuries back into pre-Christian times, the story of a relationship between the God and Father of our Lord Jesus Christ and the Israelite people whom God chose as the means of access to the world as a whole. The First Testament story has an importance for Christians that (for instance) Indian or Chinese or Greek history does not have, because this is the story of which the Christ event is the climax.

In relating Jesus' genealogy, Matthew gives us one instance of what is meant by understanding the coming of Christ in light of the story of Israel. His example also encourages us to ask with regard to other aspects of the Christ event, what light is cast on it by its background in Abraham's leaving Ur, Israel's exodus from Egypt, David's capture of Jerusalem, Solomon's building of the temple, Ephraim's fall in 722 and Judah's exile in 587, the Persians' allowing the exiles to return and Alexander's unleashing of Hellenistic culture in the Middle East, the events that make up the story that is the background to Christ's coming. The First Testament is Act I to the New Testament's Act II,[2] and as in any story, we understand the final scene aright only in light of the ones that preceded.

The converse is also true. As well as understanding Christ in light of the First Testament story, Matthew understands the First Testament story in light of the Christ event. Matthew's claim is that the story from Abraham to David to the exile to the Second Temple period comes to its climax with Christ's coming and needs to

---

2. John Bright, *The Authority of the Old Testament* (Nashville: Abingdon; London: SCM, 1967), 202.

be understood in light of this denouement. (He does not imply that Israel's history comes to an end with the exile, as Christian readers often do. He follows the First Testament itself in seeing this story continuing into the Persian and Greek periods.)

This is not the only way to read Israel's history. A non-Christian Jew will understand it very differently. Whether you read Israel's story in this way depends on what you make of Jesus. If you recognize that he is the Christ, you will know he is the climax of First Testament history. If you do not, you will not. (Conversely, for a Jew at least, whether one recognizes that Jesus is the Christ may depend on whether it seems plausible to read Israel's history in this way; a subtle dialectic is involved here.)

Once we do read Israel's history thus, it makes a difference to the way we understand the events it relates. The significance of Abraham's leaving Ur, Israel's exodus from Egypt, David's capture of Jerusalem, and so on, emerges with greater clarity when we see these events in light of each other and in light of the Christ event that is their climax.

The interpretation of the exodus provides a useful example, both because of the intrinsic importance of the exodus in the First Testament and because of interest in this event in various forms of liberation theology. On one hand, understanding the Christ event in light of the First Testament story supports the assertion that God is concerned for people's political and social liberation. The God and Father of our Lord Jesus Christ is one who is concerned for the release of the oppressed from bondage; the nature of the Christ event does not change that. On the other hand, understanding the First Testament story in light of the Christ event highlights for us the concern with the spiritual and moral liberation of the spiritually and morally oppressed that is present in the exodus story and becomes more pressing as the First Testament story unfolds. Any concern with political and social liberation that does not recognize humanity's fundamental need of spiritual and moral liberation has failed to take account of the development of the First Testament story after the exodus via the exile to Christ's coming, his death, his resurrection, and his pouring out of the Spirit.

Matthew later issues his own warning about misreading Israelite history, relating the warning John the Baptist gave his hearers: "Do not presume to say to yourselves, 'We have Abraham as our father'" (Matt 3:9). Merely having the right history does nothing for you. It places you in a position of potential privilege, but it requires that you respond to the God who has been active in that history if you are to enjoy your privilege. The story is quite capable of turning into a tragedy if you allow it. "The axe is laid to the root of the trees" (Matt 3:10). That God has been working out a purpose in history is of crucial significance for Christian faith. But it effects nothing until it leads us to personal trust and obedience in relation to God.

2. The First Testament Declares the Promise of Which Christ Is the Fulfillment (Matthew 1:18–2:23)

For most readers, Matthew really begins with the five scenes from the story of Jesus' birth in Matthew 1:18–2:23. How do these relate to the First Testament?

Each gives a key place to a reference to a prophecy that is "fulfilled" in the event related. First, Joseph is reassured that his fiancée's pregnancy results not from her promiscuity but from the Holy Spirit's activity that will bring about the birth of someone who will save his people. The point is clinched by a reference to the fulfillment of what the Lord had said by means of Isaiah concerning a virgin who would have a child called "God with us" (Matt 1:18–25; Isa 7:14). Second, the place where "the king of the Jews" is to be born is discovered to be Bethlehem, through a consideration of the prophecy in Micah concerning the birth there of a ruler over Israel (Matt 2:1–12; Mic 5:2). Third, the account of Joseph, Mary, and Jesus' sojourn in Egypt is brought to a climax by describing this event as the fulfillment of what the Lord had spoken by means of Hosea about his son having been called out of Egypt (Matt 2:13–15; Hos 11:1). Fourth, the story of Herod's massacre of baby boys is brought to a climax by its being described as a fulfillment of Jeremiah's words describing Rachel mourning for her children (Matt 2:16–18; Jer 31:15). Then, fifth, the account of the family's move back to Nazareth is clinched by describing this as a fulfillment of the statement in the prophets that the Messiah was to be called a Nazarene (Matt 2:19–23).

The reference of this last passage is unclear, there being no prophecy that says "he will be called a Nazarene." Three passages have been suggested as perhaps in Matthew's mind. Isaiah 11:1 and other passages describe a coming ruler as a branch growing from the tree of Jesse, which was felled by the exile, using the word *neser* for "branch." So describing Jesus as a Nazarene, a *nosri*, could be taken as an unwitting description of him as "Branch-man." Then the description of the servant in Isaiah 52:13–53:12 as despised and rejected could link with Nazareth's being a city in the despised and alien far north, Galilee of the Gentiles, the land of darkness (Matt 4:14–16, quoting Isa 9:1–2); it was a city proverbially unlikely to produce anything good (John 1:46). So a Nazarene was likely to be despised and rejected, as prophecy had described Yahweh's servant. A third passage is the angel's appearance to Samson's mother, when he describes Samson's calling to be a Nazirite to God from birth (Judg 13:5); the events surrounding the birth of Jesus' forerunner also recollect that angelic visitation to Samson's mother (see Luke 1:15; also 1:31).

In each of these vignettes from the opening years of Jesus' life, then, a key place is taken by a reference to a First Testament prophecy, as if to say, "You will understand Jesus aright only if you see him as the fulfillment of a purpose of God contemplated and announced by God centuries before." In particular, if you find it surprising that he should be conceived out of wedlock, born in a little town like Bethlehem rather than in Jerusalem, hurried off to Egypt at an early age, indirectly the cause of the death of scores of baby boys, and eventually brought up in unfashionable Nazareth, then consider these facts in light of what the prophets say.

Is the utilization of prophecy by Matthew and other New Testament writers in this way mere "proof from prophecy," designed to remove the scandal from the story of Jesus and to win cheap debating points over against non-Christian

Jews?[3] Matthew's use of prophecy is of a piece with his interest in other aspects of the First Testament. He is concerned with understanding Jesus and understanding the First Testament; he is not out to prove something to unwilling hearers or to explain away something to disciples of shallow faith. He knows that Jesus is to be understood in light of the promise of which he is the fulfillment, and he therefore seeks to interpret his significance in that light. This understanding of Matthew's attitude is supported by the next episode he relates, the ministry of John the Baptist (Matt 3:1–12). Here too, a passage from prophecy has a key place: John is the voice preaching in the wilderness that is spoken of in Isaiah 40:3. The idea that Matthew is utilizing apologetic "proofs from prophecy" is even less plausible here.

These passages raise a further question about Matthew's interpretation of prophecy. The modern instinct is to interpret prophecy, like other biblical material, by concentrating on the meaning the prophecy had for its author and hearers. A passage such as Micah 5 is future-oriented in its original context, and in this sense Matthew's use of it is quite in accord with its original meaning. One cannot prove exegetically that Jesus is the ruler spoken of there; Matthew's use of his text goes beyond its statements, in light of his faith in Jesus. Nevertheless, his use of his text is not alien to it. At another extreme, his appeal to Hosea 11 takes the text in a totally different way from its inherent meaning. Hosea 11 is a record of God's inner wrestling over whether to act towards Israel with love or with wrath. It opens by recalling the blessings God had given to the people, beginning by calling them out of Egypt at the time of the exodus. Hosea 11:1 is not prophecy in the sense of a statement about the future that could be capable of being "fulfilled" at all. It is history.

Between these two extreme examples there are passages among the ones Matthew quotes that are future-oriented but relate to the future within the prophet's day (Mic 5, too, may have had such a shorter-term future reference to an imminent king). Rachel's weeping (Jer 31:15) is the lament she will utter as Judeans trudge past her tomb on their way to exile. The voice in the wilderness (Isa 40:3) is a voice commissioning Yahweh's servants to prepare the road for Yahweh's return to Jerusalem. The child of Isaiah 7:14 is a more controversial figure. Let us assume that "virgin" is the right translation of the word 'almah (though that is itself a controversial question). This need not mean the girl in question will be a virgin when she conceives and gives birth. The Prince of Wales will one day rule Great Britain; this does not mean he will rule as a prince but that he will become king and will then rule. In Isaiah 7 the prophet is promising that by the time a girl yet unmarried has had her first child, the crisis Ahaz fears will be over; she will be able to call her child Immanuel, God is with us, in her rejoicing at what God has done for the people. Finally, if "he will be called a Nazarene" refers to Judges 13, this reference, too, takes up a statement

---

3. See, e.g., Friedrich Baumgärtel, "The Hermeneutical Problem of the Old Testament," in *Essays on Old Testament Interpretation* (ed. Claus Westermann; London: SCM, 1963) = *Essays on Old Testament Hermeneutics* (Richmond: John Knox, 1963), 134–59 (see 143).

about a specific imminent event; if it is an allusion to Isaiah 11 it more resembles the appeal to Micah 5. If it alludes to Isaiah 52:13–53:12, it more resembles the appeal to Hosea 11. Isaiah 52:13–53:12 is not a prophecy about the future; at least, it does not present itself to us as such. It presents itself as a vision or picture of someone whose humiliation is past and his exaltation future. Nor is it directly a portrait of crucifixion and resurrection. Nor does it prove that Jesus is the Messiah. As Jews who believe in Jesus can find Jesus in the chapter, Jews who do not believe in Jesus can point out ways in which it does not literally apply to him. Indeed, part of what happens when we study this passage is that knowing Jesus is the Messiah helps Christians make sense of this otherwise enigmatic picture.

In most if not all these cases, then, Matthew sees significance in these prophecies that they would not have had for their authors. In speaking of their prophecies as being fulfilled, Matthew means more (or less) than we would mean by it. The verb does not mean that these prophecies were statements about the future that now come true. The word usually translated "fulfilled" is *plēroō*, the regular verb meaning "fill." Applied to a prophecy, it could suggest "filled" or "filled up" or "filled out" as well as "fulfilled" in the sense of "caused to come true." The other New Testament verbs are *teleō* and *teleioō*, meaning "complete" or "accomplish." Being "fulfilled" means something like being filled out or brought to its goal. In this sense, Isaiah 53 is certainly fulfilled by Jesus' crucifixion and resurrection. And it is in this sense that one might think in terms of the New Testament revealing the "fuller meaning" of a prophecy, though the expression is misleading if it implies that the New Testament is unveiling the prophecy's inherent meaning. It is rather seeing a fuller meaning for later readers; I would rather call it a fuller significance. The First Testament prophets were a resource for the New Testament church and continue to be a resource for us, in understanding who Jesus is, and Jesus was a resource for their understanding of the prophets, and continues to be for ours.

A story in John 11 suggests the way of thinking that may lie behind Matthew's interpretation. Caiaphas declares, "It is expedient for you that one man should die for the people, and that the whole nation should not perish"; Jesus must be killed lest he continue to arouse messianic expectations and ultimately cause a revolt that the Romans would have to crush violently. John can see a hidden significance in Caiaphas's words: "He did not say this of his own accord, but being high priest that year he prophesied that Jesus should die for the nation" (John 11:50–51). Of course, Caiaphas did speak of his own accord and knew what he meant. But in light of later events (the fact that Jesus did die for the nation, in a different sense), John intuits that Caiaphas spoke the way he did by a divine prompting that gave his words a second significance. Jesus will die to avert from his people not merely Rome's wrath but God's wrath.

John's words suggest a way of understanding Matthew's assumptions about the prophets. Whatever meaning prophecy may have had historically, he finds within it particular sentences that were in a special sense not spoken by the prophets "of their own accord" but by a divine prompting that gave them a significance that the prophets and their original hearers could not have perceived but that is apparent in light of the event they refer to. All a prophet's words had a God-given historical meaning; some also had a God-given messianic significance, a way in which they illumine the significance of Jesus. It is this latter significance to which 2 Peter 1:21 refers. When New Testament writers looked back to the words of the prophets in light of Christ, sometimes they found statements so appropriate to the Christ event that this reference must have been present in them from the beginning by God's will, if not in the awareness of their human authors. Like John, they moved from some aspect of the later event back to a passage that turned out to illumine it; no one would have thought that a passage such as Hosea 11:1 was a prophecy awaiting fulfillment until someone considered it in light of what happened to Jesus. (This, incidentally, reduces the plausibility of the theory that stories in the Gospels were developed to provide fulfillments of prophecies. The hermeneutical movement is *from* the puzzle of Jesus' flight *to* a reinterpretation of Hosea 11, not from the natural meaning of Hosea 11 to a story that assures people that it has been fulfilled.)

If Matthew ignores the First Testament's historical meaning, does this undermine our conventional emphasis on texts' historical meaning? John does not suggest that every human statement, or even every statement by a high priest, or even every statement about the future by a high priest, or even every statement about the future by this particular high priest in this particular year, has a double significance. Rather, occasionally the words a particular person uses may be so striking in some other connection to raise the question of a second significance. The way he can identify this second significance is by considering what he knows about Jesus as the Christ.

Can we continue to interpret prophecy in Matthew's way? There is a possible instance in Psalm 22, the lament of someone abandoned by God and attacked by enemies; it is several times quoted in the New Testament as fulfilled in Christ. In verse 16 the suppliant says, "they pierce my hands and my feet" (so TNIV; the text and translation are problematic, but for the sake of argument we will assume a version that is most open to a prophetic interpretation). This verse is not quoted in the New Testament, but many Christians have found a prophecy of the crucifixion here. There is no hint that the psalm's author saw this lament as a prophecy or that other Israelites would have understood it so. The suggestion that it refers to Christ works back from the Christ event to the text and intuits that the facts of the crucifixion must have been in the back of God's mind when God welcomed this prayer by an afflicted Israelite into the Psalter. This seems feasible, though it is difficult to see how one can establish whether or not it was the case. Such "inspired" interpretation of Scripture is similar to other forms of inspired utterance: difficult to test, possible sometimes to disprove, but hard to prove. I accept Matthew's intuitions about the First Testament because I believe he was inspired; I could not ask you to accept mine on the same basis. Yet I do rejoice in the fact that God speaks to me and through me by means of interpretations of Scripture that do not correspond to their original meaning and that I believe come from the Holy Spirit.[4]

4. See further chapter 2 above.

The advantage of a historical approach to interpretation is that it is easier to argue for or against a historical understanding of what a text will have meant for its human author in a particular context. Theologically, the basis for an emphasis on understanding Scripture in this way is the awareness that God indeed spoke and acted in history. Some passages of Scripture may have an inspired second significance, an extra level of significance in the back of God's mind that is difficult for us to identify. All Scripture has an inspired first meaning, its meaning as a communication between God and people in a particular historical context, to which we can have access by the usual methods for interpreting written texts.

Similar considerations apply to the study of the precise form of the biblical text. In Psalm 22:16, the MT actually reads not "they pierce my hands and my feet" but "like a lion [at] my hands and my feet" (cf. TNIV margin) or "my hands and feet have shriveled" (NRSV). The familiar translation follows the Greek, Syriac, and Latin versions of the psalm. Thus the Christian textual tradition preserves a reading amenable to a Christian interpretation, while the main Jewish textual tradition preserves one that is not. It is difficult to say which is right, because either could be working back from what they believe: Jesus is the crucified Messiah, and the text can be expected to hint at that; or he is not, and the text cannot be expected to hint at it. The text's preservation can be influenced by the same factors as its interpretation; the movement is from contemporary beliefs to the text, as well as vice versa.

This post-New Testament phenomenon is paralleled within the passages from Matthew that appeal to prophecy. The quotation from Micah (Matt 2:6) instances it most clearly, since Micah's "insignificant Bethlehem" has become Matthew's "by no means insignificant," which was the result of Micah's prophecy being fulfilled. It is characteristic of textual work in New Testament times (within the New Testament and, for instance, at Qumran) to pay close attention to the text itself in the awareness that one is handling Holy Scripture; and the conviction that one now sees God acting in fulfillment of promises enables one to specify in Scripture itself the nature of the fulfillment. As with his way of interpreting prophecy, Matthew's way of handling the text of prophecy is one that we sometimes follow; we sometimes choose the translation that best makes the point we want to bring home to people. We need to be self-conscious about what we are doing and complement that with a concern to work with a text of Scripture as near as we can to the one that issued by God's providence from its human authors.

If our study of First Testament prophecy is to attend to its meaning for its authors and their hearers, our interpretation of passages such as the ones Matthew quotes will not be limited to noting the meaning he finds in them when he interprets them in light of the circumstances of Christ's coming. Isaiah 7, for instance, belongs in a context of dire peril for preexilic Judah and relates how its king was challenged to a radical trust in God despite the reality of this threat. Such a trust would issue in doing the right thing before God and before human beings, despite the temptation either to yield to Syria and Ephraim's attempts to lean on him to join their rebellion against Assyria, or to seek help against Syria and Ephraim from Assyria itself. The power of Syria and Israel threatens to destroy Judah; but within a year (says Isaiah) it will all be over, and you will know it is true that "God-is-with-us." That promise is reserved in Scripture for the impossible situations that most need it (see, e.g., Gen 28:15; Exod 3:12; Jer 1:8; Matt 28:20). In those contexts it lifts people back on their feet, promising that they do not face the future alone and that God will deal with whatever crisis threatens. So it does in Isaiah 7:14 (see also Isa 8:8, 10) and in the situation of crisis in Matthew 1:18–25.

Isaiah 9, too, needs understanding in its own right. Its context speaks of the darkness, anguish, gloom and distress of war (Isa 8:21–22), and of more than that, for these are the darkness, anguish, gloom and distress of the Day of Yahweh (cf. Amos 5:18–20), embodied in historical events for Ephraim, now the despised "gentile Galilee." But then it portrays darkness dispelled, anguish and distress comforted, the grief of a funeral replaced by the joy of a wedding (Isa 9:1–2). It goes on to speak of a son of David ruling the world by the faithful exercise of authority (Isa 9:3–7); not a vision we yet see fulfilled, but one that must be fulfilled.

What of the branch, the *neser*, in Isaiah 11:1? If a branch can grow from the trunk of a tree that has been felled, then no one and nothing is ever finished. If God says there will be new growth, there will be. For five centuries it must have seemed as if that promise was as dead as the trunk it referred to, but then there *was* new growth, in the person of the Nazarene.

To see the implications of such prophecies for the significance of the Christ event, we need to go back to the prophecies themselves. We can also take Matthew's appeal to particular aspects of particular prophecies as an encouragement to undertake a broader study of the more general pattern of God's promises in the First Testament so that we can learn more about Christ from them. Matthew's utilization of a number of specific passages (and the references elsewhere in the New Testament to other passages) hardly indicates the total range of First Testament prophecies that are to illumine the Christ event for us. They only instance the process of understanding Christ in light of prophecy, and invite us to look at the total range of these prophecies in order more fully to understand the Christ in whom all God's promises find their yes (2 Cor 1:20). These promises extend back even beyond God's promise of blessing to Abraham to the words of God about blessing in the opening chapters of Genesis.

In Genesis to Kings these promises keep receiving fulfillments, yet none is complete or final, and each experience of fulfillment or of loss stimulates renewed hope in God's overarching promise. This hope becomes more overt in the prophetic books themselves. What they offer is an updated version of God's ancient promises. It is this overarching and ever-reformulated promise that is fulfilled in Christ. He is to be understood in light of the ongoing promise, and we are encouraged to look at those promises in order to understand what he came to achieve. As much interest then attaches to aspects of those promises that did not obviously find their fulfillment in the Christ event as to aspects that did. Insofar as all God's promises are reaffirmed in him, all reveal aspects of his significance and calling. If, for instance, the hopes of a new world in which authority is exercised in faithfulness have not been fulfilled through Christ's first coming, they will be through his second coming. They must be, because (if one may put it this way) if Jesus is truly God's Messiah, he has no choice but to be the means of fulfilling all God's promises.

Matthew's example also suggests a converse of this point. As well as understanding Christ in light of prophecy, we understand prophecy in light of Christ, as the one who fulfills it. The notion of God-with-us is capable of suggesting a presence of a much fuller kind than we would have guessed from the words in their First Testament context. The darkness into which God brings light is not merely the darkness of this-worldly suffering but that of God's absence. In the person of the Branch-man, the growth from the felled tree is more extraordinary even than Isaiah pictured it.

These considerations put question marks alongside the approach to prophecy taken by the books abounding in Christian bookstores and the sites abounding on the web that refer prophecies to events in the Middle East in our own day. These ignore the meaning that their texts had for the prophet God inspired and for the readers God addressed through them. Of course Matthew does that too; the question is, Can such interpretation be acknowledged as inspired like Matthew's? It fails one test: Matthew begins from the Christ event and interprets prophecy in light of it. His interpretation has part of its justification in its faithfulness to God's revelation in Christ. The newspaper is not as inspired a starting point.[5]

3. The First Testament Provides the Images, Ideas, and Words with Which to Understand Christ (Matthew 3:13–17)

The Gospel account of John the Baptist's work closes with Jesus coming for baptism (Matt 3:13–17). At the moment when God the Holy Spirit comes to alight upon God the Son for his ministry, God the Father speaks from heaven: "This is my son, my beloved, the one in whom I delight." The words are not made up for the occasion: they are taken from the First Testament.

They combine phrases from three passages. "This is my son" recalls Psalm 2:7, part of a king's testimony to Yahweh's word to him. The king need not fear being unable to maintain control of subject nations because Yahweh has made him sovereign over them; he recalls Yahweh's words of commission and assurance, "You are my son, today I have begotten you." After the exile, when Israel had no kings, such a psalm could become linked to Israel's hope that one day it will again have a king for whom God will fulfill this commitment. In taking up these words, God the Father declares that Jesus is the anointed one ("Messiah") there spoken of (Ps 2:2).

"My beloved, in whom I delight" recalls Isaiah 42:1. Isaiah 42:1–9 describes the role Yahweh's servant is expected to fulfill. The role is in some respects quite similar to the king's calling, but the portrait of the servant in Isaiah 40–55 makes clear that this role is not fulfilled by what we normally see as the exercise of power

5. See further chapter 19 below.

but by accepting affliction and paying a huge personal price for the restoration of relationships between God and people. It is this calling that God the Father places before Jesus.

These two passages could account satisfactorily for the words that appear in Matthew 3:17. But the middle phrase "my son, my beloved" also recalls Genesis 22:2. In Genesis 22, God bids Abraham, "Take your son, your only son Isaac, whom you love" and offer him as a burnt offering. In the end this sacrifice is not exacted, but Abraham shows himself willing to make it. His action (and Isaac's implicit willingness to be sacrificed) made a deep impression on Israel, and the passage was a much pondered one among Jews of Jesus' day. It lies behind Paul's talk of God's not sparing his only Son in Romans 8:32. Its importance in Jesus' day suggests it also lies behind God the Father's words in Matthew 3:17: Jesus is the only Son whom God loves and is willing to sacrifice for the sake of the world, and Jesus is called to imitate Isaac's availability.

In Jesus' life and ministry, his baptism and the Spirit's coming on him is of key importance, and in the Gospel tradition the account of this event has a key place. In the words he hears from heaven he receives fundamental guidelines for the way he is to understand himself. He has the authority of the Davidic king, given a special relationship of sonship to the God of heaven. At the same time he has the calling of the servant with its different form of power, exercised despite or through affliction. And if that point is not explicit enough, he is the beloved Son whom the Father is willing to sacrifice for the world's sake. Here Jesus is given his fundamental theological orientation for his ministry, the key motifs that embody central aspects to his calling. They come from the First Testament Scriptures.

This passage is the only one in Matthew 1–5 that actually quotes from the First Testament to make what we might call a theological statement, but the utilization of the Scriptures in connection with making theological statements pervades the chapters' background. The vast bulk of the way the New Testament pictures God and humanity and the relationship between them assumes the way these realities are described in the First Testament. The First Testament is the New Testament's theological dictionary or its language world. What the word "God" meant was determined by what it meant in the Jewish Scriptures.

This point can be illustrated from the present context in Matthew. John the Baptist urges repentance on the grounds that the rule of heaven is at hand, exhorts people to flee from the coming wrath, warns them that trees that do not produce fruit are to be felled, and describes one who will come after him harvesting wheat and burning chaff (Matt 3:1–12). All these motifs and themes come from the First Testament. It is on the basis of people's knowledge of these Scriptures that John makes his appeal to them. (It is extraordinary how many attempts to understand "the kingdom of God" start from the New Testament; further, the "enigma" of the sense in which the rule of God is "at hand" or "has come" is less puzzling when looked at in light of First Testament speech since Amos 8:2, if not Gen 6:13.) The principle that the First Testament provides the theological framework for understanding Christian faith can easily be illustrated from elsewhere in the New Testament. It is very clear when Paul discusses fundamental questions in Romans. After stating his revolutionary gospel in Romans 3:21–26 (itself thought out in fundamentally First Testament terms), he has to face overtly the question whether this gospel is acceptable—that is, whether it is biblical enough. He approaches this question in Romans 4 by considering the key case of Abraham and maintaining that Abraham's relationship with God had a similar basis to the one he speaks of. It too involved a righteousness based on trust. First Testament theology thus supports and illumines the nature of faith in Christ. Romans 3 alludes also to the question what effect this understanding of God's ways has on the position of the Jews, and this question is taken up systematically in Romans 9–11, where the theological argument is conducted entirely in terms of the exposition of First Testament Scripture.

As in sections 1 and 2 above, there are two further points to be made. The first is that if the New Testament views the First Testament as its major resource for a theological perspective or context for understanding Christ, it directs us to a systematic study of First Testament concepts, motifs, and images. If Jesus is the Messiah, the only Son whom the Father loves, and the suffering servant, we need to investigate what these motifs mean in their First Testament context. If the First Testament provides the language world in whose terms the Christ event finds its meaning, we need to learn to think and speak in the terms of that language world. If it is the God of First Testament Israel whom Jesus calls Father (and whose fatherhood he then shares with us), we need to discover who this Father is. This takes us into a study of First Testament symbol and imagery, and also into a study of "Old Testament theology," the current version of the kind of systematic study of the First Testament to which the New Testament implicitly directs us.

Admittedly Jesus and other New Testament writers understood and handled concepts that go back to the First Testament not in their neat First Testament form but with the connotations that subsequent exegetical and theological tradition had given them. The word "messiah," which in the First Testament had referred to Israel's present anointed king (or to other anointed agents of Yahweh such as priests) now naturally referred to the future anointed king for whom Israel hoped. The human-like figure that in Daniel 7 is simply a figure in a vision, representing Israel, has become another symbolic redeemer figure, the Son of Man. Often the New Testament takes up First Testament theological motifs not in their First Testament significance, but refracted through their usage in Jewish tradition.

This makes a practical difference to the New Testament's theological use of the First Testament, though hardly a difference of principle. The New Testament is in a similar position in relation to the First Testament to that of subsequent centuries (including our own) in relation to the Bible as a whole. In both cases, it is the texts' own way of looking at reality to which we commit ourselves, even if at points we unconsciously allow our understanding of it to be influenced by subsequent semantic or theological developments.

The New Testament, then, invites us to interpret the Christ event in light of the First Testament's theological perspective as a whole, in the terms of its language world.

The converse point is that we also come to understand First Testament theology and images in light of the Christ event. No one had previously brought together the figures of the powerful king, the beloved son, and the afflicted servant. They are diverse figures, and it would have been difficult to see how one might go about relating them. They are brought together only in light of the Christ event, which enables one to look back at First Testament events or themes and see interrelationships that were imperceptible before or make relationships that were not there before, because their principle of interrelationship, the one to whom they referred in "many and various ways" (Heb 1:1) was not yet present. Jesus' baptism is a creative theological moment.

Again, if one looks once more at John the Baptist's ministry as a whole, by no means every aspect of its teaching derives from the First Testament. Baptism had no precise First Testament antecedents. The Christ event brings new religious practices and new religious language as well as new collocations of old texts. It not only supplements but also refocuses and redefines biblical faith. The incarnation does so; we have noted that "God-with-us" now means something more radical than was the case in First Testament times (though something quite consistent with the view of God and humanity stated in the First Testament). The cross does so, bringing to clearest external expression that unprecedented paradoxical collocation of kingly glory, fatherly sacrifice, and personal suffering stated at Jesus' baptism. The resurrection does so, making the hope of our resurrection central rather than marginal to biblical faith and promising a resolution of the enigma and incompleteness of human life recognized by the First Testament and instanced by Matthew's story of the death of Bethlehem's children and the prominence even in Israel's history of the likes of Herod and Archelaus. The outpouring of the Holy Spirit does so, bringing home the significance of Jesus and thus opening up new possibility of living a holy life.

When later parts of the New Testament describe the events, persons, and institutions of the First Testament as types or symbols or foreshadowings of the realities of the Christian gospel, they are themselves going about this task of understanding First Testament realities in light of the Christ event. The exodus and conquest, or the persons of Moses or Aaron, or Israelite rites of sacrifice were perfectly meaningful in their First Testament context, but in retrospect Hebrews can see them as standing for something (release and rest, leadership and priesthood, means of gaining access to God's presence) that is now a fuller reality in Christ. The First Testament realities provide the images and concepts for understanding the Christ event, and the Christ event provides more insight on the nature of salvation, in whose context First Testament institutions need to be understood.

4. The First Testament Tells Us the Kind of Life God Expects Us to Live (Matthew 4:1–11)

Immediately after his baptism Jesus is led off into the wilderness to be tempted by the devil, who offers him three suggestions of greater or lesser plausibility: to satisfy his hunger by turning stones into bread, to throw himself down from the pinnacle of the temple secure in the promise from Psalm 91 that God would keep him safe, and to secure the kingdoms of the world and their glory by submitting to the devil. Jesus refuses each of these suggestions; what is relevant to our present concern is his basis for doing so. Each time he responds, "It is written . . . ," and quotes from Deuteronomy. A person is not dependent merely on bread for life but on God's word, and Jesus must rely on that rather than unilaterally use the powers available to him as Son of God for his own benefit. He is not to put the Lord his God to the test to see whether God will keep promises of protection but rather to trust God to do so when the moment requires it. He is to worship and serve the Lord alone; it cannot be right to ignore this fundamental principle even to gain the worldwide authority and glory that do ultimately belong to him.

The quotations come from Deuteronomy 5–11 (8:3; 6:16; 6:13), the section of Deuteronomy that describes basic attitudes God expects of people as they keep their side of the covenant relationship. Jesus presupposes that his life should be shaped by these imperatives expressed in the Torah God gave Israel. Perhaps there is an implication that here in the wilderness the "one true Israelite" takes seriously that set of principles given in the wilderness to Israel as a whole but never properly observed by it.

At each point Jesus is able to draw from the stock of knowledge of the Torah that he had acquired as a Jew a passage that goes to the root of the wrong attitude to God that the devil's suggestions involve. Part of the story's challenge is our need for knowledge of the Scriptures (including the First Testament) good enough to enable us to evaluate suggestions from demonic agencies, whether or not well disguised. Often such advice may have plausibility on its side. Is it not natural, for instance, to utilize your gifts to meet your personal needs? No compromise need be involved; one has to look after one's own needs if one is to be able then to minister to others. Perceiving that plausible advice is misguided requires a profound and wide grasp of Scripture and the insight to perceive its application to us.

In connection with Scripture's application to behavior, the areas of the First Testament that will be especially significant are books in the Torah such as Deuteronomy, stories written to offer examples of how Israel should or should not behave (e.g., in Numbers), the exhortations of the prophets that often crystallize the moral attitudes to be embodied in lifestyle, and the wisdom books (especially Proverbs) that establish the links between areas often kept separate such as religion and ethics on one side, shrewdness and success on the other.

A knowledge of this material as a whole is needed in order to set in the context of the rest of Scripture's teaching on a topic an insight that taken out of that context will be misleading. Proverbs, for instance, collects a range of material on areas of life such as money or sex, and many an individual proverb (commending or downgrading riches, reminding men of their weaknesses or women of theirs) looks odd out of the context of this range of materials that as a whole recognizes the complexity of factors that need to be taken into account in coming to decisions about attitudes and behavior.

The middle of Jesus' three temptations in Matthew illustrates this point. It involves an appeal to the First Testament on the part of the devil as well as on the part of Jesus. The devil can quote Scripture, too. What is the difference between the use and abuse of Scripture?

The devil's application of Psalm 91 was entirely Christ-centered. That principle did not prevent his abusing Scripture. Perhaps he needed to be more God-centered, for Jesus responds to the devil by quoting a fundamental principle of our relationship with God: we are not to put God to the test. (It is, indeed, attitudes to God that are the concern of each of the passages he quotes: submission to God's Word, trust in God's promise, and worship of God's name.) Jesus thus sets the clear, direct demand of a fundamental passage in Deuteronomy against the devil's application of another passage to a particular set of circumstances. Personal application of Scripture is tested by being set in the context of the direct teaching of Scripture elsewhere. The need for a wide knowledge of Scripture is underlined by the nature of the devil's misuse of it.

In this particular case, further, misuse of Scripture involved taking verses out of their original context. Psalm 91 promises God's protection to "the one who dwells in the shelter of the Most High, who abides in the shadow of the Almighty." In origin it may have been a psalm of assurance for any believer, though perhaps more likely it promises God's protection to the king. If it was a royal psalm and was as such understood messianically by Jesus' time, this would give special point to the devil's quoting it. He is inviting Jesus to prove that the psalm's promise about the (coming) king is true about him. It is here that the devil's hermeneutic goes wrong. The psalm speaks of God protecting someone in whatever danger or attack comes to him. It says nothing about his courting danger or taking risks he could avoid. The devil is able to abuse the text in applying it because he has abused it in the course of his exegesis, taking particular phrases and promises out of context.

Another priority for the study of Scripture is a skill in exegesis that is able to handle particular sections of Scripture in a way faithful to their particular witness. Collections of texts in devotional books that work by drawing our attention to verses isolated from their context can express helpful devotional truths, but they risk imitating the devil's hermeneutic. The story of the man seeking God's guidance by opening Scripture at random, who found first Matthew 27:5 ("Judas went and hanged himself"), then—seeking something more congenial—Luke 10:37 ("Go and do likewise"), then John 13:27 ("Do quickly what you are going to do") contains a warning about a devotional use of Scripture that risks paralleling the devil's.

5. The First Testament Describes the Kind of Life with God That a Disciple Can Live (Matthew 5:1–12)

"Seeing the crowds, he went up on the mountain, and when he sat down his disciples came to him. He opened his mouth and taught them saying: Blessed are the poor in spirit. . ." For many readers the "Beatitudes" or blessings with which the Sermon on the Mount opens constitute a high point in the New Testament Scriptures. Here is a deep and moving account of what it means to live with God. The form and content of these blessings derive substantially from the First Testament. The declaration of blessing on people of a certain style of attitude and life recalls especially the opening psalm in the Psalter (also Ps 128). The Sermon on the Mount follows the Psalter in beginning with a blessing on those who are open to walking in God's way. The poor in spirit to whom the kingdom belongs are those to whom Isaiah 61 long ago declared good news of freedom, vindication, and restoration. Isaiah 61 was an important passage for Jesus. He quotes it in his sermon at Nazareth in a passage Luke includes at an equivalent place in his Gospel to the Sermon on the Mount in Matthew (Luke 4:16–21), and he echoes it in describing his ministry to John the Baptist (Matt 11:2–6).

Succeeding verses in Matthew 5:1–12 recall the First Testament more directly. "Blessed are those who mourn, for they will be comforted"? "Yahweh has anointed me . . . to comfort all who mourn" (Isa 61:1–2). "Blessed are the meek, for they will inherit the earth"? "The meek shall possess the land" (Ps 37:11; earth or land is the same word in Hebrew and in Greek). "Blessed are those who hunger and thirst for righteousness, for they will be satisfied"? "Everyone who thirsts, come to the waters. . . . Why do you spend . . . your labor for that that does not satisfy" (Isa 55:1–2; the gift Yahweh is offering here is righteousness in the sense of doing right by the people by delivering them from Babylon). "Blessed are the merciful, for they will receive mercy"? "With the merciful you will show yourself merciful" (Ps 18:25, following the Revised/American Standard Version translation). "Blessed are the pure in heart, for they will see God"? "Who shall ascend the hill of Yahweh? . . . The person who has clean hands and a pure heart" (Ps 24:3–4).

The depth of Jesus' insights on what it means to live with God is in large part due to the extent of his soaking in the First Testament. Psalms and Isaiah, the books most clearly reflected in these blessings, are the books most often and most widely quoted in the New Testament. Psalms is, of course, the First Testament book that most directly concerns itself with our life with God, our spirituality, our life of praise, prayer, and personal commitment, and Jesus' own example elsewhere in the Gospels directs us to Psalms as our resource for our praise and prayer. It was the interweaving of petition and praise in a lament such as Psalm 22 that provided Jesus with the means of expression for his anguish at the prospect of betrayal and abandonment (see especially Matt 27:46). In this same psalm Jesus found the psalmist's characteristic insistence on looking beyond his anguish, as well as on looking that anguish in the face. Claus Westermann exaggerated only slightly (Ps 88 seems to be an exception) when he declared that in the Psalms "there is no petition . . . that did not move at least one step . . . on the road to praise," as "there is also no praise that was fully separated from the experience of God's wonderful intervention in time of need."[6] Certainly Psalm 22 holds together an openness to God over one's feelings

---

6. *The Praise of God in the Psalms* (Richmond: John Knox, 1965; London: Epworth, 1966), 154.

and needs with a striving nevertheless to maintain faith and praise toward the God who has cared for me in the past and is still "my God" even though seeming to have abandoned me, and with an anticipation of renewed praise for God's turning to me at my moment of urgent need. The psalm's successful battle to look beyond affliction as well as looking it in the face is reflected in the reference to it in Hebrews 2:12. The anticipatory praise of Psalm 22:22–31 was found on the lips of Jesus, as well as the present lament of the opening part of the psalm.

The resources of the Psalms for our life with God are easily ignored by believers who find it difficult to get beyond the Psalms' culture-related talk of bulls of Bashan and Moabite washpots, but the effort to do so is worthwhile, for in the Psalms we are given Scripture's own collection of things that it is okay to say to God. To summarize Athanasius's exposition of this point in his *Letter to Marcellinus*, "Most of Scripture speaks *to* us while the Psalms speak *for* us."[7] Once again, however, it is a half-truth to describe the Sermon on the Mount as implying that the First Testament tells you the kind of life with God that a believer can live. While most of the raw material for the blessings comes from the First Testament Scriptures, out of this raw material Jesus creates something fresh and new and greater than the parts it incorporates. What he does theologically (or what he hears theologically) in bringing together the figures of the anointed king, the beloved son, and the suffering servant, he does devotionally in creating a new and profound whole from elements of largely First Testament origin. The blessings are not merely an anthology of half-familiar aphorisms but a profoundly ordered totality, a rounded whole that offers the listener a new total portrait of that life with God that was already the First Testament's concern.

Yet Jesus' crucial contribution to the shaping of our life with God is not his teaching but his life, and especially his death, resurrection, and giving of the Holy Spirit to his people. Insofar as the New Testament brings insight going beyond that of the First Testament, it is insight that can emerge only now on the basis of these events. The reason why new things can be said is not that the evolution of human thinking or the progress of divine revelation has developed to such a point that new statements can now be added to old less complete truths, but that new events make new statements possible and necessary. Jesus could not speak of the Spirit before the pouring out of the Spirit (John 7:39); nor could he speak of taking up the cross or enjoying resurrection life until crucifixion and resurrection were taking place. When those events have happened, the dynamics of life with God can be thought through with new depth in light of them (as happens, for instance, in Rom 3–8). It is not that life with God is different at every point (people were put right with God by grace through faith under the old covenant); rather, it is that the way in which life with God works can now be freshly conceptualized in light of realities (cross, empty tomb, giving of the Spirit) that can now be pointed to and explicated.

7. See, e.g., B. W. Anderson, *Out of the Depths* (3rd ed.; Louisville: Westminster John Knox, 2000), ix; this actual summary is not from Athanasius.

It is particularly instructive to set the "vindicatory" psalms and the Christ event alongside each other. There is a big difference between these prayers for redress for people who have wronged us (e.g., Ps 137:7–9) or who are opposed to God (e.g., Ps 139:19–24) and any prayers we are told Jesus ever prayed for such people. The psalmists were not insensitive, unspiritual, or immoral people (the rest of Pss 137 and 139 show that), nor was God's love for nations other than Israel unknown in their day (various passages at least as old as these psalms indicate that it was well known), nor did First Testament ethics allow people to do what they liked to their enemies (the context of the exhortation to love your neighbor indicates that the neighbor in question is your enemy). Theologically, perhaps prayer for one's enemies like that of Jesus on the cross is strictly possible only now, because it is the cross that makes forgiveness available to people; the Psalms' prayers for judgment on the wicked are prayers for God's justice to be at work in this world, and it is the cross that is God's yes to their prayer for wickedness to be punished.[8]

So were the Psalms' prayers for God's judgment valid before Christ but inappropriate after Christ? One should be wary of drawing too sharply the contrast between the attitude of these psalms and that of the New Testament. John the Baptist did address people as a viper's brood about to be overtaken by God's wrath, trees that have failed to fruit and will be felled and burned (Matt 3:7–10), and the Sermon on the Mount makes clear that Jesus accepts John's understanding of what Jesus' coming will bring for the impenitent (Matt 7:19). Those whose righteousness is only up to that of the scribes and Pharisees (!) will be excluded from the kingdom; anger, insults, and contempt will mean fiery judgment; adultery, lust, and divorce will mean going to hell (Matt 5:20–32). The Day of Yahweh will be the occasion of Jesus' repudiation of many who thought they belonged to him (Matt 7:21–23). Indeed (a saying from beyond the Sermon adds), it will see the sons of the kingdom cast into outer darkness where people will cry and groan in anguish (Matt 8:12). Nor is prayer for judgment like that of the Psalms absent from the New Testament: the Lord promises that such prayer for vindication will be heard (Luke 18:1–8) and reassures the martyrs that the moment of vengeance will come (Rev 6:9–11). The two Testaments dovetail and complement each other.

6. The First Testament Provides the Foundation for Christ's Moral Teaching (Matthew 5:17–48)

Christ comes not to annul the Torah and the Prophets but to fulfill them (Matt 5:17). What is this "fulfilling"? We would expect the word to have the same meaning with regard to both the Torah and the Prophets, and one suggested understanding of this kind assumes that the reference to the Torah is to passages that could be interpreted messianically (e.g., Gen 3:15; 49:9–10; Num 24:17; Deut 18:15–19). Yet

8. Cf. Dietrich Bonhoeffer, *Psalms* (Minneapolis: Augsburg, 1974), 56–60.

Matthew refers to none of these passages, though Numbers 24:17 presumably lies behind Matthew 2:2. Neither does the rest of the New Testament see Jesus as the fulfillment of these passages except for Deuteronomy 18:15–19; it refers most often to Jesus as fulfilling the promise to Abraham (e.g., Gen 12:1–3). Matthew's many quotations from the Torah, including the ones that dominate this chapter, relate to its teaching on behavior. The fulfilling of Torah and Prophets might then involve confirming them (God really made these promises and warnings, God really gave these commands), embodying them (Jesus' life puts into practice what the Torah demands and makes actual what the prophecies picture), and filling them out (Jesus will work out the deeper implications of the Torah and the Prophets). At least, this is what Jesus actually does with both Torah and prophecy.

Subsequent events and teaching will show that "not an iota" (equivalent to the smallest letter in the Hebrew alphabet), "not a dot" (the smallest part of a letter; cf. our "dotting the i's and crossing the t's") (Matt 5:18) does not mean being committed to the Torah standing forever at every point. Admittedly, most of the acts whereby Jesus offends some other Jews such as his "breaches" of the Sabbath can be reckoned to constitute a different way of understanding the Torah rather than a breaking of it. The same is true when Jesus declares that it is what comes out of our mouths not what goes into them that makes us impure, though Mark can reckon that he has hereby declared all foods pure (Mark 7:19), which points to an abrogation of the Torah itself (cf. Acts 10). In line with these characteristics of Gospel material elsewhere, Matthew 5:21–48 approaches the Torah with a "yes, but." He affirms and extends its ban on murder and adultery but undermines its acceptance of divorce and makes the same penalty apply to attitudes and apparently lesser deeds as applies to the act itself. He takes further its insistence on only true oaths and only equivalent redress: now there are to be no oaths and no redress. He implicitly thus abrogates the rule about oaths and redress. He makes explicit that its exhortation to love one's neighbor applies to one's enemy; neither the First Testament nor Jewish sources contains an exhortation to hate one's enemy, but "love your enemy" is not said in so many words in the Torah. So Jesus affirms and develops strands of First Testament attitudes as he puts a question mark by them.

What, then, is the relationship between Jesus' challenges and those that appear in the First Testament? Jesus is not merely working out the implications of the Torah but affirming some more far-reaching demands, but he is not doing so merely because the Torah was inevitably primitive in its expectations, whereas the fully mature form of Jesus' ethics could emerge only when humanity had passed through more primitive stages of thinking. The model of evolutionary development (which appears in a baptized form as the theory of progressive revelation) is misleading when applied to the Bible (and most other areas of the humanities, as far as I can tell).

Three alternative models are more helpful. One is that of foundation and superstructure. The external commands of the Decalogue provide the necessary basis for more demanding requirements that can be built on them. A second model is that of boundaries and what fills them. The negative commands of the Decalogue mark the limits of acceptable behavior beyond which one is in unequivocally foreign territory, but they are only boundary markers. When they are established, one can begin to "possess the land" by filling in the positive content of behavioral style and attitude appropriate to this country.

Given such models, it is easier to see the complementary nature of the Decalogue's negative and external commands and the demands of the Sermon on the Mount, and the continuing significance of the former in relation to the latter. The building always needs the lower courses of bricks as well as the superstructure; the land needs frontiers as well as policies for internal development. Jesus is not interested in internal attitudes rather than external actions (it is he who tells an adulteress not to sin again: see John 8:11) but in both. The New Testament writers are not interested in the law of Christ rather than the Decalogue (Ephesians supports its teaching by quoting from the latter in Eph 6:1–3, and repeats one of its prohibitions in Eph 4:28) but in both.

Jesus' own teaching suggests the third model for understanding differences in level among scriptural commands. His comments concerning divorce in the Sermon on the Mount are expanded elsewhere (Matt 19:2–9), and this further treatment of the topic offers us a clue to perceiving the significance of much of the Torah. The Pharisees ask his opinion on divorce, and he refers them to Genesis 1–2, whose account of the origin of marriage (he infers) indicates that divorce cannot really be recognized. What then of the Deuteronomic permission of divorce (Deut 24:1–4)? That was given "for your hardness of heart"; divorce and remarriage are really only a form of legalized adultery (except in the case of *porneia*, he adds: the word often means "fornication," but its precise significance here is the subject of debate). But because of human sin marriages will break down, so the Torah contains a regulation that applies to this circumstance.

Within the Torah, then, one can find both material that expresses the ultimate will of God and material that takes a realistic approach to the fact of human sin and contents itself with the attempt to control the extent to which God's ultimate will is bound to be ignored and to minimize the ill effects that issue from this. Marriage breakdown is hardly reconcilable with Genesis 1–2, but it is better to acknowledge the fact of marriage breakdown and seek to lessen the further ills to which it can lead (especially for a woman) than to refuse to recognize such realities. The "low standard" of some of the Torah issues from the fact that it comprises rules designed for sinners. Such rules contrast not only with the exalted standard of the Sermon on the Mount but also with the exalted standard of the creation story and of the challenges of the prophets. Indeed, Jesus' appeal to Genesis 1–2 reminds us that the First Testament's significance for our ethical questions emerges not exclusively (perhaps not even primarily) from the explicit commands that appear in the Torah (and in the Prophets and wisdom books), but also from the perspective on human life that appears both in the story of creation (humanity as made in God's image) and in the story of redemption (humanity as freed from bondage), from the values that are asserted especially in the Prophets and the wisdom books (values such as justice, faithfulness, and compassion), and from the concerns regarding human life that run through the whole First Testament, concern with areas such as marriage and sex, politics and land, work and pleasure, family and community.

This element of condescension in the Torah, and the background of First Testament ethics in creation as well as in redemption, point to the possibility of applying God's standards to our world. They show how in Israel God "compromised" in relating to humanity in its stubbornness rather than either insisting on a standard it would never reach or abandoning it because it would not reach this standard. It thus offers us a paradigm for our application of God's ultimate standards to the situations of humanity that we encounter. Indeed, the way the Torah applies God's standards to humanity suggests one aspect of the answer to the question whether the expectations attached to Yahweh's covenant with Israel can apply outside the covenant people. One reason they can be generally applicable is that they were given to an ordinary human people, even though they were a people invited into a special relationship with God. They can also be generally applicable because they are fundamentally teaching based on creation as well as on redemption; their background lies in the nature of humanity as humanity and in humanity's relationship with its creator. Similar considerations also suggest that it is appropriate to apply the prophets' attitudes to fairness in society to the ordinary nation today, and appropriate to apply to it promises about the blessing that can come when a people returns to the ways of God (2 Chr 7:14); indeed, the book of Jonah pictures a prophet doing this.

The element of condescension in the Torah is also present in New Testament teaching. Paul, after all, makes observations about slaves and free people that reassert their oneness before God at creation, but he nevertheless accepts that institution (in its Roman form, a much more vicious one than the debt servitude of which the Torah speaks) and bids slaves obey their masters. Indeed, perhaps compromise is present even in Matthew 19, when Jesus' ban on divorce is qualified by his making an exception in the case of *porneia*. No such qualification appears in Mark's account. Does Matthew merely make explicit what the Markan version took for granted? Or is Jesus, in Matthew's account, also condescending to the realities of human sin, failure, and suffering in the lives of his followers?

The principle of condescension may also explain the First Testament's enthusiasm over ritual regulations that Jesus turns away from in a chapter such as Matthew 15. Both the rites of sacrifice and the place of sacrifice (the temple) first appear in Scripture as human ideas that are accepted by God (with overt misgivings, in the latter case), rather than as originally divine intentions (Gen 4:3–4; 2 Sam 7). Perhaps regulations concerning cleanness and taboo have a similar status: not *ultimately* good ideas, but helpful to people in certain cultures and capable of being harnessed so as to embody real truth.

In the Bible's teaching on moral questions, then, the Scriptures written before Christ and the new insights of the Christ event complement each other. The Christian church's calling is to let its understanding of history, prophecy, theology, spirituality, and ethics be shaped by the joint witness of the two Testaments. By interpreting Christ in light of the First Testament, the New Testament invites us to take up the First Testament's own concerns in all their width of interest. By interpreting the First Testament in light of Christ, the New Testament invites us to look at all those concerns in light of his coming.

15

In What Sense Is It Appropriate to Read the First Testament Christologically?

The question is one about hermeneutics. What I mean is that we come to gain insight into things (texts or people or events) in light of the convictions, questions, and experiences that we bring to them. This need not mean we impose these convictions, questions, or experiences on them; they are our ways into gaining insight on the inherent significance of the texts or people or events. Indeed, by a feedback process such eventual insight into their inherent significance may be expected to broaden or correct our convictions and questions and our understanding of our experience.[1]

Convictions about Jesus are one set of convictions in light of which we may read the First Testament. There are then two broad aspects to relating Jesus and the First Testament. One involves using the First Testament to illumine Jesus. The hermeneutical process involved in doing so initially means letting Jesus set the agenda. Matthew 1:18–2:23 provides an example. A series of incidents associated with Jesus' birth and childhood raise questions that the First Testament helps Matthew answer. Jesus sets the agenda.[2] But if all First Testament Scripture is inspired by God and is thus useful for teaching, for reproof, for correction, and for training in righteousness (2 Tim 3:16), then this hermeneutical process also has to involve letting the First

---

1. First published in the *Journal of Theological Interpretation* 2 (2008): 7–11.
2. See further chapter 14 (section 2) above.

Testament broaden the agenda. To find out who Jesus is and what is his significance for us, we read the whole First Testament.

The other aspect to relating Jesus and the First Testament involves using Jesus to illumine the First Testament. The phrase "reading the First Testament christologically" suggests a focus lying here.

The New Testament might suggest a number of starting points for a christological reading of the First Testament. The most familiar one involves seeing Jesus as the Messiah promised there. Others involve seeing him as a priest or prophet or servant or human-like figure ("Son of Man"). There are various problems in starting with the idea of the Messiah. Within the First Testament, the person of the anointed Israelite king is of rather ambiguous theological significance. Having kings was not God's idea, and it was something God felt ambivalent about. A related problem is that the hope of a new anointed king is rather marginal to the First Testament. It is sometimes argued that it is a theme of increasing significance in the First Testament and more prominent in the First Testament's final canonical form, but this is mostly wishful thinking by Christians. In particular, there is no evidence that the Psalter was designed to be read messianically—that is, that by the time the Psalter reached its final form, people who used the psalms about the king would naturally apply them to the Messiah. While there is a strand of promise in books such as Jeremiah that thinks in these terms, Isaiah 40–55 in contrast democratizes Yahweh's commitment to David as expressed in a passage such as Psalm 89; this would mean the whole people could "claim" the psalms about the king. Again, Chronicles (written in the Second Temple period) shows how it is quite possible to remember and rejoice in the way Yahweh related to the kings without implying that one need be looking for a Messiah. Its readers might even be remembering with sadness the way Yahweh related to the kings, so that the kingship psalms become implicit laments. There are a number of attitudes to kingship in the Second Temple period, and there is no inherent reason to link the Psalter with any one of them.

From a New Testament perspective, Jesus is much too hesitant about being called Messiah for this to be a useful starting point for understanding him in relation to the First Testament. And he was not actually the anointed Israelite king. The New Testament does take up kingship and priesthood and turn them into metaphors that contribute to an understanding of Jesus, but they are of limited significance in this connection. There is only a partial overlap between the position and vocation of the Israelite king and the position and vocation of Jesus, and to say he is king and priest is not the most illuminating thing that can be said about him. To judge from his own attitude, seeing him as the servant in Isaiah or the human-like figure in Daniel (or as a prophet) is more illuminating. Because there is only a limited overlap between the application to Jesus of the metaphor of king or priest, reading First Testament references to kingship or priesthood in light of Jesus obscures them as much as it illumines them.

Jesus' hesitation about being called the Messiah links with the fact that there is insufficient basis for arguing from the First Testament that Jesus is the Messiah.

Jesus does not do the kind of things that the First Testament says the future David will do. This reflects how the logic of linking Jesus to the First Testament moves backwards not forwards. Christological reading of the First Testament issues from faith in Jesus. After the resurrection, his followers, now convinced that he was Savior and Lord, looked back to the First Testament to discover what that meant, as he himself encouraged them to do. The First Testament became a christological resource for them. But First Testament references to a future David do not point forward to Jesus. They are not like the words in 1 Kings 13 that point forward to Josiah. Neither do other First Testament motifs such as the servant or the human-like figure, even though they are illuminating with hindsight. They do not in themselves point forward to Jesus.

Thus a christological reading of the texts about the king or the human-like figure skews an understanding of their inherent meaning as much as it illumines them. It hinders our seeing what the Holy Spirit was saying in these texts when inspiring them and hinders our seeing much of what the Holy Spirit would want us to see on the basis of these texts.

A better starting point for approaching the question of a christological reading of the First Testament is the person of God.

I begin with the fact that Yahweh is God. That First Testament statement is one that the church and the Jewish community need to make if they are to be faithful to their Scriptures. Conversely, God is Yahweh. That First Testament statement is also one that the church and the Jewish community need to make if they are to be faithful to their Scriptures. If God is Yahweh and Yahweh is God, it follows that the words "God" and "Yahweh" have different meanings but the same reference, or different connotations but the same denotation. (The sense-reference distinction and the connotation-denotation distinction are matters of controversy in philosophy of language, but I assume that they can be defended.) They are like the terms "John Goldingay" and "David Allan Hubbard Professor of First Testament." In each case, both expressions refer to the same person, but they have different connotations. There is only one God, and this God's name is Yahweh. Yahweh is the only God.

Further, God is Father, Son, and Holy Spirit. That is not a statement that the Scriptures quite make, but it is a legitimate inference from the New Testament and thus a statement that the church needs to make if it is to be faithful to its Scriptures. Conversely, the Father, Son, and Holy Spirit are God. That, too, is not a statement that the Scriptures quite make, but it is a legitimate inference from the New Testament and thus another statement that the church needs to make if it is to be faithful to its Scriptures. It follows from those two statements that in Christian conviction the word "God" and the phrase "Father, Son, and Holy Spirit" have different meanings but the same reference, different connotations but the same denotation.

Yet further, since Yahweh is God, and Father, Son, and Holy Spirit are God, it follows that in Christian conviction Yahweh is the God who is Father, Son, and Holy Spirit. It then follows that whenever you read about Yahweh in the First Testament, you are reading about God the Father, the Son, and the Holy Spirit.

That is an interpretive theological observation, not an exegetical one. Many exegetical statements are theological statements in the sense that they themselves make statements about God, such as "Yahweh is a great King above all gods." These are the text's own theological statements. To say "Yahweh is God the Father, the Son, and the Holy Spirit" is an interpretive theological statement in the sense that it draws from the Scriptures as a whole an inference about objective truth, but it is not a statement that anyone reading the First Testament by itself would make.

If Yahweh is God the Father, the Son, and the Holy Spirit, it follows that Christians can read the First Testament christologically in the sense that every time it says something about Yahweh, they know it is talking about Jesus. So (for instance) Jesus is one of the persons of the Godhead who is "a great Kings above all gods."

This is again an interpretive theological statement, not an exegetical one. It is appropriate and important as a theological statement, and it signals the inappropriateness of setting up a disjunction between who Jesus is and who Yahweh is (for instance, as if Jesus were someone who forgives and Yahweh were someone who does not). Yahweh and Jesus have the same personality profile.

In light of the fact that Yahweh is God the Father, the Son, and the Holy Spirit, it is not surprising that John says that "grace and truth came through Jesus Christ," as the one who "is close to the Father's heart" and "has made him known" in the sense of making him visible (John 1:17–18). Jesus shares in the personhood of Yahweh, who is self-defined as grace and truth (Exod 34:6) and who thus naturally embodies who Yahweh has always been for Israel. Likewise it is not surprising that Hebrews begins from the assumption that God spoke identically through the prophets and by his Son (Heb 1:1–3); the former was scattergun, but the content of the two revelations was the same.

Reading the First Testament christologically then can mean letting who Jesus is give us clues to a right reading of the way the First Testament talks about God. This is not a reading that adds new meanings to the First Testament, nor is it one that approves some things the First Testament says about God and rejects others, but one that enables us to see aspects of what is present in the way the First Testament talks about God that we might otherwise miss.

The fundamental example is this. Christians commonly see the First Testament story as the story of a wrathful God at work, whereas they do not see Jesus in these terms. Jesus could not then be the embodiment of this God. Rather, Jesus is indeed the embodiment of the First Testament God of grace and truth, in being the one who sacrifices himself for the world and the one who pays the price for the world's sin. Knowing this makes one reread the First Testament story and see that this is indeed the nature of God's relationship with the world and with Israel as the First Testament portrays it. Through the First Testament story God was paying the price for sin, bearing its consequences, refusing to let it break the relationship. Through the First Testament story God was making the sacrifices that enabled a relationship to continue. Only because God continually took up the cross in an act of self-denial did God's relationship with the world and with Israel continue. The cross on Golgotha was then the logical end term of the way God had been through the First Testament story. It would be possible to see this implication of the First Testament story without knowing about the cross on Golgotha, because the point is there in the story, but that cross makes it easier to see.

The basis for such a christological reading of the First Testament thus lies in what Christians know about Jesus. Its vindication lies in its capacity actually to illumine the First Testament—not to impose a meaning on the First Testament but to draw attention to a meaning that anyone can then see.

16

What Defines Evangelical Study of the First Testament?

What are the characteristics of evangelical study of the First Testament? What follows is, of course, a statement of my personal convictions. In form it is descriptive, but its deeper structure is prescriptive. These are some of the premises that I realize are implicit in the way I approach the First Testament in living and writing, in teaching and preaching, and which I think other people should also affirm.[1]

1. It Works within the Framework of the Gospel

Evangelical study of the First Testament works within the framework of the evangel, the gospel. So what is the gospel? The gospel is the fact that God had such love for the world as to give up the only son God had, and that God did this so that people could live real life. The gospel is the fact that God has thus set about turning the world into what it was always meant to be, a world that reflects who God is. The gospel is the fact that God wanted to be in relationship with us and took the action that was needed so that nothing would stand in the way of this relationship. We study the First Testament in the light of that.

One of my delights as a teacher is getting students to read the Bible. Many come to seminary knowing that it is the inspired and infallible Word of God, yet (on their

---

1. First published in *EvQ* 73 (2001): 99–117.

own account) having a strange impression of its contents. For instance, they thought that the God of the First Testament was harsh and punitive. I send them off to read Genesis or the Psalms, and they come back wide-eyed. One student hesitatingly and tentatively commented in a class that it seemed to her that the God of Genesis was more hurt and saddened by human sin than angry about it: "Was that right?" she asked, afraid to believe what she had perceived in the text because it did not correspond to what she had been told about this God.

She had been taught to read the First Testament in the light of the gospel in a perverted sense, as if God's nature is to be angry with us, so that it was just as well that we had Jesus to placate this angry God. Reading the First Testament in the light of the gospel in the truer sense means something different.[2] It means recognizing that the God of love whom we encounter in Jesus is the God who created the world out of love and commissioned Abraham out of love and related to Israel out of love and in love. The structure of First Testament faith is itself the structure of the gospel; or rather, the structure of the gospel is the structure of First Testament faith. Like the New Testament, the First Testament is about a God of love who relates to people in grace, the grace that receives supreme concrete form in Christ's cross. Yahweh is not a God of wrath, and First Testament religion is not one dominated by legalism. Yahweh is prepared to be tough when situations require it, as Jesus is, though Yahweh does not find it first nature to be like that. As Isaiah almost puts it (Isa 28:21), it requires the expression of God's shadow side.

When I send students off to read the First Testament, as well as discovering that Yahweh is a much more interesting person than they thought, they also sometimes realize something else. They discover that the human beings in the First Testament, especially the men (people like Abraham and Jacob and Joseph), are much shadier characters than they had been told. These human characters are also more interesting, too, partly because of that. To judge from the First Testament story, David, for instance, whose name appears at the top of all those Psalms, was not a First Testament Eugene Peterson. He was more a First Testament JFK: great leader, no clue about women.

The nature of the gospel alerts us to the fact that all sinned and came short of God's glory. We can thus see the theme of the First Testament story as resembling that of a film noir, a story in which there are finally no heroes, no role models, a story in which even the goodies are flawed, often deeply flawed. It is a story that can work this way and not make you leave the cinema feeling somber as you do after *LA Confidential* or *A Simple Plan*, because you know that God is also at work in this story. God is not dependent on having flawless heroes to work with but is committed to achieving a purpose all the same. That is the gospel, and that is the nature of the First Testament. My colleague Michael Moore tells of an occasion when he was teaching an adult Bible class and inviting them to see the struggles and failures in the lives of people such as Esther, Abraham, and Joseph. Eventually a veteran Sunday

2. See further chapter 15 above.

school teacher protested. "You've got it all wrong because you fail to understand that these people aren't really like us. They have a special measure of the Holy Spirit. . . . These people are our heroes, our role models. That's why they are in the Bible." The talk had been subverting this person's deepest convictions about what the Bible is.[3] Evangelical study of the First Testament does not have to rewrite it in order to turn its heroes into saints; we can let them be the sinners we also are. We read the First Testament as the story of God's grace, not of human achievement.

Studying the First Testament in the light of the gospel means studying it in the light of the conviction that here, too, God has been especially concerned to develop personal relationships with people and that the encouragement of these relationships is one purpose of Scripture.

That was a dangerous statement. Evangelicalism has close links with pietism, and it can easily assume that developing personal relationships with us is the only thing God is really interested in. This is not so. Developing personal relationships with us may not even be the main thing God is interested in. If it were, the Bible would be a different kind of book. God has a much more varied range of concerns than that. That is why we should watch the world news.

But in reaction to a pietistic overstress on our personal relationships with God, scholarship has tended to ignore the First Testament's concern with these relationships. It has thereby missed an aspect of the First Testament itself, and failed to do its own job. It has narrowed down its interest in the First Testament to one that is a mirror image of pietism's interest.

We are fortunate to live in an age when this is no longer so, and when notable First Testament scholars write books on First Testament spirituality. Paradoxically, of course, what then happens is that we discover that the way Christians generally go about prayer and praise bears little relationship to the prayer and praise that appear in Scripture. Reading the First Testament in the light of the gospel then turns out to be a dangerous exercise. It may suggest we need to change—for instance, to change the way we pray.

Reading the First Testament in the light of the gospel means taking account of the fact that the gospel story is a continuation of the First Testament story. This does not affect the way we read individual episodes in the First Testament; it affects the way we see it as a larger whole, and as part of an even larger whole. We read it as open to closure, though recognizing that in itself it does not prescribe what this closure will look like.

The First Testament story is not one that leads inevitably to Jesus, as if it constituted Acts I to III of a drama from which you could extrapolate this Act IV. Yet it is a drama that does not reach neat closure, and it is a drama of which the Gospels are a plausible continuation. The great story from Genesis to Kings leads round in circles, taking Abraham and Sarah and their descendants from Babylon to Jerusalem

---

3. See *Reconciliation: A Study of Biblical Families in Conflict* (Joplin, Mo.: College Press, 1994; 2nd ed., 1998), 13–14.

but then taking them back again so that the story as a whole goes nowhere. It is the story of how God created the world and tried to restore it, but failed. And the slightly less great story in Chronicles, Ezra, and Nehemiah also ends with something more like a whimper than a bang. "Is that all?" one might ask as one comes to the end. Then the New Testament says, "We have good news. That is not all." Of course, as one looks at the church's story and at the church's state, one again says, "Is that all?" It seems that God has succeeded little better with the church than God did with Israel. The church's relationship with God and with life, with itself and with its future, is not as different from Israel's as has often been implied by Christian polemic against Judaism.

So reading the First Testament in the light of the gospel does not mean that we read Jesus into the First Testament. It does not mean (for instance) using artificial techniques in order to make the sacrifices of the First Testament pointers to Christ (whatever that means) that had little meaning in their own right. It does not mean finding spurious predictions of Jesus in the First Testament, as if the First Testament were a Hercule Poirot mystery in which the expert (Christian) detective can spot the clue that people such as unbelieving Jews or liberal scholars miss.

In the second Christian century, theologians such as Justin Martyr started encouraging Christians to prove the truth of the gospel by appealing to fulfilled predictions, but he thereby set the church on a false track. The New Testament does not attempt to persuade people that Jesus is the Christ on the basis of his having fulfilled predictions. There are hardly any points at which it describes First Testament passages as "predictions" of Jesus. This is good, because there are no First Testament passages that are predictions of Jesus. God does not seem to have given prophets visions of events at the manger in Bethlehem or at the cross in Jerusalem. Jewish and Christian faith does not go in for prediction much, at least not for predicting events long before they take place. If you want that, you go to the clairvoyants on Colorado Boulevard or Walnut Street in Pasadena or on equivalent streets in other cities. There was much similar predicting in the ancient world. Second Isaiah refers to it with disdain (e.g., Isa 47:13).

The nearest to an example of the First Testament going in for talk of fulfillment of predictions comes in 2 Kings 23:16. Even there the Hebrew word means "proclaim," not specifically "foretell," and the context indicates that the point being made is that a threat is being fulfilled, not merely that a prediction is coming true. Similarly, when the New Testament talks of "prediction," it usually employs the word to mean "warning." Even Acts 1:16 is an example, as the content of the "prediction" in verse 20 shows. In the New Testament as in the First Testament, when God speaks about the future, the words indicate a personal commitment to take action, which may be good news or bad news. Whether they are promises or warnings, they are designed to provoke a response from their hearers, not just to provide the curious with prognostications. They are not predictions designed to provoke a response from unbelievers living hundreds of years later, though in God's providence they may incidentally help later believers to gain an understanding of what God is doing with them.

2. It Assumes That the Whole First Testament
Issued from Acts of Communication between God and People

I hinted above that Christian prayer could be revolutionized and led into new free-dom if it read the First Testament. This leads into my second thesis. Evangelical study assumes that God gave us the Bible in its entirety and that we are supposed to take the whole of it with absolute seriousness. Every page is designed to shape our prayer, our life, our thinking.

So we read those stories about Abraham and Sarah, Moses and David, Naomi and Esther on the assumption that they are given to us to form our worldview, to form our understanding of how God relates to us and how God relates to the world, and thus to shape our lives. We read the rules in Exodus, Leviticus, Numbers, and Deuteronomy on the assumption that they are meant to influence social policy in any community that is to be shaped by God's Word. We read the reflections of intellectuals in Proverbs, Job, and Ecclesiastes and determine to think hard about life and suffering and death in the way that they do. We read the Psalms and start to pray and praise the way they do. We read the visions and the nightmares of the prophets and determine to look at the future their way.

This is not what the New Testament is doing when it refers to the First Testament, because its interest in the First Testament is focused on its need for resources to help it think through the answers to particular questions such as Who is Jesus? and What is the church? These are crucial questions, but they are not the only questions. The very fact that the first three-quarters of the Bible concerns questions other than "Who is Jesus? and What is the church? shows that God wants us to be interested in questions other than the ones that the New Testament handles.

A commitment to taking the whole Bible with absolute seriousness constitutes one link between evangelicalism and the work of Walter Brueggemann and Brevard Childs, the premier First Testament theologians in the English-speaking world. In Brueggemann's case, at least, there is admittedly a contrast (I will comment on some other contrasts later in this chapter). Brueggemann has no theory about this com-mitment to taking the whole First Testament with absolute seriousness, though he demonstrates it in practice. Evangelicalism has a theory about it but does not dem-onstrate it in practice. We know in theory that the First Testament is the authorita-tive Word of God, but having acknowledged that in theory, we ignore it. In general, if you are not an evangelical, you need have no problem when there are aspects of the Bible that you do not like, because you can simply disagree with them. If you are an evangelical, you cannot do that, so you have to find a way of reinterpreting it instead. One of the most important callings of an evangelical First Testament scholar is therefore to encourage Christians to read what the First Testament actually says, rather than reinterpreting it so that it means something that fits with what we al-ready believe. In other words, we read it also in the awareness that we ourselves are sinners and that our sin affects our interpretation. Our sin makes us avoid seeing things that we could not afford to see because we would have to change our lives if we acknowledged them. That is true of everyone who reads the Bible; it is therefore true of evangelical scholars.

One presupposition of that evangelical determination to pay attention to the whole First Testament is that we believe that the First Testament was an exercise in communication on God's part. There is a strand of current thinking about interpretation that emphasizes that it is readers who "make sense" of texts. Texts themselves do not have meaning. Originally they may have been exercises in communication between an author and an audience, but they are now independent of author and audience. When T. S. Eliot was once asked what one of his poems meant, he is said to have responded "I don't know; you tell me." How much more is it the case that we have to decide what the text means when we cannot consult the author.

One way of handling that difficulty would be to suggest that we can consult the author, because we can seek the Holy Spirit's help in interpreting Scripture. The Holy Spirit did not fall silent after inspiring Scripture. Numbers 27 tells a story about a man called Zelophehad, or rather about his five daughters. Zelophehad had had no sons, and these daughters challenged Moses to let them inherit his land rather than allow it to pass outside their nuclear family. To play for time, Moses consulted Yahweh, who like him knew it was unwise to argue with feisty women and agreed to bend the rules. Something similar happens in Isaiah 56 when the prophet is inspired to dispute the inferences his contemporaries made regarding the rules in the Torah about whether eunuchs and foreigners can come to church. It happens again in Nehemiah 8, when Nehemiah reworks the rules in the Torah in light of the situation his community finds itself in.

The Holy Spirit guides the people of God when it is engaged in its task of interpreting Scripture today and hearing the new things that God is saying today. How do we then evaluate what we and other people think the Holy Spirit is telling us about the text's meaning or about the way it applies? A key element in approaching that question is to go back to the historical meaning of the text itself. We go back to examining what was going on in the act of communication between God and people that led to these texts being preserved as of ongoing significance for the life of God's people. If some strands of scholarship will abandon the idea that texts have meanings, evangelical scholarship will not.

Evangelicals know that the First Testament resulted from a concern on God's part to communicate. God spoke in such a way as to communicate with the original audiences of the material that now appears in the Bible, and this implies that this material has its own meaning and not merely the meaning we read into it. God is also concerned to communicate with us and does so not least via those past acts of communication.

It is the same evangelical conviction about God's delight in communicating with people that makes it so difficult for an evangelical to believe that Isaiah wrote the whole of the book called Isaiah or to believe that the visions in Daniel came from the sixth century. What would God be doing giving Isaiah in the eighth century words to write down that were addressed to people two centuries later ("Comfort, comfort my people")? What would God be doing giving Daniel in the sixth century visions whose message was designed to speak to people another four centuries later? How could an evangelical ever believe that? We know that God speaks to us where we are, relates to us personally. Surely it would be the same in Scripture? How could evangelicals ever have thought anything else?

3. It Feels Free to Be Independent of Human Tradition

That rhetorical question leads into my third thesis, that evangelical study of the First Testament will feel free to be independent of human traditions in its work. The Bible itself is what counts, not human traditions that claim to interpret it.

Evangelicalism does not reject all tradition. It accepts the doctrinal traditions of the patristic period, such as the doctrine of the Trinity. We accept the Christian tradition that found itself developing a collection of new covenant Scriptures and arguing about which books belong to this collection: we assume that our Christian ancestors stumbled into the right decisions about this canon of Scripture, or we trust God's providence to have ensured that they did so, even though we cannot provide a justification for the precise bounds that the canon of Scripture has. There are traditions we accept.

Evangelicals have nevertheless reckoned it theologically important to feel free not to be bound by tradition. But evangelical scholarship has not applied the principle of freedom from tradition to our study of Scripture itself. The essential nature of biblical criticism is to be critical of tradition. It feels free to be critical of the doctrinal tradition that the church claims issues from Scripture, of traditions about the origin of the books of the Bible, of the traditional form of the text of the Bible, and of traditional understandings about the nature of the books of the Bible. Because evangelicalism knew it needed to oppose many of the results of much of that criticism, it set itself against the critical stance itself. People who questioned traditions about the Bible, such as "Moses wrote Genesis," ended up with dangerous-looking theories about the Bible's origin, its text, and its meaning. So it is better to stick with the traditional views.

Evangelical scholarship thus came to be characterized by the maintenance of certain concrete views about the authorship of the different books of the Bible and by the maintenance of traditional views about the Bible's background even when nothing hung on it. So the prophet Joel would be dated in the eighth century and Moses would be credited with the authorship of Genesis even though the books make no claims about that. This view would be maintained because it is the traditional view, and if we question that tradition, in a moment we will be questioning whether Moses lies behind the rules he is supposed to have mediated at Sinai. That was right: people who began asking questions about Moses and Genesis were soon asking questions about Moses and Deuteronomy. But that was no basis for a groundless, irrational commitment to tradition just because it was tradition. We may accept that the church's doctrinal tradition reflects the work of God's Spirit in guiding the church in God's truth, but it too remains subject to criticism, and we do not let this tradition determine our understanding of the First Testament.

So when tradition says that Moses wrote the Pentateuch, evangelical study of the First Testament is quite at home asking "Did he?" It knows that we do not need to provide God's Word with spurious support by linking it with some famous figure, as if it might lose its authority if it were of anonymous authorship. The belief that Moses wrote the Pentateuch was only a human tradition.

Tradition says that Job, Ruth, Jonah, and Esther are factual stories, but evangelical study of the First Testament is quite at home concluding that actually they are God-inspired parables.

Rather than describing them as parables, I would prefer to describe them as fictional stories, novels inspired by God, but in the end I have yielded to the persuasion of my colleague Marianne Meye Thompson. In the course of kindly attempting to help me say more clearly what I wanted to say in this chapter (which does not imply that it is what she would want to say), she urged me to take account of the fact that "fiction" suggests to people something humanly devised that is not true. I recognize that this can seem to be the word's implication, yet we also recognize that fiction can often powerfully picture truth. Many of the stories outside Scripture in which we recognize truth about God and ourselves are fictional stories, and there seems no reason why this should not be so within Scripture. Danna Nolan Fewell suggests a nice instance of the power of fiction in Scripture in a comment on Daniel 4, where Nebuchadnezzar "is made to utter praise . . . for a god for whom the historical king had no respect. In its confrontation with the historical Nebuchadnezzar, the Israelite community was impotent. But years later a member of this once impotent community played a joke on the infamous king of the exile by creating a new memory of Nebuchadnezzar. . . . The human imagination is able to overpower human history."[4]

Evangelical study recognizes that factual narrative is essential and central to the Bible because Christian faith is an evangel, a piece of news about something that happened. But it also recognizes that parable is essential to Scripture, too. Historical narrative is really important because it tells you things that actually happened. But as Aristotle almost said, the correlative limitation of factual narrative is that it can only describe what has happened; parable can describe what could happen.[5] The New Testament includes parable as well as history; Jesus needed parables. It would thus be surprising if the First Testament did not include some nonfactual narrative. To put it another way, we need vision as well as fact, and parable can express vision. That is part of what books such as Job and Ruth and Esther do. Their being factual stories is only a human tradition.

Admittedly the conviction that Jesus' parables are, on the contrary, factual has also sometimes been a tradition of interpretation, and it is still held to be important by some Christians. Whatever are the arguments that satisfy most people that the parables are fictional are also the arguments that establish that books such as Job, Esther, Ruth, Jonah, and the stories in Daniel are (largely) fictional. Admittedly

---

4. See *Circle of Sovereignty* (Sheffield: Sheffield Academic Press, 1988; rev. ed., Nashville: Abingdon, 1991), 80.

5. See *Poetics* 9 [1451ab].

one of the most difficult tasks in interpretation is to determine whether a narrative is aiming to be factual or fictional (because fiction often seeks to be realistic). But that will not lead evangelicals to assume that their default position should be that a narrative is factual unless it is proved to the contrary, as if this were equivalent to being presumed innocent until proved guilty. Fact and parable fulfill different aspects of Scripture's aims, so there is no presumption regarding which category a narrative belongs to until we have studied it to see which it might be. Both are innocent categories.

In not being tied to tradition, evangelical study of the First Testament assumes that we are always beginning afresh in our understanding of the First Testament.

The foundation documents of Princeton Seminary required first that students became well skilled in Hebrew and Greek. One reason, Archibald Alexander commented at his inaugural address there, was that translations of the Bible are not inspired, authoritative, or infallible; only the Bible is that, and presumably ordinands should be able to study what the Bible says, not only what a translator has said it says. The second reason was that they be able to explain the principal difficulties that arise in the perusal of the Scriptures. The third was that they should know about Middle Eastern antiquities, geography, and customs.[6]

The second of these requirements especially strikes me. Alexander implies that biblical study is about explaining problems, not (for instance) living with them or causing them, let alone discovering things.

Often evangelicalism has prided itself on being conservative, and we indeed want to conserve that truth that God has given us. Yet it would be at least as logical for evangelicalism to be adventurously liberal and critical as to be conservative. Evangelicalism can afford to be open-minded. We know the Bible is the Word of God; we therefore need have no fear about discovering what it says and about ignoring human traditions about what it says.

This has not been a common evangelical attitude. Instead, much so-called evangelical scholarship assumes that we already understand the Bible, that anything new that anyone says is suspicious just because it is new, and that the task of scholarship is essentially defensive, essentially to explain problems. This is not an evangelical view. The glorious prospect of evangelical study of the First Testament is to open this wonderful book confident that it is God's word, and untrammeled by theories about what it has to say. It can say what it likes.

4. It Is Interested in the Actual Text of Scripture and in the History It Refers To

Fourth, evangelical study of the First Testament is interested both in the text of Scripture as we have it and in the history it refers to.

---

6. See M. Noll, ed., *The Princeton Theology 1812–1912* (Grand Rapids: Baker Academic, 1983), 56–57, 83. I am grateful to my student John Yeo for drawing my attention to this book.

One of the first books I bought when I went to university to study theology over forty years ago was John Bright's *History of Israel*. In Britain, teachers do not make as much use of textbooks, and I do not use textbooks in California, a fact that sometimes puzzles my students, but Bright's *History of Israel* was once as near as you could get to a textbook for First Testament study. This now seems a weird fact. It implies that studying Israelite history is studying the First Testament and that if you have gained a grasp of the history of Israel, you have gained a grasp of the First Testament. This had better not be the case, given the difficulty most students have in gaining the vaguest grasp of the history of Israel. More seriously, the approach implies that the First Testament itself is about the history of Israel, as if the First Testament were a history book.

Going to a Passover meal involves taking part in the retelling of the exodus story. It is passionately vital that this retelling refers to something that actually happened, but the participants know that the story that is told is something different from a CNN video of the event. Indeed, a moment's thought will make clear that one might have a hard time turning the order of service into objective, factual history. When movies attempt to do that, even believing movies, there always seems to be something wrong with them. One leaves the theater saying, "It can't have been like that," "There must have been more to it than that." One says that because people do try to represent a wonder like the deliverance at the Red Sea, not because they avoid doing so.

The exodus story is not something that could be turned into a realistic movie script. It has been meditated on, applied, and refracted through Israel's continuing experience of God over the centuries. That this story refers to something that actually happened is passionately vital, but the story appeals to the imagination, to the heart, to the instinct to worship, to the needs, aspirations, and experience of the people who told the story over the generations. It is not pure history. (Actually Bright's *History of Israel* was not pure history; it was a "theological interpretation of history packaged as a history textbook" designed to lure conservative students like me into something that could purport to be critical study of history.)[7]

I might make the point another way. The First Testament offers us two accounts of Judah's history from David onwards, in Chronicles and in Samuel-Kings. The words in these two are sometimes exactly the same, but that makes it more striking that at other points they give a markedly different impression of what people said and did. They thus anticipate the nature of the Gospels. A synopsis of the Gospels puts the four New Testament Gospels in parallel columns and is thus hugely illuminating in allowing the reader to see what they have in common and what makes each individual Gospel distinctive and worth having. An American friend of mine went to a seminary where students were never invited to look at one of these synopses of the Gospels. It exposed what seemed to be a problem. By showing you the similarities and the

---

7. So K. L. Noll, "Looking on the Bright Side of Israel's History," *Biblical Interpretation* 7 (1999): 1–27 (see 21).

differences, it showed you how at least two of the Gospels must have rewritten the others, and how at least two of them are not giving us an exact historical account of what Jesus did and said. The same is true of Chronicles and Samuel-Kings. Of course, all four Gospels and both those First Testament narratives are proclaiming their story in a way that shows how it applies to an audience, and therefore none of them is aiming to write mere history, mere correct fact.

It passionately matters to these two First Testament writings, as it does to the Gospels, that they are talking about things that happened, but it also passionately matters to them that you see the point of the story, see the way it applies to you. They do not want to waste their time writing history. "History is bunk." It is one of the great American sayings by one of the great Americans, though the actual words of Henry Ford were apparently slightly different, like many famous "quotations": "History is more or less bunk." Interestingly, the quotation goes on, "It's tradition. We don't want tradition." While this may be a good basis for manufacturing automobiles, on my lips, at least, it is of course not a dig at church history or at any historical study genuinely worthy of the name. The concern of such disciplines is not mere antiquarianism but insight on our own lives.[8]

That desire to show people how past events impact the present is part of what makes Samuel-Kings and Chronicles the inspired and infallible Word of God. These narratives include material that is not factual, not historical. They tell us that people said and did things that they did not do and say, just as the Gospels tell us that Jesus said and did things that Jesus did not say and do (this is simply an implication of the evidence presented by a synopsis). That is so not because someone made a mistake or is deceiving us but because that is the God-inspired way to ensure that Scripture tells us the truth about David or about Jesus. It is in this way that it does the thing it was designed to do, gives us a true indication of the significance of David or of Jesus. Every word in Samuel-Kings and Chronicles, every word in the Gospels, is God-given, God-inspired, and contributes to our getting a true impression of the history, but not every word or every shot corresponds to what CNN would have broadcast if it had been there.

To be evangelical is to know that the actual books we have, Samuel-Kings and Chronicles, are the inspired Word of God. The history of Israel as someone like John Bright might reconstruct it is not what God wanted us to have in the Bible. Merely studying the history of Israel is not the way to discover what the First Testament is about.

Does the actual history matter, then? Indeed it does. The instinct that led evangelicals to enthuse over John Bright's *History of Israel* was half-right. It does matter to us to know what events happened, not because we will then understand the First Testament narrative but because without there being some events behind the narrative, the First Testament narrative could not be the Word of God.

---

8. For Ford's remark, see *The Oxford Dictionary of Quotations* (4th ed.; Oxford and New York: Oxford University Press, 1996), 289; it attributes the words to the *Chicago Tribune* of May 25, 1916.

Gerhard von Rad once described Kings as an act of praise at the justice of the judgment of God (he could say that in one word in German: it is a *Gerichtsdoxologie*).[9] What Kings does is say, "This is how we have behaved over the past four hundred years, so God has been entirely justified in letting calamity happen to us; what we need to do now is acknowledge the facts in order to cast ourselves on God's grace, because if we have any hope, that is where it lies." If the story is wrong over the way Israel has behaved over four hundred years, who knows whether God was justified in letting calamity happen and who knows what basis there might be for casting oneself on God or for any hope for the future? If that is true of Kings, it is much more true about the narratives about Abraham, Moses, or Joshua. It does matter to us that their stories have some facts behind them.[10]

In the second section above, I said I would comment further on the difference between evangelical study of the First Testament and the work of two great First Testament theologians with whom evangelicals have sensed significant commonality (I do so at this point partly because I am not aware of indications of what they would think about my fifth thesis).

I had begun in the first section with evangelicalism's emphasis on getting one's personal relationship with God right. I have the impression that Childs is more concerned with right thinking, right theology, while Brueggemann is more concerned with right behavior, and specifically with getting societal relations right. Evangelicals, Childs, and Brueggemann all care about all three, but there are differences of emphasis or profile.

My third thesis declared evangelical independence of tradition. Brueggemann is inclined to set himself over against the church's doctrinal tradition; it is a corollary of taking Scripture itself with absolute seriousness. In contrast, Childs is significantly influenced by the church's doctrinal tradition. In my judgment, that makes Brueggemann's stance resemble the one evangelicals should take, while Childs's resembles the one evangelicals actually take.

My fourth thesis was that evangelicals are interested in both history and story. Both Childs and Brueggemann have given the impression of turning their backs on history more firmly than evangelicals can afford to. Childs has emphasized that he has not turned his back on history; but that is nevertheless the drift of his emphasis on the canonical form of the text.[11] Brueggemann has declared that he is indeed interested in rhetoric not history or ontology, though amusingly Norman Gottwald has pointed out that in practice he is less rigorous in this direction than he is in theory (and rightly, Gottwald implies). Evangelicals will want to emphasize ontology, too.[12]

9. "Gerichtsdoxologie," in Gerhard von Rad, *Gesammelte Studien zum Alten Testament* (Munich: Kaiser, 1973), 2:245–54.

10. On the issues raised here, see chapter 13 above.

11. See further chapter 17 below (section 2).

12. See N. K. Gottwald, "Rhetorical, Historical, and Ontological Counterpoints in Doing Old Testament Theology," in *God in the Fray* (Walter Brueggemann Festschrift; ed. T. Linafelt and T. K. Beal; Minneapolis: Fortress, 1998), 24–37.

5. It Is Undertaken by Faith

Talk of the importance of the First Testament's factuality takes me to my fifth thesis, that evangelical First Testament study is done by faith, though perhaps not in the sense that is usually attributed to that phrase. The reason is that unfortunately First Testament study is never going to establish what events lay behind the First Testament narrative.

I exaggerate slightly. The scholarly consensus is probably still that there are good grounds for reckoning that Kings is a basically factual account of those four hundred years from Solomon to the fall of Jerusalem. It is not a universal consensus: a strong minority voice has developed the view that the entire narrative from Genesis to Kings was written much later, in the Persian period, and is in effect a piece of fiction. But at present that is mainly a view held by a small but vocal number of people in places like England.

It is otherwise with the story of Abraham, Moses, and Joshua. The confidence in their basic historicity that John Bright showed has largely collapsed. The scholarly world's confidence that it knew approximately how the books that tell their story came into being (JEDP and all that) has collapsed. The assured results of modern criticism have all ceased to be assured. Over the past century or so, First Testament study has gone full circle, the questions that everyone thought had been answered have all turned out to be open questions again, and the conclusions that everyone thought were wrong have all turned out to be open possibilities again. Scholarship has resisted conforming to Thomas Kuhn's thesis that a scholarly guild does not abandon a theory until it has a better one, even if the theory looks full of holes. The scholarly world corporately does not know anything about when those books were written or what their historical value might be. Perhaps it has moved from the premodern position (Moses wrote the Pentateuch) through the modern position (JEDP wrote the Pentateuch) to the postmodern position (we do not know who wrote the Pentateuch, and it was probably the wrong question).

Might this be good news from an evangelical perspective, if it shows that the entire historical-critical enterprise was mistaken and that we are justified in sticking by the traditional view that Moses is the key figure behind the Pentateuch? Unfortunately this does not follow. The real data in the text that led to the critical study that eventually issued in the consensus that has now shattered are still real facts. They still point to a compositional process rather than to Moses sitting down with a ghost writer during the long evenings on the way from Sinai to the Plains of Moab and wondering whether to include the account of his own death. It was indeed a compositional process; but what was its nature, how long it took, when it was completed, and how far it preserved historical information about Abraham and Sarah or Moses and Miriam, we do not know. It is for this reason that Brueggemann declares that "a theology of the First Testament cannot appeal to 'history.'"[13]

---

13. "The Theology of the Old Testament: A Prompt Retrospect," in *God in the Fray*, 307–20 (308).

The sobering fact that emerges from the story of biblical criticism over recent decades is that critical study will never come to definitive conclusions about First Testament history. The scholarly consensus that once obtained in the English-speaking world about the history of early Israel was nothing more than that, a scholarly consensus. The nature of the material on which scholars need to do their work, the nature of the books that God inspired, is such that we cannot get behind them to establish historically what events they refer to.

I have implied that we need to know that there is some history behind these books. So what we are reduced to is living by faith that this is so. That may raise a smile, for living by faith is supposed to be fundamental to evangelical faith. In our First Testament study we have to trust God that the Word of God has enough history behind it to be valid as the Word of God. And we can live with that, because we know that the First Testament is indeed the Word of God. We know it, because Jesus gave it to us (and we know that we have better historical-critical grounds for our convictions about what Jesus said and did than we have for early First Testament history; and I am prepared to see the providence of God in that). We also know that the First Testament is the Word of God because God keeps speaking to us through it.

I have hinted that there is a streak of evangelical logic that says "it is because people like Moses, David, and Solomon wrote it, and because its history is factual, that we know that the First Testament must be authentic, must be the Word of God." It transpires that this logic needs to be inverted. "It is because the First Testament is authentic, is the Word of God, that we know its history must be as factual as it needs to be (because God would not have given us a narrative without enough facts behind it); and saying that Moses wrote it is a way of giving expression to the conviction that this narrative really came from God."

I am quite relaxed about that as a way of handling the fact that the scholarly world is never going to come to any agreed conclusions about the origins of the Pentateuch and the history of Abraham and Sarah or Moses and Miriam. There is another question about which I am less relaxed. It is that as well as needing the basic First Testament narrative to be historical, we really need to know the circumstances of its origin.

In order to understand a narrative, we may not need to know whether it is history or fiction. That may not affect its meaning. Readers may disagree about whether Jonah is history or parable, but they can agree about its themes, agree that it is about how not to be a prophet, and about God's attitude to other nations, and about the possibility of repentance on humanity's part and on God's part. Those are the story's themes, whether it is history or parable. But our view on the message of a story may be affected by our view on when it was written and for whom.

Suppose that the common critical view is right that Genesis 1 was written in Babylon among people from Judah who had been transported there by the Babylonians. That chapter about creation confronts the story of creation as the Babylonians told it and brings the gospel to Judeans there who thought there was no gospel. The reason for picturing God creating the world in six days with the orderly patterning of

God's work is to declare that God is a God of order and system, not a God of mess and violence. The life of these Judeans had collapsed into mess, and the Babylonian creation story portrayed gods as messy and violent in their relationships with each other; this new creation story assures the Judeans that this is not the truth about God. Further, it portrays God as doing a week's work and then having a day off, in order to reassure the Judeans that their strange religious life that involved doing a week's work and having a day off was not just their religious peculiarity but a reflection of God's own intention. It declines to talk about the creation of sun and moon and stars until that week is half over, and even then it does not actually use the words "sun" and "moon," and it confines the stars to a delightful throwaway phrase at the end of a verse, "he made the stars, as well" (literally, simply "and the stars"). All this is for a reason: the Babylonians believed that sun, moon, and stars decided people's destinies. Genesis 1 imagines the story of creation in such a way as to confront their beliefs and to declare the gospel to Judeans who were tempted to be overwhelmed by the collapse of their own life and to be overawed by Babylonian religion.

Awareness of the historical context that a narrative addresses can thus illumine the narrative's meaning. The trouble is, I have had to choose my example carefully; there are few other stories that are thus clearly illumined by reading them against a known historical context. That may be just because we lack the historical information that enables us to see how to read the narrative. But it means we do not know what was going on between a human author and his or her readers or what was going on between God and the people God was concerned to speak to. So we have a problem in connection with my second thesis. The First Testament began as a series of exercises in communication on God's part; we are able to overhear these so as to work out their implications for us, as we listen for what God says to us on the basis of them. But understanding the original communication depends on knowing who were the audience with whom God was communicating. And generally we do not in fact know who they were.

Let me suggest another example. We know something of the altercations that took place between the prophet Jeremiah and the prophet Hananiah, though we know of these only from Jeremiah's side. We know that Jeremiah was a "true" prophet and Hananiah a "false" prophet, but they did not go about wearing tee shirts announcing which was which. Jeremiah's discussion of true and false prophecy hints at the fact that it was rather difficult to state what constituted true prophecy over against false. One reason for this is the fact that if you had heard Hananiah, he would have sounded entirely biblical. Indeed, he was entirely biblical. He would have sounded very like Isaiah, promising that Yahweh would in the end deliver Jerusalem from its attackers. There was nothing wrong with Hananiah except that he was living in the wrong century. Time had moved on, and Yahweh was no longer saying the things that Isaiah had said.

One can compare and contrast Jeremiah and Hananiah with Ezekiel and Second Isaiah a little while later. Ezekiel and Second Isaiah would be contradicting each other if it were not for the fact that there was half a century between the time when they ministered to the Judean community in Babylon. A true prophet or a true interpreter is someone who knows what time it is, knows what time it is now, and knows what time it was when the text was written.[14]

What if the interpreter does not know when the text was written, how it confronted or comforted the audience it addressed? How then can it be interpreted? If it originally brought confrontation, what if we connect it with a situation in which it would have brought reassurance, or vice versa? Exactly that problem arises with different hypotheses concerning not the creation story in Genesis 1 but the creation story in Genesis 2 and 3, for instance, and the Cain and Abel story that follows.

I do not know the way through that question, and at one level this worries me. At another level it does not worry me. I have been through this experience before, the experience of recognizing a problem of principle in connection with the interpretation of Scripture—not a problem with an individual passage but a meta-problem. I once had that difficulty over the presence of unhistorical material in Scripture, but I found my way through the problem. I once had that difficulty over the patriarchalism of Scripture, but I am now most of the way out the other side of that problem. If I were a New Testament scholar, I would be thinking furiously about the implications of postcolonial thinking for Scripture (it does not affect the First Testament quite as radically). Nor am I as far on with this other difficulty, our not having the kind of information about the origin of biblical texts that would enable us to understand them as exercises in communication between God and people. But it does not worry me because I have been this way before with difficulties over Scripture. We will solve this one (and then another will arise). It will be okay. I know I can trust God with regard to it. I know God would not have given us a book with this particular profile if there was something wrong with it.

In other words, evangelical study of the First Testament proceeds on the basis of faith. It is an aspect of the life of faith. The most basic truth about our relationship with God that evangelicals affirm is that it proceeds on the basis of trust in God, not of being able to prove God at every point, but of trusting that we have reason for living by faith. Our scholarship is an aspect of our human and Christian life, and it works on the same basis. Because we know that the First Testament is the Word of God, we know we can live with the problems it raises that we cannot at the moment solve.

The problems will not always be insoluble. To return to my starting point, we study the First Testament in the light of the gospel. One aspect of the gospel is the conviction that God is committed to bringing the gospel story to its closure. The same will be true of the story of First Testament interpretation. We interpret the First Testament by faith, and we interpret it in hope, First Testament hope. That constitutes assured expectation that God is at work, which then inspires our activity, because we know it works with the grain of God's own commitments.

---

14. Cf. Eva Osswald, *Falsche Prophetie im Alten Testament* (Tübingen: Mohr, 1962); and J. A. Sanders, "Hermeneutics," *IDBSup*, 402–7 (404–5).

17

In What Way Does Old Testament
Theology Relate to the Canon?

My title is somewhat tautologous; by definition, the Old Testament is a
canon, so Old Testament theology is bound to be canon-related. Yet
the way we speak about Old Testament theology and about the canon indicates
that actually the interrelationship of Old Testament theology and the canon can be
quite complex.[1]

We owe to Brevard Childs an emphasis on the juxtaposition of the two
expressions,[2] though I find helpful Paul House's definition of "canonical" in terms
of "analysis that is God-centered, intertextually oriented, authority-conscious,
historically sensitive and devoted to the pursuit of the wholeness of the Old Testament message."[3] And I find helpful William Abraham's emphasis that in origin
"canon" designates Scripture not as a rule or a criterion for truth but as a means of
grace, something designed "to bring people to salvation, to make people holy, to
make proficient disciples of Jesus Christ, and the like" (cf. 2 Tim 3:16).[4] He notes
that feminist theology has actually and surprisingly turned the canon back into

---

1. First published in *TynB* 59 (2008): 1–26. Whereas I usually use my preferred term "First
Testament," in this chapter where I am discussing the subdiscipline known as the study of OT
theology, I have stayed with the conventional expression.

2. See, e.g., *Old Testament Theology in a Canonical Context* (London: SCM, 1985; Philadelphia:
Fortress, 1986), 6–16.

3. *Old Testament Theology* (Downers Grove, Ill.: InterVarsity, 1998), 57.

4. *Canon and Criterion in Christian Theology* (Oxford and New York: Oxford University Press,
1998), 51.

"a means of healing and transformation" rather than a criterion,[5] though it has also rejected it as a criterion or norm. As canon, Scripture is a norm, but it is first a resource.[6] It is formative as well as normative (Moshe Halbertal).[7] Benjamin D. Sommer comments that in Judaism the Scriptures—and even the Mishnah and Gemaras—are formative *rather than* normative; it is subsequent tradition that is directly normative for behavior.[8]

I have six comments to make on the interrelationship of Old Testament theology and the canon.

1. Old Testament Theology Considers the Insight That Emerges from the Form of the Old Testament Canon

Old Testament theology takes account of the form of the canon. There are at least three senses in which it might do so. One of Childs's theses is that the individual books of the Old Testament have been "shaped to function as canon."[9] His examples vary in forcefulness. Perhaps paradoxically, they are particularly illuminating in connection with the poetic books, Psalms, Proverbs, Ecclesiastes, and the Song of Songs. But whether or not the books are so shaped, Childs is surely right that we should do Old Testament theology on the basis of the books' canonical form rather than on the basis of historical and redaction-critical hypotheses about their origins, such as the tradition that Genesis was written by Moses or the hypothesis that it was written by a committee in the Second Temple period. If we "seek to give theological autonomy to a reconstructed Yahwist source," we disregard the work of the people who made it part of the Torah and accepted it in this form as Scripture.[10] Admittedly there are historical and redaction-critical hypotheses for which the canonical text gives us significant evidence, such as the link between the book called Isaiah and both the period of Isaiah ben Amoz and that of Cyrus the Persian (Isa 1:1; 45:1). I thus find it strange that Childs argues that reference to the exilic context of Isaiah 40–55 has been almost entirely removed from these chapters.[11] It is appropriate to take into account the information the text does give us in doing Old Testament theology.

It can also be enlightening to consider the theological implications of the ordering of the books in the canon. Both Jack Miles and Stephen Dempster, for instance,

---

5. Ibid., 460.

6. Cf. John Goldingay, *Models for Scripture* (Grand Rapids: Eerdmans; Carlisle: Paternoster, 1994; Toronto: Clements, 2004), 196–97.

7. *People of the Book* (Cambridge, Mass., and London: Harvard University Press, 1997), 3.

8. See "Unity and Plurality in Jewish Canons," in *One Scripture or Many?* (ed. Christine Helmer and Christof Landmesser; Oxford and New York: Oxford University Press, 2004), 108–50 (128–30).

9. See his *Introduction to the Old Testament as Scripture* (London: SCM; Philadelphia: Fortress, 1979).

10. Childs, *Old Testament Theology in a Canonical Context*, 11.

11. *Introduction to the Old Testament as Scripture*, 325.

look at the Hebrew-Aramaic canon as if it is a narrative.[12] Yet this is a construct they bring to the text. While the Scriptures are dominated and framed by narrative, they are not actually a narrative. Both authors thus have to do considerable linking of dots and come to monumentally different conclusions regarding the dynamics of the alleged narrative: Miles sees it as relating God's gradual withdrawal, Dempster as a story that moves from Adam to David and a coming Davidic king. Less inference is involved in Marvin A. Sweeney's account of the canon as implying "the initiation of Jewish life based on the Torah, its disruption in the period of the monarchy and the Babylonian exile, and its restoration in the aftermath of the exile,"[13] or in Hans Walter Wolff's non-narrative view of the Greek canon as moving from past to present to future.[14] Or one might see this threefold canon as suggesting the definition of the community's nature in story and command, then in the discernment of the sure ordering of created reality, then in the irruption of something new in uncredentialed channels. In developing this formulation, Walter Brueggemann interestingly observes that conservative persons will be inclined to focus on the Torah, radicals on the Prophets, and people such as humanistic psychologists on the Writings.[15] At Fuller Theological Seminary, the MDiv requires a course in the Torah (students may study both Prophets and Writings but must do only one), while courses in the School of Psychology require a course in the Writings (students may study both Torah and Prophets but are not required to do so).

Brueggemann applies his formulation to the Hebrew-Aramaic canon, but I think it fits the Greek canon better. In principle, I do not think we have to choose between the Hebrew-Aramaic and Greek ordering of the books;[16] while the former was adopted by the synagogue and the latter by the church, both may be of Jewish origin. We do have to choose between the Hebrew-Aramaic list of books and the Greek one, and I choose the Hebrew-Aramaic one, though I do not think it makes a whole lot of difference except—as someone has observed—for increasing the amount of the Old Testament that the church ignores.

More important than the shaping of individual books or their order is the rhetorical form of the canon. It is dominated by narrative, in which Israel tells its story, twice, in large-scale versions that dominate the first half of the Greek Bible and that bookend and frame the Hebrew-Aramaic Bible. Yet narrative is not all. It incorporates and is accompanied by substantial speech of address, in which God or God's representatives address Israel; here narrative statements have a place but do not dominate.

12. Jack Miles, *God: A Biography* (New York and London: Simon & Schuster, 1995); Stephen Dempster, *Dominion and Dynasty* (Leicester and Downers Grove, Ill.: InterVarsity, 2003). With Miles may be compared Richard E. Friedman, *The Disappearance of God* (Boston: Little, Brown, 1995), reissued as *The Hidden Face of God* (San Francisco: Harper, 1996).

13. "Tanak versus Old Testament," in *Problems in Biblical Theology* (Rolf P. Knierim Festschrift; ed. Henry T. C. Sun et al.; Grand Rapids: Eerdmans, 1997), 353–72.

14. *The Old Testament* (Philadelphia: Fortress, 1973; London: SPCK, 1974).

15. *The Creative Word* (Philadelphia: Fortress, 1982), 11.

16. As Brevard S. Childs argues in *Biblical Theology in Crisis* (Philadelphia: Westminster, 1970), 109.

The canon also incorporates and is complemented by speech in which human beings address Yahweh in praise, protest, and penitence. Claus Westermann sees the Hebrew-Aramaic canon as following the sequence narrative-address-response, while Rolf Rendtorff comments that "in the first part of the canon *God acts*, in the second *God speaks*, and in the third part of the canon *people speak* to God and of God."[17] But this rather oversimplifies the Writings. One might indeed argue that the Hebrew-Aramaic Bible comprises a stepped structure, narrative-address-prayer-address-narrative.

The canon's being dominated by narrative signifies for Old Testament theology that Israel's faith is a gospel, a story declaring good news about what God has done.[18] It is not fundamentally a series of present-tense statements such as "God is love" or a series of imperatives such as "love your neighbor" but a series of past-tense statements such as "God so loved the world that he gave. . . ." Old Testament theology is thus first an explication of the acts of God. In fact, the much-derided biblical theology movement was not so wrong. In fact, I wonder if the biblical theology movement is due for reevaluation. By some quasi-Hegelian logic it is customary for fashions in theology to be despised in their aftermath, then to undergo rehabilitation (it happened to Barth). The biblical theology movement had its weaknesses and its blind spots, but it had its insights and strengths.

These narratives are not just one collection of liberating stories and traditions, parallel to other such collections from other cultures. They tell us *the* good news about what God did for Israel in setting about to bless the world. Their narrative form is intrinsic to their theological statement. If their gospel is true, it cannot be expressed in the form of traditional systematic theology.

The dominance of narrative in the Old Testament canon also makes it possible to discuss complex theological questions that are not open to being "solved" in the form of the discursive, analytical statement that came to dominate theology. Narrative makes it possible to discuss the relationship between divine sovereignty and human free will (in Exod 5–14), or the nature of the presence of God or the way God deals with the sin of the people of God (in Exod 32–34), or the relationship between fulfillment and nonfulfillment and between obedience and disobedience on the part of the people of God (in Joshua), or the relationship between divine politics and human politics (in 2 Kings).

So it is theologically significant that narrative opens the Old Testament and dominates it. But it is also theologically significant that these narratives both incorporate substantial instruction in non-narrative form (in the Torah) and are accompanied by further substantial nonnarrative instruction (in the Prophets).[19] Narrative is not everything. Indeed, there is a dialectical conversation between narrative and instruction. In the Torah, the conversation is symbolized by the enfolding of instruction

17. Claus Westermann, *Elements of Old Testament Theology* (Atlanta: John Knox, 1982), 10; Rolf Rendtorff, *The Canonical Hebrew Bible* (Leiden: Deo, 2005), 6.

18. See further chapter 10 above.

19. Brian Brock (*Singing the Ethos of God* [Grand Rapids and Cambridge: Eerdmans, 2007], 33) notes that it is also ethically significant.

into the narrative; in the Prophets, it is symbolized by their reference back to the narrative events. The First Testament toggles narrative and precept.[20]

So the narrative pauses to make theological statements about who God is, such as the outline Old Testament systematic theology in Exodus 34:6–7 where Yahweh offers a self-description in terms of character traits. This non-narrative description of Yahweh implicitly constitutes a theological reflection on the narrative that precedes, though in itself it constitutes a statement of who Yahweh simply *is*. Likewise Leviticus 19:18 requires that Israelites love their neighbors, especially the ones who have wronged them. The immediate basis for this is the fact that "I am Yahweh," that people are to revere Yahweh, that they are to observe Yahweh's laws, and in the slightly wider context that "you are to be holy because I, Yahweh your God, am holy" (Lev 19:2). In a much looser sense, such teaching also links with the narrative, but it stands as a statement of who Yahweh *is* and what people are supposed to *do* that is independent of such contexts. The teaching in the Prophets and Wisdom books then majors on such statements. The canonical form of the Old Testament thus does point theology toward accompanying narrative statements such as "God so loved the world" with statements such as "God is love" and statements such as "you are to love people who wrong you."

Then, as well as narrative and teaching, the Old Testament incorporates substantial material in which people speak to God in praise, protest, and penitence. Again this material links closely with narrative and instruction, which often include praise, protest, and penitence; indeed one might see the narratives as a whole as praise, prayer or protest.[21] Conversely, psalms and other prayers often take narrative form, while the Psalter is formally constructed as a book of instruction. But these psalms and prayers show that narrative and instruction are properly turned into explicit praise, prayer, and penitence; theology and ethics become doxology. And they show teaching on praise, prayer, and penitence taking the form of instances of praise, prayer, and penitence.

2. Old Testament Theology Focuses on the Canon of the Old Testament, Not the History of Israel

Old Testament theology's relationship with the canon means it focuses on the text of the Old Testament, not the history to which it refers. As Childs put it, "the object of theological reflection is the canonical writing of the Old Testament . . . not the events or experiences behind the text" and not these events or experiences apart

---

20. I derive this image from Deirdre N. McCloskey, *The Bourgeois Virtues* (Chicago and London: University of Chicago Press, 2006), 272, who in turn credits it to Richard A. Lanham, *The Electronic Word* (Chicago: University of Chicago Press, 1993), 79ff.

21. Gerhard von Rad called the books of Kings a *Gerichtsdoxologie*, an act of praise at the justice of God's judgment (*Old Testament Theology* [2 vols.; Edinburgh: Oliver and Boyd; New York: Harper, 1962], 1:343; cf. "Gerichtsdoxologie," *Gesammelte Studien zum Alten Testament* [Munich: Kaiser, 1973], 2:245–54).

from their "construal in scripture by a community of faith and practice."[22] Nevertheless he goes on to make explicit that the scriptural story needs to refer to things that actually happened. To adapt a statement by James Barr, it is no good the exodus happening canonically but not in the world outside the canon.[23]

Genesis to Joshua declares that God created, God started over, God promised, God delivered, God sealed, and God gave.[24] But did God do these things? Much Old Testament scholarship sees virtually no historical value in Genesis to Joshua. If it is right, this fatally imperils the validity of that series of theological statements. An Old Testament narrative theology is dependent on the factuality of the events it refers to. One can perhaps make definitional statements such as that God is faithful and merciful without these being dependent on particular events, and one can engage in narrative theological discussion of issues such as the relationship between divine sovereignty and human free will without the narrative being historical. One can hardly make past-tense gospel statements such as God promised and God delivered, without these being dependent on a relationship with particular events. If God did not make promises to Israel's ancestors or deliver Israelites from Egypt, it might still be true that Yahweh is a God who promises and a God who delivers, but the major content of and grounds for making those statements has disappeared. Indeed, the Old Testament builds further declarations in the realms of theology, ethics, and spirituality on Yahweh's having made these particular promises (of land, peoplehood, and blessing) and having effected this particular deliverance (from serfdom in Egypt) (e.g., Exod 23:9; Deut 26:1–14). Reckoning that Genesis to Joshua is pure fiction does not disprove its theology, ethics, and spirituality, but it does remove much of its substance as well as the basis on which the Old Testament commends it.

So the basic historicity of the events related in the Old Testament is important to the validity of its theology, and this is one reason why the study of Israelite history deserves investigation. This does not mean that our actual recognition of the Old Testament's truth and its theology is dependent on this investigation. There is a difference here between Old Testament and New Testament study, where the nature of the Gospel narratives (specifically their date) makes it reasonable to treat them as good historical sources for an understanding of who Jesus was and what he did, an understanding that does not have to presuppose their acceptance as Scripture.[25] The nature of the books from Genesis to Joshua and the state of archeological investigations of the period they cover make it impossible on purely critical grounds to treat the books as good historical sources. One can make a case for the reasonable plausibility of their being that,

---

22. *Old Testament Theology in a Canonical Context*, 6. I have paraphrased the middle part of the quotation to clarify the way I understand Childs's words.

23. See "Childs' Introduction to the Old Testament as Scripture," *JSOT* 12 (1980): 12–23 (21). On the issues raised in this section, see chapter 13 above and also chapter 16 (sections 4 and 5).

24. Cf. John Goldingay, *Old Testament Theology*, vol. 1 (Downers Grove, Ill.: InterVarsity, 2003; Carlisle: Paternoster, 2006). This chapter includes some sentences adapted from this volume and from *Old Testament Theology*, vols. 2–3 (Downers Grove, Ill.: InterVarsity; Carlisle: Paternoster, 2006, 2009).

25. See recently Richard Bauckham, *Jesus and the Eyewitnesses* (Grand Rapids: Eerdmans, 2006).

but not for the overwhelming probability of it. My conviction that they have enough historical value to justify the theology that is built on them does not come from critical study alone but from trust in Christ himself, from whom I receive these Scriptures.

The basic historicity of the Old Testament story is important to the validity of its theology. (I do not know how much historicity is enough, but I know God does, and has looked after the matter.) But it does not follow that the investigation of Old Testament history is part of doing Old Testament theology. The subject matter for Old Testament theology is the canonical writings. Insofar as "God created" is a summary of a significant Old Testament truth, it is Job, Proverbs, the Psalms, Genesis 1–2, and other Old Testament descriptions of God's creating the world that spell out that statement. Empirical scientific investigation of the process whereby the world came into being could lead to theologically significant results, but these would not be part of "Old Testament theology." Likewise, investigating the actual history of Israel's ancestors or the exodus could lead to theologically significant results, but these would not be part of "Old Testament theology." The study of Israelite history is an ancillary and supportive discipline like the study of philosophy.

Hans Frei traced the process whereby eighteenth-century scholarship came to a new realization of the difference between the story the Scriptures tell and the actual history of Old Testament and New Testament times. It then had to make a fateful decision about whether to be theologically interested in the history or the story.[26] There was no contest; history had become God by the eighteenth century, so only history could have the status of a revelation of God. Thus forty or fifty years ago, when I started studying the Old Testament, one could take it for granted that John Bright's *History of Israel*[27] was a one-stop guide to the Old Testament. But scholarship has focused for two centuries on the quest for the historical Israel and made no significant progress, and it never will. Whereas it was inevitable that scholarship made that choice two centuries ago, it was the wrong choice. This is so from a purely practical viewpoint. The history of Israel exists, but we apparently have no access to it, so we can hardly make it the locus of theological investigation (which is one aspect of or reason for what Leo G. Perdue calls "the collapse of history").[28] Yet what God has actually given us as canon is some texts, which at least do have the virtue of being accessible. The subject for Old Testament theology is the Old Testament, not the history of Israel. At this point, too, the biblical theology movement was not so wrong.

3. Old Testament Theology Lets the Canon Itself Be the Canon

Recognizing the Old Testament as canon means Old Testament theology is wary of reading the Scriptures in light of the creeds, the rule of the faith, the church's

26. *The Eclipse of Biblical Narrative* (New Haven: Yale University Press, 1974).
27. (Philadelphia: Westminster Press; London: SCM, 1959).
28. *The Collapse of History: Reconstructing Old Testament Theology* (Minneapolis: Fortress, 1994); *Reconstructing Old Testament Theology after the Collapse of History* (Minneapolis: Fortress, 2005).

theological tradition, the church's exegetical tradition, and the insights of our own age. It lets the canon itself be the canon.

The trouble with the Scriptures, theologians such as Irenaeus recognized, is that by collecting isolated verses from here and there, one can prove anything. Today we might say individual verses must be interpreted in light of their literary context and their author's intention. Irenaeus's equivalent safeguard is to measure the interpretation of individual verses by "the rule of the faith": the *kanōn* of the faith, in fact (the translation "the rule of faith" gives a misleading impression).[29] He notes that we receive this rule at our baptism, which points to the link between the rule of the faith and the creed. The creed with its summary of the biblical story in terms of the activity of Father, Son, and Spirit is an expression of the rule of the faith. Subsequent Christian faith has often operated with a related outline understanding of the Christian story in terms of creation, fall, Christ's coming, and the final judgment.

As frameworks for interpreting Scripture these comprehensively marginalize most of the Old Testament after Genesis 3 and comprehensively skew biblical theology. Old Testament theology cannot do justice to the canon if it follows the creed or the rule of the faith. I do not imply that the rule of the faith and the creed lack contextual and intrinsic merits; I say the creed every Sunday. But it is not the case that "the church's Rule of Faith constrains the theological teaching of a biblical text,"[30] at least not in a positive sense. The rule of the faith offers guidance to theological interpretation, but in the final analysis only the biblical text itself constrains its theological teaching.

Similar considerations apply to the church's broader theological tradition. B. B. Warfield defined biblical theology as "the task of coordinating the scattered results of continuous exegesis into a concatenated whole, whether with reference to a single book of Scripture or to a body of related books or to the whole Scriptural fabric."[31] William Abraham comments, "This is a preposterous undertaking. . . . One would have to be virtually omniscient."[32] He would presumably react in a similar way to Norman Gottwald's declaration that "a proper beginning point for a theology of the Hebrew Bible is to take account of everything that the Bible says about God, everything that God says, and everything that people say to God. This would be to follow radically and faithfully the course of the text. . . . Unless and until this is done . . . theological criticism will continue to build very selectively on narrow bases of God-talk."[33] Gottwald later acknowledged that this was a task of some magnitude.[34]

29. See, e.g., *Against Heresies* 1.9.4.

30. So Robert W. Wall, "Reading the Bible from within Our Traditions: The 'Rule of Faith' in Theological Hermeneutics," in *Between Two Horizons* (ed. Joel B. Green and Max Turner; Grand Rapids: Eerdmans, 2000), 88–107 (90).

31. "The Idea of Systematic Theology," *Presbyterian and Reformed Review* 7 (1896): 243–71 (256).

32. *Canon and Criterion in Christian Theology*, 326.

33. "Literary Criticism of the Hebrew Bible," in *Mappings of the Biblical Terrain* (ed. Vincent L. Tollers and John Maier; Lewisburg, Pa.: Bucknell University Press, 1990), 27–44 (39).

34. "Rhetorical, Historical, and Ontological Counterpoints in Doing Old Testament Theology," in *God in the Fray* (Walter Brueggemann Festschrift; ed. Tod Linafelt and Timothy K. Beal; Minneapolis: Fortress, 1998), 11–23 (12).

In Warfield's understanding, systematic theology's task is then to order the material in terms of its own categories. This vision might have the capacity to rescue Old Testament theology or biblical theology from unconscious assimilation to the categories of systematics; one might contrast the way the opening chapters of Childs's *Old Testament Theology in a Canonical Context* emphasize the notion of revelation, not really facing the implications of the fact that revelation is a relatively modern construct related to a relatively modern philosophical question, and not a biblical category. One distinction between biblical theology and systematics is the conscious way systematics expresses itself in terms of the philosophical questions of its day, and Old Testament theology needs to be aware of the interplay between systematics and philosophy. Both classical theism and open theism, for instance, have difficulty doing justice to aspects of the Old Testament (God must always know the future because God is omniscient; God cannot know the future at all because the future is unknowable). Old Testament theology works with the canon rather than with the church's theological convictions. Francis Watson comments that "theology may itself constitute a hermeneutic."[35] Insofar as this means the church's doctrinal tradition helps one to see things in Scripture, this is a positive notion. But like any hermeneutic, it functions properly when it is then subordinate to the text.

The link between Old Testament theology and the canon implies paying attention to the whole Old Testament. A famous shortcoming of the biblical theology movement was its neglect of the wisdom literature, a corollary of its stress on God's acts in history. Both neglect and stress reflected the theological, philosophical, historical, and cultural circumstances of the mid-twentieth century in the West. The subsequent reaction that has led to "a temptation to pan-creationism (like an earlier pan-covenantalism)"[36] also reflects theological, philosophical, historical, and cultural circumstances, along with the necessity for scholars to have something to say that differs from what the previous generation said, and for publishers to have something different to sell. The appropriate response is to acknowledge the culture-relative nature of all our work and pay special attention to theological work issuing from other contexts that may broaden our horizons and enable us to do better justice to the canon as a whole.

In seeking to develop a new biblical theology, Childs indeed urged the recovery of the church's exegetical tradition.[37] By and large and for similar reasons, what is true about the creed is true of this exegetical tradition as expressed in the work of great commentators such as Origen, Augustine, and Luther. The consistency of their christological interpretation means they fairly consistently ignore the Old Testa-

---

35. *Text and Truth* (Grand Rapids: Eerdmans, 1997), 241.

36. Walter Brueggemann, "Jeremiah: *Creatio in Extremis*," in *God Who Creates* (W. S. Towner Festschrift; ed. William P. Brown and S. Dean McBride; Grand Rapids: Eerdmans, 2000), 152–70 (153). Cf. Rolf P. Knierim, "On the Subject of War in the Old Testament and Biblical Theology," in *Reading the Hebrew Bible for a New Millennium* (ed. Wonil Kim et al.; 2 vols.; Harrisburg, Pa.: Trinity Press International, 2000), 1:73–88 (79).

37. See *Biblical Theology in Crisis*, 139–47.

ment's inherent meaning. But there is one connection in which such a recovery is desirable. Premodern commentators knew they were studying documents that were designed to be a resource or a means of grace, ones that made statements about God, not merely about Israel's faith. For these commentators, writing a commentary and preaching a sermon were not such different enterprises. Modern commentaries are short on sentences beginning with the word "God" or even containing it. Old Testament theology studies the faith of the Old Testament, not the faith of Israel, and it studies the one in whom Israel had faith (or was supposed to have faith), not merely the faith statements that Israel made. Ada María Isasi-Díaz comments on Psalm 137, "for us Christians, the important thing regarding this psalm, and all of the Bible, is that it gives voice to an authentic faith-experience."[38] Rather, the important thing about the Bible is what it says about God.

In origin, biblical criticism urged a critical stance with regard to traditional assumptions about scriptural interpretation and traditional uses of Scripture, and this continues to be a necessity if we are to let the canon be the canon. Feminist criticism offers an example as it has raised questions about traditional interpretation of Genesis 1–3 and about books such as Ruth and the Song of Songs. Postcolonial interpretation has exposed the unbalanced way Old Testament theology made much of the exodus without facing the theological and ethical issues raised by the Israelite occupation of Canaan. Again, the Old Testament sets some openness to other cultures alongside its insistence on the decisive importance of what Yahweh was doing in Israel, but in the modern missionary movement, set in the context of the European nations carving out their empires, Christian faith was identified with Western culture, and the open aspect to the Old Testament's attitudes was ignored in favor of the exclusivist one.[39]

That does also show how modern readers, too, import their own categories into Scripture, as do postmodern readers, and whereas criticism began by questioning the church's tradition of interpretation, it now must proceed by questioning criticism itself. Yet the modern tradition's commitment to understanding what texts were communicating in their historical context does give it the potential of discovering some more of what the Holy Spirit was communicating through these texts when inspiring them. A potential of our postmodern context is the possibility of recovering the strength of the premodern tradition while holding onto the strength of the modern tradition and letting each safeguard against the other's weakness.[40]

Musa Dube expresses approval of Christian readings of Scripture that "reject the privileging of biblical texts and religions above other cultural perceptions of

38. "'By the Rivers of Babylon,'" in *Reading from This Place* (ed. Fernando F. Segovia and Mary Ann Tolbert; 2 vols.; Minneapolis: Fortress, 1995), 1:149–63 (151).

39. Cf. Kwesi A. Dickson, *Uncompleted Mission* (Maryknoll, N.Y.: Orbis, 1991).

40. Contrast Childs's implicit attitude, according to John Barton, that historical criticism has been "one long bad dream": see "Canon in Old Testament Interpretation," in *In Search of True Wisdom* (R. E. Clements Festschrift; ed. Edward Ball; JSOTSup 300; Sheffield: Sheffield Academic Press, 1999), 37–52 (38); and see further chapter 2 above.

reality."[41] That open stance taken by the Wisdom literature to other peoples' learning provides a warrant for African, Asian, and Native American readers "reading biblical stories together with their native ones." But it is a different matter when this involves "a refusal to accord the biblical text the final authority it claims for itself to suppress differences."[42] The issue is not whether there is insight in other cultures' stories, or whether reading in the context of another culture helps us identify what texts have seemed to say but do not actually say, or whether they have "served imperializing nations." It is that the texts "propound imperializing ideology."[43] The Bible claims the authority to suppress differences; Dube refuses to grant it this authority, on the basis of the prior decision that colonial cultures and their stories and traditions have as much validity as imperial cultures and their stories and traditions. Yahweh's sole deity then becomes just one culture's perception (though actually it is hardly an imperial one; only for a few decades was Israel ever an imperial power, whereas for most of the Old Testament story, Egypt, Canaan, Philistia, Assyria, Babylon, Persia, and Greece are the imperial powers and Israel is resisting them—or not). Thinking in terms of Old Testament theology and the canon implies assuming the Old Testament is right in affirming that Yahweh alone is God and right in its understanding of God, and that we properly privilege the biblical narrative in relation to other cultural perceptions of reality because Yahweh was indeed undertaking something in Israel that was of supreme significance for every culture.

4. Old Testament Theology Recognizes a Canon within the Canon

The canon is the canon; but Old Testament theology recognizes that there are canons within the canon. There is something systematically ambiguous about talk of biblical criticism. It evaluates interpretations on the basis of the text itself to check whether they are imposed on the text, presupposing "the principle of charity," the assumption that the text makes sense.[44] But it comes to apply its critical principle to the text itself in light of our own (supposed) understanding of the real truth. Critical approaches work on the basis of having their principle of criticism, their canon, within themselves. Both modern and postmodern, both liberal and evangelical perspectives make themselves the criterion for truth. Readers recognize that the Scriptures are time-conditioned or culture-relative but not that they are themselves time-conditioned and culture-relative.

In describing "The Family in First Temple Israel," Joseph Blenkinsopp begins by noting that the biblical source material has the character of *"canonical* texts." He then

---

41. *Postcolonial Feminist Interpretation of the Bible* (St. Louis: Chalice, 2000), 195.
42. Ibid., 108.
43. Ibid.
44. See Willard Van Orman Quine, *Word and Object* (Cambridge, Mass.: MIT, 1960), 59; cf. Halbertal, *People of the Book*, 27–28.

infers (perhaps to one's surprise) that this means their stance was "dictated by the agenda and ideology of those who put the collection together."[45] He is thus inclined to a suspicious reading of the Old Testament regulations about the family and comments (for instance) on the ruling in Deuteronomy 22:23–29 about a woman who has been raped that "the law's indifference to her interests in general is too clearly in evidence to require comment."[46]

Whose interests do the regulations in the Torah serve? They are indeed sometimes open to a variety of interpretations in this connection, and thus to a variety of evaluations. The rules about stealing animals in Exodus 22:1–4 [21:37–22:3] can be read as in favor of the rich or the poor. They might protect the rich and penalize the poor who borrow and then cannot pay back; "this regulation may have been an important source for slavery."[47] But they might protect the poor from having anyone (including the rich) appropriate the animals that are crucial to their livelihood. Something similar is true about that ruling concerning rape. The point "too clearly in evidence to require comment" for Blenkinsopp is not at all clear to the commentators on Deuteronomy; according to one of the most rigorously historical-critical of them, the regulation "protects" the woman.[48] At the same time, it does also protect her father's interests, and regulations in the Torah commonly balance interests thus. It is the nature of law to incorporate such compromise.

Psalm 37 likewise can be read as a profound assertion of the status quo, a self-affirmation of the landed class, but also as an act of radical hope by the disenfranchised, who are confident that current unjust land distribution cannot endure and that the land eventually will be reassigned to "the righteous."[49] Qohelet can be read as reflecting the attitudes of the powerful and comfortable or as a call to oppressed people "to resist the fascinations of the dominant culture."[50]

It is therefore appropriate to utilize a suspicious hermeneutic in reading the canonical writings and to ask whose interests they serve. Identifying with the fact that the Jewish and Christian communities gave them canonical status does not exclude a suspicious reading. Jesus models this in commenting on the regulation concerning divorce. Moses gave it, Jesus says, because of people's stubbornness. It does not correspond to the way God made humanity at the beginning (Mark 10:1–9). Within Scripture, then, one can distinguish between God's will as it goes back to creation, and ways in which Scripture's teaching allows for human waywardness. God did not

---

45. In Leo Perdue et al., *Families in Ancient Israel* (Louisville: Westminster John Knox, 1997), 48–103 (see 49). Cf. J. G. McConville's comments in *God and Earthly Power* (London and New York: Clark, 2006), 3.

46. Ibid., 63.

47. So Frank Crüsemann, *The Torah* (Minneapolis: Fortress; Edinburgh: Clark, 1996), 164.

48. A. D. H. Mayes, *Deuteronomy* (London: Oliphants, 1979; Grand Rapids: Eerdmans, 1981), 313.

49. Walter Brueggemann, *The Book That Breathes New Life* (Minneapolis: Fortress, 2005), 160. Cf. Walter Brueggemann, *The Psalms and the Life of Faith* (Minneapolis: Fortress, 1995), 235–57.

50. Jorge Pixley, "Christian Biblical Theology and the Struggle against Oppression," in *Jews, Christians, and the Theology of the Hebrew Scriptures* (ed. Alice Ogden Bellis and Joel S. Kaminsky; Atlanta: SBL, 2000), 173–77 (175).

merely reveal to Israel the ultimate divine standards and then leave Israel on its own when it failed to live up to them, with the result (for instance) that women who were thrown out by their husbands were left with no evidence of their status (an issue of continuing significance for the Jewish community).[51] Notwithstanding what was so from the beginning, marriages are going to break down, and in a patriarchal world women are going to suffer. God therefore inspires a regulation to protect them from some of the consequences of their husbands' behavior.

The tension between how things were at the beginning and how things are when one makes allowance for human stubbornness runs through the Torah and the rest of the Scriptures. God's allowing for human stubbornness in the New Testament appears in its acceptance of Roman slavery, an institution that stands in much greater tension with how things were at the beginning than the temporary debt servitude of which the Old Testament speaks. In principle one can plot all the Scriptures' instructions on an axis between how things were at the beginning and how they are in light of human stubbornness. God is always concerned to pull us toward realizing the creation vision but is always starting where we are.

So there is a canon within the canon. This does not mean the outer canon ceases to be canon; we must not make the canon within the canon into the canon.[52] The material that makes allowance for human stubbornness still has Moses' authority. It is still part of Scripture that is useful for equipping the Christian community to do good work (2 Tim 3:16).

Crucially, in Mark 9 the basis for identifying the canon within the canon comes from within the Scriptures themselves, not from Jesus or from his culture. Blenkinsopp is sometimes explicit that his suspicious reading of Scripture takes as its criterion the convictions of "most modern readers."[53] Recognizing the canonical status of the Scriptures opens up the possibility of learning things that can help refine and broaden our attitudes as people who are so limited through being modern readers. Questions about ideology that generate a suspicious interpretation can coexist with a consensual interpretation that assumes the community was right to accept these texts into its Scriptures. That may also make it appropriate to prefer interpretations that cohere with this assumption.[54] A critical stance is finally subordinate to a consensual, compliant stance. Paradoxically, that is more likely to achieve one of the stated aims of ideological interpretation, which is that interpretation should be ethical.[55] If we assume ahead of time that our perspective as modern people is right and evaluate

---

51. See, e.g., Judith Plaskow, *The Coming of Lilith* (Boston: Beacon, 2005), 147–51.

52. I. Lönning, *"Kanon im Kanon"* (Oslo: Universitets Forlaget, 1972), 271; cf. John Goldingay, *Models for Interpretation of Scripture* (Grand Rapids: Eerdmans; Carlisle: Paternoster, 1995; Toronto: Clements, 2004), 106.

53. E.g., *Families in Ancient Israel*, 84.

54. Contrast Itumeleng Mosala's observation, "traditionally the biblical texts that condemn or demand relief from debt and indeed slavery are generously appraised by the readers of the texts" ("The Politics of Debt and the Liberation of the Scriptures," in *Tracking the Tribes of Yahweh* [ed. Roland Boer; London and New York: Sheffield Academic Press, 2002], 77–84 [80]). This is apparently a bad thing.

55. See. e.g., Elisabeth Schüssler Fiorenza, "The Ethics of Interpretation," *JBL* 107 (1988): 3–17.

the Scriptures in light of it, this inhibits us from changing or becoming more ethical. If we assume that the Scriptures have a positive ethical contribution to make to our understanding and lives, this opens us to change and ethical development.

Old Testament theology recognizes canons within the canon, but does not let them become the canon.

5. Old Testament Theology Treats the First Part of the Canon as Significant in Its Own Right

Old Testament theology treats the first part of the canon as significant in its own right. It does not reinterpret or reevaluate its theological insights in light of the New Testament. Specifically, it does not reinterpret Old Testament texts in light of the way the New Testament uses them. The New Testament's use of Old Testament texts has no necessary significance for what Old Testament theology does with these texts.

As the psalm most often quoted in the New Testament, Psalm 110 provides an example.[56] In light of the New Testament use of the psalm, traditional Christian exegesis took it as a messianic prophecy that Jesus fulfilled.[57] Interpreters now more commonly justify this understanding on the basis of the psalm's having come to be interpreted messianically in Second Temple Judaism. One would never guess the messianic interpretation from the psalm itself; it can only be read into it.

That also applies to a current "canonical" approach to the Psalter, which argues that in the context of the Psalter, which reached its canonical form in the Second Temple period when Israel had no kings, the psalms about the Israelite king would already be understood messianically. While it is the case that some people who used these psalms could have understood them messianically, this is by no means the only option in the Second Temple period. People who were familiar with Isaiah 55:3–5, for instance, a passage that reworks phrases from Psalm 89, could reckon that psalms about the king now apply to the whole people. The preexilic kings are also important in the Second Temple narrative of Chronicles, and there is no indication that this is a messianically inclined work. If Chronicles or the Psalter were a messianically inclined work, one would expect some concrete indication of this, but there is none, despite the fact that in other respects the Psalter shows much reworking of earlier psalms and psalm-like material (as Chronicles does in relation to Kings). We know from the *Psalms of Solomon* that Second Temple times produced messianic psalms, but the canonical Psalter does not contain any.

When Yahweh spoke the words in Psalm 110 in Old Testament times, people could not have been expected to understand them as the New Testament does.[58]

---

56. The paragraphs that follow utilize material in John Goldingay, *Psalms 90–150* (Grand Rapids: Baker Academic, 2008).

57. Derek Kidner continues to argue trenchantly for this understanding (*Psalms 73–150* [London and Downers Grove, Ill.: InterVarsity, 1975], 391–92).

58. Herbert W. Bateman thus prefers to describe the psalm as "typological-prophetic" ("Psalm 110:1 and the New Testament," *BSac* 149 [1992]: 438–53 [453]). Brock (*Singing the Ethos of God*,

The relationship between New Testament and Old Testament text is then the one that often obtains. In light of Jesus' coming, the Holy Spirit inspires people to see significance in the Old Testament that was not there before.

J. L. Mays, for instance, declares that "the psalm lets us see the enthronement of Jesus at the right hand of God as the great theological reality of the Christological present. . . . It insists that the office of Jesus concerns nations and rulers." It "puts special emphasis on the command of Jesus to the church to make disciples of all nations."[59] That is so when we look to the psalm for illumination on Jesus, but the text's inherent theological implications do not lie in its application to Jesus. That is to ignore its meaning. Its application to Jesus is part of New Testament study. For Old Testament theology, the question is, What did the Holy Spirit offer Old Testament believers in this text?[60] The psalm declares that Yahweh is on the side of the Israelite king and is involved in politics and history on that basis. Yahweh uses the king in governing the nations and acts in history with anger, energy, and violence. The king (and implicitly his people) is encouraged to live his life in light of ways Yahweh has made this work out and in light of promises Yahweh has made about how it will work out. In Israel's history that usually means believing against the odds.

Then, the particular distinctive motif of this psalm is that the king is also priest. There are things that are achieved by such combining of powers in one person. Politics and war are not allowed to escape from the context of the people's relationship with God, and the people's relationship with God is not allowed to escape from politics and war. These theological insights are unfashionable in the context of modernity and postmodernity in which Western Christians work out what they reckon is a Christian view on such topics. That Christian view often corresponds to the secular view; there is nothing very Christian about it. Interpreting the psalm in light of its use in the New Testament enables readers to neutralize its insights.

The idea of Yahweh being on the Israelite king's side against Israel's enemies does have to be set in the context of the psalm's presupposition that the enemies are resistant to Yahweh's purpose and that Israel is committed to it. But canonical interpretation must mean letting different parts of Scripture have their say, not silencing some by others that we prefer. God really was speaking and acting in Old Testament times, and therefore we should not let what God subsequently said and did overshadow what God was then saying and doing. Canonization can encourage readers to flatten the meaning of the texts in the canon, to reinterpret the different books so that they form a harmonious whole that agrees with the views of people

---

112) similarly speaks of "a logical continuity bordering on synonymity between the terms 'prophecy' and 'prefiguring'" in Augustine's interpretation of the OT.

59. *Psalms* (Louisville: John Knox, 1994), 354–55. Postcolonial interpretation would note that linking Ps 110 and Matt 28:20 would provide useful support for the historical collocation of imperialism and mission.

60. Notwithstanding his concern for seeing OT texts in light of their use in the NT, Childs makes this point in a study of Ps 8 in the context of the Christian canon in *Biblical Theology in Crisis*, 162–63.

who recognize the canon.[61] This temptation is to be resisted. (I sometimes think that in my students' eyes, their professor's job is to reassure them that Scripture does not say anything that does not fit what they already think. People of liberal Christian views do not need this reassurance; they can simply reckon that Scripture is wrong. Evangelicals cannot do that, so they have to change Scripture's meaning, to reach the same end of being able to continue to think what they have always thought.)[62]

There is a thematic as well as a textual aspect to the way the New Testament reinterprets the Old Testament. The New Testament takes Old Testament themes and uses them as metaphors for what Christ does. Through the prophets, Yahweh made various promises to Israel. In large part, these are reaffirmations of fundamental promises going back to Abraham, promises of receiving a land, becoming a flourishing people, and being a means of blessing for the world. As a result of Israel's desire for human kings and of David's desire for a fixed sanctuary, two further divine commitments get added to those original ones. The promises that appear in books such as Isaiah, Jeremiah, and Ezekiel are then substantially reaffirmations of those five fundamental promises of land, peoplehood, blessing, sanctuary, and monarchy.

The New Testament takes those promises and reworks them in expounding what Christ achieves. He is not literally Israel's anointed king, but he is that metaphorically. He is not literally a temple and neither is the church, but metaphorically his body is a temple and metaphorically the Corinthian church is God's temple. Christ is not literally a priest and his death is not literally a sacrifice, but metaphorically that is so.

To speak in terms of metaphor is not to imply that there is something unreal or artificial or untrue about what is said. Using metaphor is crucial to understanding the real significance of things, particularly new things. So when God becomes incarnate in Christ and when the incarnate one lets himself be crucified and when God becomes a reality in the life of a Gentile community such as the Corinthian church, metaphor enables the church to understand the significance of these new and unfamiliar realities by looking at them in light of realities they are already familiar with. This is the way the Holy Spirit inspires the church's understanding of Christ's significance.

But this metaphorical use of Old Testament motifs does not undo the reality of the Holy Spirit's inspiration of the original Old Testament promises, and that is the subject of Old Testament theology. When God made promises to Abraham about land, nationhood, and a ministry of blessing, and then made promises to David about monarchy and temple, this indicated that all these realities are important in their own right.

Peter Stuhlmacher urges a biblical theology of the New Testament that involves looking at the message of the New Testament in light of the Old Testament,[63] but he does not suggest that this will do as Old Testament theology or as biblical theology

---

61. Cf. Halbertal, *People of the Book*, 23–24.
62. See further chapter 5 above (section 8).
63. See, e.g., *How to Do Biblical Theology* (Allison Park, Pa.: Pickwick, 1995).

(period). The biggest significance of the work of Walter Brueggemann is that he takes the whole canon with the utmost seriousness. He is not fond of talk in terms of scriptural authority or of the canon, and he can read his own priorities into texts like the rest of us, but he shows a relentless insistence on trying to listen to every text rather than ignoring it or silencing it by means of other texts.[64] In other words, he is an Old Testament theologian who works in light of the canon and who treats the first part of the canon as significant in its own right. "Old Testament theological articulation does not conform to established church faith," and therefore the responsibility of Christian Old Testament theology is "to present to the ecclesial community not only those readings that confirm church theology, but also (and perhaps especially) those that clash with, challenge, and undermine seemingly settled church theology."[65]

6. Old Testament Theology Expects to Find the Two Parts of the Canon Illumine Each Other

A converse of the declaration that the canonicity of the Old Testament means it must not be subsumed under the New Testament is that thinking in terms of Old Testament theology does imply that Old Testament faith and New Testament faith are variants on the same reality, so that Old Testament theology expects to find that the two parts of the canon illumine each other.

Whereas the expressions "The Torah, the Prophets, and the Writings" and "the Hebrew Bible" rather imply that these collections of Scriptures stand on their own, the expression "Old Testament" (like my preferred expression "First Testament") presupposes that they are part of a larger canon. Doing Old Testament theology in light of the canon means seeing the Old Testament thus. The Old Testament and the New Testament speak in similar terms of God and of God's activity in the world. They are a two-part DVD portraying not two different persons but the same person in different situations and from different angles.

It is a common Christian assumption that there is a contrast between Old Testament and New Testament. The Old Testament God is a God of wrath, the New Testament God is a God of love. The Old Testament teaches salvation by works, the New Testament salvation by grace. I will come back to the first of those misapprehensions after commenting on the second in light of some observations by Paul. At the end of his preliminary exposition of his gospel in Romans 1–3, he has to face the question whether what he has argued is biblical. Does it fit the Scriptures? He knows that if he cannot establish this, his claims about his gospel collapse. If it is unscriptural, it cannot be true. So the question is, What does the Scripture say? (Rom 4:3). He then shows that God established a relationship with Abraham on the basis of God's gracious promise and Abraham's response of trust. This relationship became a reality before and independently of Abraham's observing the rite of circumcision,

---

64. See further chapter 16 (section 2) above.
65. *Theology of the Old Testament* (Minneapolis: Fortress, 1997), 107 (the first quotation is italicized).

and a fortiori before God gave Israel the gift of other aspects of its religious life such as Exodus-Deuteronomy prescribe. This response of trust indeed issues in a life of obedience, as Genesis 22:18 and 26:5 observe (and compare James 2:21–24), but this does not affect Paul's point.

Paul's argument issued from a hermeneutical process whereby something that happened to Paul suggested a new insight on the relationship between God and Israel, which led Paul to reread the Scriptures to try to make sense of his new insight. He now saw the significance of an aspect of the Torah, the narrative sequence of Genesis 12–15 and both Genesis 17 and the Sinai story, which he had not seen before.

His argument seems exegetically sound. He thus illustrates the way a new experience or act of God or question can indeed open up exegetical understanding. The relationship between exegesis and appropriation is a two-way, conversational one, not a one-way movement whereby we first do exegesis and then do application. Reading the Old Testament in light of the gospel (in light of the New Testament, to be anachronistic) turns out to illumine the Old Testament. While such reading can involve finding in the Old Testament a significance that in itself it does not have, in this case Paul does not rework the significance of the Old Testament; he enables one to read the Old Testament with more exegetical acumen. In theory, one might achieve this insight without the help of the Christ event, but the Christ event actually was the ultimate outworking (as opposed to reworking) of the way God dealt with Abraham, so it is not surprising that it helps to clarify the Abraham story's intrinsic nature.

Something similar is true regarding the God of wrath and the God of love. In Christ, God submitted to crucifixion by humanity and then came back to a renewed life, declining to let even humanity's execution overwhelm God's desire to be in relationship with humanity. God thus paid the price for humanity's sinfulness, made the sacrifice that dealt with that sin.

Did this mean the God of wrath had become the God of love, with that changeableness that Jack Miles traces within the Old Testament?[66] The New Testament does not think this way. Or had God always been the God of love but had concealed this through Old Testament times because of a commitment to progressive revelation? The New Testament also does not think this way. It rather sees what God did in Christ as the logical culmination to the Old Testament story. The cross makes one look back at the Old Testament to look for the footsteps of the crucified God there; and one finds them. In light of where the story of God and the world reaches its climax, one can read the earlier part of the story more clearly and see more clearly the significance of some of the scriptural comments on it.

In the Old Testament, God does from time to time act in wrath in relation to the world and to Israel, but these acts appear in the context of a story that begins and continues only because God acts in love. If the Old Testament God were essentially wrathful, the Noah flood would be a model for the way God relates to the world

66. See *God: A Biography*.

rather than a once-off event whose theological significance is precisely the fact that God has looked in the eye the logical possibility and moral appropriateness of destroying the world and has affirmed a commitment not to do so, precisely "because the planning of humanity's heart is evil from its youth" (Gen 8:21).[67] The story of humanity and of Israel continues despite their waywardness, because commitment (*hesed*, the Hebrew equivalent to *agapē*), not wrath, is the dominant principle on which God works. Like a father or mother in relation to their children, God "carries" Israel's sin (*nasa'*; the conventional translation "forgives" obscures the idea). Instead of making Israel carry it, bear responsibility for it, God does so, not in the sense of accepting responsibility for the sin happening but in the sense of accepting responsibility for dealing with it, for the consequences of it. If I wrong my wife, I might expect to pay the price; she might walk out on me. When Israel wronged God, God paid the price; God did not walk out on Israel. At least, God never definitively did that; God might storm out for a while, but always came back. Karl Barth puts it like this: the incarnation and the cross involve Christ going into the far country, like the prodigal son, in taking the form of sinful humanity. But "the God of the Old Testament . . . is already on the way into the far country to the extent that it is an unfaithful people to whom He gives and maintains His faithfulness."[68]

Love is nearer the heart of God than wrath or judgment. God first expresses the point at Sinai in that self-description that explains how it is that Yahweh stays with Israel despite its rebellion. Yahweh is characterized by compassion, grace, long-temperedness, commitment, steadfastness, a willingness to carry waywardness, rebellion, and failure, and by not remitting punishment (Exod 34:6–7). The self-description does not clarify the relationship between the long list of "positive" characteristics and the footnote describing the "negative" ones.[69] Other Old Testament passages do so. Isaiah 28:21 describes punishing Israel as "strange" or "foreign" to Yahweh. Yahweh does it, but it does not come naturally. Hosea 11 describes Yahweh as contemplating acting in wrath but resisting the inclination to do so; it is precisely because of being the holy one that Yahweh will not act in wrath. Lamentations 3:33 declares that when Yahweh afflicts or grieves people, it is not "from the heart" (translations have "not willingly"). Yahweh is capable of acting in wrath and does so, but it is not as "natural" to Yahweh as acting in compassion and mercy. Justice and love are not equally balanced in God.

The God who is inclined to carry human waywardness, who is characterized by compassion, who is prepared to act in judgment but prefers to avoid doing so, is

---

67. Not "even though" this is so (TNIV); the preposition is *ki*.

68. *Church Dogmatics*, IV/1 (repr.; Edinburgh: T&T Clark, 1961), 171. Barth later (279) describes Israel's history as "one great series of dark and heavy judgments on the part of God," so that "Israel is a people which is constantly judged by God." After its arrival in the land, are there any such dark and heavy judgments apart from the fall of Ephraim and the fall of Judah? (Even in Judges, trouble affects only individual clans or groups of clans.) Perhaps one gets that impression because the prophets issue many dark and heavy warnings of judgment, but it is those two events that are the chief fulfillment of them all.

69. Translations help it along: see, e.g., the "yet" in NRSV, TNIV, and NJPS.

exactly the God who lets people crucify him and thus pays the price for their waywardness with the aim of keeping in relationship with them (though if they insist on holding onto responsibility for their waywardness, they may do so). Looking back at the Old Testament from the New Testament makes it possible to see the pattern in these aspects of the way Yahweh acts and speaks, and the way people speak about Yahweh, which we might otherwise miss.

It is the New Testament that may help us see that in the Old Testament, but it is something that is actually there, something one can ask any interpreter to see. In principle it should be the case that Jews and Christians (and atheists or agnostics, Jewish or Gentile) interpret the Old Testament in the same way, even when they are talking about the theological implications of the text. We do not interpret canonical texts by means of different methods from ones we use for other texts, methods that involve bringing something from outside that gives us an interpretation no one else could possibly reach. I do not use a different approach for interpreting Ecclesiasticus and Proverbs, or for Judith and Esther, or for Psalms 151–155 and Psalms 1–150. I have special expectations in reading Proverbs, Esther, and Psalms 1–150, and a commitment to being open to whatever I find there.[70] Indeed, "the proper reading of Scripture depends on a repentant self-effacement before the converting power of God and his Word." Thus the problem about reading Scripture is not technical but spiritual and moral: "we refuse as sinners to be spoken to . . . and desire to live from our own word." But the process of discovering what is there is not different. Rolf Rendtorff observes, "The Hebrew Bible is itself a theological book. . . . The Bible does not become theological through interpretation through a later-elaborated theology, be it rabbinic or Christian; rather, it is possible and necessary to find the theological ideas and messages of the biblical texts themselves."[71]

The whole Old Testament "is God-breathed and useful for teaching, for rebuke, for correction, for training in righteousness, so that anyone who belongs to God may be ready, made ready for every good work" (2 Tim 3:16). God grant that Old Testament theology done in light of the canon may contribute to that.

---

70. Brock, *Singing the Ethos of God*, 63, 64, summarizing John Webster, *Word and Church* (Edinburgh: T&T Clark, 2001), 96–97, summarizing Karl Barth and Dietrich Bonhoeffer. I am not sure whether this is the kind of thing that John Sailhamer means by a sacred hermeneutic, different from the hermeneutic one applies to other texts (*Introduction to Old Testament Theology: A Canonical Approach* [Grand Rapids: Zondervan, 1995], 227–37).

71. *Canon and Theology* (Minneapolis: Fortress, 1993), 40–41.

PART 4

Concerning the Torah, the Prophets, and the Writings

18

How May We Interpret the Pentateuch?

Hermeneutics and exegesis have complementary concerns within the task of interpretation.[1] In exegesis we focus on a text's meaning in itself and aim to recover its significance for its authors and their hearers. We thus try to put on one side our own concerns and interests and concentrate on the text's objective meaning, without asking after any relevance for ourselves. Questions about hermeneutics begin from the opposite focus. In studying a text, we acknowledge that we are not merely interested in its meaning in itself but in its significance for us, and we consciously study it in light of our interests. These interests, and the commitments and experiences that we bring to the text, affect what we come to see in it. They circumscribe objective understanding, but they also contribute to it. One reason for this is that their concern with the text's appropriation in our lives corresponds to the text's own concern. "The Bible always addresses itself to the time of interpretation; one cannot understand it except by appropriating it anew."[2]

This chapter considers ten common sets of interests or commitments or convictions that both contribute to an understanding of the Pentateuch and circumscribe it in this way.

1. Christological Interpretation

According to Luke 24:27, on the way to Emmaus Jesus interpreted the things about himself in all the Scriptures, beginning with Moses. We do not know which passages

---

1. First published in *Dictionary of the Old Testament: Pentateuch* (ed. D. W. Baker and T. D. Alexander; Downers Grove, Ill., and Leicester: InterVarsity), 387–401.
2. Gerald Bruns, "Midrash and Allegory," in *The Literary Guide to the Bible* (ed. Robert Alter and Frank Kermode; Cambridge, Mass.: Harvard University Press, 1987), 625–46 (627–28).

in the Pentateuch he referred to, though elsewhere the New Testament gives us examples of such interpretation. The Son of Man must be lifted up as the serpent was lifted up by Moses in the wilderness (John 3:14; see Num 21:9). The rock from which Israel drank in the wilderness was Christ (1 Cor 10:4; see, e.g., Exod 17:6). Christ is a priest after the order of Melchizedek, the priest-king of Jerusalem (Heb 7; see Gen 14:18–20).

The chief means of christological interpretation of the Pentateuch is typology. In its full form, typology involves three assumptions. The first is that there is a consistency about God's acts that makes it appropriate to look for regular patterns in them and to picture a coming event in light of a previous one. The second is that when an event recurs, it takes more splendid form than the first event did. Both these features can be seen within the First Testament. The Pentateuch itself uses verbs to describe Abraham's journey to Egypt and back that it will later use to describe Israel's "going down" and "coming up" from Egypt (see Gen 12:10–13:1). It thus hints that Abraham's journey foreshadows Israel's. Isaiah 40–55 implies that the deliverance from Babylon will repeat the deliverance from Egypt, only this time people will not need the haste they needed before (see Isa 52:12).

When the New Testament interprets the Pentateuch typologically, it adds a third assumption, that the literal, material reality now becomes a symbol for something in the nonmaterial realm or in a nonliteral sense. The literal rock with its literal water becomes a metaphorical rock offering metaphorical water. The Pentateuch required the literal sacrifice of a literal animal by a literal priest in a material shrine. Christ is a not a literal sacrifice or lamb or priest in a material shrine, but taking these literal realities as metaphors helps Christians gain an understanding of the significance of Christ's death.

In subsequent centuries, further pentateuchal texts came to be interpreted christologically. Christ was understood to be the woman's seed of Genesis 3:15 and the one to whom the ruler's staff belongs in Genesis 49:10. This further aids Christian understanding of Jesus. He is the one through whom the snake's work is undone and the descendant of Judah who rules over the people of God as a whole. Christological interpretation of Genesis 49:10 was taking up Jewish messianic interpretation of the text. In the same way, Balaam's prophecy of a star coming out of Jacob (Num 24:17) was understood in a messianic sense before and after Christ and thus would naturally be applied to Jesus.

Christological interpretation thus starts from the knowledge that Christ is Son of God and Savior and that his people is God's chosen people. After New Testament times, christological interpretation came to be used to attempt to *prove* to people who did not believe in Jesus that he was the Messiah. It is doubtful whether this is a New Testament practice. The aim of christological interpretation was to help the community that believed in Jesus to understand more clearly who Jesus was, not to convince the non-Christian community that it should believe in him.[3]

---

3. See further chapter 14 (section 2) above.

The classic modern exposition of a christological approach to the Pentateuch is the work of Wilhelm Vischer. Vischer opens his study with the observation, "the Old Testament tells us *what* the Christ is; the New, *who* he is."[4] He goes on to declare that "all the words of the Old Testament look beyond themselves to the One in the New in whom alone they are true." If this is so, one might infer that christological interpretation will be part of all First Testament exegesis. But we have noted that the New Testament utilizes christological interpretation more to throw light on the significance of Christ than to throw light on the Pentateuch. In what sense does it fulfill the latter task?

It does this not by revealing unexpected meanings in the text itself but by setting the text in a broader context. There are few hints in the Pentateuch that an individual ruler (still less an incarnate Son of God who is crucified and rises from the dead) will eventually fulfill a crucial role in achieving God's purpose in the world, but in the event this is what actually happened, and it is always the case that earlier episodes in a story need to be read in light of later episodes and that their broader significance emerges in this context. By seeing the Pentateuch's story as one that comes to its climax with Christ, we gain a wider understanding of the significance of creation, the promise to Israel's ancestors, the deliverance from Egypt, the events at Sinai, the journey through the wilderness, and the events in the plains of Moab.

We can illustrate the point from either end of this story. First, Genesis 1 tells us of God's plan to rule the world by means of human beings made in the divine image. This intention was not wholly fulfilled. Describing Christ as bearing the divine image, in a fuller sense than human beings do, helps us see how the complete fulfillment of God's purpose in Genesis 1 is guaranteed. Second, we know that Christ is the "end" of the law (Rom 10:4), though that expression is an elusive one. Certainly Christ fulfilled the expectations of the Pentateuch, brought about the fulfillment of that which the Pentateuch itself served, and also brought to an end the time when the Torah was binding on the people of God. This awareness relativizes the significance of the reformulating of the Torah in Deuteronomy.

2. Doctrinal Interpretation

A major concern of Paul's was to establish the true relationship between divine grace and human obedience to God. Paul perceived that in Genesis God calls Abraham and gives him promises that had no preconditions—indeed, they had no post-conditions (see, e.g., Rom 5). A theological question that arose from Paul's attempt to work out the implications of the gospel thus led to his articulating a significant insight on the text of the Pentateuch.[5] At a subsequent stage in the argument of Romans, Paul comes to discuss the further theological question of the place of Israel in God's purpose,

---

4. Wilhelm Vischer, *The Witness of the Old Testament to Christ: Volume 1* (London: Lutterworth, 1949), 7. (Only volume 1 was translated into English.)

5. See further chapter 17 (section 6) above.

and what came to be known as the doctrine of election (see Rom 9). Again, his question leads him to significant articulation of the intrinsic theological implications of Genesis and of the story of Pharaoh's hardening in Exodus.

Over subsequent centuries, Christians came to interpret the Pentateuch in light of doctrinal convictions expressed in the Christian tradition as it developed over those centuries. The most subversive instance is the effect of the "rule for the faith," the outline of Christian doctrine that came to be embodied in the Apostles' Creed.[6] This allows no theological significance to the First Testament beyond the story of creation. It has been devastatingly effective in silencing the First Testament and marginalizing the place of Israel in the church's thinking.

Under the influence of Greek thought, Christian tradition came to emphasize that God was omniscient or all-knowing, omnipresent or present everywhere, and omnipotent or all-powerful. This leads to reinterpretation of the Pentateuch. There God asks questions (e.g., Gen 3:9, 11, 13). God discovers things, experiences frustration, and has regrets that lead to changes of plan (e.g., Gen 6:6–7). God declares the intention to do something and is argued out of the intention (Exod 32). In the Pentateuch, God does have extraordinary knowledge, the capacity to be in many places, and extraordinary power, and God has these in a way equaled by no other being. But the dynamic of its presentation of God's nature, God's activity, and God's relationship with the world came to be obscured when the church gave priority to a stress on God's omniscience, omnipresence, and omnipotence. If that stress is accepted, then the aspects of the Pentateuch just noted cannot be allowed to contribute to its presentation of God. God asks questions, but really knows the answers. God does not really have a change of mind, but only seems to us to do so. Prayer does not make God do anything different from what God already intended.

At a popular level, the God of the Pentateuch is often assumed to be a God of anger rather than love. This doctrinal assumption stands in tension with the fact that in Genesis God is said to be hurt but is never said to be angry. Similarly Leviticus with its regulations for sacrifice never suggests that these relate to God's being angry. Christian theology emphasizes God's being judge and emphasizes legal categories in working out God's relationship with humanity. Sacrifice then satisfies the need for retribution and satisfies God's anger. In reading the teaching about worship in Leviticus, this involves giving extra stress to its concern with sin, as well as introducing legal categories and a link between sacrifice and anger that does not appear in the text.

Christian doctrine understands sin to have come into the world as a result of the malice of a heavenly being, Satan. Revelation 12:9 identifies Satan with "that old serpent," presumably the snake of Genesis 3, and that leads Christians to assume that the snake there is a figure for Satan. This introduces some incoherence into the text, which describes the tempter as one of the creatures that Yahweh God had made. Ironically, Genesis does associate supernatural beings with the world's sinfulness, but it is Genesis

---

6. See further chapter 17 (section 3) above.

6:1–4 that does this, not Genesis 3. Theologically, it is doubtless appropriate for Christian interpretation to see Satan's activity behind the snake's work, and other parts of the First Testament do describe dynamic powers of disorder as snake-like (e.g., Job 26:13; Isa 27:1); Genesis may indeed see the snake as related to such powers of disorder. But introducing Satan into the text of Genesis 3 obscures not only the exegesis of the text but also its significance for Christian readers and for Christian doctrine.

Christian doctrine also emphasizes that God created the world out of nothing. Christian interpretation of Genesis 1 has therefore wanted to establish that Genesis 1:1–2 made this affirmation. Again, this has skewed understanding of the inherent theological significance of Genesis 1. The fact that it is not clear whether God creates "out of nothing" reflects the fact that Genesis's theological agenda lies elsewhere.

Francis Watson has argued that "an exegesis oriented primarily towards theological issues" should allow the framework of "systematic theology" or "Christian doctrine" to shape theological exegesis.[7] This introduces alien priorities and insights into the text. Like any other hermeneutical starting point, the framework of Christian doctrine may be allowed to open up questions, but must not be allowed to determine answers.

3. Devotional Interpretation

By devotional interpretation I mean an interest in the Pentateuch that focuses on its significance for people's personal lives, and especially for their personal relationship with God. The stories of Abraham, Isaac, Jacob, and Joseph have been the main focus of this interpretation, in partial correspondence to the New Testament's references to these characters. Readers have also found devotional material in Genesis 1–11 and in Exodus, though people who have sought to read through the Pentateuch with this interest in mind have usually flagged by the time they reach the middle of Leviticus. The approach thus shows that the encouragement of individual relationships with God may have been one purpose of the Pentateuch, but that it was evidently not the sole purpose. However, the approach does correspond more closely to the nature of the text than do traditional scholarly interpretations of Genesis 12–50, which have focused predominantly on questions such as the significance of the chapters for questions such as the history of (pre-)Israelite clans and the development of (pre-)Israelite religion.

Two classic Christian devotional interpretations are the works of Frederick B. Meyer and Watchman Nee (Nee To-sheng). Meyer wrote "a devotional commentary" on the whole Pentateuch, *The Five Books of Moses*,[8] and a series of studies of people such as Abraham, Jacob, Joseph, and Moses. Nee wrote an influential exposition of the lives of Abraham, Isaac, and Jacob called *Changed into His Likeness*.[9] Nee suggested

7. E.g., Francis Watson, *Text, Church, and World* (Edinburgh: T&T Clark; Grand Rapids: Eerdmans, 1994), 1.

8. F. B. Meyer, *The Five Books of Moses* (repr.; London: Marshall, 1955).

9. Watchman Nee, *Changed into His Likeness* (London and Fort Washington, Pa.: CLC, 1967).

that the lives of these three men illustrated three ways in which God works in us. More recent Jewish readings of Genesis 12–50 have read these chapters especially for their insight on personal growth in the context of family relationships.[10]

The New Testament suggests two principles of approach for devotional interpretation. In Romans and Galatians, Paul points to a key feature of the life of Israel's ancestors, and specifically of Abraham. The ancestors' relationship with God was based on God's grace. For their part, it was based simply on trust in God. In James and in Hebrews 11, the emphasis lies less on the initiative of grace than on the way in which the response of trust expresses itself in acts of commitment to God and to other people. These two emphases complement each other, and both give access to important features of the stories in Genesis.

Christian devotional reading of Genesis has often been formally committed to the conviction that grace is the founding principle of Christian living. Yet paradoxically, it has had difficulty recognizing that this makes the Pentateuch as relaxed about the weaknesses of Israel's ancestors as it is accepting of the absence of any moral basis for God's choice of Israel (see Deut 7). Indeed, the point needs expressing more radically that that. It is not merely that Genesis records the moral failings of people such as Abraham. It is that it is not very interested in moral evaluation of them at all. Thus, when Luther and Calvin offer different evaluations of Abraham and Sarah's treatment of Hagar in their commentaries on Genesis,[11] it is difficult to say which of them is right, because Genesis does not focus on this question. The mismatch between some devotional interpretation of Genesis and the text of Genesis itself draws attention to the radical nature of Genesis's understanding of God's grace.

Paul also offers what we might call a devotional reading of the stories of Israel's rebellions against God in Exodus and Numbers (see 1 Cor 10:1–11), and this draws our attention to another way in which devotional reading finds itself broadened by the Pentateuch. The Pentateuch is the story of *Israel's* origins. Its focus lies on the community. We have noted that a devotional interpretation could open up the possibility of an appropriately individual reading of Genesis 12–50. But another reason why in other respects devotional reading finds that the Pentateuch does not conform to its expectations is that the Pentateuch instinctively thinks corporately, as modern readers do not. It thus has the potential to rescue devotional reading from some of its individualism.

4. Ethical Interpretation

Instruction about behavior has a prominent place in the Pentateuch, and the First Testament suggests at least three possible approaches to such instruction. These are

---

10. E.g., Naomi H. Rosenblatt and Joshua Horwitz, *Wrestling with Angels: What Genesis Teaches Us about Our Spiritual Identity, Sexuality, and Personal Relationships* (repr.; New York: Dell, 1996); Norman J. Cohen, *Self, Struggle, and Change* (Woodstock, Vt.: Jewish Lights, 1995).

11. See Martin Luther, *Lectures on Genesis* (8 vols.; St. Louis: Concordia, 1958–1970); John Calvin, *Commentaries on the First Book of Moses, Called Genesis* (repr.; Grand Rapids: Eerdmans, n.d.).

exegetical, logical, and prophetic. We may illustrate these from the interpretation of the Sabbath command. The exegetical approach asks about the implications of the actual words in the command. Exactly what counts as work on the Sabbath? Who are the "you" who are to observe the Sabbath? Discovering the answers to such questions puts believers in a position to commit themselves to proper obedience.

The logical approach asks what principles underlie a command. The two versions of the command in Exodus 20:8–11 and Deuteronomy 5:12–15 suggest different principles, the nature of God's creative activity and the nature of God's liberation of Israel. If we understand the principles that a command embodies, we may be better able to understand a command's application in a different setting from the one in which it was uttered.

The prophetic approach is more intuitive in asking what a command means in such a new setting. Within the Pentateuch the idea of a Sabbath day stimulates the idea of a Sabbath year for the land and for the poor (Lev 25; Deut 15). Isaiah 1:12–20 declares that in some contexts the Sabbath may mean nothing because it has ceased to accompany a concern for the needy. In marked contrast, in Amos 8:5 people's opposition to the Sabbath is critiqued because it is a marker of their preoccupation with making money (cf. Neh 13). In Isaiah 56:1–8, observing the Sabbath is the very index of commitment to Yahweh (cf. Isa 58:13; Jer 17:19–27; Ezek 20). In each case, the implication of the Sabbath command seems to be perceived by inspiration rather than by the use of logic. Mere reason could not generate the insight expressed here.

All three approaches to the task of perceiving the ethical significance of the Pentateuch are still used. Jewish people still debate the implications of words such as "work" in the Sabbath command: for instance, does switching on electric current count as kindling a fire (cf. Exod 35:3)? Often the exegetical approach works backwards in the sense that Jewish people or Christians have come to believe that a certain practice is required or forbidden, and exegesis becomes the means of establishing the fact. For Jewish people, the question is, How do we know this?, the question "asked on almost every page of the Talmuds" and usually answered through exegesis of texts.[12]

One example is the conviction that people should not testify for or against their relatives, which came to be inferred (e.g.) from Deuteronomy 24:16, while another example is the variety of bases for reckoning that it is permitted to circumcise on the Sabbath.[13] For Christians, the question particularly arises in connection with largely postbiblical moral questions such as the propriety of homosexual acts or of abortion. Again people seek to justify stances by reference to biblical texts.

Such interpretation does not always work from the conclusion backwards; for instance, Jewish interpreters did not decide a priori to ban milk in coffee, or cheeseburgers. It often works from the text forwards, in this case the text prohibiting cooking a kid in its mother's milk. The threefold repetition of this text in the Pentateuch suggests it must be very important and therefore requires considerable reflection.

12. J. M. Harris, *How Do We Know This?* (Albany: State University of New York, 1995), xi–xii.
13. Ibid., 8–9, 29–32.

The logical approach has been the strength of the work of Christopher Wright on the interpretation of the Torah.[14] He takes individual biddings in the Torah as "paradigms" of the embodiment of God's will in the world. They give us concrete examples of this embodiment. He then suggests a series of questions to ask in their interpretation. Does a given bidding form part of criminal, or civil, or family, or cultic, or compassionate instruction? How does it function in the society and fit into the social system? What is its objective in that context? And how can this objective be implemented in our own social context? Applied to the Sabbath command, the logical approach generates a concern for (for example) the providing of rest for members of one's family, employees, and animals and invites us to ask what the providing of this rest looks like in our context.

The prophetic approach rather asks what other needs the Sabbath command might address in our different social context. One is the workaholism of some Western countries. As far as we can tell, this was not a feature of life in Israel, and the Sabbath command was not designed to address it, but it has the potential to do so. Another example of this prophetic hermeneutic applied to the Pentateuch was the Christian suggestion that the year 2000 should be treated as a jubilee year and marked by the remission of debts from third world countries to Western governments and banks. Neither the marking of a millennial year nor the remitting of national debts is a feature of the jubilee in the Pentateuch, but the suggestion represents a creative, intuitive perception that a practice commended by the Pentateuch could thus address needs in a very different social context.

An ethical issue that modern Western Christians often raise in connection with the Pentateuch is the question of war making. The Pentateuch does raise ethical questions about war making, but it does not see war making in itself as an ethical problem in the way that modern Western Christians do, just as traditional Christianity has not seen war making as a problem in itself. A series of hermeneutical questions are raised by this fact.

One is that modern Western Christians commonly begin their discussion of war from the just war tradition, which has little overlap with the approach of the Pentateuch. The Pentateuch thus has the potential to critique the just war approach in principle and not in detail. A second is that it is mainly Christians since the advent of modernity who have felt that war is inherently an ethical problem. The Pentateuch thus has the potential to critique modernity and help Christians see where they are shaped by the thinking of their age rather than by Scripture. A third is that it is mainly Christians within the main war making nations of the modern world who feel that war is inherently a problem. This suggests that the Pentateuch with its very different stance on this question has the potential to help them reflect on factors that have caused them to have this problem. Presumably the problem lies in their own complicity in war. Feeling uneasy about the Pentateuch's stance on war helps them to feel less guilty about the extent to which their lives are built on it.

14. E.g., Christopher J. H. Wright, *Walking in the Ways of the Lord* (Leicester: Inter-Varsity, 1995), 114–16.

5. Feminist Interpretation

Feminist interpretation starts from women's experience of life, and specifically their experience of being held down and held back by men. The starting point for feminist interpretation of the Pentateuch is the accounts of the origins of man and woman in Genesis 1–3. The fact that the woman was formed after the man and for the man had been taken to imply her intrinsic secondariness. The fact that she was the first to succumb to the snake's temptation had been taken to imply her intrinsic weakness. The declaration that after this the man would rule over the woman had been part of the justification for belief in male "headship."

Feminist interpretation begins from the conviction that women are as fully human as men and are intellectually, morally, and spiritually as strong as men. It then re-examines the biblical text and suggests that the interpretation of Scripture has been affected by patriarchalism. Patriarchalism is the assumption that human life should be lived in light of a hierarchy of relationships that gives authority to certain groups, such as the educated, or the members of certain families, or particularly the men. Patriarchal interpretation ignores the implications of the creation story in Genesis 1, which describes men and women together as made in God's image. It also reads patriarchal convictions into Genesis 2. For instance, there is no reason to infer that the creation of the woman after the man in Genesis 2 implies her inferiority. If this were so, we might have to infer that the creation of human beings after the animals in Genesis 1 implies that the human beings are inferior to the animals. Patriarchal interpretation also reads patriarchal convictions into the story of disobedience in Genesis 3, where the headship of men over women is not a divinely intended principle of creation but a regrettable consequence of human disobedience.

Feminism also resists the notion that women should be defined by their capacity to bear children, and it has thus emphasized the relational implications of the understanding of the complementarity of men and women in Genesis. But Genesis 1–3 does emphasize the significance of procreation, and it seems that here the agenda of Genesis and that of feminism diverge. One issue in the debate over feminist interpretation is thus the question how far the problem lies in patriarchal interpretation of an egalitarian text and how far the text's agenda does not correspond to feminism's.

Feminist interpretation looks more broadly at the way women feature in the pentateuchal narrative. It considers the way God relates to people such as Sarah and Hagar and observes that women play a key role in the initiation of God's deliverance of Israel from Egypt and in the response to that event (Exod 1–2; 15). Once more, it notes the potential for reclaiming the Pentateuch for women in focusing on the role of women and on the way God relates to them. It also notes the downside to the pentateuchal narrative. This involves recognizing the way women are still marginalized in the story even if they are less invisible than they have been treated. A symbol of this marginalizing is that the sign of the Abrahamic covenant is one that only men can receive. At worst, the downside involves recognizing that women are actually oppressed by the hand of heroes such as Abraham and Moses. The story of a woman such as Hagar also raises the question whether they are oppressed by God, though this same story also has God and the narrator giving Hagar a special position and a special covenantal relationship.

Feminist interpretation of the teaching material in the Pentateuch has similarly drawn attention to ways in which the account of the position of women in society accepts or encourages a situation in which women have less freedom and power than men and are subject to constraints. It also notes ways in which texts seek to offer greater scope to women and to limit the constraints that society imposes on them. Deuteronomy, for instance, keeps emphasizing that the privileges and the responsibilities of the covenant apply to mothers, wives, and daughters, as well as to fathers, husbands, and sons. Feminist interpretation has asked questions about the pollution teaching in the Pentateuch and has perceived male unease about women's sexuality in the regulations concerning menstruation and childbirth.

Feminist interpretation sometimes offers a new perspective on old problems. Genesis 12–26 includes three stories about an ancestor (conventionally known as a "patriarch"!) who passes off his wife as his sister. The possibility that a similar event simply took place three times does not explain the inclusion of the stories of all three occurrences, when many other stories from the lives of the ancestors could have been included. A feminist interpretation suggests that the stories represent male attempts to come to terms with their ambiguous feelings about their wives' sexuality.[15] This suggestion functions both exegetically, to explain the meaning of the text, and hermeneutically, to point us to the significance of the text for modern readers. Feminist approaches to the stories of Noah and his sons and Lot and his daughters offer parallel illumination on these stories from a psychoanalytic viewpoint.[16]

6. Imperialist Interpretation

Protestant Christian thinking in Britain in the sixteenth century saw Britain as inheriting the pentateuchal promises to Israel and the vocation of Israel, and it held onto these convictions in extending British rule in countries such as South Africa. There native Africans were seen as equivalent to the Canaanites. Their culture was to be destroyed, and if they resisted British rule, British troops could kill them, as Deuteronomy required the killing of Canaanites. This raises difficult questions for black African Christians today reading a book such as Deuteronomy.

European settlers in America in the seventeenth century adopted from Britain the understanding of themselves as the "new Israel." This gave them, too, a basis

15. J. Cheryl Exum, "Who's Afraid of 'The Endangered Ancestress'?," in *The New Literary Criticism and the Hebrew Bible* (ed. J. Cheryl Exum and David J. A. Clines; JSOTSup 143; Sheffield: Sheffield Academic Press, 1993), 91–113; reprinted in J. Cheryl Exum, *Fragmented Women: Feminist (Sub)versions of Biblical Narratives* (Sheffield: Sheffield Academic Press, 1993), 148–69.

16. Athalya Brenner, ed., *Genesis* (A Feminist Companion to the Bible, Second Series; Sheffield: Sheffield Academic Press, 1998), 82–128.

for annihilating Native American culture, and if they met resistance, for annihilating Native Americans. American self-understanding also inverted Britain's way of finding itself in the Pentateuch. The American Revolution was the moment when God delivered the colonies from Pharaoh Britain. As in the Pentateuch, exodus and covenant were held closely together in this self-understanding. The Mayflower group committed themselves in covenant, and the American constitutional documents of the 1780s have the same expectation.

Subsequently "Washington becomes both Moses and Joshua, both the deliverer of the American people out of bondage and the leader of the chosen people into the Promised Land of independence." This illustrates the conviction of the settlers' pastor, John Robinson, in 1620, that "the Lord hath more light yet to break forth out of his Holy Word."[17] The light of God's revelation continually breaks forth in crucial events of American history. On July 4, 1776, Congress directed Franklin, Jefferson, and Adams to design a seal for the United States. Franklin proposed a portrayal of "Moses lifting his hand and the Red Sea dividing, with Pharaoh in his chariot being overwhelmed by the waters." Jefferson suggested "a representation of the children of Israel in the wilderness, led by a cloud by day and a pillar of fire by night."[18] Both proposals illustrate the way Americans read the Pentateuch in light of their history and their convictions about their relationship with the stories.

The Civil War was then the nation's first real "time of testing," analogous to the testing that Israel underwent on the way from Egypt. On April 14, 1861, Henry Ward Beecher preached a sermon on Exodus 14:31 ("Tell the Israelites to go forward"). He retells the exodus story, comments that God's people have often been in the position of Israel before the Red Sea, and declares: "Now our turn has come. Right before us lies the Red Sea of war. . . . And the Word of God to us to-day is, 'Speak unto this people that they go forward.'"[19]

Cherry adds, "The history of the American civil religion is a history of the conviction that the American people are God's New Israel." The trouble is that this belief "has come to support America's arrogant self-righteousness. It has been all too easy for Americans to convince themselves that they have been chosen to be a free and powerful people not because God or the circumstances of history chose in mysterious ways but because they *deserve* election. The blessings of success, wealth, and power are readily taken as signs of their having merited a special place in history."[20]

In considering liberation interpretation, we will need to consider the question whether any nation has the right to see itself in the story in the Pentateuch, as if it represents a subsequent embodiment of Israel. Here we need to note especially the risks involved when a powerful nation does that. A weak nation or an oppressed group such as the American pioneers might do so in a way that indeed enabled

---

17. Conrad Cherry, *God's New Israel: Religious Interpretations of American Destiny* (Englewood Cliffs, N.J.: Prentice-Hall, 1971), 11–12.

18. Ibid., 65.

19. Ibid., 162–65.

20. Ibid., 21, 23–24.

new light to break out from God's Word, but even in the course of finding their freedom they were involved in displacing and killing other people in God's name. After a revolution, yesterday's newly freed people easily becomes today's oppressor. The process whereby British or American appropriation of the Pentateuch became ideological offers some insight on a dynamic within the First Testament itself. The Pentateuch warns Israel of the possibility that it may go through a process whereby the entity for whose sake Yahweh destroys a superior people in due course must be destroyed itself.

In turn, this may help Israelis face the question equivalent to the one that British and American people must face. The Jewish people today has more obvious right to identify with Israel in the Pentateuch, though the State of Israel is but one embodiment of the Jewish people. Neither the state nor its supporters can afford the risk of simply identifying the State of Israel theologically with the people of Israel in the Pentateuch. In 1947, Jewish refugees from the holocaust in Europe for which Britain and America must accept some responsibility again sought to find their way to the promised land. Some did so in a ship called *Exodus,* which Britain stopped landing in Palestine and sent back to Europe.[21] It would be impossible to deny such Jewish people the symbolism of seeing their escape from Europe as an exodus. However, the State of Israel half a century later has to face the question whether (in another symbolism) David has become Goliath.

To put it another way, interpretation of the Pentateuch in light of the conviction that our particular nation is an embodiment of Israel needs to be accompanied with interpretation in light of the possibility that our nation is an embodiment of Egypt.

7. Liberation Interpretation

Liberation interpretation is the mirror image of imperialist interpretation. Whereas imperialist interpretation is undertaken by people in power, liberation interpretation is undertaken by people who are not in power. Whereas imperialist interpretation identifies with Israel in its strength, liberation interpretation identifies with Israel in its weakness.

In a volume from a series on American Biblical Hermeneutics, an African American writer, Kimberleigh Jordan, thus comments that in the United States "rather than finding the freedom and liberty that the Pilgrims and Puritans understood as ordained for them, enslaved Africans and their descendants have experienced varying degrees of 'un-freedom.'"[22] Jordan suggests that people in dominant positions in the United States, especially the white men who led the journey to a new world and those who identified with them, have found that the story of Abraham illumined and validated their lives and experience. In contrast, people who were subject to

21. Conor Cruise O'Brien, *The Siege* (repr.; London: Paladin, 1988), 276–77.

22. Kimberleigh Jordan, "The Body as Reader," in *The Bible and the American Myth* (ed. Vincent L. Wimbush; Macon, Ga.: Mercer University Press, 1999), 105–21 (105).

domination, including black people who were enslaved by the people who came to this new land, and particularly black women, have found that it was the story of Hagar that rather illumined and validated their lives and experience.

It was in the exodus story that African American slaves especially found hope and inspiration. "Though these were chattel slaves, they were also aware of themselves as a separate people, strangers in a strange land, who shared a common fate. Egyptian bondage is paradigmatic for abolitionist politics, and for radical politics generally, because of its collective character. It invites a collective response—not manumission, the common goal of Greek and Roman slaves, but liberation."[23] In *Exodus and Revolution* as a whole, Walzer shows the interaction between the experience of a wide range of radical movements and each element of the pentateuchal story of bondage, exodus, wilderness wanderings, covenant making, and arrival at the edge of the promised land.

Spirituals such as "Go Down, Moses" illustrate the way African American slaves read the exodus story. Contemporary African Americans read behind the story of the exodus to the story of Joseph, asking whether Joseph's achievement in bringing all the peoples in Egypt into the position of being the Pharaoh's slaves needs to be read ironically in light of where this led. To put it another way, if an emergent black middle class forgets its poorer fellow African Americans, it has repeated Joseph's error.[24] At the moment, the African American community stands between Egypt and the promised land, no longer enslaved but not having reached the full enjoyment of God's intent.

The first influential exercise in liberation theology in Latin America, where the phrase "liberation theology" originated, was Gustavo Gutiérrez's *A Theology of Liberation*.[25] It emphasized the significance of the exodus story for people in Latin America who had insufficient food and work and no power to change their destinies. Like African American slaves, they found that the story of Israel's oppression in Egypt resonated with their experience. There too were people whose lives and work were dominated by the demands of another people. These taskmasters forced them to undertake work that was oppressive and attempted to control the size of their families. Like the Israelites in Egypt, ordinary Latin American peoples cried out to God. Liberation theologians assured them that God heard their cry as God had heard the Israelites.[26]

In seeing God's acts at the exodus as a paradigm for acts that God might be expected to undertake today, liberation theology followed an example set within the First Testament. Isaiah 40–55 had already taken events in the Pentateuch as a pattern for the deliverance that God was about to bring in restoring the people of Judah from their later bondage to the Babylonians. In this sense, Isaiah 40–55 provided a biblical precedent for liberation interpretation. But liberation interpretation did need

---

23. Michael Walzer, *Exodus and Revolution* (New York: Basic, 1985), 32–33.
24. Stephen Breck Reid, *Experience and Tradition* (Nashville: Abingdon, 1990), 62.
25. (Maryknoll, N.Y.: Orbis: 1973; London: SCM, 1974).
26. See also J. S. Croatto, *Exodus* (Maryknoll, N.Y.: Orbis, 1981).

to face a question also implicit in imperialist interpretation. The ordinary people of (say) Peru are no more God's specially chosen people than is a large, powerful nation such as nineteenth-century Britain or the United States over the subsequent century. Other peoples oppressed by the Egyptians were not delivered as the Israelites were. Can any oppressed people today "claim" the exodus story? A possible response to that question is to note that in general God's work with Israel was designed to be a paradigm of God's ways and purpose in the world. All nations were to pray to be blessed as Abraham's family was blessed (e.g., Gen 12:3). All that Latin America was asking was that God should fulfill this promise for it.

Liberation interpretation of the Pentateuch, like feminist interpretation, provides a textbook illustration of the way in which an interpretive stance or commitment both opens interpreters' eyes to aspects of the text that have been ignored and also risks assimilating the text to the commitment that the interpreters have already made. On the one hand, Christian interpretation of Exodus had long been dominated by typological and pietistic interpretation that made it possible to avoid the main thrust of the actual story. Liberation interpretation dealt with this main thrust quite literally.

On the other hand, in its determination not to subordinate the text to the religious agenda of typological and pietistic interpretation, it is subject to converse temptations. First, it could ignore the actual religious interest of the text. For instance, the story is concerned with Israel's relationship with God, with its leaving the service of Pharaoh for the service of Yahweh. And the story works with the conviction that Yahweh's direct acts fulfill an important role in this process of leaving, announced but not much helped along by Moses. Liberation interpretation wanted to emphasize human political responsibility and thus sometimes went in for a form of demythologizing in interpreting Exodus's account of events.

Second, in resisting typology, liberation interpretation also took the exodus story in isolation from the story of the exile, as well as from the story of Jesus. In due course, liberation theology had to begin to come to terms with a theology of exile and thus to affirm that we cannot interpret one act in the First Testament story in isolation from other acts. Nor can we interpret the First Testament events as a whole independently of the New Testament events, any more than vice versa.[27]

8. Midrashic Interpretation

Jewish midrash begins from gaps sensed in texts and questions that readers feel arise in them, which encourage reflection on issues that concern the readers. For instance, interpreters noted that the account of the creation of the first human couple in Genesis 1 is followed by another account in Genesis 2, and specifically by the creation of a woman who is made after Adam and from him, rather than created along with him. Interpreters inferred that something had happened to Adam's original partner.

---

27. See John Goldingay, "The Man of War and the Suffering Servant," *TynB* 27 (1976): 79–113; also at www.fuller.edu/sot/faculty/goldingay; and chapter 4 above.

They filled the gap in Genesis with the help of the enigmatic Lilith, the restless female demon in Isaiah 34:14. Her name was assumed to designate her a figure of the night (*laylah*), and her activities were known from Babylonian stories about *lilitu*. From these origins there developed the story of Lilith, Adam's first partner who rejected her position as subordinate to Adam. She was cast out for her rebellion and replaced by Eve.[28] In the traditional Lilith midrash, male reflection on the tension between the sexes and male suspicion of the opposite sex thus gains a place in the interpretation of the Pentateuch. In Judith Plaskow's modern feminist midrash on the Lilith story, the same technique utilizes the text in order to reflect on these issues from a woman's perspective.[29]

The story of Abraham's offering of Isaac has been of great importance for Jewish self-understanding, but readers also felt that it raised a number of questions. For instance, where was Sarah when the event took place, and what did she make of it? What was Isaac's attitude to the experience? Was Abraham not tempted to refuse to sacrifice his son, the one through whom the promise was to be fulfilled? And anyway, why did the all-knowing God need to test Abraham to find out how he would react? The raising of that last issue shows how it was not only Christian doctrinal interpretation of the Pentateuch that was affected by the bringing of theological convictions to the text.

Concerned about such questions, readers used material elsewhere in Scripture and material from their own theological tradition to provide clues to the answers to the questions. They noticed that the story of Sarah's death directly follows the story of Abraham's near-sacrifice of Isaac and inferred that this somehow resulted from her horror when she discovered what was happening to her son. The horror that has often come over readers of the story thus comes to be incorporated in its interpretation. They related how Satan tempted Abraham not to go through with the sacrifice, portraying his activity in light of the accounts in Zechariah and Job. They inferred that the omniscient God could indeed foreknow the result of the testing but that it was played out so that the world could know that Abraham would indeed pass the test.[30]

Such instances of midrashic interpretation illustrate two key presuppositions. One is that the Scriptures as a whole are the Word of God. The other that there is a oneness between the text of Scripture and the community that develops midrash. These presuppositions mean that other things that God has said in Scripture can be utilized in order to fill the gaps in the text in a way that coheres with the beliefs of the community.

A significant characteristic of midrash is to be relaxed about the existence of various answers to questions raised by texts. Admittedly this statement applies to haggadah rather than to halakah. Halakah ("walking") studies the Torah in order

28. Louis Ginzberg, *The Legends of the Jews* (7 vols.; reissued; Baltimore and London: Johns Hopkins University Press, 1998), 1:65–66.

29. See Judith Plaskow Goldenberg, "The Coming of Lilith," in *Religion and Sexism* (ed. Rosemary Radford Ruether; New York: Simon & Schuster, 1974), 341–43.

30. See Ginzberg, *The Legends of the Jews*, 1:270–90.

to know what is the right thing to do, what is the will of God. We have considered its concern in looking at ethical interpretation, in particular in noting the exegetical approach to interpreting texts about behavior. When we want to know what to do, there is no space for the equivocal. We need one answer.

In contrast, haggadah ("telling" or narrative or the doing of narrative theology) proceeds on an assumption that is implicit within Scripture in books such as Genesis and Exodus or Job. This presupposition is that there can be a number of illuminating answers to a question such as Why did Job suffer? or What was going on when God accepted Abel's sacrifice rather than Cain's? or What do we make of the character of Abraham or Sarah or Hagar or Jacob or Joseph or Moses? The function of such answers is more to offer resources to readers in thinking about themselves before God than to make objective statements about what went on between God and particular individuals in Genesis. The variety of answers enables readers to think about the question. Midrash thus overlaps with some forms of reader response interpretation of the text. It does not assume that there is never any such thing as objective interpretation, but it does assume that there are texts or aspects of texts that by their own nature leave space for readers to use their imagination in a way that will further their understanding of themselves and their God in their own context.

Ellen Frankel's *The Five Books of Miriam* uses the technique of midrash to expound "what the Torah means to women."[31] It thus offers a variety of comments on issues that arise in the text, in the form of a conversation between the text and its interpreters. These include traditional rabbinic interpretation and Jewish women's tradition as it developed over the centuries, the insights of contemporary scholarship and the questions and convictions of contemporary Jewish women, and the imaginary voices of great Jewish women such as Sarah, Rachel, Miriam, and Huldah. The manner of the presentation parallels that of Talmudic discussion in that often the conversation on a passage is not closed. Readers are thus drawn into it and encouraged to come to their own conclusions—or rather to add their contributions.

9. Modern Interpretation

Midrashic interpretation thus assumes that the Pentateuch is one whole, along with the rest of the Scriptures. Apparent gaps in the text are a stimulus to interpretation, which is undertaken in light of that conviction that the whole of Scripture came from one author. Confronted by the gap between Genesis 1 and Genesis 2, modern interpretation instead assumed that the two chapters issued from two authors. The question of the substantial relationship between the two texts then does not arise. The way to handle unevennesses in texts is to look behind them. Looking behind the text is also a means to discovering the text's unequivocal meaning—though actually it is the unequivocal meaning of a different text. Whereas midrashic interpretation

31. Ellen Frankel, *The Five Books of Miriam: A Woman's Commentary on the Torah* (repr.; San Francisco: HarperSanFrancisco, 1998).

assumes that unclarities are a challenge to build something onto the text, modern interpretation assumes that they are a challenge to take the text apart so as to find the unequivocal meaning that must once have been there.

Like midrashic interpretation, modern interpretation presupposes that interpretation involves treating the Pentateuch in light of our assumptions. For modern interpretation the key to interpretation is to look at the Pentateuch historically, for this is a basic principle of modern interpretation. It thus seeks to discover the different human authors of the texts and leaves aside the question of divine authorship that is a key presupposition of midrash.

The interpretation of Genesis 1–2 provides fine examples of the results of this approach. On the one hand, spectacular illumination emerges from reading Genesis 1 in the context of the stories about creation told by other Middle Eastern peoples and in light of the experience of Judean people transported to Babylon. Strictly, the results of this historical study constitute exegetical insight rather than insight on the interrelationship between Genesis and our own questions, but the historical study facilitates modern readers' reflecting on that interrelationship. On the other hand, more equivocal results have issued from reading Genesis 2–4 against the background of the early monarchy. One problem here is that the evidence for this dating is even more circumstantial than is the case with the exilic dating of Genesis 1. The other problem may be not unrelated. It is that widely different interpretations of the stories and their significance for us have been offered on the basis of a link with this period.

One key feature of the critical interpretation of Scripture that characterizes modernity is the refusal to be bound by traditions of interpretation. In this sense Reformers such as Luther and Calvin were among the first modern interpreters of Scripture, for this was their stance. It was taken up by seventeenth-century Enlightenment figures such as Thomas Hobbes and Benedict de Spinoza. The rejection of christological interpretation, doctrinal interpretation, and midrashic interpretation naturally follows.

Hans Frei's *The Eclipse of Biblical Narrative* explores another key starting point of modern interpretation of the Pentateuch.[32] Before the seventeenth century, readers of the Pentateuch made at least two assumptions about the text and about their relationship with it. First, they assumed that the Pentateuch offered a literal historical account of events from the creation of the world to the end of the life of Moses. Interpreters could thus in principle (for instance) count up the time periods in the Pentateuch and work out that the creation took place around 4004 BC. The world of the text and the real world back then were one world. Second, they assumed that this world was also one with their own world. How God related to people in the Pentateuch was also how God related to the readers of the Pentateuch. They could, indeed must, fit their world into the biblical world.

Frei shows how text and history fell apart. The world of scholarship came to recognize that there was a difference between the story the Pentateuch told and the

---

32. Hans Frei, *The Eclipse of Biblical Narrative* (New Haven and London: Yale University Press, 1974). See further chapter 2 (section 1) and elsewhere above.

actual history of creation and of early millennia in the Middle East. It then had to decide which of these two "stories" would henceforth count. There was no contest. The importance of history in modernity meant that henceforth it was the reconstructed prehistory of Israel and the world that became the focus for study of the Pentateuch, rather than the story told in the Pentateuch.

Now the Pentateuch is concerned with events that actually happened, and to this extent this decision was one that encouraged a study of the Pentateuch that went with the grain of its own agenda. But inevitably the actual investigation of that history is affected by the cultural context of the investigators. The dominance of a scientific worldview affects the study of the Pentateuch both by more conservative and by more liberal scholars. One reason why more liberal scholars may dismiss the historicity of the Pentateuch's account of events such as the plagues in Egypt, the Red Sea crossing, and the people's provision in the wilderness is that these events have no analog in our experience. Also on the basis of our scientific worldview, more conservative scholars are often attracted to explanations of such events that account for them in partly natural terms, but these are inclined to lose the mystery of the events by explaining them away.

Further, like other biblical narratives, the Pentateuch signals that an account of actual events is not all that is required in order to make a story a witness to God's acts. Words are also required, both words that announce ahead of time and words that interpret retrospectively. The Pentateuch embraces all these, but modern study of the Pentateuch focuses resolutely on history.

The attempt to reconstruct what actually happened in Moses' time and before involves first coming to some prior conclusions on the historical background of the material within the Pentateuch. Unfortunately, while from time to time there has been a scholarly consensus on some conclusions about that, the nature of the Pentateuch is such as to give few sure clues as to the date of material within it. A scholarly consensus on the questions is thus always vulnerable to collapse, and the end of the twentieth century saw such a collapse. It became impossible to make any broadly agreed statements about the origin of the Pentateuch. Some of the world of scholarship then began trying out the idea that the historical background against which to read the Pentateuch is the Persian period. But there is no more concrete reason to think that this is right than was the case with the old consensus that J should be interpreted against the monarchy.

The idea that the key to interpreting the Pentateuch is either the quest for concrete historical information within it or the dating of the material within it must be mistaken. Modern interpretation hoped to discover *the* objective meaning of the Pentateuch, but its method and its results combine subjectivity and objectivity, certainty and uncertainty, and do so as integrally as other approaches to interpretation.

10. Postmodern Interpretation

Midrashic interpretation sought to see how Genesis 1 and 2 related to each other as part of God's one Word. Modern interpretation sought to unlink them. As humanly devised stories, they are independent of each other. The only link between them is a historical one. Postmodern interpretation seeks to put the two stories in conversation with each other.

One of the characteristics of the postmodern attitude is to assume that we cannot know the whole truth about anything. Even if total, objective truth exists, the only formulations we have are partial, subjective, and provisional. Yet it is characteristic of human formulations to express themselves as if they were final and definitive. At least, they do this on the surface. But usually underneath the surface we can see the concealed other side of the coin. Thus one task of interpretation is to analyze the construction that texts place on things and to look for the other side of the coin that may lie beneath their surface.

In Genesis 1 and 2, postmodern interpretation thus perceives two different understandings of God, the world, and humanity. Another then appears in Genesis 4. Postmodern interpretation does not then claim that the truth lies in harmonizing these three or in choosing one over against the other but in letting them dialog with each other in the conviction that all contain insights.

Whereas modern interpretation abandons the tradition that Moses wrote the Pentateuch and seeks to discover who did so, postmodern interpretation perceives this question as having led to a dead end. Yet it also sees that we cannot simply revert to the premodern tradition that Moses wrote the Pentateuch, because the reasons that led to its abandoning are still compelling. Rather, it starts from the acknowledgment that we are never going to know who wrote the Pentateuch. The interpretation of the Pentateuch has to be undertaken without knowing who wrote it. Its interpretation involves reading the books. They have covered the tracks of their origins. In focusing on the history that lies behind it we are working against the grain of its own nature.

Premodern interpretation put power in the hands of the church to decide what Scripture meant. Modern interpretation took that power away from the church but gave it to the university. The authority of scholarship replaced the authority of bishops. Student papers begin sentences "most scholars say" instead of "the church teaches." Postmodern interpretation invites people to read the Bible for themselves. They do so in the company of other people who are not too like themselves, to protect them from their individualism or the idiosyncrasy of some group.

In postmodern interpretation, relational categories have priority over legal categories, and this affects the way interpreters read the stories of Adam and Eve or Abraham and other ancestors or the nature of covenants in the Pentateuch. Further, identification replaces distancing, and engagement replaces detachment; the point is to change the world as well as understand it. In this respect, postmodern interpretation again contrasts with the characteristic stance of modernity.

Believing that we cannot find the key to understanding texts by looking outside them to events of history or the lives of authors, postmodern interpretation is more inclined to look for clues in the various textual worlds to which texts belong. The study of intertextuality assumes that all texts stand in relationship to other texts.

They reflect statements made and questions raised in other texts from their culture. Perhaps implicitly and unconsciously, they stand in dialog with these other texts, affirming aspects of them but putting them in a new context, or denying aspects of them, or answering questions they raise. Because this is their origin, they are not directly portraying a world that actually exists, but taking part in a corporate creative enterprise of painting a picture of something.

There are thus links between postmodern interpretation and midrashic and other premodern forms of interpretation. Midrashic interpretation subconsciously presupposes that "the Torah, owing to its own intertextuality, is a severely gapped text," filled from within its own world and the related world of the readers.[33] The oddities, unclarities, and repetitions are all there by design, not by accident. Harris reports an argument by the nineteenth-century rabbinic writer Jacob Meklenburg.[34] God deliberately inspired the Torah in ambiguous form, because this makes it necessary for readers to work harder in order to obey it, and it gives them easy opportunity to avoid its demands. "By presenting his norms in such a way, God provides more fully for the development of the strength of character humans need to lead full ethical lives." Thus the ambiguity of the Bible is a product of God's love for humanity.[35]

As interpreters we may not wish to believe in the Pentateuch's indeterminacy, but we may believe in its polysemy.[36] It is not the case that there are really no meanings. There *are* meanings because there is someone behind these words. The mystery of truth and the richness of Torah mean it is not surprising that there are many meanings. Polysemy implies "a claim to textual stability rather than . . . an indeterminate state of endlessly deferred meanings and unresolved conflicts."[37]

The pentateuchal texts about circumcision raise historical and exegetical problems that cannot be solved by modern approaches to interpretation. We can make it possible for the texts to speak to us by beginning from our own experience in asking what might be the significance of the fact that these texts were incorporated in Scripture, in their enigmatic form. Our awareness of the need for male sexuality to be disciplined suggests the possibility of taking this as the clue to understanding the reason for preserving these texts about circumcision. It suggests that Israel had the same need for texts that raised issues about the disciplining of male sexuality, a possibility that fits a number of the accounts of male sexual behavior in the Pentateuch and elsewhere.[38] Postmodern interpretation, too, thus contributes to exegesis as well as aiding appropriation.

33. Daniel Boyarin, *Intertextuality and the Reading of Midrash* (Bloomington: Indiana University Press, 1990), 16.

34. *How Do We Know This?*, 215.

35. Harris refers to Meklenburg's *hktb whkblh* [*Scripture and the Tradition*] (4th ed.; Berlin, 1880), 1:vii–x.

36. D. Stern, *Midrash and Theory* (Evanston, Ill.: Northwestern University Press, 1996), 15–38.

37. Ibid., 33.

38. Cf. further chapter 22 (section 3) below.

19

Can We Read Prophecy in Light of the Newspaper?

I n the thinking of many Jews and Christians, the return of Jewish people to their traditional homeland from the end of the nineteenth century, and other events in the Middle East over the past century, have been the fulfillment of prophecies in the First Testament. In what sense is this so? What understanding of prophecy does it imply, and what counts as proper interpretation of prophecy?[1]

1. Prophecy as God's No and God's Yes to Israel

When people think of the prophets, they commonly have in mind the people whose words are preserved in the books called the Prophets, plus one or two illustrious others such as Elijah and Elisha, but there were many other Israelite prophets whose words never became Scripture. While some falsely claimed to speak Yahweh's words, others truly so claimed. We can only guess at the process whereby Israel came to generate the particular prophetic books we have and to preserve them so that they became Scripture. We can only guess at the criteria that led them to preserve and include these and to omit others, though I shall guess at one of these criteria in a moment, but we can see the implication of the process. While the words in these books may be no truer than the words of some other prophets and may be no more

---

1. This chapter incorporates material first published in "Palestine and the Prophets," *Third Way* 2, no. 7 (April 1978): 3–6; "Modern Israel and Biblical Prophecy," *Third Way* 6, no. 4 (April 1983): 6–8; "The Jews, the Land, and the Kingdom," *Anvil* 4 (1987): 9–22.

words of God than some other words (not all God's words and not all true words are in Scripture), they count for more in later Israel and thus in the church. They count in a way that the words of those other prophets do not. They were taken as not merely words for their own day but words for succeeding days. One New Testament way of making this point is to say that they came into being "in the Spirit": that was a way of saying that they had a mysterious capacity to speak beyond their own day, and specifically that they illumined Jesus and the life of the church. It meant that they are able to make people wise for salvation "through faith in Christ Jesus" even though they were written long before his day, and that they are able to contribute to the maturing of people who believe in him (2 Tim 3:16). That is what prophecy is designed to mean to us.

How do these prophets do this? The comment in 2 Timothy applies not only to prophecy but to the First Testament Scriptures in general, and in principle all the Scriptures fulfill their task in the same way, or in the same three ways.[2]

First, they tell us how God related to Israel in that once-for-all history that took place from Abraham to Jesus. Our life with God in the present depends on what God did back then; we can relate to God because Christ died for us and rose for us. Israel is God's people because God chose it and made promises to it back then, and the church is God's people because it became part of Israel's story. The prophets are part of that story. God's speaking to Israel through the prophets is part of that shaping of Israel through which God set about working out a purpose.

Sometimes their work contributed positively to that process: it was in part because of the prophets and their promises that there were people such as Elizabeth and Zechariah, Mary and Joseph, Anna and Simeon, ready to welcome Jesus when he came. Often they played a more paradoxical part in this process. Rudolf Bultmann has called the whole First Testament the story of the failure or miscarriage of God's plan,[3] and the prophets are key to seeing Israel's story that way. It was they who declared that God's plan was miscarrying and that Israel risked being written out of God's drama. It was in fulfillment of Yahweh's strange work through the prophets (cf. Isa 28:21) that other priests than Zechariah and other craftsmen than Joseph and other expectant people than Anna rejected Jesus and thus found themselves rejected. There are varying ways in which the prophets are part of the story of how God brought about our salvation.

Second, the Scriptures reveal to us how God regularly relates to Israel and to the world. The stories of God and Abraham, Hagar, Deborah, and David form not only part of unrepeatable history but also examples of recurrent patterns. God's relating to people in the First Testament is not random but principled, and we learn about God's relating to us through accounts of this First Testament relating. Prophecy tells us how God regularly relates to Israel and to the church in warning and promise. It

2. I here apply to the prophets a framework I apply to story in chapter 11 (section 2).
3. See "Prophecy and Fulfillment," in *Essays on Old Testament Hermeneutics* (ed. Claus Westermann; Richmond: John Knox, 1963) = *Essays on Old Testament Interpretation* (London: SCM, 1963), 50–75.

tells us how God relates to the nations in the prophets' day and gives us clues to see how God might be relating to the nations in our day.

The patterning of this promise within the First Testament reflects how God regularly relates to the world and to Israel. The prophets' warnings and promises go back to promises God made to Abraham. Humanity had set course for disaster by turning aside from God's way, but God began to put into effect a plan to restore the world by taking hold of one family. God promised to make them into a nation and give them a land to dwell in. Trouble will come on any who are against them, but God's aim for the world in general was that they should seek the blessing Abraham's family enjoys. These promises began to be fulfilled in the story told in Genesis to Joshua. Then two further promises were added. God made a commitment to be faithful to Israel's king, David, and his descendants, and to take as a home Israel's temple in Jerusalem (2 Sam 7; 1 Kgs 8). These promises lie behind the message of the prophets, who in different contexts in different ways warn of exile, decimation, shame, rejection, and the loss of king and temple, and/or promise the reversal of all these. The age-old promises are principles for God's working with Israel over the centuries.

Third, the Scriptures tell us God's expectations of Israel and of the nations. As they do this in the blocks of teaching in Exodus to Deuteronomy, so they do in the prophets. Sometimes this instruction is timeless: the worship of Yahweh alone and the refusal to misuse Yahweh's name apply straightforwardly in any century. Sometimes this instruction varies from century to century. There are differences between the expectations expressed in Isaiah and in Ezekiel or in Amos and in Haggai, reflecting the way God's challenges need to change in different circumstances. Sometimes people need to be told to focus not on worship and prayer but on caring for the poor; sometimes they need to be told to focus on worship and prayer. Sometimes they need to be told to repent, not to assume that they are all right with God; sometimes they need to be told to trust that they are all right with God and not to assume that God will always be displeased with them. The prophets' task is commonly to summon the people of God away from one set of emphases into a different set or into a more multifaceted life.

Prophecy, then, relates to us today as part of God's once-for-all relationship with Israel on which our relationship with God depends, it illustrates how God keeps working with Israel on the basis of foundational promises and commitments and with the nations, and it illustrates the kind of behavior and priorities the people of God is expected to embody in its life.

God's expectations in this connection were not fulfilled, and for much of Israel's history the prophets were busy declaring that because of this, Israel was finished. Prophecy constituted God's no to Israel. Prophets asserted that the end had come upon the people of God. Admittedly the small print in their prophecies indicated that this was not all that needed saying. Every prophetic book also refers to some positive future for the people, even if such promises are held back for the final reel (and, indeed, may come from the work of a different director from the first cut). But the bulk of the ministry of the eighth- and seventh-century prophets warns of imminent calamity that will decimate the people, devastate its land, destroy its sanctuary, dethrone its monarchy, and terminate its relationship with Yahweh.

With Ezekiel that changes. The fall of Jerusalem is the hinge of his ministry and of prophecy in general. Henceforth the minor theme in earlier prophecies becomes the major theme. The people will be restored, the land replanted, the temple rebuilt, the monarchy reestablished, the relationship renewed; all this is set in the context of the intention announced in the promise to Abraham that Israel will thereby shine God's light to the entire world. The prophets' promises are thus not random or novel. They do not come out of the blue but relate to the whole divine purpose narrated in Scripture. Ezekiel's message is a reaffirmation of these commitments, promising that Israel will be restored in such a way as to bring it to acknowledge Yahweh.

If a woman has children, she will characteristically find that the bond between her and them is so strong that there is no way she could ever throw them out or cease to care for them.[4] No matter what they do or how old they are, they remain her children, and she remains committed to them. The bond may seem even stronger than that between husband and wife. The latter relationship is created and can be uncreated (often is). The former is generated and cannot be undone. God's relationship with Israel and then with the church is like marriage in that it comes into being by conscious decision, in time, but it is like motherhood in the way it becomes integral to God's being as well as to Israel's. Perhaps it is significant that in the course of his book Hosea moves from the first image to the second, from a husband's experience (Hos 1–3) to a mother's (Hos 11). Even with the first analogy Yahweh breaks the rules, marrying the same woman for a second time. The second analogy makes it possible to indicate that Yahweh has surrendered any freedom to terminate the relationship. Yahweh is more like Israel's mother than its husband.

2. The Significance of the Prophets after Christ

In principle, then, Yahweh has said yes to Israel once and for all. "Replacement theology" or "supersessionism" (the view that the church replaced Israel in God's purpose) cannot be right.[5] In other words, the promise to Abraham stands: the people will be blessed and will become a blessing. The aspects of God's promise to Abraham, expanded to David, are an outworking of God's yes that the prophets take up and reaffirm as Israel makes the transition from being a monarchic state to being an imperial colony during the Second Temple period. The First Testament speaks of the renewing of God's special relationship with Israel and of the inner renewal of Israel, and this happens in the Second Temple period.

Do God's promises still stand when the Second Temple is on the eve of destruction? What insights on this does the New Testament offer? Without using the analogy of

4. See further chapter 22 below.
5. See further the chapter "What Is Israel's Place in God's Purpose?," in *Key Questions about Christian Faith: Old Testament Answers* (Grand Rapids: Baker Academic, 2010), 190–210.

marriage or parenthood, in Romans 11 Paul expresses the same theology as Hosea. God does not go back on calling Israel and is not finished with the Jewish people. The time will come when they acknowledge Jesus and then become the means of further blessing for the gentile world. The fundamental promise God made back at the beginning (Gen 12) still stands: God will so bless Israel that it will become a means of blessing for the entire world. Paul speaks of "Israel," but in our terms we should think of the Jewish people as the heirs of this promise and not merely the Israeli state. There are more Jews in New York than in Tel Aviv or Jerusalem, and it is to U.S. or U.K. Jews as much as to Israeli Jews that the promise belongs.

While the New Testament makes clear that God is still committed to the Jewish people, the way it talks about God's promises concerning the monarchy and the temple is rather different. It reworks those promises. The First Testament promises a new David to be king over Israel, and for short periods in the Second Temple period a descendant of David leads the people in Jerusalem, but the New Testament then sees Jesus as the fulfillment of that promise. He is a very different kind of king from the one envisaged by the promise to David, yet we look for no further fulfillment of Ezekiel 34 than the one it has received in Jesus, except the final appearing of this same Jesus.

Likewise the First Testament promises a new temple, and the temple is rebuilt after the exile and more gloriously by Herod, but Jesus subsequently speaks of his person as God's temple, as the place of God's dwelling, and the New Testament addresses Christians as the Holy Spirit's temple. Revelation in turn offers a picture colored by Ezekiel of God's dwelling in a new Jerusalem. There seems to be no room for a rebuilt stone temple here. The incarnation, the coming of the Spirit, and the new Jerusalem fulfill all that the temple stood for. Temple, like kingship, becomes a metaphor for understanding aspects of Jesus and his significance.

Yahweh's promises concerning the monarchy and the temple were the two promises that were additional to God's original commitment to Abraham. Both emerged from human desires and ideas rather than from divine initiative. Both are more dispensable than the elements in that original commitment.

What of the promise of the land? The New Testament sometimes takes up the image of land, like monarchy and temple, as a metaphor for aspects of the significance of the Christ event through which God's people enjoy the rest that never came about in Canaan (1 Pet 1:4; Heb 3–4), and it does look forward to a new Jerusalem, though a heavenly one (Rev 21). This might suggest seeing the promise about the land as fulfilled in Christ, in a metaphorical sense, like the promises concerning David and the temple. However, the way Mary and Zechariah, for instance, speak of what God will achieve through Jesus (Luke 1:46–55, 67–79) looks as if it presupposes the people enjoying freedom and blessing in their land. The New Testament never suggests questions of principle concerning the land as it does about kingship and temple. Whereas it systematically reinterprets God's commitment to David and less systematically reinterprets God's commitment to the temple, it offers relatively few hints of a reinterpretation of Israel's relationship with the land.

When it makes occasional typological use of a First Testament motif such as the land, it does so in order to utilize the First Testament material to help it answer its own theological questions, questions such as What is the significance of Jesus? and What is the church about? It is using the same methods of interpretation as other Jews of its day to find answers to other questions. Its aim is different from the aim of seeking to learn theologically from the First Testament itself, which will involve learning from the sense attaching to the First Testament when God inspired it as a means of communication with people in the time before Christ. An involvement with the First Testament in this connection will imply more than an interest in a theme such as the land as a symbol for helping Christians think through the significance of Jesus. God's original purpose involved a blessing of the people in its land that would enable it to become a blessing to others in the context of its relationship with Yahweh. That is still part of God's yes to Israel.

All this fits with the fact that land is integral to the notion of peoplehood as monarchy and temple are not. The notion of a people that does not have a relationship to a land does not make very good sense. It is for this reason that land appears in God's original promise to Abraham. In turn, this particular land became intrinsically linked to the story of this people and its Messiah. Any old land would not do as the home of the Jewish people; the story of the fulfilling of God's purpose links the people to this land. We might further then infer that the New Testament takes for granted Jewish enjoyment of the land.

In turn, that would suggest that we might indeed see the extraordinary return of Jews to the land of Palestine over the past hundred years as reflecting God's abiding intention to let Jewish people live there (ultimately as a base for their testimony to Jesus as Messiah). This return is not a mere political accident, and the parallels between this event and First Testament prophecies are not mere coincidence. First Testament prophecies were expressions of God's long-standing commitments and purposes. But monarchic statehood was not part of the promise to Abraham, and the twentieth-century reestablishment of the State of Israel is not a fulfillment of God's promise in the same sense as is the rebuilding of a Jewish population in the land. The State of Israel does not have the same theological significance as the people of Israel. The Abrahamic promise is quite compatible with Jews and Arabs both living freely in the land, especially in light of the fact that the Arab peoples trace their ancestry to Abraham and many are also the spiritual children of Abraham as they have come to believe in Jesus.

3. Foretelling and Forthtelling: Hearing Prophecy in Its Context

It is sometimes said that the prophets were forthtellers rather than or more than foretellers.[6] Their main task was not to predict events but to challenge their con-

6. See, e.g., Walter N. Owensby, *Economics for Prophets* (Grand Rapids: Eerdmans, 1988), x.

temporaries about the will of God that needed implementing in their community, to confront Israel with the demand that it should embody Yahweh's fairness and compassion in its life. This claim is right in what it affirms but wrong in what it denies, or in the strength of its denial. The prophets were both foretellers and forthtellers, and the two activities were integrally linked in a variety of ways. It was because Yahweh purposed to bless Israel (foretelling) that it was called to a life of faithfulness (forthtelling). That life was designed to embody the vision for Israel that Yahweh purposed to implement. It was also a condition of the promise coming true. Yahweh's promise and Israel's commitment could not be separated.

When we ask how the Scriptures in general and the prophets in particular are designed to address us millennia after their day, the third of the three ways I suggested they speak to us interweaves with the second.[7] The prophets' words challenge Israel, the church, and the world about their lives, as well as illustrating how God relates to them. Arguably it is not Gentile Christians' business to tell the Jewish people or the State of Israel how to run its life and how to read its prophets; if we might ever have had any such right, we long ago forfeited it. But if we are to think about prophecy's implications for Israel, we have to hold together the wondrous promises that commit God to an ongoing faithfulness to Israel with the far-reaching demands that expect of Israel an ongoing faithfulness to God expressed in a mirroring of God to the world. Further, the prophets require of us a commitment to be as concerned for the fair treatment of the non-Jewish people living west of the Jordan as we are for Israel's fair treatment. Part of the tragedy of that land is that it is loved by two peoples; the prophets refuse us the option of short-circuiting a solution to this problem by a commitment to one of these peoples that ignores the love, needs, and history of the other.

So the prophets tell forth; they also foretell. They do indeed speak about the future, so that Ezekiel (for instance) announces coming events that affect rulers such as the Egyptian Pharaoh. But there is a jump involved in reckoning that a prophet such as Ezekiel issues promises or warnings that find fulfillment in twentieth-century events. An example is the belief that the vision of the dry bones in Ezekiel 37 began to be fulfilled in twentieth-century Israel. In the vision, bones first become bodies, and then Yahweh's breath is breathed into them. In history, the nation has been brought back to political life; it will in due course be brought back to spiritual life. A more specific example that I recall from my teenage years is the prophecy envisaging the Pharaoh declaring, "My river is mine own, and I have made it for myself" (Ezek 29:3 KJV). This was said to be fulfilled in President Nasser's nationalizing of the Suez Canal in 1956. The suggestion does not work so well in modern translations, which make clear that the word for "river" is the word for the Nile, though this has also encouraged the idea that Ezekiel's prophecy refers to the building of the Aswan Dam. Rather, the coming events that Ezekiel announces relate to the people he addresses. The political events he announces are ones to unfold in his day. He speaks

7. See section 1 above.

of them in order to enable his people to respond to what Yahweh is doing in their midst. He specifically denies that he speaks about "far off days" or "distant times" (Ezek 12:21–28).

It coheres with this that prophetic books generally open with a paragraph telling us who wrote them, what period they belong to, and which countries they relate to. At the beginning they indicate that we have to understand them as God's word to particular people in particular circumstances. As the books unfold, the same fact is continually made clear by the references to specific situations, needs, and sins. Their message is one that relates to these particular people. Ezekiel could indeed have foretold the distant future. Many people have had and do have accurate previews of events to come one day, and not all such people are charlatans. The First Testament assumes that false prophets sometimes utter prophecies that come true (Deut 13:1–2). The "Mystic Meg" phenomenon (a British newspaper calls her "the world's greatest astrologer") was as familiar in Ezekiel's day as it is in ours. Ezekiel does not want to be reduced to someone who merely impresses or reassures people by predicting the distant future. He has a much more important ministry. He would not be pleased at the suggestion that his prophecies had been fulfilled 2,500 years after they were given. These prophecies were part of his ministry to the people in exile about 590 BC. He wanted *them* to hear God's message to *them*; he did not want them to push it onto some other epoch. Nor can any other generation like our own steal it from them.

The prophets' messages about coming events in their day do also speak beyond their day. They do this on the basis of the second of the three ways in which Scripture as a whole speaks. That is, they provide concrete instances of the way Yahweh related to Israel and to the world that provide us with a basis for discerning how God may be relating to Israel, the church, and the nations in other ages. If Cyrus is Yahweh's anointed (Yahweh's messiah), the chosen king through whom God's purpose is furthered in international relations for the benefit of Israel and its restoration (Isa 44–45), in our age, too, we may look for ways God is working through specific world rulers to fulfill a purpose that will bring blessing to the people of God and to the world. It is in this way that we discover from the prophets what God is doing in our world, not by treating their words as coded forecasts of events in our own century.

To discover the prophets' significance for later generations, then, we pay attention to the meaning they had in their original context. The question is what these prophecies meant for people such as Ezekiel through whom they were given and for the people whom they addressed, to whom they came as God's good news or bad news. That is true of the promises about the restoration of the land to Israel as much as any other prophecies. They are given, for instance, through Jeremiah to Judeans on the verge of exile, to assure them that God's judgment will not be the final word to them. They are given through Ezekiel to people actually in exile to reassure them that God has not finished with them.

Further, they are messages from God that have to be understood as these particular people would understand them, supposing that they had the required intelligence and spiritual insight. When a prophet promised that the desert would blossom, he was not referring to the agricultural miracles that Israelis have performed in the Negev. When a prophet spoke about the earth shaking or about fire and brimstone, he was not referring to nuclear explosions. He passed on messages that God intended to be heard and understood by people of his day, and we have to ask what such talk meant then. The chapters in Ezekiel that detail these promises are ones that have been reckoned to refer to events in the Middle East in our day, or events to come, but this understanding ignores the promises' own rationale. Our age does not see those concrete prophecies fulfilled; events in such a different context could not be the fulfillment of those prophecies. It does see the fulfillment of the same long-standing commitments and purposes on God's part. There is an inner link between First Testament prophecy and modern event, but not one that makes it possible to see the concrete details of modern history as the fulfillment of the specific details of prophecy.

The prophets also speak about another kind of future, one that we know to be far distant from their day whether or not they knew this. They speak of events to take place "in that day," the day that may come beyond the lifetime of their hearers but is relevant to these hearers because it is the day of restoration, the day of fulfillment, and therefore a day that shapes the lives of people who will not live to see it. It encourages them to live in light of the eventual consummation of God's purpose. As the New Testament emphasizes the importance of Christ's final appearing to people who will not live to see it but are called to live in light of it, so the prophets emphasize how the day of Yahweh is important to people who may not live to see it but are called to live in light of it. But this kind of envisioning of future events is very different from the way of speaking about the distant future often attributed to a prophet such as Ezekiel.

4. Finding Prophecy Fulfilled in the Newspapers

The prophets bring God's word to their day, and we learn from them by listening to them in that context as a way of seeing how it might transfer to ours. A failure to work in this way is a fundamental problem about books such as Hal Lindsey's best seller *The Late Great Planet Earth*[8] and more recent volumes of a similar kind.

These writers are right to assume that when we read the Bible, we are listening to God's words. The First Testament came into existence by God's inspiration and God's providence; its prophecies and visions were God-given, and they were not just significant for their own day. They were written down and included in God's book, and they are important far beyond their own day, important to the people of God AD as well as BC. They are indeed significant (for instance) for the Middle East today. There is no question *whether* they apply to today but only *how*. They have things to say to us about contemporary world events and contemporary church life. They

---

8. Hal Lindsey, *The Late Great Planet Earth* (Grand Rapids: Zondervan, 1970; London: Lakeland, 1971).

reveal God's will to us by revealing God's will embodied in particular contexts. The God and Father of our Lord Jesus Christ is the Lord of history, and our history is to be read in light of the Scriptures God inspired. Part of the reason why the Scriptures are given to us is to live in history and not to be overwhelmed by it.

God inspired the prophets and could have revealed to them things God intended to do in the twenty-first century. Granted that God could have done so, would God have done so? Is that the kind of thing God does? And did God do so? Is that the kind of function that prophecy fulfills? Actually, the God of the Bible is not inclined to give signs or reveal dates: see especially Jesus' teaching about the final consummation in Mark 13:32–37 and Acts 1:7. Further, when God does make statements about the future, they do not constitute detailed information on events that are predetermined to unfold, a kind of fixture list of coming events that we can tick off as they take place, but promises, warnings, and challenges designed to call people to decision now. The God of the Bible does not generally bolster people's faith by revealing to them exactly what is to come but calls them to a trusting faith and hope in the one with whom they can face an unknown future confident that they are safe in God's hands.

God does sometimes grant special revelations to people who cannot believe without them, and we could not exclude the possibility that the prophets include such revelations for us to profit from. But in his conversation with "doubting" Thomas, Jesus declared a blessing on people who would believe without such special privileges (John 20:29). That is how he usually deals with people. So we can assume that the prophets do not contain such revelations unless there is evidence in a particular case that God has here given an exceptional revelation because of some specific need.

When Ezekiel declared to the exiles that a return to the land or a particular battle was to take place, he was not telling his audience that certain events were scheduled for two and a half millennia after their day but addressing and bringing God's word to these people, warning them of calamities and promising them blessings that could come about in their time. He was not revealing a timetable of events that had to unfold over thousands of years but bringing a specific message to a particular context. The idea of a fulfillment in 1948 of a prophecy given by Ezekiel to people living in the 580s BC thus does not make sense: it is not a fulfillment of promises and warnings that were part of God's relationship with those people. The prophecies that get applied to the recent history of the Jewish people are prophecies relating to the circumstances of their ancestors in particular contexts. The words of the prophets were part of their ministry to their contemporaries.

We cannot say they are being fulfilled 2,500 years later, because they were not statements of what was bound to take place but promises or threats to particular people for particular reasons. Whether or not they actually took place would be determined (at least in part) by the response they met. Jeremiah and Ezekiel specifically indicate that their threats will not be fulfilled if people return to God, and their promises will not be fulfilled if people do not respond to them with trust and obedience (Jer 18:1–11; Ezek 33:1–20). It is not that prophets sometimes preach a message whose fulfillment depends on people's response to it. That is regularly the case, even when there are no ifs and buts in their words.[9] The story of Jonah reflects this. Jonah simply says Nineveh will be destroyed; there is no hint of escape. But when the Ninevites repent, the threat is withdrawn, as Jonah knew it would be (Jon 4:2). God's warnings of catastrophe are given to us because he wants us to accept responsibility for what happens and to act so that the catastrophes do not take place. If we assume that he has prophesied inevitable catastrophe, and expect one to happen, it probably will.

Understanding the significance of First Testament prophecy involves treating it as an act of communication between God and people in the contexts in which they lived. We have to work out its implications for us in a way analogous to the way we seek to see the significance of material in Leviticus or Deuteronomy. It does not mean treating it as a coded preview of things to take place in the far future that were not in any direct sense significant for the people to whom they were announced. It means asking how these promises and threats embodied Yahweh's purpose in the context and seeking to perceive how that purpose might then find embodiment in ours. Events of recent decades in Palestine are not directly the fulfillment of specific biblical prophecies, nor do such prophecies tell us about events of coming decades. These prophecies are part of a living relationship between God and people in the periods to which they belong. They are not forecasts of things to take place in thousands of years' time but warnings and promises about events that will affect the people to whom the prophecies are given. This means that if a prophecy does not find a fulfillment in its original context, the right inference is not that it will be fulfilled in some future day but that it never will be fulfilled, perhaps for reasons explained in a passage such as Jeremiah 18:1–11. The same considerations also work against the idea that prophecies such as Ezekiel's declaration about the river in Egypt might have a fulfillment in his own day and one in the twentieth century.

So we cannot simply assume that warnings and promises addressed to people living 2,500 years ago can be transferred directly to people living today. That is to ignore the fact that they were part of a personal, moral relationship between God and Israel. Twentieth-century Jews are a part of the same Israel as Jews of the exile and therefore have a continuing place within the people of God, but this does not mean that First Testament promises (or warnings) apply directly to them. After all, in First Testament times many different promises and warnings were given to Israel; they did not all apply to Israel at the same time. Sometimes the difference between true and false prophets (for instance, Jeremiah and Hananiah) was that the latter were encouraging Israel to trust in prophecies that did not really apply at the moment. One has to consider whether the exilic prophecies of the restoration of the land are open to being reapplied to the State of Israel or whether to do so is the act of a false prophet.

9. See further John Goldingay and Michael Moynagh, "Prophecy and Futures Studies," *Theology* 102 (1999): 416–23.

How would one decide that? The prophets assume that God deals with Israel and with the peoples it lived among on the basis of how they treated the needy and how they treated each other; whether they took people away from their homelands, whether they lived in brotherhood (see Amos 1–2). The prophets were concerned to be fair to Israel and to other people. In the twentieth-century context, that would involve considering what is fair for both Israeli Jew and Palestinian Arab. While Palestinians have been responsible for many moral atrocities within Palestine and in other parts of the world, the Israeli record in this regard is not spotless, and this does not alter the fact that a century ago the Palestinians were the long-standing legal inhabitants of this land that they viewed and still view as their historic homeland. It is difficult to imagine that God would be fulfilling promises to the Jewish people at the expense of being unfair to other peoples who were simply in the way. Indeed, the First Testament suggests that God would not do so, because it tells us that the original fulfillment of God's promise of the land was delayed for four generations to avoid being unfair to the people who inhabited the land in Abraham's day (Gen 15:16).

While God will never go back on that yes to Israel, this does not provide answers to contemporary political questions in the Middle East, certainly not by overriding questions about the destiny of other peoples who live in the land in question. While Jewish freedom to live in the land is a fulfillment of God's long-standing commitment to Israel, this is not a basis for contemporary political attitudes ("God has promised the land to the Jews, so we support their cause against the Palestinian Arabs"). The promises' concern is with blessing for other nations as well as blessing for Israel, and the prophets apply the same standards to Israel as they do to the nations. The peoples of the land west of the Jordan, like other nations, are destined to recognize that the Jewish people is in a special sense the people of God, and the Jewish people is destined to be a blessing to those peoples as to others.

5. Taking Prophecy Literally

In speaking through Ezekiel, God spoke via human words designed to make sense to Ezekiel's hearers, and when we seek to understand them, we do so as we do any other human words. We hear and obey God's word by listening to the human words God inspired. The use of prophecies in a book such as *The Late Great Planet Earth* ignores the meaning these prophecies had for their author and his audience. Ezekiel 38:14–16, for instance, "describes" how "when the Russians invade the Middle East with amphibious and mechanized land forces, they will make a 'blitzkrieg' type offensive through the area."[10] There is no comment on Ezekiel's mention of horses in this passage, which illustrates how selective this interpretation of prophecy is; one can be very impressed by particular close correspondences and not notice the elements in the prophecies and the aspects of modern history that are ignored. In

10. Lindsey, *The Late Great Planet Earth*, 157.

the verses that follow, "Ezekiel sounded the fatal collapse of the Red Army."[11] At the opening of Ezekiel 39, "the description of torrents of fire and brimstone raining down upon the Red Army, coupled with the unprecedented shaking of the land of Israel could well be describing the use of tactical nuclear weapons."[12] This is not what Yahweh was saying through Ezekiel to the people Yahweh sent Ezekiel to. Earthquake and fire is biblical symbolic language for the devastating effects that accompany and follow God's intervention in human history. It is not a picture of nuclear explosion.

Now the interpretation of prophecy is not limited to what the prophet meant. The New Testament often ignores the meaning of First Testament passages it quotes. Such prophecies turned out to have a significance for a future context that was unknown to their human author.[13] If prophetic interpreters claim similar inspiration, we shall have to test their claim, as we would test the claim of a prophet. This will not merely involve looking at whether their modern interpretation matches historical events. To meet the test for prophecy in Jeremiah 23, it will involve asking whether it fits the theological and moral test of consistency with the rest of Scripture.

Ezekiel's prophecies were given to Israel in the exile. Its relationship with God had been broken and its temple burned down. As a nation it had been defeated and shamed; its kings had been humiliated and deposed. Its land had been devastated and captured and its God apparently discredited. It was experiencing at every point the opposite to the promise of blessing to Abraham. Through Ezekiel, God asserts that nevertheless these promises are not finished. Indeed, they are reasserted in more glorious Technicolor.

These promises found some fulfillment very soon, when Cyrus defeated the Baby-lonians and encouraged the Judeans to return to Canaan to rebuild their community and their temple (see Ezra 1–6). But they were not fulfilled in the Technicolor Ezekiel suggests. So what happens to these promises? Do they stand anyway, bound to be fulfilled someday in precisely the form in which they were given? So the *Late Great Planet Earth* approach assumes. But we have noted that whether or not a prophecy is fulfilled depends at least partly on how people respond to it.

Consider a human parallel. Many years ago, I might say to my two sons on a Saturday morning, "Would you like to come swimming?" Suppose they were not interested, because they prefer to watch something interesting on television, but then on Sunday decided they now wanted to go swimming. "You said we could—can we go now?" The answer might well be, "No, that was an offer for yesterday. It doesn't apply to today." Yesterday's promises cannot be assumed to apply to today. Similarly, if a prophecy is part of a living relationship between God and Israel, we cannot as-sume that it will be fulfilled someday, if for some reason it does not find fulfillment in the day to which it originally relates.

11. Ibid., 160.
12. Ibid., 161.
13. Again, see chapter 14 (section 2) above.

However, because it was nevertheless a promise that expressed the mind of God, it will still be a significant indication of God's purpose and thus suggest events that will take place. To my boys I might well say, "No, we can't go swimming today, even though I said we could go yesterday. But we can go on Wednesday after school." The same reasons that made me make the offer in the first place make me repeat it, though in a form that is necessarily modified now that the moment of the original offer is gone. So even though we cannot assume that the actual promises in Ezekiel will be fulfilled in another age, the attitude and purpose they express may find embodiment in some way.

First Testament prophecy is not a coded preview of modern history. It is an affirmation of God's moral will, and it is as such that it needs applying to the Middle East today (as to Britain or the United States). It is a promise of how God plans to renew the Jewish people and to bless the world through the Jewish people, and the largely Gentile church can still look forward to the fulfillment of that promise. It is a warning about God's activity in judgment and a challenge to the church that does not escape the world's judgment if it is indistinguishable from the world. It is a portrait of the salvation God intends for the Jewish people and the church and an invitation to enjoy the abundance of riches that are ours now in Christ and in the Spirit and that will be ours in fullness in the new Jerusalem.

The whole story of Israel is part of the tortuous plot that will reach the denouement God planned from the beginning, whatever convolutions it may perform on the way in response to human willfulness (Israel's or that of others). It is for this reason that the same themes recur in different parts of the First Testament and that there are striking parallels between some passages in Scripture and some experiences of modern Israel. The reason is not that modern events fulfill ancient prophecy but that both are part of one overarching purpose that links the God of Israel to modern and ancient people.

20

Is There Prophecy Today?

Defining prophecy is a notoriously difficult matter. Any description of prophecy that has bite will turn out not to apply to every First Testament prophet, let alone to prophets in the New Testament. A definition that does apply to every prophet will turn out to be somewhat vacuous and/or to apply to people other than prophets.[1]

When we cannot define something or find that our attempts to do so become vacuous, then one strategy is to utilize Ludwig Wittgenstein's notion of "family resemblances."[2] A family may have a characteristic profile—a shape of nose and chin, a shape of body, a level of intelligence, a way of walking and thinking, a strength in certain emotions and a weakness in others. Individual members of the family may not have all these characteristics, but to qualify as sharing the family resemblance, they will manifest most of them. In a parallel way, we might suggest that prophets have a set of family resemblances. Individual prophets may then lack some of these without this imperiling their being identified as prophets or imperiling the accuracy of the profile. Conversely, features of character or ministry that appear in only one or two prophets may not be indications of the nature of prophecy but rather may be features of these individuals' ministry or person.

Another way to make the point would be to consider how prophets differ from other people through whom God may speak and act. In the First Testament these would include leaders (judges), kings, priests, and experts (the "wise" of Proverbs). In the New Testament, prophets appear in a list that also includes pastors, teachers,

---

1. First published in *The Spirit and Church* 3 (2001): 27–46.
2. See *Philosophical Investigations* (Oxford: Blackwell; New York: Macmillan, 1953), 65–67.

apostles, and evangelists (see Eph 4). The term "prophecy" appears in a list that also includes utterance of knowledge, utterance of wisdom, faith, gifts of healing, working of miracles, discernment of spirits, tongues, and interpretation of tongues (1 Cor 12). The complication in connection with the New Testament is that we are quite unsure of the meaning of many of these terms. In the modern church, we might ask how prophets differ from priests, pastors, worship ministers, education ministers, teachers, counselors, spiritual directors, and youth ministers—let alone social activists.

The way I therefore proceed in this chapter is by drawing up a family profile for the First Testament prophets and comment on the possible contemporary significance of each of the elements.

I make the assumption that we might reasonably expect prophetic ministry to be exercised in the contemporary church. I assume that there is no basis for the claim that the exercise of prophetic ministry was confined to the biblical period. Indeed, that seems to be in conflict with God's promise that the exercise of prophecy will be a feature of the full life that God intends for the chosen people (see Joel 2:28–29).

1. A Prophet Shares God's Nightmares and Dreams

Prophets are mediators between heaven and earth. They bring human beings a word from God that they could not have attained by ordinary means, or they bring home this word with a distinctive sharpness. They also bring a vision from God. The beginning of Isaiah 1 describes what follows as a "vision"; the beginning of Isaiah 2 describes it as a "word."

One of the First Testament words for a prophet is "seer" (e.g., 2 Kgs 17:13). Strictly there are two words, *hozeh* and *ro'eh*, but both are participles from verbs meaning "see," and they thus correspond well to the English word. Prophets are people who see things that other people cannot see. These may be realities of the present but unseen world (cf. 1 Kgs 22:15–23; 2 Kgs 2:9–14; 6:15–23). Or they may be realities of the visible but still future world (cf. the man of God in 1 Kgs 13:1–3).

Prophets such as Amos, Hosea, Isaiah, and Micah declared that political calamity was coming for the people of God, in large part because of what was wrong in their society. This might seem to suggest that they were either social reformers or astute political commentators or both. As social reformers perhaps they looked at the life of the people of God and perceived an absence of commitment to God and commitment to other members of the community, and they inferred—or were assured by God—that trouble would follow. Or as political commentators, perhaps they read the political scene more astutely than other people did. Isaiah could see that Syria and Ephraim were feebler than people in Jerusalem hoped or feared.

Yet these prophets often talked as if the process may have been the reverse of this.[3] The background of Amos's ministry was that he had seen nightmare visions such

---

3. Cf. chapter 9 (section 2) above.

as those related in Amos 7:1–9 and 8:1–3. He knew that the "Day of Yahweh" was about to happen in Ephraim, and that it was not good news, as the people thought (cf. Amos 5:18–20). Yahweh had shared this with him. The question he then had to handle was why this was so and what were its implications. Analogously, the beginning of Isaiah's ministry is his nightmare vision of the calamity that Yahweh intends to bring on Judah, and is bringing even now as the Holy One commissions him to stop up people's eyes and ears so that they cannot see or hear (Isa 6:1–13). He, too, then has to handle the question why this is so and what are its implications—questions to which Isaiah 1–5 now give the answers. It is not that the prophets' moral and social critique makes them infer that doom is coming on the people of God. It is their awareness of doom coming on the people that makes them look for the reasons in the people's life.

Politically, too, the prophets' revelations began from their mysterious knowledge of what Yahweh was planning to do. As well as knowing about that eventual calamity, Isaiah also knew that in the shorter term Yahweh was going to see to it that Assyria would defeat Ephraim and Syria, the northern neighbors who were leaning on Judah to ally with them. This had nothing in particular to do with political plausibilities. There is no reason to infer that Isaiah had more human political insight than the kings of Judah, Ephraim, and Syria and their advisers. Isaiah just knew what Yahweh was going to do. And it had nothing to do with deserve, though it did have something to do with theology. Judah deserved no deliverance; the certainty of deliverance from Ephraim and Syria derived from the faithfulness of Yahweh. These prophets sensed that calamity was coming first and asked questions about it afterwards.

Fortunately for themselves and for us, this last example shows how the prophets had dreams as well as nightmares. The most basic dream is that the decimation of the people through God's punishment, even if it is followed by further trouble for the remains of the "tree," is not the last word. "The holy seed is its stump" (Isa 6:13). Humanly speaking, a tree that has been felled and burned can hardly grow again, but the destiny of God's tree is not limited by regular rules of nature. Similar considerations emerge from Hosea. Hosea and Gomer had a nightmare marriage that ended in divorce. The Torah forbade a divorced couple from marrying each other again (Deut 24:1–4); we are not sure of the reasons for this. The existence of that prohibition adds force to the fact that Yahweh bids Hosea seek out Gomer once more and remarry her. It provides a picture of God's dream for Ephraim. Even divorce does not terminate Yahweh's concern for the people and Yahweh's commitment to it. Even while laying down a rule in the Torah about this matter, Yahweh can decide not to abide by the rule.

The prophets were people who looked at the present in light of the past and in light of the future, and also looked at the future in light of the present. They called Israel to live in the present in light of the future. They knew that God could envisage a nightmare future but also that God had that dream vision for the future, too. They pictured the dream future in light of the past; what God had done before gave God and them the ways to picture the future for people. Every element in Ezekiel's systematic portrayal of God's vision for the people in Ezekiel 34–48 involves nothing more (but nothing less) than a divinely inspired Technicolor, IMAX reworking of the key promises and key gifts that God had given the people before.[4]

The prophets thus called Israel to live in light of its own story. All the major elements in the story from creation to the fall of Jerusalem appear somewhere or other in the messages of the prophets. They see the elements in this story as providing clues for understanding God and for understanding God's people in the future. Whatever happened in their communities or was threatened for them, they kept coming back to that story and asking once more what might be its implications. They did not see themselves as great innovators, as people with a novel message. In a sense they had nothing to say that was not implicit in the story of the past. They wanted to remedy people's lack of knowledge, but this "knowledge" (*da'at*) was not a matter of mental awareness of facts. It was a matter of acknowledgment or recognition of facts that were already before them.

Prophets today will share with us God's nightmares and God's dreams for us. They will frighten us with their insight into the terrible disaster that hangs over the people of God, though if they have to do that, they will also encourage us with God's vision for our escaping disaster or finding new life the other side of disaster. If we live with the aftermath of calamity, like the church in Europe, they will thrill us with their insight into God's dreams for us. But as they do that, their encouragement will come in the context of affirming that the calamity had to be, and was deserved, and needs to be faced.

2. A Prophet Speaks Like a Poet and Behaves Like an Actor

As God's nightmares and dreams, the prophets' visions demand to be taken with absolute seriousness, but not as direct, literal portrayals of reality. Dreams and nightmares are not like that. To put it another way, the prophets were poets. While some parts of their books are prose sermons, for the most part their prophecies take the form of lines of verse, with the features of Hebrew poetry such as parallelism. They are full of imagery and symbolism, of simile and metaphor, of hyperbole and rhetorical question. Commonly they do not describe things directly, in the way that much of the teaching in the Torah does. Characteristically, their words are anything but straightforward (see, e.g., 1 Kgs 13; 22). Receiving a word from a prophet does not suddenly make life less complicated, as if we now know things we did not know before. It is more like listening to one of Jesus' parables.

We should thus expect Christian prophets to speak in pictures, as (in my experience) they commonly do. Often, receiving their revelations from God will leave us initially puzzled rather than quite clear what God is saying to us, as was the case when the disciples heard Jesus' parables. A prophet's picture may well require interpretation.

4. See further chapter 19 above.

One reason for this is that deep truths about God cannot be put in straightforward language that speaks only to the rational mind. They require imagery that can reach the whole person. Another is that we do not want to receive God's truth, and God in mercy sometimes avoids speaking to us clearly because that is to put us into a worse position than the one we already occupy. Prophets speak in pictures because we can then avoid seeing what God is saying, yet also because the picture may get underneath our guard and break through our resistance.

Prophets act as well as speak. Sometimes they act in a way that directly implements their message, even though they do not attempt to be social reformers. Like their words, their acts tend to be illustrative of their vision rather than a down-to-earth exposition of it. So Isaiah goes about naked and barefoot for three years to dramatize what Yahweh intends to do (Isa 20), and Jeremiah smashes a pitcher with the same intent (Jer 19). Such acts had various significances. They provided vivid and worrying illustrations of what the words announced. They constituted another way of getting beneath people's guard and breaking through their resistance, another alternative to straightforward words. Worst of all, they actually put Yahweh's words into effect, in the way that putting a ring on someone's finger contributes to the process of marrying him or her or returning it contributes to a breakup.

· Prophets were people with the capacity to be outrageous. This emerges in another way. In its first usages in the First Testament, the verb "prophesy" refers not to speech with identifiable content but to some unusual form of behavior that suggests that a person is under supernatural influence (see Num 11; 1 Sam 10; 18:10; 19). Prophesying functioned as a sign in the way that tongues sometimes do; perhaps it was something very like tongues. As well as providing individuals with evidence that God was indeed involved with them, prophesying could be the evidence for other people that the person's words should be heeded, though it does not constitute these words. The verb does come to be used as the regular verb to describe the delivering of a verbal message from God, and this becomes its most frequent usage. But prophesying links with an activity that the NRSV can translate as "raving" or "being in a frenzy" (though admittedly these precise translations give a misleading impression). We should not be surprised if prophets fail to observe the usual decorum of suburban congregations in the historic churches.

Prophecy will put before the church a challenge to our will, our imagination, and our insight. Perhaps God sends us prophets because we cannot respond to more straightforward address. And/or perhaps God does not send us too many prophets because we cannot respond to address that is not straightforward.

3. A Prophet Is Not Afraid to Be Offensive

Death is no joke. In our culture, the funeral is the one occasion where formality still obtains. In the First Testament, a death is the one occasion when we find David expressing his feelings, even if someone in his court ghostwrote his lament (2 Sam

1:17–27). On a later occasion Ephraimites heard a solemn prophet uttering a funeral dirge: "She has fallen, she will not rise again" (Amos 5:2). Who is this? Who has died? It is Ephraim itself. Maiden Israel turns out to be the subject of the verb. The people who overhear the dirge ask who has died and discover that they have. Yahweh likewise bids Ezekiel, "You, lead a dirge for the leaders of Israel" (Ezek 19:1). Thus Ezekiel intones an allegory about a mother who watches one of her sons be dragged off to Egypt and another one be dragged off to Babylon. The devastating and heartless picture constitutes another attempt to get the city, the leadership, and the exiles to see sense.

There is a place in Moab called Madmen (which would offer temptation to someone prophesying in English) and a place near Jerusalem called Madmenah. Fortunately or unfortunately, *madmenah* is also Hebrew for a cesspit. Isaiah thus puns on the name, promising that "the Moabites will be trampled in their place like straw being trampled in a cesspit, and they will spread their hands in the midst of it to swim as swimmers spread their hands to swim, but he will humble their majesty" (Isa 25:10–11). Moabites swimming in a cesspit? Commentators routinely critique or defend or apologize for the image, but ultimately there is nothing more violent here than appears in many other passages in the First Testament. What is noteworthy is the bad taste, by Western standards, and perhaps by Middle Eastern ones, too.

Ezekiel is the master of bad taste—oddly, perhaps, for a priest. One prize instance is his allegory about Jerusalem (Ezek 16) with its portrait of the baby wallowing in blood, then lying naked Lolita-like in puberty, which becomes a lewdly detailed account of her subsequent promiscuity and a faithlessness that involves her paying for sex rather than charging for it.

Yahweh inspires prophets to speak in the manner of late-night satellite television as well as that of BBC1.

4. A Prophet Confronts the Confident with Rebuke and the Downcast with Hope

Popular understanding assumes that the importance of the prophets lies in their anticipatory witness to Jesus. They do give such witness, but one can read page after page of the prophets without coming across any statement that directly constitutes witness to Jesus. God summoned and spoke to the prophets so that they could minister directly to the people of their day.

This indeed involved them in promising that one day God would send someone who would fulfill all the hopes attaching to Israel's anointed king, its messiah. But it is striking that they never use the Hebrew word "messiah" to refer to *the* Messiah. The word "messiah" comes only twice in the Latter Prophets (Isaiah, Jeremiah, Ezekiel, and the Twelve). Once it is a description of the Persian king Cyrus, who is God's "anointed one" in bringing down Babylon and opening up the possibility of Judah's restoration (Isa 45:1). In keeping with the common usage in other books, once it refers to Judah's current anointed king (Hab 3:13). The prophets did speak of a future figure who would fulfill God's promises to David and God's expectations of David (e.g., Jer 23:5–6), but they never use the word "messiah" of this person. That is a symbol of the fact that they do not speak much of this coming person. Their focus does not lie on that far future. In the exercise of their ministry, they focus on speaking to their own people in the present. They embody God's desire to speak to people about the realities, temptations, and pressures of their day. As God's word for us, the way they minister to God's people in their day is at least as significant as is the way they talk about the future Messiah.

When they do talk about the future, their direct reason for doing so is to help their own people live in the present. We always need to live in light of the future. Indeed, we always do live in light of the future; the question is whether it is an imagined future (feared or hoped for) or a real one.

The two halves of Ezekiel's ministry provide a noteworthy instance. Before the fall of Jerusalem in 587, people think the future will turn out all right, and Ezekiel's impossible task is to convince them that things are going to be much worse than they believe. After the fall of Jerusalem, however, people sink into despair, and Ezekiel's task is to convince them that things are going to be much better than they believe. As a prophet, Ezekiel's task was to confront the confident with bad news and the downcast with hope.

The same insight emerges from the book of Isaiah as a whole. When people were enthusiastic in their praise, generous in their giving, and fervent in their prayer, Isaiah ben Amoz told them they were a burden that Yahweh wished to cast off because their life outside church did not match their heartfelt worship (Isa 1:10–20). (We are inclined to assume that the problem is that they were not sincere in the sense that their worship was only outward, but this is not Isaiah's critique. There is no reason to doubt that they meant every hallelujah; the problem Isaiah confronts is the mismatch between their life of worship and their life in the world. They worshiped Yahweh with enthusiastic hearts, but their community life was not lived Yahweh's way.) When people despaired of their future because they knew Yahweh had brought calamity upon them, though they did not understand why, Second Isaiah told them there were grounds for hope. Yahweh is one who knows how to say that enough is enough. When trouble comes, this does not mean Yahweh has cast us off forever.

If God sends us prophets, we should expect them to confront us in the same ways. We do not need prophets to tell us what we already think or to affirm our current feelings.

Prophets may bring good news or bad news, but if it is good news, they are probably not telling the truth. It is not for nothing that Ahab calls Elijah a troubler of Israel, even if Ahab is himself Israel's real troubler (1 Kgs 18:17–18).

5. A Prophet's Task Is Mostly to Speak to the People of God

While prophets sometimes spoke *to* other nations and often spoke *about* other nations, usually they spoke *to* the people of God. As the people of God, Ephraim and Judah were also themselves nations, but the prophets addressed these nations as entities to which Yahweh was committed and addressed them concerning their commitment to Yahweh. Their primary significance for us lies in the way they addressed the people of God.

It is common to speak of the church having a prophetic ministry to society, but I am not clear that this emerges from the nature of First Testament prophecy. If we ask after the nature of Israel's vocation in relation to other peoples, it more likely lay in a vocation to be a people that embodied an alternative vision of what it meant to be a human community. It is a community with God at its center that would demonstrate the blessing that comes from having God at the center. If the church has a ministry to society, it again lies in embodying such an alternative vision. If we care to call that a prophetic ministry, we may do so. But in the absence of our *embodying* such an alternative vision, the attempt to exercise a prophetic ministry by the use of prophetic *words* is surely unlikely to have much effect. It is we ourselves who need to heed the prophetic word so that we may become the alternative community. Prophets are people who call the church to be the people of God instead of being an imitation of the world.

Similarly, it has been common to think of the prophets as social reformers, but I have noted that it is not clear that they were that. A social reformer is someone with a vision for society and some ideas about how to implement that vision, some practical policies that the reformer urges the community to adopt. Some of the prophets were indeed people who had a vision for society, though this applies in particular to prophets such as Amos and Micah; it is not a central characteristic of prophets in general. Even in the case of these prophets, their vocation was not the developing of practical plans for reform. They were usually quite general in their social vision, and when they were being specific and concrete, it was usually in critique, not in formulating positive proposals. They critiqued legal procedures that worked for the rich and powerful and against ordinary people (e.g., Amos 2:6–8), but they did not outline proposals for judicial reform to put this matter right. There were people in Israel who accepted that vocation and sought to think of ways to turn the prophets' visions into practical proposals that they could urge on the community, but they were not the prophets. They were the anonymous figures whose God-inspired work came to be incorporated in the teaching in the Torah, such as the Deuteronomists. It is these figures who were Israel's social reformers.

Yahweh's summons to the prophets was to focus on Yahweh's vision for the society as the people of God. They were to find ways of reminding people of the nature of God as the compassionate and powerful one, the committed and decisive one, the fair and just one, the faithful and authoritative one. They were to find ways of reminding the people of their vocation to image this God so that the life of the people of God spoke to the world. And they were to find ways of bringing home to the people of God the terrible cost of failing to do that. They were to draw them to turn away from wrongdoing and from other religious commitments and to turn to Yahweh.

Prophets today will then exercise their ministry to the church. It may be that they will need to speak about God's expectations of the wider society or of the nations, but there is then a trap of which they will need to be aware. It is possible to fulminate about society or about the nations in such a way as to make the church feel reassured and self-righteous. This is not the implication of the way the First Testament prophets spoke of and to the nations. Indeed, the story of Jonah warns against that trap. There it is the foreign nation that knows instinctively how to respond to a prophet. The prophets would have given their eyeteeth for a response from the people of God like the one Nineveh gave. The people of God have no room for self-righteousness over against the nations.

When prophets said that God intended to put the nations down, sometimes their aim was to deliver the people of God from a false alliance with and reliance on the nations. A modern analogy for this alliance might be the close association between church and nation in Europe and the United States. Despite the formal dissociation of church and state in the United States, there as in Europe the church's sharing the gospel with other peoples has been systematically interwoven with the nation's winning an empire. Prophets will perceive this alliance and warn the church about it.

Sometimes the prophets spoke of the destiny of the nations because the nations were a threat to the people of God. There are many countries in which this is so today. Prophets will promise the people of God that the threat will not last forever.

6. A Prophet Is Someone Independent of the Institutional Pressures of Church and State

In David's lifetime, the most prominent prophet was Nathan, and in effect he was on the king's staff. So perhaps was Gad, the only other prophet mentioned in David's story. This makes it easy for Nathan to be the king's yes-man (2 Sam 7:1–3). It also gives him chance to confront David (2 Sam 12), but one wonders whether a little more confrontation might have been appropriate throughout the story in 2 Samuel 13–1 Kings 2. Subsequently a king such as Ahab has hundreds of prophetic advisers who can be relied on to be yes-men (1 Kgs 22), as the kings of other nations had many supportive prophets.

When Amos goes around Bethel speaking of disaster to come on the nation, Amaziah, the senior pastor at Bethel, urges him to desist. He should go back to Judah and earn his living prophesying there. Judah will, of course, welcome words about disaster for the northern kingdom. In reply, Amos suggests that Amaziah has misunderstood Amos's position. He is not a prophet like Gad and Nathan who is in the king's employ and can be sent about by a royal official such as Amaziah. Nor is he a trained prophet like the people who belonged to Elisha's prophetic seminary. "I am no prophet, nor a prophet's son," he says. Admittedly the NRSV may be wrong in rendering Amos's response in the present tense. The Hebrew sentence is a noun clause, literally "I no prophet." One has to infer from the context whether such a statement refers to past, present, or future. TNIV renders it as past, which fits Amos's subsequent past-tense testimony about Yahweh's taking him and sending him to prophesy. The main point is little affected by this uncertainty. Either way, although there are prophets who work for the king and prophets who have been trained in prophetic seminaries, Amos distances himself from them. It is thus ironic that the word Amos raises questions about, the word *nabi'*, eventually becomes *the* positive word for a prophet. The word Amaziah uses to describe Amos is "seer," so evidently seers, too, can be in the service of the government (cf. 2 Sam 24:11; Mic 3:7?). The fact that they see supernaturally and accurately does not guarantee that they serve Yahweh.

Evidently there is an office of prophet, occupied by people such as Nathan and presupposed by someone such as Amaziah, but this office is not occupied by prophets such as Elijah and Elisha or Amos and Jeremiah. They are not on the payroll of the people of God, like priests. Who was king in Judah, and who were priests, was fixed. God had taken an initiative long ago with regard to kings and priests, in line with the instincts of Israel ("make us a king like the nations"). After that, normally God let things work themselves out in accordance with the rules of descent. With prophets, however, God can take an initiative and intervene. There is no parallel set of human expectations to observe or break. Thus Israel knew no women priests and few women political leaders, but it did have women prophets. And in contexts of church renewal and revival God has often used women prophets (whether or not they were called such) in churches that would not recognize women priests or pastors.

There is nothing wrong with being on the payroll; Paul argued that it was fine for a servant of Christ to be supported financially by the community. But if you are on the payroll, it is much harder for you to take a prophetic stance in relation to that community. You cannot bark at the hand that feeds you without risking its cutting off your food supply, and you may have other mouths to feed as well as your own. Your experience and that of your family may correspond to that of Micaiah, who finds himself on a diet of bread and water for bringing God's word to his people (1 Kgs 22).

To put it in modern terms, it is virtually impossible for a pastor to be a prophet. In this context, by a pastor I mean a professional, a person who receives a salary from the people whom he or she pastors, and I speak of this professional pastor's ministry to this congregation that pays this salary. It is possible for a prophet to be a pastor; Gerhard von Rad described Ezekiel thus,[5] and I would do the same for Second Isaiah. But they were on no one's payroll, as far as we know; Ezekiel would have been a priest if he had not been exiled, but there was no temple to be looked after in Babylon. There is a sad irony here that I press on ordinands, and they do not thank me for it. Many men and women go to seminary to train for the church's ministry because they have already exercised a significant informal ministry in church or parachurch contexts. They have been prophetic-type figures, one might say.

---

5. See *Old Testament Theology* (2 vols.; Edinburgh: Oliver and Boyd; New York: Harper, 1965), 2:231–32.

Their faithfulness and fruitfulness in such contexts encourages people to point them toward more formal ministry, but they then have to face the fact that they surrender the capacity to be prophetic once they are ordained and are on the church's payroll.

When we are pastoring individuals, it is necessary to be prophetic. It is therefore to be hoped that being prophetic is possible as well as necessary. This seems to have been so in Israel. The Psalms imply that there were people—presumably Levites and priests—who acted as prophetic pastors who brought the word of God to people when they came to pour out their hurt and anger to God (cf. the story of Hannah and Eli in 1 Sam 1). In this sense, a pastor who is not a prophet is not a pastor either. Indeed, in saying that a pastor cannot be a prophet, perhaps more generally I exaggerate the point, like a prophet. Perhaps one might rather say that monumental pressures not to be prophetic come upon a person who is on the church's payroll. If I am a professional pastor, the only safe stance is thus to assume that I cannot now be prophetic. I must therefore encourage the prophetic ministry of other people who are not on the payroll, who may be able to say the confrontational things that I cannot say, not least encouraging the prophetic ministry of people who may be able to say them to me.

Prophets are people who are surprised to find themselves in the role they have. You do not seek or volunteer or pray to be a prophet. Even Isaiah proves the rule. He indeed volunteers, but he does so in the context of finding that God has already drawn him into the company of heaven, where God is looking for someone to send. Being a prophet means finding yourself drawn into that company and compelled to speak for God. This experience may well contradict your life experience so far, as was the case with Amos, and you may well seek to resist the pressure, as Jeremiah did, or you may not be able to see how you can fulfill such a calling successfully, as Second Isaiah did. I once heard the principal of a rabbinic seminary commenting that when someone told him that they felt called to be a rabbi, he was inclined to send them to a psychiatrist. It is mad to want to be a prophet. Jeremiah commented on how easy it is to deceive oneself into believing that we have a message from God for people (Jer 23:25–26).

A prophet models a kind of relationship with God that is God's intention for everyone. Moses eventually found the pressure of the people to be too much and told God he could carry on no longer (Num 11:14). Yahweh's spirit came on seventy senior members of the community, apparently as a sign that the people are to take them as seriously as they take Moses (!). But two of the senior members who stayed in the camp continued to prophesy. Joshua bade Moses stop them, but Moses was unfazed by what had happened. He did not feel the need to control what Yahweh's spirit might do: "Would that all Yahweh's people were prophets, and that Yahweh would put his spirit on them."

It is intrinsic to the nature of prophecy that it is not under the control of the leaders of the community. In principle anyone may prophesy. That principle is restated in Joel 2:28–29, which makes explicit that in due course Yahweh's spirit will be poured out on people of both sexes, young and old, servants as well as masters.

Acts 2 saw this happening at Pentecost, but it has not usually characterized the church. Yet the promise suggests that it is always God's will for us and invites us to look for its fulfillment.

In our own context we might need to ask who would be the kind of people we would *not* expect to be prophets: these are the people God is likely to want to use as prophets.

7. A Prophet Is a Scary Person Who Mediates the Activity of a Scary God

One of the expressions the books of Kings use to describe prophets is "man of God." In modern parlance, "man of God" (or "woman of God") suggests someone of deep spirituality, of committed prayer life, of spiritual insight. No doubt many prophets were such people. But this is not the connotation of the term "man of God" in the First Testament. The phrase especially suggests a somewhat austere and frightening figure with mysterious powers. A man of God is someone who utters words of fearful significance that can be followed by signs that can be both destructive and constructive (see the stories in 1 Kgs 13; 2 Kgs 1; 2 Kgs 4–8; 2 Kgs 13:14–19).

Prophets are such figures because they reflect and mediate the nature of their God. Yahweh is somewhat mysterious, unpredictable, and frightening as well as consistent, reassuring, and encouraging. The man after God's heart who experienced God being full of grace and commitment through the prophet Nathan's ministry in 2 Samuel 7 also experienced God offering the choice of famine, defeat, or plague through the prophet Gad in 2 Samuel 24 (cf. also the story in 2 Sam 6). The toughness of God and prophet in these stories reminds us of the toughness of Peter and of Peter's God in Acts 5.

If prophetic ministry is exercised today, then, we should expect this to reduce the domestication of God that characterizes us.

One of the reasons why the God of the First Testament prophets is scary is that they have no one else on whom to project scary aspects of supernatural reality. Christian faith has usually been inclined to various forms of dualism, and the prophets would stand against that. Whereas we project the scary onto Satan, the prophets were insistently convinced that Yahweh was the only god who really deserved to be called God, and they denied Israel the right to treat other heavenly beings as if they had any power. Further, whereas the nations around them might assume that there were many demons that could affect the lives of people, the prophets never spoke in these terms.

We might therefore expect prophets today once again to stand against Christian inclination to think that there are demonic powers that are powerful enough to oppress people and frustrate God's purpose. They will remind us that there is only one God, only one being who has real power in heaven and on earth. If the God of love is also a scary God, at least there is no doubt that this God is in control.

8. A Prophet Intercedes with Boldness and Praises with Freedom

Prophets are mediators between God and humanity, and they mediate in both directions. We usually think of them as people who especially bring God's word to us, but they also bring our words to God. Both capacities emerge from their membership of Yahweh's cabinet. Their listening to its deliberations enables them to share the results of these with the human beings who will be affected by them. It also gives them the opportunity to take part in these deliberations in order to persuade the cabinet to come to a different decision, and this is what we see in the stories of people such as Amos (Amos 7:1–8:3). Both activities, the preaching and the prayer, have the same aim, to make it possible for Yahweh's positive purpose to be fulfilled and for Yahweh's threats to be abandoned.

The story of Jonah illustrates especially vividly one key way in which a prophet gets Yahweh's threat of punishment averted. His task is to declare that trouble is coming on Nineveh, this causes Nineveh to turn from its wrongdoing, and then Yahweh's threat can be withdrawn. Jeremiah 18 states the principle that underlies this story. It also states a correlative principle, that seeing Yahweh's promises fulfilled depends on a life of right-doing. A prophet urges people on in right-doing, in order that they may see Yahweh's promises fulfilled.

But preaching is not enough for a prophet. It is accompanied by praying, and this must be so, because praying equally emerges from that membership of God's cabinet. A person who hears that there is trouble coming on people can hardly simply accept this. Such a person would *have* to beseech Yahweh to be merciful. At least, this is the instinct of a prophet such as Amos, though the problem with Jonah is that he did not want to be the means of wrongdoers being forgiven. It is as an intercessor that Abraham is called a prophet, on the very first occasion that the word "prophet" comes in the Bible (Gen 20:7). Prophets are mediators between heaven and earth. They bring human beings a word from God that they could not have attained by ordinary means, and they also take words from human beings to God that would not otherwise reach God.

Of course there is no guarantee that Yahweh will acquiesce with the urgings of a prophet, as Amos also makes clear. Yahweh accepts Amos's first two prayers but refuses his second two. There are times when God says "Enough" and refuses to relent. Jeremiah and Hosea had the same experience (see Jer 14–15; Hos 5:15–6:6). It may be that even then a prophet does not too soon take no for an answer. The prophet's challenge is still to get God to have a change of mind, in keeping with the occasions when God does that in Scripture. The prayers of a prophet correspond to one of the three main ways of speaking to God that appear in the psalms, the laments, which cover what we call supplication (for ourselves) and intercession (for others). They ask God to do what God is not inclined to do and resist pressure to take no for an answer.

Praying in the manner of a lament is not the only way in which a prophet speaks to God on behalf of the people. The Psalms' other two main ways of speaking to God are two forms of praise, hymns and thanksgivings. Hymns praise God for who God always is and for God's great acts of salvation. Thanksgivings give testimony to what God has just done for me or for us. After Abraham, Scripture's second prophet is Miriam, and the way she acts as a prophet is in joining Moses in leading people in praise and dancing after the deliverance at the Red Sea (Exod 15:20–21). The greatest of the judges, Deborah, is also a prophet, and in an analogous way she takes the lead over Barak in praise for what Yahweh has done in delivering the people, as she does in making that victory happen (Judg 4–5). Then the opening of the story of the monarchy includes the thanksgiving of Hannah, who praises God like a prophet as she speaks of what Yahweh is doing, and as she speaks of Yahweh's "anointed," the king whom her son will anoint (indeed, two of them).

If there are prophets in our midst, they will give themselves in prayer urging God not to bring calamity on the church. They will pray not once but twice, as often as they have a sense that God plans trouble for the church, until God forbids them to pray. Even then they may wonder whether God is merely testing them, and they may not give up. They will lead us in praise and dance that speak powerfully of the nature of God as the church's formidable and generous king and deliverer and celebrate the great things God has done for us and the great things God still intends.

9. A Prophet Ministers in a Way That Reflects His or Her Personality and Time

There is a paradox about prophecy. Of all inspired Scripture, along with the revelation to Moses it is prophecy that is described most transcendently as words that come direct from God. Prophets receive God's dictation; they hear God speak and pass on God's actual words (e.g., Ezek 17:1–21). Or God's words are put in their mouth (e.g., Isa 51:16). Or God speaks "by means of them"—literally, speaks "by their hand" (e.g., Jer 37:2); their tongues are like the musical instrument that God plays.

The paradox is that the individual humanness of the prophets also comes out in their prophecy. There is little mistaking the words of Jeremiah for those of Isaiah, or the words of Ezekiel for those of Second Isaiah. *How* they speak and *what* they say reflects who they are. God uses them as the people they are to bring the message they can bring.

When we hear an alleged prophetic message today, if we know the person we may be tempted to comment, "That's just what I would have expected him or her to say." We may be right that they say what we might have been able to envisage them saying, but in itself this does not raise questions about whether God was speaking through them. Prophecy comes through the human personality. It does not bypass that personality.

There is another, related paradox about prophecy. Because Western culture has put a high value on the individual, it has appreciated the prophets because they could seem to stand like lone individuals. They could seem to have realized their own distinctive individuality in a remarkable way. Yet this likely exaggerates or misinterprets their individuality. The books of Kings speak much of those prophetic seminaries or prophetic communities referred to above. Here prophets apparently learned and ministered together, like (for instance) the groups of prophets protected by Obadiah (1 Kgs 18). Nor was it only these early prophets who worked in the midst of communities. Isaiah had a group of disciples whom he could commission to treasure his teaching (Isa 8:16). If Jeremiah was alone, he saw this as a regrettable disadvantage of his particular prophetic vocation, not as the logical fulfillment of any prophetic vocation; and even he had Baruch. Prophecy is naturally exercised in the midst of a prophetic community. Here (one might hypothesize) prophets could test out messages that might be the word of Yahweh, before declaring them to their intended audience. Here they could find encouragement to speak out and find support when they paid the price for their ministry. Sometimes they had to take a lone stand, but that was not their aim. It was not of the essence of their ministry. Most of them lived and worked in association with others. For contemporary prophets, too, that will be for their encouragement and protection and for that of the wider community of faith to which they belong and in which they minister.

10. A Prophet Is Likely to Fail

Prophets are not infallible. They make mistakes. Three notable mistake makers are Elijah, Hananiah, and Jeremiah. Elijah makes one mistake, and Yahweh meets him where he is and coaxes him back (1 Kgs 19). As far as we can tell from the book of Jeremiah, Hananiah's whole prophetic ministry was a mistake. Everything he said was scriptural, but he did not know what time it was. He was preaching from the wrong texts in the wrong century. Being scriptural does not mean you are scriptural. Jeremiah went though a number of crises in his relationship with God and found himself rebuked and offered restoration on at least one spectacular occasion (see Jer 15). If we exercise a prophetic ministry, we need to be wary of thinking that we have become infallible.

There is another sense in which prophets fail. They may make no mistakes, but they are unlikely to succeed in achieving the aim that God set before them. In this sense, by and large the great prophets all seem to have been failures. Amos and Hosea failed to halt the slide of Ephraim that hit the bottom with the fall of Samaria. Isaiah and Micah failed to halt the slide of Judah that reached new depths of apostasy in the time of Manasseh. Huldah and Jeremiah failed to halt the further slide that led to the fall of Jerusalem. Ezekiel and Second Isaiah failed to get the exilic community to look at its situation through Yahweh's eyes and to hope and prepare for the restoration of the community. Perhaps Third Isaiah, Haggai, Zechariah, and Malachi were the nearest to being successes, as the Second Temple community does seem to have learned to live with the Torah written into its heart to a much greater extent than the First Temple community. (Ironically, the very greatest of the prophetic successes was Jonah, but he only succeeded with foreigners, and only in a parable.)

Being some years out of Britain, I do not think I have a specific word for the British church, but if I were a prophet where I now live in Southern California, I would declare that the church here is on the way to the same experience as overcame the church in the Eastern Mediterranean in the first millennium and the church in Europe in the second millennium. As the heartland of the gospel moved from the Eastern Mediterranean to Europe and then from Europe to the United States, so it has now moved from the United States to the two-thirds world, to Latin America, Africa, and Asia. As the church in the Eastern Mediterranean all but died in the first millennium and the church in Europe all but died in the second millennium, so the church in the United States is dying. One way to express the inevitability of its death in Southern California is to note how comprehensively it falls into one or the other of two misunderstandings of worship. Either its worship is "moralistic, didactic, and instructive" or it is "excessively therapeutic and narcissistic." Both didactic and therapeutic tendencies are inclined "to talk about meeting with God, rather than to enact such a meeting with the one who is profoundly holy and yet genuinely present."[6]

Whether I am a prophet or not, I do declare this, though I do not expect to be heeded. Indeed, it may be that I am wrong and that God has already abandoned the church here, as God abandoned Jerusalem in Ezekiel's day (see Ezek 9–10). All that is to follow is the formal fall of the city. In Californian culture, one of the ways of denying that death is a reality is by applying vast technological resources to keeping people's bodies alive for as long as possible when the time to die has come. The culture likes to pretend that "death is optional."[7] In a parallel way, pastors spend their energy helping their churches deny that God has left them and that death is imminent. As a prophet, I would say this, but I would fail to halt this slide. But prophet or not, I pray for God not to let the church here all but die.

If I were a prophet, then, what would be the point of the declaring? If prophets (nearly) always fail, what is the point of prophecy?

First, the phenomenon of prophecy indicates that God stays ever hopeful of a response from the people. God did not cast off Israel and has not cast off the church, even if God did cast off whole generations or parts of Israel, as God has cast off whole generations or parts of the church. God kept speaking to it, ever hopeful that *this time* there might be a response. The fact that Israel and the church have never heeded prophets in the past does not close off the possibility that *this time* things might be different. Second, the phenomenon of prophecy has been far more important for other people in other times than for the people whom the prophecy directly addressed. Only a few Judeans heard the words of First Isaiah or Second

6. Walter Brueggemann, "The Book of Exodus," in *The New Interpreter's Bible* (12 vols.; Nashville: Abingdon, 1994), 1:675–981 (see 908).

7. Jane Walmsley, *Brit-Think, Ameri-Think* (repr.; New York: Penguin, 1987), 126.

Isaiah or Third Isaiah. Of the people who did hear these words, many fewer heeded. But since their day, countless millions have heard them, and some have heeded them. When the church in Southern California has died, it is possible that the church in the two-thirds world might be able to learn from its story. A prophetic word that announced the event might enable that church to reflect on the equivalent perils that might lead to its downfall in the fourth millennium.

With failure usually goes suffering. Prophets not only tend to fail to persuade their people to believe in them. The people of God tend to persecute them for bringing their offensive message (cf. Matt 5:12). This pattern appears particularly clearly in Jeremiah and in Isaiah 40–55. Solemnly, Second Isaiah tells us of realizing that the persecution that comes from the people of God (perhaps from the Babylonians, too) actually becomes God's means of ministering to them. The vision of the ultimate servant's ministry in Isaiah 52:13–53:12 reflects the prophet's own experience of being misunderstood, devalued, and persecuted. The prophet had come to see that God could use a prophet's identification with people in their suffering for their sins and a prophet's willingness to suffer even though one had done nothing to deserve it. It could bring people to their senses and enable them to perceive that they had been seeing things wrong. In accepting this suffering, one could even turn it into an offering to God that could compensate for the failures of one's people and help to put things right with God.

While Jesus is the person who supremely fulfills this vision, the New Testament also treats Isaiah 53 as a pattern by which all followers of Jesus will live (see, e.g., Phil 2; 1 Pet 2). Prophets will especially live by it. The very factors that cause God to send prophets, such as people's resistance to listening to God's word by more regular ways such as the exposition of Scripture, are also the factors that are likely to mean that prophets get rejected and persecuted. Like Second Isaiah and the servant in Isaiah 53, they will therefore have the opportunity to make their handling of that experience a means of God's reaching their people through their lives and through their silence, when they have not been able to reach them with their words. And they will have the opportunity to make their accepting of rejection and persecution an offering to God that helps to compensate for their people's resistance to God (compare Col 1:24).

Only a fool would want to be a prophet. A wise person would run away from God's summons, as Jonah did. But the person who fails to escape becomes a blessing and finds great fruitfulness.

21

How Does Poststructuralist
Interpretation Work?

Isaiah 40–55 as a Test Case

1. Deconstructing

In his epoch-making commentary whose centenary recently passed, Bernhard Duhm described the exilic Isaiah as naive and lacking in self-criticism.[1] Some of the most impressive commentaries on Isaiah 40–55, such as those of James Muilenburg and Claus Westermann,[2] have been disinclined to take up a critical stance in relation to the content of these chapters. It can seem that this material is treated as especially holy ground, or perhaps that readers agree to collude with the work's rhetoric. For Isaiah 40–55 shouts very loud, and we have laid down and surrendered. Yet a work that shouts loud may be suspected of susceptibility to deconstruction. The exposure of this susceptibility need not be a hostile act but the act of someone who appreciates the text, who more than anyone wants to understand, and who wants the object of

---

1. B. Duhm, *Das Buch Jesaja* (Göttingen: Vandenhoeck und Ruprecht, 1892; 4th ed., 1922), 307; cf. R. N. Whybray, *Isaiah 40–66* (London: Oliphants, 1975), 69. The current chapter was first published in *Biblical Interpretation* 5 (1997): 225–46.

2. J. Muilenburg, "The Book of Isaiah: Chapters 40–66," in *The Interpreter's Bible* (12 vols.; Nashville: Abingdon, 1956), 5:381–773; C. Westermann, *Isaiah 40–66* (Philadelphia: Westminster Press; London: SCM, 1969).

appreciation to be understood. There are reasons of substance for the conviction that this is holy ground, but the people and things we appreciate deserve not to be looked at through rosetinted spectacles. True honor recognizes how people oversimplify themselves (to themselves and to others) and oversimplify each other, attempting to hide from ambiguities and uncertainties but not succeeding in hiding them from the eyes of those who appreciate them.

Why does Isaiah 40–55 shout so loud? In a study of *Mark and Luke in Poststructuralist Perspectives*,[3] Stephen D. Moore applies to Mark's Gospel an observation by Paul de Man, one of the founding fathers of deconstruction: "A literary text simultaneously asserts and denies the authority of its own rhetorical mode."[4] Much of my extending of this adaptation to Isaiah 40–55 was stimulated by Moore's work.

Isaiah 40–55 keeps declaring, for instance, that the word of God is all that counts and that everything depends on God, but it does so in such a way as to presuppose that everything depends on the audience's response to it. To put the point in another way, it keeps affirming that the community is secure in Yahweh's commitment and repeatedly tells the community not to be afraid, but it also keeps assaulting it, complaining about its obstinacy, and threatening it with abandonment. Isaiah 55 will finally invite *anyone* who is thirsty to delight in the luxury of a free relationship with Yahweh, but the very next chapter begins in such a way as to query whether the invitation is real, undermining it and making the whole matter conditional: first put matters of justice right, then perhaps you may see Yahweh's deliverance. In fiction, at least, a pair of interrogators may divide between them the tasks of being "Mr. Nice" and "Mr. Nasty." The exilic Isaiah works without a partner, but by fulfilling both roles shows signs of schizophrenia. Does the velvet glove conceal an iron fist, or is the prophet all bark and no bite?

Again, the chapters keep promising a moment when all will see Yahweh's glory (Isa 40:5), when people may comprehensively recognize (four verbs are used) that Yahweh, Israel's holy one, has acted (Isa 41:20). But the moment never comes. The chapters portray an alternative world, using language designed to create before their hearers' eyes and ears a world in which these hearers can live as the real world in such a way that it becomes the real world, but they fail. One wonders why the exilic Isaiah is not put to death as a false prophet, or why, if Isaiah 52:13–53:12 reflects such an execution, the prophecies themselves are preserved rather than consumed in fire. Do they ask us to read them ironically, to recognize that they lead inexorably to the judgment that this was false prophecy?

Historically their readers have not read them so, but have rather yielded to the surface demand of their rhetoric. The chapters portray an alternative world that the believing communities have wanted to be a real world whether it is so or not. It is a

---

3. (New Haven: Yale University Press, 1992).

4. Paul de Man, *Allegories of Reading* (New Haven: Yale University Press, 1979), 17; cf. Stephen D. Moore, *Mark and Luke in Poststructuralist Perspectives* (New Haven: Yale University Press, 1992), 7. See also Moore's quotation on p. 3 from Jacques Derrida, *The Ear of the Other* (Lincoln: University of Nebraska Press, 1985), 85–87.

world in which (to consider only Isa 40) exile does not have the last word; we may pay for our failure, even to excess, but not to eternity; the plaint in Lamentations that "there is no comforter" may be true in the short term, but not in the long; God does depart, but in due course returns; outsiders may vastly outnumber insiders, but even the outsiders in due course will see; the community may be withered by the searing heat of Yahweh's breath, without this implying that Yahweh's purpose ultimately fails; the resources of the outsiders' nations, religion, political leadership, and theology may appear superabundant, but they pale into insignificance beside those of Yahweh; it may seem that Yahweh has chosen to forget the community's destiny, but actually Yahweh continues to be a God who specifically and characteristically offers renewal to the faint, weary, and resourceless.

This is an attractive world, in which people might well like to live. But the text testifies to the nagging doubts, questions, and suspicions that make hearers wisely hesitant to surrender to what may be illusory hopes. The rhetoric seeks to overcome them and gain their collusion. The repetitions, the assonance, and the accumulating, heightening parallelisms overwhelm by the force of reiteration. The rhetorical questions require the audience to involve itself by providing its own answer, yet also tell it the answer to give. The hyperbole, the irony, the ridicule, and the satire imply that only a fool would dispute the matter under discussion. Along with the explicit claim to speak the very words of God overheard in heaven are the implicit appeals to existent Scripture that dare the audience to sit in judgment on God. An escalating crescendo is created as exuberant sequences of such poetry surge relentlessly to their climax, sweeping along their audience and overwhelming resistance by their force, power, and drive. The metaphors, the similes, and the symbols appeal to the imagination. All these things combine to generate insight (not merely to ornament insight gained by some other route) in such a way as bypasses analytic, linear reason and the skepticism that asks, "But is it really so?" To adapt a phrase of Moore's, prophecy "is more like a dream than a dissertation."[5]

Suppose one could halt the poet's flow and insist on quiet reflection. Is there reason behind the rhetoric? It is nearer the surface in Isaiah 41 than in Isaiah 40. There a court scene opens with another question, about who aroused a conqueror. It is a question whose answer the prophet believes to be self-evident (even if the Marduk priests were advocating a different one). This overt question conceals a further covert one. Who is the unnamed conqueror? Ancient and modern targumists view the answer as obvious but disagree on what it is, reflecting the fact (as I believe it to be) that the audience is invited to see at least both Abraham and Cyrus here. It is the pattern of God's dealings with Abraham that reappears in apparently enigmatic or worrying recent events involving Cyrus. The audience is encouraged to see the prophetic understanding of those events as consistent with a known pattern of earlier happenings (Isa 41:1–4). Whereas other communities lack any viable way of living with these events (Isa 41:5–7), that understanding provides the prophet's audience

---

5. Moore, *Mark and Luke*, 71.

with a way of living with them (Isa 41:8–16). Its own past experience of seeking and finding provision (which I presume lies behind Isa 41:17–20) supports the point. Further, there is a pattern of Yahweh's speaking concerning the conqueror that also links Abraham and Cyrus (Isa 41:21–29). The prophet might thus claim that the argument is not in fact merely rhetoric, even if it does fall short of being conclusively compelling in itself. A leap of hope is required if people are to live in the world the prophecy lays before them, but it is not exactly a blind leap. The prophet's own leap of hope in due course finds a place in the community's Scriptures perhaps because people wanted it to be true and believed that there was enough reason behind the rhetoric to take the risk of believing that it was.

It makes a difference to an evaluation of the prophet's words that they appear in the context of Isaiah 1–39 and Isaiah 56–66. Some of the interpretive issues raised for us by Isaiah 40–55 are already implicit in Isaiah 56–66, which themselves presuppose the way chapters 40–55 deconstruct. Perhaps Isaiah 40–55 is ideological at least in the sense that it tells us what we want to hear (that pain and grief are over, that God is returning, that God's reign has begun). But the book of Isaiah could not (or at least does not) stop with chapters 40–55. It needed something else to give some consideration to the problems they raise (or the problems they seek to avoid). The exilic Isaiah may have wanted to have the last word, but could not be allowed to do so. In isolation Isaiah 40–55 might indeed be false prophecy. In cutting off chapters 56–66 from chapters 40–55, Duhm illumined both and obscured both.

2. Mystifying

Another contradiction is involved in the exilic Isaiah's repeated assertion that God's speaking is all that counts for the imminent achievement of God's final purpose (in the End is the word). In Isaiah 40–55 that word is put into writing so that it can make this point to people like twenty-first-century readers who live long after the projected End. It has to do so, for otherwise the word dies. "The mouth of Yahweh has spoken," "the word of our God will stand for ever" (Isa 40:5, 8) are large claims. "A more thoroughgoing idealization of speech can hardly be imagined. To the spoken word, that most ephemeral of substances, a status of pure transcendence is attributed," even though it falls on deaf ears.[6] This is promise about the spoken word, but it is apparently incapable of realization unless spoken word becomes written word. Moreover it is promise, but also quasi-threat, for it expresses God's determination, declaring what will happen no matter how people respond. Or will it? Like Mark, the exilic Isaiah incorporates contradiction into the body of its diction. It both idealizes speech and de-idealizes it (because it is not effective). It gives the impression that there will be achievement, closure, but there never is.

6. Moore's comment regarding an equivalent claim of Jesus, in *Mark and Luke*, 26.

Speech by its nature stands closer to its author than does writing; its meaning thus has more precision and its addressees are known. Paul Ricoeur has emphasized how writing has escaped its author's intention and meaning and has thereby gained in richness; the point was made classically by Plato in *Phaedrus* 275de.[7] Isaiah 40–55 is indeed rich and open in meaning. Whether or not it could have been so in oral form, in the only form we know it, and perhaps the only form in which it has ever existed, this rich multivalence depends on its being in written form. Yet it is a text that places much emphasis on God's speaking and that by implication shares the recurrent human antipathy towards the written. Isaiah 40–55 is presented to us as speech and therefore as clear communication; God speaks, and presumably means to communicate clearly. But it is presented to us as speech only by being presented to us as writing and thus as ambiguous and unclear, and who has the right or obligation to see themselves as addressed by it? Further, we have noted that God's speech takes up God's earlier writing (in previous chapters in Isaiah) and tends then to increase in its ambiguity—both the ambiguity of particular texts (Isa 43:1–4 is an example) and the ambiguity of its relationship with those earlier texts.

God's speech seems to be of unclear meaning not only to us but also to its original hearers/readers who do not yet know or believe or understand (cf. Isa 43:10). Some of the material's ambiguity may derive from its being designed to stimulate thought and/or to apply in several directions; that may be true of Isaiah 42:1–4. But the unclarity of our words often reflects an unclarity in our own mind, and if the prophet has little idea what God is talking about in the final servant passage in Isaiah 52:13–53:12, this would explain the apparent failure to achieve clarity there. Our philosophy of exegesis often presupposes that texts are of clear meaning and that if only we had enough information about language and context or had access to the author's mind, all would be patent. This is a fallacy.

Even when things might be viewed as exegetically clear, it is characteristic even of God's better hearers to fail to understand. This inability characterizes not only Babylonian idol makers (Isa 41:1–7) and their deities (Isa 41:21–29) but also Yahweh's own servant (Isa 42:18–25) and sometimes Yahweh's own prophet (Isa 49:4a), who has not listened to the message of earlier chapters and whose understanding at the highpoint in Isaiah 52:13–53:12 (highpoint of unclarity if of nothing else) falls significantly short of the vision that nevertheless has to be shared. The message is allegedly oral and therefore reasonably clear, but people respond to it as if it were written and therefore enigmatic: as if they are dyslexic.[8] The audience of the chapters resembles the man listening to himself read from them on a journey from Jerusalem to Gaza who needed someone to explain it all to him (Acts 8). It is as if God or prophet, too, were writing rather than speaking and no one is explaining the resultant text, and the audience is thus also reading from a written text rather than listening to a living voice. Its ears

---

7. See, e.g., Paul Ricoeur's discussion in *Interpretation Theory* (Fort Worth: Texas Christian University Press, 1976), 25–44. His work is applied to the servant in Isa 40–55 by J. S. Croatto, *Biblical Hermeneutics* (Maryknoll, N.Y.: Orbis, 1987), 25–35.

8. Cf. Moore, *Mark and Luke*, 12.

are uncircumcised or blocked, its eyes and mind closed, as was threatened in Isaiah 6:9–10, a key text that Isaiah 40–55 and Mark's Gospel have in common, though the exilic Isaiah saw it first. Indeed, enlightenment is still a matter of promise in Isaiah 61:1–2 (which I take to refer to the opening of prison rather than the opening of eyes, but Isaiah 42:16 illustrates how the two form one image; these are only examples of the prominence of the language of light, revelation, sight, concealment, darkness, splendor, knowledge, eyes and other terms from such fields within these chapters).

As well as giving us the impression that there will be closure and achievement but never quite providing it, Isaiah 40–55 also sometimes leaves things open but finds that interpreters want to close them. The wide variety of interpretations of the chapters over the centuries may suggest that most subsequent readers have misunderstood them; we are all the kind of readers it complains about. I have noted that the unclarity of the material sometimes derives from its nature, for it is capable of being allusive and ambiguous, designed to provoke thought rather than to render thought unnecessary. On its own account, however, understanding is not merely a matter of the clarity of the material. Clarity in fact develops through Isaiah 41–45 so that the allusiveness of chapter 41 has disappeared when we reach 44:24–45:8, as the prophet's point about Cyrus becomes quite explicit. But this does not mean that the time for questions is over. On the contrary, this is when the audience's questions begin (Isa 45:11). Matters can be unclear and enigmatic or clear and enigmatic. Who can understand the idea of Cyrus's being Yahweh's anointed? In other words, not everything in these chapters is allusive and ambiguous; much becomes quite clear and it is nevertheless (or rather is therefore the more) objectionable. As Mark will comment, to outsiders and insiders everything is in parables, even the things that are not. Nothing makes sense.

As is the case with Jesus' disciples, failure to understand stems from the hearers' understandable repression as well as the message's inherent ambiguity. The message attracts them by talking about good news: the third verse of Isaiah 40 reappears as the third verse of Mark's Gospel. The exilic Isaiah and the Nazarene Jesus declare that the moment of God's reign has arrived. If this is so, in the event the world looks surprisingly little different. It is not this aspect of the message's fragility that I shall consider here, but rather the fact that the declaration about good news, about the return of God, and about God's reigning lulls its hearers into a false sense of security. Prophecy and story move on from evangel to death.

It is the message about death that the disciples find particularly incomprehensible, and understandably so. Isaiah 40–55 begins from death (the people is grass withered in the searing heat of Yahweh's wind) and promises life. It transpires, however, that one can never turn one's back on death. If we are minded to be encouraged by the prospect of that withering, death-dealing wind being turned in another direction for the sake of Israel as the servant of Yahweh (Isa 40:23–24; 41:2–3, 11–12, 15–16), it is this that lulls us. No empty wind, this (contrast Isa 41:29), Yahweh's wind then returns (Isa 42:1) and—as will happen later in the story of Jesus' testing—drives the servant of Yahweh into a task that turns all that hope upside down. This servant declines to be death-dealing, to snap broken canes and quench flickering flames. But we are then reassured that he will not flicker or break, which hints at the idea that he will be subject to the same testing. The mere hint in Isaiah 42 need not be read that way, but when we return to it from the accounts of a servant's testimony in Isaiah 49–50 and of a servant's humiliation in 52:13–53:12, this seems a direction in which they suggest we read it.

On the one hand, Israel is the servant of Yahweh redeemed from death. On the other, the servant of Yahweh is on the way to death. Israel will be well advised not to listen too naively to the prophet's encouraging message about its being God's servant. They will be ill-advised to be beguiled into thinking that they can have good news without bad news. Even the good news about Cyrus, which they are not inclined to view as good news, can only lead to genuinely bad news.

When the prophet overtly addresses Babylonian gods or people, the covert intended audience is Israelite exiles. But this is only stage one in a complex process. If the prophet does mean that outsiders are to recognize the truth of the message (e.g., Isa 42:10–12, hard to confine to Israelites), in due course they will have to hear it, direct from Yahweh or via Israel or in some other unspecified way, so that the overt audience becomes the actual audience. For all Isaiah of Jerusalem's warnings that the covert Israelite audience of insiders risks forfeiting the ability ever to hear if it persists in blocking its ears, the exilic Isaiah cannot contemplate insiders ever being actually replaced by outsiders, as opposed to being joined by them. The material twice walks to the edge of such an abyss, then fences it with a "but now," we 'attah (Isa 43:1; 44:1). Looking in the face the community's blindness and deafness, the prophet nevertheless affirms its servant/witness status. The link between the end of Isaiah 42 and 43 and the beginning of chapters 43 and 44 is thus essential to their meaning (and the locating of chapter divisions at these points with their mindless or perverse obscuring of this link offers further testimony to readers' capacity for misunderstanding).

Yet the ambiguity about the community generates an ambiguity in the prophet's proclamations about everyone's coming to see (e.g., Isa 41:20; cf. 42:17; each time real disjunctions, though also obscured by the medieval chapter divisions). The "everyone" can and must include insiders in status who need to become insiders in substance, as well as others who are outsiders in both senses, and the threat about being treated as outsiders applies to insiders who open themselves to this threat. In the terms of another framework, among the reasons why the debate about nationalism and universalism in Isaiah 40–55 is misconceived is that in ways such as this the material makes a point of subverting the division between insiders and outsiders. The chapters also thus subvert their own attribution of special status to their audience on the grounds of its being ethnic "seed of Abraham."[9]

3. Intertextual

Perhaps their audience should not shoulder the entire blame for misunderstanding the prophecies, given the fact that the prophet, while explicitly claiming that the

---

9. I owe this last point to Edward Ball, for whose criticisms of this chapter I am grateful.

message is oral, also implicitly claims that it is actually written, being at least in part a mere rereading of the message of Isaiah of Jerusalem. I presume this to have reached some written form, though doubtless not a form identical with Isaiah 1–39 as we know it, and it would suffice if it were merely in reasonably fixed oral form. Either way it is already what the message of the exilic Isaiah will also have to become, independent of its speaker, no longer living speech. Of course Isaiah 40–55 is not a mere rereading of a text going back to Isaiah of Jerusalem, for if that were so it would be unnecessary; actual rereading would be enough. Without willful deafness there would be no need of prophecy; without willful dyslexia there would be no possibility of it. The implicit claim to be restating a written message is an implicit admission that this message is insufficient or multivalent or both.

Whereas Duhm viewed the two major parts of the book of Isaiah as wholly separate, the past two decades have seen increasing interest in the relationship between its different parts and between different specific texts. Intertextuality provides an alternative conceptuality for considering these interrelationships. There are, admittedly, a number of intertextualities, but they have in common the assumption that any text presupposes other texts with which it stands in dialogue. The text's historical meaning derives in significant part from its (not necessarily explicit) relationship with these other texts.

In literature and in Scriptures an allusion to another text is unlikely to be merely a formal appropriation of its language, a rhetorical flourish. It reaffirms or contests or modifies or elaborates or claims the support of this other text. We never know the entirety of a text's intertextuality; how much we know will vary. In broad terms Isaiah 1–39 is part of the intertext for Isaiah 40–55, Isaiah 1–55 as a whole for Isaiah 56–66. Insofar as in origin parts of these sections of the book belong to periods other than those implied by their literary context (for instance, parts of chapters 1–39 with material from the exile or after, or parts of Isaiah 40–55 with material from after the exile, or parts of Isaiah 56–66 with material from earlier), this means that the historical direction of the intertextuality changes, but the fact of it does not.

For different contributors to the book, the Isaiah tradition as they knew it was text they could not ignore. Indeed, it was text that in part inspired them. The new text may purport to reaffirm and reapply the old text in a new context, but it does more than merely repeat it; if that would suffice, the old text might indeed do. Particular aspects of the existent text are taken up, while as significantly other aspects are ignored, and the aspects that are taken up are themselves modified and/or transformed as they now appear in a new context. They contribute to the new prophecy by the nature of their own content that exercises substantial influence on its content. They also contribute by the resonances from tradition they give to the new text and by the authority that carries over from them to it, modifying any sense of its dangerous novelty.

Isaiah 40–55 involves a number of significant intertextualities. While I refer to some motifs that the chapters take up from other parts of the tradition, I focus on the way the exilic Isaiah claims the mantle of Isaiah of Jerusalem. I speak in those terms for convenience, not meaning to reify either person. For all I know, a score of authors may have contributed to each section of the book, and I assume we must allow for the possibility that our concern to identify material that came from a key individual is an anachronism. From time to time there is an actual "I" in Isaiah 40–55 whose importance has sometimes been underestimated, but this is no reason to see an individual's importance as all-pervasive. The text presents us with a collection of poems that refer to an individual prophet but do so only rarely. Why not at both points read with the grain?

The exilic Isaiah claims the mantle of Isaiah of Jerusalem. If Isaiah 40–55 asks us to read Isaiah 1–39 in its light, however, its claiming the support of those chapters points also to our reading Isaiah 40–55 themselves in light of them. Texts in inter-textual relationship reverberate with each other. Isaiah 40–55 cannot get away from aspects of Isaiah 1–39 that it finds troublesome. It may seek to abandon the idea of an Israelite anointed king and to democratize the idea of the servant, the chosen, the one Yahweh loves, but if the idea of an individual anointed king turns out to be difficult to evade and is thus also simultaneously applied to Cyrus, this may threaten ideologies as dangerous as the ones the exilic Isaiah is seeking to avoid. Further, the prophecy may be dangerously idealistic in its attempt to abandon the idea of the anointed king. Israel had found it could not do without one before and would be likely to find it needed one again. The community might need the harnessing of the idea of monarchy to the idea of justice as this was pressed by the kingship ideal if it was to be offered some protection from kingship without that ideal. In other words, it may be fortunate as well as inevitable that revisionist interpretations of texts do not replace their originals, even within Scripture.[10] Again, Isaiah 40–55 may seek to turn the idea of Yahweh's being Israel's holy one from threat to reassurance, but Second Isaiah cannot so easily shrug off First Isaiah's instinct to declare judgment on people who seem willfully unable to see, and this also reflects the fact that Isaiah of Jerusalem was not wrong. The nature of intertextuality is that through "the anxiety of influence" the precursors still speak even as the "strong poets" are seeking to evade or overcome their vision.[11]

Isaiah of Jerusalem had had to make a choice between death through not being written down and death through being written down.[12] The exilic Isaiah takes part in his resurrection and in his death, or perhaps in his resuscitation, his death, and

10. Cf. C. R. Seitz's comments "On the Question of Divisions Internal to the Book of Isaiah," in *Society of Biblical Literature 1993 Seminar Papers* (ed. E. H. Lovering; Atlanta: Scholars Press, 1993), 260–66 (see 266).

11. See Harold Bloom, *The Anxiety of Influence* (New York: Oxford University Press, 1973); cf. F. McConnell's comments in *The Bible and the Narrative Tradition* (ed. F. McConnell; New York: Oxford University Press, 1986), 10; and Richard B. Hays, *Echoes of Scripture in the Letters of Paul* (New Haven: Yale University Press, 1989), 16–17. I am grateful to John Kelly for reminding me of these allusions.

12. On writing and death, see H. S. Pyper, "Surviving Writing," in *The New Literary Criticism and the Hebrew Bible* (ed. J. Cheryl Exum and David J. A. Clines; Sheffield: Sheffield Academic Press, 1993), 227–49.

his resurrection, bringing him back to life by bringing his words back to people's attention, bringing him to death through making his words mean something different, and bringing him to resurrection, because the last by definition holds together revivification and transformation, the eating of bread and fish and the capacity to remain unrecognized and unconstrained. For the exilic Isaiah, too, becoming a written text is to risk death by misunderstanding. A prophetic book, unlike a prophetic speech, has no direct addressees. By its nature it thus lays itself open to the kind of redeployment that the exilic Isaiah goes in for and experiences. This happens, however, as the written text again becomes speech. It is the third section of the Hebrew canon that comprises the Writings, works that are written but not read (in the regular lectionary);[13] Isaiah becomes a writing but does not escape (mis-) reading. Speech became Scripture in order that Scripture might become speech. It lost addressees so that it might gain them again.

So there before the anonymous prophet stalk several forms of death. Yahweh "made my mouth like a sharp sword," but the sword is two-edged. Yahweh "made me like a polished arrow," but the missile launcher backfires. The prophet is the victim of friendly fire, of self-inflicted wounds. Yahweh indeed "circumcised my ear," and it meant assault and shame (Isa 50:4–6). When the chapters offer their climactic description of Yahweh's servant, it is of someone for whom shame and assault become death, though this is indeed a death followed by transformation rather than mere resuscitation. The fate of Isaiah of Jerusalem's text adumbrates the fate of Yahweh's servant, and both provide the pattern for the exilic Isaiah's own text, of which Jesus and Mark will in due course be the resuscitation, the death, and the resurrection (without Jesus and Mark many fewer people would have heard of Isa 40, but the text they have heard of is not Isa 40). What the exilic Isaiah does to Isaiah of Jerusalem, Jesus and Mark (not to mention the Qumran community and others) will do to the exilic Isaiah.

4. Sociocritical

There is another way of approaching the question why Isaiah 40–55 shouts so loud, why it seeks so hard to manipulate its hearers into compliance, whether it is an ideological text. The phenomenon raises questions about power. Consciously or unconsciously, texts are written to serve interests of their authors and their communities. That is not a total explanation of them, but it is one level of explanation. A possible question to ask of any text, then, is "Whose interest does it serve?"[14]

The sources suggest a plausible picture of the Judean community in Babylon to which the chapters refer. It comprised chiefly the religious and political leadership from Jerusalem and its families, numbering some thousands, who had been removed

13. So John Barton, *Oracles of God* (London: DLT; New York: Oxford University Press, 1986), 75–79.
14. N. K. Gottwald thus offered a study of "Social Class and Ideology in Isaiah 40–55," *Semeia* 59 (1992): 43–57.

there by the Babylonian army. A community once used to power and significance, they were people who now found themselves insignificant and powerless. They were disunited among themselves in their interpretation of their religious and political circumstances, taking different attitudes to international political prospects in Babylon and to the future of Yahwistic religion in its relationship to matters such as worship by means of images. They were thus characterized by internal and external conflict.

The nature of the contemporary community in Jerusalem and Judah is a matter of more controversy. Lamentations pictures the city as desolate and empty; Isaiah 40–55 suggests a similar understanding. This picture of an abandoned city may be an exaggeration, for rhetorical or ideological reasons or both. The surrounding Judean hills continued to be occupied by small communities of farmers and shepherds who in total numbers vastly outnumbered the exiles (see 2 Kgs 25; Jer 40–43), and it would be surprising if there was no occupation of the city.

The evidence from a slightly later period for the attitudes of Judean and Babylonian communities to each other is that the relationship involved considerable antipathy. Within each there were at least some who regarded the other as contaminated (see, e.g., Zech 3; Ezra 3–6; and the indications of conflict within Isa 56–66). It would not be surprising if the same attitude obtained in the 540s. Earlier still, on the one hand Lamentations grieves over the removal of the city's leadership (e.g., Lam 2:9; 4:13–16), while on the other it lays responsibility for the city's fall squarely at the feet of that leadership and thus at the feet of its survivors now in Babylon.

There is a similar ambiguity about the relationship of Isaiah 40–55 with Lamentations. In taking up the latter's speech and announcing a response to its pleas, Isaiah 40–55 may implicitly see itself as one in destiny with the Judean community rather than set over against it. However, Isaiah 40–55 makes much use of the terms "children," "sons," and "daughters" and refrains from describing its community as kings, princes, priests, and prophets, in the manner of Lamentations.[15] This might suggest self-effacement or might constitute an evasion of responsibility. Further, if Isaiah 40–55 treats the Judean community as nonexistent, there may be an implicitly ideological point here, parallel to one in the contemporary Middle East. "The Myth of the Empty Land"[16] facilitates the exiles' projecting of themselves as its heirs. If they represent themselves as Zion in exile,[17] this could give ideological support to a claim to be the true Israel. Representing themselves as Zion's children, entitled to return to their mother city, could have a parallel function.

Lamentations and Isaiah 40–55 may have covert concerns to justify political positions, or they may not. Perhaps the better way to put it is to grant that there may well be an aspect of self-interest in every text, but that this consideration may be a particularly significant factor in the shaping of these specific texts, or it may not. The exiles may actually be quite ignorant of the situation in Jerusalem and too

15. Cf. C. A. Newsom, "Response to Norman K. Gottwald, 'Social Class and Ideology in Isaiah 40–55,'" *Semeia* 59 (1992): 73–78 (see 74, 78).

16. The title of Robert Carroll's paper in *Semeia* 59 (1992): 79–93.

17. See P. Volz, *Jesaja* II (Leipzig: Deichert, 1932), on 40:2.

preoccupied with their own situation to reflect on that anywhere else: that is, their silence about the Jerusalem community may be significant, but there are several ways in which it could be significant. I am reminded of the hoary debate about the prophets' attitude to sacrifice, when interpreters used to keep attacking these texts to force them to give us an answer to a question they were not asking.

I have alluded to a feature running through much of Isaiah 40–55, summed up by the word "democratization."[18] Within chapters 41–42 this is represented by the treatment of Israel as God's servant. In origin or by familiar usage, expressions such as "servant," "chosen," "fear not, for I am with you," which appear in Isaiah 41:8–16, belong to the king. They are now reapplied to "Israel." The main features of the portrait of the servant in Isaiah 42:1–4 are also royal in background, and in my view they also presuppose application to Israel. What is this Israel, and over against whom is democratization asserted? Is Israel the exilic community, or is it the Judean community, or is such an antithesis not implied? Is democratization simply asserted over against the potential power of the Davidic monarchy? On the surface the prophecy's point is not that the title "Israel" belongs to the exilic community rather than the Judean community (or vice versa) but that the community addressed means something rather than nothing and that significance attaches to all of it rather than to the Davidic house alone.

In the exilic Isaiah's democratization there is a force capable of working powerfully against ideologies, for by definition it works against loci of power. It puts all human entities under the authority and protection of deity. Of course it can be subject to ideological appropriation. Yet Isaiah 40–55 seems to work against that, too. If its "Israel" (however identified) gains too unequivocal comfort from being reminded in Isaiah 41:8–16 of its high status as Yahweh's personal servant, such comfort is quickly subverted by the remainder of the vocation involved in servanthood in Isaiah 42:1–9 (if the passage may be read that way), and more explicitly and devastatingly subverted by the assessment of its servanthood offered in Isaiah 42:18–25. "This is a kind of ideological literature that incorporates a reflex of ideological autocritique."[19]

While abandoning the Davidic kingship ideal might be simply naïve, sociocritical understanding of Isaiah 40–55 is more suspicious than this, seeing the chapters as especially concerned to bolster the position of the exilic community as an aristocratic oligarchy destined to resume power in Jerusalem and as lacking any reflection on the need to safeguard against the abuse and corruption of power that characterized their preexilic predecessors.[20] The picture is a plausible one, but it remains entirely hypothetical. Aside from questions regarding the assumption of the conflict model for understanding relationships between the exilic and Judean communities rather than a consensual model, we do not even know for certain whether the material in

---

18. See G. von Rad, *Old Testament Theology* (2 vols.; Edinburgh: Oliver and Boyd, 1965), 2:240.

19. R. Alter's comment concerning the story of Jacob/Israel and Esau/Edom, in *The World of Biblical Literature* (New York: Basic Books, 1992), 68.

20. Gottwald, "Social Class," 54–55.

Isaiah 40–55 is of Babylonian background or perhaps of mixed origin.[21] The whole book of Isaiah may be of Jerusalem provenance. If so, then a quite different socio-historical understanding would be possible and necessary.

We do not have enough knowledge of the sociohistorical context of Isaiah 40–55 to provide the undergirding for a properly sociocritical interpretation; the matter is simply too conjectural. It would be regrettable if we turned out after all to have learned nothing about the hazards of setting at the heart of the interpretive task the attempt to fix the historical background of texts, so that sociocritical interpretation hastened into the same marsh as historical-critical interpretation.[22] But there may be another way of realizing the practical concerns of such interpretation.

5. Hearer-Involving

A feature of Isaiah 40–55 is a running ambiguity regarding its audience. I had some sympathy with the PhD candidate who, when asked whether he had looked at a certain question within the framework of "the implied reader," confessed that the complexities of such talk gave him a headache.[23] Nevertheless this framework does clarify some aspects of these chapters.

In general, what is the audience envisaged by these prophecies? Isaiah 40 begins by announcing a message of comfort for Jerusalem, so that in some indirect sense Jerusalem is the audience, and I believe it is the overt addressee in verses 9–11. But the matter is more complicated than that. I have referred to the view that "Jerusalem" is here a figure for the exilic community, though this in fact seems an implausible as well as unnecessary suggestion. It is implausible because everywhere else in this book so far, and demonstrably in many subsequent chapters, too, "Jerusalem" denotes the city of that name or its population. It is unnecessary because it presupposes that Isaiah 40–55 addresses the exilic community and also presupposes that a message of comfort to Jerusalem was irrelevant to that community. Both assumptions may be queried.

One basis for querying the first is the possibility we have noted that the sixth-century material in this book is of Jerusalem provenance. In German-speaking scholarship, however, there has been developing a substantial interest in the redactional

---

21. Duhm located it in Lebanon, and as his centenary approached, among others J. M. Vincent and R. E. Clements urged its partial Jerusalem background: see J. M. Vincent, *Studien zur literarischen Eigenart und zur geistigen Heimat von Jesaja, Kap. 40–55* (Frankfurt: Lang, 1977); R. E. Clements, "Beyond Tradition-History," *JSOT* 31 (1985): 95–113.

22. See G. O. West's comments in "Reading 'The Text' and Reading 'Behind the Text,'" in *The Bible in Three Dimensions* (ed. David J. A. Clines et al.; Sheffield: Sheffield Academic Press, 1990), 299–320; West, *Biblical Hermeneutics of Liberation* (Pietermaritzburg: Cluster, 1991).

23. A long list of possibilities such as W. S. Vorster's, in "Readings, Readers and the Succession Narrative" (*Zeitschrift für die alttestamentliche Wissenschaft* 98 [1986]): 351–62; see 354), hints at the reason. In her "Response" to Gottwald (73) Newsom adds the notion of "cognitive seasickness" to that of literary-critical migraine.

history of these chapters, and one contribution to their study has suggested that Isaiah 40:1–11 forms a new introduction to the exilic material, provided for the Jerusalem community after the exile.[24] This understanding suggests another basis for reckoning that there was no need to infer that the opening allusion to Jerusalem refers to the exiles. Yet it is surely unnecessary even if we reckon that Isaiah 40:1–11 was addressed to the Judean community in sixth-century Babylon, for the destiny of Jerusalem was of key importance to that community.

There are many understandings of the history of the development of the material in Isaiah 40–55 and I find that it is considering these that induces headache, or rather frustration. A number of theories are plausible, but none is compelling. We cannot attain any conviction about the audience of different stages of this redactional process, if process there was, as we cannot attain any conviction about the material's sociohistorical context and significance. Where do we go from there?

Within Isaiah 40–55 the overt audience includes both the Jerusalem community and that in Babylon. With any text it is possible that the intended audience is other than the overt audience. I presume that most of the prophecies addressed to the nations in Isaiah 13–23 were never delivered to them. Yet their value to their intended Judean audience depends on their being valid statements of what could in principle actually be said to the various nations. For prophet and audience they indicate something of the perspective Yahweh has upon the nations and the purpose of Yahweh for them. The overt audience is not the originally intended audience but it is a possible audience for Isaiah 40–55.

The overt audience of Isaiah 40–55 includes from time to time both Jerusalem and the exilic community. Even if their original covert audience was exclusively one or the other, both are possible audiences for them. Jerusalem is the explicit but indirect addressee in Isaiah 40:1–2, the explicit and direct addressee in Isaiah 40:9–11. The entirety of what follows in these chapters is implicitly of interest to the community geographically focused on Jerusalem. I am attracted to the suggestion that Isaiah 40:1–11, with its Jerusalem-Zion focus, introduces Isaiah 40:12–48:22, with its Jacob-Israel focus, while Isaiah 49:1–13, with its Jacob-Israel concern, introduces Isaiah 49:14–55:13, with its Jerusalem-Zion concern.[25] The two foci of the whole are thus bound together.

In Isaiah 40:12–31, in contrast, Jacob-Israel as a whole is the explicit and direct audience; the passage does not specify what is the referent of the term "Jacob-Israel" (e.g., whether Judean or exilic or both), and we are perhaps not to attempt to force a specific interpretation on it. Jacob-Israel is also the audience in Isaiah 41:1–20, sometimes explicitly and directly, sometimes less so. Its description as taken from the ends of the earth like Abraham (Isa 41:8–9) suggests that it is pictured in its theological location in Judah, but this might not mark that as its present geographical

24. See R. P. Merendino, *Der Erste und der Letzte* (Leiden: Brill, 1981), 13–73.

25. S. L. Stassen, "Jesaja 40:1–11 en 49:1–13 as belangrike Struktuurmerkers in die Komposisie van Jesaja 40–55," *Nederduits Gereformeerde Teologiese Tydskrif* 32 (1991): 178–86.

location. In Isaiah 41:21–42:17 the identity of the direct audience is left implicit; Jacob-Israel is not mentioned, though Zion-Jerusalem reappears as indirect audience in Isaiah 41:27.[26]

In Isaiah 42:18–44:23, Jacob-Israel is often addressed but not identified. It can be read as Babylonian or Judean, as a people in exile promised a return to its home (which therefore plays a prominent place in the rhetoric) or as a people living around a largely depopulated capital promised the restoration of its exiled population (who therefore play a prominent place in its rhetoric). Indeed, these two alternatives apply to the material as a whole. They reflect the fact that each community it envisages has things to say to the other. It implicitly invites us to read it from both perspectives (among others: that of the Babylonians, for instance, that of the Persians, and that of other peoples whom the latter might release from the former). And in doing so it may appropriately be read sociocritically in the sense of asking what praxis in community and society it warrants, appropriately not least because this concern is prominent in the book of Isaiah itself (a fact reflected in the role of the prophets as a significant intertext for Karl Marx).

The protagonists of sociocritical and of canonical interpretation have seen their work as antithetical, but here at least the one may help the other. One characteristic of prophetic hermeneutic, within writings that became Scripture and in their later appropriation, is its inclination to confront the community rather than merely confirm it in its present self-understanding.[27] Such confrontation need not always involve bringing unwelcome bad news; where the community is demoralized, it may mean bringing unbelievable good news. Where it does mean good news, it will not be a matter of mere ideology. If Isaiah 40–55 did originally function in part to offer ideological undergirding to the exilic community's aspirations to land and power in the Judean community, in more than one way its own rhetoric frustrates this aim. By speaking to the city and not merely to the exiles, it invites us to look at the situation from the city's perspective, while its claiming the mantle of Isaiah of Jerusalem and its literary setting within the book of Isaiah directs us to read it in the context of the whole book's recurrent concern with just order and decisive judgment within that city.

It could be, then, that the prophet's ministry was quite ideological, the message purporting to respond to Lamentations in order to bolster the claim that the exilic community was heir to the Jerusalem traditions and had the right to declare God's

---

26. The text is difficult but rsv, "I first have declared it to Zion, and I give to Jerusalem a herald of good tidings," likely conveys the drift.

27. See J. A. Sanders, "The Ethic of Election in Luke's Great Banquet Parable," in *Essays in Old Testament Ethics* (J. P. Hyatt Memorial Volume; ed. J. L. Crenshaw and J. T. Willis; New York: Ktav, 1974), 247–71 (see 250–53); "From Isaiah 61 to Luke 4," in *Christianity, Judaism, and Other Greco-Roman Cults* (M. Smith Festschrift, Part 1; ed. Jacob Neusner; Leiden: Brill, 1975), 75–106 (see 93–99); "Adaptable for Life: The Nature and Function of Canon," in *Magnalia Dei* (G. E. Wright Memorial Volume; ed. F. M. Cross et al.; Garden City, N.Y.: Doubleday, 1976), 531–60 (see 544–51) = Sanders, *From Sacred Story to Sacred Text* (Philadelphia: Fortress, 1987), 11–39 (see 23–30).

response to its prayers. It thus staked a claim to power in the future Jerusalem community. If so, the message has been preserved independently of such factors and without making them clear, as it has been preserved with relatively little concrete historical reference.[28]

The effect is to make questions of ideology prospective rather than retrospective. The question about ideology that the text raises by its ambiguity is the question about the audience's ideology. Why are we reading it? What do we intend to do with it other than satisfy our aesthetic, intellectual, and religious instincts and further our careers? Like historical-critical study in its concern with history, the sociohistorical quest for the ideology of the text could be a way of avoiding the ideology in ourselves. We cannot say how the material functioned historically. We can say how prophetic hermeneutic would design it to function.

A further aspect of Paul Ricoeur's work provides an alternative way of making the point. One concern of sociocritical interpretation is to aid proper praxis. Paradoxically, by conducting us into the irresolvable uncertainties of sociocritical interpretation it risks making it harder for the text to aid praxis. Ricoeur's work suggests that the question what past events the text points to can be replaced by the question what possible future events it points to.

The modern age has been instinctively inclined to privilege history over fiction, or at least has sometimes been so inclined (the seriousness with which we take drama and the novel suggests that we are schizophrenic about the matter). Fiction may have sense, but history has both sense and reference. Ricoeur has attempted to break our prejudice in favor of history, pointing out that fiction also emerges from human experience; fiction, too, has reference. But then fiction also brings out an aspect of the nature of narrative that is thus also a characteristic of history. It *redescribes* reality. Reworking Aristotle, with his linking of *mythos* and *mimesis* in *Poetics* 1448a, Ricoeur declares that "fiction is not a case of reproductive but productive imagination" and asks whether "by opening us to the different, history opens us to the possible, while fiction, by opening us to the unreal, brings us back to the essential?"[29]

If the meaning of texts lies in front of them as well as behind them, in the mode of being in the world they lay out before us, it would be as easy to suggest that fiction lays before us what is possible to complement history's account of the merely actual. Ricoeur indeed stresses the link between narrative and the passion for the possible.[30] Both history and fiction have reference, but history's reference lies behind it, fiction's in front of it. Fiction is indeed heuristic. Focusing on asking what past events generated it misses its point.

---

28. As B. S. Childs emphasizes; see his *Introduction to the Old Testament as Scripture* (London: SCM; Philadelphia: Fortress, 1979), 311–38.

29. See "The Narrative Function," in *The Poetics of Faith, Part 2* (Amos N. Wilder Festschrift; ed. William A. Beardslee; *Semeia* 13 [1978]: 177–202; see 193, 198); and, further, his *Time and Narrative* (3 vols.; Chicago: University of Chicago Press, 1984, 1985, 1988).

30. See Kevin J. Vanhoozer, *Biblical Narrative in the Philosophy of Paul Ricoeur* (Cambridge: Cambridge University Press, 1990).

Ricoeur's observation about narrative can be extended to prophecy. Compared with the two types of narrative, by its nature prophecy is more like fiction than history. In setting before us possible worlds and inviting us to go for them (or to abort them), it is not chiefly concerned with events that have (yet) taken place but with what is possible. It indeed issues this invitation with passion. In fact it does invite people to lie down (or to rather to stand up) in surrender to its rhetoric.

22

Is There Masculist Interpretation?

A
s far as I know, masculist interpretation of Scripture does not exist; indeed its birthing may be premature.[1] By masculist interpretation I mean something different from male interpretation, which is simply what nearly everyone did until a few decades ago.[2] That is interpretation undertaken mostly by males of texts written mostly by males, without the possibility occurring to anyone that this might limit or skew what the interpreter saw. Feminist interpretation drew attention to this and asked what might become visible in texts when women read them as women rather than as honorary men. Masculist interpretation is parasitic on feminist interpretation; it is by definition post-feminist. It asks what might become visible in texts when they are read in conscious awareness of maleness. Arguably, at least, masculist interpretation need not be limited to males any more than feminist interpretation need be limited to females, but in this piece I write as a man seeking to be self-aware as a man.

A passage such as Hosea 1–3 provides an obvious context for the raising of the question just noted. This is not merely because there seems no prospect of coming to agreement on an understanding of these chapters on a historical-critical basis (e.g., what are the literary relationships between the chapters and the historical

1. First published in *HBT* 17 (1995): 37–44 and in revised form in Athalya Brenner, ed., *A Feminist Companion to the Latter Prophets* (Sheffield: Sheffield Academic Press, 1995), 161–68, expanded with material from "The Significance of Circumcision," *JSOT* 88 (2000): 3–18 (also at http://www.fuller.edu/sot/faculty/goldingay).

2. But see (e.g.) the opening chapters in Elisabeth Schüssler Fiorenza, ed., *Searching the Scriptures*, vol. 1, *A Feminist Introduction* (New York: Crossroad, 1993; London: SCM, 1994), for the earlier history of feminist interpretation.

relationships between the events they refer to and between the female figures who appear?), though that is so.[3] It is because whatever the answers to these unanswerable questions, the text is overtly an expression of a distinctively male experience, and it is this experience that is then a base from which an understanding of God is expressed. There is a feminist literature that illumines Hosea 1–3,[4] but a masculist interpretation will have a different starting point and perspective, even if possibly a complementary one. If feminist interpretation uses women's experience as an aid in gaining illumination on the text's own concerns, including its implications for the nature of God, and in discovering its affirmation and challenge regarding what it means to be women (and men), masculist interpretation uses men's experience for parallel ends.

The feminist literature on Hosea 1–3 raises telling questions about the male prophet, his God, and their attitude to their partners, and a so-called masculist interpretation could be a means of avoiding those, a means of subverting the feminist agenda, of evading the challenge to patriarchy and androcentrism, and of reinstating male interpretation in new man-ish guise. It is for this reason that its birthing may be premature, and that is not my desire. A masculist interpretation does not replace a feminist one; further, the masculist interpretation of Hosea 1–3 that follows is not the only possible one. It is a conservative one, to begin with, more Phyllis Trible than Mieke Bal or Cheryl Exum. But my conviction is that something like masculist interpretation is needed to enable me to handle the theological implications of the androcentric, patriarchal aspect to Scripture and to help me come to terms with myself as a man in such a way that I may be able to change and thus respond to the feminist critique. To be post-feminist is to build on feminism, but not to attempt to leave it behind.

1. Masculinity and Genesis 1–4

So what is masculinity? The opening chapters of Genesis point to three features of maleness that resonate with the experience of many men and women today and also seem of prima facie relevance to the interpretation of Hosea 1–3. They thus make Genesis 1–4 a suggestive text to put alongside Hosea 1–3. First, men discover who they are by setting themselves over against women. It is when the man sees the woman that he knows who he is. It is enough to make him leave father and mother and want to live with her. Of course he then finds that his relationship with this wonderful creature gets him into dead trouble. For a man, at least, there is thus a

---

3. See, e.g., G. I. Davies, *Hosea* (London: Marshall; Grand Rapids: Eerdmans, 1992), and *Hosea* (Sheffield: Sheffield Academic Press, 1992).

4. See, e.g., T. D. Setel, "Prophets and Pornography," in *Feminist Interpretation of the Bible* (ed. L. M. Russell; Philadelphia: Westminster Press, 1985), 86–95; R. J. Weems, "Gomer," in *Interpretation for Liberation* (ed. Katie G. Cannon and Elisabeth Schüssler Fiorenza; *Semeia* 47 [1989]: 87–104); and other papers in *A Feminist Companion to the Latter Prophets*.

tragic ambiguity about the man-woman relationship. Women are our making: we are lonely or dissatisfied or incomplete without them, as they may not be without us (part of the background may lie in the fact that a girl's first relationship is with a person of her own sex, a boy's with a person of the opposite sex).[5] But women are also our downfall: not necessarily for reasons to do with them, but for reasons to do with us. All this is not confined to the marriage relationship. For men there can in general be a spark about their relationships with women that can be particularly creative and in which they can find themselves, though there is also the potential for big trouble, not least because men may find it more difficult than women do to avoid falling in love with women colleagues and friends (the *When Harry Met Sally* syndrome).

A second feature of masculinity reflected in the opening chapters of Genesis is that men are responsible. They rule. They have authority. To judge from Genesis 1, this is not how God meant it to be, because authority was designed to be shared by men and women, but to judge from Genesis 3 it is how it came to be. For a man that, too, has an ambiguity about it. There is great fulfillment to be gained from the exercise of responsibility, of power, and there is much good that can come from it, but there is also stress and temptation attached to it, and potential for evil.

A third feature of masculinity is relative physical strength, aggressiveness, and the capacity for violence, perhaps the inclination to violence. When the Bible first speaks of sin, in Genesis 4, what it speaks of is violence. Cain's response to disappointment with God's reaction to him is anger, and that is when sin is crouching like a demon at his door. He spurns the challenge to utilize his strength and aggressiveness to defeat this demon and instead turns them onto Abel. Henceforth Cain expects that he will live in fear of the cycle of violence he has initiated. He is a master who will be outdone by his pupils, as is illustrated in the chilling prosody of his great-great-great-grandson who is proud to multiply Cain's violence by eleven. Yet even male strength, aggressiveness, and violence are matters of ambiguity and tragedy, not merely sin. A petite feminist I know says that one thing she appreciates about men is that they are bigger than she is; they can reach things she cannot, for instance. Our aggressiveness can be a means of achievement, for the sake of others and not just for ourselves as individuals (or for our gender). In general, our strength, our aggressiveness, and our capacity for violence are gifts that can be used on behalf of the weak, but they can easily become our sin.

Male sexuality, responsibility or power, and strength or violence, might be able to form a holy trinity; they can certainly form an unholy one. Indeed, each of the three possible combinations of these three features of masculinity suggests an oppression and/or a burden. Men have commonly had to be responsible for the sexual relationship, and that becomes a problem for us as men ("Why should I always have

---

5. See V. Saiving Goldstein's classic discussion of this distinction between the sexes in "The Human Situation: A Feminine View," *Journal of Religion* 40 (1960): 100–12, reprinted in *Womanspirit Rising* (ed. C. P. Christ and Judith Plaskow; San Francisco: Harper, 1979), 25–42.

to take the initiative?") as well as for women ("Why do I have to sit here and wait?"). We have been able to combine sex and violence and have often done so; in general, it is men who commit rape. In other areas, too, we assume it is natural to exercise responsibility by force; in general, it is men who fight wars.

2. Masculinity and Hosea 1–3

What happens when we read the opening chapters of Hosea in light of its being a male text? In their preamble we are introduced to a man identified by his relationship with his father and with five monarchs who are all male. It is mostly men who get the positive opportunity to exercise power in Israel; an exception such as Athaliah in 2 Kings 11 proves the rule by behaving with the violence of an honorary man. They thus also bear the burden of guilt for the people's failure, which is commonly attributed to the leadership's failure.

When we come to the material that relates to Hosea's relationship with a woman or women and to Yahweh's analogous relationship with Israel, we begin with the assumption that the man is also responsible for the sexual relationship. It is he who has to take the initiative in wooing, and in wooing again. The ambiguity of a man's relationship with a woman comes out clearly. The relationship is characterized by love and pain; it is capable of bringing both great joy and great hurt. If most singers of blues, soul, and rock are men, and most of their songs are about the pain their relationships with women have brought them, then Hosea is their patron prophet. The potential for joy makes a man want to reach out as Hosea does; the potential for pain and rejection makes him want to lash out, an instinct only just under the surface in Hosea 2 and 3.[6] A man to whom his wife is unfaithful is torn between violence and love (see, e.g., Hos 2:2–3 and 14–15 [MT 4–5 and 16–17]). The unholy trinity are all at work.

All three features of a man's relationship with a woman reappear in the relationship Hosea attributes to Yahweh. The male prophet thinks of God as in the position of a man with a man's instincts.

First, Yahweh is incomplete without Israel as men are incomplete without women. It is he who seeks her, not she who seeks him (I usually avoid the gendered language, but here it is appropriate). The climax to his word of rejection is that she ceases to be his people and he ceases to be her God (Hos 1:9); it is a calamity for both. The climax to his indictment of her is that she forgot him (Hos 2:13 [15 MT]); to be forgotten is to be treated as a nonperson, to cease to be. The climax of his vision of a blissful future is that she should once again say "You are my God" (Hos 2:28 [MT 30]). Yahweh's self-knowledge depends on his relationship with Israel. Who is Yahweh if Yahweh ceases to be "the holy one of Israel," to use Isaiah's phrase?

---

6. On Hos 2, see Weems, "Gomer."

All this is the more interesting given that Hosea, like other prophets, declines to find sexuality within the Godhead itself. Unlike other Middle Eastern deities, Yahweh has no heavenly wife or lover. The male prophet thus finds ways both of connecting God with and of disconnecting God from sexuality with its ambiguity. To connect God with it is to affirm that God is in touch with this fundamental aspect of male being with that potential for joy and hurt. To disconnect God from it is to deny that God is affected by its negative aspect with the possible implication that its tragedy, failure, pain, and rejection are ultimate realities.

Second, Yahweh takes the initiative in the relationship. In general, the male prophet resembles other contributors to the First Testament in picturing God as bearing a man's lonely responsibility for the world and for history. Admittedly it may also be noted that the First Testament pictures God as fairly laid back about this responsibility. Yahweh has no trouble delegating and does not mind being sidelined. No doubt Yahweh can afford to take the long view in the confidence of seeing off whole sequences of uncooperative Israelite generations. As is the case with Yahweh and sexuality, though in a different way, the portrait of Yahweh as one exercising responsibility thus both reflects the nature of male experience and addresses it by offering an alternative model.

An implication of this way of looking at the gender-related element in the Bible's portrayal of God is that the Bible's emphasis on grace turns out to be a male perspective. It is a feminist commonplace that men sin by acting, women by failing to act, another difference that may have a background in girls' forming their first relationship with a person of their own sex (from whom they do not need to differentiate themselves by taking identity-forming action) and boys' forming their first relationship with a person of the opposite sex (from whom they need to differentiate themselves by taking identity-forming action).[7] In stressing God's activity in gracious initiative, the male prophet tells men what they need to hear. Everything does not depend on us; there is some responsibility being exercised on a higher plane. This provides us with another reason to be more laid back than we might be inclined to be.

Admittedly, subsequent insights in Hosea may deconstruct this suggestion. In Hosea 11 it is the powerlessness of Yahweh that speaks, which might explain part of Hosea's attractiveness for feminist interpreters, who otherwise are relatively little drawn to the prophets.[8] Yahweh is caught between love and judgment with no way out. "When God speaks through Hosea, we hear the voice of the parent, seeing the child rushing towards his downfall, and utterly powerless to do anything to stop it. . . . God has taken the risk of letting the children go, and cannot step in and sort out their mess for them," though God never gives up on them.[9] A man, then, is

7. See Saiving Goldstein, "The Human Situation."

8. So my colleague Gillian Cooper, with whom I wrote a kind of follow-up to this chapter, "Hosea and Gomer Visit the Marriage Counselor," in *First Person: Essays in Biblical Autobiography* (ed. P. R. Davies; London and New York: Sheffield Academic Press, 2002), 119–36 (also at http://www.fuller.edu/sot/faculty/goldingay).

9. G. A. Cooper, "God's Gamble," *Third Way* 15, no. 8 (1993): 20.

beguiled into trusting God as possessing the all-powerfulness that he himself often seems expected to manifest, but cannot. He is in due course drawn further on to accept the discovery that even God does not possess this quality, but models the ability to live without it.

Third, the male prophet portrays Yahweh as involved in the violence that is a characteristic of maleness. Yahweh had commissioned Jehu for the bloody coup d'état to which he was in any case inclined. Now Yahweh declares the intention to punish Jehu for it. The punishment will affect not merely the man but his entire household. One theological implication of such passages may be the conviction that Yahweh is willing to be compromised rather than stay unstained in an aseptic environment, if this is the inevitable price of being involved in history in its ambiguity.

The story and the prophecy about Jehu also point to a further element in this attribution of violence to Yahweh. John Barton has suggested that prophets did not first analyze the moral nature of their society and then infer that Yahweh must act in judgment. Rather, they first became aware that calamity was imminent and then looked at society and inferred the reasons.[10] Perhaps, then, the male prophets' preoccupation with divine violence reflects a desire that violence be explained as much as a desire that violence be inflicted. They did not invent the violent calamities; they did invent the explanations of them. Perhaps male ambiguity about violence finds expression here: we are both attracted to it and afraid of it within ourselves. We need to feel it is under control. Perhaps male awareness of responsibility for the world also finds further expression here: it is important to men that someone is in control, that things are not out of hand. In this connection, too, we can cope with violence if there is some logic to it.

As with sexuality, the male prophet both links Yahweh with violence and distances Yahweh from it. There is no violence within the Godhead, as there is among other Middle Eastern deities, but there is violence in God's relationship with the world. If men see God as involved in violence, this might (at least in theory) have the potential to protect the world a little from male violence; violence is God's business, not men's (cf. Lev 19:18; Deut 32:35; taken up in Rom 12:19). Yet even while portraying God's exercise of violence on human beings, the chapters presuppose that God is not at ease with violence, that violence does not have the last word.

3. Genesis 17

The biblical authors who are actually named in Scripture are men, and it seems likely that this was also true of most of the rest of its authors, including (for instance) those of Genesis 1–4 as well as Hosea. As writers such as Phyllis Trible have shown, these were somewhat enlightened men. To put that by means of an active verb, God enabled them to see aspects of the truth about relations between men and women

---

10. John Barton, "History and Rhetoric in the Prophets," in *The Bible as Rhetoric* (ed. M. Warner; London and New York: Routledge, 1990), 53–55; cf. chapter 9 (section 2) above.

that neither their society nor ours (still less the people of God to which they and we belong) have often been good at seeing. They portray women and men sharing in the image of God and sharing in the commission to steward the world and enjoy the blessing of fruitfulness (Gen 1:26–28). They offer no hint that the world is the man's business and the family is the woman's. They portray the first man and woman as made for partnership. While they make clear that the creature who was first made exercises authority over the one made second, they also make clear that this happens as a result of the act of disobedience in which they share, when "'to love and to cherish' is turned into 'to desire and to dominate.'"[11] Yet these authors, and other authors in Scripture, write as men. So perhaps being a man may give me aspects of the preunderstanding required to understand their work more fully.

Genesis speaks about questions of gender in ambivalent or ambiguous fashion. Alongside the declaration concerning the way men and women share in the divine image (whose implications they perhaps did not see) is the subsequent introduction of a covenant sign that is applied only to men. The Torah makes clear enough that the covenant itself also embraces women, but this makes it the odder that its sign is applied only to males.

Yet the treatment of circumcision within the First Testament makes its significance deconstruct.[12] The Abraham of Genesis 16–17 needs to have his sexual activity in connection with procreation disciplined by trust in Yahweh. For his great-grandsons, in Genesis 34 circumcision is merely a means of getting back on the men of Shechem for a lack of sexual discipline. In Exodus 4, Moses' belated circumcision is perhaps a sign of the submission of his machismo to God. The talk of circumcision elsewhere in the Torah and in the Prophets reminds men that there is a broader circumcision that they also need. Far from establishing that the males are the "real" members of the covenant community, the effect of cutting off the male foreskin is to draw attention to or establish the fact that the males embody a spiritual and moral unfitness to belong to the people of God. It is as well that this membership is not dependent on our fitness.

The Scriptures are permeated by androcentrism; indeed their (mostly, if not exclusively) male human authors sometimes (often?) consciously or unconsciously wrote in order to pursue a patriarchal agenda. The priestly writers' revisionist program for circumcision whereby this male rite becomes the sign of membership of the covenant people may be an example of their doing so, but the treatment of circumcision in the First Testament as a whole helps me to see what might have been in the back of God's mind in declining to prevent its having a place in the Scriptures. A classic New Testament passage about the Torah, the Prophets, and the Writings says that God's aim for them was and is that they should be useful for teaching, reproof, correction and training in righteousness, so as to contribute to their readers' growing

---

11. Derek Kidner, *Genesis* (London: Tyndale, 1967; Downers Grove, Ill.: InterVarsity, 1975), 71.

12. See further John Goldingay, "The Significance of Circumcision," *JSOT* 88 (2000): 3–18 (also at http://www.fuller.edu/sot/faculty/goldingay), which much of the rest of this chapter summarizes or repeats.

towards maturity (2 Tim 3:16–17). Perhaps God could see that there were various ways by which that goal could be achieved. It could have been achieved by being more interventionist and supranaturalist, but in general that does not seem to have been God's way in the world. Instead, God works towards that goal by letting the men who wrote these Scriptures expose themselves and confound themselves. Even when they were being at their most patriarchal (especially when they were being at their most patriarchal), they could not hide the way patriarchalism and androcentricity deconstruct and therefore could not but be in a position to open themselves (if someone pointed out what was going on) to insight for renewal for themselves and for women and for the world.

4. Masculist Interpretation

> The serpent . . . said to the woman . . . (Gen 3:1)
> Do not forsake wisdom, and she will protect you; love her, and she will watch over you. (Prov 4:6)
> I have found one man among a thousand, but not one woman among them all. (Eccles 7:28)
> Yahweh said to me, "Once again go and show your love to a woman." (Hos 3:1 [MT 3])
> Adam was not the one deceived; it was the woman. (1 Tim 2:14)
> A great and wondrous sign appeared in the sky, a woman clothed with the sun. (Rev 12:1)

The fact that being men played a role in the work of the writers and interpreters of Scripture is in itself nothing to be ashamed of; writers or interpreters had to be one sex or the other, and the history of culture determined what they should be. What they wrote was also shaped by their being Middle Eastern people rather than European or Antipodean, living two to three millennia ago rather than a millennium ago or at the present time, being in a culture where the relation between urban and rural was different from the one that obtains in urbanized society, living in a monarchic or hierocratic or imperial society rather than a parliamentary one. Being human involves living in history, and living in history involves accepting that people's cultures both open up varying possibilities for them and impose varying constraints on them. Part of God's living in history with us involved God in speaking (and eventually becoming incarnate) in history. Scripture is one facet of that. In inspiring the Scriptures, God worked with the positive possibilities of the cultures in which particular people lived and also with the constraints of those cultures. "Israel in 5 BC had no mass communication" (*Jesus Christ Superstar*). Living in a rural, monarchic, society means you see certain things and miss others. Being a man means that you see certain things and miss others.

Experience suggests that his relationships with women are among a man's most precious resources and among his most precious risks. I presume this underlies Genesis 3. Why is it that the story sees Eve as the one tempted and then as the first human tempter? Partly because the storyteller is a man, and for a man that is a role a woman fulfills. She is both potential partner and potential downfall. Why does Ecclesiastes feel that there is the occasional reliable man in the world but never a reliable woman? Partly because it is women who have the supreme capacity to let men down—not because they are inherently less reliable than men, but because they are the opposite sex to men and as such have most potential to hurt them. Why does 1 Timothy need to stop women exercising authority over men? Partly because they already exercise huge power over men just because they are women.

That is to take the negative side to the male Bible's talk of women. However, women and men were created for a mutual, complementary, supportive partnership. Women are among a man's most precious resources of love and creativity and insight. So if "Solomon" wants to personify wisdom, he personifies it as a woman. If Hosea wants to portray a relationship of love, he describes it in terms of a love relationship between himself and a woman. If John wants to describe the fruitfulness of Israel in bringing forth the Messiah, he does it by portraying Israel as a woman.

I would like to think of myself as a man who accepts many of the insights of feminism and their application to the Scriptures, and as a person for whom the Torah, the Prophets, and the Writings (and for that matter the New Testament) are a key religious resource that Judaism and the church possess by God's gift, or at least by God's permission, rather than by God's oversight; they are Scriptures, in fact. There is a tension between these two convictions. I was once troubled by a parallel tension between the acceptance of these writings as Scriptures and my knowledge of the implications of historical criticism. I am now comfortable with my way of handling the latter tension.[13] Having worked my way through this over the years (and through other tensions involved in being both a believer and a child of modernity), I have been less anxious about this other tension. I have traveled this way before, and if I am not sure how to handle it at the moment, this does not mean it cannot be handled. It just means that I have not yet found the answer.

The prophets' descriptions of God reflect their personalities and (for instance) their gender. Divine revelation comes via the human personality; it is because human beings are made in God's image that they can speak of God in a way that reflects who they are as human beings. But it is only when you have men and women together that you have the divine image represented, and all this therefore suggests that (for instance) male insights on God that emerge from the Bible have to be complemented by female ones. But then I would think that, being a man.

---

13. See "What Is the Relationship Between Theology and History?" above.

23

How May We Interpret Wisdom, Poetry, and Writings?

Like chapter 18 on the Pentateuch, this chapter begins from some assumptions about the relationship between exegesis and hermeneutics as complementary ways of thinking about the interpretation of texts.[1] In doing exegesis we seek to understand a text in its original context, in accordance with its own agenda and priorities; we may then move from exegesis to application. Talk in terms of "hermeneutics" recognizes that even our exegetical study is affected by who we are: by the questions that occupy us, by the culture we belong to, by the way our church has taught us, by our personal experience, by whether we are wealthy or poor, whether we are men or women, and so on. Further, the process of understanding Scripture is not linear (as the exegesis-application model implies). There is an ongoing both-ways relationship between focusing on a passage's meaning in its own right and focusing on its significance for us in light of questions that concern us. This is as true of historical and critical study as it is of other approaches, because the concerns, aims, and methods of historical and critical study come from a particular culture, and historical-critical study discovers from the text what its methods allow. All this need does not mean (or need not mean) that we find in texts only what we know already. Our perspective and experience do make it possible for us actually to discover aspects of the texts' intrinsic meaning. The trick is to see how we can utilize the positive aspects of the way subjective factors enable us to see objective

1. First published in *Dictionary of the Old Testament: Wisdom, Poetry, and Writings* (ed. Tremper Longman and Peter Enns; Downers Grove, Ill., and Leicester: InterVarsity, 2008), 267–80.

things in Scripture and to safeguard against its negative aspects, the way it limits and narrows our perspective or makes us misperceive things. A significant means of making progress in that is looking at Scripture through other people's eyes, so as to perceive and broaden the narrowness of our own vision.

In their arrangement in the printed Hebrew-Aramaic Bible, the Scriptures that Christians call the Old Testament comprise the Torah, the Prophets, and the Writings. In this chapter, I am mostly concerned with approaches to the books that comprise the first two-thirds of the Writings (they are followed there by Daniel, Ezra, Nehemiah, and Chronicles).

1. Historical Interpretation: The Writings as a Whole

Scriptural interpretation in the context of modernity emphasized understanding Scripture in light of its historical origin. This illustrates the culture-relative nature of approaches to interpretation, since many of scriptural writings give little indication of their specific historical origin; indeed, they can sometimes seem deliberately to conceal it. Thus the dating of most of the individual books will always be a matter of debate. But compared with the Torah and the Prophets, in the Writings there are more specific references to the Second Temple period. This links with their location at the end of the Hebrew-Aramaic Scriptures; they likely reached their final form as a collection later than the Torah and the Prophets. They belong distinctively to postexilic times.

We may therefore ask how an understanding of the Second Temple period helps us understand their significance. This involves a circular argument, as the books themselves are our major source for knowledge of the period, though the argument's circularity does not make it wrong.

Ezra and Nehemiah indicate that life was hard for the Judean community in the Persian period, while Esther and Daniel suggest that the position of Judeans in Persia, too, could be tough. While Persian control gave Judah more internal freedom than obtained under the Babylonians, it was a province of the Persian Empire, a little community experiencing economic difficulties, partly through the burden of imperial taxation. It existed in uneasy relations or actual conflict with surrounding Persian provinces. Further, it knew internal tensions related to its economic difficulties and to attitudes to those surrounding peoples. Its experience thus fell far short of the glorious restoration of Israel that prophets had promised, and far short of the glorious events of centuries past related in Exodus, Joshua, and 2 Samuel.

The Writings thus function as resources for a community living through tough times. How is it to survive? Continue to worship Yahweh, cast itself on Yahweh, own its sinfulness, and trust Yahweh (Psalms, Lamentations). Reflect on its human experience of life, independently of the agenda or framework set by Yahweh's activity in relation to Israel in events such as the exodus and the making of the covenant (Proverbs, Song of Songs). Face the tricky theological questions raised by its experience and think boldly about them (Job, Ecclesiastes). See Yahweh's activity behind the scenes of its experience, protecting and using it, and neither be overwhelmed by the power of foreign peoples nor dismissive of them (Esther, Ruth). Maintain confidence in Yahweh's sovereignty in the political affairs of the empire and over the broad sweep of history (Daniel). Keep telling its story with a recognition of what does get achieved (Ezra, Nehemiah). Do not undervalue the privilege of being able to worship Yahweh in the temple built by David (Chronicles).

The circumstances of post-Christian parts of the world such as Britain parallel those of the Second Temple Judean community and thus give it a way in to understanding the Writings, and their varying invitations speak to its situation. If the church in the United States continues to decline, it will share with them in the potential of this parallel.

2. Historical Interpretation: Individual Books

Most of the Latter Prophets begin with an introduction offering hermeneutical clues about how to read them. One clue is their reference to a particular human author and a particular historical context, the reign of certain kings. Interpreting them against their specific historical context is then both possible and necessary. Isaiah, Ezekiel, and Zechariah (for instance) would not have delivered the same message if they had lived in a different century. But in the case of most of the Writings, we do not know their author or what century they belong to. Interpreting them against their specific historical context is impossible and is therefore presumably (if one factors in God's providence) unnecessary.

English translations can give readers the impression that the Psalms begin in a similar way to the Latter Prophets, with the same pointer to understanding them against the background of their author and their author's day, since the expression "psalm of David" looks analogous to the expression "vision of Isaiah." Actually it is not. While "vision of Isaiah" is a construct phrase (the Hebrew equivalent of a genitive), the expression "of David" involves a preposition, *le*, and while it could mean "by David," it could as easily mean "for David" or "belonging to David." Further, many psalm headings that include the phrase "psalm of David" also describe their psalm as "psalm of the choirmaster" or by means of another such term using the same prepositional construction. This is obscured by English translations, which have phrases such as "for the choirmaster," perhaps to avoid the problem caused by implying that the psalm had two or three authors. Yet further, while "David" can denote David ben Jesse, the First Testament can also use the name "David" to refer to a subsequent Davidic king or a Davidic king to come in the future. So one way or another, there is no strong reason to take the "David" heading as an indication of a psalm's authorship and thus as an invitation to understand a psalm historically. This fits with the fact that many "David" psalms look later than the time of King David (for instance, speaking as if the temple already exists). For Chronicles, the great significance of David is as the person who under Yahweh set up the arrangements for the temple's building and worship. The heading "of/for/to/belonging to David," alongside headings such as "of/for/to/belonging to the choirmaster" might have similar significance. It affirms that these prayers and praises belong to Israel's proper, David-authorized, divinely authorized worship. The hermeneutical clue the heading offers is that readers can and should take these psalms as a guide to proper praise and prayer. (We will come back to the headings that refer to specific incidents in David's life.)

The actual contents of the Psalms also suggest that their date and origin is without hermeneutical significance. While they often refer to circumstances that suggest particular events in someone's life, such as a defeat, an invasion, a wedding, or an exile from Jerusalem, they never contain concrete information to enable readers to identify which defeat, invasion, wedding, or exile. Omitting such information makes it easier to use them; they do not give the impression of being limited in significance to one particular occasion.

Something similar is true about the Wisdom books. Job is simply anonymous, like narrative works such as Ruth and Esther. As with the Psalms, the perennial nature of its subject makes its date and authorship of little significance for its interpretation. It has been seen as the oldest book in the First Testament, and also as one of the most recent. This question affects understanding of the history of Israelite theology and religion; it makes no difference to the book's meaning.

In some contrast, Proverbs is described as "the proverbs of Solomon," using the genitive, though subsequently Proverbs 30 begins "the words of Agur" and chapter 31 "the words of Lemuel." Ecclesiastes is "the words of Qohelet, the son of David, king in Jerusalem," which both suggests associating its content with Solomon and also points away from this association by not using the actual name (*qohelet* might be a pseudonym or a description of a role). The Song of Songs uses the same preposition as the Psalms in describing itself as "of/for/by/to Solomon."

Sayings such as dominate Proverbs are usually compositions passed down in tradition; they do not exactly have "authors." But in Middle Eastern nations such as Egypt, the king is responsible for encouraging and propagating learning and education and stands as an embodiment of wisdom. In Israel, Solomon occupies that position, and his relationship with these three books is analogous to David's relationship with the "Davidic" psalms. They are Solomonic in the sense that they count as true wisdom. Like the Psalms, they have canonical authority.

In the context of modernity, interpreters emphasized a historical approach to understanding Ruth. While its story is set in the judges period, its last paragraph makes clear that it was written at least as late as David's day, and its location in the Writings suggests it comes from the postexilic period. That context highlights its emphasis on Ruth's Moabite identity and on its relating how a Moabite comes to be part of David's ancestry; it suggests a different attitude to marriage with people such as Moabites from the one implied by Ezra 9.[2] But while a historical approach thus

---

2. See §7 on "Canonical Interpretation."

illumines one aspect of Ruth, it takes attention away from many aspects. The story of Naomi and of Ruth and Naomi's relationship, for instance, becomes insignificant. Historical interpretation both enlightens and obscures.

Among the Writings, Lamentations is the book most amenable to historical interpretation, though even here the appropriateness of that approach has been questioned. The Septuagint provides Lamentations with a preface attributing it to Jeremiah in the aftermath of Jerusalem's fall in 587, and its consequent location after Jeremiah in the Christian Bible encourages the assumption that this is the context for understanding it. With hindsight one should not be surprised that this consensus assumption has been questioned in our current period in which every assumption is open to question, though there was a long time lag between scholarly abandonment of the idea of Jeremianic authorship and scholarly questioning of the dating. But Lamentations parallels the Psalms in containing no concrete indications of date and authorship. Historical criticism has stuck with the tradition of a date soon after 587 because that is the last fall of Jerusalem we know of in First Testament times. This at least gives us a context against which to imagine the book, and a historical approach thus contributes to its interpretation. But the book's lack of concrete historical reference makes it likely that this is not the only key to it.

3. Sociological Interpretation

Sociological interpretation of Scripture takes various forms, some closely related to historical interpretation. It may ask about the social location of the authors and readers of the books, even if we cannot identify their identity or historical setting, and of the way the books' content reflects the position of authors and readers in the society, and their interests. The material within Proverbs, for instance, may reflect the social contexts of the family (in many of the sayings), of the royal court (in other sayings), and of the theological school (in the expositions of the significance of Wisdom). But no doubt the social background of the book of Proverbs (like that of any biblical book, and of most books in most contexts) will be that of educated, literary, urban, professional, and well-to-do people. This may illumine aspects of its content, such as its attacks on laziness. Ecclesiastes is usually thought to have the same background, though its author then expresses disillusion with everything that educated, literary, urban, professional, powerful, well-to-do people have or value. Sociological approaches such as these suffer from the same difficulty as historical approaches; they have to connect a small number of dots, on the basis of theories that come from outside the text, and they thus produce conflicting results.[3]

---

3. See W. J. Houston, "The Role of the Poor in Proverbs," in *Reading from Right to Left* (David J. A. Clines Festschrift; ed. J. Cheryl Exum and H. G. M. Williamson; London and New York: Sheffield Academic Press, 2003), 229–40, on sociological approaches to Proverbs; and M. Sneed, "The Social Location of the Book of Qoheleth," *Hebrew Studies* 39 (1998): 38–51, on sociological approaches to Ecclesiastes.

This difficulty becomes clearer when we reconsider the process whereby Hermann Gunkel introduced sociological interpretation into the study of the poetic books.[4] He sought to redirect study of the Psalms from questions about their individual nature and their individual historical background to questions about their recurrent forms of speech and about the social context (*Sitz im Leben*) in which these belonged. This was a potentially fruitful approach, but Gunkel was prevented from realizing more of the potential of a sociological approach by assumptions about the nature of temple worship and about spirituality that he brought to his sociological study. Even the strong internal evidence within the Psalms of their intrinsic link with corporate worship did not deflect him from denying that this was their true social context. Sociological approaches to the books have a hard time attending to the content of the books themselves rather than simply reading sociological theories into them. In theory, sociological interpretation should illumine the text; in practice, we would be unwise to rely too much on its alleged results. It may illumine the interpreters more than the texts they interpret.

Asking about the social function of psalms of praise is more illuminating. In Christian worship, declaring that Jesus is Lord creates a world before us. The world and the church do not make it look as if Jesus is Lord; world and church do not live in light of this fact. Yet we know that Jesus *is* Lord, and proclaiming this reality builds up our capacity to keep believing it even though empirical evidence imperils this conviction, and also builds up our capacity to live on the basis of the statement's truth. Analogously, psalms of praise function to create a world.[5] Israel knows that Yahweh is the great God and the great King, but the facts of life in Israel often make it look as if Marduk is the great god and Nebuchadnezzar is the great king. In singing the Psalms, then, Israel affirms that the real world is the one in which Yahweh reigns, and builds up its capacity to live in light of that fact.

4. Liturgical Interpretation

Sociological interpretation thus links with liturgical interpretation. Why do the Writings, this miscellaneous collection of books, come together at the end of the Hebrew-Aramaic Bible? There may be a connection with their relationship to worship, which may even explain the puzzling title "the Writings" (this expression, *hakketubim*, could as easily be translated "the Scriptures," but the Torah and the Prophets are also part of "The Writings/Scriptures" in this sense). In synagogue worship, the weekly Scripture readings come from the Torah and the Prophets. Some of the Writings are used in other ways in worship, but not to provide the regular weekly readings. The Torah and the Prophets are read; the Writings are Scriptures that are written but not read, in this sense.[6]

4. See H. Gunkel, *Introduction to Psalms* (Macon, Ga.: Mercer University Press, 1998); *The Psalms* (Philadelphia: Fortress, 1967).
5. See W. Brueggemann, *Israel's Praise* (Philadelphia: Fortress, 1988).
6. J. Barton, *Oracles of God* (London: DLT; Philadelphia: Westminster Press, 1986).

The Five Scrolls belong together in connection with worship because they came to be used (at least in Ashkenazi communities) at five annual occasions, Passover (Song of Songs), Pentecost (Ruth), the Ninth of Av, in July/August (Lamentations), Sukkot (Ecclesiastes), and Purim (Esther). The nature of the link with these occasions varies. The Song of Songs' association with Passover presupposes the Song's interpretation as an allegory of the story of Yahweh's dealings with Israel over the centuries, beginning at the exodus. Ruth's association with Pentecost corresponds to the wheat harvest setting of a key scene in the story. Lamentations' association with the Ninth of Av is more intrinsic to the book's nature, as this fast day commemorates the fall of Jerusalem and the destruction of the temple in 587 BC and in AD 70. The link between Ecclesiastes and Sukkot is perhaps that Sukkot is traditionally "the season of our joy," and Ecclesiastes points to false and true places to locate joy. Purim's association with Esther is intrinsic to the book, which almost ends with Esther's establishing this festival to celebrate the deliverance the story tells. A liturgical approach to the Five Scrolls thus illumines aspects of some of them

The psalm headings also reflect liturgical realities and point to a liturgical interpretation of the Psalter. Paradoxically, the very fact that many of these headings are now unintelligible reflects their liturgical significance; they are the psalmic equivalents to "common meter" or "capo on second fret." For a half-century following on the work of Sigmund Mowinckel, who took forward Gunkel's work,[7] much scholarship assumed that the Psalms' use in worship was the key to interpreting them, but in the late twentieth century this assumption lost traction. Erhard S. Gerstenberger attempted to move the focus of interest from the worship of the temple to that of local communities in Judah or in the dispersion, but this also involves much reading into the texts.[8] While the general notion that the Psalms were used in Israelite worship is secure enough and significant for their interpretation, attempts to give more precision to the way they were used founder on the fact that neither their content nor their headings are specific enough in indicating the way they were used, and this focus has drawn attention away from the Psalms themselves.

5. Devotional Interpretation

There is an exception to the rule that the headings of the Psalms do not have specific hermeneutical significance. A number of these headings link psalms with specific incidents in David's life. Psalm 51, as well as being "of/for/to the choirmaster" is "of/for/to David"; this heading then adds, "when Nathan the prophet came to him as he had come to Bathsheba." Comparing these long headings with the content of their psalms reveals two features. There is a general fit between heading and psalm, and often concrete points

7. See S. Mowinckel, *The Psalms in Israel's Worship* (2 vols.; Oxford: Blackwell; Nashville: Abingdon, 1962).

8. See E. S. Gerstenberger, *Psalms, Part 1* and *Psalms, Part 2, and Lamentations* (Grand Rapids: Eerdmans, 1988, 2001).

of connection with the story the heading refers to; it would be appropriate for David to cast himself on Yahweh's mercy in the way the psalm expresses it, and appropriate for him to plead that Yahweh's holy spirit not be taken away from him. Yet other specific features stand in tension with its use by David at this point. David could hardly say that he had sinned "only" against Yahweh, and it is odd for him to look for the building up of Jerusalem's walls, with the implication that they have been knocked down.

Brevard Childs has suggested a plausible understanding of the combination of correspondence and contrast between these long headings and their psalms.[9] In effect, he suggests, they resemble the collocation of passages in a lectionary, which invites congregations to read several passages in relation to one another. The implication is not that these passages were written together or that they exactly correspond but that there is sufficient overlap between them to make it fruitful to bring them into mutual association. The analogy suggests that people who use the psalm or who read the relevant David story bring psalm and story together so as to find some indication of the way a person in David's position might pray or some indication of the circumstances in which one might pray this psalm.

These headings' presupposition may then be that David has now become not only the patron of temple worship but also a model for spirituality, as Christians have in fact regularly taken him. People read David's story to gain enlightenment on their personal walk with God. The psalms then help them relate David's story to themselves. At the same time, the incompleteness of the overlap between heading and psalm will stimulate further reflection on the ambiguities of our relationship with God. A David who actually prayed Psalm 51 in the circumstances to which the heading refers could expect a brusque response from God. Indeed, to judge from the rest of David's story as 2 Samuel tells it, he received such a response.

Something similar is true about the role of the unnamed Solomon in Ecclesiastes. The book emphasizes the way the things human beings use to bring them fulfillment and happiness cannot actually deliver. Solomon offers a model test case for this thesis, since he was in a position to realize the goals many people set for themselves. As king he was able to study all the learning that was available, to indulge himself in pleasure to excess, to bring to completion great achievements in building and creativity, to accumulate great wealth, and to build up a harem. But none of it led anywhere; all of it seemed empty. He could thus testify to that fact for ordinary people who think that these things would give meaning to their lives. So Solomon becomes instructive for ordinary people's spirituality.

The implication of the way the Psalms and Wisdom books work is that people who bring to the books their own questions about their lives and their relationship with God will discover aspects of the texts' own meaning. However, like other approaches to interpretation, this has limitations, and it is particularly inclined to narrow down what readers see in stories such as Ruth and Esther, which are about much more than individuals and their lives.

9. "Psalm Titles and Midrashic Exegesis," *Journal of Semitic Studies* 16 (1971): 137–50.

6. Canonical Interpretation: Individual Books

As well as drawing attention to their human authorship and their historical origin, the prophetic books describe themselves by means of expressions such as "the word of Yahweh." As well as being of human and historical origin, they are of divine origin.

The Writings do not take this form but present themselves as human words. The Christian description of the entire Scriptures as the Word of God implies that they are divine words just as really as the prophetic books; the difference lies in *how* God was involved in bringing them into being, rather than in *whether* God was involved. The way the Writings present themselves suggests that these are works God came to accept and authenticate rather than works that God initiated. (Theologically, we might still say that God's initiative was prior in bringing them into being; I speak here of the process as the scriptural writings themselves see it.)

When prophets describe something as "the word of Yahweh," they imply the conviction that for better or worse, this prophetic declaration will indeed come about. As Yahweh's word it demands attention if hearers want to profit from its good news or evade its bad news. Recognizing books such as Psalms or Proverbs or Ruth as the Word of God will have similar implications. It implies paying attention to them. It implies that churches should read them, whereas in practice churches rather neglect them. Where they do not simply ignore them, Christians may be inclined actively to discount them, implying that they cannot really be divine words. For instance, the Psalms say things to God that Christians rather think no one ought to think or feel or say. Ecclesiastes says things to other people that Christians would think no one ought to think or feel or say. Proverbs makes promises that Christians think cannot be relied on or that are otherwise likely to be misleading (for instance, encouraging people to believe in a prosperity gospel). It is then Christian practice to ignore these words or reinterpret them so that they fit with what Christians find acceptable.

Although they do not describe themselves as the word of Yahweh, the books implicitly anticipate and counter this attitude by suggesting a claim to something like canonical authority. These are human words that offer authoritative teaching; they are "designed to function as canon."[10] The Psalter, for instance, divides into five books, marked by doxologies after Psalms 41; 72; 89; and 106. It thus mirrors the Torah, which divides into five books (it is a Pentateuch). The Psalter is a book of teaching about praise and prayer that demands to be heeded in an analogous way to the way the Torah demands to be heeded. It decides what is proper praise and prayer.

The reference to Solomon in the introduction to Proverbs and Song of Songs implicitly ascribes quasi-canonical authority to these books, given that describing them as Solomonic claims for them the kind of authority that attaches to the teaching of someone who is the embodiment of God-given wisdom in the First Testament story.

10. See B. S. Childs, *Introduction to the Old Testament as Scripture* (Philadelphia: Fortress; London: SCM, 1979).

Ecclesiastes makes the same point in a slightly different way in beginning by describing its author as *qohelet*, from the word for the Israelite worshiping congregation, the *qahal*. This teacher is someone who represents the congregation, not some heretic. The book's closing paragraph nuances the point. It makes specific that Qohelet was indeed a wise man who taught insight to the people, one who taught truth. The description piles up words to underline the book's nature and status in these general terms. It then comes to comment on its particular nature, observing that in this case the sayings of the wise are like goads or spurs, and like nails; having them driven home is extremely uncomfortable, but they achieve things as this happens. However, the conclusion goes on, the reader needs to be wary of them, and it adds the seminarian's favorite verse, that of the making of many books there is no end and much study is a wearying of the flesh. In its context the point is that one Ecclesiastes is a good idea, but a Bible full of books like this would not be. Ecclesiastes then closes with a safe summary of the orthodox convictions whose difficulties much of the book is concerned to face.

7. Canonical Interpretation: The Collection as a Whole

The canonical placing of the books in the Hebrew-Aramaic canon and in the Greek and English canon also carries implications for their interpretation. In both orders, Genesis to Deuteronomy comes first. Then things diverge. The Hebrew-Aramaic division of the canon demarcates the first five books from what follows as the Torah over against the Former Prophets. The Greek canon does not do so and thus encourages readers to follow the narrative as it continues into Joshua, Judges, Samuel, and Kings, with Ruth inserted into this macro-narrative at an appropriate point where it provides a foil to Judges and points forward to the story of David.[11] As is the case with a historical interpretation of Ruth, the effect is to highlight certain aspects of the story and underplay others.

The Hebrew-Aramaic canon follows the Former Prophets with the Latter Prophets, Isaiah, Jeremiah, Ezekiel, and Hosea to Malachi. In the Greek canon these come at the end, with Lamentations and Daniel inserted at chronologically appropriate points, suggesting a historical approach to Lamentations by setting it in the context of Jeremiah's ministry and lifetime. In the Greek canon, further, Chronicles, Ezra, Nehemiah, and Esther follow Joshua to Kings, in that chronological order. This again emphasizes a linear, narrative reading of the books, which fits Chronicles, Ezra, and Nehemiah (not least given the overlap between the end of Chronicles and the beginning of Ezra). In Esther's case it has a parallel effect to the one it has on Ruth, making readers see it as part of a larger whole and not simply as a work in its own right, and underplaying other aspects of the story.

The placing of the Writings as a whole at the end of the Hebrew-Aramaic canon is usually reckoned to imply that they have less authority than the Torah and the

11. See D. Jobling, "Ruth Finds a Home," in *The New Literary Criticism and the Hebrew Bible* (ed. J. Cheryl Exum and David J. A. Clines; Sheffield: Sheffield Academic Press, 1993), 125–39.

Prophets; their absence from the weekly synagogue lectionary fits with that.[12] In contrast, the Greek canon's locating of Job, Psalms, Proverbs, Ecclesiastes, and Song of Songs in the middle of the collection gives these books more coherence than they have in the Hebrew-Aramaic canon. In the Greek canon, they again appear in a quasi-chronological order, as Job is traditionally assumed to be a figure from the time of Israel's ancestors, Psalms is associated with David, the last three books with Solomon. At the same time, all five books discuss perennial human issues concerning the nature and basis of human life and of a relationship with God, and they do so with little reference to God's acts in Israel's story which elsewhere define the meaning of God and the way one would understand those issues. That perhaps reflects the books' historical background in the postexilic period when the great acts of God belong in the distant past and are hard to relate to.

As a whole, the Greek canon can be seen as arranged in such a way as to relate to the past (Genesis to Esther), the present (Job to Song of Songs), and the future (Isaiah to Malachi).[13] This understanding parallels the dynamic and suggestive tensions and complementarities within the Writings and between the Writings and the other books. "Proverbs says, 'These are the rules for life. Try them and you will find that they work.' Job and Ecclesiastes say, 'We did, and they don't.'"[14] In the Psalms, suffering usually comes despite people's faithfulness; in Lamentations, it comes because of people's waywardness. Ruth suggests an open stance to foreign women who identify with Israel; Ezra urges a rigorous stance to foreign women who do not. In Exodus, God acts in interventionist fashion to bring about Israel's deliverance, and a woman or two make it possible for a man to take the human lead in this process, while in Esther Israel's deliverance comes about without divine intervention, and a man encourages a woman to take the lead. In Proverbs, right behavior is an expression of insight; in Deuteronomy it is an expression of obedience to Yahweh. In Genesis 1–2, the relationship between a man and a woman is a practical one; in the Song of Songs, it is a romantic one. We learn from the conversation within the Writings and between the Writings and other Scriptures about these questions.

8. Experiential Interpretation

While a number of the Writings do present themselves to us as texts designed to function canonically, we have noted that more prominently than the prophetic books they present themselves as human words, and this provides a significant clue for their interpretation. The human experience of readers is a key factor in thinking about hermeneutics, and more systematically than any other parts of Scripture these

12. For other interpretations of the arrangement, see Jack Miles, *God: A Biography* (New York and London: Simon & Schuster, 1995); S. G. Dempster, *Dominion and Dynasty* (Leicester and Downers Grove, Ill.: InterVarsity, 2003).

13. See H. W. Wolff, *The Old Testament* (Philadelphia: Fortress, 1973; London: SPCK, 1974).

14. D. A. Hubbard, "The Wisdom Movement and Israel's Covenant Faith," *TynB* 17 (1966): 3–33.

books appeal to and speak in terms of human experience. While Ruth and Esther relate the experiences of certain ordinary individuals, the Psalms, Lamentations, Proverbs, Job, Ecclesiastes, and the Song of Songs give prominence to first-person expressions of praise, prayer, insight, pain, questioning, and enthusiasm. All human writing reflects human experience, and in the scriptural writings as a whole God speaks through that experience, but these books reflect human experience in a particularly explicit and systematic way.

The experiential aspect to hermeneutics is the focus of a significant nineteenth-century tradition of hermeneutics that saw interpretation as aiming to share or repeat the experience of the writers of a work, our own analogous experience being our way in to being able to do that.[15] We come to these books as people who ourselves praise God, pray, reflect, doubt, suffer, and love. If we do not do those things, it is unlikely that we would have a starting point for understanding them. To do so, we have to put ourselves empathetically into the position of people who do them. In principle that is possible because we are human beings like them and have the potential for those experiences if not the experiences themselves. It means we can understand something of what the books mean when they express their enthusiasm in praise, their pain in prayer, their agonizing about injustice in the world, and the thrill of their love.

At the same time, we then recognize that much of their praise, prayer, agonizing, and thrill is different from anything we experience. Our own experience both opens up the possibility of understanding and draws attention to our need to go beyond our own experience if we are to understand the texts. We are thus introduced to the "hermeneutic circle," or better, "hermeneutic spiral," and the notion of the merging of horizons.[16] It is possible to settle for affirming the features that gel with our own experience and ignoring the rest; the hermeneutic process then becomes a vicious circle. Even the recent renewed appreciation of lament psalms reflects something about us as readers, in a way analogous to the more traditional Christian emphasis on penitential psalms.[17] Growing in our understanding involves starting from the overlap between our experience and the experience reflected in the text and letting that be a way into appreciating the aspects of the text that we have not experienced.

9. Narrative Interpretation

Ruth and Esther are short stories. This description does not beg the question whether they are more factual or more imaginative stories (my assumption is that both

15. See F. D. E. Schleiermacher, *Hermeneutics* (Missoula, Mont.: Scholars Press, 1977); W. Dilthey, *Selected Writings* (Cambridge and New York: Cambridge University Press, 1976); Dilthey, "The Understanding of Other Persons and Their Life-Expressions," in *The Hermeneutics Reader* (ed. K. Mueller-Vollmer; New York: Crossroad, 1985; Oxford: Blackwell, 1986), 152–64.

16. See H.-G. Gadamer, *Truth and Method* (New York: Crossroad, 1982); A. C. Thiselton, *New Horizons in Hermeneutics* (Grand Rapids: Zondervan, 1992).

17. H. P. Nasuti, *Defining the Sacred Songs* (JSOTSup 218; Sheffield: Sheffield Academic Press, 1999).

historical facts and divinely inspired imagination have contributed to them). But even if they are purely factual stories, they use the techniques of creative writing, and approaches to interpretation that are honed to the nature of creative writing contribute to their understanding.

a. Character. Character plays a key role in both stories, in the persons of Naomi, Ruth, Boaz, Ahasuerus, Vashti, Mordecai, Haman, and others. Some of these are well-rounded characters with the complexity of human personality; Naomi is an example. Others are simpler characters presented in plain, black-and-white fashion; Ahasuerus is an example. This is not to say that the real Ahasuerus was any less complex than Naomi but to comment on the role of the character within the story and the questions that are appropriate to understanding their role. Some characters (such as Boaz) are portrayed with sympathy, some (such as Haman) without. Interpreters vary in the way they understand the portrayal of Vashti. People who favor women's subordination are negative about Vashti; people who oppose it are positive about the stance she takes. The presuppositions people bring to characters influence their interpretation.

b. Plot. The framework of Ruth is the way a family from Bethlehem become the ancestors of Israel's greatest king, from Bethlehem. Events at the beginning of the story threaten to derail this possibility as the family has to leave Bethlehem for Moab, where all the men in the family die. The plot then has to get the family's mother back to Bethlehem and make it possible for her to have a child who can turn out to be David's grandfather. Like many plots, it involves a series of points where everything could go wrong (for instance, what if Naomi succeeds in persuading Ruth to stay in Moab?) and coincidences (Boaz is a member of Naomi's extended family!). The framework of Esther is the way the Jewish people in Persia escape a pogrom. In the background is some indulgent and then angry action on the part of the Persian king, interwoven with some assertiveness on the queen's part, which leads to a Jewish girl becoming queen. The more direct background is a Jewish man's resistance to bowing down to one of the king's officials, which provokes the official to manipulate the king into authorizing the pogrom. Again coincidence plays a role (a Jewish girl becoming queen, Mordecai discovering a plot against the king, the king being unable to sleep one night), and again, everything could go wrong (what if Esther had not bravely urged the king to reverse his action?). Like Ruth, Esther follows the standard linear plot form: the exposition of a problem, the complexities of events and actions it leads to, and its eventual resolution.

c. The viewpoint from which the story is told. In Ruth and Esther the story is told in the third-person (contrast, in part, Nehemiah). Thus we do not discover as much about the thinking of these lead characters as we might if Ruth or Esther told the story in the first person. But the narrator can tell us things that no individual character in the story can know. The narrator knows things that members of the Persian court say to one another as well as things that ordinary members of the Jewish community say to one another. Indeed, the narrator sometimes knows what people are thinking, though this is only occasionally the case; the narrator does not know everything. It is more characteristic of First Testament narrative to leave the reader to infer from people's words and actions what was going on inside them. Nor does the narrator know what God is thinking; at least, the story does not tell us. Nor does the narrator offer evaluative comments on people's actions (hence the fact that readers may understand Vashti's actions affirmatively or critically). This makes Ruth and Esther contrast with some other First Testament narratives. The effect is to tell a story that resonates with regular human experience, in which we regularly do not know what other people are thinking or what God is thinking. We have to work out whether and where and how God is involved in the story. But, even though told in the third person, the story sometimes adopts the perspective of one of the characters, as if we are looking over their shoulder even though not looking into their mind. Much of Ruth is told from Naomi's angle; the book might more accurately have been called "Naomi and Ruth." Much of Esther is told from Mordecai's angle, or Haman's.

There are broader aspects to the notion of viewpoint. Together the books imply that any activity of God that people in their context can look for takes place behind the scenes of history and human experience, not in the interventionist fashion of the stories in Exodus and Judges with which in other ways Esther and Ruth have points of contact. Associated with that is their shared conviction that Israelites, and specifically Israelite women, must take responsibility for their destiny and take bold action in relation to the men who hold power in their contexts, using their femininity as they do so.

d. Ambiguity and irony. Ambiguity and irony play a part in the stories, related to questions about character, plot, and viewpoint. In Genesis, Judges, or 2 Samuel, we may reckon that the narrator and/or author and/or God disapproves of many of the actions that the people undertake, though the narrative does not make this explicit. On the basis of information that the story as a whole conveys regarding the narrative's viewpoint, it assumes that readers can make the right inferences, but it leaves them to do so. On the other hand, in some stories there is room for debate about whether the narrator approves of what happens, and/or whether the author does, and/or whether God does. Both kinds of ambiguity (resolvable and irresolvable) appear in Ruth and Esther.

Ruth makes no comment on the death of the three men in the story. Is this Yahweh's judgment for the sons' marrying Moabites? Does Ruth's audacious courting of Boaz relate to Israelite perceptions (or fantasies) of Moabite women? By the end of the story, it is at least clear that the narrator affirms Ruth precisely as a Moabite and believes that Israel should be open to members of other races who come to believe in Yahweh. The stance of the story as a whole in relation to Ruth as a Moabite rules out the pejorative interpretation of the opening events. It is nevertheless an irony that it is a Moabite who provides David with his grandfather. Further, the story leaves ambiguous what precisely happened on the threshing floor, rather in the style of an old-school Hollywood movie; and the question "Was Naomi a Scold?" (someone who is always complaining) could become the subject of a scholarly debate.[18]

18. D. Nolan Fewell and D. Gunn, "'A Son Is Born to Naomi," *JSOT* 40 (1988): 99–108; P. W. Coxon, "Was Naomi a Scold?" *JSOT* 45 (1989): 25–37; D. Nolan Fewell and D. Gunn, "Is Coxon a Scold?" *JSOT* 45 (1989): 39–43.

In Esther, in light of other parts of the First Testament one might wonder whether Jews had any business staying in places such as Susa and not returning to Jerusalem; the narrator presupposes that it is acceptable for Jews to let exile become dispersion and that they can expect to find themselves preserved and even successful there. While the narrative makes no evaluative comment on the Persian men's concern that Vashti's action will encourage other Persian women's insubordination, its portrayal of the king's general capacity for stupidity and manipulation points to sympathy for Vashti rather than for the king and his fellow husbands. With irony, it is the king's next wife who is the means of reversing his edict. With deeper irony the Jews finally indulge in the pogrom that they had themselves escaped; the narrative at least leaves open the question whether the Jews had any business killing more than 75,000 people. Disapproval of the book for this action misses the book's own implicit questioning or critique as the Jews end up behaving like Persians at the moment when many Persians have become Jews.[19]

10. Postmodern Interpretation

Beneath the surface of Ruth and Esther are some more elemental relationships or motifs that also underlie the other books, such as can be examined by structuralism. Stories also presuppose antinomies and take sides with regard to them; deconstruction brings these to the surface and questions their easy resolution.[20]

Ruth and Esther also have in common that they manifest illuminating links with other First Testament material. Esther makes for comparison with the Joseph story as well as the exodus story, while Ruth makes for comparison with the story of Tamar as well as other characters in the First Testament story and other parts of the First Testament such as Isaiah 40–55.[21] The Psalms have multiple such intertextual relationships with other parts of the First Testament,[22] such as the retelling of Israel's story in different psalms. Within the Psalter one can trace the way similar phrases or lines or sequences of lines recur, in varying forms and combinations. Often it may be difficult to know whether such links or similarities are deliberate or coincidental, and if they are deliberate, to know which text came first, but the framework of intertextuality makes it possible to consider their significance without knowing the answer to those questions. Juxtaposing the texts still illumines each of them.

Such awarenesses are an aspect of postmodernity, one of whose features is the recognition that truth is more complicated than it used to be. Christians did once

19. S. Goldman, "Narrative and Ethical Ironies in Esther," *JSOT* 47 (1990): 15–31.

20. For Ruth, see E. L. Greenstein, "Reading Strategies and the Story of Ruth," in *Women in the Hebrew Bible* (ed. A. Bach; New York and London: Routledge, 1999), 211–31; for Esther and Job, see David J. A. Clines, *On the Way to the Postmodern* (2 vols.; Sheffield: Sheffield Academic Press, 1998); also F. W. Bush, *Ruth/Esther* (Dallas: Word, 1996), for Ruth and Esther.

21. See K. Nielsen, *Ruth* (Louisville: Westminster John Knox, 1997).

22. See B. L. Tanner, *The Book of Psalms Through the Lens of Intertextuality* (New York: Lang, 2001).

recognize that we actually understand only the hem of God's garments, and some Christian theologians have wondered whether theology best focuses on saying what God is not (for instance, God is not a created being, God is not located in space, God is not within time, God is not human). Postmodernism reminds us about mystery and complexity. Some of the Writings recognize the complexity of who God is and how we relate to God, and/or recognize the limitations in what we can say about these matters.

While Job begins from the question why bad things happen to good people, this question raises more radical ones about God and humanity and their relationship. Using the form of a dramatic dialogue allows the book to look at the problem from a series of different angles and to propound a series of answers to these questions. It does not survey a number of answers and finally declare that one of them is right. All its answers have some truth in them, though they vary in their relevance to Job. Even Yahweh's response does not have the final word, as the end of the story implies a different perspective.

Job may have undergone a process of redaction (for instance, the prose framework of the story may be older than the poetic speeches, and the Elihu speeches may be a later addition). It may also have been subject to some accidental disordering, particularly in the third set of speeches between Job and his friends. But one implication of approaching the book in light of postmodern insights is that we are unwise to try to simplify or tidy the book. Its complexity and untidiness are one way its message is conveyed.

Ecclesiastes' postmodernity is expressed in its reaction to the difficulty of handling those big questions, not by sharing as many partial insights as possible but by emphasizing how few things we can say.

11. Feminist Interpretation

The Song of Songs and Ruth were among the first books of the Bible that attracted feminist approaches to interpretation.[23] Feminist interpretation asks what happens when women (or men) attempt to read Scripture in conscious awareness of distinctive features of women's lives (or of men's), such as their bodily experiences and their experience of subordination to men (or as men, of the subordination of women to them). Contemporary Western women's insistence on seeing themselves as fully human and standing alongside men rather than as inferior to them opened up the possibility of recognizing the egalitarian aspect to the relationship portrayed in the Song of Songs, where the woman speaks first and longest and the man is not portrayed as the active "lover" and the woman as the acted-upon "beloved." It

---

23. See P. Trible, *God and the Rhetoric of Sexuality* (Philadelphia: Fortress, 1978; London: SCM, 1992); Athalya Brenner, ed., *A Feminist Companion to Ruth* (Sheffield: Sheffield Academic Press, 1993); *A Feminist Companion to the Song of Songs* (Sheffield: Sheffield Academic Press, 1993); A. Bach, ed., *Women in the Hebrew Bible* (New York and London: Routledge, 1999).

thus lets the Song speak to subordinationist attitudes in the church. It opened up avenues of analyzing the relationship of Ruth and Naomi and the way they discover how to live as women in a men's world. Similar dynamics were perceived in Esther, the story of the radical feminist Vashti and the liberal feminist Esther[24]—though they are still, like Ruth and Naomi, finally subordinated to men. In reverse fashion, feminist interpretation raises questions about the aphorisms in Proverbs and their understanding of women and men, and about the figure of the "strange woman," though noting how the aphorisms are set in the context of the different way womanhood features in the book's opening and closing chapters, which form a frame for understanding it.[25] Feminist interpretation inquires further after the significance of the apparent absence or near-absence of women from works such as Psalms and Job, though also of the potential of reading psalms as women's texts.[26]

12. Typological, Allegorical, and Christological Interpretation

It became customary in Judaism to interpret the Song of Songs as a figurative account of Yahweh's relationship with Israel. Successive chapters describe the love relationship between Yahweh and Israel, with its ups and downs, in the exodus period, at Sinai, in the wilderness, in the promised land, and so on. Christian interpretation from Origen onwards similarly interpreted the Song as a figurative account of Christ's love for the church or of God's love for the Virgin Mary or of Christ's love for the individual believer. Such understandings illustrate the process of interpreting a text in light of convictions that come from outside it.

Premodern reading of the passages in Job about a mediator, an advocate on high, and a redeemer (Job 9:33–34; 16:18–20; 19:25–27) referred these passages to Christ. This came decisively to determine popular Christian understanding through the use of the last passage in Handel's *Messiah*. Like much New Testament reading of the First Testament, this made use of verbal points of connection that enabled the First Testament text to help people understand the significance of Christ, but it did not significantly open up the meaning of the First Testament itself. Indeed, there is a substantial gap between the inherent meaning of the passages and the significance of Christ (for instance, Job wants a mediator who will establish his innocence, not deal with his sin). The intuitive or occasional nature of such interpretation is reflected in the fact that Christian interpretation can also see Job as a type of Christ. He is supremely committed to God, profoundly tested by the will of both the Adversary and God, loudly crying out to God in his affliction, let down by his friends, required to sustain devastating suffering because of God's purpose, but finally restored.

24. See Clines, *On the Way to the Postmodern*, 1:3–22.
25. See C. V. Camp, *Wisdom and the Feminine in the Book of Proverbs* (Sheffield and Decatur, Ga.: Almond, 1985).
26. See M. V. Rienstra, *Swallow's Nest: A Feminine Reading of the Psalms* (Grand Rapids: Eerdmans, 1992).

Traditional Christian interpretation read the Psalms as Christ's praise and prayers. This could take as its starting point the New Testament's use of some passages from the Psalms to interpret the significance of Christ. This was facilitated by a process of reinterpretation of the Psalms that had already taken place within Judaism. Some psalms refer explicitly to the king or the anointed one, and when Israel had no anointed king these could be understood to refer to the king Israel would surely again have one day, to a coming Messiah. Given that the Psalms in origin are not prophecies but declarations relating to Israel's actual kings, we might call the New Testament's adoption of this approach a typological understanding.[27]

We might also think in typological terms about the way Lamentations has been related to Christ's suffering. Lamentations is used in Holy Week in the service of Tenebrae ("Darkness"); Jerusalem's suffering, particularly as expressed in the protest of a male individual in Lamentations 3, can thus illumine Christ's suffering: "Is it nothing to you, all you who pass by?" (Lam 1:12).

The picture of God's Wisdom in Proverbs embodied as a person standing alongside God is not explicitly quoted in the New Testament, but its language and conceptuality underlie the way the New Testament speaks of Christ as God's Word and God's Wisdom, and it thus facilitates the New Testament's articulating the idea that Christ could be both divine and preexistent and also distinguishable from the Father. The relationship between the First Testament passage and the significance of Christ again involves overlap rather than identity, and when Christian interpretation sought to read Proverbs 8:22–31 as if it is actually about Christ, it found itself in trouble: reading the First Testament in Greek, the Arians could make better sense than the Nicene fathers of the fact that the passage speaks of God's Wisdom as *created* by God.

13. Post-Holocaust Interpretation

Christian and Jewish reading of Esther was decisively changed by the Holocaust. For Christians, the key interpretation is that of Wilhelm Vischer, who in the 1930s saw the need to read Esther in light of the Nazi persecution of the Jewish people.[28] He attempted but failed to get the church to take seriously Esther's implications for the church's understanding of the Jewish people (and of itself), not least in light of Romans 9–11, and thus to commit itself to the Jewish people's defense. Richard Bauckham revisited this reading of Esther when, decades later, Jews and Christians began to face the questions raised by the Holocaust.[29] Among Jewish scholars, Sandra Beth Berg comments that "the rampant destruction of European Jewish communities in the recent past is similar to a threat described, but not fulfilled, in Esther. Haman's spiritual descendants proved more successful in attaining their goal

27. H. W. Bateman, "Psalm 110:1 and the New Testament," *BSac* 149 (1992): 438–53.
28. See "The Book of Esther," *EvQ* 11 (1939): 3–21.
29. See Richard Bauckham, *The Bible in Politics* (London: SPCK; Louisville: Westminster John Knox, 1989).

of genocide. . . . One message of the Book of Esther, with its emphasis upon Jewish solidarity and human responsibility and action, remained unheard by Mordecai's and Esther's descendants."[30] Michael V. Fox similarly prefaces a study of Esther with an account of how the pogroms of a century ago as well as the Holocaust influence his reading of the book.[31]

In related fashion, Mirish Kiszner comments that Lamentations comes "hauntingly alive" in light of the Holocaust.[32] Tod Linafelt suggests that one reason Lamentations continues to haunt readers is that the book reaches no closure; it is full of protests to God that receive no response.[33] Reading Lamentations in light of the Holocaust illustrates a difficulty that appears in connection with other approaches to interpretation. Either one assimilates Lamentations to the reading context and underplays the emphasis on the way it was Jerusalem's rebellions that led to its fall; or one assimilates Jewish suffering in the Holocaust and elsewhere and implies that it happened through the Jewish people's sins.

14. Postcolonial Interpretation

The "wind of change" that a British prime minister recognized blowing through Africa in 1960 eventually issued not only in the political independence of former European colonies but also in the 1990s in the two-thirds world's quest for hermeneutical independence. As happened with feminist interpretation, this involved looking at the Scriptures through new eyes and seeing things that Eurocentric interpretation had not perceived or seeing how Eurocentric interpretation had skewed things. Eurocentric interpretation thus has the man in the Song of Songs addressing the woman as "fair," which rather presupposes that being "lovely" (*yapah*) involves being white rather than black, while also (paradoxically) it has the woman declaring, "I am dark *but* beautiful." Is she suntanned or is she an African, and is it "but" or "and"? The Psalms are illumined by awareness of African culture and traditions rather than simply the assumptions of Western scholarship, and by awareness of the experience of exile.[34] The traditional negative Christian interpretation of Esther might be seen in colonizing terms.[35]

---

30. *The Book of Esther* (Missoula, Mont.: Scholars Press, 1979), 183, 184.

31. See *Character and Ideology in the Book of Esther* (2nd ed.; Grand Rapids and Cambridge: Eerdmans, 2001).

32. M. Kiszner, "Holocaust Lamentations," http://www.aish.com/jewishissues/jewishsociety/Holocaust_Lamentations.asp.

33. See *Surviving Lamentations* (Chicago: University of Chicago Press, 2002).

34. See D. T. Adamo, "The Use of the Psalms in African Indigenous Churches in Nigeria," in *The Bible in Africa* (ed. G. O. West and M. W. Dube; Boston and Leiden: Brill, 2001), 336–49; Ada María Isasi-Díaz on Ps 137 in *Reading from This Place* (ed. F. F. Segovia and Mary Ann Tolbert; 2 vols.; Minneapolis: Fortress, 1995); and more generally D. Patte et al., eds., *Global Bible Commentary* (Nashville: Abingdon, 2004).

35. See T. K. Beal, *The Book of Hiding* (London and New York: Routledge, 2002).

The period during which much of the material in these books grew or reached its final form was the time when Judah lived in a quasi-colonial relationship to the Babylonian and Persian empires.[36] Lamentations is then the hurt prayers of a people living under colonial domination, Esther the story of the relationship to the empire of members of a colonized people who live in the imperial capital.

Postcolonial perspectives throw light on Ruth (and vice versa) in paradoxical fashion, because of their implications in relation to both Ruth the Moabite and Naomi the Israelite, let alone Elimelech and their sons. Elimelech, Naomi, and their sons are forced to become immigrants in a foreign country with which Israel had often had a hostile relationship. Ruth in due course commits herself to Naomi in a way that involves her becoming an immigrant in a foreign country and unconsciously challenging its people about what attitude they will take to this foreigner. Or is this people like a colonizing power taking away her identity?[37] Women of African descent in the United States or in Europe and black women in South Africa have a way in to appreciating her story and may read it either way, as is also the case with Esther.[38]

36. See N. K. Gottwald, *The Politics of Ancient Israel* (Louisville: Westminster John Knox, 2001).
37. See J. McKinley, *Reframing Her* (Sheffield: Sheffield Phoenix, 2004).
38. See M. W. Dube, ed., *Other Ways of Reading* (Atlanta: SBL, 2001).

Index of Modern Authors

Index of Ancient Sources